D1035622

ESSAYS ON ADAM SMITH

THE GLASGOW EDITION OF THE WORKS AND CORRESPONDENCE OF ADAM SMITH

Commissioned by the University of Glasgow to celebrate the bicentenary of the Wealth of Nations

I

THE THEORY OF MORAL SENTIMENTS
Edited by A. L. MACFIE *and* D. D. RAPHAEL

II

AN INQUIRY INTO THE NATURE AND CAUSES OF THE WEALTH OF NATIONS
Edited by R. H. CAMPBELL *and* A. S. SKINNER; *textual editor* W. B. TODD

III

ESSAYS ON PHILOSOPHICAL SUBJECTS
(and Miscellaneous Pieces)
Edited by W. P. D. WIGHTMAN

IV

LECTURES ON RHETORIC AND BELLES LETTRES
Edited by J. C. BRYCE
This volume includes the *Considerations concerning the First Formation of Languages*

V

LECTURES ON JURISPRUDENCE
Edited by R. L. MEEK, D. D. RAPHAEL, *and* P. G. STEIN
This volume includes two reports of Smith's course together with the 'Early Draft' of the *Wealth of Nations*

VI

CORRESPONDENCE OF ADAM SMITH
Edited by E. C. MOSSNER *and* I. S. ROSS

Associated volumes:

ESSAYS ON ADAM SMITH
Edited by A. S. SKINNER *and* T. WILSON

LIFE OF ADAM SMITH
By I. S. ROSS

ESSAYS ON ADAM SMITH

EDITED BY

ANDREW S. SKINNER

AND

THOMAS WILSON

CLARENDON PRESS . OXFORD

1975

Oxford University Press, Ely House, London W. 1

GLASGOW NEW YORK TORONTO MELBOURNE WELLINGTON
CAPE TOWN IBADAN NAIROBI DAR ES SALAAM LUSAKA ADDIS ABABA
DELHI BOMBAY CALCUTTA MADRAS KARACHI LAHORE DACCA
KUALA LUMPUR SINGAPORE HONG KONG TOKYO

ISBN 0 19 828191 9

Printed in Great Britain by
William Clowes & Sons, Limited,
London, Beccles and Colchester

Acknowledgements

THE publishers are indebted to the following for permission to reprint a number of articles in this volume. In Part I, Professor Cropsey's article is reprinted through the generosity of Rand McNally and originally appeared in *History of Political Philosophy*, ed. Strauss and Cropsey (1963). Professor Howell's piece is reprinted with the permission of Princeton University Press, and appeared in his *Eighteenth Century British Logic and Rhetoric* (1971). Professor Raphael's article is reprinted (with slight revision) by kind permission of the British Academy, from their *Proceedings*, vol. lviii (1972). Professor Stigler's article has appeared in abbreviated form in *History of Political Economy*, vol. iii (Fall, 1971).

In Part II, the first article is based on pp. 133–43 of Professor Hollander's *Economics of Adam Smith* (1973) and is reprinted by kind permission of the University of Toronto Press and Heinemann Educational Books Ltd. Article VI, by Professor Rosenberg has been published in the *Journal of Political Economy* (1974). Article VIII is adapted from pp. 165–6, 168–9, 177–9 in *On Economic Knowledge* by Adolph Lowe. Copyright 1965 by Adolph Lowe. Reprinted by permission of Harper and Row, Publishers, Inc.

Contents

PART II

Abbreviations

Corr.	*Correspondence*
ED	'Early Draft' of *The Wealth of Nations*
EPS	*Essays on Philosophical Subjects* (which include:)
Ancient Logics	'History of the Ancient Logics and Metaphysics'
Ancient Physics	'History of the Ancient Physics'
Astronomy	'History of Astronomy'
English and Italian Verses	'Of the Affinity between certain English and Italian Verses'
External Senses	'Of the External Senses'
Imitative Arts	'Of the Nature of that Imitation which takes place in what are called the Imitative Arts'
Music, Dancing, and Poetry	'Of the Affinity between Music, Dancing and Poetry'
Stewart	Dugald Stewart, 'Account of the Life and Writings of Adam Smith, LL.D.'
FA, FB	Two fragments on the division of labour, Buchan Papers, Glasgow University Library.
LJ (A)	*Lectures on Jurisprudence*: Report of 1762–63
LJ (B)	*Lectures on Jurisprudence*: Report dated 1766
LRBL	*Lectures on Rhetoric and Belles Lettres*
TMS	*The Theory of Moral Sentiments*
WN	*The Wealth of Nations*

Editorial Note

REFERENCES to Smith's published works are given by citing part, section, and paragraph number. For example, the reference 'TMS I.iii.2.2' indicates a reference to Part I, section iii, chapter 2, paragraph 2. The statement 'WN I.x.b.1' indicates a reference to the WN Book I, chapter x, section b, paragraph 1. Astronomy, I.4 refers to section I, paragraph 4.

The Table of Corresponding Passages which is appended to this volume identifies the sections into which the WN is divided and provides the page references for each paragraph in the Cannan editions of 1930 and 1937. It should thus be possible to trace references to either of these editions, and to the Glasgow edition. Unless otherwise stated, references in the text are to the 1930 edition.

In the case of the lecture notes we have followed the following practice: references to the LRBL are given in the form 'LRBL 2.8', indicating a reference to lecture 2, paragraph 8. In the *Lectures on Jurisprudence* we have cited the volume and page reference from the original manuscripts (all of which will be included in the new edition) while retaining page references to the Cannan edition as supplied by the contributors. References to the *Correspondence* give date of letter and letter number from the new edition.

PART I

Analytical Table of Contents of Part I

The nature of Smith's 'whiggery' is subjected to closer scrutiny. It is argued that Smith is to be regarded as a 'sceptical whig' because he was, like Hume, a political scientist; that he was not a 'vulgar' whig is shown by reference to the fact that he rejected the cherished idols of the latter position: the contract theory of government, the unique perfection of English institutions, the view that absolutism was not a proper form of government. *The processes of history* were admittedly associated with the growth of personal freedom, as noted in the two preceding papers, but it is argued that Smith's account is so complex as to cast doubt on any assertion of a *necessary* connection between the two.

Smith's attitude to the American colonies is examined and, while due weight must be given to economic constraints, the author emphasizes that Smith's preferred solutions for the current crisis reflect his own acceptance of contemporary British constitutional practices of the kind confirmed by the Revolution Settlement.

While more explicitly concerned with the mercantile system as a whole, the examination of Smith's views on this subject is set within the framework of his theory of politics with particular reference to the four-stage theory. It is also argued that Smith's strictures on the mercantile system in England were qualified by his grasp of her unique constitutional position, especially with regard to the liberties of the subject. The political role of the merchants and the influence of sectional groups on legislation is also considered.

Smith gave relatively little attention to the working of political processes, and there is a paradox that while self-interest dominates economic life, Smith apparently rejected this motive as a general explanation for legislation. It is held that Smith seems to have given a 'larger role to emotion, prejudice and ignorance in political life than he ever allowed in economic affairs'.

Introduction

THIS volume is published in conjunction with a new edition of all the works of Adam Smith, commissioned by the University of Glasgow to celebrate the bicentenary of *The Wealth of Nations*. As a part of the celebrations, it was also felt appropriate to publish a series of essays by contemporary students of Smith which would cover the main areas of his work, as distinct from simply concentrating on the economics. To this end, the first part is mainly concerned with the broadly 'philosophical' and political aspects of Smith's contribution, the second, with the subject-matter (by no means entirely economic) of *The Wealth of Nations* itself.

I

Although not unusual at the time, the sheer width of Smith's knowledge is particularly striking in a period where the division of labour has enhanced the difficulty of mastering a wide range of subjects. We know, for example, that Smith had an extensive knowledge of contemporary work in the natural sciences and the arts. As Professor of Logic in Glasgow in the session 1751–2, he seems to have drawn heavily on his successful Edinburgh lectures of 1748–51 in delivering what his pupil, John Millar, described as a 'system of Rhetoric and Belles-lettres'. Significantly, Millar pointed out that this represented something of a departure from current practice and that Smith considered that:

The best method of explaining and illustrating the various powers of the human mind, the most useful part of metaphysics, arises from an examination of the several ways of communicating our thoughts by speech, and from an attention to the principles of those literary compositions which contribute to persuasion or entertainment. By these arts, everything that we perceive or feel, every operation of our minds, is expressed and delineated . . .

(Stewart, I.16)

When Smith moved to the Chair of Moral Philosophy in the following session, he divided his lectures into four parts: Natural Theology, Ethics, Jurisprudence, and Economics. As Millar pointed out, the second section formed the basis of the *Theory of Moral Sentiments* (1759), while the fourth 'contained the substance of the work' later published as *The Wealth of Nations*. The *Considerations concerning the First Formation of Languages*, which seems to have been an extension of one section of the *Lectures on Rhetoric*, was first published in 1761.

Both major books proved to be extremely successful and continued to attract a good deal of Smith's attention: the WN, for its part, went through five editions in his life time (the last major revision was for the third edition of 1784); the TMS appeared in six editions, with the last major revision in 1790, the year of Smith's death. Yet Smith evidently hoped to write more. For example, in Letter 248 addressed to Rochefoucauld, dated 1 November 1785, Smith referred to his continuing work on the TMS and added that he had:

two other great works upon the anvil; the one is a sort of Philosophical History of all the different branches of Literature, of Philosophy, Poetry and Eloquence; the other is a sort of theory and History of Law and Government. The materials of both are in a great measure collected, and some Part of both is put into tollerable good order.

Although Smith doubted his ability to complete this programme, some parts of the first work were published in 1795, edited by Joseph Black and James Hutton, under the title of *Essays upon Philosophical Subjects*. This work contained such wide-ranging pieces as a history of astronomy, and of ancient logics, together with essays on the *Imitative Arts* and *English and Italian Verses*.

But perhaps Smith's most consistent ambition was to publish a version of the material contained in the third part of his lectures: that on Jurisprudence, a desire expressed in the closing sentences of the first edition of the TMS. Writing in the advertisement to the sixth edition of 1790 he remarked that with the publication of the WN he had partly executed the original promise:

What remains, the theory of jurisprudence, which I have long projected, I have hitherto been hindered from executing, by the same occupations which had till now prevented me from revising the present work. Though my advanced age leaves me, I acknowledge, very little expectation of ever being able to execute this great work to my own satisfaction, yet, as I have not yet abandoned the design, I have allowed the paragraph to remain as it was published more than thirty years ago, when I entertained no doubt of being able to execute everything which it announced.

Fortunately the two sets of lecture notes (for 1762–3 and 1763–4) now available to us provide some idea as to the outlines of a plan, partially incorporated in the third book of the WN, which seems to have included a global history linking ancient Greece and modern Europe.

II

However, despite his range of interests, Adam Smith was no mere essayist and it may be said that his various and diverse contributions are all linked together in point of doctrine and method.

To begin with, it is evident that Smith's works are informed by three major propositions. First, by the characteristic Humean argument that the study of human nature is a necessary precondition for the study of all forms of activity. Secondly, by the view that the science of man can only be properly developed by using the 'experimental' method as evolved by Newton. Thirdly, Smith accepted Hume's view that the study of man, thus constituted, would yield the conclusion that in all nations and ages human nature remains still the same in its principles and operations.

As Dugald Stewart was to point out, the assumption that human nature could be regarded as a constant became one of the most characteristic features of contemporary philosophy in all its branches. In Smith's case, it is essential to his economic analysis where he makes use of the hypothesis that man is motivated by a desire to seek pleasure and avoid pain; that he is self-regarding and possessed of certain propensities (for example 'to truck and barter') together with particular objectives (for example to 'better his condition'). Similarly in his work on morals, it is argued that all men possess by nature certain faculties and propensities, such as reason, imagination, and fellow-feeling, on whose exercise moral judgement depends.

The fact that human nature (as distinct from experience or environment) could be regarded as a constant made it possible for writers such as Smith to conceive of the social sciences as being on a par with the natural (a point of view which Newton had encouraged), and also to accept another doctrine associated with Newton, namely, that of 'the argument from design', or 'unintended social outcomes'. In Smith's hands, the argument involved a distinction between efficient and final causes (TMS II.ii.3.5), and prompts the conclusion that in every field, whether natural philosophy, linguistics, morals, economics, or history, man in following his natural propensities produces results which were no part of his original intention, and thus contributes to give substantial expression to some aspect of the Divine Plan.

A second link between the main parts of Smith's work is to be seen in the fact that all are prompted by common motives, and made to conform to common requirements, with regard to structure and organization; motives and requirements which are discussed at some length in Smith's treatment of the 'principles which lead and direct philosophical enquiries' and in a theory of rhetoric which includes some account of the proper organization of didactic (or scientific) discourse.

In the first case, Smith argued (in the essay on Astronomy) that the thinker is normally stimulated to inquire into the causes of observed events as a means of escaping the subjective discomfort which arises from contemplating the unexplained, thus restoring the mind to a state of tranquillity; a condition which can only be attained where the explanation offered is coherent, capable of accounting for the observed phenomena, and stated in terms of familiar (or plausible) principles. Smith also argued that there was a positive pleasure to be derived from effort of a philosophical kind and that the greatest achievement of science was to expose the 'connecting principles of nature'; to elucidate the hidden laws which 'govern' and 'explain' what would otherwise be a chaos of unconnected appearances in the world at large.

Smith also emphasized that scientific work represented in itself a source of pleasure and made much of the idea of beauty in referring to the attraction of systematical arrangement and to the choice of what he called the 'Newtonian method'. In the *Lectures on Rhetoric*, for example, he pointed out that in scientific work there are two possible 'methods': in the first we assign a principle, 'commonly a new one', for every phenomenon; in the second we may 'lay down certain principles, [primary?] or proved, in the beginning, from whence we account for the several phenomena, connecting all together by the same chain'. He added:

> This latter, which we may call the Newtonian method, is undoubtedly the most philosophical, and in every science, whether of Morals or Natural Philosophy, etc., is vastly more ingenious, and for that reason more engaging, than the other. It gives us a pleasure to see the phenomena which we reckoned the most unaccountable, all deduced from some principle (commonly, a well known one) and all united in one chain, far superior to what we feel from the unconnected method . . .
>
> (LRBL 24.7; Lothian 140)

In the same vein it is interesting to recall that Smith should have referred to a *propensity*, natural to all men, to account for 'all appearances from as few principles as possible' (TMS VII.ii.2.14).

It is, of course, quite possible that arguments such as these may reveal a great deal as to Smith's own drives and preferences as a thinker, and that these drives and preferences may find some reflection in the structure of his main works. Perhaps it may be stated with even greater confidence that these works all conform to his own requirements for didactic discourse, and that they all aspire to account for a wide range of 'appearances' in terms of a small number of basic and familiar principles, such as, for example, the constant principles of human nature.

III

Although it is interesting to recall the similarities which exist between the various areas of Smith's thought with regard to form, motive, and method, the analytical connections between the different aspects of his study of social science may be still more striking.

It is particularly noteworthy in this connection that Smith should have regarded Ethics and Jurisprudence as the separate branches of a *single* subject, where the latter included not only a historical account of law and government but also of 'police, revenue and arms'. As he himself said in the introduction to the sixth edition of the TMS, the WN represented only a *partial* fulfilment of his original plan; a plan which, as we have already seen, he still hoped to finish. In short, Smith himself regarded his major works not as separate enterprises but as parts of a single whole.

Some pattern of interconnection should, therefore, be evident between them, and is, in fact, not difficult to find if we approach Smith's plan in the order of subjects which he originally proposed: ethics, law, and economics.

Thus the TMS was mainly concerned with the question of the means by which the mind comes to form a judgement as to what is worthy of approval, and what is not. It is argued that our perception of the propriety or impropriety of the actions taken, or feelings expressed, by another person is central to the decision, and that we can only reach this decision by conceiving what we ourselves should feel in a like situation. At the same time, however, Smith showed that the psychology of man was complex and that it included self-regarding as well as other-regarding propensities. A major task of the TMS thus emerged as being to explain the way in which men erect barriers against their own self-regarding propensities; a task which is fulfilled in so far as Smith was able to state that all societies feature certain general rules of justice and morality; rules which in effect express accepted patterns of behaviour, or 'values', which may be taken as data, at least at some point in time. Smith was careful to argue in this connection that accepted rules were in effect the by-product of our ability to frame judgements in particular cases:

> It is thus that the general rules of morality are formed. They are ultimately founded upon experience of what, in particular instances, our moral faculties, our natural sense of merit and propriety, approve, or disapprove of. We do not originally approve or condemn particular actions; because, upon examination, they appear to be agreeable or inconsistent with a certain general rule. The general rule, on the contrary, is formed, by finding from experience, that all actions of a certain kind, or circumstanced in a certain manner, are approved or disapproved of.
>
> (TMS III.4.8)

The argument has a number of interesting features, four of which may be noticed here. First, there is the weight of emphasis which Smith gave to self-regarding (not necessarily selfish) motives; indeed he argued that 'regard to our own private happiness and interest' were often 'very laudable principles of action' and went on to suggest that: 'Carelessness and want of economy are universally disapproved of, not, however, as proceeding from a want of benevolence, but from a want of the proper attention to the subjects of self-interest' (TMS VII.ii.3.16).

Secondly, it is interesting that Smith should have drawn so careful a distinction between the rules of justice and other rules of morality, in arguing that our ability to perceive and conform to the latter represents a higher level of moral experience than the former. At the same time, however, he made it clear that justice is the minimum condition which must be satisfied if any organized social grouping is to be possible. Beneficence thus emerges as the 'ornament which embellishes, not the foundation which supports, the building' whereas:

> Justice, on the contrary, is the main pillar that upholds the whole edifice. If it is removed, the great, the immense fabric of human society, that fabric which to raise and support seems in this world, if I may say so, to have been the peculiar and darling care of Nature, must in a moment crumble into atoms.
>
> (TMS II.ii.3.4)

Thirdly, while Smith makes much of our desire to attain the approval of our fellows, and to be worthy of that approval, in explaining our willingness (in general) to observe the rules of justice and morality, he also links this desire to many other activities, including the economic. Thus, for example, he remarked that the 'rich man glories in his riches, because he feels that they naturally draw upon him the attention of the world' (TMS I.iii.2.1) and went on to note that:

> Though it is in order to supply the necessities and conveniences of the body, that the advantages of external fortune are originally recommended to us, yet we cannot live long in the world without perceiving that the respect of our equals, our credit and rank in the society we live in, depend very much upon the degree in which we possess, or are supposed to possess, those advantages.
>
> (TMS IV.i.3)

In short, Smith suggests that in some spheres of activity we are likely to be motivated by a desire, not necessarily for ease and tranquillity, but for that particular form of pleasure which comes from the attainment of social status. For what, he inquired, 'are the advantages which we propose by that great purpose of human life which we call bettering our condition? To be observed, to be attended to, to be taken notice of with sympathy, complacency, and approbation, are all the advantages which we can propose to derive from it' (I.iii.2.1). Smith went on to suggest that the means to this end, namely the qualities of prudence and frugality, were themselves 'apprehended to be very praiseworthy qualities, which deserve the esteem and approbation of everybody' (VII.ii.3.16), and indeed that it is 'the consciousness of this merited approbation and esteem which *alone* is capable of supporting the agent in this tenor of conduct' (IV.i.2.8, italics supplied).

Finally, it is worth noting one further distinctive feature of the TMS, namely, that while Smith ascribes a central role to the rules of justice and morality, he does not seek to define their content in anything other than the most general terms. The point is, of course, that since these rules are represented as the products of our experience it follows that they may vary with that experience; a point which drew from Edmund Burke the perceptive comment that: 'A theory like yours, founded on the nature of man, which is always the same, will last, when those that are founded upon his opinions, which are always changing, will and must be forgotten' (Letter 38 addressed to Smith, dated 10 September 1759).

Smith's was an age dominated by consciousness of the variety of human experience and it is significant that, in addressing himself to this problem and to the wider problem of historical change, Montesquieu should have exerted so important an influence. As Millar told Dugald Stewart, in the third part of his lectures, Smith

> treated at more length of that branch of Morality which relates to *Justice*, and which, being susceptible of precise and accurate rules, is for that reason capable of a full and particular explanation.
>
> Upon this subject he followed the plan that seems to be suggested by Montesquieu; endeavouring to trace the gradual progress of jurisprudence, both public and private, from the rudest to the most refined ages, and to point out the effect of those arts which contribute to the subsistence, and to the accumulation of property, in producing correspondent improvements or alterations in law and government.
>
> (Stewart, I.19)

It was in this connection that Smith developed his four-stage theory of economic development (hunting, pasture, agriculture, commerce); a theory which is probably at its most successful in explaining the transition from the destruction of Rome to the emergence of the exchange economy, with its more liberal patterns of social dependence and distribution of political power.

The links between Smith's economic analysis and the other areas of his thought need not be laboured and are probably obvious enough. It can be plausibly argued, for example, that in the WN Smith was concerned with a particular institutional framework, namely the exchange economy or 'commercial' stage, where productive activity was characterized by the division of labour and featured the use of three distinct factors of production (land, labour, capital). As far as the TMS is concerned, it is equally plausible to suggest that Smith's economic analysis presupposes some degree of social order and that it takes as one of its essential premises the minimum condition required, namely justice. At the same time it is evident that the WN employs at least a part of the psychology set out in the older work, especially with regard to the drive to better our condition, and the associated (morally approved) virtues of prudence and frugality.

IV

Points such as those which we have just noticed are useful, perhaps, in that they remind us of the degree of abstraction involved in Smith's formal economics, where he was concerned with a part only of the range of experience which had been delineated in the TMS and in his (historical) work on jurisprudence. This was unquestionably a conscious act on Smith's part. It is also one which represents a considerable intellectual achievement in its own right, while possessing a certain historical significance in that it helped to confirm the differentiation of economics from other studies. Since Smith's contribution to individual areas of economic analysis are examined at some length in the second part of this book it would be inappropriate to devote any significant amount of space to them here. But perhaps two points should be noticed.

To begin with, it is of course entirely proper to examine Smith's economic work in terms of his contributions to a number of separate problems, such as the theory of value or economic growth. Yet at the same time it is now widely recognized that a major source of Smith's originality lies in the fact that he succeeded in producing a systematic treatise which made it possible to grasp the interconnection between a number of separate problems such as price, allocation, or distribution, and thus the interdependence of economic phenomena. It was in part the recognition of this point that prompted Dugald Stewart to remark that:

> Besides the principles which Mr. Smith considered as more peculiarly his own, his *Inquiry* exhibits a systematical view of the most important articles of Political Economy, so as to serve the purpose of an elementary treatise on that very extensive and difficult science. The skill and the comprehensiveness of mind displayed in his arrangement, can be judged of by those alone who have compared it with that adopted by his immediate predecessors. And perhaps, in point of utility, the labour he has employed in collecting and methodising their scattered ideas, is not less valuable than the results of his own original speculations: for it is only when digested in a clear and natural order, that truths make their proper impression on the mind, and that erroneous opinions can be combated with success.
>
> (Stewart, IV.27)

On the other hand it would be misleading to concentrate on Smith's theoretical economics to the exclusion of all else since it is obviously true that the WN was also concerned with matters of policy. Thus, for example, Smith's emphasis on the importance of the activities of individuals working within a competitive environment led to the conclusion that they should work in freedom from the impertinent regulations of the state if the maximum benefit was to be obtained. The state emerged as being ideally responsible only for essential services such as justice, defence, and those public works which could never repay the expense of any individual or small number of individuals. Such services must, Smith insisted, be organized in such a way as to take account of the basic (self-interested) principles of human nature in this sphere, and designed to create an environment which would best enable the people to better their condition, by virtue of their own efforts. Simple as it is, the programme of action is quite ingenious when looked at from one point of view; ingenious in that the discussion of the public sector and of the principles on which public goods should be provided is essentially part of Smith's economic model and quite consistent with its premises.

But, of course, Smith went much further than this and in ways which often remind us of his awareness of the complexities of other areas of experience. For example, he was well aware of the interplay between past, present, and future, and often pointed out that institutions frequently outlast their usefulness and that they may thus become constraints on the present. In this connection he cited a large number of examples such as the laws of primogeniture and entail, the statute of apprenticeship, the poor laws, and the privileges of corporations. In almost all these cases Smith felt able to state that they were unjust in that they infringed the liberty of the subject, and *impolitic* in that they impeded the effective working of the economy. In the same vein Smith objected to current mercantile policy, and its chief engine, monopoly power, in calling for nothing less than a reform of national policy—again with the object of freeing individuals from restraint and regulation and with a view to improving economic welfare (as measured by the level of real income per head).

Yet, as a student of history and of politics, Smith was well aware that such programmes of reform are rarely if ever fully acted upon and he noted that to 'expect, indeed, that the freedom of trade should ever be entirely restored in Great Britain, is as absurd as to expect that an Oceana or Utopia should ever be established in it' (WN IV.ii.43).

Smith clearly recognized the inherent difficulties of the tasks which governments must face before the 'obvious and simple system' of perfect liberty was established—and also made the point that governments in a mercantile state such as Great Britain were likely to be subject to a good deal of sectional (economic) pressure. For all that he showed considerable confidence in the type of socio-economic system currently manifested in Britain, at least from the standpoint of economic growth, arguing as he did that the system of liberty and security established at the revolution of 1688 had made it possible for individuals effectively to pursue the drive to better their condition, and thus overcome the 'impertinent obstructions with which the folly of human laws too often encumbers its operations' (WN IV.v.b.43).

From other points of view Smith is known to have sounded a more cautionary note, particularly with regard to the social consequences of the division of labour; an institution on which the process of economic growth largely depended, and yet one which at the same time caused 'mental mutilation' by adversely affecting the intellectual powers and sensibilities of the individual. The point was almost a commonplace among many of Smith's friends and is repeated in a variety of forms in the works of Lord Kames, Adam Ferguson, and John Millar, to name but three. But Smith's statement is perhaps particularly striking, partly because as an economist he had already made so much of the institution, and partly because it is as a moralist that the real importance of his argument emerges. For Smith was in effect suggesting that unless steps were taken to prevent it, the large mass of mankind might well acquire great material benefits on the one hand, and, on the other, decline in their ability to exercise those faculties and propensities such as reason, imagination, and fellow-feeling, on which the process of moral judgement depended and on which moral experience must rest. Such points can be multiplied to an extent which makes it reasonable to assert that if the WN contains the basis of modern economics, it also embraces a much wider subject for which Smith's other writings are a necessary preparation.

A.S.S.

I

Adam Smith's Lectures on Rhetoric: an Historical Assessment*

WILBUR SAMUEL HOWELL

BEFORE the summer of 1958, historians of eighteenth-century British rhetoric were unable to connect Adam Smith with the drastic changes that took place in rhetorical theory in Britain during the 1700s. They knew that Smith delivered a course of lectures on rhetoric in Edinburgh during the fall and winter of 1748–9, and that, according to some authorities, he repeated those lectures at the same place and during the same seasons in 1749–50 and 1750–1.[1] They also knew that Smith continued to deliver those lectures, or revisions of them, as part of his duties as professor of logic and later as professor of moral philosophy at the University of Glasgow from October 1751 to December 1763. But Smith's biographers had made it clear to everyone that, as he saw death draw near, he gave orders to have all his papers destroyed, except for some which he judged ready for publication, and that two of his friends accordingly burned sixteen volumes of his manuscripts, the lectures on rhetoric among them.[2] That event has been a source of frustration for all students of Smith's influential career, but it was particularly damaging to the attempt of historians of British rhetoric to evaluate in any substantial way what Smith may have contributed to their subject. They were to have no choice, it appeared, but to confine themselves to what Smith's contemporaries had said about his rhetorical theory and to leave unanswered the question of his connection with the changes which that theory was undergoing in his lifetime.

Unsatisfactory as that situation was, it seemed upon examination to fall short of being completely hopeless. Three unusually well-qualified witnesses among Smith's contemporaries had taken pains to make written comments

* Professor of Rhetoric and Oratory, Emeritus, at Princeton University. This essay first appeared in *Speech Monographs*, xxxvi (Nov. 1969), 393–418. It was later published as a section of Chapter 6 in its author's book, *Eighteenth-Century British Logic and Rhetoric* (1971).

[1] See Alexander Fraser Tytler, *Memoirs of the Life and Writings of the Honourable Henry Home of Kames* (1814), i.266; also John Rae, *Life of Adam Smith* (1895), 30, 36. William Robert Scott, *Adam Smith as Student and Professor* (1937), 50–5, considered Smith's lectures in 1750–1 to be on jurisprudence instead of rhetoric, but, of course, Smith might have given both courses of lectures in that last year at Edinburgh.

[2] Rae, 32, 434. See also Francis W. Hirst, *Adam Smith* (1904), 19.

upon his lectures on rhetoric, and their testimony was readily available to all scholars. Those three contemporaries were John Millar, James Wodrow, and Hugh Blair. What they had to say holds interest for any of the connections in which Smith's life could be viewed. But to all with my present interests, those three witnesses made a shadowy matter emerge in some semblance of outline.

John Millar heard Smith's original lectures on rhetoric in Edinburgh, and he heard them again during Smith's first year at Glasgow. After Smith's death in 1790, Millar gave Dugald Stewart his impressions of the Glasgow lectures, and Stewart incorporated them into his 'Account of the Life and Writings of Adam Smith, LL.D.', which he read at meetings of the Royal Society of Edinburgh on 21 January and 18 March 1793. Here are some of Millar's observations:

In the Professorship of Logic, to which Mr Smith was appointed on his first introduction into this University, he soon saw the necessity . . . of directing the attention of his pupils to studies of a more interesting and useful nature than the logic and metaphysics of the schools. Accordingly, after exhibiting a general view of the powers of the mind, and explaining so much of the ancient logic as was requisite to gratify curiosity with respect to an artificial method of reasoning . . ., he dedicated all the rest of his time to the delivery of a system of rhetoric and belles lettres. The best method of explaining and illustrating the various powers of the human mind, the most useful part of metaphysics, arises from an examination of the several ways of communicating our thoughts by speech, and from an attention to the principles of those literary compositions, which contribute to persuasion or entertainment. . . .

It is much to be regretted, that the manuscript containing Mr Smith's lectures on this subject was destroyed before his death. The first part . . . was highly finished; and the whole discovered strong marks of taste and original genius. From the permission given to students of taking notes, many observations and opinions contained in these lectures, have either been detailed in separate dissertations, or ingrossed in general collections, which have since been given to the public. But these, as might be expected, have lost the air of originality and the distinctive character which they received from their first author . . .[3]

Millar's judgement of Smith's lectures is not unlike James Wodrow's. Wodrow was serving as Library Keeper at the University of Glasgow when Smith went there to be professor of logic. In a letter written sometime after 1776 to the Earl of Buchan, Wodrow spoke thus with Smith's lectures on rhetoric at Glasgow in mind:

Adam Smith delivered a set of admirable lectures on language (not as a grammarian but as a rhetorician) on the different kinds or characteristics of style suited to different subjects, simple, nervous, etc., the structure, the natural order, the proper arrangement of the different members of the sentence etc. He

[3] *Transactions of the Royal Society of Edinburgh*, vol. iii, pt. I (1794), 61–2. Tytler, i.267, listed Millar among those who attended Smith's original lectures on rhetoric in Edinburgh.

characterised the style and the genius of some of the best of the ancient writers and poets, but especially historians, Thucydides, Polybius etc. . . ., also the style of the best English classics, Lord Clarendon, Addison, Swift, Pope, etc.; and, though his own didactic style in his last famous book (however suited to the subject)—the style of the former book was much superior—was certainly not a model for good writing, yet his remarks and rules given in the lectures I speak of, were the result of a fine taste and sound judgement, well calculated to be exceedingly useful to young composers, so that I have often regretted that some part of them has never been published.[4]

As for Hugh Blair, he, like Millar, heard Smith's original lectures on rhetoric in Edinburgh and, like Millar and Wodrow, made a comment upon the content of the manuscript from which the lectures issued. His comment appeared first in 1783 in the earliest edition of his own *Lectures on Rhetoric and Belles Lettres* in a footnote connected with his discussion of the plain style:

On this head, of the General Characters of Style, particularly, the Plain and the Simple, and the characters of those English authors who are classed under them, in this, and the following Lecture, several ideas have been taken from a manuscript treatise on rhetoric, part of which was shewn to me, many years ago, by the learned and ingenious Author, Dr. Adam Smith; and which, it is hoped, will be given by him to the Public.[5]

These testimonials are useful as a sketch of the content and value of Smith's lectures on rhetoric, even if they are so generalized as to prevent us from judging whether Smith's approach was definitely anti-traditional. They certainly suggest that the lectures were important. Nevertheless, Francis Hirst spoke disparagingly of them in his book on Smith in the series devoted to English men of letters. After noting that the manuscript of the lectures was destroyed shortly before Smith's death, Hirst loftily concluded that 'the world is probably not much the poorer' (Hirst, 19). These words are particularly unimaginative in the light of Hirst's own lively account of the way in which a student notebook containing a transcript of Smith's other lectures at Glasgow in 1762–3 on the subject of justice, police, revenue, and arms had been recovered from an attic in 1876 by Charles Maconochie and published at Oxford in 1896 under the editorship of Edwin Cannan, after having been regarded for more than a century as a casualty of Smith's request in 1790 that his manuscripts be burned (68–71). If the recovery and publication of that notebook were instruments, as Hirst jubilantly declared them to have been, in disposing

[4] Scott, 51–2. Wodrow's reference to Smith's 'last famous book' dates his letter after the publication in 1776 of *The Wealth of Nations*.

[5] (1783), i.381. Tytler, i.267, listed Blair as a member of Smith's audience when the lectures on rhetoric were first delivered in Edinburgh. See also Robert M. Schmitz, *Hugh Blair* (1948), 20.

of the legend 'that Adam Smith was little more than a borrower from the French school, a mere reflector of the Reflexions of Turgot' (71), might not Hirst have deemed it possible that the discovery of a student notebook containing a transcript of Smith's lectures on rhetoric could become instruments in disposing of the legend that Smith's opinions on this subject were almost worthless?

At any rate, that possibility existed, and it became a reality as the year 1958 was advancing from summer to autumn. The scholar responsible for bringing this reality about was John M. Lothian, Reader in English in the University of Aberdeen, and one-time professor of English literature in the University of Saskatchewan. In the newspaper, *The Scotsman*, for Wednesday 1 November 1961, under the headline, 'Long-Lost MSS. of Adam Smith/Literature lectures found in Aberdeen', Lothian announced his discovery of a notebook containing a student's transcript of Adam Smith's lectures on rhetoric. Here is part of what Lothian wrote on that occasion:

> It was with a kind of solemn jubilation that I realised, in the later summer of 1958, that certain volumes of manuscripts, which I had purchased at the sale of books from a manor house in Aberdeenshire, were indeed the long-lost lectures on Rhetoric and Belles-Lettres of the great Adam Smith, which his friends had frequently urged him to publish and which he had been so resolutely determined to destroy.

In that article in *The Scotsman*, Lothian also announced the discovery of another student notebook containing a more detailed transcript of the lectures which Cannan had edited in 1896 from the notebook recovered by Maconochie; and he indicated that his findings made a very considerable addition to the known corpus of Smith's writings. 'Between 70 and 80 thousand words of Adam Smith's hitherto unknown lectures on literature,' he declared, 'and about 170,000 of a new version of his views on the philosophy of history, law, and economics, had suddenly become available for the student and the scholar, and would certainly be put to use by all those in any way interested in the man and his period.' Jacob Viner has calculated that this new version of Smith's lectures on philosophy, law, and economics contains 'substantially over 50 per cent more matter' than did the version edited by Cannan.[6] But its discovery, even so, is not likely to yield richer results than those which we can expect from Lothian's discovery of a really substantial version of Smith's lectures on rhetoric.

Lothian himself as the first scholar to put this latter discovery to use achieved mixed results. In 1963 he brought out an excellent edition of Smith's lectures on rhetoric as they were recorded in the transcript which a student in the University of Glasgow had presumably made when he

[6] See his 'Guide to John Rae's *Life of Adam Smith*', 11, published as the Introduction to the facsimile reprint (1965) of the 1895 edition of Rae's *Life*.

heard Smith deliver them in the academic year 1762–3.[7] But Lothian's attempt in the introduction to that edition to evaluate Smith's contribution to rhetorical theory fell considerably short of success. So far as it supplies an account of the Scottish milieu in which Smith's lectures were delivered, it performs a necessary service for scholars interested in Smith's life and in British rhetoric. But it gives no adequate insight into the nature and quality of Smith's work with rhetorical theory. If Lothian had interpreted Smith's lectures as the outcome of immediately previous developments in British rhetoric and logic, he would have seen that a new view of rhetoric had been gaining headway in Britain in the century before 1748, thanks to such effective critics of the old rhetoric as Boyle, Sprat, and Locke;[8] and he would have been forced to conclude that Adam Smith's lectures gave that new rhetoric its earliest and most independent expression. A judgement of this kind could not have been substantiated at any time before 1958, but it can be substantiated now, and Lothian, who edited the materials on which it rests, was not aware that it should be pronounced.[9]

My present purpose being to set forth the facts which support this judgement, I shall proceed first to clarify the relation of Smith's lectures to his own life and to the cultural life of Scotland.

Smith entered the University of Glasgow in 1737 at the age of fourteen and graduated with great distinction as master of arts in 1740 (Scott, 36, 136–7, 392). For the next six years he held the Snell Fellowship at Oxford, where he was a member of Balliol College, his studies being mainly in the field of Greek, Latin, French, Italian, and English literature (Rae, 22–4; Scott, 40, 42). His future plans as of that time could have been deduced from the terms of the Snell Fellowship; it required its Scottish beneficiaries to prepare at Oxford to take orders in the Church of England under the solemn promise that they would later become practising clergymen only in Scotland (Scott, 42–3). But something caused Smith to change those plans and to return to Scotland in 1746 with at least four years of his Fellowship still unexpended.

[7] Lothian's work is entitled *Lectures on Rhetoric and Belles Lettres Delivered in the University of Glasgow by Adam Smith Reported by a Student in 1762–1763* (1963).

[8] See Robert Boyle, *Some Considerations Touching the Style of the H. Scriptures* (1663), 147–247; Thomas Sprat, *The History of the Royal-Society of London* (1667), 61–2, 111–15; and three articles of mine, 'The Plough and the Flail: The Ordeal of Eighteenth-Century Logic', *The Huntington Library Quarterly*, xxviii (1964–5), 63–78; 'John Locke and the New Rhetoric', *The Quarterly Journal of Speech*, liii (1967), 319–33; 'John Locke and the New Logic' in *Action and Conviction in Early Modern Europe: Essays in Memory of E. H. Harbison*, ed. T. K. Rabb and J. E. Seigel (1969), 423–52.

[9] For three other appraisals of Smith's lectures on rhetoric, see Vincent M. Bevilacqua, 'Adam Smith's Lectures on Rhetoric and Belles Lettres', *Studies in Scottish Literature*, iii (1965–6), 41–60; Frank Morgan, Jr., 'Adam Smith and Belles Lettres' (Unpubl. diss., 1966)—described in *Dissertation Abstracts*, xxvii (1967), 3846A; Vincent M. Bevilacqua, 'Adam Smith and Some Philosophical Origins of Eighteenth-Century Rhetorical Theory', *The Modern Language Review*, lxiii (1968), 559–68.

From 1746 to 1748 he lived quietly with his mother at Kirkcaldy, thinking no doubt that he would one day acquire a professorship in a Scottish university or gain employment as tutor and travelling companion of a nobleman's son (Rae, 30). In that period he made the acquaintance of Henry Home, who in 1752 would become Lord Kames. Kames had visions of creating in Scotland a growing community of speakers and writers of distinguished and correct English, and he was so far successful on the literary side of this aspiration as to have Adam Smith say later of the famous Scottish authors of the generation to which Smith himself belonged that 'we must every one of us acknowledge Kames for our master' (Tytler, i.218, 219–66). It was Kames who, having been made aware of Smith's six-year residence at Oxford and of his accomplishments in ancient and modern literature, proposed that Smith deliver a course of public lectures in English on rhetoric and belles-lettres for the benefit of any interested students at the University of Edinburgh and for the improvement of literary taste among any subscribing citizens of the surrounding city. Lectures on literary subjects were of course being delivered regularly at that time in the University, and John Stevenson, who was an early Scottish disciple of Locke and the teacher of Dugald Stewart, made literary subjects a part of his academic course in logic, as Smith was later to do at Glasgow, and William Barron at St. Andrews.[10] But Stevenson's lectures were not available to the townsmen of Edinburgh, and besides, like most academic discourses of that time and place, they were pronounced in Latin.[11] Thus to Kames they would probably not have been considered competitors of the English lectures which would be needed if Scotland were to become the centre of correct English speech and style. At any rate, Kames, in association with James Oswald and Robert Craigie, two other friends of Smith, joined in urging Smith to deliver a course of public lectures on rhetoric and belles-lettres, and he yielded to their solicitations (Scott, 48).

His lectures were accordingly delivered in the late fall and winter of 1748–9, as I said above; and they were probably not held at a location within the University, as Rae thought, but at the quarters of the Philosophical Society of Edinburgh (Scott, 49–50; Rae, 32). This Society, which had been founded in 1731, and which numbered Kames among its members, did not hold regular meetings during the years in which Smith delivered his Edinburgh lectures, and thus its quarters would have been open to such events as the lectures represented.[12] Students of law like John Millar, lawyers and sponsors of an improved English speech like Kames and

[10] For an account of Stevenson's academic course at Edinburgh, see *The Scots Magazine*, iii (1741), 373. See also Alexander Bower, *The History of the University of Edinburgh* (1817–30), ii.269–81.

[11] Bower, ii.275. See also Thomas Somerville, *My Own Life and Times 1741–1814* (1861), 12–14.

[12] Tytler, i.256–9. This Society grew into The Royal Society of Edinburgh.

Alexander Wedderburn, students of theology and rising young preachers like Hugh Blair, present and future members of parliament like James Oswald and William Johnstone, and various other groups interested in matters of literary taste and fashion, made up the audience of some hundred or more persons to whom Smith lectured that first year (Tytler, i.266–7; Rae, 32; Scott, 46). His discourses were a financial and literary success, and he repeated them during the fall and winter of one and possibly both of the two following years.

They contributed to his own career by leading directly to his appointment in 1751 to the professorship of logic and in 1752 to the professorship of moral philosophy at Glasgow, these two positions being flexible enough to allow him to continue his lectures on rhetoric and belles-lettres in connection with the subjects which his academic titles required him to teach. But they also contributed a new institution to the cultural life of Edinburgh. That is to say, they led to Robert Watson's being named to continue the public lectures on rhetoric after Smith departed for Glasgow, and to Hugh Blair's assignment to the same duties after Watson departed for St. Andrews (Tytler, i.272–5; Schmitz, 62–3). And they led as well to Hugh Blair's later appointment as professor of rhetoric and belles-lettres at the University of Edinburgh. In other words, after having been instituted as a course of extra-academic lectures in English on the subject of rhetoric, they so far proved their value as to lead the University to give a place in its curriculum within a few years to what had grown out of them. While this new development was taking place, John Stevenson is said to have protested against it on the ground that Hugh Blair was usurping a function that had long been performed within his own course in logic.[13] His complaint had some foundation, of course, but in 1760 he was sixty-five years old, and the educational reforms which he had introduced as a youth were becoming obsolete. Thus his case against Blair was not strong enough to carry the day.

Even though Lothian's edition of the student notebook brings us much closer to Smith's actual accomplishments as a rhetorician than we have ever been before, we must keep in mind that it does not enable us to speak with finality of this part of his career or even to be sure that a given opinion ascribed to him in the notebook is his. Here are the difficulties. First, there is a possibility that our student will have distorted Smith's opinions by condensation or will have made errors in hearing and recording what Smith said. Secondly, there is a possibility that our student would have turned his notes over to an unknown copyist, and that what Lothian edited is not what the student heard and recorded, but what the copyist found implied in the student's notes. Thirdly, there is a possibility that the notebook will be occasionally misinterpreted by a modern scholar seeking to make it suitable for publication. And lastly, there is a possibility that a course of

[13] *The Scots Magazine*, lxiv (1802), 22.

lectures pronounced in any given year of a professor's academic career will be lower in quality than that course in earlier or later years, and that Smith's lectures in his penultimate year at Glasgow may not have represented him at his best.[14] But when we have acknowledged that each of these limitations may weaken our evaluations of his rhetorical theory to an unknown and incalculable degree, we still have to try to make them anyway, recognizing as we must that Smith was a man of real genius, that he actually lectured on rhetoric, that his contemporaries were impressed by his lectures, and that at last we have access to a substantial and no doubt largely accurate version of what he said. Under these circumstances we shall proceed to pass judgement upon Smith's theory of rhetoric as best we can, and to see whether he made as large a contribution to the development of the new rhetoric as I just now said he did.

One important statement should be made once more about these particular lectures: Smith intended them, not as discourses on ancient and modern literature, but as discourses to expound a system of rhetoric. He made this point clear as he was lecturing on the tropes and figures. After taking the grammarians to task for arguing that these contrivances of language are the cause of any stylistic beauty that a literary work may have, Smith spoke as follows:

> It is, however, from the consideration of these figures, and divisions and subdivisions of them, that so many systems of rhetoric, both ancient and modern, have been formed. They are generally a very silly set of books and not at all instructive. However, as it would be reckoned strange in a system of rhetoric entirely to pass by these figures that have so much exercised the wits of men, we shall offer a few observations on them, though not on the same plan as the ordinary writers proceed on.
>
> (LRBL 6.4; Lothian, 23–4)

The significance of these words is that they add Smith's authority to that of Millar, Wodrow, and Blair in identifying rhetoric as the subject of his lectures.

In the twentieth century, rhetoric has so far lost its respectability as to be thought an unseemly study for a first-rate mind. Accordingly, Smith's modern admirers have often felt constrained to retitle the lectures under consideration here. Thus Rae and Hirst spoke of Smith's first discourses at Edinburgh as 'lectures on English literature' (Rae, 36; Hirst, 19). Scott said that 'the subjects of the Edinburgh lectures may be taken, at least provisionally, to have been two courses on Literature and Literary Criticism, followed by a final course on Jurisprudence' (Scott, 51). Lothian, who as a rule uses 'rhetoric' to characterize the subject of these lectures,

[14] For a most thoughtful analysis of the problems confronting Lothian in his edition of Smith's *Lectures on Rhetoric and Belles Lettres*, see Ernest C. Mossner's review of that work in *Studies in Scottish Literature*, ii (1964–5), 199–208.

and who says that the two volumes of the notebook containing them 'carried on the spine of each volume in neat hand-writing the inscription, "Notes of Dr. Smith's Rhetorick Lectures"', nevertheless refers in his article in *The Scotsman* to 'Adam Smith's hitherto unknown lectures on literature', and on another occasion he quotes Smith's remark that elaborate treatises on the figures are silly and not at all instructive, but he omits that part of the passage in which Smith identifies his subject as rhetoric (Lothian, xii–xxxii). Finally, Ernest C. Mossner, in his review of Lothian's edition, says that '"Dr. Smith's Rhetorick Lectures", as they were called by the copyist, might with some justice be called Lectures *against* Rhetoric, taking rhetoric as the ancient logic of multiplicity of divisions and sub-divisions.'[15]

But despite modern opinions to the contrary, the historian of rhetoric is forced to insist that the tradition of a respectable and learned rhetoric flourished in the 1700s, and that Smith not only identified himself with it but also through his efforts sought to bring it into partnership with the needs of his day. His 'antirhetoric' is therefore not in truth the opposite of rhetoric, but the very essence of rhetoric as he conceived of it in its modern form.

One other important thing has now to be said about Smith's lectures: he brought rhetoric and belles-lettres together, not in line with the plan of previous writers like Rapin, Bouhours, and Rollin, but on a plan quite his own.

Rapin had conceived of rhetoric as that branch of the belles-lettres which taught how to compose traditional orations or how to judge the classical orations of such masters as Cicero and Demosthenes; and in his view, rhetoric is what it had been in the systems of Aristotle and the major Latin rhetoricians.[16]

Bouhours had considered logic and rhetoric to be the disciplines associated with the composition and criticism of all literary works, with logic the guide to thought, and rhetoric, to style.[17] This position, of course, is vaguely Ramistic, although Bouhours hardly did more than suggest to the initiated that Ramus's way of separating logic from rhetoric was an influence upon him.

[15] *Studies in Scottish Literature*, ii (1964–5), 206.

[16] See René Rapin, *Les Comparaisons des grands hommes de l'antiquité, qui ont le plus excellé dans les belles lettres*, and *Les Rèflexions sur l'éloquence, la poétique, l'histoire, et la philosophie. Avec le judgement qu'on doit faire des auteurs qui se sont signalez, dans ces quatre parties des belles lettres* (1684). (Translated into English and published in London in 1706 as *The Whole Critical Works of Monsieur Rapin.*)

[17] See Dominique Bouhours, *La Manière de bien penser dans les ouvrages d'esprit* (1687). (Published in an English translation in London in 1705 as *The Art of Criticism*, and in London in 1728 as *The Arts of Logick and Rhetorick*, the latter translation being the work of John Oldmixon.) For Bouhours's distinction between logic and rhetoric, see *La Manière de bien penser dans les ouvrages d'esprit* (1715), vi.

As for Rollin, he had regarded rhetoric as one of the five components of the belles-lettres, its purpose being the preparation of students for careers at the bar or in the pulpit, and its means, the study of the precepts of classical rhetoric, the assiduous practice of composition, and the thorough mastery of literary works renowned for eloquence.[18] In other words, he, like Rapin, was essentially an eighteenth-century Ciceronian, even if he especially admired Cicero's most famous disciple, Quintilian.

Adam Smith's system of rhetoric and belles-lettres differs in at least two ways from those just mentioned. First, he made rhetoric the general theory of all branches of literature—the historical, the poetical, the didactic or scientific, and the oratorical. And secondly, he constructed that general theory, not by adopting in a reverential spirit the entire rhetorical doctrine of Aristotle, or Quintilian, or Ramus, but by selecting from previous rhetorics what he considered valid for his own generation, and by adding fresh insights of his own whenever he saw the need to do so. As a result, his system of rhetoric is on the one hand more comprehensive and on the other hand more independent than are those of his French predecessors.

Lothian is right in observing that Smith's lectures on rhetoric 'were the first of their kind, as far as we know, to be given in Great Britain' (xxiii). But he errs when he qualifies this observation by adding, 'though something similar had been given by Rollin in the University of Paris'. Rollin's lectures at Paris have their parallel in Great Britain, not in Adam Smith's lectures at Glasgow, but in John Ward's lectures at Gresham College.[19] Like Rollin, Ward was dedicated to the rhetoric of Cicero and Quintilian. But Adam Smith, as I said earlier, was dedicated to the rhetoric of Boyle, Sprat, and Locke. Between his outlook and that of Rollin were the differences which divide the modern from the ancient rhetoric. And those differences become fully visible for the first time in the history of rhetorical theory when we study Adam Smith's rhetoric in detail and see how far he was justified in saying that he was not following 'the same plan as the ordinary writers proceed on'. Let us now inspect the extraordinary plan that he chose to follow instead.

In that course at Glasgow in 1762–3, Smith delivered thirty lectures on rhetoric and belles-lettres. The first lecture is unhappily not recorded in our student's notebook, and therefore, in undertaking to assign terms to the major subjects discussed in the series as a whole, we cannot take advantage of any hints that Smith's introductory discourse would have made in this direction. The other twenty-nine lectures, however, may reasonably be said to fall under one or the other of two heads of doctrine. We could give

[18] For Rollin's lectures on rhetoric, see Charles Rollin, *De la manière d'enseigner et d'etudier les belles lettres* (1726–8), ii. (Translated into English and published in London in 1734, this work went through ten editions in Britain in the eighteenth century.)

[19] See John Ward, *A System of Oratory* (1759).

titles to these heads by using the terms proposed for them by Millar, but in the interests of brevity and precision I propose that we use the term 'communication' and the term 'forms of discourse' to identify them. To the subject of 'communication' Smith devoted ten lectures, and to that of the 'forms of discourse', nineteen. As we proceed to discuss the lectures dealing with each of these subjects, what I said a moment ago will become increasingly clear. In other words, it will be seen that Smith was not attempting to look at rhetoric through the eyes of Aristotle, Cicero, and Quintilian, although he could have expounded their doctrine adequately if he had wanted to do so. What he did instead was to see rhetoric not only as the theoretical instrument for the communication of ideas in the world which Locke had done so much to render intelligible to itself, but also as the study of the structure and function of all the discourses which ideas produce as they seek passage from person to person and from age to age. If Adam Smith drew his rhetorical system from the past, he drew it from the past which is always seeking to prepare for the future rather than from the past which is always seeking to preserve itself against change.

The ten lectures devoted by Smith to the first of his major subjects make two significant points about rhetoric. One is that communication is the fundamental process that rhetoric studies. The ancients had made persuasion the goal of rhetorical discourse, and Smith did not set out to quarrel openly with that particular way of formulating the end sought by oratory and its companion forms of literary composition. He proceeded instead to stress repeatedly that discourse takes place in order to transfer ideas and attitudes from speaker to audience. Thus his system of rhetoric takes the position that persuasive discourse is the species, and communicative discourse the genus, in the classification of the functions of literature, and that persuasion is to be understood more properly as a subordinate than as a generic function, if rhetoric is to achieve its true status among the learned disciplines. The other significant point made by Smith in the ten lectures is that the only acceptable modern style for a rhetoric committed to the goal of communication is the plain style. John Locke would have particularly approved of this point and of the one which defined rhetoric in terms of its communicative function. Indeed, Locke himself made analogous points about the art of speaking.[20] Let us now turn to Smith's ten lectures in order to see how far he develops these two points as continuing themes. We shall find that he develops them, not as separate propositions, but as different aspects of the same proposition.

In the second, and again in the sixth, the seventh, the eighth, and the eleventh lectures, Smith took pains to state and repeat the doctrine that discourses have communication as their main function and plainness of

[20] For details, see my article, 'John Locke and the New Rhetoric', *The Quarterly Journal of Speech*, liii (1967), 328–30.

style as their chief means. He introduced this doctrine in connection with his discussion of such other subjects as perspicuity, the tropes and figures of speech, and the practices of modern English authors.[21] Perhaps his best statement of the doctrine occurred in his sixth lecture, as he was preparing to treat the tropes and figures, those immensely popular ingredients of traditional rhetoric. As he approached them, he observed that they came into being whenever 'an expression is used in a different way from the common' (LRBL 6.5; Lothian, 24). By this he meant, of course, that the tropes and figures are so many repudiations of the ordinary ways of saying things; they are examples of the plain style in reverse. Recalling that the traditional rhetoricians like Cicero and Quintilian had found in these figures 'all the beauties of language, all that is noble, grand, and sublime, all that is passionate, tender, and moving', Smith offered the following comment:

> But the case is far otherwise. When the sentiment of the speaker is expressed in a neat, clear, plain, and clever manner, and the passion or affection he is poss[ess]ed of and intends, *by sympathy*, to communicate to his hearer, is plainly and cleverly hit off, then and then only the expression has all the force and beauty that language can give it. It matters not the least whether the figures of speech are introduced or not.
>
> (LRBL 6.2; Lothian, 22–3)[22]

At this point, our student's notebook has an insertion which contains an alternative statement of the passage just cited, as if Smith had said it in one way in one year, and in another way in another year, with the result that our student had access to two versions of it and chose to include both to emphasize the importance that Smith attached to the doctrine involved. The insertion reads as follows:

> When your language expresses perspicuously and neatly your meaning and what you would express, together with the sentiment or affection this matter inspires you with, and when the sentiment is nobler and more beautiful than such as are commonly met with, then your language has all the beauty it can have, and the figures of speech contribute or can contribute towards it only so far as they happen to be the just and natural forms of expressing that sentiment.
>
> (6.2; Lothian, 23)

Still another form of this doctrine concerning the communicative function of discourse and the consequent necessity of plainness in style occurs in the eighth lecture, and on this occasion both sides of the doctrine are stressed once more, as they were in the earlier of the two passages just quoted:

[21] See the following passages of LRBL: 2.11; 6.2; 7.1; 8.1; 11.1. Lothian, 4 (lines 25–9), 22 (lines 26ff.), 29 (lines 10–16), 36 (lines 1–8), and 51 (lines 1–8).

[22] The bracketed syllable is Lothian's. Unless otherwise noted, the use of brackets follows Lothian's usage.

Having in the foregoing lecture made some observations on tropes and figures, and endeavoured to show that it was not in their use, as the ancient rhetoricians imagined, that the beauties of style consisted, I pointed out what it was that really gave beauty to style, that when the words neatly and properly expressed the thing to be described, and conveyed the sentiment the author entertained of it and desired to communicate to his hearers, then the expression had all the beauty language was capable of bestowing on it.

(8.1; Lothian, 36)

And in the eleventh lecture, Smith once again laid stress upon the communicative function and the plain style of rhetoric, as he was about to enter upon his analysis of the second of the two major heads of his rhetorical system. He said:

In some of our former lectures we have given a character of some of the best English prose writers, and made comparisons betwixt their different manners. The result of all which, as well as the rules we have laid down, is that the perfection of style consists in express[ing] in the most concise, proper, and precise manner the thought of the author, and that in the manner which best conveys the sentiment, passion, or affection with which it affects—or he pretends it does affect—him, and which he designs to communicate to his reader. This, you'll say, is no more than common sense: and indeed it is no more. But if you will attend to it, all the rules of criticism and morality, when traced to their foundation, turn out to be some principles of common sense which every one assents to: all the business of those arts is to apply these rules to the different subjects, and shew what the conclusion is when they are so applied.

(11.1; Lothian, 51)

As these words indicate, comparative comments upon English prose writers were a continuing feature of Smith's first eleven lectures. It is now time to observe that those comments enabled Smith to establish Swift as the still unappreciated but nevertheless fully qualified master of the best modern style, and to establish Lord Shaftesbury as a prime example of the writer who, though widely admired, was in fact a representative of outworn stylistic conventions. In his eighth lecture, Smith first dwelt in detail upon the differences between these two writers, although he made frequent mention of both on earlier and later occasions. The eighth lecture immediately followed those in which Smith had discussed the figures of speech and had vigorously asserted that these devices, founded as they were upon the notion that good literary style must involve a systematic repudiation of the ways of common speech, should not in fact be regarded as the indispensable conditions of stylistic beauty. With that denial fresh in his students' minds, Smith applied it to the literary fashions of their day, and he made it obvious to his hearers that the current admiration for Shaftesbury and the current disrespect for Swift merely equated stylistic beauty with figurative language and with very little else. Here are a few of his observations on these subjects:

We in this country are most of us very sensible that the perfection of language is very different from that we commonly speak in. The idea we form of a good style is almost contrary to that which we generally hear. Hence it is that we conceive the further one's style is removed from the common manner, it is so much nearer to purity and the perfection we have in view. Shaftesbury, who keeps at a vast distance from the language we commonly meet with, is for this reason universally admired . . . Swift, on the other hand, who is the plainest as well as the most proper and precise of all the English writers, is despised as nothing out of the common road: each of us thinks he would have wrote as well. And our thoughts of the language give us the same idea of the substance of his writings.

(8.7; Lothian, 38)

Smith went on to emphasize, however, that Swift was the exemplar of the modern and Shaftesbury of the outmoded style, not simply because the one avoided and the other adopted the tropes and figures, but because the one was profoundly and the other superficially learned. This point emerges only when we probe more deeply than we have done hitherto into the great contrast which Smith drew between these two writers. Shortly after he expressed the sentiments just quoted, Smith laid down the rule that a good writers must meet the following conditions: 'first, that he have a complete knowledge of his subjects; secondly, that he should arrange all the parts of his subject in their proper order; thirdly, that he paint [or] describe the ideas he has of them several in the most proper and expressive manner—this is the art of painting or imitation (at least we may call it so)' (ibid.). Then he stressed at once that Swift met these three criteria beyond question. He spoke thus in this connection:

Now we will find that Swift has attained all these perfections. All his words shew a complete knowledge of his subject. He does not, indeed, introduce anything foreign to his subject, in order to display his knowledge . . .; but then he never omits anything necessary . . . One who has such a complete knowledge of what he treats will naturally arrange it in the most proper order. This we see Swift always does . . . That he paints but each thought in the best and most proper manner, and with the greatest strength of colouring, must be visible to anyone at first sight.

(8.8–9; Lothian, 38–9)

In direct contrast to his view of Swift, Smith emphasized later that Shaftesbury's greatest defect consisted in his failure to meet the first of these three criteria. In the eleventh lecture, Smith subjected Shaftesbury to a penetrating analysis, and therein the theme recurs several times that Shaftesbury's style stems from his feeling of insecurity about his own learning. Smith mentioned that Locke was Shaftesbury's tutor, but that

Shaftesbury preferred rather to follow his own whims than to master the metaphysical profundities of his preceptor. Thus Shaftesbury cultivated the fine arts, spoke with some show but with no true distinction in both Houses of Parliament, indulged himself in the pleasures of the imagination, allowed the delicacy of his sentiments to alienate him from his bent towards Puritanism, found Hobbes and the scholastics almost equally disagreeable, and finally embraced Platonism as the main guide to what he hoped to establish as the best modern philosophy (11.5–6; Lothian, 52–4). At the same time, however, Smith noted, Shaftesbury found 'abstract reasoning and deep searches' too fatiguing for his delicate frame (11.5; Lothian, 52). Natural philosophy he did not seem 'to have been at all acquainted with'—indeed he showed 'a great ignorance of the advances it had then made, and a contempt for its followers', no doubt because 'it did not afford the amusement his disposition required, and the mathematical part particularly required more attention and abstract thought than men of his weakly habit are generally capable of' (11.5; Lothian, 53). And, after having arranged this balance sheet of Shaftesbury's liabilities and assets, Smith drew a very revealing conclusion, which deserves to be identified as a reflection of the dislike of the new rhetoric for superficiality of subject-matter and the ornate style as its necessary concomitant. He spoke thus of Shaftesbury as he was preparing to take leave of the themes of his first eleven lectures: 'As he was of no great depth in reasoning, he would be glad to set off by the ornament of language what was deficient in matter. This, with the refinement of his temper, directed [him] to make choice of a pompous, grand, and ornate style' (11.9; Lothian, 54).

In his twelfth lecture, as he took up the discussion of the forms of discourse, Smith proposed that every written composition intends either to relate some fact or to prove some proposition, in connection with its basic communicative function; and that, as a result, discourses must have one of three forms. The first form, which emerges from the attempt to relate facts, he decided to call narrative discourse. The two other forms he decided to call didactic discourse and rhetorical discourse, although on another occasion he was to change his mind and call the latter form the oratorical (12.1, 22.1; Lothian, 58, 124). Didactic discourse, he said, emerges from the attempt to prove a proposition when proof can be accomplished by putting both sides of a question before an audience, and by giving each side its true degree of influence. Rhetorical or oratorical discourse emerges from the attempt to prove a proposition when proof can be accomplished only by magnifying one side and by diminishing or concealing the other. Didactic discourse seeks conviction, rhetorical discourse, persuasion. Smith clarified this distinction thus:

Persuasion, which is the primary design in the rhetorical, is but the secondary design in the didactic. It endeavours to persuade us only so far as the strength of the argument is convincing: instruction is the main end. For the other, persuasion is the main design, and instruction is considered only so far as it is subservient to persuasion, and no further.

(12.1; Lothian, 58)

At this point Smith paused to comment upon the analogy between his three forms of discourse and the three forms of ancient oratory. But he developed the analogy in such indefinite terms as to lead us to suppose that the student's notebook may not here be an accurate guide to what he actually had in mind (12.5–7; Lothian, 59–60). It seems obvious, from his final nineteen lectures as a whole, that his classification of discourses, so far as he had thus far permitted it to emerge, is like the ancient classification of orations more by reason of its threefold structure than by reason of its actual contents and intentions. I mean that Smith intended narrative discourse to cover historical writings, and didactic discourse to cover philosophical argument and scientific exposition, while oratorical discourse was limited to deliberative, forensic, and demonstrative speeches in their ancient and modern forms. Thus rhetoric, as he was thinking of it in the twelfth lecture, was the theory of all kinds of non-poetical discourse. In fact, if we were to attempt to develop an analogy between his theory and its parallels in the ancient world, we would have to say that his rhetoric embraced what ancient rhetoric and dialectic were severally designed to control, and that in addition it continued onward so as to bring within its province the works of ancient and modern historians.

As his lectures proceeded, Smith widened his conception of the forms of discourse so that it included poetic composition. Thus in its fullest extent his system of rhetoric assumed jurisdiction not only of histories but also of what the ancients had considered the separate disciplines of dialectic, rhetoric, and poetics. Smith's treatment of poetics as part of his system occurred in his twenty-first lecture. He had just finished his analysis of narrative discourse, and didactic discourse should by rights have been his next subject. But he was arrested by the thought that historical narratives and poetical narratives had much in common, and that the rules governing the historian and biographer often applied to the poet, too. For what is it that makes up the essential differences between history and historical poetry? 'It is no more than this,' he declared, 'that the one is in prose, and the other in verse' (21.2; Lothian, 113). His momentary preoccupation with this difference led Smith to say that poetical compositions were designed not to relate facts and not of course to prove propositions but rather to afford pleasure and entertainment (21.2; Lothian, 113–14). Thus it turned out that his nineteen final lectures dealt with four kinds of communication —instruction, entertainment, conviction, and persuasion—and with four resulting forms of discourse—history, poetry, didactic writing, and oratory. And it turned out, too, as these concepts were substituted for those of traditional rhetorical theory, that rhetoric for the first time measured itself against the needs of the modern world and became fully and triumphantly responsive to those needs. Nothing quite like this had ever happened to rhetoric before.

To historical discourse Smith devoted nine lectures, and he made this part of his discussion unfold under five heads (12–20; Lothian, 58–112). Thus he spoke first of the kind of facts that entered historical narration, and he proceeded next to comment upon the historian's manner of narration, his methods of arranging his work, and his style of writing. Finally he spoke of ancient and modern historians. As a rhetorician seeking to make a distinctively rhetorical contribution to the work of any future historian among his hearers, Smith aimed his discussion of these five heads at the problems involved in the literary presentation of historical materials. For example, in respect to the methods of arranging a historical work, he said that, 'In general, the narration is to be carried on in the same order as that in which the events themselves happened' (18.2; Lothian, 93). But this rule should not be followed if the historian is tracing a series of events in one locality and a simultaneous series in another locality. The best method here would be to narrate those events 'that happened in the same place for some considerable succession of time, without interrupting the thread of the narration by introducing those that happened in a different place' (18.3; Lothian, 93). And in addition to considerations of time and space as determinants in the ordering of a work of history, Smith recommended that the order of cause and effect is often highly successful. As for historical style, Smith discussed it also with reference to the problems of future historians. In fact, he succeeded in making this part of his discussion helpful alike to young historians and orators:

> An historian, as well as an orator, may excite our love or esteem for the persons he treats of: but then the methods they take are very different. The rhetorician will not barely set forth the character of a person as it really existed, but will magnify every particular that may tend to excite the strongest emotions in us. He will also seem to be deeply affected with that affection which he would have us feel towards any object . . . The historian, on the contrary, can only excite our affection by the narration of the facts and setting them in as interesting a view as he possibly can. But all exclamations in his own person would not suit with the impartiality he is to maintain and the design he is to have in view, of narrating facts as they are, without magnifying them or diminishing them.
>
> (18.9; Lothian, 96)

Under his fifth head, Smith discussed in some detail the ancient and modern historical classics, and this subject occupied him for two lectures. He had spoken earlier of the design of historical writing, and had said then that the historian's aim as an author consisted, not in seeking to entertain the reader, as an epic poet might do, but rather in offering him instruction, so that mankind, by coming to know the more interesting and important events of human life, and by coming to understand what caused them, could learn the means by which good effects might be produced and evil effects avoided in human affairs (17.6; Lothian, 85). This definition of the historian's design became one of Smith's themes when he discussed the historical classics. In fact, he mentioned that Thucydides was the first historian to recognize this aim as the proper goal of historical authorship. Thucydides tells us, Smith remarked, of his having undertaken his history of the Peloponnesian War so that, 'by recording in the truest manner the various incidents of that war, and the causes that produced [it], posterity may learn how to produce the like events or shun others, and know what is to be expected from such and such circumstances' (19.5; Lothian, 101–2). 'In this design', Smith added, 'he has succeeded better perhaps than any preceding or succeeding writer.' Smith went on, however, to pay his respects to other distinguished historians of antiquity—Herodotus, Xenophon, Caesar, Polybius, Livy, and Tacitus. As for the moderns, he thought that Machiavelli surpassed Guicciardini among the Italians, and indeed that Machiavelli surpassed all moderns in having dedicated himself in the true spirit of history 'to relate events and connect them with their causes, without becoming a party on either side' (20.10; Lothian, 110–11). And Smith proceeded next to observe that Britain's two leading historians, Clarendon and Burnet, did not measure up to Machiavelli's standard, inasmuch as both of them had written not to present the facts but to praise or denounce parties (20.13–14; Lothian, 111–12).

In a brief concluding paragraph of his second lecture on the great historians, Smith remarked that Paul de Rapin-Thoyras's *L'Histoire d'Angleterre* was the most candid of all historical accounts of England, but that Rapin had been guilty of entering too much into the private lives of monarchs and too little into the affairs of the body of the people (20.15; Lothian, 112). Lothian tells us in a footnote that our student's notebook contains in the margin against this reference to Rapin an annotation reading, '10 years ago. A better now', and he indicates without comment that the first volume of what came finally to be called David Hume's *History of England* had appeared in 1754, and the last volume in 1761.[23] It seems obvious, indeed, that the student's marginal annotation refers to Hume's *History*. But, if the annotation came from the student, and not from something Smith said in the lecture that day in January 1763, it suggests that Smith did not change his lectures from year to year, and that his reference to Rapin rather than to Hume helps to attach the date of composition of this lecture, and perhaps of many of the others, to the period in which he first

[23] See T. E. Jessop, *A Bibliography of David Hume and of Scottish Philosophy* (1938), 28–30. Jessop correctly gives 1762 as the date of the final volume.

delivered them in Edinburgh.[24] At that time, the earliest instalment of Hume's *History* was six years in the future, and Rapin's *L'Histoire d'Angleterre*, which very probably figured in Smith's wide reading in history and literature at Oxford, had appeared almost a quarter of a century before.

Poetical composition, the second of the four forms of discourse involved in Smith's system of rhetoric, was treated in a single lecture, the twenty-first in the series, and it was placed immediately before didactic and oratorical and immediately after historical composition by virtue of the narrative element which it shared with history. As we have seen, Smith considered that history, didactic discourse, and oratory were designed to produce a composite effect upon mankind, and that the ingredients of this effect entitled it on some occasions to be called instruction, on other occasions, conviction, and on still other occasions, persuasion, according as the author's purpose required him to be a neutral expositor or an active advocate. Moreover, these forms of discourse were bound by their mission to a common set of resources. That is to say, they were to confine themselves to facts and actualities; they were to keep to prose as their natural medium of communication; they were to reconcile themselves to their inherent inability ever to arouse the highest degree of attention or the deepest degree of feeling in the audience; they were always to seek to achieve a full measure of unity of thought; and they were to establish their separate identities by calling themselves histories, or philosophical dissertations, or scientific treatises, or orations, in proportion as they found themselves differing from each other in respect to natural gradations in their content and aim. But poetical compositions, in Smith's critical philosophy, were set apart from all other writings by virtue of their having a special function of their own—that of affording mankind pleasure or entertainment. As the means to this end, poetical compositions were to exercise licence in inventing their stories; they were to choose to express themselves in verse that would delight the ear; they were to take special pride in their inherent ability to surpass the other forms of discourse in beauty, strength, and conciseness; they were always to seek to achieve propriety in character portrayal and unity of interest, time, and place; and they were to establish their separate identities by calling themselves tragedies, comedies, epics, odes, elegies, or pastorals, in recognition of the differences that inhere in changes from the mood of grief to that of laughter, from the technique of direct presentation to that of narrative, and from a subject involving many events to that involving only a single action. These distinctions and terms form the outline of the single lecture devoted by Smith to poetical com-

[24] See Lothian, xii, xvii, for evidence to suggest that Smith's lectures on rhetoric at Glasgow were repetitions of those presented in Edinburgh. But not all evidence points in that direction. For example, Smith's twenty-first lecture ends with a reference to Gray's 'Elegy written in a Country Church-Yard', first published on 15 February 1751, when the final repetition of the Edinburgh lectures had probably just ended.

positions (21). A further analysis of that lecture can hardly be undertaken here. But as we take leave of it, we should remember that it has presented us with the opportunity of seeing the new rhetoric undertake to present the theory of poetical literature as one of the natural responsibilities of rhetoric in its endeavour to make itself into a general theory of discourse for the modern world.

As I said earlier, Smith intended to treat didactic composition immediately after he had finished the last of his nine lectures on the writing of history, but he suspended that plan in order to deliver a single lecture on poetry instead. When the latter discourse had been pronounced, and didactic composition had again emerged for consideration, he disappointingly remarked that, since its rules were very obvious, he would pass them over so as to allow himself to give attention at once to the forms of oratory (22.1; Lothian, 124). In line with this new plan, he devoted his next two lectures to demonstrative or epideictic eloquence, and he seemed now to be bent upon continuing in this vein until deliberative and judicial eloquence had also been covered. In fact, it appeared quite possible that he had decided to omit didactic composition altogether from his system of rhetoric in line with his earlier remark that its rules could be easily deduced from what had been said of historical composition (21.1; Lothian, 113). Such a decision would have meant that the earliest British treatise on the new rhetoric was to fail to bring within its jurisdiction what had formerly been the property of dialectic. It would also have meant, of course, that didactic composition, which was already being rejected as an object of doctrinal concern by the new logic, had not yet been declared eligible for admission within the new rhetoric and so was drifting along by itself without any affiliation whatever with its traditional associates in the enterprise of communication. Fortunately, however, Smith's decision to forgo the discussion of didactic composition did not prove final. In fact, he openly revoked it at the beginning of his twenty-fourth lecture, and what he then said upon didactic composition gave rhetorical theory a refreshing new dimension.

Didactic composition has two aims, said Smith in the course of that twenty-fourth lecture: it seeks to prove a proposition to an audience that needs only to be convinced; or it seeks to deliver a system of science to the community of learning (24.1, 5; 12.1; Lothian, 136, 138, 58). Thus in its rhetorical aspect it must provide doctrine that looks towards the effective literary presentation of philosophical argument or scientific knowledge. In other words, rhetoric at this point interests itself in discourse addressed to the learned audience, and its mission is to provide a theory to guide the literary endeavours of philosophers and scientists. Smith's discussion of this theory is obviously designed to offer concrete advice to future authors in these two fields, as his lectures on history and on poetry had been designed with future historians and poets in mind.

In proving a proposition, Smith remarked, the young philosopher or scholar should state what he wishes to have his audience accept. Then he should do one of two things: if his task is relatively uncomplicated, he should proceed immediately to advance the arguments which his proposition needs for its support; but if there are complications, he may have to proceed to advance several subsidiary propositions, and to offer argumentative support for each, on his way towards proof. The more complex method Smith found to be illustrated by Shaftesbury's *Inquiry into the Nature of Virtue*, but he took pains to point out that this illustration was meant to endorse the perfection of Shaftesbury's method rather than the soundness of his reasoning (24.2; Lothian, 136). In words reminiscent of those used in a similar connection in the *Rhetorica ad Herennium*, Smith then advised the young philosopher that three was a very proper limit to set upon the number of subordinate propositions which might be advanced in support of a major one, for the reason that 'Three is the number of all others the most easily comprehended: we immediately perceive a middle and one on each side.'[25] Indeed, Smith added, 'There are more sermons and other discourses divided into this number of heads than into any other.' But he argued that there could safely be five heads, too, and he commented upon differences between the problem involved in comprehending at a glance the number of windows in one of the walls of a building and that involved in seeing in the mind's eye the number of propositions in a discourse. This part of his discussion he brought to a close with the remark that the divisions, subdivisions, and subsubdivisions employed by Aristotle in the *Ethics* 'are carried so far that they produce the very effect he intended to have avoided by them, viz. confusion' (24.4; Lothian, 138).

When didactic composition undertook to fulfil its second aim, that of delivering a system of science to the learned public, it had a choice of either of two methods. Smith indicated that the first method had originated with Descartes, but that it was nevertheless entitled to be named after Newton. It consisted in advancing one or a very few principles at the beginning of a discourse and in using them thereafter to explain the natural connection among the rules or phenomena under discussion. The second method, which Smith associated with Aristotle, began by enumerating the subjects one had to explain and proceeded to take up each subject in turn so as to reduce it to its essential principles but to make no attempt to reconcile one principle with another. Smith illustrated this second method by commenting thus upon what Virgil had done in composing the four books of his *Georgics*:

His design is to give us a system of husbandry. In the First he gives us directions

[25] 24.3; Lothian, 137. Cf. *Rhetorica ad Herennium*, 1.10.17.

for the cultivation of corn; in the Second, of trees; in the Third, of cattle; in the Fourth, of the insects called the bees.

(24.7; Lothian, 139)

And how would the *Georgics* have had to be changed in order to become an illustration of the first method? What would the method of Descartes and Newton have done to it? Smith addressed himself directly to these questions in the following words:

If Virgil had begun with inquiring into the principle of vegetation, what was proper to augment it, and *ex contra*, in what proportion it was in different soils, and what nourishment the different plants required, and, putting all these together, had directed us what culture and what soil was proper for every different plant, this would have been following the first method, which is, without doubt, the most philosophical one.

(Ibid.)

In seeking somewhat later to clarify in other terms the differences between the Newtonian and the Aristotelian methods, Smith remarked that 'It gives us a pleasure to see the phenomena which we reckoned the most unaccountable, all deduced from some principle (commonly, a well-known one) and all united in one chain, far superior to what we feel from the unconnected method, where everything is accounted for by itself, without any reference to the others' (24.7; Lothian, 140). We need not be surprised, Smith went on, that Descartes, whose philosophy contains hardly a word of truth, could yet have gained an almost universal acceptance among the learned men of Europe. For here was a case where a philosophic method was so good as to be able to survive in spite of the weaknesses of the philosophy within which it was woven. 'The great superiority of the method over that of Aristotle, the only one then known,' said Smith with a touch of sportive mockery, 'and the little inquiry which was then made into those matters, made them [that is, European scholars] greedily receive a work which we justly esteem one of the most entertaining romances that have ever been wrote.'[26]

The Newtonian and the Aristotelian methods thus recommended by Smith to students interested in didactic composition were borrowed from the old logic, as he himself made no effort to conceal. In fact, what the old logic tended prevailingly to call the method of analysis became in Smith's system the Aristotelian method; and the Newtonian (or Cartesian) method as set forth by him was what Ramus had called the method of science and what Ramus's immediate successors had tended to call the method of synthesis. Interestingly, Ramus had cited Virgil's arrangement of the *Georgics* as an example of the method of science, whereas Smith, as we have seen, considered that the *Georgics* could be made to illustrate that method

[26] 24.7; Lothian, 140. The bracketed phrase is mine.

only if the work were completely rewritten and rearranged.[27] Since Ramus flourished almost a century before Descartes, it is obvious that Smith was historically inaccurate in making Descartes appear to be the originator of the Newtonian method. Indeed, Smith would only have been on safe ground in this instance if he had said that the Newtonian and the Aristotelian methods, as he described them, were derived from concepts quite familiar in Plato's time, and that those concepts had had an active history from that date to Smith's own epoch.[28] But I mention this inaccuracy without intending to suggest that it is important. What seems to me to be important is that rhetorical theory under Smith's inspired leadership borrowed from the old logic the doctrines and methods which guide the literary presentation of scientific knowledge, and made those doctrines and methods its own, thereby giving itself the opportunity to be to the modern world what dialectic and rhetoric had together been to the ancients. Rhetoric had always had the capacity to meet a challenge of this kind, simply because the theory and practice of addressing the popular audience teach much that is necessary, and little that is irrelevant, to the task of addressing men of learning. But it was not in a position to meet the challenge while logic retained control of the theory of learned communication, and while rhetoric itself was blind to anything but its ancient rituals. It was Smith who taught rhetoric to see beyond those rituals and to assert jurisdiction over what logic no longer wanted to control.

Oratorical composition, the fourth form of discourse in Smith's system of rhetoric, brought him and his hearers to what had formerly been the sole concern of the rhetorician. It also brought him and his hearers into contact with the whole of the ancient rhetorical tradition. Here would have been the place for a display of conservatism on Smith's part, if he had been disposed to concentrate upon past glories and hallowed principles rather than upon present exigencies and new challenges. Here would have been the place where the spirit of the antiquarian might well have prevailed over that of the creative scholar. For was not traditional rhetoric an impressive structure? Had it not been given its great ancient authority by Aristotle himself, and had it not acquired from the eloquent Cicero the right to be regarded as the only avenue to eloquence? Had it not accommodated itself to Christianity and become the long-drawn aisle to greatness in the pulpit and to blessedness in the sight of God's vicars upon the earth? Was it not worthy of adaptation to modern times with only the few modifications that might be necessary to make it responsive to recent

[27] For Ramus's views on Virgil's *Georgics* as an illustration of the method of science, see his *Dialectique* (1555), 124–5. See also my *Logic and Rhetoric in England, 1500–1700* (1956), 163.

[28] See Plato, *Phaedrus*, 265–6; Neal W. Gilbert, *Renaissance Concepts of Method* (1960), 3–4, 110, 171–2, 184; my *Logic and Rhetoric in England, 1500–1700*, 21–2, 160–5, 289–91, 297, 306–8, and *passim*.

regrettable lapses in the standards of culture? These questions have caused twentieth-century rhetoricians to hesitate to raise too many objections to the old rhetoric of Aristotle and Cicero, and they caused eighteenth-century rhetoricians to hesitate even more. But they did not prevent Adam Smith from exercising his independent judgement or from offering severe criticisms of ancient doctrine.

As I have already indicated, Smith made the three kinds of oratory the subject of his last nine lectures, although he interrupted himself long enough to devote a large part of one lecture to didactic discourse. His announced plan was to deal with each oratorical kind by speaking successively of its ends, its means, its structure, its style, and its distinguished practitioners (22.4, 25.1, 28.1; Lothian, 124, 142, 164); and speak he did in these very terms when he treated demonstrative oratory. Thereafter he adhered to his plan with much less strictness. He spoke of deliberative oratory largely with its practitioners in mind, doing little with the other four of his promised heads; and he spoke of judicial oratory under all of his promised heads except style. His observations throughout these lectures are fresh, astute, and never commonplace, despite the losses which they must have suffered in the process of being transmitted to us through someone else's interpretations. But a complete discussion of those observations need not be undertaken here. What I shall do instead is to comment upon Smith's attitude towards the nature of oratorical composition in modern rhetoric and towards the traditional rhetorical doctrine that lay behind the orator's work.

First of all, Smith indicated that, so far as the later stages of civilization are concerned, demonstrative oratory must be considered less important than either of its companion forms. Audiences found pleasure in listening to it, but it never gave them sound argument. Speakers used it presumably to praise someone else but in reality to glorify themselves, without being able to connect it with the conduct of public business. Primitive man, Smith argued, sharply differentiated between the necessary labours of his daylight hours and the recreation which he sought in the evenings when his work was done (23.3; Lothian, 131–2). For these latter times he devised dancing, music, song, and poetry. Panegyrics, or hymns to his gods and heroes, became a part of his recreation, and thus in its origin demonstrative oratory had no connection with workaday occupations. At a later state of society, as commerce developed, and riches and opulence appeared, man began to cultivate prose, which 'is naturally the language of business, as poetry is of pleasure and amusement' (23.3; Lothian, 132). Panegyrists turned away from poetry and accommodated themselves to prose, seeking meanwhile to perfect this new medium by embellishment; but panegyrics still endeavoured not only to afford pleasure to their hearers, but also to commend men and institutions and to glorify the panegyrist himself. Said Smith:

Men would much sooner consider what was to be done, or consider the merit of those actions that have been done, than they would think either of commending men and actions, or of discommending them, and consequently would sooner apply themselves to the cultivation of the Deliberative and Judicial eloquence than of the Demonstrative. Their subjects are such as would be interesting both to speaker and hearers, whereas that of the latter could interest neither; for though the speaker gave out that his design was to commend some person or nation, yet the motive was the advancement of his own glory.

(23.1; Lothian, 130)

In this context Smith discussed three of the leading panegyrists of antiquity, but he mentioned none of his own time. 'There have been but very few', he said, 'who have turned their thoughts this way' (ibid.). And he cited Brutus's disapproval and Cicero's admiration of Isocrates, as expressed in Cicero's *Orator*, to suggest to his own Scottish audience that they would waste their time if they read Isocrates 'to discover the truth of the matter in question' or to be instructed 'in order, method, argument, or strength of reasoning'.[29] 'But if we expect entertainment and pleasure from an agreeable writer,' he added, 'we will not be disappointed.'

The second point concerning Smith's attitude towards oratorical composition is that to his mind the authors of ancient textbooks in rhetoric made far too narrow an application of their highly schematized doctrine. Smith allowed this attitude to be expressed so much by implication, however, that it would probably not be noticed by anyone not closely familiar with Latin rhetoric in the form which it had in Cicero's *De Inventione*, in the anonymous *Rhetorica ad Herennium*, and in Quintilian's *Institutio Oratoria*. These elementary treatises taught that the exordium of the classical oration involved either of two procedures, the *insinuatio* or the *principium*, that is to say, the ingratiating approach or the direct opening.[30] The former of these was to be used in addressing an initially hostile, the latter in addressing an initially friendly, audience. Smith gave these two procedures new names and treated them, not as strategies limited to a speaker's introductory remarks, but as methods applicable to the conduct of the entire deliberative oration. He spoke of these methods as he was finishing his account of didactic composition:

The first may be called the Socratic method, as it was that [of] which, if we may trust the dialogues of Xenophon and Plato, that philosopher generally made use. In this method we keep as far from the main point to be proved as possible, bringing on the audience by slow and imperceptible degrees to the thing to be proved, and by gaining their consent to some things whose tendency they cannot discover, we force them at last either to deny what they had before agreed to,

[29] 23.7; Lothian, 134–5. See *Orator*, 13.40.

[30] See *De Inventione*, 1.15.20; *Rhetorica ad Herennium*, 1.4.6–11; *Institutio Oratoria*, 4.1.42.

or to grant the validity of the conclusion. This is the smoothest and most engaging manner.

The other is a harsh and unmannerly one, where we affirm the things we are to prove boldly at the beginning, and when any point is controverted, begin by proving that very thing; and so on. This we may call the Aristotelian method, as we know it was that which he used.

(24.9–10; Lothian, 140–1)

Smith's immediate explanation of the circumstances in which these two procedures were to be used broaden the textbook doctrine of the exordium so that it becomes applicable to the speech as a whole. He spoke thus:

These two methods are adapted to the two contrary cases in which an orator may be circumstanced with regard to his audience. They may either have a favourable or an unfavourable opinion of that which he is to prove: that is, they may be prejudiced for, or they may be prejudiced against. In the second case we are to use the Socratic method; in the first, the Aristotelian.

(24.11; Lothian, 141)

The third point to be mentioned as we assess Smith's attitude towards oratorical composition involves us in the problem of reconciling an inconsistency between one part of his system and another. In his discussion of deliberative oratory, Smith would have us believe that 'in general, in every sort of eloquence, the choice of the arguments and the proper arrangement of them is the least difficult matter', and that Cicero and Quintilian had accordingly treated 'the invention of arguments, or topics, and the composition or arrangement of them, as very slight matters and of no great difficulty' (25.1; Lothian, 142); but in his later treatment of judicial oratory, he indicated his awareness of the elaborate ancient machinery for the invention of arguments in legal and deliberative cases (28, 29.6; Lothian, 164–71, 175–6), and he said at one point that 'It is in the proper ordering and disposal of this sort of arguments that the great art of an orator often consists' (28.7; Lothian, 167). Here, then, we have on the one hand Smith's denial that the invention and arrangement of arguments are important matters in modern oratorical practice or in ancient rhetorical theory; and on the other hand we have his later affirmation that these two processes are important to the practising speaker and that the ancients expended a great deal of effort in reducing them to rule and method. In his recent study of Smith's lectures on rhetoric, Vincent M. Bevilacqua, taking cognizance only of Smith's denial of the importance of invention and arrangement in ancient rhetorical theory, argues that the denial is based upon Smith's misunderstanding of the rhetorical works of Cicero and Quintilian; and that, 'in accord with his misinterpretation, Smith proposed not a traditional theory of rhetoric, which included the classical arts of invention, arrangement, style and delivery, but a stylistic-belletristic one'.[31] 'Indeed,' adds Bevilacqua, 'in Smith's lectures style alone is the pressing concern of rhetoric and the area of greatest artistic latitude.' But the charge that Smith did not understand the ancient doctrines of invention and arrangement is destroyed by Smith's whole discussion of judicial oratory; and, as I have shown, the assertion that style alone is in his view the pressing concern of rhetoric would hardly serve to express what he conceived the pressing concerns of rhetoric to be.

What led Smith, then, to belittle in one place and to emphasize in another the importance of invention and arrangement in the theories of Cicero and Quintilian? This question cannot be given a final answer at this time. But a plausible hypothesis is that our student's notebook, in recording the earlier of these inconsistent statements, omitted some of Smith's oral elaborations or misstated some of his essential doctrine, and that therefore at this particular point the notebook does not bring us into contact with what Smith actually thought. At any rate, we should not allow a patently erroneous view of the position of invention and arrangement in Ciceronian rhetoric to stand as Smith's final opinion when it is obvious that he has given us later a more complete and a much more accurate opinion upon the same matter. I would not want to argue that Smith accepted the ancient doctrines of rhetorical invention or disposition in their totality. Indeed, it is obvious that he did not. What I am arguing is that those doctrines were heavily stressed in Cicero's *De Inventione*, in the *Rhetorica ad Herennium*, and in Quintilian's *Institutio Oratoria*, and that Smith knew from his reading of the *Institutio Oratoria* and possibly of the other two works, as his discussion of judicial oratory proves, that ancient rhetoric had not regarded those doctrines as 'very slight matters'.

Another point to be emphasized in this analysis of Smith's view of oratorical composition is that he regarded the oratory of one cultural establishment to be unsuited to a different establishment, and that, as a consequence, the rhetorical theory calculated to produce oratory under one set of conditions would not necessarily be the theory which ought to prevail when the conditions change. This idea is a characteristic of the new rhetoric, and Boyle had already stressed it effectively in his argument that the rhetorical theory meant to explain the orations of Cicero was not the sort needed to explain the Holy Scriptures. The idea also means, of course, that the rhetoric of pre-scientific times should not be made a law unto scientific times, and that, if Ciceronian rhetoric fitted the former of these epochs, it need not therefore bend the latter one to its inexorable will. Smith did not commit himself to these particular propositions in these exact terms. What he did rather was to show that deliberative oratory in ancient

[31] 'Adam Smith's Lectures on Rhetoric and Belles Lettres', *Studies in Scottish Literature*, iii (1965–6), 52.

Athens was different from that of Rome, and would in all probability not have succeeded in Rome, and that judicial oratory in ancient Athens and Rome had proceeded on a set of assumptions no longer valid for judicial oratory in London.

In speaking upon the deliberative oratory of Cicero and Demosthenes, Smith emphasized the contrast between patrician Rome and democratic Athens. The Roman orators spoke as superiors to inferiors, the Athenian orators as equals to equals:

In the one country the people, at least the nobles, would converse and harangue with dignity, pomp, and the air of those who speak with authority. The language of the other would be that of freedom, ease, and familiarity. The one is that where the speaker is supposed to be of superior dignity and authority to his hearers, and the other is that of one who talks to his equals. Pomp and splendour suit the former well enough, but would appear presumption in the other.

(26.10; Lothian, 153)

'These considerations', continued Smith, 'may serve to explain many of the differences in the manners and style of Demosthenes and Cicero. The latter talks with the dignity and authority of a superior, and the former with the ease of an equal.' And later he spoke thus upon this matter: 'Such, then, are the different manners of Demosthenes and Cicero, both adapted to the state of their country; and, perhaps, had they been practised in the other countries, they would have been less successful' (26.16; Lothian, 155).

The case is the same, Smith argued, when we compare the forensic orators of Greece and Rome with those of modern Britain. Here is part of what he said upon this matter:

I shall now give ye some account of the state of the Judicial eloquence of England, which is very different from that either of Greece or of Rome. This difference is generally ascribed to the small progress which has been made in the cultivation of language and style in this country, compared with that which it had arrived to in the Old World. But [though] this may be true in some degree, yet I imagine there are other causes which must make them essentially different. The eloquence which is now in greatest esteem is a plain, distinct, and perspicuous style, without any of the floridity or other ornamental parts of the Old Eloquence. This and other differences must necessarily arise from the nature of the country and the particular turn of the people. The Courts were then much in the same manner as the Jury is now. They were men unskilled in the law, whose office continued but for a very short time, and were often in a great part chosen for the trial of that particular cause, and not from any particular set of men, but only by ballot and rotation from the whole body of the people, and of them there was always no inconsiderable number. The Judges in England, on the other hand, are single men who have been bred to the law, and have generally, or at least are supposed to have, a thorough knowledge of the law, and are much versed in all the different circumstances of cases, of which they have attended many before, either as judges or pleaders, and are supposed to be acquainted with all the different arguments that may be advanced on it. This therefore cuts them out from a great part of the substance of the old orations.

(30.19; Lothian, 190)

Smith's modernity of outlook towards rhetoric is nowhere seen to better advantage than in the words which followed these observations:

There can here be no room for a narration, the only design of which is, by interweaving those facts for which proof can be brought with those for which no proof can be brought, that these latter may gain credit by their connection with the others. But as nothing is now of any weight for which direct proof is not brought, this sort of narration could serve no end. The pleader, therefore, can do no more than tell over what facts he is to prove . . . And if he should assert anything for a fact, as the old orators frequently did, for which he can bring no proof, he would be severely reprimanded. The pleader has here no opportunity of smoothing over any argument which would make against him, as the judge will perceive it and pay no regard to what he advances in this manner. Nor can he conceal any weak side by placing it betwixt two on which he depends for the proof of it . . . All these were particularly directed by the ancient rhetoricians. The inattention and ignorance of the judges was the sole foundation of it: as this is not now to be expected, they can be of no service.

(30.19; Lothian, 190–1)

The next point to need attention concerns Smith's theory of oratorical structure. His modernity in this matter has two aspects: his rejection of the classical doctrine that an oration has five or six parts, each elaborately conceived; and his assertion that, when everything has been taken into account, the orator must state his proposition and prove it, while giving heed to whatever his speech may require in the way of a simple introduction and conclusion. The first statement of this theory occurred in his seventeenth lecture, when he paused in his analysis of historical writing to emphasize the difference between the structure of a historical work and that of an exposition or oration. 'The didactic and the oratorical compositions', he declared on that occasion, 'consist of two parts; the proposition which we lay down, and the proof which is brought to confirm this, whether this proof be a strict one, applied to our reason and sound judgement, or one adapted to affect our passions and by that means persuade us at any rate' (17.4; Lothian, 84–5). An extended form of this same idea appeared in his later discussion of forensic oratory, where he spoke thus of ancient rhetoricians:

They tell us that every regular oration should consist of five parts. There are, it is true, two chief parts, the laying-down the proposition, and the proof. But in the connecting these two properly together and setting them out in the brightest light, the oration, they say, naturally divides into five parts. The *first* of these is the Exordium, in which the orator explains briefly the purpose of his discourse and what he intends to accuse the adversary of, or to acquit his client of. The *second* part is, according to them, the Narration . . . In the practice of the modern Courts of Judicature the narration is never introduced . . . The other three parts are the Confirmation, the Refutation, and the Peroration . . . The Peroration contains a short summary of the whole arguments advanced in the preceding part of the discourse, placed in such a way as naturally to lead to the conclusion proposed. To this the Roman orators generally added some arguments which might move the judge to decide in one way rather than in another, by either showing the enormity of the crime, if the person accused be his opponent, and setting it out in the most shocking manner; or, if he is a defendant, by mitigating the action and showing the severity of the punishment. This latter the Greeks never admitted of: the other is the natural conclusion of every discourse.

(29.2, 6, 8; Lothian, 172, 175, 176)

Smith's mention of the Greek orators in the passage just quoted should remind us that Athenian oratorical practice was simpler than Rome's and that Smith, in rejecting the elaborate Ciceronian theory of the oration, was in part endorsing the simpler theory set forth in Aristotle's *Rhetoric* (1414^{a}30). Thus the new rhetoric, so far as its theory of speech composition is concerned, turned away from the elaborate Ciceronian ideal and adopted the earlier and plainer formula of Aristotle. But it did so, not in a spirit of reverence for a greater as distinguished from a lesser figure of the past, but in a genuine search for an oratorical form that would best fit the needs of the modern world. Classical scholars who consider the ancients more perfect than the moderns, and who among the ancients prefer the Greek to the Roman orators and philosophers, should not be misled by Adam Smith's preference for Demosthenes and Aristotle over Cicero. For Smith was not an apostle of Demosthenes and Aristotle in a situation in which he thought them giants towering above the puny men of Rome. He was their apostle only when they spoke to his own time with more relevance than Cicero could command. And when their words ceased to be relevant on any issue, he was their apostle no further.

A matter upon which Smith was the apostle of neither Aristotle nor Cicero involved the utility of the topics in the invention of oratorical proofs. Aristotle and Cicero had considered the invention of artistic proofs to be the heart of their theories of rhetoric, and they had lavished their energies upon creating a system of topics to assist the orator in devising these proofs. Smith did not flatly reject this system. He discussed it in part, and it is plain that he did not find it altogether useless. But he spoke slightingly of it on occasion, and in general he expected the modern orator to rely upon direct proofs rather than upon those that issued from mere conjectures and suspicions.

One expression of this expectation occurs in a passage already quoted, where, after showing how the classical *narratio* was suited to the situation in which established facts could be mixed with mere unsubstantiated allegations so as to give the speaker's argument some degree of credibility, Smith said that in modern times, only direct proof being admissible, the classical *narratio* was no longer employed. But the best expression of this expectation occurs when Smith was discussing proof as one of the two indispensable parts of the modern oration. On that occasion he revealed his basic attitude towards the topical devices which classical rhetoric had recommended for the discovery of rhetorical arguments:

The Confirmation consists in the proving of all or certain of the facts alleged, and this is done by going through the arguments drawn from the several topics I mentioned in the last lecture; and the Refutation, or the confuting of the adversaries' arguments, is to be gone through in the same manner. The later orators adhered most strictly to the rules laid down by the rhetoricians. We see that even Cicero himself was scrupulously exact in this point, so that in many, indeed most, of his orations, he goes through all of those topics. It would probably have been reckoned a defect to have omitted any one, and not to have led an argument from the topic *De Causa, Effectu, Tempore*, etc. This may serve to show us the low state of philosophy at that time . . . In his oration in defense of Milo he has arguments drawn from all the three topics with regard to the cause; that is, that he had no motive to kill Clodius; that it was unsuitable to his character; and that he had no opportunity. These, one would have thought, could not take place in this case, and yet he goes through them all. He endeavours to show that he had no motive, though they had been squabbling and fighting every day—he had even declared his intention to kill him; that it was unsuitable to his character, although he had killed twenty men before; and that he had no opportunity, although we know he did kill him.

(29.6; Lothian, 175–6)

Notice how Smith balanced the known facts of Milo's case against the glib conjectures which Cicero drew from the topic of cause. Notice how poorly the conjectures fare when the known facts confront them. Notice how Smith's analysis of this part of Cicero's famous speech is itself a witty exposure of the sterility of artistic arguments in a case where the non-artistic arguments directly controvert them. There can be little doubt that the students who heard Smith deliver this lecture would never have been able in their later lives to restrain their smiles when they thought of Smith's mocking comments upon Cicero's defence of Milo. Nor would they ever have been likely in their own practice as speakers or writers to prefer arguments drawn from the topics to arguments based upon the facts. As the expounder of the new rhetoric, Smith was never more effective than he was on this particular occasion.

In concluding this assessment of Smith's system of rhetoric and belles-lettres, I should like to re-emphasize that Smith's rhetorical theory is remarkable for its originality, its validity, and its timeliness. It took the position that the new rhetoric must define its function as broadly communicative rather than narrowly persuasive and hence must assert jurisdiction over the forms of historical, poetical, and didactic composition not less than over the traditional kinds of oratory. It asserted that the new rhetoric must teach the eloquence of plainness, distinctness, and perspicuity. It decreed that the new rhetoric must abandon the ritualistic form of the Ciceronian oration and must adopt the simpler pattern of proposition and proof. And it required the new rhetoric to turn away from the artistic proofs and the topical machinery of the old rhetoric, and to adapt itself to non-artistic arguments and direct proofs instead. Only in two respects was Adam Smith silent upon the issues confronting the new rhetoric: he did not openly condemn the syllogistic orientation of ancient rhetorical theory or propose inductive procedures in its place; nor did he stress that probable arguments, as ancient and modern phenomena in popular discourse, must learn in the new age to conform to higher standards of validity than they had done before. These two issues were to be squarely faced and creatively resolved by George Campbell and were to produce Campbell's major contributions to the new rhetoric.[32] But surely Adam Smith implied his endorsement of the position that Campbell was later to take on these issues, and thus he is not to be counted an opponent of the new rhetoric in respect to them.

In one sector of his rhetorical theory Smith showed himself seriously weak; that was in his willingness to accept pleasure or entertainment as the sole distinguishing characteristic of poetical composition. Surely poetry gives its readers pleasure, but so on occasion does history or oratory or even didactic discourse. Thus Smith's theory of the distinction between poetical and non-poetical composition does not meet the most elementary standard of adequacy, and it could not survive comparison with a really effective standard like that, for example, which Aristotle developed in his *Poetics*. Aristotle's distinction depended upon the existence of the principle of mimesis in all the forms of poetry, and upon the non-existence of that principle in historical writing, didactic writing, and oratory.[33] Smith was deeply interested in the principle of artistic imitation, and wrote a short treatise upon that subject;[34] but his treatise did not apply the principle to poetical composition in any sense that would allow poetry to emerge as distinctively mimetic.

Aside from the inadequacy of his theory of poetry, however, Smith may

[32] See George Campbell, *The Philosophy of Rhetoric* (1776), i.103–85.

[33] For a discussion of this matter, see my essay 'Aristotle and Horace on Rhetoric and Poetics', *The Quarterly Journal of Speech*, liv (1968), 325–39.

[34] For it, see 'Of the Nature of that Imitation which takes place in what are called the Imitative Arts', in *Essays on Philosophical Subjects*, by the late Adam Smith, LL.D. (1795), 131–84.

confidently be called the earliest and most independent of the new British rhetoricians of the eighteenth century. It is a calamity indeed that the destruction of his manuscripts by his own request prevented his excellence as a rhetorician from being recognized and acclaimed until he had been dead for almost two hundred years. Rhetorical theory in the nineteenth century might have taken a better turn than it did, had Adam Smith's lectures been available to stand beside the works of Campbell and Blair when the latter authors became the leading exponents of the new rhetoric against Archbishop Richard Whately's successful revival of the rhetorical doctrines of Aristotle. Smith's steadily growing posthumous fame, and the distinction of his rhetorical teachings, might have helped the new rhetoric to prevail over Whately's Aristotelianism, even as the genius of John Stuart Mill decisively helped the new logic of Thomas Reid and Dugald Stewart to prevail over Whately's attempt to convert the nineteenth century to the Peripatetic logic of Dean Aldrich.

II

Adam Smith and the History of Ideas[1]

W. P. D. Wightman*

I

In a letter (248) addressed to the Duc de la Rochefoucauld, dated 1 November 1785, Adam Smith announced that he then had 'two other great works upon the anvil' of which the one with which we are primarily concerned was 'a sort of Philosophical History of all the different branches of Literature, Philosophy, Poetry and Eloquence'.[1] The materials were 'in a great measure collected and some part of both put into tolerable order'; but though he 'struggled against the indolence of old age' (he was then 62) he doubted whether either work would ever be completed. So far were they from being completed that shortly before his death Smith could find no peace of mind until his friends could assure him of the destruction of all his papers—all, that is, except, apparently, those that under the editorship of his friends Joseph Black and James Hutton, were published in 1795. Of these *Essays* only three could be described as a 'history', whether 'philosophical' (see below, 46) or otherwise; and of these, two were little more than fragments. The third—the *History of Astronomy*—placed first in the published collection—is, however, a work of 91 pages showing—for that age—a remarkable grasp of the subject and of central importance for our discussion. In Letter 137 addressed to David Hume, dated 16 April 1773, Smith himself had suggested that of all his then extant papers this piece alone might be worthy of publication; subsequent testimonies from various quarters prove that it was later enlarged (and perhaps 'corrected') and

* Sometime reader in the History and Philosophy of Science at the University of Aberdeen.

[1] The subject of this essay was suggested by studies undertaken in connection with the editing of the volume on Adam Smith's *Essays on Philosophical Subjects* and is best read in conjunction with that volume. In order to render the present essay as nearly self-contained as possible some repetition of matter presented in the Editorial Introduction to that volume has been unavoidable, the guiding-line being in general to state the various relevant conclusions arrived at in the Introduction with such references as may enable the interested reader to find the evidence presented therein. Without Mr. Andrew Skinner's opening of my eyes to wider horizons it could never have been started and without his constant encouragement and guidance it would never have been finished. To Professor David Raphael I owe the correction of some howlers, and the suggestion to renew, and this time with more circumspection, my acquaintance with David Hume; with some of the consequent second thoughts Professor Raphael would almost certainly disagree. A hint from Dr. Eric Forbes prompted me to make a more searching study of Descartes than I had contemplated.

suggest that Smith never changed his estimate of its quality. To what I have called the 'fragments'—the histories of the *Ancient Physics* and *Ancient Logics and Metaphysics*—Smith never specifically alluded. It is certainly a reasonable inference that they were also 'fragments' of the intended 'juvenile work' mentioned in the letter to Hume; nevertheless, even if 'in tolerable order', of neither could it be said that 'the materials were in a great measure collected'. The only other candidate for inclusion in the 'great work' is the essay on *The Nature of that Imitation which takes place in what are called the Imitative Arts*. On both stylistic and external grounds it would appear to have been composed much later than the 'histories'—probably about 1777, though with some subsequent correction and possible enlargement. Whether Smith himself intended it to be part of the 'great work' we do not know. If so, he must have greatly enlarged the original compass of his inquiries at the cost (see below, 52) of confusion of his original aim as set out in his letter to Rochefoucauld; the inclusion of 'Poetry and Eloquence' in the scheme outlined in the letter to Rochefoucauld supports this view.

What then had become of the 'great work'? On the most optimistic evaluation, including the *Imitative Arts* despite the latter's lack of any historical sequence, the conclusion seems inescapable that starting as a 'young man's vision' it ended as an 'old man's dream'. If correct, this is a paradoxical development: more usual is it for the generous ambition of youth to be refined and circumscribed by the discipline found to be necessitated by the humbling experience of age. But Adam Smith was no ordinary man. To the confusion of thought and equivocal terminology characteristic of the so-called 'Age of Reason' he added, as his contemporaries were not slow to note,[2] disconcerting quirks of behaviour amounting almost to what might now be called a benign schizoid state. Joseph Schumpeter found it hardly credible that *The Wealth of Nations* and the *History of Astronomy*, so utterly diverse in subject-matter, could be the products of the same mind.[3] Even less credible on a superficial view is the fact that the same mind could acquire and master the immense mass of objective detail forming the core of *The Wealth of Nations* and yet be apparently satisfied with the monumental nonsense that passes for a 'history' of education in the medieval universities (WN V.i.f.19–31). On the superficial view, yes indeed; but it will be one aim of this essay to show that though perhaps regrettable this discordancy was in the existing climate of opinion almost inevitable. Our first task, however, is to explicate what I have called the 'young man's vision'. For however inflated and confused it ultimately became as Smith's darting intelligence lighted on one field of interest after another, Andrew Skinner and others have given

[2] See E. C. Mossner, *Adam Smith, the Biographical Approach* (1969), 7.
[3] *History of Economic Analysis* (1954), 182.

incontestable evidence of the abiding influence—even sometimes reflected in almost identical phraseology—of the vision expressed in the titles of the historical *Essays*: 'The Principles which lead and direct Philosophical Enquiries; illustrated by the History of Astronomy'. Compare for instance: 'The great phenomena of nature . . . are objects which, as they necessarily excite the wonder, so they naturally call forth the curiosity of mankind to inquiries into their causes' (WN V.i.f.24) with sections 1 and 2 of the *Astronomy* which are respectively entitled 'Of the effect of Unexpectedness' and 'Of Wonder or of the effects of Novelty'. Or again, 'As those great Phenomena are the first objects of human curiosity, so the science which pretends to explain them must naturally have been the first branch of philosophy that was cultivated' (WN ibid.) with 'Of all the phenomena of nature the celestial appearances are, by their greatness and beauty the most universal objects of the curiosity of mankind' (Astronomy, IV.1). Surprise, Curiosity, Wonder—these were the feelings that moved men to become philosophers. In using the term *philosophy* as a synonym for *natural philosophy* Smith was only following the custom of the time: though his immortal work was entitled *Philosophiae naturalis Principia mathematica* Newton in his *Preface* refers simply to 'philosophy'. So long as the context left no cause for misunderstanding there could be no objection to this practice; but this proviso must not be forgotten. Elsewhere Smith had written 'The ancient Greek philosophy was divided into three great branches; physics or natural philosophy; ethics or moral philosophy; and logic' (WN V.i.f.23). Though a distinction between the genus and its species is here indicated, failure at times to make clear whether it is to the former or the latter that reference is being made adds considerably to the modern reader's difficulty in assessing Smith's progress towards the coming distinction between *philosophy* and *science*—a difficulty apt to be increased in such passages as: 'The science which pretends to investigate and explain those connecting principles is what is properly called philosophy.' On one notable occasion in the *Astronomy* Smith is caught by the net of his own loose terminology into an unrecognized contradiction that makes nonsense of his argument (Astronomy, IV.18).

My concern with linguistic usage must not be regarded as mere pedantry: it is intimately bound up with the title of this essay, a title consciously adopted instead of the more usual 'Philosophy of Science'.[4] At the purely linguistic level the ascription to Adam Smith of a 'philosophy of science' is clearly unhistorical: to him and his contemporaries such an expression would have been tautologous if not meaningless. This is of course in no way to impute lack of understanding to those recent writers to whom I have

[4] e.g. O. H. Taylor, *A History of Economic Thought* (1960), Ch. 3; Herbert F. Thomson, *Quarterly Journal of Economics*, lxxix (1965), 212–33. Cf. T. D. Campbell, *Adam Smith's Science of Morals* (1971).

referred, each of whom puts forward a reasoned, though I think hardly convincing, claim for the importance of Smith's contribution to what is *now* regarded as 'philosophy of science'. Unfortunately there is still no general agreement as to what constitutes the *philosophy* of science, not to mention the still vigorous, even violent, disagreements on whether a particular body of knowledge qualifies as a 'science'. For these reasons I have thought it worth while, though far less versed in Smith's other works than these and other contributors to the discussion, to take a leaf out of Smith's book, or what I conceive to be his 'book', and consider his place in the *history of ideas*. Though the term itself did not exist, Smith's 'juvenile' aim was I think rather to discover the *history* of the *idea* of science, or 'philosophy' as he would synonymously have called it. His partial success in this aim enabled him to apply the result to the fields of inquiry—the *Imitative Arts*, the *First Formation of Languages*, the *Theory of Moral Sentiments*, and finally the *Nature and Causes of the Wealth of Nations*—that at different times filled the first place in the field of his interests.

In referring for convenience to the *History of Astronomy* etc. we must not lose sight of the fact that these 'histories' are as it were chapters of a work whose title was *The Principles which lead and direct Philosophical Enquiries*; it is only as *illustrations* of these 'Principles' that the histories are to be considered. Only if what we should call the psychological (and perhaps sociological) conditions of the advancement of the sciences are regarded as part of the 'philosophy' of science is Smith's endeavour certainly part, but perhaps the lesser part, of that philosophy. Since *faute de mieux* and in view of the lack of any general agreement as to details I prefer to regard *any* reasoned and critical talk *about* science as constituting its 'philosophy', I should be very willing to concede that Smith had made an important contribution thereto. That in the course of his investigation (see below, 52) he made some striking and novel observations that went beyond mere illustration and involved hypotheses of a bold and controversial nature I should not deny; but it is the absence of any overt recognition that any problems (other than historical) are involved that would I think exclude the possibility of his acceptance as a 'philosopher' of science by those who take a narrower view of the connotation of the term than I do. What they might be willing to concede is that only after the distinction between 'philosophy' and 'science' had been introduced (as it was during the decades following Smith's death in 1790) could a separate discipline called 'philosophy of science' emerge, and that towards this clarification Smith had, albeit unconsciously, made a significant contribution. Such is my justification for attempting to estimate Adam Smith's place in the history of ideas.

If we have had to take careful account of the present uncertain boundaries of the 'philosophy of science' we are met with a historically much more subtle and extensive conceptual range in respect of the 'history of ideas'. For the public recognition of this conveniently vague field of endeavour we can give a precise date—January 1940—when the first number of the *Journal of the History of Ideas* appeared under the editorship of Arthur O. Lovejoy, who also contributed a substantial introductory memoir setting forth the aim of the new periodical to encourage investigation in what might be called the 'interstices' or 'frontiers' of history and philosophy. Unlike some enthusiasts for new 'disciplines' Lovejoy provided in a separate publication a masterly example of the need for, and achievement of, such investigation in the form of his famous work on *The Great Chain of Being*—an 'idea' that had in varying degrees been potent in European literature from the time of Plato into the nineteenth century, but of which no history had ever been written. As a record of the changing application of this pervasive 'idea'—sometimes expressed in the form of *plenitude*—and of the esteem in which it was held Lovejoy's work was unquestionably *history*; yet it was history not of what men had *done* but of what they had *thought.* Unfortunately categorization was not facilitated by the fact that in the years immediately following Lovejoy's William James Lectures at Harvard (1933, published 1936) R. G. Collingwood was developing his philosophic theory that 'the historian must re-enact the past in his own mind', from which Collingwood inferred that 'chronicles' of what men *did* become 'history' only in terms of what they *thought.*[5] If this influential but not universally accepted judgement is true, then *all* history is of 'ideas'. Since despite the difficulties it involves I have found no more satisfying characterization of history I must emphasize that for me the label 'history of ideas' *tout court* is no more than a denotatory sign for the study of one aspect of history. That this difficulty was so to say 'felt' rather than formulated by the eighteenth-century *soi-disant* historians is suggested by their introduction of qualifying expressions indicating at least a new approach to history.

II

Though we have every reason to believe that it was in the *History of Astronomy* that Adam Smith first set down his aim to 'illustrate the principles which lead and direct philosophical inquiries', his first essay in 'philosophical history' to be published was the *Considerations concerning the First Formation of Languages and the Different Genius of Original and Compounded Languages*, which was bound with the third edition of the *Theory of Moral Sentiments* in 1761. Despite his having given the wrong title and number of editions, Dugald Stewart's subsequent remarks could hardly be bettered as an introduction to this 'particular sort of enquiry,

[5] *The Idea of History*, ed. T. M. Knox from Collingwood's literary remains (1946), Editor's Preface, v and text, 282f.

which, so far as I know, is entirely of modern origin, and which seems in a peculiar degree to have interested Mr. Smith's curiosity. Something very similar to it may be traced in all his different works, whether moral, political, or literary . . .' (Stewart, II.45). What this 'sort of enquiry . . . entirely of modern origin' is about Stewart proceeds to reveal in the next paragraph, namely, 'by what gradual steps', in respect of 'our opinions, manners, and institutions', 'the transition has been made from the first simple efforts of uncultivated nature, to a state of things so wonderfully artificial and complicated'. As an example of such fields of inquiry he cites language; the origin of the different sciences and arts; the 'astonishing fabric of political union'. 'On most of these subjects very little information is to be expected from history; for long before that stage of society when men begin to think of recording their transactions, many of the most important steps of their progress have been made.' To an analytical philosopher of our time the above formulation of the enterprise will appear to involve circularity; his scepticism as to the validity of the procedure to be employed would be greatly enhanced by the uncritical assumptions that allowed it to be set in motion and which will appear in our subsequent more detailed consideration of Adam Smith's individual essays. Nevertheless, confused and even naïve as much of it may appear to our 'superior intelligence', a start had to be made some time, not only that the mind might be 'to a certain extent satisfied', but that a check might be given to that 'indolent philosophy, which refers to a miracle whatever appearances, both in the natural and moral worlds, it is unable to explain' (Stewart, II.48). Surely it is as right to applaud this dual aim as it would be wrong either to accept uncritically the proposed methods for its attainment or to despise these pioneer venturers into the uncharted past merely on the ground of the inadequacy of their instruments. The discovery of America was motivated by just such false assumptions and achieved despite the incompetence of Columbus to use such instruments as were available. That the urgency of the aim was widely felt Stewart proceeded to show by reference to 'Mr. Hume', the 'late M. d'Alembert', and Montesquieu. To the 'species of philosophical investigation', specimens of which these three men had published shortly before Smith's *First Formation of Languages*, Stewart proposed to give the name '*Theoretical or Conjectural History*; an expression which coincides pretty nearly in its meaning with that of *Natural History* [*of Religion*] as employed by Mr. Hume, and with what some French writers have called *Histoire Raisonnée*' (Stewart, II.48). Of these, Stewart's 'Conjectural History' seems to me the only one free from confusion—at any rate from the point of view of today.

Stewart's reference to d'Alembert is of special significance for Smith's *History of Astronomy*, a fact that Stewart himself was quick to note in a paragraph that is worth quoting in full:

The mathematical sciences, both pure and mixed, afford, in many of their branches, very favourable subjects for theoretical history and a very competent judge, the late M. d'Alembert, has recommended this arrangement of their elementary principles, which is founded on the natural succession of inventions and discoveries, as the best adapted for interesting the curiosity and exercising the genius of students. The same author points out as a model a passage in Montucla's *History of Mathematics*, where an attempt is made to exhibit the gradual progress of philosophical speculation, from the first conclusions suggested by a general survey of the heavens to the doctrines of Copernicus. It is somewhat remarkable, that a theoretical history of this very science (in which we have, perhaps, a better opportunity than in any other instance whatever, of comparing the natural advances of the mind with the actual succession of hypothetical systems) was one of Mr. Smith's earliest compositions, and is one of the very small number of his manuscripts which he did not destroy before his death.

(Stewart, II.50)

In a letter to the editors of the *Edinburgh Review* (1755), Smith himself referred to the excellence of d'Alembert's *Discours préliminaire* in the *Encyclopédie* (1751) but with no hint of its significance for 'conjectural history'. To Montucla he could not of course refer since the *Histoire des mathématiques* was not published until 1758. Before attempting an independent assessment of the attitude of d'Alembert (and of Montucla) I shall first give an outline of Smith's 'principles' as they are formulated and 'illustrated' in the three 'historical' *Essays*.

It was, it will be recalled, to the quality of 'unexpectedness' in certain natural phenomena that Smith attributed the feeling of 'wonder'; and it was 'wonder' that first drove men to seek out the causes of things. Before embarking on the history of astronomy that is to 'illustrate' this view he sums up his thesis as follows:

Their [*sc.* 'those of liberal fortunes'] imagination, which accompanies with ease and delight the regular progress of nature, is stopped and embarrassed by those [*sc.* astronomical] incoherences; they excite their wonder, and seem to require some chain of intermediate events, which, by connecting them with something that has gone before may thus render the whole course of the universe consistent and of a piece. Wonder, therefore, and not any expectation of advantage from its discoveries, is the first principle which prompts mankind to the study of philosophy...

(Astronomy, III.3)

Taken as a sample of 'conjectural' history, as a 'theory' as to how eighteenth-century (natural) philosophy *could* have been set on its course in earlier times, this passage shows remarkable insight that is not without significance for recent dissensions on the nature of scientific investigation. The subsequent account of the course of scientific astronomy most plausibly 'illustrated' its essential relevance. As an account of the origin of natural philosophy as such, and not of the highly sophisticated astronomy already current in Smith's day, it is vitiated by a number of *historical* assumptions to question which does not seem to have occurred to Smith or to any of the engaging 'amateurs'[6] whose elegant fictions passed for 'history' at the time that he was writing. How for instance, could Smith *know* that 'wonder and not any expectation of advantage' was the *first* 'principle' to prompt mankind to the study of 'philosophy'.[7] Had Ludwig Wittgenstein been available to fill the idle hours at Oxford he might have been able to persuade Smith that what he was doing was less 'history' than seeking a definition of his term 'philosophy'. When he speaks about mankind being prompted to a *study* of philosophy did he realize that 'philosophy' was not something 'there', like the apparent movements of the planets, but a new way of *looking* at what was 'there'? His intuition, here and elsewhere, was, I fancy, sounder than his forms of expression, in which he had failed to break out of the rigid formulas of the schools which in other contexts he so roundly condemned. Though in general he adhered to the current fashion for rhetorical elegance he showed in his enthusiastic response to Berkeley's sign-theory (*The External Senses*) a readiness to take an analytical approach to language. For this reason I think he would have been willing to agree about the misleading nature of such latter-day clichés as 'science says', 'modern science', and the 'endowment of science'; all three are latent in 'Science moves but slowly, slowly', though this poetic licence may have hidden Tennyson's recognition that what the physicist and influential philosopher of science, P. W. Bridgman, called 'sciencing' is the fundamental nature of 'science'. 'Modern science' viewed as a corpus of information of a certain kind differs in no essential way from Wisden (though it is probably less reliable!). Nor of course does science 'say' anything; only individual scientists do so, even granting that the *relatively* universal agreement is one of the defining characteristics of at least some sciences. Science in the sense of Smith's 'philosophy' is essentially *action* whether in the mode of material instruments or in the manipulation of ideas according to certain rules, conventions, and 'models'. But whereas the generic term *Wissenschaft* signals the relative independence of this kind of action with respect to the matter to which it may be applied, the Anglo-Saxon mistranslation of the Latin *scientia* is the source of ridiculous brawls as to pecking order, not of course restricted to the Anglo-Saxon world. Despite its clumsiness I prefer Bridgman's 'sciencing' to the more recent 'doing science' exemplified in Professor J. H. Hexter's recent *Doing History*

[6] Rousseau seems to have been an exception. See J. I. MacAdam, 'The Discourse on Equality and the Social Contract', *Philosophy*, xlvii (1972), 309.

[7] Cf. J. S. Mill (a great admirer of *The Wealth of Nations*): 'In every department of human affairs Practice long precedes Science: systematic enquiry into the modes of action of the powers of nature is the tardy product of a long course of efforts to use those powers for practical ends', *Works* (1965), ii.2.

(London, 1971) in which he makes out a strong case against the distortion of 'science' by the separation of the practice of investigation from the 'rhetoric' most appropriate to the expression of the results: a sense in which 'the medium is the message'. My preference is based on the desirability of removing the last traces of the hangover from the 'substantival' theory of knowledge in which the latter is envisaged as something 'out there' waiting to be 'discovered'.

That Smith might have been sympathetic to this point of view is suggested by his emphasis on 'wonder'; the suggestion is strengthened by his insistence on the 'imagination' being 'shocked and embarrassed by those incoherencies' that seem to require a chain of intermediate events; and finally by the standard by which he proposed to judge of the quality of the suggested 'chains'—less their 'agreement or inconsistency with truth or reality' than 'how far each was fitted to sooth the imagination, and to render the theatre of nature a more coherent, and therefore a more magnificent, spectacle, than otherwise it would have appeared to be' (Astronomy, II.12). Even allowing for the rhetorical expressions natural to an enthusiastic student of the drama, this passage, though not at all inconsistent with a philosophy of 'positive' science, excites our interest much more by presenting a view of the 'idea of nature', if not wholly novel, at least standing out strongly against the background of his age. It will be necessary to comment more narrowly on some particular features of this view but it is convenient at this stage to contrast Smith's ideas with those of his contemporaries—d'Alembert, Montucla, and David Hume—and also with those of the originators of the ensuing debates—Francis Bacon and René Descartes. To maintain direction in our survey I shall commence with d'Alembert's definitive statement perused by Smith not later than 1755.

III

To do justice to d'Alembert's remarkable manifesto would of course demand a whole article—it is comparable in length to Smith's three 'historical' *Essays* taken together. It must have been written at about the same time as most likely was that of Smith's composition of all but the 'Newtonian' addition (Astronomy, IV.67–76, and editors' note) to the *Astronomy*; but d'Alembert was six years older than Smith. The author's aim—a 'philosophical' history of the progress of the human spirit since the rebirth of letters—strongly resembles Smith's subsequent *description* of his 'great work' but the outcome was totally different: the former a masterly and systematic survey of the field proposed; the latter—the *Astronomy* and the *Imitative Arts* excepted—no more than a noble dream. Yet the exceptions are sufficiently complete monuments to enable us to make profitable comparisons between the two styles.

Most striking of all perhaps is that the 'conjectural history' ingeniously employed by both writers led them to almost diametrically opposite conclusions: for Smith the origin of 'philosophy' was 'wonder, not any expectation of advantage'; for the Frenchman the discovery of the use (*usage*) to which bodies could be put—'the discovery of the mariner's compass is no less advantageous to the human race than would be to physics the explanation of the properties of that needle'. The nearest approach to 'wonder' is the admission that 'amusement' might have played some part. The reader may have been struck by the fact that the comparison of the invention of the compass with theory is a paraphrase of a similar passage in the *Advancement of Learning*[8] where the mariner's needle is compared with the sails. The *Discours* is in fact so permeated with the spirit of 'l'immortel Chancellier d'Angleterre' that Smith, in his *Edinburgh Review* letter (1755) had no more to say of the *Discours* than that 'Mr. Alembert gives an account of the connection of the different arts and sciences, their genealogy and filiation as he calls it, which, a few alterations and corrections excepted, is nearly the same as that of my Lord Bacon.' Maybe it was; but the 'genealogy or filiation' occupies a small part of the whole *Discours*. Of Bacon's works d'Alembert made the well-known judgement 'si justement estimés et plus estimés pourtant qu'ils ne sont connus, méritent encore plus notre lecture que nos éloges'. Whether through relative ignorance of his works or because of the studied rejection of Bacon's pragmatic view of 'philosophy' Smith seems to have been one of the first of those, still too numerous, who fail to do justice to Bacon's combination of universality and cautious reservations. Only in the *Moral Sentiments* is there a hint that Smith may have realized that a highly abstract science such as astronomy provides a very powerful 'illustration' of only one branch of 'philosophy'. Astronomy in his day presented a 'theatre' of unparalleled grandeur, precision, and economy only because, in Whitehead's phrase, it 'ignored everything which refused to come into line'. It consisted of little more than the correlation of rates-of-change of angles ('positions') with rates-of-change of other angles ('clocks'—the mechanical clocks being ultimately correlated with the 'stellar' clock): it was in fact little more than applied mathematics, having little relation, except as a 'model', to 'Nature'. D'Alembert was himself a leading mathematician in an age that included Clairaut, Euler, and Daniel Bernoulli, and to the end of his life insisted on the *ideal* of expressing all knowledge in terms of pure mathematics. Nevertheless he expressly stated, as Smith did not, that 'les abstractions mathématiques nous en facilitent la connaissance; mes elles ne sont utiles qu'autant qu'on ne s'y borne pas.' He soundly rates 'nos médicins algébristes' for treating the immensely complex human machine as if it were one of the simplest and the easiest to decompose. If in demanding the accumulation of as many facts as possible he lays himself open to

[8] *Philosophical Works*, ed. J. M. Robertson (1905), 99.

the charge of being a 'Baconian' (in the derogatory sense still popular in some quarters) he redeems it, as of course if less formally did Bacon himself (e.g. on the 'double scale', op. cit. 92–3), in emphasizing that it is necessary 'les rappeler a un certain nombre de faits principaux dont les autres ne soient que des conséquences'. Here he restores the emphasis proper to many areas of 'philosophy' as displayed in the axiomatic structure of Newton's *Principia* (N.Princ., 1–28). The logical form was not of course originated by Newton, as might perhaps be inferred from an uncritical reading of much of the secondary literature; and in the youthful Hume's exuberant optimism concerning the 'experimental philosophy' it is 'my Lord Bacon' who is taken as the milestone; Newton is not mentioned (*Treatise*, ed. Selby-Bigge, 1896, xxi). But of this more later (p. 64).

Fundamentally as the two thinkers (d'Alembert and Smith) differed as to aim and emphasis there was a great deal of common ground. One characteristic that they shared both with one another and with the great majority of their learned contemporaries was an ignorance of even relatively recent history as exemplified in d'Alembert's remark that Bacon was born *dans le sein de la nuit la plus profonde*. Such 'invincible ignorance' could only be the result of deeply ingrained prejudice: 'terms like religion, priest, Middle Ages, barbarism were for such persons not historical or philosophical or sociological terms with a definite scientific meaning . . . but simply terms of abuse' (Collingwood, *Idea of History*, 77). More excusably, where evidence was lacking they supplied a 'likely story'; in itself this, the essence of 'conjectural history', was a valuable extension of the device employed by Thucydides, of concocting speeches for the principal actors to lend to the well-attested historical events a dramatic appeal such as his readers were accustomed to in the theatre. What puzzles the modern reader is the willingness of men of intellectual power and general integrity, as were Smith and d'Alembert, to leave him in doubt as to where 'fact' ended and fiction began: the conjecture 'Les langues nées avec les Societés n'ont sans doute été d'abord qu'une collection assez bizarre des signes de toute espèce . . .' is on the following page developed, even in respect of details, as if it were an established fact. Ingenious and fascinating as were Smith's *Considerations* (above, p. 48) he nevertheless *assumes* that association of 'new instances' with the 'name of the correspondent idea' could not fail to take place. Nor does it seem to have entered his head that the advanced and specialized Latin language, in terms of which nearly all the examples of development of grammatical form are expressed, was almost totally irrelevant to the 'First Formation of Languages'. Similarly in his elegant 'account' of Ionian natural philosophy ('Ancient Physics') he gives the reader no guidance as to how much this is merely his own conjecture. In his lectures on rhetoric and belles-lettres (below, p. 62) he goes so far as to urge that since 'those facts of whose truth we are altogether satisfied' are more 'interesting' than those about which there is some doubt 'it would be more proper to narrate these facts [*sic*], without mentioning the doubt, than to bring in any long proofs' (LRBL 18.13; Lothian, 97). History is to be subservient to 'Rhetoric' as is, in other contexts, 'Philosophy'. About fifty years later ('An VII') than the *Discours préliminaire* Montucla admitted in the *Preface* to his greatly enlarged *Histoire des mathématiques* that he sometimes substituted for a 'developpement inconnu un de fictice et probablement peu différent du véritable'; the 'probablement' is significant, and the fiction more likely to be 'true' in a reconstruction of the development of mathematics than in that of language.

Mention of Montucla directs us to the more pleasant task of admiring the new style of 'intellectual history' that these men were calling for and in part supplying. In explicating the history of astronomy in terms of a response to 'wonder', 'surprise', and the need for a 'chain' or 'bridge' Smith set an example that, had it been followed, would have rid subsequent 'histories' of the bald lists of names and dates of the principal practitioners, and which in the case of science have only recently disappeared. Montucla categorically deplored such treatment; rather, he urged, should the attempt be made to present a 'tableau' revealing the 'esprit' of successive discoveries and the part played by those who had made them. In support he quoted the mathematician, Rémond de Montmort (not to be confused with the founder of the earlier 'Montmort Academy'), who in a letter to one of the Bernoullis had called for a history of mathematics to set beside those on painting, music, and medicine, which 'pourrait être regardé comme l'histoire de l'ésprit humain'. De Montmort did not live to complete his own considerable effort (referred to in 1721, but now no longer extant) to achieve this; but in thus categorizing such a history he seems to be the first to have sensed the significance of the history of *science* as a fundamental component in the history of ideas. The influence of Bacon (*si voisin des tenèbres*!!) on Montucla is evident in his 'second thoughts' to include in his history the 'mixed mathematics' of navigation, optics, and astronomy.

Since, however much and however late Smith may have 'corrected' his *History of Astronomy*, there can be no doubt that he had formulated the 'principles that lead and direct philosophical enquiries' before he could have known of d'Alembert's and Montucla's similar conjectures; the same conclusion can not of course apply to Descartes, whose *Passiones sive Affectus Animae* had been available for nearly a century, and to whose writings Smith made specific reference in the *Lectures on Rhetoric* as well as in the *Astronomy*. In the *Order and Enumeration of the Passions*[9] Descartes argued for *Admiratio* being 'prima omnium Passionum'. It is clear from the context that 'admiratio' is the equivalent of Smith's 'wonder'; in a

[9] *Opera philosophica*, editio ultima (the 'corrected' edn. published by Elsevir, Amsterdam 1677), Passiones Animae Art. LIII. Tr. Haldane and Ross (1931), 358.

rather inadequate preamble Smith does indeed admit that 'admire' has been used by good writers in the sense of 'wonder' or 'surprise'. Since the use to which 'wonder' is applied by Smith seems to me his most important contribution to 'philosophy of science' *sensu lato* (see p. 47) it is interesting to conjecture what part if any Descartes's emphasis on the primacy of *admiratio* may have played in suggesting this approach to the problem of discovery.

In developing his ideas on *admiratio* Descartes first correlates the psychic experiences with the supposed motion of 'spirits' in the nerves and cavities of the brain. Since Smith never exhibited any interest in such 'metaphysical' speculations I pass on to Art. LXXV (Haldane and Ross, 364): 'In what wonder particularly consists':

> it is useful inasmuch as it causes us to learn and retain in our memory things of which we were formerly ignorant; for we shall only wonder at that which appears rare and extraordinary to us, and nothing can so appear [unless] we have been ignorant of it, or also because it is different from the things which we have known; for it is this difference which causes it to be called extraordinary. Now although a thing which was unknown to us presents itself anew to our understanding or our senses, we do not for all that retain it in our memory, unless the idea which we have of it is strengthened in our brain by some passion or else by the application of our understanding which our will determines to a particular retention and reflection . . .

What seems to be common to Smith's and Descartes's account is that if we may assume that 'retention in the memory of a thing' is a necessary condition of knowledge then a further necessary condition is 'wonder' at its first perception. Descartes categorizes 'wonder' as the 'prime mover' of all passions; Smith does not in fact categorize it as a passion at all, but the whole tenor of his long introduction is to treat it as such. And in so doing he is setting himself apart from the position taken up by Hume, whose list (*Treatise*, 276–7) contains no suggestion of 'wonder'.[10]

The chances of discovering a direct 'influence' of Descartes on the 'juvenile' Smith are very small: Smith's earliest public expression of his views on related matters was his lectures on rhetoric and belles-lettres in Edinburgh in the period 1748–51 of which no trace remains. They are, however, believed to have been incorporated into his lectures from the chairs of logic and moral philosophy to which he was appointed at Glasgow in 1751 and 1752 respectively: but in the transcript of a student's notes for the academical year 1762–3 there is no reference to Descartes's views on the passions. As primarily a historian of ideas I am concerned less with tracing 'influences' and establishing 'priorities' than in 'conjecturing' why certain interpretations of ideas were current at particular epochs even, or perhaps

[10] Compare however 'As this difficulty excites the spirits, it is the source of wonder, surprise, and of all the emotions which arise from novelty.' *A Dissertation on the Passions, Philosophical Works* (1826), iv.231.

more so, if they were 'absorbed', perhaps unconsciously, from unacknowledged common sources. Once more we find d'Alembert walking as it were on a parallel road to Smith's; he ranks 'curiosité' as a passion and characterizes it as a 'désir inquiet . . . animé par une sorte de défit de ne pouvoir entièrement se satisfaire'. Linking the two men as they search for the springs of discovery is Descartes's emphasis on the need to find a 'chain'. I pass now to examine a rather more technical relationship between Descartes's and Smith's scheme of ideas.

The relationship I have in mind is that not only were both Descartes and Smith concerned at some stage (Smith near the beginning, Descartes near the end, of his philosophical enterprise) with the psychology of discovery as distinct from the grounds of knowledge, but each was at pains to refer it to some *mechanism*. This aspect of their relationship has been obscured, as has already been hinted at, by the fact that they approached the problem from what may be described as opposite ends: Descartes by the creation of a detailed mechanical model of how the passions 'worked', Smith by showing that the model of a 'celestial machine' had been created in order to 'sooth the imagination' and satisfy the craving for a 'bridge' or 'chain' between apparently disparate phenomena. Exasperating as the ramifications of Descartes's vortices, first and second elements, celestial matter, *et hoc genus omne* may be, no less than the psycho-physical demon controlling the flow of animal spirits through the pineal gland, it must never be forgotten that they were, he believed, based on *verae causae*, the 'occult powers' and ill-defined 'sympathies' of the pseudo-Aristotelians being summarily rejected. Though recognizing that the actual model had been superseded by the Newtonian system Smith readily accepted that

> Des Cartes was the first who attempted to ascertain, precisely, wherein this invisible chain consisted, and to afford the imagination a train of intermediate events, which succeeding each other in an order that was of all the others the most familiar to it, should unite those incoherent qualities, the rapid motion, and the natural inertness of the planets. Des Cartes was the first who explained wherein consisted the real inertness of matter; that it was not in an aversion to motion, or in a propensity to rest, but in a power of continuing indifferently either at rest or in motion, and of resisting, with a certain force, whatever endeavoured to change its state from one to the other.
>
> (Astronomy, IV.61)

It may be interesting to observe that the Paris 1647 edition of Descartes's *Principes de la philosophie* is included in the catalogue of the Bodleian Library for 1738—ten years before Smith was in residence at Balliol College.[11]

[11] Professor Mossner could find no evidence in the archives of the Bodleian Library that Adam Smith had ever borrowed there; Mr. Quinn, Librarian of Balliol College Library has kindly informed me of a similar lack of evidence at Balliol. Since W. D. Mackay

Descartes recognized that there is not much difference between the Copernican system and that of Tycho Brahe except that the latter had rejected the former's assumption of the motion of the Earth as 'absurd'. But Brahe's rejection, Descartes averred, was 'pource qu'il n'a pas assez consideré quelle set la vraye nature du mouvement'. He himself preferred the Copernican system as a whole but would retain a stationary Earth though for better reasons than those given by Brahe: these 'better reasons' were of course Descartes's postulation of the principle of inertia subsequently formulated as the First Law of Motion by Newton who wrongly attributed it to Galileo. The 'straight line' envisaged by the latter, who had not freed himself from Aristotelian concepts as completely as he supposed, was a circle centred at the Earth's centre—*observationally* indistinguishable from a Euclidean straight line. Descartes's final comment on his own system is in our context the most important of all: 'Et cependant j'advertis que je ne pretens point qu'elle soit recevé comme entièrement conform a la verité, mais seulement comme une hypothese ou supposition qui peut estre fausse.' How does this view stand in relation to Smith's assertion that the adequacy of the 'chains' or 'bridges' supplied by 'philosophy' must be judged by criteria 'without regarding their absurdity or probability, their agreement or inconsistency with truth and reality'?

A full consideration of this question would outstrip the available space and the competence of the author; but without entering into current controversies as to the meaning of 'truth and reality' it is important and possible to place Smith's judgement firmly in the history of ideas, Descartes's being taken as a special case. The *locus classicus* concerning the 'truth' of astronomical systems is in the commentary of Simplicius on Aristotle's *Physics* where, allegedly quoting earlier authorities, Simplicius himself emphasizes that while 'the physicist will, in many cases, reach the cause by looking to creative force', 'it is no part of the business of an astronomer to know what is by nature suited to a position of rest, and what sort of bodies are apt to move, but he *introduces hypotheses* under which some bodies remain fixed, while others move and then considers to which hypotheses the phenomena actually observed in the heaven will correspond' (quoted from T. Heath, *Greek Astronomy*, London, 1932, 124–5, italic added). When Descartes wrote: '. . . les astronomes ont inventé trois [*sc.* Ptolemaic, Copernican, Tychonic] differentes hypotheses ou suppositions, qu'ils ont seulement tasché de rendre propres a expliquer tous les phainomenes sans s'arrester particuliement à examiner si elles estoient avec cela conformes à la verité', he had a sound historical precedent. How far he was aware of

(*Annals of the Bodleian Library*, 1890, 208) states that at that time the recorded *withdrawals* seldom amounted to more than one a day and often none, it does not follow that Smith never *consulted* books there. For Professor Mossner's suggestion of alternative sources used by Smith see his *Adam Smith—the Biographical Approach*.

this is uncertain; but he was very well aware that it was the prudent line to take in his *own* historical circumstances since this was what Galileo's condemnation by the Holy Office was all about. If that pugnacious 'astronomer' had, as Cardinal Bellarmino tried to persuade him to, restricted his claim to the *astronomical* superiority of the system of Copernicus (whose great work, *De Revolutionibus Orbium Coelestium*, 1543, was of course dedicated to Paul III) he might have remained an ornament instead of a condemned heretic of the Church of which he was almost certainly a devoted son. But the 'physicist' kept on breaking in.

In fact, in almost every quarter the 'bloodless categories' attributed to the 'astronomers' were no longer fashionable: despite the Foreword to the *De Revolutionibus* written anonymously by its (Lutheran) editor, Andreas Osiander, Copernicus unquestionably regarded the motion of the planet Earth as a real motion; half a century later Kepler, the first to break through the Platonic demand for uniform circular motion as alone appropriate to 'things divine', was motivated by physical ('or if you like metaphysical') conceptions. As a stage in the march of ideas, the confrontation between Galileo and the Church of Rome (Kepler being similarly threatened by the Reformed Church) was inevitable; but it was no simple issue of 'truth and reality'. The Church did its best to provide a scientifically respectable escape-route; Galileo, for scientifically untenable reasons, insisted on the 'truth' of the Copernican system instead of merely, as the evidence of the phases of Venus justified his doing, on the 'falsity' of the Ptolemaic. On the advantages of the Tychonic system, *not* falsified by the telescopic evidence, he maintained a discrete, or rather indiscrete, silence. By the time that the youthful Smith was willing to settle for a 'chain' irrespective of its 'truth' there was no such dilemma as Descartes had had to face: the Kirk of Scotland, though hardly 'liberal' in its attitudes, had more fundamental 'deviations' to 'correct', as Smith had not much later to warn his friend, David Hume.

IV

From what has been said it begins to look as if the usual view that the 'method' adopted by the 'Scottish School' in constructing their 'Science of Man' was 'Newtonian' is at least in need of qualification. Before we attempt to assess how much of it was in fact 'Cartesian' it is important to take both a broader and deeper look into the 'Newtonian Age' itself than has, I believe, yet been done in this connection. I use the term 'Newtonian Age' as a flag of convenience to cover both Newton's own attitude to his achievement and the latter's reception by his contemporaries, which was far from being that appropriate to the 'tutelary deity' he became for Smith's contemporaries. It is convenient to start with Smith's own admission that though Descartes had been the 'first' to provide a 'chain', yet by the time (at latest 1758) he was writing his account of the Newtonian system the latter 'prevails over all opposition'. Though there is evidence that the Cartesian philosophy was taught in Edinburgh at a relatively early date, there is no doubt that David Gregory was expounding the Newtonian some time before 1692[12] when he left to become Savilian Professor of Astronomy at Oxford. So in Great Britain at least the Newtonian system was largely effective half a century before Smith could have made his judgement and, *a fortiori*, before he showed himself to have a pretty good idea of its nature. Newton himself, despite his *caveat* about 'hypotheses' (an observation still misinterpreted out of context—it refers not to 'gravity' but to the *cause* of gravity) insisted that 'gravity does really exist and act according to the laws which we have explained and abundantly serves to account for all the motions of the celestial bodies and of our sea'. If pressed, Smith would, I think, have accepted without hesitation the first and probably the second of these propositions, the third only with some reservations; all would turn on the meaning of 'account for'. For those—and in the course of two centuries they became the great majority—natural philosophers who regarded Newton as the *beau idéal* of what later came to be called 'positivism' the famous paragraph on gravity and hypotheses remained in 'splendid isolation': 'particular propositions are inferred from the phenomena and afterward rendered general by induction'[13]—what could be more 'positive', even if no one was quite sure what Newton meant by 'induction'? In recent times, however, more attention has been paid to the paragraph of the *General Scholium* that follows, and to the four pages that precede, the 'positive' one (N.Princ. 543–7). The concluding paragraph opens: 'And now we might add something concerning a most subtle spirit, which pervades and lies hid in all gross bodies . . .', by the action of which attractions and repulsions—gravitational, electrical, and cohesive (i.e. chemical)—would be explained, together with heat, light, sensation, and 'the members of animal bodies move at the command of the will' (N.Princ. 547). But perhaps to amplify and 'correct' the ambiguous passage on 'hypotheses' he continued: 'we are not furnished with that sufficiency of experiments which is required to an accurate determination and demonstration of the laws by which this electric[14] and elastic spirit operates'. There seems to have been no doubt in Newton's mind of the *existence* of this 'spirit'; but he would not commit himself to a dogmatic statement in the absence of knowledge of 'the laws by which it acts'. Was Newton then tied to a 'real' mechanical explanation of the universe like Descartes? There is no 'metaphysical' difference between Newton's 'spirit' and Descartes's

[12] For a recent assessment see P. D. Lawrence and A. G. Molland, 'David Gregory's Inaugural Lecture at Oxford', *Notes and Records of the Royal Society*, xxv (1970), 143–78.

[13] All quotations from the *Principia* are taken from Motte's translation in the edition of F. Cajori (1934), hereinafter cited as 'N.Princ.', Newton's *Opticks* are cited as 'N.Op.'

[14] The word 'electric' was added (quite plausibly) by Motte.

'ether'; there was, however, the immense pragmatic difference that in respect of the planetary (and cometary) motions the laws of its action 'worked', whereas those of Descartes did not. But that is not the end of the matter: the four pages preceding the 'positive' manifesto demand our attention.

Smith, it will be recalled, laid great stress on his claim that Newton's 'greatest and most admirable improvement that was ever made in philosophy' was that 'he could join together the movements of the planets by so familiar a principle of connection which completely removed all the difficulties the imagination had hitherto felt in attending them'. If all the difficulties were removed from Smith's imagination, this was far from being the case with the continental philosophers, notably Leibniz. No one could quarrel with Smith's insistence on the 'familiarity of gravity', or with the justice of the analogy between the inverse square law of its action and the experimentally demonstrated law in respect of light proceeding from a centre. What was *not* 'familiar' was the assumption that in respect of the celestial motions gravity must act *instantaneously* (which light did *not*) *through immense distances in empty space.* On the physical level Newton's system rested on an assumption of baffling difficulty—if indeed such an 'action at a distance' was not a 'philosophical' *contradiction* demanding a return to the Aristotelian 'occult powers' that Newton and his contemporaries flattered themselves they had expelled for ever. But there was another assumption that shocked many contemporaries even more: it is sometimes forgotten that the seventeenth-century mind—unlike that of Smith's day—was at least as deeply concerned with theology as it was with the 'new experimental philosophy'. Newton had to admit (N.Op. Query 31) that owing to the mutual gravitation of the planets on each other 'some inconsiderable irregularities' from the calculated orbits had already arisen and 'which will be apt to increase till the system wants a reformation', to restore the cosmic harmony. It was presumably with this passage in mind that Leibniz wrote in 1715 that 'according to the doctrine of Sir Isaac Newton and his followers', 'God Almighty wants to wind up his watch from time to time' and more in the same vein. (Quoted from *The Leibniz-Clarke Correspondence*, ed. H. G. Alexander, Manchester 1956, 11.) It was left to the atheist, Simon Laplace, to demonstrate mathematically that owing to internal compensation within the solar system no such 'rewinding' is necessary; but this was some time after the latest date at which Smith was at all likely to have written on Newton.

Thus far we have been concerned mainly with Smith's attitude to Newton's conclusions—both what we might call epistemological and metaphysical in character. It is true that for the eighteenth century the former term did not exist and the latter was on the whole a dirty word; furthermore, as Glenn R. Morrow noted (*Adam Smith: Moralist and Philosopher* . . .

1776–1926, University of Chicago, 1928, 8), Smith himself was one of the least metaphysical persons of his century. But, as has already been suggested (61), it is Smith's *reasons* for preferring Newton's system beyond all others that gives his views their special interest—reasons which combined the *Cartesian* 'conventionalism' in respect of 'truth' with moral ('soothing the imagination'), aesthetic (providing a more dramatically effective 'spectacle'), and even, as (personal communication) Andrew Skinner has suggested, 'economic' in that it removes the 'disutility' of moral 'uneasiness'. There is nothing 'Newtonian' about these *attitudes*: in his *Rules for Philosophising* and elsewhere Newton insists on his system being accepted as 'accurately or very nearly true . . . till such time as other phenomena occur by which they may either be made more accurate or liable to exceptions' (N.Princ. 409). For Newton himself its chief merit was that in Dryden's words it 'publishes to every land the work of an almighty hand'.

Though Smith's recognition that the Newtonian system could admirably *illustrate* his 'juvenile' views on philosophical inquiries was a remarkable achievement I must enter a *caveat* against the too literal acceptance of Dr. T. D. Campbell's recent claim (op. cit. 21) that '*The Wealth of Nations* and even more the *Moral Sentiments* are attempts to apply his understanding of Newtonian scientific methods to the study of society'. Without being merely captious it would, I think, be a more acceptable judgement to refer to it as his (Smith's) *mis*understanding, or at least misdescription; Smith, it is true (LRBL 24.7; Lothian, 139–40) stated that '. . . we may lay down certain principles primary [reading uncertain] or proved, in the beginning from whence we account for the several phenomena connecting all together by the chain. This . . . we may call the Newtonian method.' But with a characteristic eighteenth-century *non sequitur* he proceeds to admit that 'Descartes was in reality the first who attempted this method'. Smith's loose description of this 'method' is perhaps sufficiently near to Descartes's (in his *Principia*), who was of course not the first to use it; but it was not much more than a shadow of Newton's. In the *expository* demonstration of his *Principia* Newton employs a method very closely resembling that used and published ten years previously by Spinoza in his *Ethica ordine geometrico demonstrata*, so-called since it followed the style of Euclid's *Elements* of geometry, the propositions or theorems (Newton draws a perhaps rather pedantic distinction between these) being derived deductively from a set of *definitions* and *axioms*. Newton differs from Spinoza in that the three 'axioms or laws' of motion are rooted in experience and the theorems deduced by highly ingenious mathematical techniques. The sequential form of the argument was called (e.g. by Descartes) *synthetic* and was closely related to the *methodus compositiva* familiar for centuries to the despised 'medievals' and traceable through Galen and Cicero to Aristotle's *Posterior Analytics*—a fact that Smith, in comparing what he called the 'method of Aristotle', completely ignores. Thus Newton's *demonstration*. But before demonstration can even begin the 'principles' 'from whence we account for the several phenomena' have to be *discovered*; where Newton's 'method' differed from Smith's and Descartes's is revealed in a letter (6 July 1672) to Henry Oldenburg: 'You know the proper method for inquiring after the properties of things is to deduce them from experiments' (*The Correspondence of Isaac Newton*, i, Cambridge 1959, 208). This was fifteen years before the appearance of the *Principia*; but thirty years *after* its appearance Newton remained of the same opinion: 'As in mathematics so in natural philosophy, the investigation of difficult things by the method of analysis ought ever to precede the method of composition (or synthesis). This analysis consists in making experiments and observations and in drawing general conclusions from them by induction' (N.Op. Query 31).

There is of course no logical term about which less agreement has been reached than 'induction'. What Newton meant by it is still disputed, but it certainly differs from Bacon's whose 'induction', once hailed as the foundation of 'modern science', it is still fashionable in some quarters to reject with contempt. That Bacon mixed with sound logical theory a great deal of extraneous by-play is beyond question; but in rejecting 'induction' as playing no part in scientific investigation Sir Karl Popper (than whom no one has done more to clarify the problem) misses an essential factor that Adam Smith, at least implicitly, did not. This is the element of 'surprise', also stressed by Descartes and Hume. Now 'novelty' and its concomitant 'wonder' can arise only in relation to a content already supposed exhaustively subsumed by 'custom': in Whitehead's telling phrase 'We habitually observe by the method of difference. Sometimes we see an elephant and sometimes we don't' (*Process and Reality*, Cambridge, 1929, 5). Of course such a simple inductive procedure plays little or no part in those 'advanced' sciences that are the most frequent examples studied by 'philosophers of science'; but even in these a new branch (e.g. cosmic rays, radioactivity) may be born by the shock of the unexpected without any 'hypothesis' or attempt at 'falsification' being involved. Perhaps the supposed *primary* necessity for *hypothesis* has been confused with *intentionality*; but that is another story.

If we examine Smith's actual practice, for example in Chapter vii of *The Wealth of Nations*, accounted by Joseph Schumpeter (op. cit. 189) the best piece of economic theory produced by Smith, we do find a certain parallelism to the *Principia*; but we have to look for it. 'Average rates of wages, profit; and of rent; natural rates; natural price'—these are introduced as *definitions*. 'The commodity is then sold for precisely what it is worth' might be called the First Law of Exchange. It arises, like Newton's First Law, from experience, and (though this was hardly recognized before Ernst Mach's critical analysis in the *Science of Mechanics*, 1883, Engl. ed. 1893) embodies in effect a *definition* of 'real cost', hence of 'exchange worth'. It differs from Newton's Law in involving the deductive argument by which the introduction of these concepts is justified. It necessarily differs, as does the whole of Smith's *corpus*, from the 'Newtonian' method *sensu strictu* in not being based on *experiment*. The practice of the mature Smith may be compared with that of the youthful Hume: the latter explicitly refers to the 'application of experimental philosophy to moral subjects' (*Treatise*, xx–xxiii); reveals an adequate insight into the 'method' of this philosophy even to a clear recognition of the 'peculiar disadvantage' in moral philosophy 'which is not found in natural'; proceeds with characteristic Humean double-think to confound experiment and observation; and finally (332f.) sets out as 'proofs' of his 'hypothesis' eight 'experiments' that are in fact mere exemplifications. In extenuation it must be recalled that in 1775 Hume publicly repudiated the *Treatise*;[15] but in the introductory chapter of the *Enquiry* (1.10.16) his delineation of the style of 'abstruse, profound philosophy', whose 'abstractness' he proposes to 'surmount by care and art', follows the Newtonian inductive line of 'proceeding from particular instances to general principles'. The taint of 'enthusiasm' has, however, been expunged; the great revolution in thought to be expected by application of the 'experimental philosophy' to the science of man is no longer referred to.

V

Though any conclusion can be no more than tentative I must now attempt to formulate a personal assessment of *Adam Smith and the History of Ideas*. Since I have neither the space nor the competence to appraise the adequacy of Smith's actual practice—a question with which most of the writers on his 'method' have been concerned—I shall confine myself to the two historical questions: (i) what contribution, if any, did Smith make towards the subsequent recognition of the *idea* of the History of Ideas, and (ii) how does he stand in relation to such history?

The writing of this essay was prompted by the suspicion that whereas Smith was but one of several thinkers who saw the necessity for enlarging the boundaries of history to include the development of the 'different branches of Literature, Philosophy, Poetry and Eloquence', he alone combined a fairly detailed knowledge of the history of the ideas of an 'exact' science (astronomy) with the subsequent recognition of the significance of this critical historical method to effect a better understanding of the most diverse areas of human knowledge—a significance admirably expressed by one whose own significance Smith never seems to have recognized: 'We

[15] The possible reason for this is discussed by J. O. Nelson, *Philosophical Review*, lxxi (1972), 333.

shall not obtain the best insight into things until we actually see them growing from the beginning.'[16] The supposition that such a task lay within the compass of a single human mind—even in 1750—was of course absurd; but the vision represents a landmark in the progress of the human spirit.

This claim as to Smith's place in the emergence of the History of Ideas can not be wholly separated from the quality and circumstances of his achievement. Though in the first three *Essays* he claimed to be writing history, the quality of the historical achievement cannot be rated very high: his allusions—unlike Hume's in the *Natural History of Religion*—are hardly ever backed by references to sources; he has no *chronological* sense of growth—the admirable analysis of the late development of languages, though forming the greater part of the essay, is wholly irrelevant to the *First Formation*. It might indeed be argued that his skilful use of the 'history' of astronomy to 'illustrate' a *philosophical* thesis is a paradigm of the 'contrived' history that has been the bane of the history of science down to our own day.[17]

A more cogent claim might be put forward for his application to human experience in general of the philosophical method more rigorously grounded by Edmund Husserl under the name of 'transcendental phenomenology'. Already in the *Treatise* Hume had made a similar effort (e.g. the recognition of the incorrigibility of 'feelings' as such, but one which was vitiated by his inability to reject the phenomenological blunder of *assuming* psychological atomism). Smith 'transcends' the vicious abstraction latent in the *universal* application of the 'machine' analogy by insisting on the necessity for *constant* properties. Left to itself the socio-economic 'machine' is self-adjusting towards equilibrium (WN I.111); it may even be 'manipulated' as *a whole*; but 'the man of system seems to imagine that he can arrange the different members of a great society with as much ease as the hand arranges the different pieces on a chess-board; he does not consider that the pieces on a chess-board have no other principle of motion besides that which the hand impresses upon them; but that, in the great chess-board of human society, every single piece has a principle of motion of its own altogether different from that which the legislature might choose to impress upon it' (TMS VI.ii.2.17).

In his published works Smith both acknowledged and criticized Hume.

[16] It is difficult to imagine on what grounds Smith could have concluded that Aristotle 'appears to have been as much superior to his master Plato in everything but eloquence' (Ancient Logics, 3 note) in view of the fact that on the rare occasions when he refers to Aristotle it is in the most superficial terms.

[17] An example is the persistent myth that James Watt owed the idea of the separate condenser to his association with the 'academic' Joseph Black. The most recent assessment is W. A. Smeaton, 'Some Comments on James Watt's Published Account of his Work on Steam and Steam Engines', *Notes and Records of the Royal Society*, xxvi (1971), 35–42. An earlier cruder example is that the 'Industrial Revolution' had been 'caused' by the invention of the steam engine.

After Smith's death John Millar, who had been his pupil and then occupied the chair of law at Glasgow, wrote 'I should like to see his powers of illustration employed upon the true old Humean philosophy', implying that Smith had read at least the *Treatise* at the time of writing the *Philosophical Essays* (See below, 84 n.4). If there is such a thing as the 'true old Humean philosophy' a fairly extensive study of his philosophical works has failed to reveal it to me; nevertheless such striking passages as: 'Admiration and surprise have the same effect as the other passions' (*Treatise*, 120) cannot be ignored. Admittedly this has to do with 'belief' rather than 'invention'; but when Hume's magic wand, the 'imagination', is first waved (*Treatise*, 6) to remove an incongruity in his theory it is to fill a 'gap' observed in a discontinuous colour-scale. By being less 'metaphysical' than Hume Smith was able to avoid the 'twists and turns'[18] the latter had to resort to in order to escape contradictions he had correctly deduced from his over-simplification of the 'data of the understanding'. A parallel of a more general nature depends on the extent to which Smith's what we may call 'criterion of acceptability' of an 'improvement in philosophy' may be regarded as a claim on 'belief'. Hume's conclusion that 'belief is more properly an act of the sensitive, than of the cogitative part of our natures' (*Treatise*, 183) would then afford a striking parallel. Smith's criterion of 'soothing the mind' is readily related to Hume's claim that when 'the attention is on the stretch' the 'posture of the mind' is uneasy and 'straining of the imagination always hinders the regular flowing of the passions and sentiments' (*Treatise*, 185). That Smith regarded 'philosophical enquiries' as actuated, and their results as evaluated, by the 'sensitive part of our natures' is further strengthened by his appeals to aesthetic criteria—'. . . to render the theatre of nature . . . a more magnificent spectacle'.

Partaking of both 'sensitive' and 'cogitative' elements was Smith's hint that the progress of understanding could be regarded as the successive refinements of a *language* appropriate for describing and explicating the observed complexities of nature. His strongly worded approval of Berkeley's 'semantic' theory of perception in which adequate 'signs' need not be 'like' the objects signified shows that his mind was still running on this comparison some years after the greater part of the *Astronomy* had been written[19] (External Senses, 44, 63).

In making a final estimate of Smith's significance in and for the History of Ideas we should avoid the tendency to exaggerate, such as in my view somewhat reduces the impact of some of the earlier writers on his 'scientific method'. As a historian he was no more than a well-read amateur; in this

[18] The expression is Professor J. A. Passmore's to whose *Hume's Intentions* (1952) I am greatly indebted.

[19] For a detailed exposition of this point of view the reader is referred to Professor Ralph Lindgren's article, 'Adam Smith's Theory of Enquiry', *Journal of Political Economy*, lxxvii (1969), 897–915.

he was no worse than his contemporaries with the possible exception of Hume, whose essay 'Of the Rise and Progress of the Arts and Sciences' (first published anonymously in *Essays Moral and Political*, Edinburgh 1741, nearly ten years before the likely date of Smith's early *Essays*) casts a revealing light on this situation. 'It is more easy', Hume wrote, 'to account for the rise and progress of commerce in any kingdom, than for that of learning . . . there is no subject in which we must proceed with more caution, than in tracing the history of the arts and sciences; lest we assign causes which never existed, and reduce what is merely contingent to stable and universal principles.' All unconsciously he proceeds to exemplify this danger by arguing—very effectively, indeed—for the prior necessity of free institutions. Within a few pages he does not even argue but announces the 'utter depravation of every kind of learning' in—of course—the Middle Ages. All the critical historiography of Camden, Spelman, Dugdale, Selden, and the Bollandists had evidently been in vain; the just previous epoch-making *Scienza nuova* (1725) of Giambattista Vico, though probably known in France, was ignored. Instead of carefully defined concepts a few 'resounding commonplaces' as Professor E. Smith Fussner cruelly calls them (*The Historical Revolution*, London 1962, 320), like 'Nature' and 'Reason' were held to have 'established strict rules of criticism to try the truth of fact, but after all "Reason" was no more a scientific term than "Nature"'. Those who used Reason as the touchstone for truth and value and who survived until 1789 saw their ideal vanish in the flames of the Bastille: thereafter, for a generation, not reason but blood was men's argument. Smith in the *Moral Sentiments* must be credited with breaking new ground in relying more on establishing a 'test-situation', a kind of 're-thinking' through the medium of an ideal spectator, than on mere conjecture from 'Reason' and the 'Unalterable facts of Human Nature'.

Though by his historical *naïveté* Smith is precluded from ranking as a *founder* of the History of Ideas his work, as I have tried to show, forms a reservoir of ideas which such historians would be unwise not to explore: the vigorous new shoots of growth in the social sciences among his successors in Scotland provide the first evidence of their value.[20]

At the last Memorial Celebration of the appearance of *The Wealth of Nations* Professor Viner said '. . . how refreshing it is to return to *The Wealth of Nations* with its eclecticism, its good temper, its commonsense, and its willingness to grant that those who saw things differently from itself were only partly wrong' (in *Adam Smith . . . 1776–1926*, University of Chicago Press, 1928, 155). In those areas I have been able to study, and aided by nearly half a century of research by many hands, I have found no reason to refrain from extending this appraisement to the book's author.

[20] See e.g. Andrew Skinner, 'Natural History in the Age of Adam Smith', *Political Studies*, xv (1967), 32–48.

III

Scientific Explanation and Ethical Justification in the *Moral Sentiments*

T. D. Campbell*

ADAM SMITH'S *Theory of Moral Sentiments* is to be interpreted and admired principally as a pioneering venture in the scientific study of morality,[1] but it can also be read as a vindication and, to some extent, as a critique of normal moral attitudes. That Smith usually shares the moral sentiments which he analyses is clear enough; what is less often remarked upon is Smith's conviction that his causal explanations of the origin and development of moral opinions make a positive contribution both to the defence and to the refinement of those opinions. Certainly he sees no incongruity in adding prescription to description or in following an explanation of a moral attitude with an hortatory aside. Yet his characteristic method is not to pass *from* causal explanation *to* moral justification but rather to combine the two enterprises, working on the assumption that scientific explanation constitutes the core of any adequate justification of moral attitudes.

Thus, in talking of the judgements of the impartial spectator as 'natural', Smith implies both that these judgements express the average reactions of normal human beings who are in the position of observing the behaviour of others, and that they are, for this reason, morally correct. A similar coalescence of descriptive and prescriptive modes occurs in Smith's use of the term 'ideal spectator'. On the one hand the ideal spectator is simply the imagined as distinct from the actual spectator of conduct, but on the other hand, Smith notes that where the views of the ideal spectator are in conflict with those of the normal impartial spectator, the judgements of the ideal spectator are usually taken to be morally superior to those of the ordinary impartial spectator, a practice which he endorses. However, since the attitudes of the ideal spectator—as well as those of actual impartial spectators—are in principle explicable within the terms of his scientific theory, it is apparent that the ideal spectator is primarily a scientific concept, developed, in fact, to explain the origin and operation of conscience, which Smith then uses to make moral assertions underwriting the authority of conscience. And the evidence which he uses to explain why

* The author is Professor of Philosophy in the University of Stirling.

[1] This is the main theme of my book *Adam Smith's Science of Morals* (1971).

the ideal spectator represents a source of moral sentiments which are in fact regarded as more authoritative than the moral judgements of the ordinary spectator is, as we shall see, substantially the same evidence which he considers relevant to showing that the attitudes of the ideal spectator ought to be regarded as superior.

Summarizing the normative aspect of Smith's moral theory in the words he uses to describe the 'science of Ethics', we can say that, in so far as it is a study of the attitudes of the average impartial spectator, Smith presumes that, by drawing our attention to our ordinary moral sentiments, it will 'inflame our natural love of virtue, and increase our abhorrence of vice', and, in so far as it is a study of the attitudes of the ideal spectator, he hopes that it will serve 'to *correct* and to ascertain our natural sentiments with regard to the propriety of conduct' (VII.iv.6; italics supplied), and so contribute to the improvement of ordinary moral standards.

It is obvious that Smith took the transition from descriptive to prescriptive statements with less self-consciousness than would be the case with a present-day naturalist, but he was not unaware of the importance of the distinction between 'is' and 'ought',[2] and it is possible to elicit from the *Moral Sentiments* an indication of the sort of consideration which gave him the confidence to combine his dominant role of scientist with his secondary one of moralist. In so doing there is a danger that more will be read into his passing methodological comments than is strictly warranted by them. But, despite the dangers inherent in addressing a typically twentieth-century philosophical question to an eighteenth-century text, I intend to examine, in general terms, the assumptions and arguments which lie behind Smith's conviction that his science of morals reinforces rather than undermines normal moral attitudes and, more particularly, to ask what it is about the 'ideal spectator' which leads Smith to regard his judgements as morally superior to those of the real spectator.

Most critics of Smith's moral theory have failed to appreciate the extent to which he saw himself as applying the methods of Newtonian Science to the study of morals.[3] Newton, in Smith's view, by employing the 'simple and familiar fact of gravitation' (Astronomy, IV.67), had established a natural philosophy which not only satisfied all the imaginative or aesthetic criteria of a good explanatory theory (such as comprehensiveness, simplicity, and familiarity), but whose truth had been demonstrated by its capacity to predict, with great accuracy, the detailed movements of physical bodies. Smith hoped to do the same in moral philosophy. In this case it was the simple and familiar fact of sympathy by which he sought to provide a

[2] Cf. TMS II.i.5.10: 'Let it be considered too, that the present inquiry is not concerning a matter of right, if I may say so, but concerning a matter of fact.'

[3] The main evidence for Smith's theory of scientific method is to be found in his essay 'On the History of Astronomy'.

comprehensive explanation of moral phenomena, arguing that 'Nature . . . acts here, as in all other cases, with the strictest economy, and produces a multitude of effects from one and the same cause' (VII.iii.3.3), namely sympathy. This was his scientific aim.

But, just as the explanatory power of the scientific laws which are based on the application of the concept of gravity to the study of astronomical occurrences draws from him the admission that Newton had discovered, not just a psychologically compelling theory, but one which laid bare 'the real chains which Nature makes use of to bind together her several operations' (Astronomy, IV.76), so, in a roughly comparable way, Smith, I shall argue, thought that his theory of sympathy, by demonstrating in detail that men *necessarily* approve and disapprove of certain types of behaviour, thought that he had discovered a key to moral 'reality' in the sense of the morally proper standard of human conduct.

For, as well as exhibiting how normal unreflective moral judgements are caused by the interaction of human faculties with the social environment, he sought to demonstrate how reflective moral judgements, which are also a product of these same faculties and social environment, are rightly accepted as having a higher moral status than unreflective ones. He argued that, since all moral judgements presuppose reference to the feelings of spectators, moral justification must terminate in an appeal to those feelings of which we as reflective spectators cannot divest ourselves. This may be called his metaphysic of morals.

I

Briefly stated Smith's moral theory is that men approve of the conduct and character of another person if, when they imagine themselves to be in that person's situation, their 'sympathetic' feelings accord with those which they observe to motivate the person's behaviour; and, similarly, men disapprove of actions or attitudes which they cannot enter into by this sort of imaginative change of situation. The analysis is complicated by the fact that, in assessing an action, men also consider its consequences for persons other than the agent, and moral approval and disapproval are affected by whether or not they can enter into the emotions of gratitude or resentment felt by persons who have, or might have, enjoyed or suffered the consequences of the action in question. Reasoning comes into the process in so far as men form, by induction, general rules which serve as everyday moral guides as to the sorts of conduct which are generally approved and disapproved of, but, in the end, all moral judgements are based on that species of 'immediate sense and feeling' (TMS VII.iii.2.7) which is the product of the imaginative consideration of specific actions.

The moral sentiments are, therefore, those sentiments felt by the spectator of human behaviour, the spectator being the ordinary person when he is in the position of observing the behaviour of any person with whom he has no special connection and whose behaviour does not affect him any more or less than it affects anyone else. Such a spectator is impartial only in the limited sense that he has no personal involvement in the situation which he is observing. He is, as Smith says, a 'bystander' who has all the feelings and limitations of any ordinary human being. The impartial spectator represents, therefore, in the first instance at any rate, the average reactions of ordinary observers of human conduct. I will call this, Smith's main use of the term, the 'ordinary' spectator.[4]

Smith argues that the approval and disapproval of the spectator depends on his capacity to imagine what it is like to be in situations other than the one which he is at that time experiencing. He attempts to reduce the operations of the imagination to empirical laws of universal human application. For instance he points out that men can more readily imagine pleasure than pain and common rather than unusual circumstances; similarly they can imagine mental more easily than bodily pleasures and pains. By reference to these 'laws of sympathy' Smith explains such alleged facts as that men approve of the expression of emotions, like love, which are pleasant to experience, more than of emotions, like anger, which are unpleasant for the person who has them, that men disapprove of those who complain of physical pains more than those who complain of mental ones, and that they approve of behaviour which is normal for a society more than that which is unusual or idiosyncratic.

One of the main grounds for Smith's contention that the moral norms of a society can be explained as the products of spectator attitudes is the manner in which his theory can account for the basic similarities and detailed variations in the moral rules of different societies. The dominant influence of the attitudes of ordinary spectators in the determination of a society's moral norms is explained by two postulates: firstly that the desire for harmony or agreement of sentiments, and so for mutual approval, is an irreducible and universal feature of human nature, and secondly that it is only by adopting the standpoint of impartial spectators that men can achieve the coincidence of sentiments which they desire. The feelings of impartial spectators tend to agree, those of agents and persons particularly affected by the actions of agents tend to conflict; the impartial spectator represents the common denominator which unites men in their attitudes towards conduct and to which men approximate in their pursuit of the 'pleasures of mutual sympathy', the awareness of sharing the sentiments of others and so enjoying their approval.

It is to the agent's desire to obtain the approval, or at least to avoid the

[4] Smith has many alternative descriptions of the impartial spectator: a third person, mankind, other men, society, or simply 'everybody but the man who feels it', cf. TMS I.ii.2.1.

disapproval, of the spectators of his conduct that Smith traces the origin of conscience. Conscience, on his theory, originates in the maturing individual's attempts to 'observe' his own behaviour for the purpose of anticipating how other people will react to it. By imagining how his conduct must appear to a spectator the agent learns to act in such a way as to avoid criticism and gain approval. However, in this process the agent does, to some extent, actually become the spectator of his own behaviour and consequently he shares the feelings of those who approve or disapprove of his actions, with the result that he is led to pronounce judgement on his own conduct. Thus a man approves of his own behaviour when his feelings as the imagined spectator of his own conduct coincide with those which actually characterize his actions and he disapproves when they do not, and he praises or condemns himself according to whether or not the feelings which he imagines to be those of persons affected by his conduct are ones of gratitude or resentment.

By habitually taking up the position of a spectator of his own conduct the individual develops 'the representative of the impartial spectator, the man within the breast' (VI.i.11), as an internal monitor of his behaviour. This is the ideal spectator; 'ideal' because he is not the actual but the imagined spectator of conduct. This does not imply, however, that the feelings which arise from the individual imagining himself to be the observer of his own conduct do not have a powerful influence on his conduct. It is an important part of Smith's theory that men desire the approval not only of actual spectators but of the 'ideal man within the breast', the approval of their own conscience. The former he calls the love of praise, the latter he calls the love of praiseworthiness. Conscience, which has its origin in the first, comes to provide the standards for the second.

In speaking of praiseworthiness Smith is not appealing to some moral norms other than those produced by imaginative sympathy. He is simply contrasting the feelings which men have as observers of the conduct of others with those which they have when imagining themselves to be the spectators of their own actions. The imagination has a different task in the two types of judgement but the principles on which it operates are the same in both cases.

Nevertheless the judgements of the actual spectators and those of the ideal spectators do not always agree because although the same laws of sympathy apply to both, they are not in the same situation. For instance the ideal spectator has more knowledge about the behaviour of the agent, that is of his own behaviour, than does the actual spectator, but, on the other hand, the ideal spectator's feelings, being sympathetic feelings, will not be so intense as the feelings of the actual spectators of his conduct. Moreover, since it takes some effort for the agent to adopt the position of observing his own conduct, there is always a tendency for him to fail to be as impartial as the actual spectator, especially when impartiality is likely to lead to self-condemnation, so that the man within has a propensity towards self-partiality which is constantly requiring correction by the influence of actual spectators.

It might be thought that in so far as the attitudes of the ideal spectator conflict with those of ordinary spectators they would be rejected by the agent, for, after all, if the purpose of conscience is to anticipate the reactions of actual spectators, then, in so far as it fails to perform this function, it would appear to be defective. But Smith argues that, although conscience originates in the desire to please others, it develops a certain autonomy in that men come to desire their own approval as much as, and sometimes more than, the approval of others. A person may morally approve or disapprove of his own conduct whether or not it is approved or condemned by any actual observers of his behaviour; a point which is often missed by Smith's critics.

Indeed Smith goes on to argue that the ideal spectator, despite an initial bias towards self-partiality, is capable of becoming less partial than actual spectators and in fact where conscience does become relatively autonomous in relation to the judgements of actual spectators it tends to represent a less partial standpoint than that of the ordinary spectator. This is because, in the course of moral argument, the individual appeals to his conscience against the partial views of his critics, and in so doing he counters their criticisms with claims about what their views would be were they less partial and better informed. In this way he tends to get the support of the minority of actual spectators[5] who are markedly more impartial and knowledgeable than their fellows, and this, plus the approbation of his own conscience, is sufficient compensation to balance the unfavourable judgements of his fellows.

It is this impartial and well-informed manifestation of the ideal spectator that Smith has in mind when he states, with clearly implied approval, that conscience is regarded as a 'higher tribunal' than the judgements of the ordinary spectator, and as the 'vicegerent of God' within us (III.2.31; III.5.6). He considers that the man within, by reflection on the conduct of himself and others, develops a model of 'perfect' conduct which goes beyond anything which is expected of him by his fellows, but which he sets himself as the standard by which to measure his own behaviour. The imaginative mechanisms developed through the operations of the maturing conscience, by directing the individual's attention to the nature of his own behaviour, result in each person forming a picture of what he regards as proper behaviour, first for himself and then for others, on the basis of

[5] In contrast to the 'ordinary' spectator Smith often refers to that minority of spectators who are 'humane', 'candid', 'generous', 'wise', or, frequently, 'well-informed', cf. TMS II.iii.3.6 and III.2.5.

which he can then criticize the attitudes of ordinary spectators. So, in Smith's words: 'There exists in the mind of every man, an idea of this kind, gradually formed from his observations upon the character and conduct both of himself and of other people. It is the slow, gradual, and progressive work of the great demigod within the breast, the great judge and arbiter of conduct' (VI.iii.25).

The ideal spectator thus appears in two forms. Firstly, and originally, as the internalization of the attitudes of ordinary spectators, and secondly as the expression of those attitudes which are the product of the individual's attempts to view conduct in an impartial and informed manner. In the latter form the ideal spectator comes to represent, for Smith, the attitudes of the minority of persons who undertake extensive reflection about human behaviour. These reflective attitudes are those which, Smith sometimes suggests, *ought* to characterize the reactions of the ordinary spectator in that they are the attitudes which the ordinary spectator would have were he well-informed, imaginative, impartial, and so on (III.2.5). Our task is to consider how Smith's basically scientific approach to the study of morality is used to justify this preference for the judgements emanating from the more reflective version of the ideal spectator, the attitudes which are characteristic of the autonomous moral conscience.

II

To some extent Smith's justification for his valuation of the ideal over against the ordinary spectator is an extension of the arguments which he uses to back up his endorsement of normal attitudes, namely that they have beneficial, usually unintentionally beneficial, consequences for the general happiness. Normal moral sentiments prompt men to act spontaneously in a manner which coincides with the sort of conduct of which an all-seeing utilitarian would approve. The attitudes of the ideal spectator support and supplement this process and can therefore be justified on the same grounds as those of the ordinary spectator. They support it because the ideal man within is, to a large extent, simply an internalization of the ordinary impartial spectator. The presence of the ideal man within has the effect of making men genuinely rather than merely prudentially concerned to act in accordance with the wishes of their fellows. Conscience, therefore, gives men a commitment to social co-operation which would not result from external sanctions alone (III.2.7).

But we have seen how the point of view of the ideal spectator also enables men to form an idea of moral conduct which goes beyond and 'perfects' the norms of conduct which are approved of by the ordinary spectator. In this respect the ideal spectator supplements the attitudes of the ordinary spectator, for 'he' allows individuals, on the basis of more extensive reflection and more adequate information about human conduct, to correct some of the less fortunate consequences of ordinary moral sentiments, for these sentiments are not in every way and in every case completely adapted to the maximization of human happiness. For instance, the ordinary impartial spectator places little emphasis on the distinction between the intentional and the unintentional infliction of injury on another person, and this has, on the whole, the beneficial consequence of making men take care not to cause injury to others. But some unforeseen and unintended consequences of acts are not the result of lack of care and the more refined principles of the ideal spectator take this into account so that, in so far as the principles of the ideal spectator are adopted, there is less likelihood of unnecessary suffering being inflicted in the form of punishment of those who cause injury in unforeseeable ways. Moreover, the ideal spectator, either in the form of the man within or in the form of the minority of well-informed, attentive, and exceptionally impartial spectators, can be an important source of consolation to those persons who are adversely criticized by ordinary spectators (II.iii.3.6), and a means of attaining inner tranquillity for those whose morally praiseworthy behaviour fails to obtain the recognition of their fellows (III.2.5).

Such arguments are all part of Smith's thesis that the mechanisms of sympathy work out for the well-being of men, and they fit in with his total scheme for exhibiting the 'economy of nature' as a system which works for the preservation and happiness of the human species. Ordinary moral sentiments, including those which are 'corrupt' and 'irregular', facilitate the smooth operation of the social system by encouraging the social passions and repressing the anti-social ones (VI.iii.15), and so contribute to the happiness of men as social beings, although, of course, this is not the intention of those who act in accordance with them. The attitudes of the ideal spectator, particularly those manifested in the judgements arising from the relatively autonomous activities of individual consciences, correct some of the anomalies and shortcomings of the system and so make it a more effective means to the general happiness. Smith, therefore, approves of the fact that the judgements of the ideal spectator are usually accorded greater weight than those of the ordinary spectator because this tends to perfect rather than replace a system of social relationships founded on ordinary unreflective moral sentiments.

Arguments of this sort illustrate one way in which Smith thought that scientific explanation and moral justification are part of the same process. His accounts of the functional utility of the moral sentiments in general, and of conscience in particular, have the consequence of commending them by showing that they are essential for social harmony and so for the preservation and happiness of mankind. This is the way in which 'philosophical researches . . . when they came to take place, confirmed those original anticipations of nature' (III.5.5). But such justifications do, of course, presuppose the validity of the utilitarian maxim that morally right action maximizes happiness and minimizes pain, and it is to Smith's proof of this principle that we must turn our attention.

It needs to be stressed that Smith does not wish to justify the principle of utility as a guide to everyday moral choices. He does not think that men have the time, the ability, or the information to make the necessary utilitarian calculations. Nor does he think, as against Hume, that considerations of utility have any significant influence in determining the content of any widely accepted moral principles. But Smith does assume that utility is the standard by which to assess the good and bad qualities of a total way of life. I call this contemplative utilitarianism to indicate that utility is, for Smith, the standard by which to appreciate the qualities of an entire social system. Contemplative as distinct from practical moral attitudes are concerned with the evaluation of the desirability of a situation without relating this to questions about how an individual ought to act. Universal benevolence is for Smith a contemplative principle because although he did not think that anyone ought to attempt to further the happiness of all men he did think the goodness or desirability of a society should be assessed in terms of the happiness of its members.

Part of Smith's appreciation of the unintended utility of the moral sentiments is to be interpreted in terms of an aspect of utility on which he himself lays some stress. Smith basically accepts Hume's analysis of utility as having to do with furthering the general interest, but he observes that men find pleasure in contemplating the efficiency of a complex mechanism whatever its products might be. The exact adjustment of means to ends is, he points out, a source of admiration and wonder and this is part of the reason why 'utility pleases' (IV.i.1.1). This 'aesthetic' aspect of the appreciation of utility does contribute to Smith's readiness to endorse ordinary moral sentiments on the grounds that the ways in which they work for the welfare of men in general is exceptionally intricate and effective (VII.iii.1.2). This is, after all, one of the things which his moral theory is designed to demonstrate.

But the principle of utility is primarily about the value of ends rather than the way in which means achieve these ends, so that we cannot look to Smith's analysis of aesthetic utility for a proof of the supreme value of human happiness as an end in itself. In so far as Smith does provide such a proof it arises out of his contention that benevolence or concern for human happiness is the contemplative moral principle which *must* be accepted by all reflective persons. Thus, in discussing universal benevolence, he argues that 'we cannot form the idea of any innocent and sensible being, whose happiness we should not desire, or to whose misery, when distinctly brought home to the imagination, we should not have some degree of aversion' (VI.ii.3.1). This is a subjunctive rather than an imperative use of 'should' and what he means is that, when reflecting on particular cases, any person who brings himself to imagine the happiness or misery of another human being cannot help but be pleased by the first and distressed by the second. And, since this is so in each individual case, by extrapolation, any person, when contemplating the situation of humanity as a whole, comes to desire that all men should be happy.

Generalizing this mode of argument we can say that Smith believed that, after reflection, certain feelings have a necessity which serves to justify the moral judgements which follow from them, for 'it is impossible that we should be displeased with the tendency of a sentiment, which, when we bring the case home to ourselves, we feel that we cannot avoid adopting' (II.i.3.3). And, since contemplative moral principles are based on the most extensive reflection, they are the ultimate test for assessing the moral desirability or otherwise of practical moral principles. Therefore the fact that universal benevolence is the necessary contemplative principle is the basis of Smith's proof of utility.

But why should 'necessary' feelings be the ultimate criteria of moral judgements? Is this not a simple confusion of causal and moral necessity? To answer these questions we must first be clear that it is only necessary *sympathetic* feelings to which Smith ascribes final moral authority. For, while all feelings, when felt, 'seem reasonable and proportioned to their objects' (III.i.4.3), it is only on the basis of sympathetic feelings that men make moral judgements. Indeed he claims that there is a necessary connection between possessing a sympathetic feeling and approving of those who act on the basis of the original feeling. Sometimes he presents this as a logical connection, asserting that to sympathize is the same thing as to approve, but most of his arguments treat it as a causal connection, in that sympathetic feelings always do, in fact, give rise to judgements of approval and disapproval. This empirical generalization has, for Smith, the necessity of a scientific law since it is an integral part of his moral theory which, as a whole, he believes, satisfies all the canons of scientific proof. This objectively, in the sense of scientifically, established necessity manifests itself subjectively in men's inability to conceive that it is possible to sympathize without at the same time approving.[6]

Further, certain sympathetic feelings, like contemplative benevolence, are themselves necessary, and since men must make moral judgements in accordance with their sympathetic feelings, it is inevitable that these necessary sympathetic feelings be accepted as the final moral authority. The sympathetic feelings which Smith regards as necessary are those felt by all men in imagining a certain type of situation. Following Hume's analysis of causality Smith regarded the constant conjunction of certain

[6] Cf. TMS I.i.3.2. This psychological necessity is explained, by Smith, in terms of the association of ideas.

imaginative acts with the occurrence of certain sympathetic feelings as sufficient to establish a relationship of causal necessity. Thus each individual, on the basis of his own experience of the repeated conjunction of such imaginative acts and sympathetic responses, comes to feel that the relationship between them is a necessary one in that he cannot help associating the two events. And, as this experience is shared by all other men who perform the same imaginative acts, such responses are regarded as causally necessary, and hence, in Smith's view, obligatory for all men. Because of the constitution of human nature all men are bound to adopt certain attitudes towards each other and, for Smith, this is equivalent to saying that they are obliged to do so.[7]

It should be noted that Smith's belief in 'necessary' sympathetic emotions does presuppose a basic uniformity in human nature. His position on this may be regarded as that of an empirical natural law theorist, for he takes for granted that there exist certain 'natural sentiments of all mankind' (II.iii.2.9) which properly directed observation can discern behind the complex variety of human behaviour. This applies to moral as well as to other sentiments, for our sympathetic emotions are the combined effect of our 'original passions' and the laws of sympathy. Such variations as there are in human sentiments, Smith thinks, can be explained by reference to the ways in which the natural sentiments, such as the love of praise, manifest themselves in different circumstances, particularly different economic circumstances. The discovery of necessary sympathetic feeling depends partly on our knowledge of the 'laws of sympathy' from which we can deduce the extent to which spectators can enter into the different types of original emotions as felt by the agents themselves. But it also depends on our knowledge of which original or agent's sentiments are necessary, for, aside from the laws of sympathy, the spectator's imaginative feelings are determined by his past experience of how he as an agent has felt and behaved in such situations. In consequence, although there may be a few exceptions, Smith doubts whether 'any sentiment could be regarded as unjust, to which we are by nature irresistibly determined' (I.iii.1.15). Since it is the social scientist's task to demonstrate this basic uniformity of human behaviour and since the uniformity of human nature constitutes Smith's grounds for accepting that there are feelings which are necessary to men, and which are therefore justified, it is not surprising that Smith could regard his scientific moral theory as establishing normative conclusions. For, if a necessary feeling must be accepted as a correct one, then science, by discovering which sympathetic feelings are necessary, is at the same time telling us which feelings are the measure of right conduct.

[7] For Smith's equation of necessity and obligation see TMS I.ii.4.1.

III

To give ultimate moral authority to those sympathetic feelings which are necessary would seem to rest justified normative preferences on the claim that the sympathetic feelings in question are felt by all men. This would make the universality of a sympathetic emotion the test of its moral correctness. But, as we have seen, Smith indicates that the more reflective and informed moral judgements are superior to the less reflective and informed ones, and these are the judgements which are characteristic of the ideal spectator rather than the ordinary spectator and they are not therefore to be observed as actually occurring in all men. In fact it turns out that there is an important hypothetical qualification in his equation of necessary sympathetic feeling with those which are universal or common to all men. The ultimate moral authority, in the sense of the standard by which common moral sentiments are judged to be on the whole morally good but in need of revision in minor particulars, is the feelings which all men would have *if* they were well-informed, impartial, and accurate in their imaginative representation of the situations being assessed; the attitudes of the ideal spectator considered simply as representing individual conscience are in fact morally superior only because or in so far as they are well-informed, impartial, and imaginatively accurate.

Smith recognizes that, after reflection and discussion, all men change some of their spontaneous emotional responses to imagined situations. Some sympathetic emotions do not 'bear any serious examination' (III.2.5) and are abandoned or radically modified, most are reinforced by the process of reflection. But in each case the eventual basis for accepting or modifying sympathetic feelings is comparison with those sympathetic feelings of which a person cannot divest himself after having subjected them to various forms of examination.

This claim amounts to something more than an appeal to the fact that men do in fact alter their sympathetic responses in the light of extensive reflection, for Smith implies that such reflection carries with it, not just a feeling that certain emotions are necessary because we cannot rid ourselves of them, but a sense of rational conviction. In some ways the use of the term 'rational' here is out of place since Smith usually equates rationalism in moral theory with the views of those intuitionist philosophers who held that reason 'pointed out the difference between right and wrong, in the same manner in which it did that between truth and falsehood' (VII.iii.2.5). His own position is that, strictly speaking, reason enters into moral judgements only with respect to the inductive reasoning which is involved in formulating moral rules on the basis of regularities in our 'immediate sense and feeling'. However, he does talk of the judgments of a 'refined and enlightened reason' (II.ii.3.5), and by this he means not only a judgement that takes into account inductively obtained knowledge but one which makes judgements which carry with them a sense of intellectual satisfaction.

There are parallels which can be drawn here between what Smith has to say about moral and scientific reasoning. A good scientific theory is psychologically compelling but also intellectually authoritative. Newton's theory of gravity certainly pleased the imagination but it did so in such a way as to satisfy the intellect as well. And similarly, in the field of ethics, Smith seems to have assumed that in the end causal and rational necessity coincide in the judgements of a 'refined and enlightened reason'.

For instance the tests which Smith thinks of as being employed in the examination of sympathetic feelings are in many ways similar to those which he applies to the critique of scientific theories, although there are, of course, important differences between them as well. Thus moral judgements which are based on a more comprehensive consideration of the causes and consequences of an action are preferred to those which are less inclusive. Humanity should not be 'weak and partial' but 'generous and comprehensive' (II.ii.3.7). Impartiality, which in the case of ordinary moral judgements Smith regards as involving only the absence of particular personal interests, is, in the case of the ideal spectator and even more so with respect to contemplative moral attitudes, given a more positive meaning to include the requirement that the spectator take into account the interests of all men who are or might be involved in the situation in question. The more comprehensive the view of the spectator the more authoritative his moral judgements are to be regarded. This is why there is a sense in which contemplative moral principles, which are those based on the most extensive view of human life, are the highest moral norms. This acceptance of comprehensiveness as a test of moral attitudes echoes what Smith has to say about the advantages of a scientific theory which is more comprehensive in that it accounts for a larger number of phenomena than any competing theory (Astronomy, IV.16,32).

The sort of examination of sympathetic feeling which Smith stresses most relates to the accuracy of the imaginative act on which the moral judgement is based. A moral judgement is considered to be defective if it follows from inaccurate or insufficient information (TMS VI.iii.25). If a person's imaginative picture on the basis of which his sympathetic feelings arise is at variance with the realities of that situation (cf. III.4), for instance if he imagines that the life of wealthy persons is substantially more pleasant than that of ordinary persons, then he is in error and his moral judgements will be in need of revision. Similarly if a man does not attend to a situation or neglects to envisage certain aspects of it, then his judgement is suspect because he cannot be said to have an adequate awareness of the situation which he is assessing.

The assumption that justifiable moral attitudes must be based on a correct imagining of the action being assessed is, perhaps, Smith's most fundamental test for the acceptability of a sympathetic feeling, and this may be paralleled by his insistence that a scientific theory, as well as satisfying psychological or aesthetic criteria, must fit the observed facts (Astronomy, IV.68,76). Smith allows that, with ordinary moral judgements, sentiments based on illusory imaginings, such as imagining what it is like to be a small child, or to be lying in your grave (TMS II.i.2.5; I.i.1.2), may be reliable moral guides in that they prompt us to act in ways which can be justified in utilitarian terms. But the contemplative moral judgements which enable us to judge that some illusions are beneficial cannot themselves be based on illusions of the imagination. Accuracy of observation is in this way a moral as well as a scientific virtue since a man who makes moral judgements based on erroneous imaginings is mistaken in the same sort of way as a man who makes observational statements based on erroneous sense-perceptions.

All these factors compel men to change their judgements in that if they attain a point of view which is more comprehensive, more consistent, and leads to more accurate imaginative portrayal of actual behaviour, they cannot help altering their sympathetic responses. And Smith assumes that these responses will be common to all reflective persons. But he regards this as a compulsion which, because it is the consequence of extensive examination, must seem reasonable to those who experience it. In contrast to the original passions which are the spontaneous expressions of human nature and are therefore non-rational brute facts about mankind, the moral judgements of an extensively well-informed reflective person have been subjected to these processes of critical scrutiny, and are therefore properly regarded as rational and enlightened.

If this convergence of causal, rational, and moral necessity seems unsatisfactory Smith's remaining argument must be the theological one that a necessary sympathetic feeling is a manifestation of the intention of God. The ideal man within is, for Smith, the voice of God, not only because of the force with which he 'overawes' our selfish passions (II.ii.3.4), but because, as Smith deduces from the fact that sympathetic feelings are unique in that they alone are used to judge conduct, it is God's intention that the ideal spectator should guide our behaviour (cf. III.5.5). Moreover, Smith argues that the supreme contemplative principle of benevolence by reference to which we judge that creation is good is the principle which determines the acts as well as the thought of God. In both ways insight into necessity is insight into the mind of God.

Although these theological considerations infuse Smith's whole functionalist approach to the study of society it is only rarely that he makes any direct appeal to them. As arguments they are, of course, unsatisfactory not only because they presuppose the existence of God but also because they assume that God is morally good. Yet, although Smith does not consider how we can know that God is good, he does subscribe to the view that the existence of God can be inferred from the evidence of design in the universe. The precise adjustment of means to ends, where this is not simply a human product, is attributed to the action of God. And the more precise and intricate the mechanisms by which these ends are produced the greater the strength of the argument from design. Moreover, his own theories, in exhibiting the functional unity of human societies, including the role of imaginative sympathy in producing this unity, offer important examples of the 'wisdom of God' and so provide grounds for the deistic belief which lies behind his conviction that what is necessary is right. Social science, by contributing to natural theology, helps to establish the context in which it is plausible to regard the imperatives of conscience as the commands of God. This is the metaphysical background for Smith's moral philosophy and provides my final example of the close ties which exist between Smith's scientific and normative purposes in the *Moral Sentiments*.

IV

The Impartial Spectator

D. D. RAPHAEL*

THIS article was originally written as a Dawes Hicks Lecture on the history of philosophy. Adam Smith is in one respect particularly fitted to be the subject of such a lecture because he was himself one of the first students of the history of philosophy. For an eighteenth-century writer the term 'philosophy' meant philosophy and science. Smith's three essays on the history of astronomy, of ancient physics, and of ancient logic and metaphysics are, I believe, the remains of his earliest project for a book. Towards the end of his life he thought of putting this together with his literary studies in 'a sort of Philosophical History of the different branches of Literature, of Philosophy, Poetry and Eloquence'.[1] 'Philosophical history'[2] had a special appeal for Adam Smith. His lectures on moral philosophy included a substantial treatment of the history of the subject; and his lectures on jurisprudence were basically a history of law within the framework of a history of forms of government and forms of society.

Smith's practice of philosophical history was much akin to our modern British approach to the history of philosophy. His interest was no less philosophical than historical. He studied the history of thought for the purposes of criticism and of building more soundly than his predecessors. While his historical researches were certainly designed to discover historical truth, he believed that there was also a philosophical truth to be found and that attention to history could help find it. Thus his essays on the history of astronomy, etc., were intended to confirm a theory of scientific method, and his survey of earlier theories of moral philosophy included critical appraisal, carrying the suggestion that his own theory was less defective. Intentions of course can differ from actual consequences. (No one knew that better than Adam Smith, who in two celebrated passages wrote of men being led by an invisible hand to produce effects which they had not intended.) Smith went into the history of jurisprudence in the hope of

* Professor of Philosophy in the University of London.

[1] Letter 248 addressed to the Duc de La Rochefoucauld, dated 1 Nov. 1785.

[2] Some modern students of Smith's work have been captivated by the name of 'conjectural history' coined by Dugald Stewart. (He in fact suggested 'the title of *Theoretical* or *Conjectural History*'.) In my opinion the adjective 'conjectural' is seriously misleading when applied to most of the historical interests of Adam Smith.

'establishing a system of . . . natural jurisprudence, or a theory of the general principles which ought to run through, and be the foundation of, the laws of all nations'.[3] He never succeeded in producing a theory of natural jurisprudence, but instead his inquiries led him to write the *Wealth of Nations.*

No doubt that is a symptom of the fact that Adam Smith's bent was scientific rather than philosophical. Despite his philosophic interests, shown in a tendency to make connections and to raise general questions, Smith was in one way markedly unphilosophical: paradoxical metaphysics left him cold. In an essay on the external senses he applauded Berkeley's interpretation of vision in terms of touch, but there is not the ghost of any reference to Berkeley's general idealism, though Smith must surely have read the *Principles of Human Knowledge* as well as the *New Theory of Vision.* Similarly with Hume. Adam Smith was one of the few people of his time who took the measure of Hume's positive achievements in philosophy; Smith's emphasis on the constructive role of the imagination in his theory of scientific method,[4] and the function which he assigned to nature in his ethical theory, must both have come from an appreciation of Hume. Yet the sceptical and paradoxical side of Hume's treatment of metaphysical problems such as causation, substance, and identity, simply flowed off Smith's mind like water off a duck's back.

None the less it would be a mistake to dismiss Adam Smith from the history of philosophy as a great economist who happened to be a professor

[3] TMS VII.iv.37. This is in fact the last paragraph of the book.

[4] I am thinking of Smith's essay on the history of astronomy, the lengthiest of his 'illustrations' of 'the principles which lead and direct philosophical enquiries'. Section ii is thoroughly Humean in its account of the imagination at work in the association of ideas, especially when the imagination 'endeavours to . . . fill up the gap' if the 'customary connection be interrupted'. Some of Smith's closest associates must have thought so too. His heir, David Douglas, evidently sent to John Millar a description of Smith's remaining manuscripts, and Millar, in his reply of 10 Aug. 1790, wrote: 'Of all his writings, I have most curiosity about the metaphysical work you mention. I should like to see his powers of illustration employed upon the true old Humean philosophy.' W. R. Scott, who printed this letter in *Adam Smith as Student and Professor* (1937), 311–13, added a note at p. 313: 'There is no trace of this MS.' Elsewhere in the same book (115, note 3) Scott surmised that the 'metaphysical work' might be the 'Principles which direct Philosophical Enquiries' or else 'an unknown manuscript'. To my mind there is not the slightest doubt that it is the former. The titles of all three of the essays concerned state that the principles are 'illustrated' by the history of astronomy, etc., and this is clearly picked up in Millar's phrase 'his powers of illustration'.

It is, I think, commonly supposed that Hume's contemporaries fastened upon the sceptical side of his theory of knowledge and failed to appreciate his positive doctrine of naturalism and the role which he assigned to the imagination, so well brought out in our own day by N. Kemp Smith, *The Philosophy of David Hume* (1941), and H. H. Price, *Hume's Theory of the External World* (1940). One is not surprised to find that Adam Smith's reaction to Hume differed from 'the Reid–Beattie interpretation' (Kemp Smith's phrase). It is, however, interesting to observe that Smith's friends, Douglas and Millar, not only recognized Smith's essays as having a Humean basis but were ready to speak of 'the *true* old Humean philosophy'.

of philosophy before he found his true *métier*. Certainly Smith himself never thought that he had abandoned philosophy, and according to Sir Samuel Romilly he 'always considered his *Theory of Moral Sentiments* a much superior work to his *Wealth of Nations*'.[5] He spent his last years revising and expanding the *Moral Sentiments* to such an extent that the resulting sixth edition, published shortly before his death, was virtually a new book. The fact is that a man can be a philosopher of distinction without reaching eminence in both main branches of the subject. A Berkeley, a Russell, a Wittgenstein can count for much in the philosophy of knowledge and for nothing in the philosophy of practice. Conversely, a Rousseau, an Adam Smith, a Bentham can count for nothing in the philosophy of knowledge and for much in the philosophy of practice. The positive advance that Smith made in moral philosophy was as great as Hume's (though he could not match the negative force of Hume's assault on ethical rationalism) and represents the culmination of an important movement of empiricist ethics.

Smith's main contribution to this movement lies in two things, his theory of imaginative sympathy and his notion of the impartial spectator. Each of these he developed from ideas that he had found in Hume, but in each the development was touched with a subtlety that makes the result original. The name of Adam Smith in the history of ethics is chiefly associated with the concept of the impartial spectator because the phrase sounds so distinctive.[6] His concept of sympathy is in fact equally distinctive and differs from the notion of sympathy in ethics employed by Hume before him and other writers after him.

A theory of moral judgement based upon the feelings of spectators is found in the three Scottish philosophers, Hutcheson, Hume, and Adam Smith. Rationalist theories of moral judgement begin from the standpoint of the moral agent. So do those empiricist theories that presuppose an egoistic psychology. Francis Hutcheson was not the first empiricist philosopher to question an egoistic psychology, but he probably was the first to insist upon disinterested judgements as well as disinterested motives. Lord Shaftesbury and Bishop Butler both argued for disinterested motives, but neither of them could fully shake off the conviction that in the last resort an agent must justify an action on grounds of self-interest. At any rate, whether or not influenced by this conviction, Shaftesbury and Butler gave accounts of moral judgement in terms of the psychology of the moral agent alone. They spoke of the agent reflecting upon his motives and thereby forming a judgement. Shaftesbury used the *phrase* 'moral sense', but

[5] *Memoirs of Sir Samuel Romilly* (1840), i.403; quoted by John Rae, *Life of Adam Smith* (1895), 436.

[6] Smith may have taken it from the opening words of Addison's deducation of vol. i of *The Spectator*: 'I should not act the part of an impartial spectator, if I dedicated the following papers to one who is not of the most consummate and most acknowledged merit.'

not to express the moral sense theory proper, which was invented by Hutcheson.

The moral sense, as understood by Hutcheson, is a disinterested feeling of approval naturally evoked when we come across the disinterested motive of benevolence (and a feeling of disapproval for motives with a tendency opposed to that of benevolence). Hutcheson compared the moral sense with the disinterested feeling of love or admiration aroused by objects that we call beautiful. This was not to say quite that beauty and virtue are in the heart of the beholder, for the *objects* of moral approval and aesthetic liking respectively have their own particular character; moral approval is directed upon benevolence, and aesthetic admiration is directed upon unity-in-variety. Nevertheless benevolence alone does not constitute virtue for Hutcheson, and unity-in-variety alone does not constitute beauty. Virtue is benevolence approved, and beauty is unity-in-variety admired. The reaction of a spectator is a necessary though not a sufficient condition. Since Hutcheson was at pains to stress the disinterestedness of moral approval and disapproval, he had to concentrate on the reaction of a spectator; approval of benevolence by the agent himself may well be, and approval by the beneficiary is almost bound to be, an interested approval. It is not surprising, then, that Hutcheson should often refer to 'spectators' or 'observers' in explaining his views. (I have added the italics in the quotations as given here.) 'Virtue is then called amiable or lovely, from its raising good-will or love in *spectators* towards the agent';[7] 'does not *every spectator* approve the pursuit of public good more than private?'[8] 'it is more probable, when our actions are really kind and publicly useful, that *all observers* shall . . . approve what we approve ourselves';[9] 'do these words [merit, praiseworthiness] denote the quality in actions, which gains approbation from *the observer*, . . . or . . . are these actions called meritorious, which, when *any observer* does approve, *all other observers* approve him for his approbation . . . ?'[10]

Hume added to this theory an explanation of the moral sense or 'moral sentiment' of approval and disapproval. It is, he said, a feeling of pleasure and displeasure of a particular kind, and it arises from sympathy with the pleasure or pain of the person affected by the action judged. Benevolence pleases the observer because it brings pleasure to the beneficiary. Hume did not follow Hutcheson in confining virtue to benevolence. That was too simple a scheme, and Hume saw that a satisfactory theory needed to give a more complex account of what he called the 'artificial' virtues, notably justice. Essentially, however, he founded all moral approval on sympathy.

[7] *Inquiry concerning Virtue* (ed. 4), I.viii; D. D. Raphael, *British Moralists 1650–1800* (1969), §314.

[8] *Illustrations upon the Moral Sense* (ed. 3), I; Raphael, §362.

[9] *Illustrations*, IV; Raphael, §370.

[10] *Illustrations*, V; Raphael, §373.

For the same reasons as Hutcheson he analysed moral judgement from the point of view of a spectator. 'The hypothesis which we embrace . . . defines virtue to be *whatever mental action or quality gives to a spectator the pleasing sentiment of approbation*; and vice the contrary.'[11] Hume distinguished the language of morals from the language of self-love, The language of morals, in being disinterested, expresses feelings common to all mankind. When a man speaks the language of self-love he expresses sentiments 'arising from his particular circumstances and situation'; but when he speaks the language of morals he must 'depart from his private and particular situation, and must choose a point of view, common to him with others: he must move some universal principle of the human frame, and touch a string, to which all mankind have an accord and symphony'.[12] The 'sentiments' that Hume's spectator feels are impartial and (in a sense) rational; impartial because disinterested, and rational because universal. In one place Hume wrote of 'a judicious spectator',[13] and elsewhere of 'every spectator'[14] or 'every bystander'.[15] The concept, though not the precise name, of an impartial spectator is there already in Hume.

What is original in Adam Smith is the development of the concept to explain the judgements of conscience made by an agent about his own actions. A spectator theory accounts most easily for judgements made in the third person and well enough for second-person judgements, but is apt to be in difficulties with judgements made in the first person. It is also more comfortable with passing verdicts on what has been done in the past than with considering and deciding what should be done in the future. Ethical rationalists concentrated on the idea of duty and on a criterion for determining one's duty. Hutcheson and Hume thought more of virtue and the assessment of virtue by third parties; on the idea of duty or obligation they were decidedly weak.

Smith's theory of the impartial spectator did not, like Athena, spring fully armed at its first appearance from the head of its creator. A distinct development can be seen in changes made both in the second edition of the *Moral Sentiments*, published a couple of years after the first, and in the sixth edition, published thirty years later. A recently discovered letter shows that the relevant new material added in the second edition was in answer to a criticism made privately to Smith by Sir Gilbert Elliot of Minto. I believe there is evidence enough to say that the earliest version of Smith's lectures on moral philosophy did not contain the theory at all.

[11] *Enquiry concerning Morals*, Appendix I; ed. Selby-Bigge (2nd ed., 1902), §239.

[12] *Enquiry*, IX.i; ed. Selby-Bigge, §222.

[13] *Treatise of Human Nature*, III.iii.1; ed. Selby-Bigge (1896), p. 581. So did Hutcheson in his lectures, published posthumously in 1755 as *A System of Moral Philosophy* (i.235).

[14] *Treatise*, III.iii.1; ed. Selby-Bigge, p. 591: *Enquiry*, V.i; ed. Selby-Bigge, §172.

[15] *Enquiry*, Appendix III; ed. Selby-Bigge, §260.

Glasgow University Library possesses a short manuscript[16] which is unquestionably, in my opinion, the latter part of one of Smith's lectures on ethics from which he later composed the *Theory of Moral Sentiments.* (Indeed the manuscript contains that expression as his name for the subject.) In this fragment there is no mention of the impartial spectator although much of the discussion is concerned with reactions that go to form the sense of justice and the measure of just punishment. Smith spoke of what 'we' feel, of 'our heart' or of 'mankind' naturally applauding a punishment. In one place he wrote that the magistrate who hears a complaint of injustice 'promises . . . to give that redress which to any impartial person shall appear to be just and equitable'; and when he reproduced this passage in the *Moral Sentiments*[17] it became simply 'the magistrate . . . promises to hear and to redress every complaint of injury'. The word 'impartial' in the manuscript is significant only of its normal usage in a context of justice and equity. Since Smith wrote 'any impartial *person*' he clearly had not, at this date (*c.* 1752), formulated the doctrine of the impartial spectator. Nor had he done so when he first wrote the shorter form of words that eventually appeared in the *Moral Sentiments.* In the lecture Smith said that there was no precise rule for determining the proper degree of resentment or punishment, and that this aspect of justice (though not others) was loose and indeterminate, like beneficence. By 1759, when the *Moral Sentiments* was first printed, he had reached the view that there was a precise criterion: the proper or just degree of resentment or punishment was that degree which had the sympathy of the impartial spectator (II.ii.2.1–2).

In the course of editing the *Theory of Moral Sentiments* I have spent a good deal of time collating the text of all editions published in Adam Smith's lifetime and working out the exact nature of the revisions he introduced. That kind of exercise gives one an eye for spotting earlier and later composition. There are many passages in the *Moral Sentiments* which appear to me to come from an early draft and which, like the manuscript lecture on justice, speak of moral judgements as expressing the feelings, not of a 'spectator', but of 'us' or 'mankind' or 'other people' or 'the company' or 'strangers'. ('We' and 'mankind' are especially common.) The theory, no less than the theories of Hutcheson and Hume, begins from the spectator's point of view, but it does not need to stress the word 'spectator' at that stage. Nor does it need Adam Smith's special concept of the *impartial* spectator so long as it is confined to judgements made in the second or the third person. The spectator is 'indifferent' in the sense of not being an interested party, and he expresses a universal point of view in being

[16] I have published the text, and have discussed several questions affecting the manuscript, in an article entitled 'Adam Smith and "the infection of David Hume's society"', *Journal of the History of Ideas*, xxx (1969), 225–48.

[17] VII.iv.36. The reference is to the sixth and subsequent editions, but the words were written for the first edition and remained unchanged.

representative of any observer with normal human feelings. For Adam Smith, however, the theory of Hutcheson and Hume could as well be stated in terms of 'mankind' or 'us' or 'strangers'.

Smith began to stress the impartiality of the spectator only when he came to theorize about the *effect on the agent* of the reactions of spectators. Smith's spectator is first called 'impartial' in the chapter that distinguishes between 'the amiable and the respectable virtues', the virtues of humanity on the one hand and of self-command on the other. Humanity is a more than average degree of sympathetic feeling and is the result of an effort by the spectator to heighten his sympathy so as to match the experience of 'the person principally concerned'. Self-command is conversely a virtue of 'the person principally concerned' and is the result of an endeavour to control natural emotion and to lower its pitch to that which the ordinary (not the especially humane) spectator feels by sympathy. It is in this latter context that Smith first used the phrase 'the impartial spectator' (I.i.5.4). Humanity and self-command together constitute for Smith 'the perfection of human nature', a combination of Christian and Stoic virtue. 'As to love our neighbour as we love ourselves is the great law of Christianity, so it is the great precept of nature to love ourselves only as we love our neighbour, or, what comes to the same thing, as our neighbour is capable of loving us.' (I.i.5.5) Self-command is essentially to feel for ourselves only what we see others can feel for us.[18]

So too, according to Adam Smith, the approbation and disapprobation of oneself that we call conscience is an effect of judgements made by spectators. Each of us judges others as a spectator. Each of us finds spectators judging him. We then come to judge our own conduct by imagining whether an impartial spectator would approve or disapprove of it. 'We examine it as we imagine an impartial spectator would examine it.'[19] Conscience is a social product, a mirror of social feeling. Without society, Smith wrote (III.i.3), a man 'could no more think of his own character, . . . of the beauty or deformity of his own mind, than of the beauty or deformity of his own face'. For both he needs a mirror. The mirror in which he can view his character 'is placed in the countenance and behaviour of those he lives with'. We are all anxious to stand well with our fellows. 'We begin, upon this account, to examine our own passions and conduct, and to consider how these must appear to them. . . . We suppose ourselves the spectators of our own behaviour, and endeavour to imagine what effect it

[18] In III.4.6. Smith writes of seeing ourselves 'in the light in which others see us, or in which they would see us if they knew all'. Professor A. L. Macfie, *The Individual in Society* (1967), 66, has remarked that this must surely have inspired Burns's 'To see oursels as others see us' since Burns knew and valued Smith's book.

[19] III.1.2, but with the wording of eds. 1–5. Ed. 6 expands the sentence to: 'We endeavour to examine our own conduct as we imagine any other fair and impartial spectator would examine it.'

would, in this light, produce upon us. This is the only looking-glass by which we can, in some measure, with the eyes of other people, scrutinize the propriety of our own conduct.' (III.i.5)

The 'supposed impartial spectator', as Smith often called him, is not the actual bystander who may express approval or disapproval of my conduct. He is a creation of my imagination. He is indeed myself, though in the character of an imagined spectator, not in the character of an agent.

To judge of ourselves as we judge of others . . . is the greatest exertion of candour and impartiality. In order to do this, we must look at ourselves with the same eyes with which we look at others: we must imagine ourselves not the actors, but the spectators of our own character and conduct. . . . We must enter, in short, either into what are, or into what ought to be, or into what, if the whole circumstances of our conduct were known, we imagine would be the sentiments of others, before we can either applaud or condemn it.[20]

On revising this passage for edition 2, Smith was more explicit:

When I endeavour to examine my own conduct, . . . it is evident that . . . I divide myself, as it were, into two persons; and that I, the examiner and judge, represent a different character from that other I, the person whose conduct is examined into and judged of. The first is the spectator. . . . The second is the agent. . . .

(III.i.6)

The impartial spectator, 'the man within', may judge differently from the actual spectator, 'the man without'. The voice of conscience reflects what I imagine that I, with all my knowledge of the situation, would feel if I were a spectator instead of an agent.

It is easy to miss this distinction and to suppose that conscience for Smith is purely a reflection of actual social attitudes. The misunderstanding is especially easy if one concentrates on a passage that in edition 1 appeared at an early stage in the discussion:

To be amiable and to be meritorious; that is, to deserve love and to deserve reward, are the great characters of virtue; and to be odious and punishable, of vice. But all these characters have an immediate reference to the sentiments of others. Virtue is not said to be amiable, or to be meritorious, because it is the object of its own love, or of its own gratitude; but because it excites those sentiments in other men. The consciousness that it is the object of such favourable regards, is the source of that inward tranquillity and self-satisfaction with which it is naturally attended, as the suspicion of the contrary gives occasion to the torments of vice.

(III.i.7)

The view that conscience reflects actual social attitudes faces a difficulty: if this view were correct, how could conscience ever go against popular

[20] This passage appeared in ed. 1 following what is now III.1.3.

opinion, as it clearly sometimes does? This must have been the objection put to Smith by Sir Gilbert Elliot in a letter written soon after the publication of the first edition of the *Moral Sentiments*. Smith replied on 10 October 1759 (Letter 40) and sent Elliot a copy of a lengthy revision obviously written as an instruction to the printer. He said in his letter that the revision was 'intended both to confirm my Doctrine that our judgements concerning our own conduct have always a reference to the sentiments of some other being, and to shew that, notwithstanding this, real magnanimity and conscious virtue can support itselfe under the disapprobation of all mankind'. The revision differs in some slight details from that which was subsequently incorporated in edition 2 of the book, published late in 1760 (and imprinted 1761). In principle, however, the development of the doctrine of the impartial spectator in edition 2 was due to the objection made by Elliot.

On the one hand Smith wanted to retain the traditional view that the voice of conscience represents the voice of God and is superior to popular opinion. On the other hand he believed that conscience is initially an effect of social approval and disapproval; in the first instance, *vox populi* is *vox Dei*. 'The author of nature has made man the immediate judge of mankind, and has, in this respect, as in many others, created him after his own image, and appointed him his vicegerent upon earth to superintend the behaviour of his brethren.'[21] Although the developed conscience is a superior tribunal, 'yet, if we enquire into the origin of its institution, its jurisdiction, we shall find, is in a great measure derived from the authority of that very tribunal, whose decisions it so often and so justly reverses.'[22]

How, then, does the superior tribunal acquire its independence? We find by experience that our first fond hopes of winning everyone's approbation are unattainable; 'by pleasing one man, we . . . disoblige another'. In practice bystanders tend to be biassed by partiality and ignorance. And so we imagine an impartial spectator. 'We conceive ourselves as acting in the presence of a person quite candid and equitable, of one who has no particular relation either to ourselves, or to those whose interests are affected by our conduct, who is neither father, nor brother, nor friend either to them or to us, but is merely a man in general, an impartial spectator who considers our conduct with the same indifference with which we regard that of other people.' Smith then went on to describe the impartial spectator as 'this inmate of the breast, this abstract man, the representative of mankind, and substitute of the Deity'. As in perception, true judgements require the use of imagination. Smith illustrated the analogy with his perception of distant hills through the windows of his study. To the eye the

[21] III.2.31, but as it appears in the draft sent to Elliot and in ed. 2.

[22] This quotation, and the two that follow it, occur shortly after the preceding one in the draft sent to Elliot and in ed. 2, but were removed from ed. 6. See below.

hills are enclosed within the small space of the window-frame; in order to obtain a true judgement of the relative sizes of the vista and the window, one needs to imagine oneself at roughly equal distances from both.[23]

It is significant that at one place edition 2 dropped a paragraph which had appeared in edition 1 about the unreliability of the imagination as a 'moral looking-glass'. After speaking of the function of the imagination as the mirror in which we see our own character, Smith had added that, while ordinary mirrors can conceal deformities, 'there is not in the world such a smoother of wrinkles as is every man's imagination, with regard to the blemishes of his own character'.[24] In the second edition he trusted the imagination more and society less.

This process was carried farther still in edition 6, where Smith wrote that it was the mark of vanity to be flattered by the praise of society and to ignore the truer judgement of conscience. Evidently Smith still felt the force of the objection that conscience was independent of social attitudes. Experience of the world had in fact made him more distrustful of popular opinion. He was especially moved by the fate of Jean Calas, unjustly condemned at Toulouse in 1762 to torture and execution for the alleged murder of his son. Any educated European would have heard of the case from the prolonged advocacy of Calas's innocence by Voltaire; but Adam Smith knew more than that. He spent eighteen months at Toulouse in 1764–5 and must have heard much discussion of the city's *cause célèbre*. Smith referred to Calas in the course of a virtually new chapter added to edition 6 of the *Moral Sentiments* (III.2), distinguishing the love of praise from that of praiseworthiness and the dread of blame from that of blame-worthiness. Such a distinction was implicit in edition 2, where the approval and disapproval of actual spectators may be opposed by the judgement of conscience that one does not merit approval or disapproval. But whereas in edition 2 Smith had said that the jurisdiction of conscience 'is in a great measure derived from that very tribunal, whose decisions it so often and so justly reverses', in edition 6 he withdrew that statement and wrote instead that 'the jurisdictions of those two tribunals are founded upon principles which, though in some respects resembling and akin, are, however, in reality different and distinct' (III.2.32). He was even ready to reverse the causal relationship in some instances. 'The love of praise worthiness is by no means derived altogether from the love of praise.' The happiness which we receive from the approval of conscience is confirmed when actual spectators also approve. 'Their praise necessarily strengthens our own sense of our own praise worthiness. In this case, so far is the love of praise worthiness from being derived altogether from that of praise; that the love

[23] In ed. 6 this comparison appears at III.3.2.

[24] The paragraph followed what is now III.1.5.

of praise seems, at least in a great measure, to be derived from that of praise worthiness.' (III.2.2–3)

Adam Smith added some further elaboration of his theory in other new passages written for edition 6. As I have noted earlier, he first spoke of the 'impartial' spectator when describing the Stoic virtue of self-command, which he placed on a par with the Christian virtue of love. In edition 2 he followed up his reply to Sir Gilbert Elliot's objection with a discussion of the necessity of conscience to counter the force of self-love.[25] The Christian virtue of love or benevolence or humanity, he said, is not strong enough for this purpose. (The words 'benevolence' and 'humanity' suggest an implicit criticism of the theories of Hutcheson and of Hume.) 'It is reason, principle, conscience, the inhabitant of the breast, the man within. . . . It is from him only that we learn the real littleness of ourselves, . . . and the natural misrepresentations of self-love can be corrected only by the eye of this impartial spectator.' This function of conscience is closely akin to self-command, and in edition 6 Smith proceeded in the same chapter to explain the origin and development of self-command in terms of 'that great discipline which Nature has established for the acquisition of this and every other virtue; a regard to the sentiments of the real or supposed spectator of our conduct' (III.3.21). A child, Smith wrote, first learns to control emotion in order to gain the favour and avoid the contempt of his schoolfellows. A man of weak character is like a child; in misfortune he can control his feelings only when others are present. A man of greater firmness remains under the influence of the impartial spectator at all times, so much so that the division of the self into two persons, the imagined spectator and the agent, almost disappears; imagination virtually takes over from reality. 'He almost identifies himself with, he almost becomes himself that impartial spectator, and scarce even feels but as that great arbiter of his conduct directs him to feel.' (III.3.25) But even the most stoical of men cannot altogether escape self-interested feelings in 'paroxysms of distress', such as losing a leg in battle. 'He does not, in this case, perfectly identify himself with the ideal man within the breast, he does not become himself the impartial spectator of his own conduct. The different views of both characters exist in his mind separate and distinct from one another, and each directing him to a behaviour different from that to which the other directs him.' (III.3.28) Yet agony does not last for ever, and in due time the man who has lost a leg recovers his equanimity. He identifies himself again with 'the ideal man within the breast' and no longer laments his loss. 'The view of the impartial spectator becomes so perfectly habitual to him, that, without any effort, without any exertion, he never thinks of surveying his misfortune in any other view.' (III.3.29)

Here, as elsewhere, Smith distinguished the impartial 'supposed'

[25] To be found, with some revision, at III.3.3-5 of ed. 6.

spectator from the 'real' one. The rudimentary stage of the virtue of self-command, found in the child or the man of weak character, depends on the feelings of actual spectators. The higher stage, reached by the man of constancy, depends entirely on conscience. What is new in this passage is the view that the agent can identify himself with the imagined spectator to the extent of obliterating the natural feelings of self-regard.

Smith returned to self-command in a later section also added in edition 6, and here he wrote of two different standards of moral judgement concerning ourselves. 'The one is the idea of exact propriety and perfection. . . . The other is that degree of approximation to this idea which is commonly attained in the world, and which the greater part of our friends and companions, of our rivals and competitors, may have actually arrived at.' (VI.iii.23) The first is the judgement of the impartial spectator. 'There exists in the mind of every man an idea of this kind, gradually formed from his observations upon the character and conduct both of himself and of other people. It is the slow, gradual, and progressive work of the great demigod within the breast, the great judge and arbiter of conduct.' (VI.iii.25) The second standard is reached from observing the actual behaviour of most people. Smith's distinction in this passage between two standards of judgement is not quite the same as the earlier distinction between the judgement of conscience and that of actual spectators, for the second standard discussed here is derived from the practice of others, not from their reaction as spectators of practice. Still, this distinction is like the earlier one in contrasting the normative ideals of conscience with the positive facts of social life.

Throughout the development of Smith's concept of the impartial spectator, his fundamental position was unchanged. In the first edition he stressed the effect of men's social situation more than the work of the imagination; in the second and the sixth editions he reversed the emphasis. But both were elements in his theory at all stages. Even before any sharp contrast between the man within and the man without, Smith's view was that an agent can judge his own character and conduct only if he imagines *himself* in the position of a spectator. And even in his latest thoughts on self-command added to edition 6, Smith wrote of 'a regard to the sentiments of the *real or supposed* spectator of our conduct' and said that the child and the man of weak character acquire self-control from adjusting their feelings to those of actual spectators.

The impartial spectator has been mentioned in some modern discussions of ethical theory. The ideal observer theory of Professor Roderick Firth and others has been, understandably enough, compared with Adam Smith's theory of the impartial spectator. More recently Professor John Rawls in his important book *A Theory of Justice* (1971–2) has written of the impartial spectator as a device of utilitarian theory for regarding the interest of society as if it were the interest of a single person. It is, however, a mistake to suppose that either of these conceptions comes near to Adam Smith's theory of the impartial spectator.

Differences between Professor Firth's ideal observer and Adam Smith's impartial spectator have been admirably brought out by Professor T. D. Campbell in his *Adam Smith's Science of Morals* (1971, ch. 6). According to Professor Firth, moral judgements are to be analysed as statements of the hypothetical reactions of an observer who is ideal in being omniscient, omnipercipient, disinterested, and dispassionate. As Professor Campbell says (133), this theory makes the ideal observer more like a god than a man and revives some of the difficulties that face a Christology. Adam Smith's impartial spectator is disinterested, but neither omniscient nor omnipercipient, and he is certainly not dispassionate. He has the normal feelings of a normal human being. He approves and disapproves according to his sympathies with or antipathies to the feelings of agents and of people affected by action. So far as judgements about others are concerned, Adam Smith's spectator simply *is* any normal observer who is not personally affected.

But what of the later development of Smith's theory when dealing with judgements about ourselves? What of the description in edition 2 of 'this abstract man, the representative of mankind, and substitute of the Deity', or of the phrases used in edition 6, the 'ideal' man or 'demigod' within the breast? There is an element of rhetoric here, designed to emphasize the superior authority of conscience when opposing the judgement of actual spectators. The impartial spectator is still a man, not a god, and indeed a perfectly normal man. The 'substitute of the Deity' in edition 2 is also 'the representative of mankind'. The metaphorical 'demigod' or 'ideal man within the breast' of edition 6 is given a literal interpretation in another late passage added to that edition, where Smith wrote of 'the approbation of the impartial spectator, and of the representative of the impartial spectator, the man within the breast' (VI.i.11). The man within is 'ideal' because he seeks to be praiseworthy more than to be actually praised by 'the man without'. The judgement of conscience is superior to that of actual spectators simply because the agent can know better than bystanders what he has done or not done, and what was his motive for acting as he did. He is 'well informed' but he is not omniscient. His superior knowledge is a matter of common experience.

If the man without should applaud us, either for actions which we have not performed, or for motives which had no influence upon us; the man within can immediately humble that pride and elevation of mind which such groundless acclamations might otherwise occasion, by telling us, that as we know that we do not deserve them, we render ourselves despicable by accepting them. If, on the contrary, the man without should reproach us, either for actions which we never performed, or for motives which had no influence upon those which we may have performed; the man within may immediately correct this false judgment, and assure us, that we are by no means the proper objects of that censure which has so unjustly been bestowed upon us.

(III.2.32; added in ed. 6)

For Professor John Rawls, the concept of the impartial spectator is a device of utilitarian theory. 'Endowed with ideal powers of sympathy and imagination, the impartial spectator is the perfectly rational individual who identifies with and experiences the desires of others as if these desires were his own. (*A Theory of Justice*, 27) He can thus organize the interests of society into a single system analogous to the system of self-interested desires which everyone constructs for himself. In working out this notion Professor Rawls was probably influenced more by Hume than by Adam Smith, though he has described his account as 'reminiscent' of both these thinkers (184) and has included both in his list of classical utilitarians (22, note 9).

Far from being a utilitarian, Adam Smith was a severe critic of utilitarianism in many parts of his ethics and jurisprudence. Of course he wrote in the *Wealth of Nations* about a natural harmony of individual and social interests, but there he was abstracting economic activity from the whole of social life, and in any event that harmony owed nothing to sympathy. In Adam Smith's theory of approval, the spectator's sympathy is concerned first with the motive of the agent. The spectator imagines himself in the shoes of the agent, and if he finds that he would share the agent's feelings, the correspondence of sentiments constitutes his 'sympathy' (as Smith used the term) and causes him to approve the agent's motive as right and proper. In some circumstances a second species of sympathy may be added to this first one. If the agent's action benefits another person, the spectator may find that he sympathizes with the beneficiary's gratitude as well as with the agent's benevolence. This double sympathy causes the spectator to approve of the action as meritorious. That is Smith's theory of approval in a nutshell. He agreed with Hume that utility pleases a spectator through sympathy with the pleasure given to the direct beneficiary, but he entirely disagreed with Hume's view that this kind of sympathetic pleasure is the sole or main constituent of moral approval. In his final account of the matter Smith listed four grounds or 'sources' of moral approval, and made a regard to utility the last and the least of these.

What sort of thing was Adam Smith's theory of the impartial spectator meant to be, and what was it meant to do? It was meant to be a sociological and psychological explanation of some moral capacities. Not a task that any modern philosopher would attempt; but philosophical theories continue to be rather odd, and it is as well to observe the glass houses of the modern counterparts before throwing stones at Adam Smith's construction.

Professor Firth proposes his ideal observer theory as an analysis of the *meaning* of moral judgements, and as such it is surely incredible. The suggestion is that when you or I say that an action is right, we mean, we intend to assert, that it would evoke a favourable reaction in a hypothetical observer who was omniscient, omnipercipient, disinterested, and dispassionate. We have all been making moral judgements happily—or unhappily—from early youth, but it is a safe bet that none of us had the remotest thought of connecting them with an omniscient and dispassionate observer until we heard of Professor Firth and his theory. Professor Rawls is doing something different. He presents the impartial spectator version of utilitarianism as a possible alternative to his own, contractual, theory of justice. He does not regard either theory as an analysis of meaning. Rather he thinks of them as hypotheses of what logically could have produced our present thoughts, though he does not for a moment suppose that either of these possible causes was an actual cause. Like Hobbes, Professor Rawls evidently thinks that one can explain something by reasoning from known effects to *possible* causes. Such a procedure may possibly improve our understanding, but it seems no less bizarre than Professor Firth's interpretation of the ideal observer hypothesis as an analysis of meaning. Adam Smith at any rate did not anticipate either of these modern theorists. He was certainly not giving an analysis of the meaning of moral judgements, nor was he putting forward a hypothesis of a purely *possible* cause. He was presenting a hypothesis of the actual causal process whereby judgements of conscience are formed. No doubt this is a scientific rather than a philosophical function. Fortunately the division of labour had not been carried that far in Adam Smith's time.

Adam Smith's theory can certainly stand comparison with the best known of modern psychological explanations of conscience, Freud's account of the super-ego. This is similar to Smith's view in taking conscience to be a second self built up in the mind as a reflection of the attitudes of outside persons. Freud's hypothesis is presumably helpful in the diagnosis and treatment of certain neuroses. But if regarded as a general theory of the formation of conscience, normal as well as abnormal, it is less satisfactory than Adam Smith's account because it takes too narrow a view of the causal agencies. Freud concentrated (though not exclusively) on the attitude of parents, while Adam Smith spoke of the reaction of society in general and mentioned the influence of teachers and schoolfellows as well as parents when referring to the growth of conscience in children. A more important difference is that Freud emphasized the negative attitudes of disapproval on the one side and fear of punishment on the other, and so he represented the super-ego as predominantly (though again not exclusively) a restrictive or censorious element in the mind. He accounted for the excessively rigid conscience produced by a repressive upbringing but not for the more liberal kind produced by an affectionate upbringing. Adam Smith, unlike Freud, did not stress the force of disapproval and fear. He spoke of both favourable and unfavourable attitudes on the part of society as having a place in the formation of conscience.

What was Smith's theory meant to do? It was meant to provide a satisfactory alternative to *a priori* accounts of conscience and morality generally. Like Hutcheson and Hume before him, Smith was a good empiricist. They all aimed at giving an explanation of ethics in terms of 'human nature'—empirical psychology, we should say today. But Adam Smith appreciated that the theories of Hutcheson and Hume were inadequate to account for the peculiarities of conscience. Hutcheson in his later years accepted Bishop Butler's description of the authority of conscience, but without explaining how this could be fitted into the moral sense theory. At first Adam Smith followed the example of his teacher. There is one passage in the *Moral Sentiments* (III.5.5–6) where Smith wrote as if he were unconsciously quoting Butler, even to the extent of inferring divine intention from the character of moral judgement. This is a relic of the earliest version of Smith's lectures, written before he had developed his own theory of conscience. In due course he came to see (no doubt influenced by Hume) that the use of empirical method required one to explain, not just to assert, the existence of peculiar qualities. Hutcheson had not been empirical enough in regarding the moral sense as an original endowment of human nature; and Butler had not been empirical enough in taking the authority of conscience to be a simple datum, intelligible only by reference to theology. Both phenomena could be explained as the natural effects of ordinary experience.

In evaluating Adam Smith's theory, the first question that arises is whether Smith, any more than Butler, remained true to the empirical method. He wanted to explain ethics in terms of empirical psychology and sociology, yet he ended up with the apparently conventional thesis that moral rules are equivalent to divine laws and that conscience has an authority superior to social approval and disapproval. The reader is apt to think that about half way through the book Smith abandoned empiricism and slipped into the traditional views of theists and rationalists without noticing the inconsistency. A more careful scrutiny of his theory shows that this is not so. His concept of the impartial spectator remained empirical throughout, as I hope will be clear from what I have said. It would need another lecture to show that the same thing is true of Smith's account of moral rules, an account that is no less ingenious, but perhaps less impressive, than his theory of conscience.

A second question that arises is whether it is reasonable to attribute greater complexity to moral judgements made about ourselves than to those made about others. If Smith had been giving an analysis of meaning, this would be a fair criticism. There is no reason to suppose that the statement 'I ought to pipe down' has a more complicated meaning than the statement 'You ought to pipe down'. Smith's theory does not have that implication. His view was that the making of the first statement has a more complicated history. Still, if he were right, might we not expect to see some traces of a difference of character between first-person moral judgements and the rest? Well, there is one respect in which we do differentiate between them. We not only recognize that an agent's judgement about himself may be independent of the judgement of others about him. We also accept the principle (with some reservation, I think, for social contexts in which the rights of others are affected) that it is a man's moral duty to follow his conscience even though it may be misguided. The judgement of conscience in directing one's own conduct is given a priority over the judgement made by other people. This does nothing to confirm Adam Smith's particular theory, but it does rebut the suggestion that an account of moral judgements concerning ourselves should be on all fours with an account of moral judgements concerning others.

Finally, however, I wish to pose a criticism of a different kind about the complexity of Adam Smith's hypothesis. It seems to me that his concept of the impartial spectator is too complicated to be acceptable when one works it out fully in terms of his general theory of approval. An ordinary spectator approves of an agent's conduct if he finds that, after imagining himself in the agent's shoes, he would feel and act as the agent does. An agent who consults his conscience has to imagine himself in the position of an uninvolved spectator while retaining his present knowledge of the facts. He has to imagine that he is an uninvolved spectator who in turn imagines himself to be in the position of the involved agent; and having performed this feat of imagination doubling back on its tracks, the agent has to ask himself whether the feelings that he imagines he would then experience do or do not correspond to the feelings that he actually experiences now. The process is not impossible but it seems too complicated to be a common occurrence.

W. R. Scott once suggested that Adam Smith had exceptional powers of imagination himself and 'as a Moral Philosopher he insisted in crediting everyone with his own genius' (*Adam Smith: An Oration*, 1938, 11). That too is not impossible but again unlikely if only because the quoted words imply that Smith was rather unimaginative in his social observation. I prefer to think that Smith, like anyone else, could make a mistake in the details of his theory. The difficulty which I have described becomes apparent only when one spells out Smith's theory of conscience in terms of his theory of approval. The idea of the impartial spectator seems persuasive when taken by itself, with an unanalysed notion of approval. This suggests that the trouble lies in Smith's initial theory of approval. But that is another story.

V

The Topicality of Adam Smith's Notion of Sympathy and Judicial Evaluations

LUIGI BAGOLINI*

I

To act often implies making decisions. Making decisions often implies making choices regarding the purposes of the actions and the means necessary to achieve those purposes. This seems to be true on the basis of normal common sense. This seems to be a kind of common denominator on which most of the so-called philosophers from Aristotle to our day agree. The analysis of the elements of human action contained in the third Book of the *Nicomachean Ethics* is still topical. Consider, for example, the notions of προαίρεσις, of βούλησις, of βούλευσις, that is purpose, will, desire, appetitive spontaneity, deliberation, etc., that seem even today effectively usable. The disagreement among philosophers begins when it is a question of considering the relations between choices of means and choices of purposes. The disagreement involves especially the nature of the choice of purposes. The problem of the choice of purposes implies the problem of evaluating these purposes. The problem of evaluating purposes exists for those who do not consider the choice of purposes as quite identical with certain so-called physical or biological events such as, for example, the breaking away of a piece of rock from a mountainside, or the formation of a glaucoma in an eye. The disagreement becomes even greater when it is a question of choices and of evaluations of final purposes. We understand, with Hans Kelsen, as final purposes those which (at the moment when they are chosen) are chosen independently of the fact of their being capable of serving as suitable means for the achievement of ulterior purposes.[1]

If we wish, for the sake of brevity, to draw up a scheme (be it purely conventional but, as I think, useful), the disagreement is determined by and converges on two extreme positions which manifest themselves in contemporary culture, too. On the one hand, the choice of purposes is thought of as rational. On the other, the choice of purposes is thought of as tending

* Professor of Political Philosophy at the University of Bologna.

[1] 'A judgment of value is the statement by which something is declared to be an end, an ultimate end which is not in itself a means to a further end. Such a judgment is always determined by emotional factors.' Thus H. Kelsen, 'The Metamorphoses of the Idea of Justice', in *Interpretations of Modern Legal Philosophies, Essays in Honor of Roscoe Pound*, edited with an Introduction by P. Sayre (1947), 394.

to be irrational, emotional, and arbitrary.[2] These two opinions, at first sight contrasting one with the other, express two dogmatic attitudes that I would call respectively the dogmatism of the rational and the dogmatism of the irrational. By a dogmatic attitude I mean here a standpoint that is not sufficiently demonstrable nor plausible.

Against the dogmatism of the rational it is sufficient to observe that any formulation of a purpose of human action to which one attributes a value (that is rational, *a priori*, universal, and absolute) does not serve in itself as a guide to action. For example, we use the word 'justice' to indicate a purpose of human action. We say that it is 'just to give to each his own'. We say that this criterion is rational, *a priori*, and absolute. We must, however, observe that this criterion does not serve, alone and in itself, as a practical and real guide to action. Since, in the determination of what is mine, of what is yours, and of what is his, there enter choices that are dependent on variable elements that cannot be expressed by means of a formulation that is abstract, *a priori*, and immutable. We have here individual, subjective, social, cultural, and ideological elements that vary historically. No concept with which one wishes to express the purpose of human action is free from such variable elements. Neither the concept of happiness nor that of the common good, which have a variable content, is free of such variable elements; nor is that of utility (useful for what?); nor is that of normality, since, for example, what is normal for the many may not be so for the few; what may be normal in one situation may not be so in another; what is normal in one historical period and in a particular country may not be so in another historical period and in a different country. Not even reason, understood in an empirical and inductive manner, serves practically and alone in determining the choice and the evaluation of purposes. Reason, understood empirically, serves to determine the fitness of the means with respect to the achievement of the purposes; that is, the relation of means to purpose. But the relation of means to purpose presupposes the choice of the purpose.

On the contrary, against the dogmatism of the irrational it suffices to observe that in admitting that the choice of a purpose is absolutely irrational, there arises the problem of distinguishing between a so-called irrationality that is identical with what we call madness and an irrationality that is not madness. Now, a search for the distinction between so-called irrationality and madness goes, I think, beyond the bounds of the so-called irrational.

Speaking abstractly and elliptically, the irrational implies the rational.

[2] I have given various examples of the two extreme positions in the introduction to my book *La simpatia nella morale e nel diritto* (2nd edition, 1966), 11–19. See the introductory essay by M. Reale to the Portuguese edition of this work, *Moral e direito na doutrina da simpatia* (1952), 7–20.

The irrational cannot be stated in absolute terms as the only constitutive condition of the choice of a final purpose. In other words, in order that the purpose chosen shall not be pure fancy, my choice cannot be simply irrational but must also imply a rational limit. This limit consists in the conditions of possibility of realization of the purpose and may be expressed by means of judgements concerning the relationships between means and purposes.

Following these brief considerations, it seems to me that the merit of the doctrine of sympathy, from Hume to Smith, lies in offering us the possibility of escaping from both the above-mentioned dogmatisms. That is, in David Hume's theory of sympathy, and to a greater extent in Adam Smith's, we find, I think, a very original integration of rational and emotional elements involved in moral evaluations and decisions. This is true, I think, in contrast with many partial analyses that have been made and some of which I listed in a book first published in 1950.[3] This corresponds to that need of synthesis or unification which is characteristic of Smith's theory of sympathy, and on which, quite rightly and very well, Professor Macfie has recently insisted.[4]

Here I am interested in the synthetic core of the theory of sympathy propounded by Smith, leaving aside certain difficulties and contradictions into which both Hume and Smith may have fallen.[5] I think that as regards the fundamental core of the doctrine of sympathy Smith, in spite of his criticism of Hume, incorporates Hume's doctrine.[6] In relation to the synthetic core I think the doctrine of sympathy is still topical and usable from the point of view of certain problems of the philosophy of law,[7]

[3] *La simpatia nella morale e nel diritto*, especially 133ff., where various interpretative points of view are discussed concerning Smith's theory.

[4] 'Smith was by nature a synthetic thinker (*rara avis*) always seeking a systematic explanation for many factors.' Thus A. L. Macfie, *The Individual in Society, Papers on Adam Smith* (1967), 91–2. For some elements which appear in all areas of Smith's work see the Introduction by A. Skinner to *The Wealth of Nations*, Books I–III (1970), 15–29.

[5] See P. S. Árdal, *Passion and Value in Hume's Treatise* (1966), 133ff.

[6] Cf. A. Giuliani, 'Adamo Smith filosofo del diritto', *Rivista internazionale di filosofia del diritto* (1954), 505–38 and P. Stein, 'Osservazioni intorno ad Adamo Smith filosofo del diritto', *Rivista internazionale di filosofia del diritto* (1955), 97–100.

[7] Hume had written to Smith: 'I am told that you are preparing a new Edition, and propose to make some Additions and Alterations, in order to obviate Objections. I shall use the Freedom to propose one, which if it appears to be of any Weight, you may have in your Eye. I wish you had more particularly and fully prov'd, that all kinds of Sympathy are necessarily Agreeable. This is the Hinge of your System, and yet you only mention the Matter cursorily . . . Now it would appear that there is a disagreeable Sympathy, as well as an agreeable: And indeed, as the Sympathetic Passion is a reflex Image of the principal, it must partake of its Qualities, and be painful where that is so. Indeed *when we converse with a man with whom we can entirely sympathize*, that is, where there is a warm and intimate Friendship, the cordial openness of such a Commerce overpowers the Pain of a disagreeable Sympathy, and renders the whole Movement agreeable. But in ordinary Cases, this cannot have place. An ill-humored Fellow; a man tir'd and disgusted with every thing, always *ennuié*; sickly, complaining, embarass'd; such a one throws an evident

especially with reference to the nature of the judge's decision in Court, as I shall mention at the end of this paper. It is interesting to see how and in what senses the sympathetic process, as outlined by Smith, is applicable to the decision of a judge. This might constitute a proof of a certain contemporary validity of Smith's doctrine, from which emerge certain notions that have a judicial sense.[8] I refer, for example, to the notion of the impartial and well-informed spectator. On the other hand, all Smith's theory, as Professor Macfie says, 'is much more convincingly and consistently worked out on its objective, social and institutional side than on its subjective-conscience side' (loc. cit.). 'The main stress is Smith's insistence on the development of sympathy through social contacts with the moral standards sustained by social institutions.' 'Smith's exploration of society's ethical development is his *major* achievement.' It is 'an exploration in social ethics (though in individual ethics he cuts as deeply and as deftly as any of his Scottish contemporaries)' (op. cit. 100).

Any moral judgement, any proper attribution of praise or blame could be only relative to the individual 'situation', in his historical society. It could therefore be assessed only through a careful estimate of these relevant social influences. But this is the antithesis of an immediate moral sense declaring spontaneously yea or nay. At this level Smith is poles apart from the intuitive view.[9]

All this, from my point of view, could mean that moral evaluations cannot be based exclusively on either the immediacy of a 'moral sense' or on an

Damp on Company, which I suppose wou'd be accounted for by Sympathy; and yet disagreeable . . . It is always thought a difficult Problem to account for the Pleasure, receiv'd from the Tears and Grief and Sympathy of Tragedy; which would not be the Case, if all Sympathy was agreeable . . . You say expressly, *it is painful to go along with Grief and we always enter into it with Reluctance.* It will probably be requisite for you to modify or explain this Sentiment, and reconcile it to your System.' Hume expressed himself thus in Letter 36 addressed to Smith, dated 28 July 1759 with reference to the first edition of *The Theory of Moral Sentiments.* The second edition did not appear till 1761, *The Letters of David Hume* ed. J. Y. T. Greig (1932), i.312, 6 and 313. Smith's reply to Hume is contained also in the 6th edition of *The Theory of Moral Sentiments* (printed for A. Strahan, T. Cadell, W. Creech, and J. Bell, 1790): 'I answer that in the sentiments of approbation there are two things to be taken notice of; first, the sympathetic passion of the spectator; and, secondly, the emotion which arises from his observing the perfect coincidence between this sympathetic passion in himself, and the original passion in the person principally concerned. This last emotion, in which the sentiment of approbation properly consists, is always agreeable and delightful. The other may either be agreeable or disagreeable, according to the nature of the original passion, whose features it must always, in some measure, retain' (I.iii.1.9, note). See, for example, the comment of P. Salvucci in *La filosofia politica di A. Smith* (1966), 127ff., to which I refer the reader also for bibliographical references, and E. Mossner, *Adam Smith: The Biographical Approach* (1969), 12–14.

[8] Cf. A. L. Macfie, op.cit. 49.

[9] Macfie, op.cit. 87. '. . . sympathy is not a bare feeling, as Hume evidently thought, but is, as Adam Smith seems to have realized in developing his theory, a highly complex state of mind involving thought and imagination.' Thus D. D. Raphael, *Moral Judgement* (1955), 108.

immediate *a priori* rational intuition. The moral evaluation is a sympathetic process in which the activity of reasoning is involved, not *a priori* but inductive reasoning, connected with concrete situations and social circumstances.

II

Sympathy is a process that includes (1) the mental representation of the situation of others and (2) the emotional and imaginative attitudes that consist in the placing of oneself in the situation of another person.

The mental representation of another person's situation is the work of inductive reasoning. On the other hand, the placing of oneself in the situation of another is an imaginative process. As such this process is not reducible to terms of inductive reasoning; moreover, from the point of view of inductive reasoning it is in itself illusory. Smith speaks literally of 'illusion of the imagination' (TMS I.i.1.13).

For example, the inductive representation of the situation indicated by a certain common use of the word 'death' is complex and may be made up of a number of elements, among which the cancellation of all the prerogatives of human existence that death brings, oblivion on the part of the living, the perception of the disintegration of corpses in tombs. Here, I repeat, there enters the rational inductive representation of a certain complex situation. On the other hand, we may add to this representation the imagination of the effect that this situation would produce on our feelings if we, though living and reasoning as living beings, should be able paradoxically to find ourselves in the situation indicated by what we mean when we say that a person is dead (I.i.1.13). At this point it seems easy to object to Smith because if So-and-So is dead then he no longer exists and it is absurd and irrational to speak of So-and-So's situation; that is, it is not possible to place oneself in the situation of the deceased because if he no longer exists, his situation no longer exists either. But the critical validity of such a possible objection seems to me to be greatly weakened by the following two considerations: (1) Sympathy as moral evaluation is not immediate sympathy, like the correspondence of the feeling of one person with the feeling of another person. 'Sympathy', says Smith, 'does not arise so much from the view of passion, as from that of the situation which excites it.'[10] Consequently there is no question here of sympathy with the feelings of a dead

[10] I.i.1.10. In attempting to bring out the importance of the element 'situation' in Smith's conception, I had already discussed and criticized the interpretations of L. Limentani, *La morale della simpatia* (1914), 95ff.; cf, W. Eckstein (in the introduction to his valuable German edition of the *Theory*, I.lviiiff.; J. Bonar, 'The Theory of Moral Sentiments by A. Smith', *Journal of Philosophical Studies*, i (1926), 339. I refer the reader to my *La simpatia nella morale e nel diritto*, 38, 147, 149, 152 and to the works of G. Marchello: *L'utilitarismo simpatetico di Adamo Smith* (1953), 6, and Salvucci, op.cit. 121.

person but of placing oneself in the situation that is expressed in the representation of death. (2) Smith himself, when he speaks of a person placing himself imaginatively in a situation different from his own, while remaining in his own situation, speaks, as I have said, of illusion. He observed, however, that this type of illusion is often necessary to moral evaluations in which sympathetic participation is involved. Hume, too, speaks of the 'imagination', which, for example, 'enables us to sympathise with an unfelt feeling' and which converts an idea into an impression in sympathy.[11] But Smith has developed and enriched with new elements Hume's doctrine of sympathy: first, in a 'constant emphasis on the situation in which sympathy occurs, and secondly, insisting in the actual operation of sympathy through the mediation of the partial and well-informed spectator'.[12] Situation, impartiality, and information are, therefore, elements that from Smith's point of view integrate one with the other in the complexity of the moral–evaluative process. This process is therefore a kind of dynamic synthesis.

The placing of oneself imaginatively in the situation of another does not suffice to constitute a moral evaluation. The direct sympathetic participation in the situation of another is not sufficient. It is necessary that the evaluation should imply the point of view of an impartial and well-informed spectator. Direct sympathy does not suffice, in so far as experience demonstrates that it is possible to sympathize even with the vices of persons who are involved in certain determinate situations. In fact it is also possible to sympathize with the vices of persons who occupy a certain social position such, for example, as that founded on wealth (I.iii.2.7).

In order that sympathy should function as a condition and within the ambit of a moral evaluation it is necessary to pass from direct to indirect sympathy. While direct sympathy is a participation in the situation of the person who acts, indirect sympathy is an imaginative participation in the situation of the person who is the recipient of the action to be judged (II.i.5.1,2).

III

I think that Smith's theory can be utilized and developed in the following manner. It is not necessary that indirect sympathy should involve imaginative participation in the situation of a really existent person who is really subjected to the effect of the action to be judged. It is sufficient that the indirect sympathy should involve participation in the situation of a hypothetical person who would receive the effects of the action to be judged.

[11] See D. Hume, *A Treatise of Human Nature* (1739), II.ii.7,9 ed. L. A. Selby-Bigge (1946, 1st ed. 1888), 371, 385, 386. It is to this edition of the *Treatise* that I refer here and in other quotations that follow.

[12] See, for example, TMS III.2.5,31. Cf. Macfie, op.cit. 94.

For example, in the instant when I act, I believe I am acting well, and I give a positive evaluation to the effects of my action, in that I imagine myself to be in the situation of somebody who, in a more or less near future, may receive the effects of my action. This does not in any way eliminate the necessity of the inductive reasoning through which the situation in which I imagine placing myself can be expressed. It is a situation that I represent to myself rationally, recognizing it from the elements of the social and cultural environment in which I live in relation to others. In order that an action of mine, in the instant that I am about to accomplish it, should appear to me to be commendable, it is necessary that I imagine myself to be in the situation of the real or hypothetical recipients of my action and that, at the same time, I should maintain my awareness of the situation in which my action develops or has developed. In this way I make myself an impartial spectator of my action. The point of view of the impartial spectator coincides with that of the 'man within' as distinct from the 'man without' in the metaphorical terminology of Smith (III.2.31–5). The same person may be both the 'man without' and the 'man within'. It is a question of two attitudes that can coexist in the same person. The jurisdiction of the 'man without' is founded directly on the desire to receive the praise of others at once and, correspondingly, on the desire to avoid the immediate condemnation of others. It is an immediate judgement of first instance. The jurisdiction of the 'man within', on the contrary, is based on the desire to possess those qualities and to achieve those actions that the judging subject himself admires in others. Conversely it is based on the fear of possessing those qualities and of perpetrating those actions that the judging subject condemns in others. Precisely, while the 'man without' aims in the first place at the praise of others, the 'man within' aims at the consciousness that he is worthy of it by making himself the impartial spectator of his own actions.

One criticism of this doctrine is that of those who say that the impartiality of the spectator is illusory, that there is nothing objective in it, that it is purely subjective, that it depends on individual tastes and tendencies that vary from one person to the next and that therefore it is quite arbitrary. But this criticism, in my opinion, is not valid. It depends on a purely individualistic and abstract view of Smith's doctrine, it depends on an incorrect reduction of Smith's theory to terms of dogmatism of emotion, it does not take into account the element of inductive reasoning present in Smith's theory of sympathy. It does not take account of the fact that the impartial spectator of Smith is the well-informed spectator of the situations from which emerge the motives, the causes, and the purposes of the actions to be judged. He is also the spectator of the situations in which the suitable means to the achievement of such purposes are realized and of the situations on which bear the effects of the actions to be judged. The inductive knowledge of the causes, of the motives, of the purposes, and of the effects of the actions to be judged enters in the inductive knowledge of social situations in which such elements (causes, purposes, and effects) manifest themselves. Such knowledge makes it impossible to reduce the moral evaluation to terms of pure emotional individuality. Such knowledge is that which ensures that sympathetic evaluation will express more or less the meaning of the social, legal, and moral standards at the moment and in the place in which the evaluation itself occurs. The judgement of the impartial spectator does not express an absolute criterion of good, that is a criterion *a priori* deducible from a rational faculty that is superimposed on the changes in the historical situation. The judgement of the spectator is so much less partial, the better, I repeat, he is informed of the social situations in which his judgement is uttered. Impartiality is not absolute but relative to the social standards of conduct. These standards may assume, in a given historical moment, the character of norms resulting from sympathetic processes that have previously determined the formulation of such norms.

Any criterion of evaluation that is determined through sympathy (and that shall imply both the judgement of the 'man without' as well as of the 'man within') may assume furthermore the character of a directive influence on the behaviour of others and consequently the character of a tendency towards persuasion.[13] I sympathize with the action of another to the extent to which I am, more or less, persuaded that I should act in the same manner if I were to find myself in his situation; I judge my action more or less worthy of approbation to the extent to which the purpose of my action is more or less suitable to function as a criterion capable of influencing the conduct of the person who should find himself in an analogous situation. From this point of view my practical and moral evaluation acquires a social objectivity that, as such, is not, I repeat, an absolute objectivity deducible from an individual reason independent of the changes in historical and environmental situations. It is, on the contrary, a synthesis emerging from such situations, that is a synthesis of inductive reasoning and imaginative processes. In themselves imaginative processes may appear, as we have seen, purely illusory if they are considered independently of the inductive representation of the situations to which in actual fact they are linked. From another standpoint one can say that the choice, the determination, and the evaluation of purposes is implied in the rational and inductive representation of the means suitable to the achievement of the purposes.

[13] See TMS VII.iv.25–8, and LRBL. Also A. Giuliani, 'Le "Lectures on Rhetoric and Belles Lettres" di Adamo Smith', extract from the *Rivista critica di storia della filosofia*, xvii (1962), 328–36.

IV

Though Smith criticized Hume, as I have pointed out above, he substantially completed Hume's philosophy.

In Hume's opinion 'the usefulness' of a behaviour, of a 'character', of an 'action' consists in its tendency to realize a 'certain purpose' that may be considered in some way 'agreeable'. Most works of art, says Hume in his *Treatise*, are esteemed beautiful in proportion to their fitness for the use of men, and even many of the productions of nature derive their beauty from that source. Handsome and beautiful, on most occasions, is not an absolute but a relative quality, and pleases us by nothing but its tendency to produce an end that is agreeable. And he continues in a note quoting a Latin writer: 'Pulcher aspectu sit athleta, cujus lacertos exercitatio expressit; idem certamini paratior. Numquam vero *species* ab *utilitate* dividitur' (III.iii.1).

'Usefulness', Hume goes on to say in his *Enquiry concerning the principles of morals*, 'is agreeable and engages pure approbation. This is a matter of fact confirmed by daily observation. But useful? For what? For somebody's interest, surely. Whose interest, then? Not our own only; for our approbation frequently extends farther. It must, therefore, be the interest of those who are served by the character or action approved of; and these we may conclude, however remote, are not totally indifferent to us.' 'By opening up this principle, we shall discover one great source of moral distinctions.'[14] That is what Hume says. Well, Smith, in criticizing Hume, sets propriety against the 'utility' and the 'usefulness' of Hume. 'Propriety' is, for Smith, an attitude in which the consideration and the pleasure deriving from the well-balanced organization of the means suitable to the achievement of a purpose prevail over the consideration and the pleasure connected with the realization itself of the purpose. Smith says that from the point of view of the spectator and of the 'man within' those actions and behaviours can be worthy of approbation in which the realization of a future purpose implies the sacrifice of a present pleasure. Prevalence of the future over the present. But I believe that such possibility of prevalence is not even excluded by Hume, as may be found, though implicitly, in the passage referred to here and in the whole of Hume's theory of justice; and may also be derived from Hume's objections to the two fundamental criticisms of sympathy (*Treatise*, III.iii.1). In my opinion, it is not possible to give up Hume's 'utility'; and the deeper value of Smith's philosophy consists, in my view, on this point, in proceeding to that integration of 'utility' and 'propriety' which is implicit, but not quite explicit in Hume's philosophy. The conclusion is that 'utility' has significance only within

[14] Hume, *An Enquiry Concerning the Principles of Morals* (1777), s.v. Pt. I, ed. L. A. Selby-Bigge (2nd ed. 1902), 218.

the ambit of a sympathetic process in which the realization of 'propriety' is implicit.

V

Any evaluation in terms of utility acquires a concrete sense only through the sympathetic process. 'Utility' is not a principle that can replace sympathy in the manner of Bentham.[15] Looking at the question from the Hume–Smith standpoint, we can say that Bentham did not take into account all the positive elements of the sympathetic process as they had been expounded by Smith, without which the principle of 'utility' remains indeterminate in the sense that it cannot function as a guide to action. As regards the calculation of the so-called pleasures considered by Bentham, it has been also recently shown that it is not realizable.[16] According to Bentham, with the principle of utility accepted independently of any sympathetic process, I must choose those actions from which the greatest pleasure and the least pain will result. But how is it possible to calculate pleasure in relation to pain? It has been said that in spite of the impossibility of calculating pleasures in relation to pains—and vice versa—Bentham offers us a principle that functions as a guide to action and that can be formulated by saying that those actions are useful that in a given society contribute most to the happiness of its members (Ayer, op. cit. 259). Now I think that, even formulated in this way, this principle is of little value as a guide to action of an individual. This because (1) there are actions that contribute to the happiness of some and cause unhappiness to others; (2) the desire which in this moment may move me to act in a given manner cannot always be verified as an exact repetition of the desires felt by others; (3) it may be that the desire that urges me to act is considered good by some people and bad by others (the same thing may happen in the effects of the action that I am about to perform); (4) the action that I am about to perform is not always necessarily comprised within a class of my past actions or of those of others whose consequences have already been verified. It is true, I think, that the principle of 'utility' may assume contents different and contrasting one with respect to another; and it cannot serve as a principle of rational discrimination in terms of 'yes or no', of useful or useless, as occurs in the field of that which is rationally verifiable as true or false. I think that perhaps within the ambit of moral evaluations the logic of 'yes or no' is not always of value. A moral evaluation is not rationally true or false; it is not the alternative of 'yes or no' that is appropriate to it, but the character of being more or less reasonable and plausible. From this point

[15] See, for example, J. Bentham, *An Introduction to the Principles of Morals and Legislation*, II. 11–19, ed. W. Harrison (1948), 136–46.

[16] See A. J. Ayer, *The Principle of Utility of Jeremy Bentham and the Law: A symposium*, ed. G. W. Keeton and G. Schwarzenberger (1948), 258.

of view Smith's position, by which both 'utility' and 'propriety' are synthetically implied in moral evaluations, seems valid; both emotion and reason, both the imaginative transposition from one situation to another and an inductive representation of the respective situations are also implied. And the result of this synthesis has precisely the character of reasonableness and of persuasiveness, by which the moral evaluation is determined, but not the character of pure and exclusive rationality.

VI

Following Smith's train of thought, one can say that sympathetic evaluation does not claim to eliminate the arbitrariness of a decision but to limit it as much as possible. Let us think, for example, of the decision of the judge who has to apply a statute. Let us accept for the sake of argument the distinction that some theories of law make between the interpretation of a statute as a rational and theoretical activity on the one hand, and decision as a volitive, practical activity on the other hand. Let us accept for the sake of argument what those jurists say when they affirm that generally no concrete situation allows only one application of the law. 'This is true' (Professor Alf Ross, for instance, goes on to say) 'even in those cases where a definite rule exists, expressed in relatively fixed terms; and it is certainly true to an even higher degree when the case is judged according to legal standards or even by discretion.'[17] There is always a margin of variable width in which the decision moves, there is a penumbra, as Professor Hart says.[18] That is, different decisions are possible. Which is the least arbitrary? In Professor Ross's opinion the decision is not arbitrary, 'but is objective ('just' in the objective sense) when it is covered by such principles of interpretation and such evaluations as are current in practice. When it is not in contrast to what is typical of the judges as a whole' (Op. cit. 285). However, this point of view of Professor Ross is not, in my opinion, satisfactory. The cases and complex situations of the so-called 'crises in normality' remain outside Ross's perspective. In these cases and situations the current evaluations of practice can be different from and in contrast with one another, and it is not possible to speak comprehensively of what is 'typical of judges as a whole'. Nowadays, for example, this crisis in normality appears in Italian legal activity especially concerning questions that involve trade unions and conflicts between employers and workers. It is a crisis that is influenced also by the ideological tendencies of the judges. The problem arises once again of limiting as much as possible the arbitrariness of the decisions.

The German philosopher, Leonard Nelson, in his *Kritik der praktischen*

[17] See, for example, A. Ross, *On Law and Justice* (1958), 284.

[18] H. L. A. Hart, 'Positivism and the Separation of Law and Morals', *Harvard Law Review*, 71, No. 4 (1958), 607ff.

Vernunft of 1917, proposed a 'Gedankenexperiment', that is a 'thought-experiment'. Namely, according to Nelson, in order that the decision concerning a conflict of interests should have as little arbitrariness in it as possible, it is necessary that it be conditioned by the equal balancing of all the interests affected by the decision. This seems to correspond, in Nelson's view, to the general juridical and moral feeling. He went on to say that in order that such a comparison of all the interests affected by the decision should, in its turn, be possible, it is necessary for the judge to imagine that all the interests affected by the decision are his own interests.[19] Now in Ross's opinion, Nelson's thought-experiment is unrealizable for the following reason: 'Whereas I can easily imagine myself wearing somebody else's hat, fully realizing that the hat belongs to someone else, the same thing is not possible in the case of an interest. I cannot experience an interest and at the same time regard it as not mine but as another person's.'[20] Nevertheless, from the point of view of Smith's theory of sympathy I think that Nelson's thought-experiment can be reconsidered and modified, taking into account Ross's objection. It is a question of replacing in Nelson's statement the notion of interest and introducing elements of Smith's theory. It is perhaps true that I cannot experience a wish (or an interest) and at the same time consider it not mine but another person's; however, from the standpoint of Smith's theory I can on the contrary imagine myself to be in the situation of another person, though being fully aware that I am in my own.

The greater the participation of the judge is in the situation of the persons involved in a conflict of interests, the greater is the possibility that the judge's arbitrariness will be limited and that in his decision an objectivity even if relative and socially relevant will be expressed.

The decision is so much the less arbitrary the more it is preceded by a comparison and an equilibration of the situations of the persons involved in the conflict on which the judge is called upon to make his decision. Certain critics of sympathy have continued to say that sympathy is devoid of all objectivity because the more I find a person likeable the more drawn I am to make a decision in his interests.[21] But this, I repeat once again, is an opinion that does not allow for indirect and mediate sympathy which is completely different from direct and immediate sympathy with the feelings of others. Only indirect and mediate sympathy renders comparison possible.[22] For example, So-and-So is in conflict with

[19] L. Nelson, *Vorlesungen über die Grundlagen der Ethik*, i, *Kritik der praktischen Vernunft* (1917), 133ff.

[20] Ross, *Kritik der sogenannten praktischen Erkenntnis. Zugleich Prolegomena zu einer Kritik der Rechtswissenschaft* (1933), 533ff., and op. cit. 227ff.

[21] See, for example, among various writers, R. A. P. Rogers, *A Short History of Ethics* (1945), 161.

[22] See from a legal point of view M. Reale, *Dos estados de necessidade* (1971), 48.

another and I am a judge. I must compare and balance the various situations involved in the conflict between So-and-So and the other. And I must also introduce into this comparison my own situation as judge. Well, I must not only put myself in the situation of So-and-So but in the situation also of the other. I must take So-and-So's situation into account by putting myself in the situation of the other and I must take the situation of the other into account from the standpoint of So-and-So. But this is not sufficient. Before deciding I must also consider the effects of my possible decisions both from the standpoint of So-and-So's situations and that of the other, as well as the standpoint of other real or hypothetical persons who may have an interest in evaluating my possible decision. The more numerous the situations are, of other individuals distinct from myself, in which I imaginatively place myself, so much the more effective will be the equilibration and the comparison of the interests in conflict before my decision. Only thus, I repeat once more, is it possible to speak of a comparison of the situations and of the corresponding interests in conflict, which limits the arbitrariness of the decision to the minimum. If I were drawn only by the situation of So-and-So there would be no comparison.

It may still be objected that the comparison of the situations has no need of sympathy just as there is no need of sympathy in order to discover the differences and similarities between so-called material objects. But the objection is not valid because here there is no question of a simply empirical verification or of a simple intellectual act. It is a question of evaluations. Furthermore, in the decision of a judge there is expressed an 'ought' and not an 'is' or the bare description of a fact or of an event. An 'ought' cannot be considered as a material object. The specific sense of an 'ought', in so far as it is distinct from a simple object, and from a material object, cannot be detached from the manner in which it is regarded and evaluated by those who find themselves in the situations to which the 'ought' refers. That is to say 'ought' has an inner sense with respect to such situations. For that reason it is necessary to place oneself imaginatively, by means of sympathy, inside these situations in order to evaluate the 'ought' of a decision that the judge must deliver. From another aspect, the more the decision of the judge is prepared by a sympathetic comparison of the situations involved in a conflict of interests on which the judge is to make a decision the more equitable the decision itself may be said to be and equity as an evaluative attitude does not seem reducible to a simple fact, to an 'is', but, it seems to me, to imply, precisely, an 'ought'.

VII

The greater the participation of the judge in the various situations of the persons, even merely hypothetical, who directly or indirectly, totally or in part receive the effects of his decision, the more equitable the judge's decision may be said to be. I refer to a notion of equity that is not exclusively reducible to the notion of indulgence as distinct from the notion of justice as at some points in the *Rhetoric* of Aristotle. I refer instead to the meaning that the word equity (the Greek ἐπιείκεια) acquires within the limits of a broad meaning of the word justice (τὸ πρῶτον δίκαιον), that is natural, fundamental, and primal justice, as distinct from τὸ νομικὸν δίκαιον, that is legal and conventional justice. This is the meaning of equity that we find in the fifth book of *The Nicomachean Ethics*[23] where equity indicates the realization, in particular concrete human situations, of that need of universality which is implied in the idea of justice. Equity is in fact the realization and particularization of justice. This corresponds to a need implied both in the fifth book of *The Nicomachean Ethics* and perhaps in the theory of Smith, even setting aside any difference between the basic conceptions of justice in the two philosophies.[24]

[23] See, for example, R. A. Gauthier, *L'éthique à Nicomaque*, ii, *Commentaire*, *Livres I–V* (1959), 432–4.

[24] 'As our sense of the impropriety of conduct arises from a want of sympathy, or from a direct antipathy to the affections and motives of the agent, so our sense of its demerit arises from what I shall here too call an indirect sympathy with the resentment of the sufferer' (TMS II.i.5.4). And here, also as regards 'resentment', there opens up the possibility of a more extensive discussion that is beyond the limits that I proposed to myself for the present article.

VI

Moral Philosophy and Civil Society

HIROSHI MIZUTA*

SINCE the predominance of the principle of self-love or self-preservation in human actions was noted by Machiavelli, and defined by Hobbes as a right of nature, philosophers have been trying to justify it either morally or through an analysis of the structure of civil society.[1] Needless to say any moral justification will be most powerful where it is accompanied by an objective analysis of the social structure. But on the other hand, before one can produce an objective analysis of a society one must see it at least to a certain extent before one's eyes, and before one can see it a mass of human beings supported by a sort of moral philosophy must have constructed it. This is the way in which the moral philosophy and political economy of the Enlightenment, especially in the case of Adam Smith, strengthened each other through being united into a system of social philosophy.[2]

The aim of the present essay is to give an outline of the social philosophy of Adam Smith mainly by locating it in the history of social thought.

I

For Hobbes, the *right* of nature was the right to do whatever one thinks necessary for self-preservation, and he concluded that the *state* of nature is necessarily a state of war. Men thus have to agree to set up an absolute sovereign power to keep the peace, although Hobbes does admit that everyone has a right of resistance.[3] One reason for this conclusion may be that Hobbes assumed that the quantity of necessities of life was fixed so that a struggle for survival was inevitable.

Locke, however, in discussing the concept of private property, suggests

* Professor of the History of Social Thought at the University of Nagoya, Japan. The author wishes to thank Mr. Andrew Skinner for his help in improving his English style.

[1] As far as Hobbes and Machiavelli are concerned, I have discussed the matter in my book, *Kindaijin no keisei* (*The Formation of the Modern Concept of Man*) (1954). For a wider perspective, see Franz Borkenau, *Der Übergang vom feudalen zum bürgerlichen Weltbild* (1934). There were some contemporary critics who insisted on the sociable and benevolent nature of man. Cf. J. Bowle, *Hobbes and his Critics* (1951), and S. I. Mintz, *The Hunting of Leviathan* (1962).

[2] The civil society is almost identical with the civilized society or the commercial society in Smith's terminology. It is not the civil society of Hobbes with an absolute sovereign power nor that of Hegel and Marx with such an unconquerable contradiction as the class struggle.

[3] Hobbes, *Leviathan* (1651), 66 and 111.

the possibility of a peaceful coexistence, even in the absence of some supreme power, and made a great step forward in constructing a science of civil society.[4] He steps even further toward an economic analysis of it, even though the fact that he put private property in land and its product at the basis of civil society means that those who had no such property were effectively excluded.[5] Moreover, his economic analysis is made only by way of discussing such current problems as the rate of interest, so that compared with his political analysis of civil society, the contribution to economics was more practical and fragmented. In other words, the introduction of the product of labour did not, as far as Locke was concerned, lead to anything like a systematic economic analysis of civil society.

Locke's effort to establish and justify the passions and actions of individuals in civil society also falls short in the field of moral philosophy. For example, his ambiguous and relativist concept of the law of opinion and reputation[6] is far from strong enough to justify the activities of embryonic industrialists. The task of justifying their activities through an economic analysis of civil society was left to Adam Smith, although that of supplying some moral justification was taken up by philosophers immediately after Locke—despite the weakness of having no objective analysis of society as a whole. Thus, for example, certain Deists[7] at the turn of the century tried to restore Hobbes and the principle of self-love, arguing that reason is the supreme conductor of every man's actions and passions, so that even religion has to pass through the examination of reason before it is admitted to be true. The fact that Hobbes was a man of virtue was used as evidence to suggest that his philosophy of reason and self-preservation was morally justifiable. Such a justification of the principle of self-love does not, however, provide any guarantee that a multitude of people acting on the same principle can coexist. The attempt made by some of the Deists to restore Hobbes was thus only a first step; further and more substantial advances were to be made by Mandeville and Hume[8] apart from the French thinkers (including Voltaire, under the strong

[4] J. Locke, *The Treatises of Government* (1690), II, sect. 27.

[5] Accordingly, he makes two different proposals on education, one for the gentry and another for the labouring poor. Cf. J. Locke, *Educational Writings*, ed. J. W. Adamson (1922), which contains Locke's plan of education for the labouring poor.

[6] J. Locke, *An Essay concerning Human Understanding* (4th edition, 1690), II, Ch. XXVIII, Sect. 10.

[7] e.g. A. Collins, *A Discourse of Free-thinking* (1713), 170–1.

[8] In the preface to the *British Moralists 1650–1800* (1969), D. D. Raphael writes as follows: 'I felt that the new selection should start quite firmly with Hobbes, who gave the initial impetus to the lively controversies of the British Moralists. (The very title of the greatest work in British philosophy, Hume's *Treatise of Human Nature*, was suggested, I, believe, by the use of the phrase in the body of Hobbes's brilliant little book, *Human Nature*.)'

influence of the Deists).[9] A different attempt was made by Shaftesbury, writing immediately after Locke, who, unlike the restorers of Hobbes with their emphasis on self-love, stressed the benevolent and social nature of mankind, while admitting self-love to a certain extent.

The way in which Shaftesbury tries to build a bridge between man and society,[10] or self-love and love of society, is as follows.[11] Human passions or affections as causes of human actions are divided into three classes: the first class contains in natural (social) affections, the second, self-affections, and the third, non-natural affections, which may be harmful to either society or self. Leaving aside the latter, both of the first two sorts of passion should be kept within a certain limit to make the social life of men possible. Even a strong benevolent passion can be harmful to society, when, for example, a man is too benevolent to take care of himself. Extremes would make society impossible, and to avoid them there are two things which the human mind can do: the moral sense innate to every human being can keep a balance of the social and private affections; and starting with self-love everyone can extend his affection gradually from self to family, friends, community, and ultimately to the nation to which he belongs. However, in either case Shaftesbury's way of building the bridge between man and society applies only to men of sense and culture, namely, aristocrat-philosophers like himself, and this is just the point raised by Mandeville when he criticizes Shaftesbury. 'If the vulgar are to be all excluded from the social virtues, what rule or instruction shall the labouring poor, which are by far the greatest part of the nation, have left them to walk by?'[12]

Mandeville's criticism is sharp but double-edged. Even in his world of grumbling bees where everybody is said to be free to promote his self-interest, the labouring poor are to be driven to work by necessity.[13] And the ruling and middle classes themselves are not so free as they may seem at first sight. In the world of bees, self-love must be bound by justice (*Fable of the Bees*, i.37) and 'private vices by the dextrous management of a skilful politician may be turned into publick benefits' (i.369). Mandeville makes it quite clear that Shaftesbury's aristocratic, though enlightened philosophy falls short of justifying or analysing the autonomous structure of the newly emerging civil society, by pointing out that the labouring poor cannot control themselves as Shaftesbury's men of culture do, and that even among

[8] See Voltaire's picture of the Royal Exchange in *Lettres philosophiques* (1734), Lettre VI, which suggests that the religious and moral unity of men is unnecessary for their economic prosperity. For Smith's idea of the diversity of religious opinion see the WN V.i.g.8–9.

[10] According to the nominalist–empiricist tradition of the British philosophy, the wording should be 'among individuals in society'.

[11] Earl of Shaftesbury, *Characteristicks of Men, Manners, Opinions, Times*, 3 vols. (3rd ed. n.p., 1723), i.1–176. (Treatise IV, viz. an inquiry concerning virtue, or merit.)

[12] Mandeville, *The Fable of the Bees* (6th edition, 1732), ed. F. B. Kaye (1924), ii.47.

[13] The necessity-driven labouring poor and the omnipotent statesman is a characteristic contrast common to the majority of mercantilist thinkers.

the latter sort of men the management of a skilful politician is necessary to keep the society going. By this able criticism itself, Mandeville also shows at the same time that he too is not equipped with a social philosophy which can cope with the problem.

However, the 'never-to-be-forgotten' Hutcheson[14] appeared in Shaftesbury's defence against the criticism of Mandeville. In one of his earliest works[15] Hutcheson starts with pointing out the ambiguity of Mandeville's wording of 'private vices public benefits' and proceed to state that:

> The world is so well provided for the support of mankind, that scarce any person in good health need be strained in bare necessaries. But since men are capable of a great diversity of pleasure, they must be supposed to have a great variety of desires, even beyond the necessaries of life. . . . The universal gratification is plainly impossible, and the universal suppressing or rooting them out a vain attempt. What then remains, in order to publick happiness after the necessary supply of all appetites, must be to study, as much as possible, to regulate our desires of every kind, by forming just opinions of the real value of their several objects, so as to have the strength of our desires proportioned to the real value of them. . . . Now all men of reflection . . . have sufficiently proved that the truest, most constant, and lively pleasure . . . consists in kind affections to our fellow creatures, gratitude and love to the deity . . .

Thus self-preservation and self-love are allowed to exist at the level of subsistence but beyond that men have to regulate their various desires so as to keep them in a good order corresponding to the hierarchy of virtues which ranks the love of fellow creatures and God as the highest of them.

In his later works, where he is repeating the formula of Shaftesbury on the extension of self-love to the love of universe, and giving the same limitation as to the validity of this formula, Hutcheson puts more stress than Shaftesbury does on the fact that the multitude of men live without philosophical reflection. 'The greater part of mankind, by the necessary avocations of life, are incapable of very extensive design',[16] or in other words, incapable of loving any systems greater than oneself or the small community to which one belongs. Among those people 'the righteousness or goodness' of actions is not indeed the same notion with their tendency to universal happiness, nor does it flow from the desire of it. Our moral sense has also other immediate objects of approbation, many narrower affections, which we must immediately approve without thinking of their tendency to the interest of a system (*System*, i.253–4). This is apparently

[14] The phrase occurs in Adam Smith's letter of acceptance of the office of rector. W. R. Scott, *Adam Smith as Student and Professor* (1937).

[15] An anonymous letter 'To Hibernicus' published in the *Dublin Journal* (4 Feb. 1726). *A Collection of Letters and Essays on Several Subjects, Lately Publish'd in the Dublin Journal*, 2 vols. (1729), i.370–4.

[16] *A System of Moral Philosophy* (1755), i.243.

not the world of men of culture. This is the world of the populace and this is the world which the new science of civil society has to be confronted with. 'The populace often needs . . . to be taught, and engaged by laws, into the best methods of managing their own affairs . . . and in general, civil laws should more precisely determine many points in which the law of nature leaves much latitude.'[17] However, the actions of a populace taught by civil laws are not always exactly consistent with the moral virtue of the wise. 'From the very best body of civil laws certain external rights must arise, which tho' no man can insist upon with a good conscience, yet if the persons to whom they are granted claim them, they must hold them with impunity.'[18] In this world of civil laws, especially 'in all matters of commerce, contracts in which men sin against some general law may be obligatory' even if they are 'of some detriment to the publick'. He added: 'The allowing men to recede from all imprudent contracts would be of far greater detriment, as it would obstruct all commerce' (*System*, ii.4).

Thus Hutcheson begins the analysis of civil or commercial society and suggests that the industry of people (*System*, ii.318) may be promoted not by moral teaching but by economic policy. Although Hutcheson also saw that the division of labour would increase the skill and dexterity of men (*System*, i.288–9), it would be wrong to say that he is now concerned with the civil society of Adam Smith. Although he sees clearly such advantages to society as division of labour and the exchange of products, the second part of his description of exchange shows clearly that his idea is quite different from that of 'a mercenary exchange of good offices according to an agreed valuation'.[19] Hutcheson says that ''tis obvious that we cannot expect the friendly aids of our fellows, without, on our part, we be ready to good offices, and refrain all the selfish passions . . . so that they shall not be injurious to others' (*System*, i.290). Another point of contrast is found between their ideas about the relation of contract and morality. According to Hutcheson certain contracts should be valid regardless of whether they should be morally approved or not. According to Smith, on the other hand, frequent and regular contracts create by themselves a new morality among people (LJ (B) 327–8; Cannan, 254–5). While Smith did make allowance for contracts extorted by force, it is evident that he goes far beyond Hutcheson; at the same time, however, it should not be overlooked that Hutcheson paves the way for his great pupil though he himself stays in the framework established by Shaftesbury.

The advance which Hutcheson makes in his later works may have been promoted at least partly by Hume who criticized the former in a number

[17] Hutcheson, *A short introduction to moral philosophy* (1747), 325.

[18] Ibid. 325–6. A similar passage appears in his *System*, ii.328.

[19] Adam Smith, *The Theory of Moral Sentiments* (1759), 189. Cf. *The Wealth of Nations*, I.ii.

of letters,[20] saying in short that benevolence is neither natural nor fundamental for human nature and human society. But since Hume could not find how it is possible to construct an orderly society from human beings acting on the principle of self-love, he has to recourse to the idea of public utility to realize that idea by regulating human nature. Although this is apparently a sort of compromise of individual and society, Hume shows more clearly than does Hutcheson the problem which the young Adam Smith had to tackle.

II

In one of the early works of Adam Smith which is said to have been written before 1758, he refers to the bulk of mankind, the generality of mankind, and the vulgar, in distinction from philosophers and scientists (Astronomy, II.11, 12). These words may be the remnants of the Shaftesbury–Hutcheson dichotomy which are still to be found in the *Moral Sentiments*, although in the latter work the change in the meaning of the word 'vulgar' is far more decisive than we see in Hutcheson. Smith says that

> the amiable virtue of humanity requires, surely, a sensibility, much beyond what is possessed by the rude vulgar of mankind. . . . Virtue is excellence, something uncommonly great and beautiful, which rises far above what is vulgar and ordinary. . . . Upon many occasions, to act with the most perfect propriety, requires no more than that common and ordinary degree of sensibility or self-command which the most worthless of mankind are possessed of.
>
> (TMS I.i.5.6–7)

It is not so much the excellent virtues as ordinary propriety that Smith is trying to explain as the main subject of his book. The vulgar who are given a relatively small but independent territory in Hutcheson's later works are now allowed to occupy the major and most important part of the human world in Smith's early work.

But one can ask here the old question once more. How is it possible to find or establish any social order among the vulgar, who combine a limited degree of sensibility with the principle of self-love? A few years before the publication of the *Moral Sentiments*, Rousseau had given his answer, starting from the basis established by Hobbes.[21] Admitting that the principle of self-love is the basic and most important principle of human nature, Rousseau proposed three ways to integrate the particular wills or particular self-loves into the general will. The first is by law, the second is by education, and third is through the control of self-love by pity.

[20] *The letters of David Hume*, ed. J. Y. T. Greig, 2 vols. (1932), i.33, 39–40, and 47–8.

[21] J. J. Rousseau, *Discours sur l'origine et les fondemens de l'inégalité parmi les hommes* (1755). Idem, *Discours sur l'économie politique*, *Encyclopédie* (vol. 5, 1755). For Hobbes's influence, see Derathé's notes to the Pléiade edition of Rousseau's work.

The first two can also be found in Helvétius,[22] though built on a less democratic base. In the first two cases, self-love is regulated more or less externally, even if everybody while acting on the principle of self-love participates in legislation and education. But in the third, both self-love and pity belong to the same individual. Thus the human society of Rousseau which seems to be an autonomous organization based on the free pursuit of self-interest is, in reality, just an assembly of self-controlled individuals quite similar to the benevolent men of culture to be found in Shaftesbury and Hutcheson.

Nevertheless, it must be said that Rousseau puts the specific modern problem of the individual and society, or self-love and social order, in the most clear and dramatic form, and by doing so helps Smith to make a great step forward. It is perhaps for this reason that Smith expressed a very high opinion of Rousseau's *Inégalité* and the French *Encyclopédie* which contains his article *Économie politique*.[23]

How is it possible to construct a peaceful social order from a number of individuals acting on the principle of self-love? Shaftesbury and Hutcheson put the stress on the social, while Hobbes, Mandeville, and Hume, emphasized the selfish aspect of the problem. Rousseau stops short of making a synthesis, or at best produces a peculiar synthesis which gave birth to a continuing controversy as to whether he is totalitarian or individualist. Adam Smith gives his own synthesis first in terms of moral philosophy and then in terms of political economy, and shows finally that they are inextricably linked.

Shifting the focus from the wise few to the vulgar multitude, Smith brings the greater and selfish part of mankind to the foreground of his picture of that form of civil society which he calls also the commercial society. Since this is a great society in which the multitude go beyond narrow circles of friendship and kinship even in their daily life, nobody can expect excellent virtues of sympathy and benevolence among them. They are not wise enough to see a great society, or the society is too great for their understanding. Even according to the philosophy of benevolence associated with Shaftesbury and Hutcheson, sympathy becomes weaker as society becomes greater and the distance to the object greater. And for this very reason it is only the wise few who can see society as a whole, and feel sympathy toward those who are at a distance. By shifting the focus in this way, Smith denies that sympathy or benevolence is the main connecting principle of a great society which consists mainly of the vulgar. In this society, however, sympathy prevails in a way quite different from the one

[22] C. A. Helvétius, *De l'ésprit* (1758), esp. disc. 2, Ch. 24.

[23] Adam Smith, 'A letter to the authors of the Edinburgh Review', *Edinburgh Review* (no. 2, 1756), 73ff. The date of publication suggests the possibility that Smith has in mind *Économie politique* too when he refers either to Rousseau or *Encyclopédie*.

which is recommended by Shaftesbury and Hutcheson. Although there is no predominance of the virtue of being sympathetic toward people at a great distance, there is a universal tendency among the multitude to recognize the propriety of being sympathized with by those people. As we see in the passages quoted above, Smith thinks that an unusual degree of sympathy is necessary for the virtue of benevolence but that a usual and weaker degree of sensibility is enough for the multitude to act with complete propriety. And this weak sympathy does exist universally among the multitude.

The multitude, with its weaker degree of sensibility, and the propriety of action and passion, provides three elements which make Smith's picture of human society completely different from any of those drawn by his predecessors.

According to Smith, the propriety of passions and actions consists in the degree to which other members of society, whom he calls spectators, can sympathize with them. As it is impossible for spectators to have the same degree of passion as the person principally concerned, the effort to produce a concord must be made from both sides. 'In order to produce this concord, as nature teaches the spectators to assume the circumstances of the person principally concerned, so she teaches this last in some measure to assume those of spectators' (I.i.4.8). In this sense both parties must be attentive and imaginative. But the concord does not involve *agreement* of the passions of both sides; indeed this is clearly denied when Smith states that: 'After all this [imaginative effort], however, the emotions of the spectator will still be very apt to fall short of the violence of what is felt by the sufferer. Mankind, though naturally sympathetic, never conceive, for what has befallen another, that degree of passion which naturally animates the person principally concerned' (I.i.4.7). It is not an *agreement* but a *concord* of emotions which the person principally concerned can expect from the spectator ('Compassion can never be exactly the same with original sorrow'), and even this 'he can only hope to obtain . . . by lowering his passion to that pitch, in which the spectators are capable of going along with him' (ibid.). Moreover, this concord principally depends on the effort of the agent to moderate his feelings. In a sense, the effort to sympathize is more laudable but less important for Smith's society than the effort to be sympathized with, just as virtue is more laudable but less important than propriety. The effort to be sympathized with by moderating the individual's own emotion should be increased as the society in which he lives becomes greater and as the distance between him and the spectators increases. 'The company of a friend will restore it [the mind] to some degree of tranquillity' which may be lost when we are alone. 'We expect less sympathy from a common acquaintance than from a friend . . . we assume, therefore, more tranquillity before him. . . . We expect still less sympathy from an assembly of strangers, and we assume, therefore, still more tranquillity before them.' The cooling effect of the spectator is greatest and best when he is at the greatest distance from the person principally concerned.

But who is this stranger-spectator? It is true that the word 'stranger' means a person who has a very remote relation with us and whom we have never met before and may never meet again. But the point is that as soon as we enter into civil society, leaving the small circle of kinship and friendship, we meet stranger after stranger on the street. Although we may see any particular stranger only once in our lives, we always see some strangers. It is in the civil or commercial society that men meet each other without any special relation but as strangers.[24]

> Society and conversation, therefore, are the most powerful remedies for restoring the mind to its tranquillity . . . as well as the best preservatives of that equal and happy temper, which is so necessary to self-satisfaction and enjoyment. Men of retirement and speculation, who are apt to sit brooding at home over either grief or resentment, though they may often have more humanity, more generosity, and a nicer sense of honour, yet seldom possess that equality of temper which is so common among men of the world.
>
> (I.i.4.10)

The constancy or equality of temper which is more valuable for Smith than virtues like humanity, generosity, etc., is obtained through a society where everyone has continuously tried to moderate his emotions. Thus in society everyone is enabled to keep the pitch of his emotion as low as he can; everyone is accustomed to think how others will judge his action and passion and to act accordingly.[25]

Smith goes on to argue that every man who is accustomed to act by considering how strangers look at him forms a general idea about the judgement of strangers, which takes the form of general rules or guidelines concerning what is fit to be done or to be avoided. Now man can consult his conscience *before* he really acts, that is to say before he is actually judged by strangers in society or by public opinion. Up to this point Smith may seem to be standing not so far from Shaftesbury, Hutcheson, and Rousseau, while his emphasis on the importance of self-command recalls the 'love of system' in Shaftesbury and Hutcheson, and the pity of Rousseau. But it must be repeated that self-control in Smith cannot be established without the judgement of strangers. It means also that there may be some possibility of conflict between a man's conscience and public opinion.

[24] The stranger is not a friend from whom we can expect any special favour and sympathy. But at the same time he is not an enemy from whom we cannot expect any sympathy at all. Everyone in society is as independent of every other as a stranger, and is equal with every other as they can exchange the situations. The famous impartial spectator is no one else but the spectator who is indifferent to, and does not take the part of either side.

[25] In this sense 'the book is an essay supporting and illustrating the doctrine that moral approbation and disapprobation are in the last analysis expressions of sympathy with the feelings of an imaginary and impartial spectator'. J. Rae, *Life of Adam Smith* (1895), 141. To make the meaning clearer 'feelings' should be replaced by 'sympathies'.

III

It would be better to discuss the conflict mentioned above after a closer examination of the character of self-command, since Smith mentions three sorts of self-command without making a clear distinction between them. As self-command means control by conscience, one cannot discuss the conflict of conscience and public opinion before understanding fully what self-control means.

The three sorts of self-control are the self-control of men of the world in civil society, as discussed to a certain extent already; the self-control of savages, and the self-control of the Stoic philosophers of whom Smith had a high opinion.

The Stoic apathy or self-control differs from that of the generality of men in society, first because the former state is reached only by 'the wise' and not by 'the giddy multitude':

> He [the Stoic wise man] enters . . . into the sentiments of that Divine Being, and considers himself as an atom . . . of an immense and infinite system, which must, and ought to be disposed of, according to the convenience of the whole. Assured of the wisdom which directs all the events of human life, whatever lot befalls him, he accepts it with joy, satisfied that, if he had known all the connexions and dependencies of the different parts of the universe, it is the very lot which he himself would have wished for.
>
> (VII.ii.1.20)

He can almost identify his will with the benevolent divine providence or at least completely rely on it regardless of whether he actually is in adversity or in prosperity.[26] He is not included in the people who value the means much more than the ends, and in so doing promote the wealth of society. 'It is well that nature imposes upon us in this manner. It is this deception which rouses and keeps in continual motion the industry of mankind' (IV.i.1.10). This exemption being the second, the third difference is that the self-control of the Stoic and all other similar philosophers of the ancient world is a product of tyranny, faction, and war, all of which tend to deprive men of the hope of enjoying their lives and tend to drive them to resignation, self-denial, and even to suicide as an extreme form of the self-control.[27] The following passage shows clearly that the self-control of men of the world does not reach by any means to self-denial.

> The qualities most useful to ourselves are first of all superior reason and understanding, by which we are capable of discerning the remote consequences of all

[26] In an addition made for the sixth edition (VI.ii.3). Smith mentions both the 'perfect confidence in that benevolent wisdom which governs the universe' and the 'entire resignation to whatever order that wisdom might think proper to establish'.

[27] The Stoic idea of suicide appears for the first time in the addition (Part VI) to the sixth edition. However, according to the author in his advertisement, there was no fundamental change of his opinion about the Stoic philosophy.

our actions, . . . and secondly, self-command, by which we are enabled to abstain from present pleasure or to endure present pain, in order to obtain a greater pleasure or to avoid a greater pain in some future time. In the union of those two qualities consists the virtue of prudence, of all the virtues that which is most useful to the individual.[28]

Thus self-command in this sense is a quality with which man can live better in the long run than without, whereas self-command as a product of turbulent ages and its tendency toward self-denial and suicide can be mentioned as the third and fourth characteristics of the Stoic concept of self-control.

As to the self-control of savages, Smith describes it as a characteristic observed mainly among 'the savages in North America' and also among the 'negro[es] from the coast of Africa'.[29]

Among civilized nations, the virtues which are founded upon humanity, are more cultivated than those which are founded upon self-denial and the command of the passions. Among rude and barbarous nations, it is quite otherwise, the virtues of self-denial are more cultivated than those of humanity. The general security and happiness which prevail in ages of civility and politeness afford little exercise to the contempt of danger, to patience in enduring labour, hunger, and pain . . . Among savages and barbarians it is quite otherwise. Every savage . . . by the necessity of his situation is inured to every sort of hardship. He is in continual danger. . . . Before we can feel much for others, we must in some measure be at ease ourselves. If our own misery pinches us very severely, we have no leisure to attend to that of our neighbour: And all savages are too much occupied with their own wants and necessities, to give much attention to those of another person. A savage, therefore, whatever be the nature of his distress, expects no sympathy from those about him, and disdains, upon that account, to expose himself, by allowing the least weakness to escape him.

(V.i.2.9)

A savage cannot expect any sympathy even from the members of his own clan owing to the severe conditions of life. Sympathy is a product of a society which has attained a certain standard of living. In addition, there is another reason for the higher degree of self-control found among savages. A savage's life is precarious not only because he cannot expect any help or sympathy from his friends but also because he is always exposed to the danger of being attacked by his enemy. 'When a savage is made prisoner of war, and receives, as is usual, the sentence of death from his conquerors, he hears it without expressing any emotion, and afterwards submits to the most dreadful torments, without ever bemoaning himself, or discovering any other passion but contempt of his enemies' (ibid.).

[28] IV.i.2.6. Self-command here is one of the component parts of the virtue of prudence. A somewhat different explanation is given in VI.iii.

[29] Incidentally, this is evidence of Smith's interest in the natives and slaves of North America.

Admitting thus that there is a higher degree of self-control among savages than among civilized peoples, and calling it 'heroic and unconquerable firmness', Smith, however, does not conclude that the civilized man is inferior to the savage in all respects. 'Thus rules of decorum among civilized nations, admit of a more animated behaviour than is approved of among barbarians. The first converse together with openness of friends; the second with the reserve of strangers.' Although the words 'of strangers' may sound odd, in this context, it means that they are as alien as an enemy. Therefore, the contrast is shown as follows.

> A polished people being accustomed to give way in some measure to the movements of nature, become frank, open and sincere. Barbarians, on the contrary, being obliged to smother and conceal the appearance of every passion, necessarily acquire the habits of falsehood and dissimulation. . . . The passions of a savage too, tho' they never express themselves by any outward emotion . . . are, notwithstanding, all mounted to the highest pitch of fury. Tho' he seldom shows any symptoms of anger, yet his vengeance, when he comes to give way to it, is always sanguinary and dreadful. The least affront drives him to despair. . . . In civilized nations the passions of men are not commonly so furious or so desperate. They are often clamorous and noisy, but are seldom very hurtful; and seem frequently to aim at no other satisfaction but that of convincing the spectator.
>
> (V.i.2.10)

In the last quotation Smith stands with civilization. His belief in the progress of mankind prevents him from sharing fully the idea of 'bon sauvage' with some contemporary French thinkers, and although the chapter is entitled 'of the influence of custom and fashion upon moral sentiments' (V.i.2), he is not a mere relativist.

Through the comparison of self-command among the ancient, savage, and modern nations, it can be seen clearly that the last sort of self-control differs from the first in its attitude to worldly affairs. Whereas the last is a rational calculation to achieve the greatest pleasure in the long run, the first is resignation. Although Smith admits that the turbulent world is useful for the formation of self-control, he does not approve the transformation of it into complete self-denial. As to the second, its main difference from the third is the great fluctuation of emotion among savages from concealment and suppression to explosion, also including suicide. Here too Smith admits the importance of the continuous state of war among the savage. In short, Smith thinks that a man of self-control in civilized society has the constancy of emotion found in the Stoic, and the fighting spirit of the savage. In so far as they are struggling to live through tyranny, faction, and war, both the Stoic and the savage provide a good example of self-control for men in civil society. That is to say, Smith is more favourable to the fighting spirit of the savage than to the resignation of the Stoic, to say nothing of the self-denial of medieval Christianity. The place of religion and especially of Christianity in the world of Smith will be discussed later, in so far as it is relevant to the present question.

Smith's favourable view of the fighting spirit of the savage is based on the parallel he sees between war and business activities.

> A person appears mean-spirited, who does not pursue these [the more extraordinary and important objects of self-interest] with some degree of earnestness for their own sake. We should despise a prince who was not anxious about conquering or defending a province. . . . Even a tradesman is thought as a poor-spirited fellow among his neighbours, who does not bestir himself to get what they call an extraordinary job. . . . This spirit and keenness constitutes the difference betwixt the man of enterprize and the man of dull regularity. Those great objects of self-interest, of which the loss or acquisition quite changes the rank of the person, are the objects of the passion properly called ambition; a passion, which when it keeps within the bounds of prudence and justice, is always admired in the world, and has even sometimes a certain irregular greatness, which dazzles the imagination, when it passes the limits of both these virtues, and is not only unjust but extravagant. Hence the general admiration for heroes and conquerors, and even for statesmen, whose projects have been very daring and extensive, tho' altogether devoid of justice.
>
> (II.6.7)

The parallel is confirmed in one of the additional passages for the sixth edition. 'The man of real constancy and firmness, the wise and just man who has been thoroughly bred in the great school of self-command, in the bustle and business of the world, exposed, perhaps, to the violence and injustice of faction, and to the hardships and hazard of war, maintains this control of his passive feelings upon all occasions' (III.3.25). Business, faction, and war are the great schools of self-command which is, however, far from denying self-interest and ambition. In this sense, Smith's savage can enter into civil society, and in this particular sense Smith has his own idea of the 'bon sauvage'. But it must be noted that Smith's savage does not become a man of the world in civil society by degeneration, at least in the *Moral Sentiments*.[30]

The self-command of the man of the world is a result of schooling in the business of the world and also an inheritance from the warrior-savage with a certain modification. On the other hand, there is an inheritance from the Stoic too. The Stoic self-command tends to become, as mentioned above, resignation and self-denial which Smith refuses to consider as a suitable character for civil society. But there remains an inheritance which can be called a love for greater systems and which plays a particular role in

[30] In *The Wealth of Nations*, Smith says that 'in the progress of improvement the practice of military exercises . . . goes gradually to decay, and, together with it, the martial spirit of the great body of the people' (V.i.f.59). However, in spite of his regret for the decay of the martial spirit, Smith despises national prejudice. Cf. TMS VI.ii.2.

integrating men who are self-interested and assertive. Since there is no space to explain the point in detail, I have to confine myself to reminding the reader that the Shaftesbury–Hutcheson formula which connects self-love with benevolence is used by Smith to merge the latter in the former through the Stoic idea of a benevolent God.

IV

As the strangers in civil society show the character of sympathy in Smith's moral philosophy, so the savages in it show the character of self-command. Both sympathy and self-command are based on the desire for self-preservation of equal, independent, and competitive men of the world. Those activities are kept in balance not only through the *change* of situations which makes sympathy among strangers possible but also the *exchange* of commodities of equal values. But as Smith entered deeper into the analysis of the commercial or civilized society as he calls it, and as the society itself developed, he evidently realized that it was not so harmonious nor so homogeneous as he had thought in 1759.

When he considered the formation of man's conscience in the first edition of the *Moral Sentiments*, he saw no possible contradiction between conscience and public opinion. If we regularly 'examine our own conduct, and endeavour to view it in the light in which the impartial spectator would view it. . . . It is thus that the general rules of morality are formed' (III.4.8). He added: 'Those general rules . . . are all formed from the experience we have had of the effects which actions of all different kinds naturally produce upon us' (III.4.9). Again: 'Those general rules of conduct, when they have been fixed in our mind by habitual reflection, are of great use in correcting the misrepresentations of self-love concerning what is fit and proper to be done in our particular situation' (III.4.12). Conscience appears here as the general rules which are extracted from experience and which are to be obeyed without question.

However, in the second edition of 1761, Smith established a superior court which he calls also the man within, the inmate of the breast, the abstract man, the representative of mankind, and the vicegerent of the Deity (1761 ed., 205, 208). When men feel that the inferior court of public opinion judges unjustly, they think they should appeal to the superior court of conscience. Those who are contented 'with the decision of the inferior tribunal . . . never think of appealing to the superior court. . . . When the world injures them, therefore, they are incapable of doing themselves justice, and are, in consequence, necessarily the slaves of the world' (TMS, 1761 ed., 208–9). Although Smith thus declares that the court of conscience is superior to that of public opinion, he admits that the former cannot be completely independent of the latter and that it cannot unconditionally overrule its decisions. Some difference between the two may occur but scarcely any fundamental contradiction.

Though this tribunal within the breast be thus the supreme arbiter of all our actions, though it can reverse the decisions of all mankind with regard to our character and conduct, and mortify us amidst the applause, or support us under the censure of the world; yet, if we enquire into the origin of its institution, its jurisdiction we shall find is in a greater measure derived from the authority of that very tribunal, whose decisions it so often and so justly reverses.

(TMS, 1761 ed., 206–7)

The discrepancy between those two courts appears decisively in the sixth and last edition of 1790, especially when Smith refers to the case of Jean Calas, the Protestant merchant of Toulouse executed in March 1762, who believed in the judgement of his conscience and who died protesting calmly against the unjust sentence of the judiciary. In this case the discrepancy between the two courts is that of life and death.

To persons in such unfortunate circumstances, that humble philosophy which confines its views to this life, can afford, perhaps, but little consolation. . . . Religion can alone afford them any effectual comfort. She alone can tell them, that it is of little importance what man may think of their conduct, while the all-seeing Judge of the world approves of it. She alone can present to them the view of another world.

(III.2.12)

Whatever reason one may assume, the changes from the first to the second edition and from the second to the sixth edition are undeniable. Starting from the homogeneous and harmonious structure of civil society which is outlined in the first edition, Smith approaches gradually the heterogeneous structure as a result of a widening and deepening of his analysis, and also as a result of the historical development of the society itself.

I think we may isolate three elements which are chiefly responsible for the changes between the second and sixth editions. The first is the growth of political economy in the form of *The Wealth of Nations* published in 1776, and which enabled him to make a full analysis of the heterogeneous class structure of civil society. The second is the impact of the Calas case itself whose rehabilitation campaign was fought by Voltaire and others when Smith was in Toulouse from March 1764 to August 1765. The rehabilitation was declared in March 1765, although public opinion in Toulouse was said to be still against it. The third reason was the French Revolution of 1789 which occurred at a time when Smith was working hard on the last edition. Although he did not live long enough to see the tragic outcome of the Revolution, he was able to read the news of 'the Revolution in France' which appeared in the Edinburgh newspapers almost every day even before 14 July. It may have been that the impact of the

French Revolution reminded Smith of the case of Calas; if so, nobody can blame him for making no distinction between the character of the two popular movements, the radical and the conservative.

Reading the last passage quoted above, one may be inclined to think that Smith in his declining years had turned his mind towards traditional religion, but the fact is that he sees the matter with the eyes of the author of *The Wealth of Nations*. In Book five of *The Wealth of Nations* Smith severely attacked the traditional moral philosophy of self-denial as preached by monks, in remarking that:

> In the ancient philosophy the perfection of virtue was represented as necessarily productive, to the person who possessed it, of the most perfect happiness in this life. In the modern [i.e. medieval] philosophy it was frequently represented as generally . . . inconsistent with any degree of happiness in this life; and heaven was to be earned only by penance and mortification, by the austerities and abasement of a monk; not by the liberal, generous, and spirited conduct of a man. . . . By far the most important of all the different branches of philosophy [i.e. moral philosophy], became in this manner by far the most corrupted [and unsuitable] for the education of gentlemen or men of the world.
>
> (WN V.i.f.30)

In the new passages included in the sixth edition of the *Moral Sentiments*, and in the chapter in which he refers to Calas, he criticized the ascetic philosophy in exactly the same tone. Quoting from one of Massillon's sermons as an example of this kind of philosophy, Smith says that

> to compare, in this manner, the futile mortifications of monastery, to the enobling hardships and hazards of war; to suppose that one day, or one hour, employed in the former should, in the eye of the great Judge of the world, have more merit than a whole life spent honourably in the latter, is surely contrary to all our moral sentiments; to all the principles by which nature has taught us to regulate our contempt or admiration. It is this spirit, however, which, while it has reserved the celestial regions for monks and friars, or for those whose conduct and conversation resembled those of monks and friars, has condemned to the infernal all the heroes, all the statesmen and lawgivers, all the poets and philosophers of former ages; all those who have invented, improved or excelled in the arts which contribute to the subsistence, to the conveniency, or to the ornament of human life; all the great protectors, instructors, and benefactors of mankind; all those to whom our natural sense of praiseworthiness forces us to ascribe the highest merit and most exalted value.
>
> (III.3.35)

Calas's appeal to the superior court and his expectation for rehabilitation in another world is by no means connected to the God of the traditional religion.

Smith sees the importance of religious feelings even in the first edition of the *Moral Sentiments* when he refers to the role of religion in making men more obedient to the general rules of conduct as a result of a constant regard to the sympathy of strangers. This religious attitude, which leads men to obey, constantly and regularly, general rules only because of their being the general rules and not for any possible benefit expected from obedience, reminds us of the Weberian concept of the Protestant ethics of 'calling'.[31] And this is developed in *The Wealth of Nations* into 'the austere system of morality' of the religious sects of the common people (WN V.i.g.11). In this case too, austere morality does not mean self-denial or asceticism. If this can be called ascetic, it is exactly the same as Weber's 'asceticism in the world' (secular asceticism). The particular reason which Smith mentions to explain this character of the religion of the common people is worth quoting.

A man of low condition . . . is far from being a distinguished member of any great society. While he remains in a country village his conduct may be attended to, and he may be obliged to attend to it himself. . . . But as soon as he comes into a great city, he is sunk in obscurity and darkness. His conduct is observed and attended to by nobody, and he is therefore very likely to neglect it himself, and to abandon himself to every sort of low profligacy and vice. He never emerges so effectually from this obscurity, his conduct never excites so much the attention of any respectable society, as by his becoming the member of small religious sect. . . . All his brother sectaries are, for the credit of the sect, interested to observe his conduct, and if he gives occasion to any scandal, . . . to punish him.

(WN V.i.g.12)

The religious sects are regarded as an intermediate stage for the common people from the rural small group, in which they can regulate their conduct quite easily under the eyes of their acquaintances, to a great society of civilization and commerce where they will learn to examine their conduct in the light in which they imagine strangers regard them. It is true that the ignorant vulgar still exist in the rural part of the world of Adam Smith. But they are not confined to that part of life. They flow into towns or a commercial society where they have to learn 'in the great school of self-command, in the bustle and business of the world'. The religious sects are preparatory courses to that great school, not to the world to come.

And then, in an addition to the 1790 edition, Smith remarks of those people that:

In the middling and inferior stations of life, the road to virtue and that to fortune, to such fortune, at least, as men in such stations can reasonably expect to acquire, are happily, in the most cases, very nearly the same. In all the middling and inferior professions, real and solid professional abilities, joined to prudent, just, firm, and temperate conduct, can very seldom fail of success. . . . Men in the inferior and middling stations of life . . . can never be great enough to be above the

[31] Max Weber, *Die protestantische Ethik und der Geist des Kapitalismus*, in *Gesammelte Aufsätze zur Religionssoziologie*, Bd. 1 (1920).

law . . . The success of such people . . . almost always depends upon the favour and good opinion of their neighbours and equals; and without a tolerably regular conduct these can very seldom be obtained. . . . In such situations, therefore, we may generally expect a considerable degree of virtue; and, fortunately for the good morals of society, these are the situations of by far the greater part of mankind. (TMS I.iii.3.5)

Such laudable virtues as humanity and benevolence are not mentioned here. The vulgar multitude of Shaftesbury and Hutcheson are transformed into those people by Adam Smith who takes their side and constructs a moral and social philosophy both of them and for them.

Smith knows the class structure, if not the fatal antagonism, of the society he analyses, and the new sort of ignorance caused by the division of labour, but without seeing any unconquerable disorder in civil society. The conflict of conscience and public opinion also is by no means a fatal one, though it shows that the complete and unconditional identification of man and society which we see in small groups or in the earlier stages of history is no longer possible in a civil society which is being transformed into a capitalist system.

VII

Adam Smith and Political Philosophy

JOSEPH CROPSEY*

THE major writing of Adam Smith is contained in two books, *Theory of Moral Sentiments* (1759) and *An Inquiry into the Nature and Causes of the Wealth of Nations* (1776), to which may be added the posthumously published *Essays on Philosophical Subjects*. His major professional employment was to serve as professor of moral philosophy from 1752 to 1763 in the University of Glasgow, following the single session in which he held the chair of logic and belles lettres. His fame now rests upon the foundation he laid for the science of economics. In all of this there is not much of political philosophy to be seen, even allowing for the inclusion of jurisprudence in the Morals course. Smith's contribution to economics, however, has the character of a description and advocacy of the system now called liberal capitalism; and the ligaments between the economic order and the political system, close under any circumstances, are exceptionally broad and strong in the world as seen and moulded by Adam Smith. The close conjunction of economics and political philosophy, even or perhaps especially if tending toward the eclipse of the latter, is a powerful fact of political philosophy; the men, like Smith, who were responsible for it would have a place in the chronicle of political philosophy on that ground alone.

Smith is of interest for his share in the deflection of political philosophy toward economics and for his famous elaboration of the principles of free enterprise or liberal capitalism. By virtue of the latter, he has earned the right to be known as an architect of our present system of society. For that title, however, he has a rival in Locke, whose writing antedated his own by roughly a century. Our thesis will be that, although Smith follows in the tradition of which Locke is a great figure, yet a distinct and important change fell upon that tradition, a change that Smith helped bring about; that to understand modern capitalism adequately, it is necessary to grasp the 'Smithian' change in the Lockean tradition; and that to understand the ground of engagement between capitalism and post-capitalistic doctrines —primarily the Marxian—one must grasp the issues of capitalism in the altered form they received from Adam Smith. To state the point in barest simplicity: Smith's teaching contains that formulation of capitalist doctrine

* Professor of Political Science at the University of Chicago.

in which many of the fundamental issues are recognizably those on which post-capitalism contests the field.

It would be vastly misleading to suggest that the initiative in modifying the classic modern doctrine was Smith's. To avoid that intimation, we must cover all of what follows with a single remark on the obligation of Smith to his senior friend and compatriot, David Hume. Smith's moral philosophy, as he in effect admits, is a refinement upon Hume's which differs from it in respects that, although very significant, are not decisive.[1] A thorough study of the relation between the doctrines of Smith and Hume would disclose in full the connection between liberal capitalism and the 'sceptical' or 'scientific' principles upon which Hume wished to found all philosophy. The broadest conclusions that would emerge from such a study can be deduced from an examination of Smith's doctrines alone; precisely those which do reflect so deeply the influence of Hume.

Many of Smith's fundamental reflections are contained in the *Theory of Moral Sentiments*, wherein he sets forth his important understanding of nature and human nature. He does this in the course of answering the following question: What is virtue, and what makes it eligible? The premise of his answer is that, whatever virtue may turn out to be, it must have very much in common with, perhaps it must simply coincide with, that by reason of which men or their actions deserve approbation. The question, What is virtue? is never distinct from the question, What deserves approbation? Approbation and disapprobation are bestowed upon actions. The spring of any action is the sentiment (or emotion, or affection, or passion—they are synonymous) which is the motive for committing the act. Approbation of any action must ascend to the passion which truly explains the action.

> The sentiment or affection of the heart from which any action proceeds, and upon which its whole virtue or vice must ultimately depend, may be considered under two different aspects, or in two different relations; first, in relation to the cause which excites it, or the motive which gives occasion to it; and secondly, in relation to the end which it proposes, or the effect which it tends to produce.
>
> In the suitableness or unsuitableness, in the proportion or disproportion which the affection seems to bear to the cause or object which excites it, consists the propriety or impropriety, the decency or ungracefulness of the consequent action.
>
> In the beneficial or hurtful nature of the effects which the affection aims at, or tends to produce, consists the merit or demerit of the action, the qualities by which it is entitled to reward, or is deserving of punishment.
>
> (TMS I.i.3.5–7)

[1] *Theory of Moral Sentiments* (1759), VII.ii.3. Comparison of such a representative passage from Hume as part V of *An Enquiry Concerning the Principles of Morals* with, for example, part I of *Theory of Moral Sentiments* will suggest the broad agreement between the two doctrines.

Propriety and merit are thus the attributes of the passion behind each action that determine the virtuousness of the action. These bear a certain similarity to the 'agreeable and useful' of Hume, but Smith believed his own doctrine to be original in that it avoids the final reduction of all approbation to utility, which Smith rejected on the Humean ground that 'utility' is not as such recognizable by immediate sense and feeling, but only by a sort of calculation of reason. Smith believed he had been able to ground morality on a phenomenon of the passions alone, a belief to which the name of his book testifies. If sense and feeling are indeed immediate—unmediated in the sense that nothing is between them and the root of the fundamental self—then there is considerable value in bringing down the analysis of the virtues to its true bottom in the passions. In Smith's doctrine, the clue to that reduction is in the phenomenon of Sympathy, the criterion of propriety and merit.

Sympathy is a word used by Smith in its literal meaning, an etymological parallel of compassion: 'feeling with', or a fellow feeling. It is a fact, of which perhaps no further mechanical account can be given, that the passions of one human being are transferred to another by the force of imagination at work in the recipient. The man who sees or merely conceives the terror, hatred, benevolence, or gratitude of another must to some extent enter into that passion and experience it himself, for he must imagine himself in the other's circumstances, and therefrom everything follows. Of chief importance in the foregoing is the qualification 'to some extent'. If the impartial spectator, cognizant of what stimulated the terror, hatred, or other passion of the agent, feels in his own breast the same measure of that passion as moved the agent to his action, then the spectator literally sympathizes with the agent and approves his act as consistent with 'propriety'. The spectator experiences sympathetically the passion of the agent; and if he experiences it in the same degree, he further experiences the 'sentiment of approbation'—for that, too, is a passion.

Propriety, however, is not the only ground of moral virtue. Not only the suitableness of the agent's passion to its cause, but the aim or tendency of that passion, its effect, has a bearing on the moral quality of the act in question. Smith refers to 'the nature of the effects which the affection aims at, or tends to produce'. The 'or' is disjunctive, and we must later discuss the important difference between the effects that the sentiment aims at and those that the act it inspires actually tends to produce. For the present it is enough to note that when an action falls upon some human being, it will cause him to feel gratitude or resentment because it will be either beneficial or harmful, pleasurable or painful. If an impartial spectator, informed of all the circumstances, would sympathize with the gratitude felt by the object human being, then the spectator would judge the agent's act to be meritorious, and the second condition of moral virtue would have been met. In brief: if the actual or supposed impartial spectator should sympathize with the passion both of the agent (propriety) and of the patient (merit), then the agent's act may be pronounced virtuous on the basis of the spectator's feeling of approbation.

If Smith's elaboration of the sympathy mechanism did nothing more than show how a rather strict morality could be educed from the passions and the imagination alone, it would have a certain interest. In fact, it points toward a much wider circle of consequences. Sympathy cannot be separated, in Smith's formulation, from imagination. Together they define an undoubted natural sociality of man. By the exercise of two sub-rational capacities, sympathy and imagination, each man is by his nature led or compelled to transcend his very self and, without indeed being able to feel the other man's feeling, is able and is driven to imagine himself in the place of that other and to participate, how vicariously is a matter of indifference, in the feelings which are the fundamental phenomena of the other's existence. Smith, it will be recalled, wished to know not only what virtue is but what makes it eligible. Why—in principle—do men choose to be virtuous, when to be virtuous means to be deserving of approbation? Smith's answer is that it is of the nature of a human being to desire the approbation and love of his human congeners.[2] The first sentence of the *Theory of Moral Sentiments* intimates the withdrawal that is in progress from the doctrine of the war of all against all: 'How selfish soever man may be supposed, there are evidently some principles in his nature, which interest him in the fortune of others, and render their happiness necessary to him, though he derives nothing from it except the pleasure of seeing it.' The combination of imagination, sympathy, and the need for the love and approbation of other men is the ground for Smith's asseverations that nature formed man for society.[3]

Not only does Smith thus teach a natural sociality of man, but also the natural character of the moral law. He can with ease refer to 'the natural principles of right and wrong' (TMS V.i.2.2), understanding by 'right' not merely what benefits or avoids bringing harm to the agent. He can do so because the ground of moral action and perception is the inner constitution of human nature; not in the antique sense of man's highest possibilities, it is true, but in the sense of human psychology—the instincts, sentiments, mechanisms of sympathy that are the efficient causes of human behaviour. These are perfectly natural, and the sentiments of approbation are equally so; hence the principles of right and wrong are incontestably natural.

Smith's version of natural right depends very heavily upon the construct of the 'impartial spectator', the imaginary being who is supposed to

[2] 'The chief part of human happiness arises from the consciousness of being beloved' (TMS I.ii.5.1).

[3] For example, TMS III.i.2.6–7.

represent all mankind in viewing and judging each individual's actions. Judgement rendered from such a point of view implies that no man may rightly prefer himself to the extent of making exceptions from the general rule in his own behalf. 'As to love our neighbour as we love ourselves is the great law of Christianity, so it is the great precept of nature to love ourselves only as we love our neighbour, or what comes to the same thing, as our neighbour is found capable of loving us' (TMS I.i.5.5). Recourse to the imagined judgement of general humanity at the same time directs conscience toward the imagined surveillance maintained over each man at all times by a supposed all-seeing humanity. The constructive standard of 'universal mankind' is fundamental to the version of natural right and natural sociality taught by Smith. It is also a premonition of the post-capitalistic construct of 'all mankind' as the focus of right and history.

It is true that Smith taught the natural sociality of man and the natural basis of the moral law, but this modification of the modern natural law doctrine did not mean a return to antiquity. It must be repeated that natural right for Smith rests upon the primacy of the sub-rational part of the soul, and that natural sociality as he understood it is not an irreducible principle of man but the product of a mechanism at work. Later on, Kant was to speak of the same phenomenon as man's asocial sociality. Natural sociality in this sense does not, as it did for Aristotle, point toward political society. It rather resembles gregariousness. It is a compassion with one's fellow species-members that has everything in common with the alleged unwillingness of horses to tread upon a living body (of any species) and the distress of all animals in passing by the cadavers of their like.[4] To claim on the basis of it that man is by nature a social animal is by no means to claim equally that he is a political animal. Man is tied to humanity by the bonds of immediate sense and feeling, but he is tied to his fellow citizens as such by the weaker, superinduced, bonds of calculation or reason, derivative from considerations of utility. As we have seen, the viewpoint of moral judgement for Smith is that of 'man' or universal mankind, the homogeneous class of species-fellows. The moral law is natural in such a sense as to overleap the intermediate, artificial frontiers of political society and regard primarily the natural individual and the natural species. Under that law, the perfection of human nature is 'to feel much for others and little for ourselves, . . . to restrain our selfish, and to indulge our benevolent affections . . .' (TMS I.i.5.5).

Political society, however, is not directed toward this humane perfection of human nature but toward the safeguard of justice very narrowly con-

[4] From Rousseau, *Discourse of the Origin of Inequality*, First Part. Readers of Rousseau's two *Discourses* will be struck by the similarity of themes and views between them and the *Theory of Moral Sentiments*. The division of human nature between self-love and compassion, and the qualified goodness of civil society are but instances.

ceived. 'Mere justice, is upon most occasions, but a negative virtue, and only hinders us from hurting our neighbour. The man who barely abstains from violating either the person, or the estate, or the reputation of his neighbours, has surely very little positive merit.' Justice means to do 'every thing which [a person's] equals can with propriety force him to do, or which they can punish him for not doing' (TMS II.ii.1.9). Justice, in brief, closely resembles compliance with the law of nature as seen by Hobbes and Locke. Smith understood it so himself. He concluded the *Theory of Moral Sentiments* with a passage on natural jurisprudence, justice, and the rules of natural equity, meaning by all of them 'a system of those principles which ought to run through, and be the foundation of the laws of all nations'. (He closes by promising to take up this theme in a later work. His only other book is *The Wealth of Nations*.)[5]

We shall not sufficiently understand Smith's version of man's natural sociality if we do not grasp thoroughly the difference between man conceived as a social animal and as a political animal. It is helpful for this purpose to consider further the problem of justice, the singularly political virtue which might even be synonymous with obeying the positive law. Justice, in the context of Smith's moral theory, is a defective virtue. He prepares for the exceptional treatment of justice by dividing moral philosophy into two parts, ethics and jurisprudence, the subject of the latter being justice. The defence of justice means the punishment of injustice; and the punishment of injustice is based upon the unsocial passion of resentment, the desire to return evil for evil, the command of 'the sacred and necessary law of retaliation' which 'seems to be the great law which is dictated to us by Nature' (TMS II.i.2.5, cf.II.ii.2). Political society is based upon a moral paradox, one of many we will encounter: sociality rests upon latent animosity, without which the state could not exist.

In the second place, justice, equal to rendering another no less (or more) than what is his due, does not command gratitude and therefore in Smith's system is not attended with merit—or with 'very little'. Considering both the nature of justice and the safeguard of it, it is a defective virtue in that it cannot, or almost cannot, deserve fullest approbation, on the grounds of merit as well as propriety.

In the third place, although there is a sense in which political society is natural, it is a weak sense. The national society is indeed the protector and the matrix of ourselves, our homes, our kin, our friends, and Smith does not for an instant dream of the withering away of the state. 'It is by nature endeared to us.' But 'the love of our own nation often disposes us to view,

[5] In Letter 248 addressed to Rochefoucauld, dated 1 Nov. 1785 Smith indicated that he still had two works 'upon the anvil': 'the one is a sort of philosophical history of all the different branches of literature, of philosophy, poetry and eloquence: the other is a sort of history of law and government.' The advertisement to the 6th edition of the *Moral Sentiments* repeats the promise made at the close of the first, despite Smith's advanced age.

with most malignant jealousy and envy, the prosperity and aggrandisement of any other neighbouring nation' (TMS VI.ii.2.3).

The love of our own country seems not to be derived from the love of mankind. The former sentiment is altogether independent of the latter, and seems sometimes even to dispose us to act inconsistently with it. France may contain, perhaps, near three times the number of inhabitants which Great Britain contains. In the great society of mankind, therefore, the prosperity of France should appear to be an object of much greater importance than that of Great Britain. The British subject, however, who, upon that account, should prefer upon all occasions the prosperity of the former to that of the latter country, would not be thought a good citizen of Great Britain. We do not love our country as a part of the great society of mankind: we love it for its own sake, and independently of any such consideration.

(TMS VI.ii.2.4)

These reservations and qualifications upon political sociality deserve notice. They will appear in a swollen incarnation conjured by Marx a century later, when the replacement of political man by the species-animal reaches a climax.

It would be misleading to suggest that Smith's doctrine of man's sociality was a relapse into the Middle Ages or into antiquity. It would be more misleading to suggest that, in Smith's view, human nature is simply dominated by a natural sociality of any description. We have given attention to the mechanical or psychological bond of sympathy, at the basis of Smith's moral theory, in order to show the change in emphasis between the preparation of capitalism in Locke's doctrine and the elaboration of it in Smith's. But the theme of man's natural directedness toward preservation is not by any means made to languish by Smith. On the contrary: 'self-preservation, and the propagation of the species, are the great ends which Nature seems to have proposed in the formation of all animals' (TMS II.i.5.6n). There is no reason to doubt that Smith meant this in all its force. We are able to gather, therefore, that if we use 'altruism' and 'egoism' in their literal sense, man can be described, according to Smith, as being by nature altruistic and egoistic—a species-member moved by love of self and fellow feeling with others.

It is one of the outstanding characteristics of Smith's system that sociality, withal of a certain description, and self-centred concentration upon preservation are shown as profoundly combined in a natural articulation of great strength; and this is achieved simultaneously with a rehabilitation of morality upon natural grounds: 'Nature, indeed, seems to have so happily adjusted our sentiments of approbation and disapprobation, to the conveniency both of the individual and of the society, that after the strictest examination it will be found, I believe, that this is universally the case' (TMS IV.i.2.3). When it is borne in mind that Smith's teaching aims at the articulation of morality and preservation, and that the practical fruits of his doctrine are intended to be gathered by emancipating men, under mild governement, to seek their happiness freely according to their individual desires, the accomplishment as a whole commands great respect. The reconciliation of the private good and the common good by the medium not of coercion but of freedom, on a basis of moral duty, had perhaps never been seen before.

In this wide and symmetrical edifice Smith perceived what appeared to him to be an irregularity or a class of irregularities. He observed that at certain points a disjunction develops between what man would by nature be led to approve as virtuous and what he is led by nature to approve as conducive to the preservation of society and the human species; and this notwithstanding the over-all truth of the passage quoted immediately above. It will be recalled that the elements of a virtuous act are propriety and merit, and that both rest upon a ground of sympathy. If men did not desire the sympathy of others, as well as respond to the impulse to sympathize with them, there would be no morality and no society. But the natural tendency of men is to sympathize especially with joy and good fortune; and it goes without saying that men not only desire to be sympathized with but to be sympathized with by reason of their prosperity, not their adversity. But the wish to be sympathized with on the grandest scale becomes, as a consequence, the foundation of ambition, which is the aspiration to be conspicuous, grand, and admired. To this aspiration the multitude of mankind lends itself, for it naturally sympathizes with eminence, that is, wealth and rank. But wealth and rank are not, as Smith occasionally said, necessarily conjoined with wisdom and virtue. He remarks, 'This disposition to admire, and almost to worship, the rich and the powerful, and to despise or, at least, to neglect persons of poor and mean condition, though necessary both to establish and to maintain the distinction of ranks and the order of society, is, at the same time, the great and most universal cause of the corruption of our moral sentiments' (TMS I.iii.3.1).

Merit, we remember, is the quality of an act that the impartial spectator would pronounce worthy of gratitude. The decisive quality of such an act is the propriety of the agent's passion in committing it, his benevolent intent toward the patient, and the patient's pleasure in the benefit conferred, in consequence of which he desires to reciprocate a benefit to the agent. The conjunction is perhaps complicated, but through it all one condition stands out clearly: benefit must be conferred on the patient. Now Smith observes that there is a gap of sorts between the intention and the consummation. That gap is Chance. Because of mere chance good will miscarries, and the benevolent agent produces nothing or worse than nothing for his intended beneficiary. On other occasions the agent, intending nothing or possibly worse than nothing, happens to be the source of a benefit to the patient. Contrary to sound morality, the first agent's act goes without the approval of sympathy and the stamp of virtue, while the second agent's act wins applause and gratitude. The universal tendency of men to regard the issue rather than the intention is said by Smith to be a 'salutary and useful irregularity in human sentiments', for two reasons. In the first place, 'to punish . . . for the affections of the heart only, where no crime has been committed, is the most insolent and barbarous tyranny'. To try to live a common life while holding men culpable or laudable for their secret intentions would mean that 'every court of judicature would become a real inquisition'. In the second place, 'Man was made for action, and to promote by the exertion of his faculties such changes in the external circumstances both of himself and others, as may seem most favourable to the happiness of all. He must not be satisfied with indolent benevolence, nor fancy himself the friend of mankind, because in his heart he wishes well to the prosperity of the world' (TMS II.iii.3.3). Smith goes on to speak of the utility to the world of the cognate inclination men have, to be troubled in spirit even when the ill they have wrought is wholly unintended, a subject that he illuminates with some healthy remarks upon the fallacious sense of guilt, illustrated by the 'distress' of Oedipus. In sum, nature has wisely provided that our sentiments direct us toward the preservation of our kind where a conflict between preservation and either moral virtue or sound reason is brought on by the divergence of intent and issue.

Further in the same vein, Smith notes that when a man conquers fear and pain by the noble exertion of self-command, he is entitled to be compensated with a sense of his own virtue, in exchange for the relief and safety he might have had by giving way to his passions. But it is the wise provision of nature that he be only imperfectly compensated, lest he have no reason to listen to the call of fear and pain and to respond to their promptings. Fear and pain are instruments of preservation; a man or a species indifferent to them would die. The self-command that dominates them does not, as it ought not, bring with it a sense of self-esteem sufficient to outweigh the anguish of suppressing those violent passions (TMS III.i.3). Evidently moral virtue neither is nor ought to be simply its own reward; nor therefore can it be unqualifiedly eligible or eligible for its own sake. It must yield, according to the dictate of nature, a certain precedence to preservation.

In an important passage, Smith unfolds further the paradox of natural morality as he conceives it. He is led to contrast 'the natural course of things' with 'the natural sentiments of mankind' (TMS III.i.5.10). It is in the natural course of things that industrious knaves should prosper while indolent men of honour starve, that great combinations of men should overweigh small ones, and finally that 'violence and artifice prevail over sincerity and justice'. The natural sentiments of man, however, are in rebellion against the natural course of things: sorrow, grief, rage, compassion for the oppressed, and at last despair of seeing the condign retribution of vice and injustice in this world—these are man's natural sentiments. The natural course of events, though, for all its offensiveness, has something weighty to recommend it. In allotting to each virtue, without favour or accommodation, the reward proper to it, nature has adopted the rule 'useful and proper for rousing the industry and attention of mankind'. Toil and moil happen to be indispensable to human survival, and the only way to draw them forth is by appropriate reward and punishment. The natural course of events supports the preservation of the race at the expense of precise morality; the natural sentiments of mankind are stirred by 'the love of virtue, and by the abhorrence of vice and injustice'. Nature is divided, but not equally divided against itself. The cause of unmitigated virtue can be heard only upon a change of venue to a jurisdiction in a world beyond nature.

Smith pursues his theme of the price in goodness and reason that must be paid to get the world's fundamental business done. He takes up the question, of much importance to his doctrine, whether the utility of actions is the basis of their being approved. If the answer were a simple affirmative, then it would follow that the principle of virtue (approbation) is rational: the calculation of usefulness. But we know that in his view the principle of virtue and approbation is not reason but sentiment and feeling, via sympathy. Yet it is evident that mankind exhibits a steady tendency toward those measures of labour and government which are the supports for the preservation of the race. Smith explains this by recurring to a delusion imposed upon men by nature, a delusion that does the work of reason better than reason could have done it. When we look upon the power or wealth in a man's possession, our minds are led in imagination to conceive the fitness of those objects to perform their respective functions. At the same time we sympathize with the imagined satisfaction of the possessors of those prizes. It is only a step from that to desiring ourselves to be happy in greatness, and thence to putting forth the immense exertions that eventuate in wealth and government. Upon consideration, it appears that we are led to pursue prosperity and power by a psychological motive, and thus to generate wealth and order among men as by-products of subjective 'drives', as we would say. Moreover, and conjunctively, we act under the influence of the appetite for the means to gratification, not even for the gratification itself, when we seek after wealth and power. Both are desirable for the happiness they supposedly give their possessors. In fact, happiness is not at all, or very little, promoted by the possession of power and riches, those 'enormous and operose machines contrived to produce a few trifling conveniencies to the body, consisting of springs the most nice and delicate, which must be kept in order with the most anxious attention, and which in spite of all our care are ready every moment to burst into pieces, and to crush in their ruins their unfortunate possessor' (TMS IV.i.1.8).

Smith's reason for depreciating distinction of wealth and place is of interest: 'In what constitutes the real happiness of human life, [the poor and obscure] are in no respect inferior to those who would seem so much above them. In ease of the body and peace of the mind, all the different ranks of life are nearly upon a level, and the beggar, who suns himself by the side of the highway, possesses that security which kings are fighting for' (TMS IV.i.1.10). It is in this context that Smith announces, in the *Theory of Moral Sentiments*, the notion of the expression of the 'invisible hand', very famous from its elaboration through the central argument of *The Wealth of Nations*. The passage deserves extensive quotation:

And it is well that nature imposes upon us in this manner. It is this deception which rouses and keeps in continual motion the industry of mankind. It is this which first prompted them to cultivate the ground, to build houses, to found cities and commonwealths, and to invent and improve all the sciences and arts, which ennoble and embellish human life: which have entirely changed the whole face of the globe, have turned the rude forests of nature into agreeable and fertile plains, and made the trackless and barren ocean a new fund of subsistence, and the great high road of communication to the different nations of the earth. The earth by these labours of mankind has been obliged to redouble her natural fertility, and to maintain a greater multitude of inhabitants. It is to no purpose, that the proud and unfeeling landlord views his extensive fields, and without a thought for the wants of his brethren, in imagination consumes himself the whole harvest that grows upon them. The homely and vulgar proverb, that the eye is larger than the belly, was never more fully verified than with regard to him. The capacity of his stomach bears no proportion to the immensity of his desires, and will receive no more than that of the meanest peasant. The rest he is obliged to distribute among those, who prepare, in the nicest manner, that little which he himself makes use of, among those who fit up the palace in which this little is to be consumed, among those who provide and keep in order all the different baubles and trinkets which are employed in the oeconomy of greatness; all of whom thus derive from his luxury and caprice, that share of the necessaries of life, which they would in vain have expected from his humanity or his justice. The produce of the soil maintains at all times nearly that number of inhabitants which it is capable of maintaining. The rich only select from the heap what is most precious and agreeable. They consume little more than the poor, and in spite of their natural selfishness and rapacity, though they mean only their own conveniency, though the sole end which they propose from the labours of all the thousands whom they employ, be the gratification of their own vain and insatiable desires, they divide with the poor the produce of all their improvements. They are led by an invisible hand to make nearly the same distribution of the necessaries of life which would have been made, had the earth been divided into equal portions among all its inhabitants, and thus without intending it, without knowing it, advance the interest of society, and afford means to the multiplication of the species.

(TMS IV.i.1.10)

Beyond this there is no advantage in multiplying the evidence of Smith's belief that the dominant end of nature with respect to man, namely, the prosperity of the species as a whole, is achieved by mitigations of morality and reason. Since this is a point which post-capitalistic thought was to take up polemically and against which it was to bring its ultimate, most ambitious dialectic, it deserves to be examined with some attention.

That nature's end for man is advanced by the guidance of his sentiments rather than his reason follows from the premise that the passions are more governing than the mind, and every animal persistently desires its own uninterrupted being. A man's nature is more immediately reflected in what he feels than what he thinks; moreover, the difference between the two is not the profound one anciently conceived but is rather such as can be composed by their being both subsumed under 'perceptions'. Smith does not employ the language of 'impressions and ideas' used by Hume in the enterprise by which the operation of the mind was given a unified appearance as the distinctions among sensation, emotion, and reason were blurred. If Smith had done so, he would more explicitly have concurred in Hume's definition of the self as 'that succession of related ideas and impressions, of which we have an intimate memory' and of 'ideas [as] the faint images of [impressions] in thinking and reason'.[6] The reduction of the self, the ego or the real man, to his actuality or to the traces of what he has actually perceived rather than to his soul and its powers or 'faculties' is part of the doctrine that rejected innate ideas and therewith all but the nominal essences. This doctrine, with its echoes of Hobbes and Locke, is interlaced with the view that the lines of force along which nature produces and communicates its motions penetrate him and govern him more through his passions than through his reason.[7]

In any event, Smith's formulation is that nature did not leave it to man's feeble reason to discover that and how he ought to preserve himself, but gave him sharp appetites for the means to his survival as well as for survival itself, thus ensuring his preservation. But it is this same primacy of sentiment over reason, or at least the equal subsumption of them both under something like perception, that is the basis for the concessions which must be made against morality on behalf of preservation.

[6] Hume, *A Treatise of Human Nature*, I.I.i. and II.I.ii.

[7] Hume's remark is characteristically uncompromising: '[the reason] can never oppose passion in the direction of the will' (Ibid. II.III). Smith makes two remarks, in the form of allusions, which deny man's unique rationality: 'mankind, as well as . . . all other rational creatures' (TMS III.i.5.7) and the great society of all 'rational and sensible beings' (VI.ii.3.6).

It will be recalled that Smith's moral doctrine begins with approbation: the virtuous is so because it is in fact or in principle approved by the sentiment of mankind. We now understand that a difficulty exists because nature teaches man to approve both what conduces to morality and what conduces to preservation. The instruction of nature is occasionally equivocal. Evidently the attempt to derive the Ought from the Is is vexed by the fact that, although what is virtuous is actually approved, it does not follow either that everything which is approved is virtuous or that everything which is virtuous is approved. It is from this circumstance that the 'irregularities' or concessions previously mentioned have their origin. What, then, is to be gained by the psychological or 'behavioural' derivation of a natural morality? It is that by this method, moral virtue may be deduced from the character of 'man as man', i.e. in abstraction from his character as a political being and attentive only to his character as a 'natural' one. Smith's moral philosophy aims at comprehending the basis of virtue as that basis may be said to exist in a fully actual state at every moment in 'the bulk of mankind' (TMS III.i.5.1) as such. That is to say, Smith's starting-point is the natural equality of men in the sense elaborated by Hobbes. The contrast with classical antiquity throws light on the modern position. The famous scheme of Plato's *Republic* makes a high principle of the division of labour or distribution of functions in the political society because virtue in one social class could not well be measured by the same rule against which it must be measured in another class. Aristotle's *Politics* distinguishes the virtue of slaves, freemen, and men of excellence; the *Nicomachean Ethics* cannot be regarded as a manual of the excellence of the bulk of mankind. The ancient moralists coldly concentrated upon the distinction between the politically weighty people and the entire populace that dwelt within the frontiers. Only democracy has the merit of making possible the effacement of that distinction, and we are entitled to deem the 'humanization' of moral virtue—its universalization or reference to what is actually present in 'all men as men'—as the democratization of morality.

Democracy is the regime that minimizes the distinction between rulers and ruled, the fundamental political phenomenon; and in that sense it can be said that democracy or liberal democracy tends to replace political life by sociality (private lives lived in contiguity) at the same time as it diffuses political authority most widely. The abstraction of morality from the demands of political life proper is in a way impossible: political life has to be lived, and support for it must be provided in the form of economic organization, the use of force for suppressing crime and rebellion, the legitimation of conventional inequalities in the interest of order, and so on. Where morality is radically 'human' or 'natural' in the sense of those words that is opposed to political, the indispensable provision for political life will have the character of an inroad on morality, or an irregularity. It is not our contention that the moral basis of Smith's social doctrine is contrived to produce an abstraction from the conditions of political existence. It is rather, on the contrary, that in order to mitigate or forestall that abstraction, which his premises threaten to enforce, he must have recourse to 'irregularities' of nature or exceptions to his premises.

There is hardly a better way of illustrating the elusive relation between rectitude and politics than by the following passage from Churchill's *Marlborough*:

> The second debate in the Lords . . . drew from Marlborough his most memorable Parliamentary performance. It is the more remarkable because, although he had made up his mind what ought to be done and what he meant to do, his handling of the debate was at once spontaneous, dissimulating, and entirely successful. As on the battlefield, he changed his course very quickly indeed and spread a web of manoeuvre before his opponents. He made candour serve the purpose of falsehood, and in the guise of reluctantly blurting out the whole truth threw his assailants into complete and baffling error. Under the impulse of an emotion which could not have been wholly assumed, he made a revelation of war policy which effectively misled not only the Opposition but the whole House, and which also played its part in misleading the foreign enemy, who were of course soon apprised of the public debate. He acted thus in the interests of right strategy and of the common cause as he conceived them. He was accustomed by the conditions under which he fought to be continually deceiving friends for their good and foes for their bane; but the speed and ease with which this particular manoeuvre was conceived and accomplished in the unfamiliar atmosphere of Parliamentary debate opens to us some of the secret depths of his artful yet benevolent mind.[8]

It is apparent that dissimulation cannot be made the principle of morals; it is also apparent that morality which makes no serviceable distinction between dissimulation in a noble cause and common mendacity will end either in the precisianism that condemns it all as vice or in the latitudinarianism that peers unsuccessfully for the line between vice and virtue. Ancient moral philosophy could in this respect be described as very politic. It recognized in prudence a subtle virtue that animated the others from its seat in the mind. In palliation of the Odysseanism of the ancients' moralizing, it should be said that departure from the straitest morality was countenanced by them in the ultimate interest of something higher, for they did not conceive moral excellence to be the greatest of all excellences. The Smithian subtractions from morality cannot be in the interest of anything higher, for there is nothing higher: 'The most sublime speculation of the contemplative philosopher can scarce compensate the neglect of the smallest active duty' (TMS VI.ii.3.6). 'The man who acts solely

[8] Winston S. Churchill, *Marlborough: His Life and Times* (4 vols. in 2 books, 1947), vol. III, book II, 303. Reproduced by permission of Charles Scribner's Sons and George Harrap & Co., Ltd.

from a regard to what is right and fit to be done, from a regard to what is the proper object of esteem and approbation, though these sentiments should never be bestowed upon him, acts from the most sublime and godlike motive which human nature is even capable of conceiving' (TMS VII.ii.4.10). To state the case somewhat simplistically, the ancients and the moderns alike conceded something in mitigation of strict moral virtue, the ancients without repining because they had in view a higher excellence, Smith with mixed feelings because his aim could not exceed moral virtue in worth.

Smith's aim, a free, reasonable, comfortable, and tolerant life for the whole species, found its hope, its basis, and its expression in the science of economics as he to a considerable extent launched it. Anything like a detailed account of Smith's economics would be far out of place here, and we shall confine ourselves to selected themes. His teaching in *The Wealth of Nations* is above all famous for its defence of free enterprise on a broad and simple line: The welfare of the nation cannot be separated from its wealth, which he conceives in the modern mode as the annual national product. But the annual product of the nation is the sum of the annual products of the individual inhabitants. Each inhabitant has an undying interest in maximizing his own product and will do everything possible to accomplish this if left in freedom. Thus all should be accorded this freedom, and they will simultaneously maximize the aggregate product and keep each other in check by the power of competition. His renowned attack on mercantilistic capitalism—the system of invidious preference for the merchant interest—is part of his argument that the common interest is served not by differential legislative stimulation of enterprises but by allowing nature automatically to convert the individual self-interest into the good of all:

As every individual, therefore, endeavours as much as he can both to employ his capital in the support of domestic industry, and so to direct that industry that its produce may be of the greatest value; every individual necessarily labours to render the annual revenue of the society as great as he can. He generally, indeed, neither intends to promote the public interest, nor knows how much he is promoting it. By preferring the support of domestic to that of foreign industry, he intends only his own security; and by directing that industry in such a manner as its produce may be of the greatest value, he intends only his own gain, and he is in this, as in many other cases, led by an invisible hand to promote an end which was no part of his intention. Nor is it always the worse for the society that it was no part of it. By pursuing his own interest he frequently promotes that of the society more effectually than when he really intends to promote it. I have never known much good done by those who affected to trade for the public good. It is an affectation, indeed, not very common among merchants, and very few words need be employed in dissuading them from it.[9]

[9] *An Inquiry into the Nature and Causes of the Wealth of Nations* (1937), IV.ii.9. All references are to this edition.

We have no difficulty recognizing the natural reconciliation of the individual and common interest for which the *Theory of Moral Sentiments* has prepared us. Nor are we unprepared for the moral 'irregularities' that Smith conceived to be incidental to that reconciliation. They fall under two or three main heads in the argument of *The Wealth of Nations*. In the first place, the prosperity of each and all cannot be disconnected from their productivity, and their productivity rests upon the division of labour. But the division of labour inevitably stultifies the working classes, much if not the bulk of mankind. The labourer's 'dexterity at his own particular trade seems . . . to be acquired at the expense of his intellectual, social, and martial virtues. But in every improved and civilized society this is the state into which the labouring poor, that is, the great body of the people, must necessarily fall, unless government takes some pains to prevent it' (V.i.f.50). In his discussions he tries not to exaggerate the likelihood that the government will succeed.

In the second place, a large part if not the preponderant part of the economic life of the nation must come under the regulation of the class of merchants and manufacturers. His animadversions upon them as a body of men are sometimes shockingly severe. The burden of his objection against them is that their preoccupation with gain puts them in illiberal conflict with the other orders of society and with the nation as a whole—except by inadvertence (I.xi.p.10; IV.iii.c.9). The wisdom of government is necessary to prevent their mischief, i.e. their interested interference, and to give free rein only to their useful activities, i.e. their productiveness. Smith was not the dogmatist that some advocates of *laissez-faire* were later to become.

In the third place, the annual addition to product is believed by Smith to be generated by labour. The 'exchangeable value' or price of each commodity, once land has been made private property and capital has been accumulated, 'resolves itself' into wages, rent, and profit. In this way, landowners and the employers of labour 'share' in the produce of labour. Smith is at pains to argue that the profits of capital are not a wage for the 'supposed labour of inspection and direction', which he said is often 'committed to some principal clerk' (WN I.vi.6). He was far from attempting to conceal the contribution to output that results from the accumulation of capital. On the contrary, he dwelt upon it; but he described it as taking effect by an 'improvement in the productive powers of labour' (WN II.ii.7 etc.). In the course of his investigations into what we now call national income accounting, he certainly gave later generations some reason to regard him as holding a labour theory of value, with concomitant beliefs about distribution. As for rent, that is 'a monopoly price' (WN I.xi.a.5) for the use of land, by the exaction of which the owner is enabled to share in the annual product of labour. We cannot fail to notice how little trouble Smith gave himself to justify this 'sharing' and this 'resolving'. On the contrary, by a certain invidiousness of expression—'As soon as the land of any country has all become private property, the landlords, like all other men, love to reap where they never sowed, and demand a rent even for its natural produce' (WN I.vi.8)—he indicates a reserve as to its perfect propriety. He seems to think, it is true, that when the facts of distribution are recited, the intimation of possible inequities may be fully balanced by a statement of the broad, compensatory benefits: he speculates whether it might not be true 'that the accommodation of a European prince does not always so much exceed that of an industrious and frugal peasant, as the accommodation of the latter exceeds that of many an African king, the absolute master of the lives and liberties of ten thousand naked savages' (WN I.i.11). But Smith manifestly did not imagine himself to be addressing the multitude of labouring poor in detailed defence of capitalism, as Marx was to address them in detailed denunciation. Smith freely hinted at his notion that something like one of his moral 'irregularities' lay around the root of the distributive order, but it was much outweighed by the correlative advantages for all—and he loathed the men of 'system' who would be incapable of grasping such a simple computation.

Smith did not refer to the complex of free enterprise as 'capitalism' but as 'the system of natural liberty', or the condition in which 'things were left to follow their natural course, where there was perfect liberty' (WN IV.ix.51; I.x.a.1). Nature meant for Smith the humanly unhindered or unobstructed, and this more amply means what is not confounded by the misplaced interventions of human reason: letting nature take its course, letting men do as they are instinctively prompted to do, as far as that is compatible with 'the security of the whole society' (WN II.ii.94). It is easy to conceive and to grant that natural is in distinction to artificial, human, or constrained to obey a forecontrived design. Thus freedom is all on the side of nature, as opposed to constraint on the side of human reason. At the same time, however, nothing in the world is so unyielding and hence constraining as the necessary dictate of deaf and dumb nature, while the source of man's freedom resides in his power of reason, the origin of his various contrivances.[10] Smith's manner of confronting this difficulty is in effect to declare for the freedom of reason harnessed in the service of the more binding freedom of nature: calculation at the command of passion. Smith's doctrine is pervaded by the consequences of the fact that the superordinate element, nature conceived as the free motive of passion, is the symbol of man's unfreedom, as Kant was to emphasize so elaborately.

It is a distinguishing characteristic of Smith's doctrine and of liberal

[10] Smith commonly juxtaposes 'naturally' and 'necessarily', the latter often used apparently as an intensified form of the former. Cf., e.g., ibid. I.i.7, I.viii.57, III.i.2, IV.i.30, IV.ii.4,6; IV.vii.c.80; V.i.6.12, V.i.f.23, V.i.g.23.

capitalism at large that they do not conceive freedom to be important primarily because it is the condition for every man's existence as an individual moral being, the ground of his self-legislating will in action or of his humanity. Liberty continued to mean for Smith what it had meant to Locke, to Aristotle, and to the long tradition of political philosophy: the condition of men under lawful governors who respect the persons and property of the governed, the latter having to consent to the arrangement in one way or another. This view of liberty is primarily political and belongs to the libertarianism of Locke, not of Rousseau. The capitalistic project is not animated by a search for methods of institutionally liberating the inner drives of every man in the interest of the moral will. It is animated by a search for methods of institutionally liberating every man's natural instinct of self-preservation in the interest of external, politically intelligible freedom and peaceful prosperous life for mankind as a whole. Therefore Smith had no difficulty in conceiving man as free while both in thrall to nature and subject to forms of law which guarantee his external freedom but can scarcely aim to be the basis of his internal emancipation from that same nature.

Smith is thus at liberty to repose his trust in a wisdom of nature that shows itself even or especially in the folly and injustice of man: the moral hygiene that produces a multitude, in fact a race of self-legislators, was not indispensable to his plan, nor was political life a species of psychotherapy for bringing on man's subpolitical emancipation. Smith was thus resigned to receive the benefits of civil society even if they must be mediated by certain undoubted ills, and he was prepared to do so indefinitely if the benefits are vast and the ills unavoidable. In this respect he anticipated the mechanisms of philosophy of history as it would emerge, but not its ends: good through ill and reason through folly, but no Elysium at a rainbow's end.

It is important for us to see more exactly what Smith's doctrine has in common with philosophy of history as that was later to develop. There is, to begin with, his belief in a 'natural progress of things toward improvement'—animated by 'the uniform, constant and uninterrupted effort of every man to better his condition', bettering his condition being understood in 'the most vulgar' sense (WN II.iii.31). Smith illustrates this in an account of the progress of Europe from medieval disorder to the comparative regularity of modern times. The anarchy of old persisted because the great landed proprietors had troops of retainers who comprised, in fact, private armies. Nothing could produce order which did not dissolve those armies. The basis for their existence was the fact that the grandees had abundant income in kind which, under the primitive conditions of commerce then prevailing, they could not dispose of by exchange or sale. They accordingly were compelled to feed it to crowds of men who became their dependents and inevitably their soldiers. What brought down the entire system was the enlargement of trade, which enabled the magnates to convert their produce into money and thence into luxuries for their personal delectation instead of into the military basis of their political power.

A revolution of the greatest importance to the public happiness, was in this manner brought about by two different orders of people, who had not the least intention to serve the public. To gratify the most childish vanity was the sole motive of the great proprietors. The merchants and artificers, much less ridiculous, acted merely from a view to their own interest, and in pursuit of their own pedlar principle of turning a penny wherever a penny was to be got. Neither of them had either knowledge or foresight of that great revolution which the folly of the one, and the industry of the other, was gradually bringing about. (WN II.iv.17)

Smith speaks of the ascendancy of the Roman Church from the tenth to the thirteenth century. He regards it as signalized by the temporal power of the clergy, and that in turn as resting upon the influence of the clergy with the multitudes of men. The inferior ranks of people were bound to the clergy by ties of interest, the multitudes depending upon a charity which was bestowed freely because, once again, the clergy had no other means of disposing of an enormous produce from their lands. When such means presented themselves, the constitution of the Catholic Church underwent a profound alteration:

Had this constitution been attacked by no other enemies but the feeble efforts of human reason, it must have endured for ever. But the immense and well-built fabric, which all the wisdom and virtue of man could never have shaken, much less overturned, was by the natural course of things, first weakened, and afterwards in part destroyed . . .

The gradual improvements of arts, manufactures, and commerce, the same causes which destroyed the power of the great barons, destroyed in the same manner, through the greater part of Europe, the whole power of the clergy. (WN V.i.g.25)

By these same instrumentalities, the species of mankind at large is drawn together, probably upward as well as onward. Smith regards the geographical discoveries as of unparalleled significance for the species: 'The discovery of America, and that of a passage to the East Indies by the Cape of Good Hope, are the two greatest and most important events recorded in the history of mankind.' The communication and commerce of the species as a whole was thereby in principle achieved for the first time in the memory of man, and with that epochal event came the supreme occasion for enabling all mankind reciprocally 'to relieve one another's wants, to increase one another's enjoyments, and to encourage one another's industry' (WN IV.vii.c.80, IV.i.32).

Smith believed that, to a large extent, nature speaks to history in the language of economics, and that the broad course of history so instructed is probably toward an easier, more cultivated, more rational, and secure life for the generality of mankind. At the same time, he imagined that the advance of civilization was synchronous with the generation of a tremendous industrial mob, deprived of nearly every admirable human quality. Civilization is not an unqualified good, or more accurately, it comes at a price. This famous theme, of which Rousseau was the virtuoso, was developed by Smith with concern but without agitation. He proposed to palliate the ill with a wide system of almost gratis elementary schooling for the masses and with the encouragement of an unheard-of number of religious sects (as many as three thousand), each necessarily to be so small that every member of it would be conspicuous to the surveillance of his fellow communicants. All would maintain a vigil upon each other's morals that, far from being in any danger of flagging through lack of interest, would itself require to be moderated by febrifuges: courses of education in science and philosophy and artistic spectacles such as theatre (WN V.i.f.52–55, V.i.g.12–15). Smith repeatedly recommends the intellectual and moral state of much of industrial mankind to the most serious attention of government, not only out of philanthropy but for obvious reasons of state.

Our thesis, with a summary of which we shall now conclude, has been this: Within a short time of the completion of Locke's work, intelligent men began to reflect on and to draw out what would today be called the 'moral implications' of his doctrine.[11] How far he had mitigated Hobbes's teaching of the natural ferocity of man and thereby turned political philosophy in the direction of economics has been described elsewhere.[12] But the chief teaching of the modern school of natural law was not thereby impaired: nature continued univocally to mean preservation, with the supporting rights to whatever pertains thereto. Now this came to be regarded as insufficient, and the reduction of man to his affections was thought to imply that man is affected not only toward himself but toward his species. Perhaps Locke was not given enough credit for the important mitigation mentioned above, which is in this direction, but in any event the theme was made emphatic by Smith (at about the time of Rousseau's

[11] The reader's attention should be drawn to the work of Bernard Mandeville (*c.* 1670–1733) whose *The Fable of the Bees* (1714) had the subtitle 'Private Vices, Public Benefits'. Controversy raged around him, and Smith added his rebuke by dealing with him in a chapter 'Of Licentious Systems' (TMS VII.ii.4), at the same time admitting that Mandeville was not mistaken in all respects.

[12] For example in 'John Locke' by Robert A. Goldwin, in *History of Political Philosophy*, ed. Leo Strauss and J. Cropsey (1963).

Second Discourse). The reduction of human life to its emotional foundations was enlarged to become the ground of duties as well as rights. It cannot be denied that those duties were consciously made to revolve about the preservation of the species; but it cannot either be denied that duties are different from rights, and the two require somehow to be reconciled with one another. In the course of reconciling the duties of moral virtue with the rights of nature, which is to say preservation, Smith had recourse to the tension between nature and the moral order derived from it, leaving the reconciliation inevitably imperfect. From this germ grew the teaching as to the moral imperfection of the natural or best order of society—the free, prosperous, and tolerant civil society. In its self-understanding, capitalism thus anticipated the chief post-capitalistic criticism of capitalism: civil society is a defective solution of the human problem.

Our second point, inseparable from the first, is that the self-understanding of capitalism also anticipated an astonishing proportion of what was to be proposed by the nineteenth century as the alternative to capitalism. We have tried to show how the direction of capitalism was toward the construction of a universal mankind, both as the ground of duty (the universal spectator) and as the ultimate beneficiary of economic progress—thus as the ultimate society. The engine of that progress was the ignoble desires and strivings of man, channelled through the economic institutions of production and distribution that opened up to him from time to time. An expectation of good through evil, reason through unreason, progress, a belief in the tendency of the interest of mankind to supersede that of particular political society, in the preponderance of economic influence on human affairs, in the primacy of labour in the process of production, in the preoccupation of civil society with the defence of property, this and more which Marxism would trumpet was present to the doctrines of capitalism in one measure and form or another, as it has been our purpose to show. A strange light is cast on Marx's theory that capitalism contains the seed of its own negation. It might perhaps be said that according to its own self-understanding, the ground of capitalism coincides to a remarkable degree with the seed-bed of its own negation; but the seed itself is an alien thing, namely, philosophy of history, something that was generated not by the working of any economic institutions but by an act of human speculation.

Perhaps Smith is to be blamed for not having extracted a metaphysic from that 'wisdom of nature' which he believed to guide the human process and to which he so often recurs, a metaphysic that would historicize the consummation of the whole human career. Perhaps he ought to have perceived the potency in such a metaphor as the 'wisdom' of nature and gone on to postulate still higher wisdoms by which the laws of nature itself might be brought under orders. He never reached that point, however, for he did not question the belief that there is an unchanging horizon within which all change takes place, that horizon or framework being Nature.

Philosophy of history is outside our scope. For the present we may observe that when Rousseau's teaching of the malleability of human nature received its due cultivation and enlargement, it proved to be the little leaven that leavened the whole lump. The paradoxes and irregularities that liberal capitalism was willing to abide because of their origin in man's nature could not be tolerated by the nineteenth century since it no longer saw a need to tolerate them. The nature that gives rise to inconveniences must away, and itself submit to be superseded by the law of the change of nature, namely, History. It is this fissure, narrow but bottomless, that divides capitalism from communism.

VIII

Adam Smith: an Economic Interpretation of History

ANDREW S. SKINNER*

I

WHILE an interest in the past informs all Smith's works, there can be no doubt that he regarded the study of history as a separate subject in its own right. However, the kind of history in which Smith was interested was not wholly conventional, being described by Dugald Stewart as 'theoretical or conjectural' in order to distinguish it from the 'orthodox' or 'vulgar'. While the term 'philosophical history' is probably to be preferred,[1] Stewart was undoubtedly correct in stating that this sort of study 'seems, in a peculiar degree, to have interested Mr Smith's curiosity' and that 'something very similar to it may be traced in all his different works, whether moral, political, or literary' (Stewart, II.43).

Smith's work on the history of civil society is particularly noteworthy, and among the first subjects to which he appears to have addressed himself. It is known for example that he lectured on the 'progress of society' while in Edinburgh between 1748 and 1751, since we have it on the authority of Callander of Craigforth that 'Dr Robertson had borrowed the first volume of his History of Charles V from them [i.e. from these lectures] as every student could testify' (Scott, 55). We also know, from the account supplied by John Millar, perhaps Smith's most distinguished student at Glasgow, that the third part of his lectures while in the Chair of Moral Philosophy had been concerned with 'that branch of morality which relates to justice' and that:

> Upon this subject he followed the plan that seems to be suggested by Montesquieu; endeavouring to trace the gradual progress of jurisprudence, both public and private, from the rudest to the most refined ages, and to point out the effect of those arts which contribute to subsistence, and to the accumulation of property, in producing correspondent improvements or alterations in law and government.
>
> (Stewart, I.18)[2]

* Senior Lecturer in the Department of Political Economy, the University of Glasgow.

[1] See below, p. 169.

[2] In Letter 116 addressed to Lord Hailes, dated 5 Mar. 1769, Smith made the interesting comment that he had 'read law entirely with a view to form some general notion of the

Smith himself also indicated his intention to provide 'an account of the general principles of law and government, and of the different revolutions they have undergone in the different ages and periods of society, not only in what concerns justice, but in what concerns police, revenue, and arms, and whatever else is the object of law' (TMS VII.iv.37). More than thirty years later, Smith allowed this paragraph to stand in the hope that he might still complete a plan which had been only partially fulfilled by the publication of the *Theory of Moral Sentiments*, and *The Wealth of Nations*.

While Smith did not in fact manage to fulfil his original promise, the lectures on justice do provide us with a clear picture of its broad outline; with the sketch of a history which begins with the rise and fall of Greece and Rome before proceeding to offer some account of the progress of society in Europe after the collapse of the Western Empire.[3] Much of this material also appeared in *The Wealth of Nations*: in Book V, and especially Book III, which contains in fact a particularly elaborate explanation of the origins of the 'present establishments' in Europe.

The latter subject is intrinsically interesting not only to the student of history, but also to those concerned with the problems of economic development. The analysis of Book III also attracts attention because of its polished style and the high level of formality with which it unfolds, while the argument as a whole is remarkable for the almost Marxian reliance which is placed on economic forces. Indeed, it may be said that Smith's historical work in this sphere rests on three distinct propositions:

First, that social change depends on economic development, the latter taking place only in such areas as Attica or Europe, which satisfy the physical preconditions of growth.[4]

Second, that man is self-regarding in all spheres of activity, more especially the economic and political, thus explaining his pursuit of security, wealth, and that form of satisfaction on which the development of productive forces may be seen to depend.

Third, that the normal processes of development will generate four distinct economic stages, each with a particular socio-political structure reflecting the mode of subsistence prevailing. In Smith's words: 'The four

great outlines of the plan according to which justice has been administered in different ages and nations; and I have entered very little into the detail of particulars of which I see your Lordship is very much master.'

[3] The most complete and elaborate account of the whole argument is to be found in the fourth volume of LJ (A), which corresponds to the briefer treatment 'Of Public Jurisprudence' offered in LJ (B), Part I. It is interesting to note that while LJ (A) deals with Private, Domestic, and Public Law in that order, LJ (B) reverses the sequence.

[4] The main preconditions of economic growth which Smith cited are: ease of defence, fertility, and ready access to water transport. The argument is considered at some length in LJ (A) iv, for 23 Feb. 1763, and LJ (B) 30–31; Cannan, 21–2. Similar arguments appear in WN I.iii and FB.

stages of society are hunting, pasturage, farming and commerce' (LJ (B) 149; Cannan, 107).[5]

In what follows we shall examine each of these stages in turn with a view to elucidating their main features and the causes of transition between them, before going on to consider some of the methodological and analytical implications of the argument.

II THE STAGES OF HUNTING AND PASTURAGE

The first stage of society was represented as the 'lowest and rudest' state, 'such as we find it among the native tribes of North America' (WN V.i.a.2). In this case, life is maintained through gathering the spontaneous fruits of the soil, and the dominant activities are taken to be hunting and fishing—a mode of earning subsistence which is antecedent to any social organization in production. In consequence of this, Smith suggested that hunting communities would tend to be small in size, characterized by a high degree of personal freedom on the part of their members, and by the absence of private property other than that involved in the possession of the instruments or fruits of the 'chace'.[6] Under such economic and social conditions, it was suggested, there would be no need for any permanent system of magistracy, since the only injuries which were inflicted or suffered would affect the person or reputation of the individual.[7] Smith recognized of course that it would be necessary on occasion to have some means of resolving disputes between members of the group and also that in the event of war the whole people would have to act in concert—thus requiring a willingness to obey. Smith argued, however, that willingness to obey in this kind of society would depend solely on the individual's perception of the *utility* of so doing and added that 'Universal poverty establishes there universal equality, and the superiority, either of age, or of personal qualities, are the feeble, but the sole foundations of authority and subordination. There is therefore little or no authority or subordination in this period of society' (WN V.i.b.7).

The second stage is that of pasturage, which Smith represented as 'a more advanced state of society, such as we find it among the Tartars and Arabs' or the Hottentots at the Cape of Good Hope.[8] While Smith did

[5] The same division of stages appears in LJ (A) i.27.

[6] Similar arguments may be found in John Millar's *Historical View of the English Government* (1803, hence cited as 'HV'), i.61; Adam Ferguson's *History of Civil Society* (1767, ed. Forbes, 1966) Part II; Robertson, *Works* (1808), ii.100–47; Lord Kames, *Sketches of the History of Man* (1774), XII.

[7] See for example LJ (A) i. 33 and iv. 4.

[8] It is emphasized in FA that the economy of this shepherd nation was sufficiently far advanced as to admit of some degree of the division of labour. See for example, R. L. Meek and A. S. Skinner, 'The Development of Adam Smith's Ideas on the Division of Labour', *Economic Journal*, lxxxiii (1973), 1109, 1113.

make allowance for the existence of 'stationary shepherds' as found in the Highlands of Scotland,[9] he argued that:

Such nations have commonly no fixed habitations, but live, either in tents, or in a sort of covered wagons which are easily transported from place to place. The whole tribe or nation changes its situation according to the different seasons of the year, as well as according to other accidents. When its herds and flocks have consumed the forage of one part of the country, it removes to another, and from that to a third . . .

(WN V.i.a.3)

While the nomadic life is, typically, a consequence of the mode of subsistence, Smith also emphasized that larger numbers would be possible in this stage as compared to the preceding (WN V.i.a.5), and that the emergence of a form of property which could be accumulated and transmitted would generate new sources of distinction:

Birth and fortune are evidently the two circumstances which principally set one man above another. They are the two great sources of personal distinction, and are therefore the principal causes which naturally establish authority and subordination among men. Among nations of shepherds both those causes operate with their full force.

(WN V.i.b.11)[10]

Elsewhere he stated that in fact 'there is no period of society in which the superiority of fortune gives so great authority to those who possess it' (WN V.i.b.7). At the same time Smith took note of the point that a distinction in terms of fortune would generally involve a division between those who owned the means of subsistence and those who must acquire it—in this case through the exchange of personal service and at the price of dependence on their superiors:

A Tartar chief, the increase of whose herds and flocks is sufficient to maintain a thousand men, cannot well employ that increase in any other way . . . The thousand men whom he thus maintains, depending entirely upon him for their subsistence, must obey his orders in war and submit to his jurisdiction in peace. He is necessarily both their general and their judge, and his chieftainship is the necessary effect of the superiority of his fortune.

(WN V.i.b.7)

Smith went on to notice a further point of contrast with the previous period in remarking that the advent of property in a permanent form gave rise not

[9] Smith commented on the attention given to kindred in pastoral economies in TMS VI.ii.1.12 and added that 'It is not many years ago that, in the Highlands of Scotland, the chieftain used to consider the poorest man of his clan, as his cousin and relation.'

[10] It is remarked in TMS VI.ii.1.20 that 'Nature has wisely judged that the distinction of ranks, the peace and order of society, would rest more securely upon the plain and palpable difference of birth and fortune, than upon the invisible and often uncertain difference of wisdom and virtue.'

only to a pattern of authority and subordination, but also to government properly so called: 'The appropriation of herds and flocks, which introduced an inequality of fortune, was that which first gave rise to regular government. Till there be property there can be no government, the very end of which is to secure wealth, and to defend the rich from the poor' (LJ (B) 20; Cannan, 15).[11]

The hunting and shepherd communities thus differ with regard to their mode of subsistence, their size, and with respect to the sources of subordination or authority which prevail within them. These are important differences, although Smith did draw attention to two important areas of similarity. First, he suggested that in both cases such government as did exist would be of a broadly democratic character, in the sense that judicial and executive power would continue to rest, ultimately, with the whole body of the people.[12] Secondly, he noted that in both cases, the manner of life would ensure that a high proportion of each community would be fitted and available for war. It thus followed that if the impact of a hunting community was limited because of the small numbers involved,[13] 'Nothing, on the contrary, can be more dreadful than a Tartar invasion has frequently been in Asia. The judgement of Thucydides, that both Europe and Asia could not resist the Scythians united, has been verified by the experience of all ages' (WN V.i.a.5). As Smith went on to argue, the power of the nomadic hordes, which reflected the mode of subsistence which prevailed among them, was to have a dramatic impact on the course of civilization.

III AGRICULTURE: ALLODIAL AND FEUDAL

The nations which overran the Western Empire were represented by Smith as having been at exactly the state of development which we have just described. Primitive peoples whose military power was of the awesome proportions appropriate to the second stage are thus shown to have come in contact with a much more sophisticated society, but one whose power was already on the decline.[14] The result, as Smith duly noted, was the destruction

[11] It is also stated in LJ (A) iv. 22–3 that 'Laws and government may be considered in this and indeed in every case as a combination of the rich to oppress the poor, and preserve to themselves the inequality of the goods which would otherwise be soon destroyed by the attacks of the poor; . . .' Cf. LJ (B) 11; Cannan, 8, and Hume, *A Treatise of Human Nature*, III.2.viii.

[12] This subject is considered at length in LJ (A) iv.1–35 and LJ (B) 18–30; Cannan, 14–21.

[13] LJ (A) iv.39 states with reference to the North American Indians that: 'there can be no great danger from such a nation. And the great astonishment of our colonies in Am. are in on account of these expeditions, proceeds intirely from their unacquaintedness with arms, for though they may plague them and hurt some of the back settlements, they could never injure the body of the people.' Cf. LJ (B) 27–8; Cannan, 20.

[14] As Smith represents the case in his lectures, both Greece and Rome had already passed through the stages of hunting and pasturage in reaching a stage of development

of civilization as then known; in a sense, a step backwards. As Smith put it:

When the German and Scythian nations over-ran the western provinces of the Roman empire, the confusions which followed so great a revolution lasted for several centuries. The rapine and violence which the barbarians exercised against the ancient inhabitants, interrupted the commerce between the towns and the country. The towns were deserted, and the country was left uncultivated, and the western provinces of Europe, which had enjoyed a considerable degree of opulence under the Roman empire, sunk into the lowest state of poverty and barbarism.

(WN III.ii.1)

At the same time however, Smith argued that the domination of the barbarian nations had generated not only a desert, but also an environment from which a higher form of European civilization was ultimately to emerge.[15]

Smith's explanation of this general trend begins with the fact that the primitive tribes which overran the empire had already attained a relatively sophisticated form of the pasturage economy, with some idea of agriculture and of property in land.[16] He argued therefore that they would naturally use existing institutions in their new situation and that in particular their first act would be a division of the conquered territories: 'the chiefs and principal leaders of those nations, acquired or usurped to themselves the greater part of the lands. . . . A great part of them was left uncultivated; but no part of them, whether cultivated or uncultivated, was left without a proprietor. All of them were engrossed, and the greater part by a few great proprietors' (WN III.ii.1). In this way we move in effect from a developed version of one economic stage to a primitive version of another; from the state of pasture to that of 'agriculture' which features a settled abode,

which was more sophisticated than the agrarian, but without attaining all the characteristic features of the commercial stage. The economies which he described certainly featured developed patterns of trade for example, and to this extent fit rather uneasily within the fourfold classification with which Smith is usually associated. On point is clear, however: the decline in the power of both Greece and Rome was attributed to common causes: to 'improvements in the mechanic arts, commerce, and the arts of war' (LJ (B) 43; Cannan, 30). Smith specially emphasized the importance of commerce and luxury as an explanation for decline in military power, in arguing that the fall of Rome was attributable to internal weakness of such an order as to oblige her to hire for her defence the very forces which were to prove the sources of her dissolution. See LJ (A) iv. 75–114; LJ (B) 32–49; Cannan, 23–34; WN V.i.a 'Of the Expence of Defence'. In the WN V.i.a.44 it is pointed out that in modern times the position of the barbarous and civilized had been reversed owing to the expense of fire-arms.

[15] Almost exactly this point was made by Dugald Stewart in *Works*, x.147.

[16] Smith commented further on the implied sequence of stages in stating that men would 'naturally turn themselves to the cultivation of land' once the growth of population had put pressure on supplies derived from pasturage. He added that 'The only instance that has the appearance of an objection to this rule is the state of the North American Indians. They, tho they have no conception of flocks and herds, have nevertheless some notion of agriculture' LJ (A) i. 29. Similar points are made in LJ (B) 150, Cannan, 108.

property in land, and some form of rudimentary tillage. Under the circumstances outlined, property in land becomes the great source of power and distinction, with each estate assuming the form of a separate principality. As a result of this situation, Smith argued, a gradual change took place in the laws governing property, featuring the introduction of primogeniture and entails, designed to protect estates against division and to preserve a 'certain lineal succession'. The basic point emphasized was that in such periods of disorder 'The security of a landed estate, . . . the protection which its owner could afford to those who dwelt on it, depended upon its greatness. To divide it was to ruin it, and to expose every part of it to be oppressed and swallowed up by the incursions of its neighbours' (WN III.ii.3).[17]

Such institutions as these quite obviously reflect a change in the mode of subsistence and in the form of property, thus presenting some important contrasts with the previous stage. At the same time, however, Smith emphasized basic similarities: for example, property remains the basis of power in that there is still a division in society between those who own the means of subsistence and those who must somehow acquire it. As in the previous case, the great proprietor has nothing on which to expend his surpluses other than through the maintenance of dependents—and at the same time has a positive incentive to do so since they contribute to his own security and military power. Once again, the individual who lacks the means of subsistence can only acquire it by becoming the servant of some great lord and therefore his dependent, thus becoming members of a group who 'having no equivalent to give in return for their maintenance, but being fed entirely by his bounty, must obey him, for the same reason that soldiers must obey the prince that pays them' (WN III.iv.5). While Smith carefully distinguished between *retainers* and *cultivators* in this context, he took pains to emphasize that the latter group were in every respect as dependent on the proprietor as the first, and added that 'Even such of them as were not in a state of villanage, were tenants at will, who paid a rent in no respect equivalent to the subsistence which the land afforded them' (WN III.iv.6).[18]

In short, the period was marked by clear relations of power and dependence—but above all by disorder and conflict, and it was from this source that the first important changes in the outlines of the system were to come. As Smith put it by way of summary:

[17] Smith provides a homely example based on the Gordon and Douglas Estates at LJ (A) i.133. Cf. LJ (B) 161–62; Cannan, 118.

[18] It is pointed out in LJ (A) i. 119 that those who used the land initially 'paid a small rent to the possessor, rather as an acknowledgment of their dependence than as the value of the land'. Sir James Steuart affords an interesting parallel with Smith's general line of argument; *Principles of Political Oeconomy* (1767, ed. Skinner, 1966), i. 208 and note. See generally i. 206–17 and lxiii–lxviii.

In those disorderly times, every great landlord was a sort of petty prince. His tenants were his subjects. He was their judge, and in some respects their legislator in peace, and their leader in war. He made war according to his own discretion, frequently against his neighbours, and sometimes against his sovereign. (WN III.ii.3)

It was this state of conflict, Smith suggests, which gave the proprietors some incentive to alter the pattern of landholding, in two quite different ways. First, Smith argued that the heavy demands which were inevitably made on their immediate tenants (as distinct from villeins) for military service would inevitably change the quit-rent system in terms of which land was normally held. Smith argued in effect that the great lords would naturally begin to grant leases for a term of years, and then in a form which gave security to the tenant's family and ultimately to his posterity. In this way, land came to be held as *feuda* rather than *munera*, designed to give both parties a benefit: the lord, in terms of the supply of military service, and the tenant, security in the use of the land. Smith also noted certain consequential developments which reflected the basic purpose of the arrangement, namely to improve and protect the power of the great proprietor, in describing what he called the feudal *casualities*.[19]

Secondly, Smith argued that the same need for protection which altered the relationship between the great lord and his tenants would also lead to patterns of alliance between members of the former groups and, therefore, to arrangements which gave some guarantee of mutual service and protection. It was for these reasons, Smith argued, that the lesser landowners entered into feudal arrangements with those greater lords who could ensure their survival (thus enhancing their ability to do so), just as the great lords would be led to make similar arrangements amongst themselves and with the king. These changes took place about the ninth, tenth, and eleventh centuries, and by imposing some shackles on the free enterprise of the proprietors contributed thereby to the emergence of a more orderly form of government.

However, while Smith did describe the feudal as a higher form of the agrarian economy, he also took some pains to emphasize the limited possibilities for economic growth which it presented; limitations which were themselves the reflection of the political institutions now prevailing. For example, he pointed out that the laws of primogeniture and entail hindered the sale and division of lands, and therefore their acquisition by those who might have sought to improve them. He also argued that the quit-rent system, so far as it survived, gave no incentive to industry and that the institution of slavery ensured that it was in the interest of the ordinary individual to 'eat as much, and to labour as little as possible' (WN III.ii.9). In the same way he also cited the disincentive effects of the

[19] See LJ (A) iv. 127ff; LJ (B) 53–7; Cannan, 36–40; WN III.iv.9, V.ii.h.5,6.

arbitrary services and feudal taxes which were imposed at this time.[20] But undoubtedly, Smith placed most emphasis on the continuing problem of political instability:

> The authority of government still continued to be, as before, too weak in the head and too strong in the inferior members, and the excessive strength of the inferior members was the cause of the weakness of the head. After the institution of the feudal subordination, the king was as incapable of restraining the violence of the great lords as before. They still continued to make war according to their own discretion, almost continually upon one another, and very frequently upon the king, and the open country still continued to be a scene of violence, rapine, and disorder.
>
> (WN III.iv.9)

Once again, a state of instability was to produce some change in the outlines of the social system, and once again the motive behind it was political rather than economic—this time with the kings rather than the great lords as the main actors in the drama.[21]

IV EMERGENCE OF THE EXCHANGE ECONOMY

The kind of economy which Smith described as appropriate to the agrarian state is fundamentally a simple one. It consists of the usual division between town and country, that is, between those who produce food and those who make the manufactured goods without which no large country could subsist (WN III.iii.17). The cities which Smith described were, however, small, and composed of those merchants, tradesmen, and mechanics who were not bound to a particular place and who might find it in their (economic) interest to congregate together (WN III.ii.4).[22] Smith had in fact relatively little to say about the historical origins of such groupings, but he did emphasize that the inhabitants of the towns were in the same servile condition as the inhabitants of the country, and that the wealth which they did manage to accumulate under such unfavourable conditions was subject to the arbitrary exactions of both the king and those lords on whose territories

[20] This analysis appears in WN III.ii. It finds a close counterpart in ED, and LJ (B) 285–98; Cannan, 223–36 (where Smith also considers the causes of the slow progress of manufactures). When he came to write or rather rewrite this section of the WN Smith must have decided to integrate the discussion of the 'slow progress of opulence' with his general account of the feudal state which had been developed earlier.

[21] Smith also stressed the importance of the Church as a source of political instability, for example, in WN V.i.g.17,22.

[22] Smith emphasized the different origins of modern and classical cities in WN III.iii.1, in pointing out that in the former case the inhabitants were mainly tradesmen and mechanics, whereas the latter were mainly composed of the owners of land who congregated together for the purposes of defence. See also LJ (A) iv. 143 where Smith comments on the small size of towns at the time of William the Conqueror, and explains this in terms of the very low level of demand for manufactured products which prevailed.

they might happen to be based on through which they might pass (WN III.iii.2).

But evidently some development must have been possible, for Smith examines the role of the city from that period in time when three distinctive features of royal policy with regard to them were already in evidence. First, Smith noted that cities had often been allowed to farm the taxes to which they were subject, the inhabitants thus becoming 'jointly and severally answerable' for the whole sum due (WN III.iii.3). Second, he noted that in some cases these taxes, instead of being farmed for a given number of years, had been 'let in fee', that is 'forever, reserving a rent certain, never afterwards to be augmented' (WN III.iii.4).[23] Third, Smith observed that the cities 'were generally at the same time erected into a commonality or corporation, with the privilege of having magistrates and a town council of their own, of making bye-laws for their own government, of building walls for their own defence, and of reducing all their inhabitants under a sort of military discipline, by obliging them to watch and ward . . .' (WN III.iii.6).

It was as a result of following these policies that some kings had achieved the apparently remarkable result of freezing the very revenues which were most likely to increase over time, and at the same time effectively curtailing their own power by erecting 'a sort of independent republics in the heart of their own dominions' (WN III.iii.7). Smith advanced two main reasons to explain the paradox: first, that by encouraging the cities the king made it possible for a group of his subjects to defend themselves against the power of the great lords where he personally was unable to do so, and, secondly, that by imposing a limit on taxation 'he took away from those whom he wished to have for his friends and if one may say so, for his allies, all ground of jealousy and suspicion that he was ever afterwards to oppress them, either by raising the farm rent of their towns, or by granting it to some other farmer' (WN III.iii.8).

The encouragement given to the cities represented in effect a tactical alliance which was beneficial to both parties, and in speaking of the burghers, Smith remarked that 'Mutual interest, . . . disposed them to support the king, and the king to support them against the lords. They were the enemies of his enemies, and it was his interest to render them as secure and independent of those enemies as he could' (WN III.iii.8). Smith also noted that this development was directly related to the weakness of kings so that it was likely to be more significant in some countries than in others, and that in general the policy had been successful where employed.[24]

[23] Smith also comments on this point in LJ (A) iv. 144–5, 151 and LJ (B) 40; Cannan, 40.

[24] In LJ (A) iv. 154, Smith also associated this trend with the military ambition of certain kings such as Edward I and Henry IV, 'the two most warlike of the English Kings'. It is also pointed out in WN III.iii.11 that while the cities in England did not become so powerful as to be virtually independent (as in Italy and Switzerland, where the physical

He also remarked that the granting of powers of self-government to the inhabitants of the cities had set in motion forces which were ultimately to weaken the authority of the kings through creating an environment within which the forces of economic development could, for the first time, be effectively released. In Smith's own words:

Order and good government, and along with them, the liberty and security of individuals, were, in this manner, established in cities, at a time when the occupiers of land . . . were exposed to every sort of violence. But men in this defenceless state naturally content themselves with their necessary subsistence; because to acquire more might only tempt the injustice of their oppressors. On the contrary, when they are secure of enjoying the fruits of their industry, they naturally exert it to better their condition and to acquire not only the necessaries, but the conveniences and elegancies of life.

(WN III.iii.12)

The stimulus to economic growth and to further social change was thus seen to emanate from the cities; institutions which had themselves been developed and protected in an attempt to solve a political problem. From this point, Smith's attention shifted to the analysis of the process of economic growth in the manufacturing, before going on to examine its impact on the agrarian, sector.

Smith clearly recognized that growth was limited by the size of the market and that since the agrarian sector was relatively backward, the main stimulus to economic growth would have to come from foreign trade. He therefore concluded that cities such as Venice, Genoa, and Pisa, all of which enjoyed ready access to the sea, had provided the models for the process, while noting that their development had been further accelerated by particular accidents such as the Crusades.[25] In general, however, Smith laid most emphasis on three sources of encouragement to the development of trade and manufactures. First, he argued that in many cases agrarian surpluses could be acquired by the merchants and used in exchange for foreign manufactures, and suggested as a matter of fact that the early trade of Europe had largely consisted in the exchange 'of their own rude, for the manufactured products of more civilised nations'. Secondly, he argued that over time the merchants would naturally seek to introduce manufactures at home (with a view to saving carriage). Such manufactures, it was suggested, would require the use of foreign materials, thus inducing an important change in the general pattern of trade. Thirdly, he argued that

size and nature of the country made this possible) yet 'They became, however, so considerable, that the sovereign could impose no tax upon them, besides the stated farm rent of the town, without their own consent. They were, therefore, called upon to send deputies to the general assembly of the states . . .'

[25] Smith also comments on the position of the Italian cities in LJ (A) iv. 111 and added that 'Milan too, though no sea-port, had great commerce'.

some manufactures would develop 'naturally', that is, through the gradual refinement of the 'coarse and rude' products which were normally produced at home and which were, therefore, based on domestic materials. Smith suggested that such developments were normally found in those cities which were 'not indeed at a very great, but at a considerable distance from the sea coast, and sometimes even from all water carriage' (WN III.iii.20). That is, he suggested that manufactures might well develop in areas to which artisans had been attracted by the cheapness of subsistence, thus allowing trade to develop within the locality. Once some progress had been made in this way foreign trade becomes possible:

> The manufacturers first supply the neighbourhood, and afterwards as their work improves and refines, more distant markets. For though neither the rude produce, nor even the coarse manufacture, could, without the greatest difficulty, support the expence of a considerable land carriage, the refined and improved manufacture easily may. In a small bulk it frequently contains the price of a great quantity of rude produce.
>
> (WN III.iii.20)

Smith cited the silk manufacture at Lyons and Spitalfields as examples of the first category; the manufactures of Leeds, Halifax, Sheffield, Birmingham, and Wolverhampton as examples of the second, the 'natural offspring of agriculture' (WN III.iii.19, 20). He also added that manufactures of the latter kind were generally posterior to those 'which were the offspring of foreign commerce' and that the process of development just outlined made it perfectly possible for the city within which growth took place to 'grow up to great wealth and splendour, while not only the country in its neighbourhood, but all those to which it traded, were in poverty and wretchedness' (WN III.iii.13).

In the next stage of the analysis, however, it was argued that this situation as outlined was unlikely to continue indefinitely; that the development of manufactures and trade within the cities was bound to impinge on the agrarian sector and, ultimately, to destroy the service relationships which still subsisted within it:

> commerce and manufactures gradually introduced order and good government, and with them, the liberty and security of individuals among the inhabitants of the country, who had before lived in a continual state of war with their neighbours, and of servile dependency upon their superiors. This, though it has been the least observed, is by far the most important of all their effects.
>
> (WN III.iv.4)[26]

[26] Smith went on to add that 'Mr Hume is the only writer who, so far as I know, has hitherto taken any notice of it'. See especially Hume's essay 'Of Refinement in the Arts' and Duncan Forbes's introduction to Hume's *History* (Pelican, 1970), 38–43. Smith's statement is interesting when we recall that Steuart, Ferguson, Millar, and Kames, had all published prior to the appearance of *The Wealth of Nations*. Since Smith can hardly have been unaware of the fact, it seems likely that his citation of Hume alone simply provides further evidence as to the age of this section of the work.

Essentially, this process may be seen to stem from the fact that the development of trade and manufactures had given the proprietors a means of expending their wealth, other than in the maintenance of dependents. The development of commerce and manufactures, in short, had 'gradually furnished the great proprietors with something for which they could exchange the whole surplus of their lands, and which they could consume themselves without sharing it either with tenants or retainers. All for ourselves, and nothing for other people, seems, in every age of the world, to have been the vile maxim of mankind' (WN III.iv.10).[27]

This situation generated two results. First, since the proprietor's object was now to increase his command over the means of exchange, it would be in his interest to reduce the number of retainers: 'till they were at last dismissed altogether. The same cause gradually led them to dismiss the unnecessary part of their tenants. Farms were enlarged, and the occupiers of land, notwithstanding the complaints of depopulation, reduced to the number necessary for cultivating it, according to the imperfect state of cultivation and improvement in those times' (WN III.iv.13).

Secondly, since the object was now to maximize the disposable surplus, it was in the proprietor's interest to change the forms of leasehold in order to encourage output and increase his returns. In this way, Smith traced the gradual change from the use of slave labour on the land,[28] to the origin of the 'metayer' system where the tenant had limited property rights, until the whole process finally resulted in the appearance of farmers properly so called 'who cultivated the land with their own stock, paying a rent certain to the landlord' (WN III.ii.14). Smith added that the same process would tend over time to lead to an improvement in the conditions of leases, until the tenants could be 'secured in their possession for such a term of years as might give them time to recover with profit whatever they should lay out in the further improvement of the land. The expensive vanity of the landlord made him willing to accept of this condition . . .' (WN III.iv.13).

As a result of these two general trends, the great proprietors gradually lost their powers, both judicial and military,[29] until a situation was reached where 'they became as insignificant as any substantial burgher or tradesman

[27] At the same time Smith emphasized the importance of the expenditure of the 'rich' in LJ (A) iii.135 and LJ (B) 139–40; Cannan, 100. See especially TMS IV.i.i.10.

[28] Smith argues in effect that slavery was undermined because of economic forces and thus rejected the claims of the Church (WN III.ii.12). See also LJ (A) iii.121. He also pointed out that slavery still subsisted in large parts of Europe, especially 'Russia, Poland, Hungary, Bohemia, Moravia, and other parts of Germany. It is only in the western and south-western provinces of Europe, that it has gradually been abolished altogether.' See also LJ (A) iii.122 and LJ (B) 134; Cannan 96.

[29] In WN V.i.g.25 Smith ascribed the decline in the temporal powers of the clergy to the same basic forces. In this connection he pointed out that although the clergy as a group had exerted greater power than the lords, as a result of their greater cohesion, none the less their authority declined rather sooner owing to the fact that in general the benefices of the clergy were smaller than the fortunes of the barons.

in a city. A regular government was established in the country as well as in the city, nobody having sufficient power to disturb its operations in the one, any more than in the other' (WN III.iv.15).

Smith thus associated the decline in the feudal powers of the great proprietors with three general trends, all of which followed on the introduction of commerce and manufactures: the dissipation of their fortunes,[30] the dismissal of their retainers, and the substitution of a cash for the service relationships which had previously existed between the owner of land and those who cultivated it. As a result, we face a system where the disincentives to 'industry' had been removed from the agrarian sector, and where both sectors were, for the first time, fully interdependent at the domestic level.

Smith argues in effect that the *quantitative* development of manufactures based on the cities eventually produced an important *qualitative* change in creating the institutions of the exchange economy, that is, of the fourth economic stage. It is in this situation that the drive to better our condition, allied to the insatiable wants of man, provides the maximum possible stimulus to economic growth, and ensures that the gains accruing to town and country are both mutual and reciprocal.

> The great commerce of every civilised society, is that carried on between the inhabitants of the town and those of the country. It consists in the exchange of rude for manufactured produce, either immediately, or by the intervention of money, or of some sort of paper which represents money . . . The gains of both are mutual and reciprocal, and the division of labour is in this, as in all other cases, advantageous to all the different persons employed in the various occupations into which it is subdivided.
>
> (WN III.i.1)

It is, moreover, a situation which effectively eliminates the direct dependence of the previous period; where each productive service commands a price and therefore ensures that while the farmer, tradesman, or merchant must depend upon his customers, yet 'Though in some measure obliged to them all, he is not absolutely dependent upon any one of them' (WN III.iv.12).[31]

[30] Smith did note, however, that this general trend had not been matched in Germany because of the size of the country and the extent of the estates which were held by individuals. As he pointed out in LJ (A) iv.166 the German nobles 'could not possibly, by any personal luxury, consume all their revenues; they therefore contrived to have a great number of retainers and dependents, and have accordingly become absolute.' Similar points are made in LJ (B) 60–1; Cannan, 43.

[31] Smith also pointed out in the WN V.i.b.7 that 'In an opulent and civilised society a man may possess a much greater fortune, and yet not be able to command a dozen of people. Though the produce of his estate may be sufficient to maintain . . . more than a thousand people, yet as these people pay for everything which they get from him, as he gives scarce anything to anybody but in exchange for an equivalent, there is scarce any body who considers himself as entirely dependent upon him, and his authority extends only over a few menial servants.'

It may now be apparent that Smith's argument is very largely concerned with the analysis of the nature of the agrarian economy and with the causes of transition from it to the fourth economic stage; that stage with which the economic analysis of *The Wealth of Nations* was formally concerned. Smith's argument taken as a whole has three characteristic features which are worthy of note. First, he consistently argues that the whole process of change depends on the self-interest of individuals: for example, it is this motive which is seen to lie behind the alliances formed by the great proprietors, the protection given to cities by kings, and the activities of the merchant classes. Secondly, it is evident that the motivation behind many of the most important changes was in fact political rather than simply economic: for example, the alliances formed by the great proprietors had a political object, as did the royal encouragement given to the cities themselves. Thirdly, it is argued that the whole process of change, and especially that involved in the transition from the feudal to the commercial state, depends on the activities of individuals who are themselves unconscious of the ultimate ends towards which such activities contribute. Or, as Smith put it in reviewing the actions of the proprietors and merchants during the latter stages of the historical process which we have outlined:

> A revolution of the greatest importance to the public happiness, was in this manner brought about by two different orders of people, who had not the least intention to serve the public. To gratify the most childish vanity was the sole motive of the great proprietors. The merchants and artificers, much less ridiculous, acted merely from a view to their own interest, and in pursuit of their own pedlar principle of turning a penny wherever a penny was to be got. Neither of them had either knowledge or foresight of that great revolution which the folly of the one, and the industry of the other, was gradually bringing about. (WN III.iv.17)

It is principles such as these which Smith used in explaining the rise of the classical civilizations and their decline, and which are employed in tracing the gradual process which had brought mankind from the primitive hunting economies (still to be found among the American Indians) through many vicissitudes to the relatively sophisticated social forms which the European nations had assumed in the eighteenth century. Smith took a vast historical sweep and produced a theory (admittedly incomplete) which was designed to give coherence and order to what otherwise appeared as a chaos of unconnected events. To this extent the description once offered of John Millar's teaching would also seem to apply to that of his master, for he too taught that we should not gaze 'with stupid amazement on the singular and diversified appearances of human manners and institutions' but rather 'consider them as necessary links in the great chain which connects civilized with barbarous society'.[32]

[32] Francis Jeffrey, in the *Edinburgh Review* (1803), 157.

V CONCLUSIONS

While it is hoped that the brief account which we have offered of Smith's argument is sufficient to delineate its major features, it may be appropriate to add some words of comment with regard to its general character and content in terms of two broad areas.

I. *Methodological.* Perhaps the most striking feature of the analysis which we have considered is that it purports to place the study of history on the same level as other social sciences and to apply to history the methodology of Newton whereby we 'lay down certain principles, primary or proved, in the beginning, from whence we account for the several phenomena, connecting all together by the same chain' (LRBL 24.7; Lothian, 140). The point is important for a number of reasons. First, we are reminded that this kind of study is only conjectural in the sense that there are some occasions on which principles which are derived from known facts must be applied to situations where facts are lacking. Or, as Dugald Stewart put it in discussing the problems of pre-history:

> In this want of direct evidence, we are under a necessity of supplying the place of fact by conjecture; and when we are unable to ascertain how men have actually conducted themselves upon particular occasions, of considering in what manner they are likely to have proceeded, from the principles of their nature and the circumstances of their external situation.
>
> (Stewart, II.45)

Secondly, we are reminded that the claims of 'science' often implied that philosophical history was in some respects superior to other forms of historical writing—and in particular to the orthodox or narrative type. The terms used often invite this conclusion, as for example, when Dugald Stewart referred to the 'habits of scientific disquisition' which were required of the natural historian, while expressing regret that William Robertson, perhaps the leading orthodox historian of his own time and country, had not prepared himself more for his incursions into this field. A rather similar impression is left by John Millar's statement that he would seek to 'point out the chief incidents of a constitutional history, lying in a good measure beneath the common surface of events which occupy the details of the vulgar historian' (HV iv.101).

But whatever points Stewart or Millar may have intended to convey in making such remarks, it should be noted that Smith himself was very careful in his comments—as befits one who broke new ground in lecturing on the history of historians.[33] While space precludes an extensive examination of

[33] See LRBL, lectures 16 to 19 and especially the latter. Smith's classification of types of historical writing affords an interesting parallel with Hegel's introduction to his lectures on the philosophy of history.

these lectures, it should be noted that Smith at no time expressed contempt for those historians who worked in different fields. He pointed out for example that the first historians, the poets, who had concerned themselves with the 'marvellous' provide valuable evidence as to the times in which they lived, and went on to argue that if Herodotus had many defects as an historian, yet 'We can learn from him rather the customs of the different nations and the series of events . . . in this way too, we may learn a great deal' (LRBL 19.4; Lothian, 101). Smith also observed that historians such as Thucydides and Tacitus were also particularly informative not only because of the way in which they recorded facts but also because they tended to emphasize the psychological pressures to which the main figures involved were subjected. He added that 'though this perhaps will not tend so much to instruct us in the knowledge of the causes of events, yet it will be more interesting and lead us into a science no less useful, to wit, the knowledge of the motives by which men act' (LRBL 20.4; Lothian, 111). Smith, in short, quite clearly recognized that the narrative historian often supplied the materials on which the work of the philosophical historian was based.

Thirdly, we should recall that Smith did not himself claim that philosophical history had an exclusive title to be described as scientific in character. For example Smith referred to the objectivity or 'impartiality' which the orthodox historian has to maintain, in remarking that he fulfils his duty only when he 'sets before us the more interesting and important events of human life, points out the causes by which these events are brought about, and by this means points out to us by what manner and method we may produce similar good effects or avoid similar bad ones' (LRBL 17.6; Lothian, 85). In short, the historian must bring to his study a critical awareness of facts; he must study these facts objectively, and he must seek to elucidate their causes—qualities which led Smith to give particular praise to Thucydides (who reported events of which he was the witness) and Tacitus (who recorded the history of a nation). Of the modern historians, Smith considered Machiavelli to be incomparably the best, in the sense that he was the only one 'who has contented himself with that which is the chief purpose of history, to relate events and connect them with their causes, without becoming a party on either side' (LRBL 20.10; Lothian 110–11).

Machiavelli is an interesting choice in that his example also reminds us that use of the 'constant principles of human nature' in the interpretation of events was not of itself the distinguishing feature of 'philosophical history' as written by Smith. For Machiavelli too employed exactly this hypothesis in seeking to provide a science of history. As he put it in a characteristic passage: 'If the present be compared with the remote past, it is easily seen that in all cities and in all peoples, there are the same desires and the same passions as there always were.'[34] We may therefore conclude that philosophical history has no special claim to be regarded as more *scientific* than any other form of historical investigation, and that it cannot be regarded as the first exercise in writing a *science* of history. The distinguishing features are rather to be found in the particular hypotheses used and in the *nature* of the question asked; a question which was stated very neatly and exactly by Dugald Stewart (surely the most perceptive of contemporary commentators) when he remarked:

When, in such a period of society as that in which we live, we compare our intellectual acquirements, our opinions, manners, and institutions, with those that prevail among rude tribes, it cannot fail to occur to us as an interesting question, by what gradual steps the transition has been made from the first simple efforts of uncultivated nature, to a state of things so wonderfully artificial and complicated. Whence has arisen that systematical beauty which we admire in the structure of a cultivated language. . . . Whence the origin of the different sciences and of the different arts . . . Whence the astonishing fabric of the political union, the fundamental principles which are common to all governments . . . ?

(Stewart, II.44)

Finally, we should recall, as the last point implies, that philosophical history is in no sense confined to the particular area of inquiry which has been the main subject of this paper. Thus for example Smith himself referred to his interest in 'a sort of philosophical history of all the different branches of literature'[35] and his editors, Black and Hutton, to 'a plan he had once formed for giving a connected history of the liberal sciences and elegant arts'. In the same way Dugald Stewart mentioned Smith's essay on the *Formation of Languages* as 'a very beautiful specimen of theoretical history' (Stewart, II.54) and took notice of the fact that the mathematical sciences 'afford very favourable subjects' for treatment of this kind (Stewart, II.48). Indeed it is probably true that Smith's history of astronomy is one of the most perceptive and complete versions of the thesis which Smith left us, starting as it does from a statement of the principles of human nature as relevant for the work of scientific or speculative thought, before tracing the development of knowledge in terms of four major astronomical systems, which culminate in the work of Newton.[36]

[34] *The Discourses of Niccolò Machiavelli*, ed. L. J. Walker (1950), i.302. Cf. Montesquieu, *Considerations of the Causes of the Greatness of the Romans and their Decline*, ed. Lowenthal (1965), 26.

[35] See Letter 248 to Rochefoucauld, dated 1 Nov. 1785. In Letter 276 addressed to Cadell, dated 15 Mar. 1788 Smith also mentioned 'several other works which I have projected and in which I have made some progress', while expressing doubt that he would live to complete them.

[36] See for example, A. Skinner, 'Adam Smith: Science and the Role of the Imagination' in *Hume and the Enlightenment: Essays in Honour of Ernest Mossner*, ed. W. B. Todd (1974); and from the standpoint of the historian of science the article by Dr. Wightman which is published in this volume.

II. *Analytical.* The point which we have just discussed raises an issue of some importance in that Smith's early interest in mathematics and natural science may have had an important influence on the way in which he handled certain social questions. It is also noteworthy that Smith had a very wide knowledge of the scientific work which had been done subsequent to Newton, especially in the field of biology. It may be recalled that Smith purchased the *Encyclopédie* for Glasgow University Library and that he personally owned the works of D'Alembert, Diderot, Buffon, and Maupertius—some of which he admiringly reviewed in an article of 1755.[37] The type of work done in biology by such writers was particularly important, linked as it has been to the entrance of 'historicism' into the European outlook in the late 1740s and 1750s. As Lester Crocker put it: 'The rise of relativism in ethics and social thought as evidenced in the writings of Montesquieu, Diderot and others, is a complementary part of a general evolutionist view of the universe, which embraced the cosmos, life, and societies.'[38] Smith's interest in the general problem of historical change was clearly not a pecularly Scottish phenomenon.[39]

Secondly, we should recall that Smith's specific interest in *social* history also found precedents and parallels on the Continent, and that once again he can be said to have been well aware of the fact. It is interesting to note in this connection that as Quaestor for the University Library his purchases included the works of Giannonne, Daniel, and Brosse, and that he owned copies of Fenelon, Fontenelle, Rollin, Raynal, Mably, Duclos, and Chastellux, to name but a few.[40] In many cases such writers are associated with something of a revolution in historical writing; a revolution whose nature is aptly expressed in Voltaire's comment that: 'My principal object is to know as far as I can, the manners of peoples and to study the human mind. I shall regard the order of succession of kings and chronology as my guides, but not as the objects of my work.'[41] Writing much earlier, the Italian Giannonne felt able to state that his

[37] In a *Letter to the Authors of the Edinburgh Review* (1755). Smith also frequently cited Linnaeus, the Swedish naturalist, in his essay *Of the External Senses.* As Dugald Stewart pointed out with reference to the former work, Smith's observations 'on the state of learning in Europe are written with ingenuity and elegance; but are chiefly interesting, as they show the attention which the Author had given to the philosophy and literature of the Continent, at a period when they were not much studied in this island' (Stewart, I.25).

[38] *Forerunners of Darwin*, ed. Glass, Strauss and Timken (1959), 143. See especially the articles by Crocker, Glass, and Lovejoy together with the latter's *Essays in the History of Ideas* (1948).

[39] See for example H. R. Trevor-Roper, 'The Idea of the Decline and Fall of the Roman Empire', in *The Age of Enlightenment*, ed. W. H. Barber (1967); 'The Scottish Enlightenment', in *Studies on Voltaire and the Eighteenth Century*' lviii (1967).

[40] See for example, Carl Becker, *The Heavenly City of the Eighteenth Century Philosophers* (1932), lecture III.

[41] Quoted in J. B. Black, *The Art of History* (1926), 34. See also J. H. Brumfitt, *Voltaire: Historian* (1958).

History of Naples, 'wherein the Polity, Laws and Customs of so noble a Kingdom, shall be treated separately', could be regarded for this reason as being altogether new.[42] But of course it was Giannonne's disciple, Montesquieu, who 'first showed that laws were not the arbitrary fiat of their makers' and who now seems to stand at the beginning of a major change in historical writing.[43] As John Millar often said, it was Montesquieu who first pointed out the way, and the acknowledgement finds an echo in Dugald Stewart's generous assessment of his influence (Stewart, II.49).

Thirdly, it is appropriate to observe that the interest which Smith showed in economic forces also featured largely at the time. For example, Harrington was widely recognized as a 'profound political writer' and as one who showed a 'thorough acquaintance with the true principles of democracy'.[44] Montesquieu too had shown an interest in the role of time in his *Considerations* (1752)[45] and had given some attention to economic factors in the *Esprit*, especially in Book XX where he examined the problem of 'How commerce broke through the barbarism of Europe'. The same basic theme is featured in Rousseau's *Origin of Inequality*, in Hutcheson's *System*, and especially in Hume's *History*, where he relates the increasing significance of that middling rank of men 'who are the best and firmest basis of public liberty' to the growth of commerce and industry.[46] Another notable figure in this general area is Lord Kames, who as early as 1747 had quite unequivocally linked the decline of feudal institutions to the appearance of arts and industry in remarking that 'after the arts of Peace began to be cultivated, Manufactures and trade to revive in Europe, and Riches to increase, this Institution began to turn extremely burdensome. It first tottered and then fell by its own Weight, as wanting a solid foundation.'[47]

[42] Pietro Giannonne, *The Civil History of the Kingdom of Naples:* Where the Author Clearly Demonstrates, That the Temporal Dominion and Power exercis'd by the Popes, has been altogether owing to the ignorance, and Connivance of, or Concessions extorted from Secular Princes during the dark Ages (translated by James Ogilvy, 1729). The introduction is especially informative; for comment see Trevor-Roper, op. cit. 1653.

[43] Kingsley Martin, *French Liberal Thought in the Eighteenth Century*, ed. J. P. Mayer (1954), 152. In Scottish circles at least, the emphasis given to physical factors was widely discounted. See for example, Hume's essay 'Of National Characters' and John Millar's introduction to his *Origin of the Distinction of Ranks* (1771, ed. W. C. Lehmann, 1960).

[44] Kames, *Sketches*, II, Millar, HV iii.286. Harrington's *Oceana* (1656, 3rd ed. 1747) was also praised in Hume's essay on 'The Idea of a Perfect Commonwealth' and was given considerable attention by Francis Hutcheson in his *System of Moral Philosophy* (1755), Book 3, Ch. 6, 'The Several Forms of Polity, with their Principal Advantages and Disadvantages'.

[45] Perhaps the best example of a truly dynamic theory of historical change is provided by Vico's remarkable *New Science* (1725). This work does not, however, seem to have had much direct impact at least in this country.

[46] For comment, see Forbes, op. cit. 39.

[47] *Essays Upon Several Subjects concerning British Antiquities* (1747). For comment see I. S. Ross, *Lord Kames and the Scotland of his Day* (1972).

While it is not our purpose here to assess the extent of Smith's intellectual debts, so much as to report on the existence of a climate of opinion, it should also be noted that the idea of distinct socio-economic stages was also entering the literature on quite a wide front. It is found, for example, as early as 1750 in Turgot's (unpublished) notes for a *Universal History*, in Sir James Steuart's *Principles*,[48] first published in 1767 but completed in outline by 1758, and also in Kames's *Historical Law Tracts*, printed in the same year.[49]

However, it would appear that Smith must be regarded as a particularly influential figure in the development of this general line of thought; one which appears to have been especially dominant among Scottish writers at this time. It was in recognition of this point that Dugald Stewart felt moved to remark, in the course of an address to the Royal Society of Edinburgh, that:

> It will not, I hope, be imputed to me as a blamable instance of national vanity, if I conclude this Section with remarking the rapid progress that has been made in our own country during the last fifty years, in tracing the origin and progress of the present establishments in Europe. Montesquieu undoubtedly led the way, but much has been done since the publication of his works, by authors whose names are enrolled among the members of this society.
>
> (*Works*, x.147)

Fourthly, it may be noted that even if the work done by Smith and his contemporaries finds parallels and precedents, nevertheless it does appear to have been remarkable for the *weight* of emphasis which was placed on economic factors. As we have seen, there were really two applications of the general thesis: First, the argument that the development of productive forces ultimately depended on the 'natural wants' of man; the point being that man is first subject to certain basic needs which, once satisfied, allow him to pursue more complex goals (WN III.iii.12). The same point was made by Adam Ferguson in remarking that 'refinement and plenty foster new desires, while they furnish the means, or practice the methods, to gratify them'.[50] John Millar also linked these natural and insatiable desires to the development of productive forces, and even went so far as to argue that the

[48] These points are made in Steuart's *Principles*, ed Skinner, at lxiii and note; R. L. Meek 'Smith, Turgot, and the Four Stages Theory', *History of Political Economy*, iii (1971) and in his introduction to *Turgot on Progress, Sociology and Economics* (1973).

[49] The stadial argument figures especially in Tract I 'Criminal Law' and Tract II 'Promises and Covenants'. Dugald Stewart considered that Kames's *Law Tracts* provided some 'excellent specimens' of philosophical history (Stewart, II.50).

[50] *History of Civil Society*, ed. Forbes, 216–17. See also the same author's *Principles of Moral and Political Science* (1792), Ch. 3, section ix. The thesis is a feature of Smith's lectures (for example, LJ (B) 206–11; Cannan, 157–61) and the TMS IV.i.i 'Of the Beauty which the Appearance of Utility bestows upon all the Productions of Art, and of the extensive Influence of this Species of Beauty'.

latter would emerge in a sequence which corresponded to the four socio-economic stages.[51]

The second application of the thesis is of course to be found in the link which Smith established between economic organization and the social structure, particularly with regard to the classes involved and the relations of power and dependence likely to exist betweeen them. As we have seen, the link which was established between the form of economy and the social structure was remarkably explicit, so much so indeed as to permit William Robertson to state the main propositions which were involved with great accuracy and economy. As he put it, in a passage which is an apt summary of Smith's general position: 'In every enquiry concerning the operations of men when united together in society, the first object of attention should be their mode of subsistence. According as that varies, their laws and policy must be different.'[52]

No doubt some of the writers who employed these propositions in the interpretation of the history of civil society could be accused of vulgar 'marxism' in the sense that they were occasionally guilty of employing the arguments in an unqualified form. But Smith did not commit any such 'error' and would appear to come close to Engels's general position in arguing that the economic finally asserts itself as the 'ultimate', rather than as the sole, determining factor.[53] This carefully qualified view can be seen in many ways and is nowhere more obvious than in Smith's use of the economic stages which are offered as general categories in terms of which the experience of different peoples can be interpreted rather than as templates to which that experience must be made to conform.

Finally, it is worth observing that while Smith did regard the processes of history as inherently complex, he did none the less associate these processes with certain definite trends. As we have seen, the growth of 'luxury and commerce' is represented as the inevitable outcome of normal human

[51] *Origins*, ed. Lehmann, 176, cf. 224.

[52] *Works*, v.111 and 128. For comment on the work of what is in effect a Scottish Historical School, see especially the pioneering article by Roy Pascal, 'Property and Society: The Scottish Historical School of the Eighteenth Century', *Modern Quarterly* (1938). This was followed by Gladys Bryson's *Man and Society: The Scottish Inquiry of the Eighteenth Century* (1945). Three notable contributions which followed are: R. L. Meek, 'The Scottish Contribution to Marxist Sociology' (1954), reprinted in *Economics and Ideology and Other Essays* (1967); Duncan Forbes, 'Scientific Whiggism: Adam Smith and John Millar', *Cambridge Journal*, vii (1953–4), and W. C. Lehmann *John Millar of Glasgow* (1960). For more recent comment on related subjects see L. Schneider, *The Scottish Moralists on Human Nature and Society* (1967), and J. R. Lindgren, *The Social Philosophy of Adam Smith* (1973).

[53] In a letter to J. Bloch, dated September 1890, Engels wrote that 'According to the materialist conception of history, the *ultimately* determining element in history is the production and reproduction of real life. More than this neither Marx nor I have ever asserted. Hence if somebody twists this into saying that the economic element is the *only* determining one, he transforms that proposition into a meaningless, abstract, senseless phrase' (*Marx-Engels, Selected Works* (1958), ii.488).

drives, and associated with the appearance of new sources of wealth together with a particular type of economy: an economy composed of interdependent sectors within and between which all goods and services command a price. These new forms of wealth allied to the higher degree of personal liberty appropriate to the new patterns of dependence also brought with them a new social and political order—a form of 'constitution'[54] which was often cited as an explanation for, and in defence of, the English Revolution Settlement. In this way Whig principles could, apparently, be put on a sound historical basis; a point which is neatly illustrated by Ramsay's comment on Lord Kames's abandonment of his early Jacobite leanings. Ramsay expressed no surprise that Kames should have finally concluded that the Revolution was 'absolutely necessary' after 'studying history and conversing with first rate people'—no doubt including Smith![55] Rather similar sentiments were expressed by John Millar when he remarked that 'When we examine historically the extent of the tory, and of the whig principle, it seems evident, that from the progress of arts and commerce, the former has been continually diminishing, and the latter gaining ground in the same proportion' (HV iv.304).[56] There is little doubt that Smith shared such opinions, or that he rejoiced in a situation where the personal liberty of the subject had been confirmed at the expense of the absolutist pretensions of kings. However, there are perhaps three points which should be made by way of qualification to this simple view.

First, while Smith did argue that the 'commercial' stage of socio-economic growth would have certain recognizable features, he did not suggest that it was incompatible with 'absolutist' government. For example both France and Spain could be regarded as 'developed' economies from an historical point of view, yet both were associated with monarchical systems which pretended to be absolutist.[57] Smith also made this point with respect to England, in arguing out that the first effect of a developing manufacturing sector had been to *increase* the power of her kings (for example, the Tudors) at the expense of the Lords;[58] the point being that

[54] 'Upon the manner in which any state is divided into the different orders and societies which compose it, and upon the particular distribution which has been made of their respective powers, privileges, and immunities, depends what is called the constitution of that particular state' (TMS VI.ii.2.8).

[55] Ramsay, *Scotland and Scotsmen*, ed. Allardyce, from the Ochtertyre MS. (1888), i.191.

[56] In LJ (A) v.124, Smith associated the 'bustling, spirited, active folks' with the Whig interest, and the 'calm contented folks of no great spirit and abundant fortunes' with the Tories. He also argues in this place that while the Tories favour the principle of authority, the Whig interest favoured that of utility in matters of government.

[57] Smith comments in WN I.xi.n.1 that though 'the feudal system has been abolished in Spain and Portugal, it has not been succeded by a much better'.

[58] This point is made in LJ (A) iv.159 and LJ (B) 59–60; Cannan, 42, where is it stated that as a result of the growth of manufactures etc. 'the power of the nobility was diminished, and that too before the House of Commons had established its authority, and thus the

the decline in the power of the Lords had taken place before the same underlying causes elevated the Commons to a superior degree of influence.[59]

Secondly, Smith argued that England was really a special case, and that she *alone* had escaped from absolutism.[60] To a great extent this was the reflection of her own natural economic advantages (WN III.iv.20), but Smith also emphasized other factors many of which were of an extra-economic type. For example, he argued that the solution to the Scottish problem (brought about by union), allied to Britain's situation as an island, had obviated the need for a standing army, and thus denied her kings an important instrument of oppression. He added that Elizabeth I had also contributed to weaken the position of her successors by selling off crown lands; a policy which was not unconnected with the fact that she had no direct heir. As Smith presents the case, it was the growing weakness of the Stuart kings (reflecting in part their own peculiarities of character), and the growing significance of the Commons, which had ultimately combined to produce that particular system of liberty which was now found in England.[61] In England alone, he emphasized, liberty is secured by 'an assembly of the representatives of the people, who claim the sole right of imposing taxes' (WN IV.vii.c.51).

Thirdly, it should be recalled that Smith rejoiced in the system of security which had been established in England 'and perfected by the revolution' (WN IV.v.b.43) on moral, political, and economic grounds. Indeed he quite clearly believed that the natural effort of every man to better his condition, allied to the security given him under the law had 'maintained the progress of England towards opulence and improvement in almost all former times, and . . . it is to be hoped, will do so in all future times' (WN II.iii.36). Yet Smith was very far from arguing that personal freedom, in the sense of security under the law, was incompatible with absolutism, and if he preferred the English model, he did not suggest that that experience represented the best of all possible worlds. In his *Early Draft* especially, Smith adverted to the 'oppressive inequality' of the modern economy,[62] and elsewhere drew attention to the fact that the House of Commons,

king became arbitrary. Under the House of Tudor the government was quite arbitrary, the nobility were ruined, and the boroughs lost their power.'

[59] Smith considers the rise of the House of Commons in LJ (A) iv.148ff., LJ (B) 58–9; Cannan, 40–1.

[60] Smith emphasized England's position as a special case at some length. See especially LJ (A) iv.167 where it is stated that 'In England alone a different government has been established from the naturall course of things. The situation and circumstances of England have been altogether different.' Cf. Millar, HV iv.102–4 and Forbes, op. cit., 23.

[61] The same arguments are considered in LJ (A) v.1–16 where Smith also includes a review of the constitutional guarantees of English liberties. Similar arguments are stated in LJ (B) 61–4; Cannan 43–6, although at rather less length.

[62] The *Early Draft* opens chapter 2 with a long statement concerning the problem of inequality in the modern state.

whose power provided the foundation and protection of the liberty of the subject, could easily become a clearing house for those sectional interests on which that power was collectively based (WN I.xi.p.10). Smith was also well aware of the problem of corruption in politics and of the fact that the institutions of British Government were markedly unrepresentative. 'It is in Great Britain alone that any consent of the people is required and God knows it is but a very figurative metaphoricall consent which is given here. And in Scotland much more so than in England, as but a very few have a vote for a member of Parliament who give this metaphoricall consent' (LJ(A) v.134).

Yet if Smith did notice many of the defects of modern society, and some of the problems which were to arise in the future, the general tenor of his argument must be said to be broadly optimistic with regard to the possibilities of economic and political development. In this respect his position is perhaps adequately summarized in the remarks of his pupil, Millar, who wrote that when we contemplate the 'crowds of people . . . daily rising from the lower ranks . . . how habits of industry have banished idleness . . . and have put it in the power of almost every individual to earn a comfortable subsistence', then 'We cannot entertain a doubt of their power to propagate corresponding sentiments of personal independence, and to instill higher notions of general liberty' (HV iv.124). The point was not lost on the French revolutionary, Barnave, who, writing quite independently of Smith and his contemporaries, reached the conclusion that:

As soon as the arts and commerce succeed in penetrating the life of the society, and of opening up a new source of wealth for the labouring class, a revolution is prepared in political laws; a new distribution of wealth produces a new distribution of power. Just as the possession of land created aristocracy, so industrial property gives rise to the power of the people. It acquires liberty, it grows in numbers, it begins to influence affairs.[63]

[63] Quoted in Laski, *The Rise of European Liberalism* (1930), 232. The socio-economic content of Steuart's *Principles* prompted the editor of the French translation (1789) to remark that of the advantages to be derived from reading the book: 'Le premier sera de convaincre, sans doute, que le révolution qui s'opere sous nos yeux était dans l'ordre des choses nécessaires' (Steuart, op. cit. 24n).

IX

Sceptical Whiggism, Commerce, and Liberty

DUNCAN FORBES*

It has been usual, when discussing the politics of Smith and Hume, to describe one as Whig and the other Tory, as though this needed no further argument.[1] One is expected to nod assent to a use of terms which, whatever else it may mean, is presumably designed to convey some considerable contrast, something more than a nuance or question of degree. It may seem pedantic to ask what is meant precisely; in the smoke-filled rooms of politics everyone 'knows'. But this is hardly the right atmosphere in which to consider seriously the politics of two such absolutely dedicated 'philosophers' as Smith and Hume, and when their political views are closely examined and taken down to their roots, especially Hume's alleged Toryism, the gap between them narrows interestingly until one begins to wonder not only whether the labels serve any useful purpose at all in this context, but even whether they may not be positively harmful. To persist in thinking of the two men in this way is to deprive oneself of the illumination and understanding of Smith's politics—direct evidence of which is somewhat scanty anyway—that can be got by considering them as in essence Humean, and seeing both men not as though they were on different sides of some political valley, which raises the awkward question which one?, but as flying high above all political valleys whatever, observing everything but doing nothing, as Smith said was the task of the philosopher (LJ (B) 217; Cannan, 167–8; WN I.i.9).[2]

Halévy refused to think of Smith as a Whig, and says that if what Rae asserts is true, that Smith remained throughout his life a faithful Whig of the Rockingham party, he must have been, 'to use one of Hume's expressions . . . the most sceptical of the Whigs'.[3] Halévy proceeds to give a brief list of Smith's sceptical Whiggisms, and concludes that in general Adam Smith was a sceptic in political affairs, 'above all'. For Halévy, Smith was a sceptical Whig because he was a political sceptic altogether, not interested

* Fellow of Clare College, Cambridge.

[1] e.g. L. Robbins: 'They varied greatly in political outlook: Hume was a Tory; Smith, Senior and Malthus were Whigs . . .' *The Theory of Economic Policy in English Classical Political Economy* (1953), 3.

[2] I have not made use of the forthcoming second and fuller version of the *Lectures on Police etc.* It will be interesting to see how much this new version differs from that published by Cannan.

[3] E. Halévy, *The Growth of Philosophic Radicalism* (1934), 141.

in a science of politics, or the political bearing of his economic doctrines. This view of Smith is a section of the great rift valley that runs all through Halévy's book, between 'rationalism' and naturalism', Smith's economics belonging to the former, his politics to the latter. What truth there is in describing Smith as a political sceptic will, it is hoped, appear in due course, but Halévy did not get anywhere near the heart of the matter. Ignoring Smith's lifelong concern to establish the 'science of politics' on a proper basis, he made the fatal mistake of equating sceptical Whiggism with political scepticism generally, so that Smith emerges from Halévy's consulting-room as neither a Whig nor a political scientist in any real sense. In fact, Smith, like Hume, was a 'sceptical' Whig because he was a political scientist, or 'philosopher' in politics.

Hume was called a Tory, or worse, because he was a sceptical Whig, and in a simple black-and-white world, what else could a sceptical Whig be? Smith did not publish anything bearing so directly on the explosive political or party-political topics of the day as Hume did in some of his *Essays* and parts of his *History*. Had he done so, the same cry might have been raised and Smith might now be numbered among the Tories. Hume's 'scepticism' was the attitude of the scientist, but how could a good orthodox Whig, say Horace Walpole, seeing the resulting slaughter of holy cows and the questioning of the most indubitable truths, such as the justness of the Revolution, the wickedness of the Stuart kings, the enormous and unbridgeable gulf between English freedom and French slavery, be expected to appreciate the difference between downright perverse scepticism, playing to the gallery, at best, and the scepticism of the philosopher or scientist, applying the experimental method fearlessly to moral subjects and in duty bound ignoring the dangers and the accusation of iconoclasm? Applying 'experimental' philosophy to morals, observing political phenomena with the cool detachment and neutrality of the impartial spectator, was bound to lead to the destruction of many of the cherished idols of what one may perhaps be allowed to call, for short, 'vulgar Whiggism': a 'Whiggism' which does not exclude commonwealthmen, republicans or democratic radicals or even Tories, and which cuts deeper than any distinction between 'court' and 'country', and is also something more than the merest chauvinism and Francophobia. This may lack precision, but Hume's politics are more deeply penetrated and properly understood by the use of the dichotomy of 'scientific' or 'sceptical' and 'vulgar' Whiggism than that of Whig and Tory, and it has the advantage of bypassing the warnings and counter-warnings of the historians of eighteenth century British politics as to the proper use of the latter. And it is suggested that this might be a fruitful approach also to the politics of Adam Smith.[4]

[4] In his lectures on rhetoric at Glasgow, Smith asked why Swift was so generally underestimated as a writer. And the first reason he suggested was that although Swift was

The first idol to be destroyed was what Hume called the 'fashionable system' of political obligation: the contract theory of government. In his lectures on jurisprudence at Glasgow, Smith simply took over Hume's arguments (LJ (B) 15–18; Cannan, 11–13), and the young reporter wrote them down, blow by blow, when he could have saved himself trouble by making a note like 'see Hume's *Essay on the Original Contract*'. At this crucial juncture, the two thinkers are in wholehearted agreement and for the same reasons: the contract theory, besides being faulty in reasoning, and not empirically grounded, was parochial, though both men were wrong in fact to regard it as a doctrine 'peculiar to Great Britain' (LJ (B) 15; Cannan, 11). (What they should have said, and perhaps what they really meant, was that the doctrine was parochial as used by Locke and others, in so far as it led to the denial of absolute monarchy as a legitimate form of government.)

The political philosophy which Hume built on the ruins of the contract theory and Locke's theory of consent had one rather curious feature: it could not be used to justify the Revolution at the time it occurred, and Hume's attempt to do this in Book III of the *Treatise of Human Nature* is inconsistent with his main line of reasoning; no such attempt is made in the essay on the Protestant Succession, which was so sceptical that it had to be held back, in Hume's own interests, for three years. In fact it was in connection with this essay that Hume called himself a sceptical Whig. As against this, Smith in his lectures on jurisprudence concludes the section dealing with the limits of sovereign authority and the right of resistance by saying that James II 'was with all justice and equity in the world opposed and rejected', on account of his 'encroachments on the body politic' (LJ (B) 98–9; Cannan, 72). The reporter presumably got this right, but the whole section is rather breathless and garbled, an extraordinary but rather fascinating mixture of history, theoretical history, law, political theory, natural law, and Smith's own theory of sympathy (e.g. James turned to the army but found that they did not sympathize with him, and he in return 'told them that he would never any more bring down his sentiments to theirs ...'). One may suspect that Smith was at times talking over the heads of his audience, trying out ideas of his own on his way to a 'philosophical' account and justification of 1688 based on the principles of human nature: a lecturer's 'green plums', as Professor Brogan once described them, in the midst of the accepted historical and legal commonplaces which included something similar to the argument Hume used, inconsistently, in the *Treatise* in terms of the illegal encroachment by one part of the government on another in a regular, mixed monarchy. The whole question is a large and complicated one; there is, for instance, the problem of the

no friend to tyranny, religious or civil, he 'never has such warm exclamations for civil or religious liberty as are now generally in fashion' (LRBL 8.5; Lothian, 37).

rights and wrongs of excluding James II's innocent heirs—Hume thought the purely legal aspect of this questionable: in the *Treatise* he presents a psychological explanation as justification. Smith seems to have been satisfied that the law of forfeiture of a private estate by the heirs applied also to the Crown. Without going into further learned detail and conjecture, perhaps one can say that Smith's account of the Revolution would not have been wholly 'fashionable',[5] but what we have, such as it is, is less sceptical than Hume's. But one is here confronted with the difficulty that dogs any attempt to compare the political science of Adam Smith with that of Hume, or Montesquieu, or anyone else: we do not have a version of it published by Smith himself, only oblique references and hints in other works, mostly *The Wealth of Nations*, and the lecture notes edited by Cannan, and these, suggestive as they are, often give one the merest outline, and are full of gaps and obvious slips. The nature of the evidence must not be forgotten when one tries to discover to what extent Smith agreed with Hume's account of the British Constitution and British liberty.

Whereas vulgar Whiggism gloried in the unique perfection of the English constitution, Hume's science of politics revealed the 'unavoidable disadvantages' and dangers in the institutions necessary to sustain a degree of liberty such as the world had never seen: for example a system of management of the House of Commons, described and attacked by the opposition as 'corruption' and 'dependence'; 'court' and 'country' parties, at a time when parties were generally regarded as a pathological symptom; and an absence of discretionary powers in the executive greater than in any other form of government, monarchical or republican. Scientific or sceptical Whiggism in fact involved an attitude of clinical detachment towards British liberty and the 'matchless' constitution which Hume himself could not always sustain. No such elaborate and detailed account of the pros and cons of the British government as can be gathered together from Hume's writings is to be found in Adam Smith. In the lectures on jurisprudence (11) there is, as Cannan pointed out in a footnote, an echo of Hume's account of the psychological origin of the two parties in a mixed government—'the factions formed some time ago, under the names of Whig and Tory' were influenced by the principles of utility and authority respectively. Smith's account suggests that some such parties are to be expected in such a government. Elsewhere he says or implies that parties were a necessary feature of all 'free governments',[6] but that is too general

[5] For example, he does not say that it was wrong to try to change the religion of the country. He stresses the difficulty of such an undertaking. 'It is necessary before a religion be changed that the opinion of the people be changed, as was done by Luther, Calvin, John Knox . . .' This is rather detached and cool.

[6] For example LJ (B) 113; Cannan, 81: when men have no trust nor dependence on each other, they cannot form into parties, and therefore the government must always be arbitrary, as in Turkey.

to be specifically Humean, and of course there is nothing specifically Humean or even 'philosophical' about any of his remarks which reveal a dislike of parties or 'factions' as such. (The same could be said of those remarks that show his distrust of the people's judgement, or anti-democratic sentiment generally—e.g. WN IV.v.b.40.)

In *The Wealth of Nations*, there are two references to the 'management' of Parliament, which suggest that Smith took Hume's point that this was a necessary feature of the British mixed government. The Stuart kings tried violence sometimes, without success. 'The parliament of England is now managed in another manner . . .' (WN V.i.g.19). What this means is made clear elsewhere. It was a long time, Smith writes, before the parliament of England could be brought under a system of management. It was only by distributing among the particular members of parliament a great part either of the offices, or of the disposal of the offices arising from the civil and military establishment (WN IV.vii.c.69). On the other hand, there is an implied criticism of this system in Smith's remark that the legislative assemblies of the English colonies in America, though not always a very equal representation of the people, are more representative than the House of Commons, because the executive power has neither the means nor the need to 'corrupt' them (WN IV.vii.c.51).

On the question of discretionary powers, Smith openly disagreed with Hume. In his attitude to standing armies, Hume had always shown himself as a man of 'republican principles', to use Smith's phrase, and in the last edition of his *History*, in the Appendix to the reign of James I, he had added a remark to the effect that it seemed 'a necessary, though perhaps a melancholy truth, that in every government, the magistrate must either possess a large revenue and a military force, or enjoy some discretionary powers, in order to execute the laws and support his own authority'. Smith countered by arguing that where you had a well-regulated standing army, a degree of liberty approaching licentiousness could be tolerated, and the public safety did not require that the sovereign should be entrusted with any discretionary power 'for suppressing even the impertinent wantonness of this licentious liberty' (WN V.i.a.41). Standing armies were a defence of liberty and not necessarily a menace to it, provided they were properly constituted and not 'overgrown',[7] and Hume's 'melancholy truth' was a chimera. Halévy regarded this as an outstanding example of Smith's sceptical Whiggism; if one agrees, then Hume is here the less sceptical Whig, the more republican of the two thinkers. But Smith was not opposed to militias: the martial spirit of the people 'would diminish very much the dangers to liberty, whether real or imaginary, which are commonly apprehended from a standing army' (WN V.i.f.59)—imagined dangers were a political reality to be reckoned with and catered for.

[7] An 'overgrown standing army' is 'formidable to the government' (WN IV.ii.43.).

It was the lack of discretionary powers in the British government that caused Hume to say, at the time of the popular Wilkite disturbances, that the English had too much liberty. Given his theory of standing armies, Smith presumably did not agree. But in the lectures on jurisprudence he is reported as saying that 'nothing is more difficult than perfectly to secure liberty'; in this country no magistrate has an arbitrary power of imprisonment, in spite of the fact that it is 'reasonable' that he should have, where there is ground of suspicion, even if an innocent man may suffer a little by it (LJ (B) 191; Cannan, 144). A faintly heard harmony, perhaps, which seems to sound a bit louder and in a different key in another passage, singled out by Halévy, in which Smith contrasts the fuss over General Warrants with the resigned acceptance of the law of settlements, which in Halévy's words, 'paralysed the world of labour', as though Smith was only or predominantly interested in the economic paralysis, and not at all in the cruel oppression felt in some part of his life by nearly every poor man over forty in England, as a result of such 'an evident violation of natural liberty and justice'. But though the common people of England are so jealous of their liberty, they, like the common people of most other countries, never rightly understand wherein it consists (WN I.x.c.59), and with this remark we begin to get nearer to the heart of the matter. Because, as Dugald Stewart pointed out in his 'Account of the Life and Writings of Adam Smith', although the progress of political science has so far been inconsiderable, it has been sufficient to show that the happiness of mankind depends, not on the share which the people possess, directly or indirectly, in the enactment of laws, but on the equity and expediency of the laws that are enacted (Stewart, IV.4). This is wholly in the tradition and spirit of the political science of Hume and Smith: what matters, and the true end of government, is liberty, but liberty in the sense of the Civilians and Grotius, Pufendorf, and the authoritative exponents of natural law: the personal liberty and security of individuals guaranteed by law, equivalent to justice, peace, order, the protection of property, the sanctity of contracts. In so far as 'liberty' is for Hume the object of government, it means this; any other, more political, sort of liberty being a means to this end. It is what Hume called 'Justice', in a political philosophy which, unlike that of Locke and vulgar Whiggism, did not result in the parochial absurdity of declaring that absolute monarchy could not be a proper form of government. Hume expressly declared that the absolute monarchies of Europe also, for all practical purposes, realized the ends for which government was instituted; they too were a 'government of laws, not men'; to pretend otherwise, to talk of tyranny and slavery in this context, as vulgar Whiggism did, was so much 'high political rant'. (See the essays on *Civil Liberty*, and *The Rise and Progress of the Arts and Sciences*.) There is implied in this some sort of distinction, which Hume does not make verbally, between 'civil' and 'political' liberty, since it is possible in what Hume calls the 'civilized' absolute monarchies, to have the former without the latter, whereas presumably behind vulgar Whiggism was the unquestioned assumption that without political liberty civil liberty was so insecure as to be virtually non-existent—hence the talk of 'slavery'. The gravitational pull of this attitude was so powerful that even Hume could talk like a vulgar Whig, and possibly even think like one, at times. After all, there is the quotation from Tacitus on the title-page of the *Treatise*, and Hume, glorying in the name of North Briton, could sing the praises of the Hanoverian regime as loudly as anyone. In fact the tension between sceptical and vulgar Whiggism is found in the writings of both Hume and Smith, and is needed sometimes as an aid to interpretation.

A liberty which was not Anglocentric but which applied to all civilized Europe was also the main axis of the political thought of Montesquieu, who was not, in spite of much popular belief to the contrary, a vulgar Whig. Vulgar Whiggism naturally seized on anything in *De l'esprit des lois* which could, taken out of context, be used to show that for this great writer the British Constitution was a light shining in the darkness of absolutism and a model for all governments, thereby distorting the whole trend and spirit of Montesquieu's political science. For Montesquieu, as for Hume, the 'singularity' of the mixed government of Britain was something to arouse the philosopher's curiosity rather than an object of admiration. For Montesquieu, the paradox of this constitution was that in taking liberty as its direct object, it had destroyed those intermediary powers, mainly of the nobility, which were the firmest and most natural support of liberty. The result was an extreme liberty (and for Montesquieu extremes are always to be avoided), maintained only by the famous separation of powers, which went along with a harsh climate and an equally harsh, anti-social, unpolished national character, or style of life. In France a very much more sociable and civilized people enjoyed—or should have enjoyed, because of course Montesquieu's point was that it was threatened—a more moderate and for that reason sounder liberty, which was not the immediate object of the constitution, but the by-product of 'manners' and other institutions, especially the all-important division of the executive and judicial powers. This is not the place to unpack all the evidence of Montesquieu's sceptical as opposed to vulgar Whiggism. What needs to be noted is that for Montesquieu, as for Hume, 'political liberty' is opposed to the 'natural liberty' of the 'state of nature', hypothetical, or actual in primitive conditions, and means essentially the liberty and security of the individual guaranteed by regular government and the rule of law, so that although France is not a 'free state' (*état libre*), the citizens of France nevertheless enjoy 'political' and 'civil' liberty. It is possible therefore to have 'political liberty' in a state that is not free, which is not a contradiction in terms provided one remembers what Montesquieu means by 'political liberty', and that the essential mark of a 'free state' is the separation of the legislative and executive powers of government. As political liberty consists in security, or in the belief that one has security, the crucial test of liberty is the state of the law, especially the criminal law, so that it is possible to be free in a state that is not a 'free state', and also unfree in a 'free state'. As an example of the latter, Montesquieu refers to the legal powers of a father in the Roman republic and the cruelty of the laws against debtors at Athens and Rome. He might have mentioned the press-gang in England, as Hume did. 'Political liberty' is found in all moderate states, and only in *états modérés*, but this means states that are not despotically governed, i.e. purely arbitrarily and without law, and therefore includes the French monarchy.

Smith presumably had a good working knowledge of *De l'esprit des lois*. In fact his science of politics was described by Millar as combining Grotius and Montesquieu. The projected science was never completed, but there is enough to show that it was on the same wavelength as that which has just been briefly sketched. The ground of this science was natural jurisprudence; the crucial thing in any government was the state of the law; the science of politics was concerned first and foremost with the fundamental principles of all law. As Dugald Stewart, describing Smith's science of politics, said: the only infallible criterion of the excellence of any constitution is to be found in the detail of its municipal code (Stewart, IV.5). In general, one can say that Smith's conception of the end of government is the same as Hume's: justice, the protection of property from the 'injustice' of those who would invade it (WN V.i.b.2 LJ (B) 210; Cannan, 160), the liberty and security of the individual under the rule of law. In so far as Smith was interested in a more political sort of freedom than that of the 'natural system of liberty', it was mainly freedom in the sense of law and order; 'all the liberty and security which law can give' (WN III.iii.19), 'order and good government, and along with them the liberty and security of individuals' (WN III.iv.4), the regular and impartial administration of justice securing freedom from that continual fear of the violence of their superiors, which in feudal Europe and in most of the governments of Asia caused men to bury their treasure (WN II.i.31), and from that 'dependency' of which Smith said, echoing Rousseau, that 'Nothing tends so much to corrupt mankind' (LJ (B) 204; Cannan, 155), (but unlike Rousseau, he taught that this 'dependency' was destroyed by the progress of civilization which brings with it freedom of which the badge is taxation, denoting that a man is subject to government, indeed, but cannot himself be the property of a master (WN V.ii.g.11)); freedom 'in our present sense of the word' (III.iii.5)—which incidentally reveals the same sensitiveness to historical relativism that is so striking in Smith's essay on the 'History of Astronomy'—and the context is the contrast with what Smith called elsewhere 'the ancient state of Europe before the establishment of arts and manufactures' (WN V.i.g.22), 'the barbarous times of feudal anarchy' (WN V.ii.k.20), when the regular administration of justice, abandoned by the king to the great lords, was interrupted and a scene of raging violence and disorder ensued in which no sovereign in Europe was able to protect the weaker part of his subjects from the oppression of the great lords (WN III.iv.9), a contrast still reflected in the difference between London and Paris, a much more disorderly city owing to the crowds of idle and demoralized dependents, and even Glasgow and Edinburgh (LJ (B) 204; Cannan, 155). Another contrast lies behind this notion of freedom with its emphasis on the security and protection provided by law and order against the violence of feudal superiors: that between Scotland, where the middling and inferior ranks of people had only been delivered by the Union from an aristocracy which had always oppressed them (WN V.iii.89) and an always 'freer' and more democratic England, for the government of England 'all along favoured democracy, and that of Scotland aristocracy' (LJ (B) 171; Cannan, 126), 'freer' that is, from the shackles of feudalism and feudal law.

The impetus of his dislike of hereditary aristocracy in general, and the Scottish nobility in particular, with its 'unnatural' law of primogeniture, once functional, now a harmful historical survival, and its large unimproved, entailed estates, contrasted with the freedom which England has almost uninterruptedly enjoyed (LJ (B) 242; Cannan, 188), could carry Smith into the sort of vulgar Whiggism which believed in a primeval or Saxon English liberty, lost and restored.

Hume had paid lip-service to the freedom-loving Germans of Whig and republican myth, but *qua* scientist he knew that this was not freedom in our present sense of the word, because that involved the established law and regular government that was the product of advancing civilization. Smith, in whose science of politics the progress of society was of considerable importance, is reported as explaining in his lectures how liberty was 'restored' after the Tudor despotism (LJ (B), 61; Cannan, 43) in spite of Hume's *History*, which must have been fresh in his mind, and of whose argument he must have had as good a grasp as anyone (not that that is saying very much). And in *The Wealth of Nations*, after demonstrating how the progress of wealth and prosperity has on the long view been continuous in England from the earliest times, Smith says that the effort of every man to better his own condition, 'protected by law and allowed by liberty to exert itself in the manner that is most advantageous . . . has maintained the progress of England towards opulence and improvement in almost all former times' (WN II.iii.36). The qualifying 'almost' barely covers the nakedness of this piece of 'vulgar Whig' rhetoric, because although there is nothing in Smith's teaching to prevent the effort and the improvement being there in the absence of law and liberty, though hindered and slower, in fact law and liberty are modern, not ancient, only 'perfected' by the Revolution (WN IV.v.b.43), as the reader who turns to Smith's famous account of the growth of commerce and liberty in Europe quickly discovers. Independence began earlier in the towns than in the country, but the inhabitants of both were for long at the mercy of the violence of great lords, and there was certainly no pristine Saxon 'liberty' in the conditions prevailing. Nor can Smith be making a distinction between freedom 'in the present sense of the word' and the freedom enjoyed by the barons—English liberty being ancient and continuing in a more philosophical sense, as seen in Millar—because the latter was not conducive to economic progress, which began—at least the increase of Europe's manufactures and agriculture began—with the fall of the feudal system.

And at first glance the dead hand of vulgar Whiggism appears to be present when we find Smith, in *The Wealth of Nations*, describing the government of the absolute monarchies as 'despotic'. Hume had done it, but in later editions of his essays he had corrected himself, writing 'absolute government' for 'despotism'. Smith continued to use 'depotism' in this context. So here we seem to have something more than a slip of the pen caused by the tyranny of old usage and the gravitational attraction of vulgar Whiggism. Montesquieu, and other French writers before him, Bossuet, for example, had distinguished between absolute monarchy, a government which respected rights and was exercised according to the laws, and despotism, or arbitrary government, which did not;[8] a crucial distinction in Montesquieu's tripartite classification of the forms of government: republic, including democracy and aristocracy, monarchy, despotism. His description of despotism was attacked, by Voltaire for example, for not being empirical, for being a caricature of the actual governments of Turkey and Asia; though in fact Montesquieu's account of depotism belonged as much to political propaganda and rhetoric as to descriptive science and was designed accordingly. In any case, Smith, when he made his classification of the types of government at the beginning of his Glasgow lectures, did not adopt it, though he must have been very conscious of Montesquieu's scheme, so striking and original in its rejection of the old classical formula. It looks as though Smith was trying to be more scientific according to his own notion of what constituted a good scientific system: viz. an explanation, which satisfied the imagination, in Hume's use of the word, of the largest number and variety of phenomena by the fewest and simplest and most familiar principles, which in moral science would be psychological principles of human nature.[9] Accordingly Smith,

[8] E. Carcassonne, *Montesquieu et le probleme de la constitution française au XVIIIe siècle*, (1927) 3.

[9] An excellent account of Smith's scientific method is given by T. D. Campbell, *Adam Smith's Science of Morals* (1971).

inspired by Hume's two psychological types, the republican lovers of liberty and the monarchical lovers of peace and order, reduced all the various kinds of government to two basic ones: monarchy and republic, derived from the two principles of human nature, 'authority' and 'utility' respectively, with the British government a mixture of the two (LJ (B), 12–15; Cannan, 9–11). This is both simpler and truer to experience than Montesquieu's scheme. Depotism in Smith's science of politics, no longer a particular form of government, means arbitrary rule, and is a question of degree; Montesquieu's despotism, in so far as it is not simply a symbol or idea of negation, is included under monarchy. In the *Lectures*, Smith does not describe the governments of Asia as despotisms, but as 'military monarchies' (in *The Wealth of Nations* they are not given any particular definitive term), but they are distinguished from the military monarchies of the Roman Empire and Cromwell, which is 'monarchy or something like it' (LJ (B) 37; Cannan, 26) in so far as in the latter there is the strictest admininstration of justice according to settled laws, whereas in the military monarchies of the East, life and fortune are altogether precarious, depending on the caprice of the lowest magistrate (LJ (B) 46; Cannan, 31–2).[10] We have what in *The Wealth of Nations* Smith calls a 'gradation of despotism' (V.i.g.19). But this is a gradation which includes France, and it is not simply a question of the 'mildness' or otherwise of the government, because the context is concerned with the personal liberty and rights of a class of people, the clergy, who are respected 'even in the most despotic governments', not only the 'gentle and mild' government of Paris, but 'every gradation of despotism', even the 'violent and furious' government of Constantinople. This looks as though 'despotic' government begins on the other side of the Channel, in the style of vulgar Whiggism.

But at least there is a 'gradation of despotism', and the French government, 'though arbitrary and violent in comparison with that of Great Britain, is legal and free in comparison with those of Spain and Portugal' (WN IV.vii.c.52). France, in spite of its bad taxation system, 'is certainly the great empire in Europe which, after that of Great Britain, enjoys the mildest and most indulgent government' (WN V.ii.k.78). But what Smith says about standing armies would apply to France, though he does not actually say so, and gives Caesar and Cromwell as his examples: that they are a danger to liberty where the military force is not placed under

[10] In his classification and history of governments in the *Lectures*, there is no mention of France or any of the absolute monarchies of modern Europe. In the *Lectures on Rhetoric* given at Glasgow at about the same time (1762–3), Smith is reported as saying that 'the French monarchy is in much the same condition as the Romans under Trajan . . .' As there was great tranquillity and security, with the most advanced state of luxury and refinement of manners, and no political activity, people 'with nothing to engage them in the hurry of life' naturally turned their attention 'to the motions of the human mind'. The context is the sort of history written by Tacitus (LRBL 20.2, Lothian, 108).

command of those who have the greatest interest in the support of the civil authority, because they themselves have the greatest share of that authority (WN V.i.a.41). And the French *parlements* are not properly 'managed', because 'such is the natural insolence of man', that if a government can use force and violence, the worst and most dangerous instruments of government, it will (WN V.i.g.19). But what above all makes the French government 'despotic' is the delegated power and authority of the Intendants (cf. WN V.ii.j.7), because although the sovereign in an absolute government 'can never have either interest or inclination to pervert the order of justice, or to oppress the great body of the people' (WN IV.vii.b.52), because it is in his own interest to ensure their prosperity (WN V.ii.k.73), the delegated discretionary powers of his officers are sure to be oppressive. 'Under all absolute governments there is more liberty in the capital than in any other part of the country' (WN IV.vii.b.52). That is why the colonies belonging to absolute monarchies are oppressively governed. In France, under the administration of the Intendants, the Corvée is 'one of the principal instruments of tyranny' (WN v.i.d.19), and in this context of the powers of the Intendants, Smith says, discussing the upkeep of roads, that 'in the progress of despotism, the authority of the executive power gradually absorbs that of every other power in the state . . .' (WN V.i.d.16), which was the teaching of *De l'esprit des lois* as a work of political propaganda for home consumption.

In *The Wealth of Nations*, the word 'civilized' is used to mean sometimes the degree of economic improvement, sometimes that, with in addition, the degree of 'liberty'. It is possible to have a considerable degree of wealth and improvement without a corresponding degree of liberty, but not vice versa. (The word 'civilized' is never used in connection with India and China, although these countries are said to be almost as economically advanced as the nations of Europe, and even wealthier than some.) Thus France, which, with a better soil and climate (WN V.ii.k.78) is 'not altogether so prosperous' as Britain[11] is less civilized in both senses of the word.

Nor does one get the impression in Smith that one gets in Hume, that France, though 'perhaps' less prosperous economically, is catching Britain up in political civilization. Smith is gloomier, for example, about the possibility of tax reform. (WN V.ii.k.77; cf. the penultimate paragraph of Hume's essay on *Civil Liberty*.) Spain, Portugal, and Poland are relatively uncivilized. Poland, 'where the feudal system still continues to take place', is 'as beggarly a country as it was before the discovery of America'; in Portugal and Spain, 'after Poland, the two most beggarly countries in Europe', the feudal system has been abolished, but 'it has not been succeeded by a much better' (WN I.xi.m.1), and bad economic policy is not

[11] Inferior to England in opulence and improvement 'perhaps' (WN I.i.4).

'counterbalanced by the general liberty and security of the people' (WN IV.v.b.45). Owing to the irregular and partial administration of justice, industry is neither free nor secure in those violent and arbitrary governments (WN IV.vii.b.6,53). In fact, one gets the impression that Smith would have applied to these governments what T. H. Green said of the Russian empire: that it is only by courtesy that it is counted among the civilized states at all.[12]

One might be tempted to say that these examples show that Smith was less of a 'sceptical' Whig than Hume. But this may largely be due to the fact that there is more descriptive detail in Smith's account of what Hume called the 'civilized monarchies'. Hume's is, as usual, brief and elliptical; he does not consider Poland, Spain, and Portugal in this context. It seems to be France that he has in his sights, and even so his scientific sceptical Whiggism does not deny the very considerable superiority of the English constitution, with all its dangers and disadvantages, to any other; vulgar and sceptical Whiggism had this much in common. Hume said himself in the essay on *Civil Liberty*, that the absolute monarchies were 'still much inferior'. (In the edition of 1770, 'much' was withdrawn.) Smith's more elaborate variations on this theme do not necessarily represent any radical disagreement. The point Hume was making aginst Locke and vulgar Whiggism was the parochial absurdity of a theory of political obligation which excluded the civilized, absolute monarchies of modern Europe, especially France; against this he insisted that the purpose of government was for practical purposes realized in all the civilized states, free or absolute. Smith took the point and accepted this view of the 'civilized monarchies'.[13] They had a high degree of liberty, as well as all the other marks of a civilized society: an established order of ranks, a highly developed division of labour, opulence, and so on.

Thus, in the chapter on public debts in *The Wealth of Nations*, Smith explains how the same cause, the progress of society, which makes it necessary for governments to borrow money, produces an ability and inclination in subjects to lend, because commerce and manufactures 'can seldom flourish in any state in which there is not a certain degree of confidence in the justice of government" (WN V.iii.7). The same confidence which disposes great merchants and manufacturers to trust their property to the protection of government disposes them to lend, where there is 'universal confidence in the justice of the state'. Since 'all the great nations of Europe' have enormous national debts, it must follow that this confidence in the regular administration of justice must apply to them all. Again, the

[12] Smith says of Russia, that it enjoys a 'degree of order and peace' which is due to a well-regulated standing army (WN V.i.a.40). It is not quite clear where Russia stands in Smith's league of civilized nations.

[13] WN V.ii.a.15,16. The 'civilized' are contrasted with the 'ancient monarchies of Europe'.

separation of powers which Smith, like Montesquieu, considers crucial is the separation of the judicial from the executive power.[14] On this depends the impartial administration of justice, and on that 'depends the liberty of every individual, the sense which he has of his own security . . .' This is the spontaneous result of the progress of society and applies to 'the European monarchies'' (WN V.i.b.24,25). The French *parlements* may not be very convenient courts of justice, and are inferior to 'the present admirable constitution of the courts of justice in England', but they have never been accused, and not even been suspected of corruption (WN V.i. b.21).[15] Further, arguing that primogeniture and entails have no longer the function they had in the disorderly times when land was considered the means not of subsistence merely but of power and protection, Smith says: 'in the present state of Europe, the proprietor of a single acre of land is as perfectly secure of his possession as the proprietor of a hundred thousand' (WN III.ii.4). In 'the present state of Europe . . . small as well as great estates derive their security from the laws of their country' (III.ii.6).

These references show that one can have freedom 'in the present sense of the word', the freedom which is the end of government as such and the ground of political obligation, in a government which is not a 'free government'. (As has been seen, there is more 'liberty' at the centre than at the circumferences of absolute monarchies.) And 'despotic government' cannot mean, in *The Wealth of Nations*, what it is said to mean in the *Lectures*: in 'despotic' as opposed to 'free' governments, 'the will of the magistrate is law' (LJ (B) 191; Cannan, 144). What we must have here is either loose talking, loose reporting, or a change of opinion, vulgar Whiggism being involved in all three possibilities.[16] What is needed to save the phenomena, as well as Smith's use of 'despotic' in *The Wealth of Nations*, is a gradation of despotism (and freedom) which applies to any government whatever: all governments, including the freest, having an element of arbitrary authority, and none, including the most despotic, being wholly arbitrary. This tallies with Smith's account of the facts,[17] as well as with the point

[14] 'This is the great advantage which modern times have over ancient, and the foundation of that greater security which we now enjoy, both with regard to liberty, property and life' (LRBL 28.12; Lothian, 170).

[15] The sentences of the judges in England are greatly more equitable than those of the Parlement of Paris or other Courts which are severed from censure by their number. LRBL 28.10, Lothian, 169.

[16] In the *Lectures*, 'absolute', meaning arbitrary and tyrannical, is used for the Tudor monarchy, but that was not 'civilized'. (LJ (B) 60–61; Cannan, 42–3). But Smith is also reported as saying that the right of resistance is 'more frequently exerted in absolute monarchies than in any other . . . In Turkey eight or ten years seldom pass without a change of government' (LJ (B) 59–61; Cannan, 69). 'Absolute monarchies' here is loose language. Smith should have said, perhaps did say, 'Eastern military monarchies', or 'some absolute monarchies'.

[17] e.g. 'even in Britain it is but a very figurative consent that we have (to taxation), for the number of voters is nothing to that of the people' (LJ (B) 94; Cannan, 69).

made by Hume in the essay on the *Origin of Government* written in 1774, towards the end of which he asks in effect: what, if all governments are more or less absolute, more or less free, is commonly meant by a 'free government', and answers that it is one in which there is a partition of power between bodies whose united authority is greater than that of any monarch, but who rule by known equal laws, which is roughly Montesquieu's definition of an *état libre*.

Smith uses terms like 'free governments', 'free countries', a 'free people', 'every system of free government', without offering definitions. A 'free government' seems to be one in which the whole people, or a majority, or the 'natural aristocracy' of leading men, have the whole or a large share in the government of the country. On the whole, these terms do not refer to absolute monarchy,[18] especially 'free government', which applies only to the English mixed government and republics, and this is not inconsistent, always provided that it is possible to have freedom in a government which is not free. This, which was foolishness to vulgar Whiggism, was, as has been seen, the teaching of Montesquieu: it makes sense if one keeps apart the legal and political meaning of freedom. Smith knew that in Rome and all the other ancient republics, the poor people were constantly in debt and in a state of subjection to their creditors, 'the rich and the great' (WN V.iii.61), whereas in the 'military monarchy' of the Roman Empire there was a strict and impartial administration of laws which, though Smith does not say so, but he must have known, were much less harsh (LJ (B) 45; Cannan, 31).

As in Hume, so in Smith, the progress of commerce and manufactures and 'order and good government, and with them the liberty and security of individuals', is the great theme of European history, embracing the absolute as well as the free governments, and in *The Wealth of Nations*, Hume is said to have been 'the only writer' so far to have noticed the vital connection. (WN III.iv.4. This is unfair to Millar, whose *Origin of Ranks* had been published in 1771. Considering that Millar was Smith's pupil and friend, it is in fact a rather curious remark.) In two well-known sections of *The Wealth of Nations*, which together constitute a *locus classicus* of the theme of commerce and liberty,[19] Smith describes how baronial and ecclesiastical power and authority were undermined and destroyed by economic progress without anyone willing or planning it. It is Hume's

[18] One cannot always be quite sure. See, e.g. WN V.i.f.61: 'In free countries, where the safety of government depends very much upon the favourable judgement which the people may form of its conduct . . .' Is this meant to apply to the civilized monarchies, or not? France? Since the previous sentence had mentioned 'faction' and 'opposition', it might not. Hume's famous remark about all government being founded on opinion is not relevant here. The context is the need to educate the population of an advanced commercial state rendered stupid by the effect of the division of labour.

[19] Book III, and Book V, Ch. I, Part III, article III (V.i.g).

thesis, but Smith gave the theme of commerce and liberty a philosophical foundation in the nature of man which it does not have in Hume, for whom it is a historical event, something which the philosopher, looking back, can observe to have happened. To appreciate the difference, to understand why Millar described Smith and not Hume as the 'Newton' of the history of civil society, it is necessary to remember not only the motive of progress which is stressed in *The Wealth of Nations*, man's constant desire to better his condition, but also the socio-psychology of *The Theory of Moral Sentiments*; ultimately it seems that the most important psychological factor in social progress is the fact that men are highly sensitive to the opinions and feelings of others and desperately want to be loved and approved of. Or one may have to go further back still, but this is not the place to do so.[20] The question is: does this more 'philosophical' approach imply that there is a natural and necessary connection between the progress of improvement and liberty? Granted that there is a 'natural progress of opulence', and a 'natural progress of things toward improvement' in the economic sense, is there a natural progress of civilization in the full sense, which includes liberty? Does 'the natural progress of law and government' (WN IV.vii. b.2), whatever else it may mean, mean this? Such a connection formed part of one of the most powerful and stimulating studies of Adam Smith's thought to have appeared in recent years; in which the author, most decisively rejecting the view of Smith as politically sceptical and indifferent to forms of government, endeavoured to show how a deterministic idea of nature, as a system whose end is self-preservation, ministers to Smith's 'overmastering goal' of free, secular society.[21] There is a necessary connection between commercial civilization, *laissez-faire* capitalism, and liberty, and liberty is the higher purpose and meaning of Smith's advocacy of the former. 'If the advantages of commerce can be sufficiently impressed upon the general mind, freedom and civilization will automatically follow in its train, and mankind will perhaps even be disposed to defend civilization, not necessarily out of love of freedom but out of love for commerce and gain' (op. cit. 95). It is because of its power to generate civilization that Smith can conscientiously advocate commerce in spite of what he takes to be its radical defects. (Hume incidentally was far less sceptical about the all-round benefits of commercial civilization than Smith; he could see no flaws,[22] whereas Smith has lately been attracting attention from those who are interested in Marx's theory of alienation. But surely it is not necessary to point out the enormous gulf that divides Smith and Marx on the subject of the division of labour? Can one not take that for granted, and still suggest

[20] I suspect that Malebranche had more to do with some aspects of Smith's philosophy than is commonly appreciated.

[21] Joseph Cropsey, *Polity and Economy* (1957).

[22] Unless one regards the national debt as a necessary feature of commercial civilization.

that there is something like a theory of alienation or a premonition of one, not necessarily Marx's, in Smith?)

In the interpretation of Smith just mentioned, the freedom generated by commerce is not just the rule of law and the freedom and security of individuals, not the 'political' or 'civil liberty' of Hume and Montesquieu, or Smith's freedom 'in our present sense of the word', but democratic institutions, 'the institutions of free polity'. In recommending *laissez-faire* capitalism, Smith is said to be indirectly condemning and rejecting absolutism in favour of free government: that Smith rejects absolutism is taken for granted. His philosophy is geared to the substitution of the just for the benevolent society, because the latter demands the strictest control, and justice, as defined by Smith, 'requires the freest republican government'. This is why there is 'considerable evidence of Smith's preference for "republicanism" above all other regimes', especially his 'reiterated praise of those aspects of Dutch life which were supposedly assignable to republican institutions', though this does not mean that Smith was advocating a republican regime for his own country, and in fact his conception of republicanism seems 'tantamount to constitutional monarchy' (Cropsey, 65, 66, 68, 94).

Certainly to describe Smith, as Rae does, as 'always theoretically a republican',[23] is not saying very much. The same could be said of Hume. But what was 'constitutional monarchy' for Smith? Rae's remark is given some content by a quotation from the Earl of Buchan, who wrote that Smith 'approached to republicanism in his political principles, and considered a commonwealth as the platform for the monarchy . . .' But the evidence suggests that Smith subscribed to the commonplace Blackstonian view of the British constitution as a 'happy mixture of all the different forms of government properly restrained, and a perfect security to liberty and property' (LJ (B) 63; Cannan, 45). It was not a question of a commonwealth forming a platform for monarchy; the English government was a mixed government (LJ (B) 14; Cannan, 11) and it was a question of maintaining the balance between 'the influence of the crown' and the 'force of the democracy', between the 'monarchical and democratical parts of the constitution' (WN IV.vii.c.78).[24] In these circumstances, being a 'republican' would imply that the equilibrium had been disturbed in favour of monarchy, and this was the intellectual ground or justification of Millar's militant Whiggism after the constitutional crisis, as he saw it, of 1784. There is not enough evidence to show how far or when Smith veered in this direction also.

[23] John Rae, *Life of Adam Smith* (1895), 124.

[24] 'We on this side of the water, are afraid lest the multitude of American representatives (in any parliamentary union of Britain and the colonies) should overturn the balance of the constitution' etc.

What 'republicanism' seems to mean, above all, in *The Wealth of Nations* is the 'equality' which is the result of freedom from aristocratic privilege and oppression, and along with this goes a more representative or democratic or 'republican' government. The manners of the English colonists in America and their governments are more 'republican' than in the mother country: the descendant of an old family is more respected than any 'upstart', but 'he has no privilege by which he can be troublesome to his neighbours' (WN IV.vii.b.51). 'No oppressive aristocracy has ever prevailed in the colonies' (WN V.iii.90). One has the impression that a privileged aristocracy is always oppressive, as in Scotland, and it is difficult to accept the view that the hereditary nobility has the role, in Smithian society, of guaranteeing the general liberty by standing between the monarch and absolute power (Cropsey, 68). This is Montesquieu, and Burke, but surely not Smith? In fact, as suggested, if Smith's 'republicanism' means anything, it means precisely the opposite of this. In the *Lectures* (LJ (B) 116; Cannan, 84), there is a remark to the effect that hereditary nobility is the great security of the people's liberty, but the context indicates that by 'people's liberty', Smith meant national independence.[25] For Hume the chief support of liberty was the middling rank, and it seems unlikely that Smith would be more 'feudal' than Hume. 'The stability and duration of every system of free government' depends on the power of the 'leading men, the natural aristocracy of every country' to preserve their importance (WN IV.vii.c.74; V.i.a.41) but apart from the fact that old families are more respected than upstarts, for psychological reasons explained in the *Theory of Moral Sentiments*, Smith's 'natural aristocracy' is very different from Burke's, because Burke's is precisely a hereditary nobility in which there is the minimum of meritocracy. The context of Smith's remark is the American colonies: his 'natural aristocracy' is perfectly compatible with his 'republicanism'. That is why Holland's 'republican form of government' would be overthrown if the great mercantile families were deprived of their share in the government, and the whole administration thrown 'into the hands of nobles and of soldiers' (WN V.ii.k.80). Holland being almost wholly a mercantile state, this would destroy 'equality'; the merchants forming the 'natural aristocracy', or a great part of it, of 'principal men'.

But if Smith was, in the sense indicated, a man of republican principles, it does not mean that he had any special admiration for actual republics

[25] The remark is thrown out in a discussion of the disadvantages of polygamy; where there is polygamy, there can be no hereditary nobility, and a country can be easily conquered. Into the flow of his ideas and words at the rostrum Smith has woven something remembered from Montesquieu or Machiavelli, to make another 'point'. He may also have been thinking of the role of the medieval barons in Hume's *History* (the Tudor despotism rose on the ruins of the nobility, LJ (B) 60; Cannan, 42), but they were not defending freedom as we know it.

and republican regimes; at least there is considerable evidence that his admiration was severely qualified, and that includes the Dutch republic, quite apart from the fact that the modern world was a world in which great monarchies were the order of the day and set the tone (LJ (B) 79; Cannan, 55, cf. 274), and the republic was not a suitable form of government for a large commercial state. Rae mentions Smith's admiration for Geneva, but he does not remind the reader that for Smith all the republics of the ancient world were nations of oppressed debtors, that it was the Italian republics that began the ruinous system of national debts (WN V.iii.57), or that 'some modern republics' without a standing army had to thole a 'troublesome jealousy' which 'seems to watch over the minutest actions, and to be at all times ready to disturb the peace of every citizen'; (WN V.i.a.41) a point which Hume had made in his essay on the liberty of the press. Nor did Rae mention that Smith wanted to absorb the 'small democracies' of America in a parliamentary union, thus delivering them from 'those rancorous and virulent factions which are inseparable from small democracies' and which, if they separated from Britain, would probably destroy them (WN V.iii.90) or that thoughtless extravagance is a feature of democracies (WN V.ii.a.5). As for Holland (which means sometimes the province, sometimes the United Provinces), it is, unlike Britain or France, a nation of merchants and manufacturers so that whereas in the latter 'liberality, frankness and good fellowship naturally make a part of the common character', in the former, 'narrowness, meanness and a selfish disposition, averse to all social pleasure and enjoyment' (WN IV.ix.13), though no doubt there is more honesty and punctuality (LJ (B) 326; Cannan 253). Merchants and manufacturers 'neither are, nor ought to be, the rulers of mankind" (WN IV.iii.c.9). In Holland they only have a share in the government, and this is what is meant by Dutch republicanism accounting for the country's 'present grandeur' (WN V.ii.k.80). The context makes it clear that 'present grandeur' is a purely neutral term and does not mean greatness: it is the merchants' share in the government which satisfies their self-importance and prevents them from leaving and ruining completely a country enfeebled by debt (WN V.iii.57) and oppressive taxes (WN V.ii.k.78)—more than once Smith makes the point that the 'wise republic' of Holland has had to adopt a ruinous system of taxation in order to defend itself, thereby, one might add, paying the penalty of being a small republic in a world of large monarchies.[26]

[26] On the other hand, in WN I.ix.10, Smith suggests that there is no 'general decay' of trade in Holland. But it is not clear whether this refers to the province or the United Provinces. There is also some ambiguity whether Smith's troublesome discretionary powers in 'some modern republics' is meant to apply to Holland. It does specifically in Hume. It does not in Smith, if or in so far as 'Holland' does have a properly constituted standing army. (In LJ (B) 332; Cannan, 258, there is a reference in passing to 'the standing army of the Dutch' at the beginning of the century.)

But consideration of Smith's 'republicanism', and what it amounted to, does not affect the main issue. Smith, like Hume, preferred 'free government' to 'despotic' or absolute government, however mild, and thought it superior. The question is whether this preference is reflected in his science of politics in such a way that there is a necessary connection between economic progress and 'free government', between justice and 'the freest, republican government'.

The answer to the second half of the question has been suggested already. The connection is between justice and civilized states, which include absolute monarchy; what matters is not the form of government, whether free or absolute, but the degree of civilization. This is the element of truth in the view of Smith as indifferent to forms of government. If Smith's system was designed to exclude absolute monarchy, assuming that 'liberty' was impossible without 'free government', so that neither is found in the absolute monarchies, which are thus equated with the governments of Asia, we have what Hume called 'high political rant', and I have called 'vulgar Whiggism'. But although Smith said that representative institutions were a necessary security for free government,[27] he is not on record as saying that free government is a necessary security of freedom 'in our present sense of the word'. It would have been flying in the face of the facts of European society as observed by Smith himself.

As for the effect of economic progress on the development of free government, political liberty in that sense, Smith commended Hume for seeing that commerce and manufactures had brought good government and the liberty and security of individuals; this applied to all civilized Europe. But Hume's *History* showed how the uniquely free British constitution was the result of peculiar circumstances and historical accident; its history was as 'singular' as the thing itself. And Millar, in his manner, agreed. In the *Origin of Ranks*, Millar discussed the effect of economic progress on the power of the sovereign and the emergence of popular government, and showed how economic progress, in itself, does not tend automatically towards popular government, but leads naturally in two opposite directions. It increases the sovereign's power and influence, and much more so in a large than in a small state, but at the same time it increases the wealth and independence of the lower ranks in society. The conflict between these two natural and opposite tendencies is resolved by 'a variety of accidents', and in a large state the struggle is likely to terminate in absolute government as it did in nearly all the large states of modern Europe. Thus in a large state the natural tendency of economic progress is towards the absolute authority

[27] WN IV.vii.b.51 '. . . the liberty of the English colonists to manage their own affairs their own way is complete. It is in every respect equal to that of their fellow-citizens at home, and is secured in the same manner, by an assembly of the representatives of the people, who claim the sole right of imposing taxes for the support of the colony government.'

of government.[28] Smith, in his published writings, did not discuss this question directly, though the fact that China and India are economically very advanced, though stationary and not improving, and politically very backward, would not support the idea of a necessary connection between commerce and manufactures and liberty in either sense of the word, civil or political, not to mention the improving state of the greater part of Europe. In his Glasgow lectures, economic progress brings about the dissolution of the republics of antiquity, but this is due, or partly due, to the absence of properly constituted standing armies (LJ (B) 40; Cannan, 28). But the creation of a standing army has to be a conscious act of wisdom on the part of the state; it cannot be left to the silent operation of the division of labour;[29] and to that extent the maintenance and defence of liberty is not automatic, the unconscious by-product of men seeking to better their condition. There is a brief reference to the peculiar advantage of Britain being an island and the king not needing a standing army in the seventeenth century (LJ (B) 62; Cannan, 28); otherwise there is not enough in Smith's *Lectures* to show to what extent he agreed with Millar's thesis as just outlined. Fundamental disagreement on such a crucial issue seems unlikely, without leaving some ripples on the surface.

However, one can go still further, and carry out a flanking movement, by asking whether not just political liberty—free institutions—but liberty in the broader sense of the rule of law is the natural and necessary result of economic progress. It happened in Europe, but only in modern Europe has it happened, and Smith does not suggest that this is for reasons of climate —there is a 'variety of climate' in China (WN IV.ix.41)—so that the theme of commerce and liberty seems to belong to European and not 'natural' or 'theoretical' history. Millar's *Origin of Ranks* also supports this interpretation, but this time one does not have to rely so heavily on Millar. Because although there is, in Smith's science of man, a principle of human nature, man's unfailing desire to better his condition, which leads naturally to increasing opulence, there is another unfailing principle, man's desire to dominate others and enforce his will, which brings it about that the progress of opulence will not diminish but tend to increase and worsen slavery. Man's arrogance is a very conspicuous feature of Smith's science of man, as any reader of *The Wealth of Nations* knows: it overrides considerations of real self-interest and prudence; for example, the fact that slavery is uneconomical, wasteful, and inefficient.[30] Consequently 'even at present',

[28] It is part of Cropsey's thesis that Smith favoured large, populous states.

[29] WN V.i.a.14 '. . . it is the wisdom of the state only which can render the trade of a soldier a particular trade separate and distinct from all others . . . and states have not always had this wisdom.'

[30] In the *Lectures on Rhetoric* this 'inhumanity which disposes us to contempt [*sic*] and trample underfoot our inferiors' is used to explain why our social inferiors are the best characters for comedy. We do not laugh at the misfortunes of kings and nobles (LRBL 21.12, Lothian, 120).

slavery 'is almost universal. A small part of the West of Europe is the only portion of the globe that is free from it . . .' (LJ (B) 134; Cannan, 96). It is in fact more 'natural' than in Montesquieu. It is found 'in all societies at their beginning, and proceeds from that tyrannic disposition which may almost be said to be natural to mankind' (LJ (B) 134; Cannan, 96), and though it may be 'softened' in a monarchy, it becomes more severe 'in proportion to the culture of society', especially in free governments. 'Freedom and opulence contribute to the misery of the slaves. The perfection of freedom is their greatest bondage; and as they are the most numerous part of mankind, no human(e) person will wish for liberty in a country where this institution is established'' (LJ (B) 137–8; Cannan, 99). Its abolition in Europe was a unique event, due to very special and exceptional circumstances, and Smith's account in *The Wealth of Nations* is an expanded version of that given in the *Lectures*. And this famous story of the destruction of baronial and ecclesiastical power needs to be looked at more closely before one generalizes about it. In Europe the natural progress of improvement was reversed as a result of the Germanic invasions and the conditions which followed: the engrossing of all the land by a few great proprietors and the legal perpetuation of this unnatural state of affairs. The land was cultivated by serfs, or 'slaves' as Smith calls them. How this species of servitude 'gradually wore out' is 'one of the most obscure points in modern history'; it was gradually abolished by the joint operation of the interest of the proprietor and that of the sovereign, who was jealous of the great lords and always ready to encourage their villeins against them (WN III.ii.12). The inhabitants of the towns, originally in an equally servile condition, arrived at liberty and independence much earlier as a result of their alliance with the Church and the Crown against the lords (WN III.iii.3). As a result of this political move 'improvement' started in the towns, not, as it naturally should, in the country, and led eventually to the unlooked for result of the destruction of baronial and ecclesiastical power and authority, and the emancipation of the inhabitants of the country also. Surely no 'law' of commerce giving rise to liberty could be drawn from such peculiar conditions?

Millar's account is similar to Smith's and is clearly derived from his lectures, and endorses the view that economic progress naturally leading to freedom is not part of his political science. In the *Origin of Ranks*, Millar discusses the effect of economic progress on various types of power and authority. Progress naturally leads to the emancipation of women and children (from the power of the *paterfamilias*); but diminution of the power and authority of the sovereign, as seen already, and the emancipation of slaves are not the natural result of economic progress. As regards the latter, Millar's account follows Smith's very closely; though it was published first.

It seems then that although in Europe commerce and liberty have advanced together, and the process once started has gone on without anyone consciously willing it, it is only an abridged account of Smith's philosophy that can maintain that there is a necessary and natural connection between them. One cannot have freedom without commerce and manufactures, but opulence without freedom is the norm rather than the exception.[31] No doubt Smith had his absolute values, his 'overmastering goal' of free, secular society, his preference for 'free government'. But it does not seem that he can offer us these things *qua* 'philosopher', or scientist. But should not science be the more sceptical, the more desperately we want it to give us something nice?

[31] Opulence without freedom is less exceptional than opulence and commerce without 'the improvement of arts and refinement of manners'. Opulence and commerce 'commonly precede', in fact are a 'necessary requisite' of the latter, but the Dutch and Venetians show that the latter are not 'the necessary consequences of commerce' (LRBL 23.3, Lothian, 132).

X

Adam Smith and the Colonial Disturbances

DAVID STEVENS*

I

On 9 March 1776, *An Inquiry into the Nature and Causes of the Wealth of Nations* was published in London by Strahan and Cadell. On 4 July the Second Continental Congress meeting in Philadelphia approved without dissent the Declaration of Independence. The two events are separate yet linked since it cannot be doubted the Smith's knowledge of America had a great influence upon his work.

In his earlier days as Professor in Glasgow (1751–64) Smith was made aware of America by the merchants of that city, many of whom amassed fortunes as a result of their commercial relations with the American colonies. During his period of seclusion at Kirkcaldy, the newspapers in Scotland were greatly expanded in number and they gave the developing difficulties in the colonies extensive coverage.[1]

From 1773 until 1776 Smith remained in London. He was admitted to the Royal Society in May 1773, attended Lord Wedderburn's weekly dining club, and was admitted to Johnson's Literary Club,[2] where the American problem would almost inevitably be discussed.

His fellow Scot, Adam Ferguson, who was in London in 1775, was also active in American affairs, while in addition Benjamin Franklin was resident in the city during the last two years of Smith's stay.[3] Indeed, their respective biographers, Parton and Rae, were later to report that:

* The author is Roger and Davis Clapp Professor of Economic Thought at Whitman College, Walla Walla, U.S.A.

References to *The Wealth of Nations* are to the Cannan edition (1937).

[1] Dalphy I. Fagerstrom, 'Scottish Opinion and the American Revolution', *William and Mary Quarterly* (April 1954), 252–75.

[2] Johnson condemned the American 'Zealots of Anarchy': Samuel Johnson, *Taxation No Tyranny: An Answer to the Resolutions and Address of the American Congress* (1775). In his reply to the so-called 'Suffolk Resolves' of The First Continental Congress (1774), Johnson says, 'We are told, that the subjection of Americans may tend to the diminution of our own liberties; an event, which none but very perspicacious politicians are able to foresee. If slavery be thus fatally contagious, how is it that we hear the loudest yelps for liberty among the drivers of negroes?'

[3] Many of Franklin's works, including *The Interest of Great Britain Considered, With Regard to Her Colonies* (1760) were in Adam Smith's library. See Hiroshi Mizuta, *Adam Smith's Library: A Supplement to Bonar's Catalogue, with a Checklist of the whole Library* (1967), 95.

[Dr. Franklin] once told Dr. Logan that the celebrated Adam Smith, when writing his *Wealth of Nations* was in the habit of bringing chapter after chapter, as he composed it, to himself, Dr. Price and others of the literati; then patiently hear their observations, and profit by their discussions and criticism—even sometimes submitting to write whole chapters anew, and even to reverse some of his propositions.[4]

Evidence seems to indicate that this story is based on the weakest of evidence, but it is at least probable that Smith discussed American affairs with so obvious an authority.[5]

Smith also had an interest in military developments and in 1775 his friend John Roebuck sent a lengthy first-hand account by Walter Lowne of the Battle of Breeds (Bunker) Hill and a somewhat unflattering description of the 'Character of the Boston Patriots'.[6] With this background it is very probable, as Rae suggests, that Smith should have been busy revising his treatment of the American problem in the very year of the Declaration of Independence. Indeed, there is evidence to suggest that publication may have been delayed as a result. In February 1776 Hume wrote to complain: 'By all acounts your book has been printed long ago; yet it has never yet been so much as advertised. What is the reason: If you wait till the Fate of America be decided, you may wait long . . .'[7]

II

Opinions and attitudes concerning the American problem were widely divided during the period in which Smith was writing *The Wealth of Nations*, and especially among those who were opposed to the government's policy. Doubtless, Smith had particular interest in two of the major, yet differing, objections to the government's policy of forced colonial

[4] John Rae, *Life of Adam Smith* (1895), 264–5; and Parton, *Life and Times of Benjamin Franklin* (1864).

[5] Thomas D. Eliot, 'The Relations Between Adam Smith and Benjamin Franklin Before 1776', *Political Science Quarterly*, xxix, no. 1 (March 1924), 67–96, is an excellent analysis not only of the relations between Smith and Franklin before 1776 but also gives a careful evaluation of this particular story.

[6] Unpublished manuscripts in the Bannerman Collections, University of Glasgow Library. Letter 147 addressed to Adam Smith, dated 1 Nov. 1775. In the 'Character of the Boston Patriots', Lowne says of John Hancock, '. . . a man once of worth in trade . . . but of a weak ambition—is a necessary and generous dupe to another of deeper designs, to the utter ruin of his private fortune.' Of Samuel Adams, 'a malster by profession, but of little reputation, until he made himself conspicuous in political disputes—a man of superior cunning and abilities was made collector of the town taxes, for a support, in which capacity, he in a most notorious manner, cheated the town of a sum not less than £2,000 sterling which after his influence with the community was established, he had the boldness to get spunged off, in consideration of secret services—has since been subsisted in a very ambiguous way, and is now the principal Delegate at the grand American Congress' (1775).

[7] Letter 149 addressed to Adam Smith, dated 8 Feb. 1776; in *The Letters of David Hume*, ed. John T. Y. Greig (1932), ii. 308.

compliance as typified by the positions held by Edmund Burke and Josiah Tucker, Dean of Gloucester.[8]

The views of Burke were essentially Lockian in character, believing as he did that '. . . no man ought to be subject to any government, or to any mode of taxation, which he himself had not, by some explicit and personal engagement chosen for that purpose'. This position is reflected in his speech on *Moving Resolutions for Conciliation with the Colonies*,[9] where Burke reminded Parliament that the colonists 'complain that they are taxed in a Parliament in which they are not represented. If you mean to satisfy them at all, you must satisfy them with regard to this complaint . . .'[10]

But Burke wanted to preserve the ties of the colonies to the mother country within an empire which he defined as 'the aggregate to many states under one common head, whether this head be a monarch or a presiding republic'. He was not, however, willing to give up faith in the old commercial system. To Parliament he had said,

> Leave America, if she has taxable matter in her, to tax herself . . . Leave the Americans as they anciently stood, and these distinctions, born of our unhappy contest, will die along with it . . . Be content to bind America by laws of trade; you have always done it. Let this be your reason for binding their trade. Do not burthen them with taxes, you were not used to do so from the beginning.[11]

The colonies were to be freed of taxation and were to be given representation, but the old restrictions on trade were to be maintained. The member from commercial Bristol felt that the mother country could offer a political solution, but could not afford to lose its profitable commercial ties with America. While Smith would have some points of agreement with this argument, the call for continued commercial restrictions could not fit into his plan of economic liberty. It was probably only as Burke's mercantilistic views moderated with the passage of time that Smith could say, 'Burke is the only man I ever knew who thinks on economic subjects exactly as I do, without any previous communications between us.'[12]

Josiah Tucker forms the other extreme of opposition to the government's colonial policy in this period. He had no sympathy for the colonists, but nevertheless believed in a policy of separation as best suiting British interests. The colonists were an 'ungrateful, ungovernable and rebellious people' and would remain so whether they gained independence or not.

[8] *Political Pamphlets*, published from 1768 to 1775. Seven pamphlets on political and American affairs bound together (from Adam Smith's library) in Glasgow University Library. This volume contains two pamphlets by Burke and two by Tucker.

[9] Edmund Burke, *Speech of Edmund Burke, Esq. On Moving His Resolutions for Conciliation with the Colonies* (1775). Included in *Political Pamphlets* (supra).

[10] Ibid. 49.

[11] Edmund Burke, *Speech on American Taxation*, 19 Apr. 1774 (1775), 89–90.

[12] John Rae, *Life of Adam Smith*, 387–8.

The elaborate system of commercial regulations which were typical of the old commercial system did not effectively control colonial trade in the interest of the mother country.

> Nor was it in our power, even when we were strongest, and they in the weakest stage of their existence . . . to compel them to trade with us to their own loss. Mutual interest was the only tie between America and Great Britain at all times and seasons . . . As to the planting of colonies for the sake of a monopolizing or exclusive trade, it is the arrantest cheat, and self deception, which poor, short-sighted mortals ever put upon themselves.[13]

The American colonies were a 'millstone hanging about the neck of this country'. They had benefited the mother country little in either trade or tax revenue, but as a burden they were great.[14] British goods could be sold anywhere, even in America, without the preferential treatment of the old commercial system. Britain's source of raw materials would not be endangered by separation since the Americans would depend upon their former mother country for a market. Britain then would be not only free of the many expenses of governing and protecting the colonies but would be free to purchase in the least expensive market. Thus in 1774 Tucker had said that the only solution to the colonial problem was 'to separate entirely from the North American colonies, by declaring them to be free and independent people, over whom we lay no claim'.[15]

Burke and Tucker stood at opposite poles as to the degree of conciliation that should be offered; the opinion of others opposed to the Government's policy ranged between these extremes. Thomas Pownall, former governor of Massachusetts and generally considered a spokesman for the colonies in Parliament, held a position close to that of Burke. Parliament, he thought, should not immediately declare the colonies independent, but should form a commission to 'consult, and finally to agree, and acknowledge the Americans as independent; on condition, and in the moment, that they will, as much, form a federal treaty, offensive and defensive and commercial'.[16] In the same debate William Pulteney typified the *naïveté* of Parliament when he argued: 'Secured from taxation; relieved from the fear of having any share in the burthen of our debts; protected during war by our

[13] Josiah Tucker, *Four Letters on Important National Subjects Addressed to the Right Honourable The Earl of Shelburne* (1783). Quoted in Schuyler, *The Fall of the Old Colonial System* (1945), 45–6.

[14] Cf. Josiah Tucker, Letter to Lord Kames, dated 16th June 1782. Included in Tytler, *Memoirs of the Life and Writings of Lord Kames* (1807), ii, Appendix, 18–21.

[15] Josiah Tucker, *The True Interest of Great Britain Set Forth in Regard to the Colonies*, published as a separate tract and as Tract IV of *Four Tracts Together with Two Sermons* (1774).

[16] Thomas Pownall as quoted in *Parliamentary Debates in the Parliamentary Register or History of the Proceedings and Debates of the House of Commons During the Fourth Session of the Fourteenth Parliament of Great Britain*, (1778), ix. 58.

strength, and cultivated during peace by our arts—with these advantages joined to dependency, could they wish to be independent?'[17]

Lord Kames, the distinguished Scottish judge, friend and correspondent of Smith, Hume, Franklin, and Tucker, was sympathetic with the colonist's cause and Burke's arguments, but rejected them for constitutional reasons. David Hume was early to take a position similar to that of Tucker, but on somewhat different grounds, that is, he thought the present union was futile. In 1771 he wrote to William Strahan of 'our union with America, which in the nature of things, cannot long subsist'.[18] In October 1775 Hume made his position clear: 'Let us, therefore lay aside all Anger; shake hands, and part Friends. Or if we retain any anger, let it only be against ourselves for our past Folly; and against that wicked Madman, Pitt; who has reduced us to our present Condition.'[19]

It was against such a background that Smith developed an original analysis of, and solution for, the colonial problem.

III

Initially Smith indicated a preference for a political solution close to that of Burke and even closer to that of Governor Pownall. (The publication of *The Wealth of Nations* predated Pownall's suggestion to Parliament of a Treaty of Federation by a year.) Smith was willing to grant the colonies their independence, but he pleaded that a better solution, for both the colonies and the mother country, was one of imperial union. This was to serve as the centre-piece of his colonial policy.

The political problem of the colonies, according to Smith, was from some points of view, largely illusory:

In every thing, except their foreign trade, the liberty of the English colonists to manage their own affairs their own way is complete. It is in every respect equal to that of their fellow citizens at home, and is secured in the same manner, by an assembly of the representatives of the people, who claim the sole right of imposing taxes for the support of the colony government. The authority of this assembly over awes the executive power, and neither the meanest nor the most obnoxious colonist, as long as he obeys the law, has anything to fear from the resentment, either of the governor or any other civil or military officer in the province.

(WN IV.vii.b.51)

In fact, Smith pointed out that the colonial assemblies had more equal representation than the inhabitants of the mother country and that there was little influence exerted by the governors and none by a class of nobles (ibid.). Nor was the regulation of trade a major problem; the difficulty lay rather in Britain's insistence on her right to tax the colonies. Smith

[17] William Pulteney, ibid. 147.
[18] David Hume, *Letters of David Hume*, ii. 237.
[19] Ibid. 300–1.

believed that if Parliament established the right of taxation, the importance of the colonial assemblies and the colonial leaders would be diminished,[20] and, since, 'Men desire to have some share in the management of public affairs chiefly on account of the importance which it gives them . . . They have rejected, therefore, the proposal of being taxed by parliamentary requisition, and like other ambitious and high-spirited men, have rather chosen to draw the sword in defence of their own importance' (WN IV.vii.c.74).

Dean Tucker's idea of voluntary separation is considered by Smith and then rejected as impractical. 'To propose that Great Britain should voluntarily give up all authority over her colonies . . . would be to propose such a measure as never was, and never will be adopted, by any nation in the world' (WN IV.vii.c.66). Even while rejecting this solution out of hand, Smith somewhat wistfully sees that it is compatible with his general philosophy. If separation were adopted, the mother country would at least be freed of the expense of defending the colonies and could well settle for a free trade treaty that would benefit all. 'By thus parting good friends, the natural affection of the colonies to the mother country, which, perhaps, our late dissensions have well nigh extinguished, would quickly revive' (ibid.).

The colonial problem was clear, that is, 'The parliament of Great Britain insists upon taxing the colonies; and they refuse to be taxed by a parliament in which they are not represented' (WN IV.vii.c.75). To Smith the solution was equally clear. It was not, as Burke suggested, to remove the onerous taxes but rather to grant the colonists representation to Parliament in proportion to what the colonies contribute in taxes to the new empire. In return they should be granted the same rights of free trade as their fellow subjects at home. This was to be no federation, but a complete political union, with Parliament being the 'assembly which deliberates and decides concerning the affairs of every part of the empire' (WN IV.vii.c.77). A year after publication of *The Wealth of Nations*, in a memorandum to Wedderburn, Lord North's solicitor-general, Smith clearly states the type of union he had in mind. 'The Americans, I imagine, would be less unwilling to consent to such a Union with Great Britain as Scotland made with England in 1707 . . .'[21] The colonial representation in Parliament would grow as the colonies' contribution to general taxation also grew. There need be no fear in the mother country that the balance of government would be overturned since the representation would always be in proportion to the tax contribution. On the other hand, the Americans should not fear oppression since their representatives would feel that they

[20] Cf. John Maurice Clark, 'Adam Smith and the Currents of History', in *Adam Smith 1776–1926* (1966), 67. Clark suggests that Smith implied these were 'natural leaders', a concept that fits in well with his general philosophy.

[21] Published by G. H. Gutridge in *American Historical Review*, xxxviii (July, 1933), 714–20.

owed their seat in Parliament to their constituents and thus would complain, with all the force of a member of Parliament, of any outrage perpetrated against any constituent 'in those remote parts of the empire'. Furthermore, the Americans should not feel that they would be disadvantaged by their distance from the seat of government since they might well believe, 'with some appearance of reason too', that this condition would not long continue. 'Such has hitherto been the rapid progress of that country in wealth, population and improvement, that in the course of little more than a century, perhaps, the produce of American might exceed that of British taxation. The seat of empire would then naturally remove itself to that part of the empire which contributed most to the general defence and support of the whole' (WN IV.vii.c.79).

To Smith the political problem of the colonies was closely tied to the continuing fiscal problem, that is, that the taxes levied upon the colonies, 'have seldom been equal to the expence laid out upon them in time of peace, and never sufficient to defray that which they occasioned in time of war' (WN IV.vii.c.13). Thus the colonies have not been a source of revenue but an expense to the mother country. Smith clearly states a number of times that it is fiscally irresponsible not to levy upon the colonies their share of responsibility for revenue. He stands firm against the somewhat more politically astute position of Burke and his followers in Parliament that the colonial disturbances could be ameliorated by not taxing the colonies. Smith's plan of empire is generally presented in his lengthy chapter 'Of Colonies' (Book IV, Ch. vii) but it is significant that he returns to the political problem and its solution in the last few pages of *The Wealth of Nations* in his discussion 'Of Public Debts' (Book V, Ch. iii). Smith saw the colonial political problem and its solution as being closely tied to the fiscal problem and its solution.

In his discussion of 'public debts', Smith repeats with somewhat less hope of achievement the necessity for and the advantages to be achieved by an imperial union. But, 'it is not contrary to justice' that America should contribute toward the public debt of Great Britain. The debt was contracted not so much in the defence of Great Britain, but in defence of America. It is to the mother country that the colonies of America owe the 'liberty, security, and property which they have ever since enjoyed' (WN V.iii.88). It was because the colonies were considered provinces of the British empire that these expenses were contracted. But colonies which contribute neither revenue nor military assistance to the support of the empire cannot be considered provinces. 'They may perhaps be considered as appendages, as a sort of splendid and showy equipage of the empire.' (WN V. iii.92) To Smith empire was more than it was to Burke, whose empire was merely several countries with one head. Smith's empire was to be an economic union as well as a political one. He points out:

The rulers of Great Britain have, for more than a century past, amused the people with the imagination that they possessed a great empire on the west side of the Atlantic. This empire, however, has hitherto existed in imagination only. It has hitherto been, not an empire, but the project of an empire; not a gold mine, but the project of a gold mine; a project which has cost, which continues to cost, and which, if pursued in the same way as it has been hitherto, is likely to cost, immense expence, without being likely to bring any profit.

(WN V.iii.92)

If the project of union, which alone could bring reality to 'this golden dream' of empire, proved illusory, 'it ought to be given up'. If the provinces of the empire cannot be made to contribute toward the support of the entire empire, then Britain should free herself of the expense of maintaining the colonies. In the end, Smith had moved far from the position of Burke and almost, but not quite, surrendered to the separatism of Tucker. With resignation, Smith gave his final word, if Britain does not accept a plan of union and empire, she must 'endeavour to accommodate her future views and designs to the real mediocrity of her circumstances' (ibid.).

IV

If Smith wavered in his political proposals, there is no doubt as to his position concerning the economic and commercial factors underlying the American problem. Here, he is more original and clearly superior analytically to his contemporaries.

It can be hypothesized from nothing more substantial than the order and unity in the development of his arguments, that most of the material on America, as opposed to his discussion of the American problem, was not a last-minute addition to *The Wealth of Nations*. America was a land where his thesis of economic liberty could be demonstrated, and Koebner was surely correct in stating that:

Adam Smith took care to have his reflections on the American problem organically woven into the context of his great systematic work. They could appear at first sight as 'unavoidable inferences of the consistent and comprehensive argument which generation after generation accepted as the elementary approach to reality.'[22]

In America all the ingredients were there: 'plenty and cheapness of good land', an educated leadership, a growing (as the result of high wages) labour force, but above all, because of their distance from the mother country the colonists were less in her power and could pursue 'their interest their own way'. 'Plenty of good land, and liberty to manage their own affairs their own way, seem to be the two great causes of the prosperity of all

[22] Richard Koebner, *Empire* (1961), 227.

new colonies' (WN IV.vii.b.16). America was only waiting for the addition of capital, either from the mother country of from the colonies themselves. Since the colonies never have sufficient capital it most likely will come from the mother country, but with liberty to handle their own economic affairs the colonists only had to use it in such a manner as to increase 'most the annual produce of the land and labour of that country'.[23] For the American colonies the proper use of capital was a physiocratic one. 'It has been the principal cause of the rapid progress of our American colonies toward wealth and greatness', Smith notes, 'that almost their whole capitals have hitherto been employed in agriculture.' This was in the natural order of things; it was only in subsequent stages of development that a country could move to manufacturing and finally to commerce.

The model could be destroyed by depriving the colonies of the freedom to manage their affairs in their own way or by ill-advised commercial or political policies by the mother country, and the fact that the colonists thought that this was exactly what the mother country was doing clearly contributed to the current disturbances.

The British government's commercial policy, according to Smith, restricted the colonies by restricting their manufacturing and monopolizing their trade. Manufacturing was limited to the 'first stage' of production. 'The more advanced or more refined manufactures even of the colony produce, the merchants and manufacturers of Great Britain chuse to reserve to themselves, and have prevailed upon the legislature to prevent their establishment in the colonies, sometimes by high duties, and sometimes by absolute prohibitions' (WN IV.vii.b.40). By prohibiting trade in certain commodities, by prohibiting manufacture of certain goods for distant sale, and by prohibiting certain productions, e.g. 'steel furnaces and slit-mills', the mother country effectively confined colonial industry 'to such coarse and household manufactures, as a private family commonly makes for its own use' (WN IV.vii.b.42,43). Smith admits that because land is so cheap and labour so dear, the colonists can import from the mother country more cheaply than they could produce themselves. Even if most refined and advanced manufacturing were not prohibited, the colonists would be and were guided by their own self-interest to buy from the mother country. But, nevertheless, these restrictions 'are impertinent badges of slavery imposed upon them without any sufficient reason, by the groundless jealousy of the merchants and manufacturers of the mother country'. Then somewhat prophetically he points out, 'In a more advanced

[23] One recent study indicates that during the entire eighteenth century, and particularly during the period from 1768 to 1772, there was little or no deficit on the colonial balance of payments and from this the authors arrive at the contention that British long-term investment in the colonies was negligible during this period. See James F. Shepherd and Gary M. Walton, *Shipping, Maritime Trade, and the Economic Development of Colonial North America* (1972), 154–5.

state they might be really oppressive and insupportable' (WN IV.vii.b.44).

Smith would not be Smith, however, if he did not denounce the principle behind these limitations on man's freedom. 'To prohibit a great people, however, from making all that they can of every part of their own produce, or from employing their stock and industry in the way that they judge most advantageous to themselves, is a manifest violation of the most sacred rights of mankind' (ibid).

It is, however, in the monopoly of trade that Smith sees the greatest disadvantages to the colonies (as well as the mother country) and by implication a basic cause of the colonial disturbances. 'The exclusive trade of the mother countries tends to diminish, or, at least, to keep down below what they would otherwise rise to, both the enjoyments and industry of all those nations in general and of the American colonies in particular' (WN IV.vii.c.9). The exclusive trade privilege 'cramps' the industry of the colonies and raises the price in the colonies of goods produced in other countries. The policy is a 'clog' which 'encumbers the industry of all other countries; but of the colonies more than any other' (ibid.). Smith carefully enumerates the disadvantages of the monopoly of trade to the mother country and the advantages of free trade. Trade with the colonies, Smith admits, had been beneficial to Britain, not because of the monopoly, 'but in spite of it'. The expenses of maintaining the colonies had been enormous, and although at first the acquisition of exclusive trade privileges with America seemed to be of the highest value, it actually had been a cause of difficulty and strife. Rising to rhetorical heights, Smith says, 'To the undiscerning eye of giddy ambition, it [the American trade monopoly] naturally presents itself amidst the confused scramble of politics and war, as a very dazzling object to fight for . . . The dazzling splendour of the object, however, . . . is the very quality which renders the monopoly of it hurtful' (WN IV.vii.c.85). While advantageous to a 'single order of men', that is, the merchants, it is in many ways 'hurtful to the general interest of the country'. 'To found a great empire for the sole purpose of raising up a people of customers, may at first sight appear a project fit only for a nation of shopkeepers. It is, however, a project altogether unfit for a nation of shopkeepers; but extremely fit for a nation whose government is influenced by shopkeepers' (WN IV.vii.c.63). When an unnaturally overgrown system of commerce suffers even a small stoppage, Smith points out, it 'is very likely to bring on the most dangerous disorders upon the whole body politic. The expectation of a rupture with the colonies, accordingly, has struck the people of Great Britain with more terror than they ever felt for a Spanish or a French invasion. It was this terror, . . . which rendered the repeal of the stamp act . . . a popular measure . . .' (WN IV.vii.c.43).

To deliver Great Britain from the possibility of dangerous disorders, Smith states that there must be 'some moderate and gradual relaxation of the laws which give to Great Britain the exclusive trade to the colonies, till it is rendered in a great measure free . . .' (WN IV.vii.c.44). It is to be remembered that a major feature of Smith's plan of union was to be that in return for sharing the tax burden with the mother country the colonies would be given the same freedom of trade as their fellow citizens in the homeland. Smith's commercial policy was as much a part of his plan of union as its political aspects, and he correctly prophesied that: 'Our colonies, unless they can be induced to consent to a union, are very likely to defend themselves against the best of all mother countries, as obstinately as the city of Paris did against one of the best of kings' (WN IV.vii.c.76).

V

America had been virtually in a state of war for about a year by March 1776, when *The Wealth of Nations* was published. It is interesting to speculate as to whether this work, which was subsequently to have such great impact upon both Great Britain and America, had any direct effect upon the thought of the colonists during the Revolution or in the period immediately following the war. In this context the important question is not whether the American colonies were actually suffering from the policies of the British mercantilistic system, but rather whether they thought they were and, if the achievement of economic liberty was a goal of the Revolution, whether their thought was influenced by Smith's work.

The question as to whether the mercantilistic policies of Great Britain were actually damaging to the American colonies has been discussed widely by economic historians, and, while their opinions are widely diverse, the generally accepted opinion today seems to be that on balance they had little detrimental effect upon the colonists.[24] A few of the colonial leaders may have thought that the policies were economically damaging but all of them resented the restrictions and taxation as infringements of their liberty. They resented the enforcement of the old restrictions even more

[24] Among the many excellent works on the effects of Great Britain's economic regulations on the colonies are Oliver M. Dickerson's *The Navigation Acts and the American Revolution* (1951); Lawrence A. Harper, 'The Effect of the Navigation Acts on the Thirteen Colonies', in *The Era of the American Revolution: Studies Inscribed to Evarts Boutell Greene* (1939), 1–39; and 'Mercantilism and the American Revolution', *Canadian Historical Review*, xxxii (Mar. 1942), 24–34. An attempt to reconcile the divergent views of Harper and Dickerson in a somewhat more theoretical manner may be bound in Robert Paul Thomas's 'A Quantitative Approach to the Study of the Effects of British Imperial Policy Upon Colonial Welfare: Some Preliminary Findings', *Journal of Economic History*, xxv (Dec. 1963), 615–38. Peter D. McClelland in 'The Cost to America of British Imperial Policy', *The American Economic Review*, lix (May 1969), 370–81, argues that the earlier work by Harper and the more recent work by Thomas are theoretically defective and that the burden of the Acts on American income and economic welfare was small—less than 3 per cent of colonial income. Douglass C. North, *Growth and Welfare in the American Past: A New Economic History* (1966) discusses the approaches taken by Harper and Thomas, and the reasons for the burden and finds it to be relatively small in relation to colonial income.

than they resented the restrictions themselves. This, it will be remembered, is exactly the position which Smith took, that the restrictions were not oppressive to the colonists, but were 'impertinent badges of slavery imposed upon them without sufficient reason'. This feeling was particularly true of the Sugar Act of 1764, the Stamp Acts, and the Townshend duties. While these taxes were not intended to force the Americans to share the burden of the Seven Years War, they were intended to have the colonists share in the peacetime colonial financial burden (including a large peacetime army). Smith had maintained that his was a just position on the part of the mother country. It was, however, the attempt of Parliament to impose these taxes (both internal and external) without consent, and more particularly their attempts to strengthen the customs service and make the new regulations effective, that were considered 'badges of slavery'. As George Washington was to write in 1765,

> The Stamp Act, imposed on the colonies by the Parliament of Great Britain, engrosses the conversations of the speculative part of the colonists, who look upon this unconstitutional method of taxation, as a direful attack upon their liberties and loudly exclaim against the violation.[25]

Throughout the American colonial period there were objections to the commercial restrictions placed upon the colonies by the mother country, but it was not until 1763 and the years following that the new regulations and taxes imposed upon the colonies, together with the concerted effort to enforce both old and new regulations, began to bring forth more loudly voiced objections from the colonial merchants.[26] Even when the First Continental Congress convened in 1774, the delegates, whom Dr. Johnson was to call 'croakers of calamity' and 'demigods of independence', showed little opposition to the old system. In Resolve No. 4 of the Suffolk Resolves, they said, '. . . we cheerfully consent to the operation of such acts of the British Parliament as are bona fide, restrained to the regulation of our external commerce, for the purpose of securing the commercial advantages of the whole empire to the mother country, and the commercial benefits of its respective members, excluding every idea of taxation internal or external, for raising a revenue on the subjects without their consent'.

There is no evidence that *The Wealth of Nations* had any direct effect on the Declaration of Independence. If nothing else, the proximity of their

[25] George Washington, 'Letter to Francis Dandridge' (20 Sept. 1763), *The Washington Papers: Basic Selections from the Public and Private Writings of George Washington*, ed. and intro. by Saul K. Padover (1955), 121.

[26] See Thomas C. Barrow, *Trade and Empire: The British Customs Service in Colonial America, 1660–1775* (1967). Barrow suggests that in the early years of the colonies (1673 to the rise of Walpole) there was stubborn and general resistance to the old mercantilist system. Under Walpole and succeeding Whig ministries (until 1763) a policy of 'salutary neglect' allowed the colonies to develop in relative freedom.

mutual publication dates would make this doubtful. By the time *The Wealth of Nations* was published the colonists were far beyond any plan of union or economic solution. Furthermore, the interests of Smith and the framers of the Declaration of Independence were not the same. Smith was interested in the welfare of the empire and particularly the mother country, and by 1776 influential colonists saw any connection with the mother country as a hindrance. In any event, their concern was more political than economic. The common influence of Locke on both works seems obvious, although he was far from the sole root of either and was not a major influence upon *The Wealth of Nations*. Jefferson, claiming no originality in writing the Declaration of Independence, drew heavily from Locke whose treatise *On Civil Government* was a commonly accepted authority on the right of revolution. Smith was, to some extent at least, directly influenced, and indirectly through Burke, by Locke. But Locke's philosophy was one which would reflect on an entire age rather than on any one or two individual works. There is no indication that Franklin, who of all the colonial leaders was most familiar with Smith's thesis of economic liberty and who made minor changes in Jefferson's draft of the Declaration, considered the need for commercial liberty as appropriate to the document.

The Revolutionary spirit had progressed so far by the publication of *The Wealth of Nations* that Smith was not particularly considered a friend of American liberty and may well have been resented for his justification of British taxation of the colonies. Arthur Lee, brother of Richard Lee, was to write from London in August of 1776,

> . . . the fact is as Dr. Smith, a Scotchman, *and an enemy to American rights*, has stated it in his late laboured and long-expected book on the Wealth of Nations. 'Whatever expense,' says he, 'Great Britain has hitherto laid out in maintaining this dependency has really been laid out in order to support their monopoly.' Speaking of the debt incurred last war, he says, 'This whole expense is, in reality, a bounty, which has been given in order to support a monopoly. The pretended purpose of it was to encourage the manufactures and to increase the commerce of Great Britain.' The operation of this monopoly against the colony he states thus: 'The monopoly of the colony trade, therefore, like all the other mean and malignant expedients of the mercantile system, depresses the industry of all other countries, but chiefly that of the colonies.'[27]

Lee goes on to warn Congress of the danger of Smith and his fellow Scots: 'When you write to the Congress, it would be well, I think, to mention that, as all the evils have been produced by Scotch counsel and those people prosecute the business with more rancor and enmity, a distinction

[27] Arthur Lee, 'Letter from Arthur Lee to M. Charles Dumas', *The Revolutionary Diplomatic Correspondence of the United States*, ed. Francis Wharton (1889), ii. 110–11. Italics supplied.

ought to be made between the treatment of them and other people when made prisoners.'[28]

Following the war, Smith's work was considered somewhat more sympathetically but it cannot be said to have been more influential. Jefferson praised it as 'the best book extant' on political economy. His writings on the economic development of America follow in some degree those of Smith, but his arguments seem to be more physiocratic than Smithian. The doctrine of *laissez-faire* appears as part of Jefferson's natural order as it does in Smith. The American government, he was to write, '. . . is a composition of the freest principles of the English constitution, with others derived from natural right and natural reason'.[29] Like Smith, Jefferson believed in the advantage of agriculture to the colonies, but for somewhat different reasons. Smith has espoused the cause of manufacturing in countries where land was in short supply and labour plentiful, but for America, since the reverse was the case, agriculture seemed the most efficient manner in which to increase the annual revenue.

Franklin maintained his faith in Smith's principles and he as much as any of the colonial leaders spread the 'true gospel' in America. On the eve of the Revolution he had written, 'Perhaps, in general, it would be better if government meddled no farther in trade, than to protect it, and let it take its course . . . When Colbert assembled some wise old merchants of France, and desired their advice and opinion, how he could best serve and promote commerce, their answer, after consultation, was in three words only, *Laissez-nous faire*; "Let us alone".' He goes on to say in very much the tone and style of Smith, 'It was therefore to be wished, that commerce was free between all nations of the world, as it is between the several counties of England; so would all, by mutual communication, obtain more enjoyments. Those counties do not ruin one another by trade; neither would nations. No nation was ever ruined by trade, even seemingly the most disadvantageous.'[30] By 1784, soon after the peace treaties were signed at

[28] Arthur Lee was appointed in Dec. 1775 secret agent in London for the Committee of Secret Correspondence. He seemed to be a man of strong personal dislikes, e.g. his jealousy of Franklin, but he reserved special hatred for the Scots. Wharton notes, 'We have already incidentally noticed Arthur Lee's transfer to the Scotch in America of Junius' attack on the Scotch in England . . . Yet by Arthur Lee those cries of "Beware of the Scotch" had been caught up long after Junius had ceased to utter them, and were hurled at Congress with a constant vehemence which shows how unaware he was of their utter want of appropriateness and of propriety. Thus he tells Congress in his dispatch of June 3, 1776, to beware of "the Scots, whose perfidy you know can never be trusted", Scots being "to a man treacherous and hostile"; and on September 23, 1776 the "principles of a Scotchman" make him 'subtile, proud, tyrannical, and false." ' In *The Revolutionary Diplomatic Correspondence of the United States*, i. 535.

[29] Thomas Jefferson, *Notes on Virginia*, included in *The Writings of Jefferson* (1905), ii. 120.

[30] Benjamin Franklin, 'Principle of Trade' (1774) in *Essays on General Politics, Commerce and Political Economy*, ed. Jared Sparks (1836, 1971), 401,

Versailles, Franklin, in his continuing role as America's first propagandist, was to publish in London several pamphlets on America. He follows Smith closely in describing America as a model for economic development, that is, cheapness of land, an industrious, well paid (and pious) labour force, and those 'encouragements' which are 'derived from good laws and liberty'. Franklin, if anything, goes even further than Smith in opposing the old mercantilistic practices and in calling for free trade without limitation. Even the infant industry argument is discarded when he states, '. . . if the country is ripe for the manufacture, it may be carried on by private persons to advantage; and if not, it is a folly to think of forcing nature' (ibid. 474).

Other statesmen of the new America obviously read Smith, but his, and Franklin's, arguments were generally rejected as not appropriate for America. Alexander Hamilton was clearly typical of this opinion. In his 'Report of Manufactures'[31] to the House of Representatives (1791) Hamilton, as Secretary of the Treasury in the new governemnt, presented a broad sweeping plan for the economic development of America. Throughout the *Report* he often closely paraphrases *The Wealth of Nations* and in one instance quotes (without credit) a lengthy passage from Smith.[32] Although as one commentator states, 'the whole cast of Hamilton's argument seems to have been affected by the study which he made of *The Wealth of Nations* . . .' (ibid. 233), he rejects Smith's economic plan. Hamilton admits the proposition that the 'cultivation of the earth . . . has intrinsically a strong claim to pre-eminence over every other kind of industry. But, he says, 'that it has a title to anything like an exclusive predilection, in any country, ought to be admitted with great caution' (ibid. 249). Then, by paraphrasing Smith, Hamilton uses Smith's own arguments to refute the very physiocracy which Smith had advocated for an undeveloped America:

> The labor of Artificers being capable of greater subdivision and simplicity of operation than that of Cultivators, it is susceptible, in a proportionately greater degree of improvement in its productive powers, whether to be derived from an accession of skill, or from the application of ingenious machinery, in which particular, therefore, the labor employed in the culture of land can pretend no advantage over that engaged in manufactures . . .
>
> (Ibid. 250–1)

America, states Hamilton, must not be dependent upon Europe for manufactured goods since an agrarian economy is a sign of weakness. Thus to induce manufacturing in the United States, Hamilton called upon Con-

[31] Alexander Hamilton, 'Report on the Subject of Manufactures' (1791) in *Industrial and Commercial Correspondence of Alexander Hamilton*, ed. Arthur H. Cole (1968). *The Reports of Alexander Hamilton*, ed. by Jacob E. Cooke (1964) correlates the 'Report' with *The Wealth of Nations*.

[32] Alexander Hamilton, *Industrial and Commercial Correspondence*, 233.

gress to enact a series of mercantilistic measures, that is, protective duties, prohibition of the importation of rival products, prohibition of the exportation of raw materials, bounties, premiums, the encouragement of new inventions, etc. *The Report on Manufactures* was never accepted by Congress, but its spirit of mercantilism was victorious over the freedom and physiocracy of Jefferson and the economic liberty of Franklin and Smith. While a true protective tariff was not imposed until 1816, the continuation and expansion of state bounties and loans, the establishment of a national bank, the levying of duties that were at least somewhat protective in effect were all examples of the victory of Hamilton's programme over *The Wealth of Nations*.

VI

When *The Wealth of Nations* was published in March of 1776 the time was not propitious for Smith's solutions of political union and economic equality between America and the mother country. It was too early for Parliament to listen to his proposals, and it was too late for Congress to want to listen to them. As for his 'simple system of natural liberty' it was too late to influence British commercial policy toward her American colonies, and it was not particularly compatible with the philosophy of the colonists which was basically nationalistic–mercantilistic after the revolution as it had been mercantilistic before the revolution. The colonists took Smith's doctrine of equal burden of taxation as a political infringement upon their rights. Smith probably was not greatly concerned by the failures of his proposals in America since America still remained an integral part of his system as an illustrative model. It was not until some sixty-five years later, with the advent of the Industrial Revolution in the United States that the essential message of *The Wealth of Nations* was given consideration. It was only then that the rising American industrialist discovered in it a 'compatible philosophy'. In America as in Great Britain, more than half a century before, they read and misread *The Wealth of Nations* as their declaration of independence.

XI

Adam Smith and the Mercantile System[1]

A. W. COATS*

I

It has often been remarked that a great author has something fresh and significant to offer each succeeding generation of readers, and in Adam Smith's case this truism is especially apt. Quite apart from the multitude of ideologists and propagandists who have cited him in support of their polemical campaigns, innumerable scholars have sought to comprehend the meaning of his writings and to assess their significance for Smith's own and subsequent epochs. In recent decades there has been a considerable debate about the interrelationships between the various component elements in Smith's works, especially his conception of scientific method, his moral philosophy, his view of the process of historical change, and his contributions to economic analysis.[2] The present essay is designed to place his treatment of economic policy in this broader intellectual context, by reconsidering his account of the mercantile system in relation to his theory of history and politics and his view of long-run socio-economic development.

This is, admittedly, a bold undertaking, for the range and variety of relevant issues is far too large to be treated adequately in a single essay. Nevertheless there are some compensations, for this topic does not lend itself to definitive treatment, since certain features of Smith's style and mode of presentation make it virtually impossible to determine the precise meaning and significance of his ideas. Among these is the conspicuous lack of that species of small-mindedness which makes a virtue of consistency—although Jacob Viner no doubt exaggerated when he remarked of Smith's *magnum opus* that 'traces of every conceivable sort of doctrine can be

* Professor of Economic and Social History at the University of Nottingham.

[1] This paper has been substantially revised, following trenchant criticisms of an earlier draft by a number of readers. Although I cannot name them all, I am especially indebted to Samuel Hollander, Neil de Marchi, and Andrew Skinner. They cannot, however, be held responsible for the remaining deficiencies. A first draft of this paper was completed and presented at the University of Sheffield in May 1972.

[2] Andrew Skinner's editorial introduction to *The Wealth of Nations* (Penguin Books, 1970) contains a valuable survey of these issues. See also A. L. Macfie, *The Individual in Society, Papers on Adam Smith* (1967) and the works by Campbell and Meek referred to below. My debt to these secondary sources will be obvious enough in the following pages. I have also benefited greatly from reading Samuel Hollander's important book, *The Economics of Adam Smith* (1972).

found in that most catholic book, and an economist must have peculiar theories indeed who cannot quote from *The Wealth of Nations* to support his special purposes.'[3] But in addition to the specific problems of interpreting that work, there is also the problem of relating *The Wealth of Nations* to the *Theory of Moral Sentiments*, a task which no serious student of Smith's economic ideas and policy can now avoid. Consequently there is added force in Viner's criticism that while 'the system of natural liberty' is much in evidence among Smith's interpreters, 'that natural harmony which should also result is strikingly lacking' (ibid. 216).

II

Despite its prominence in *The Wealth of Nations*, Smith's attack on the 'Mercantile System' has too often been considered only *en passant*, possibly because his admirers have been embarrassed by its decidedly polemical tone and orientation. Yet this phase of Smith's work exemplifies the subtle combination of analysis, historical insight, and policy recommendations which is to be found throughout his writings, and it also illustrates the difficulties involved in disentangling these closely interwoven strands of his thought. Although his treatment of the mercantile system has been correctly characterized as 'an emphatic piece of free trade propaganda',[4] it is also much more than this. As is well known, Smith condemned mercantilist regulations because they led to a serious misallocation of scarce resources and consequently inhibited economic growth; more fundamentally, such policies conflicted with 'the obvious and simple system of natural liberty', an ideal which Smith consistently advocated. This ideal was expressed in his unpublished Edinburgh lectures of the late 1740s and early 1750s,[5] and was anticipated by his 'never-to-be-forgotten teacher', Frances Hutcheson, and his lifelong friend David Hume, who published an outspoken critique of mercantilist policies more than twenty years before *The Wealth of Nations* appeared in print. Nor did Smith's central allegiance weaken in later life, despite his readiness to admit exceptions to the general principle of governmental non-interference in economic and social affairs. On the contrary, successive editions of *The Wealth of Nations* reveal Smith's determination to reinforce his anti-mercantilist position. Even in the first edition the seven chapters of Book IV devoted to the mercantile system occupied nearly a quarter of the whole work, while in the enlarged third edition he added a further chapter and

[3] Jacob Viner, 'Adam Smith and Laissez-Faire', originally published in 1928 and reprinted in his collected essays, *The Long View and The Short* (1958), 221.

[4] Eli Heckscher, *Mercantilism*, revised ed. (1955), ii.332. For the sake of convenience I shall treat the modern term 'mercantilism' as equivalent to Smith's usage.

[5] Cf. W. R. Scott, *Adam Smith as Student and Professor* (1937), 54, 111, where he draws on the opinion of Dugald Stewart.

several additional paragraphs. These additions contain few, if any, novel arguments; but they include much new factual material on such matters as duties, bounties, and drawbacks which is probably a by-product of Smith's experience as Commissioner of Customs, a post he assumed in 1778.[6] Also noteworthy is the intensification of his attack on trading companies in the third edition, which contains a lengthy new section in Book V, Chapter I, entitled 'Of the Expenses of the Sovereign or Commonwealth'. Smith described this as 'a short but, I flatter myself, a complete history of all the trading companies in Great Britain'.[7]

Smith employed the term 'mercantile system' broadly, applying it both to economic doctrines and to policy practices, though he was primarily concerned with the latter. In commenting on economic ideas he occasionally mentioned the best English writers who, he said, 'were apt to forget their own principles in the course of their reasonings and fall into confusion'; but he was far more interested in the beliefs of practical men than in intellectual achievements as such. Indeed, he maintained that self-interested merchants and manufacturers had been the 'principal architects' of the mercantile system.[8] His preoccupation with policy practice—rather than simply policy recommendations—followed directly from his definition of political economy as 'a branch of the science of a statesman or legislator'. Of 'the two different systems of political economy' which had been devised to enrich the people, namely, the mercantile system (or 'system of commerce') and the 'agricultural system', the former was the more 'modern', and it was 'best understood in our own country and our own times' (WN IV.2). As will be seen later, this reference to the national and temporal context is of special interest in any study of the relationship between Smith's view of economic policy and his conception of long-run socio-economic development, since it illustrates his practice of combining the analytical and historical dimensions of a given problem. He treated the mercantile system on two distinct, but interrelated levels: in terms of his atemporal ideal system of natural liberty, and by reference to the actual past and current practices of various European nations. This two-dimensional approach has been largely overlooked, or at least ignored, by many historians of economics, who have been concerned with the analytical aspects of *The Wealth of Nations*, such as the theories of value and distribution, the price mechanism, and the allocation of resources. As a result they have focused their attention on the first two Books, which contain 'the central part of Smith's work as a

[6] Adam Smith, *The Wealth of Nations*, ed. Cannan (1930), ii.160, n. 1. There was also a broader empirical justification for this shift of emphasis. See Ralph Davis, 'The Rise of Protection in England, 1689–1786', *Economic History Review*, xix (1966), 306–17.

[7] Letter 222 addressed to his publisher, T. Cadell, dated Dec. 1782, quoted in John Rae, *Life of Adam Smith* (1895), 362. Also in Cannan, op. cit. xvi.

[8] WN IV.vii.54. For an elaboration of this point see J. A. La Nauze, 'The Substance of Adam Smith's attack on Mercantilism', *The Economic Record*, xiii (June 1937), 90–3.

theoretical economist',[9] while neglecting the remainder of the volume—some of which is, admittedly, tedious and longwinded. This preoccupation has encouraged the habit of viewing Smith's attack on the mercantile system simply and solely as an analysis of impediments to the smooth functioning of the competitive market economy, rather than an integral part of a larger system of moral, socio-philosophical, historical, and political ideas. Yet Smith's profound impact on his own and subsequent generations was not merely due to his analytical ability. It was mainly attributable to his exceptional skill in combining analysis with empirical data, with historical examples, and with direct and incisive comments on the conditions and tendencies of his own times. In his treatment of the mercantile system the combined force of these disparate elements is well nigh irresistible; and they are so exquisitely interwoven that it is extraordinarily difficult to disentangle them for the purposes of historical reappraisal.

In recent years there has been a discernible shift of scholarly interest away from Smith's economic analysis towards his sociological and historical ideas, and it is now especially appropriate to re-examine his attack on the mercantile system in the light of his conception of the 'natural history of society'. It has long been recognized that Smith's *Lectures* embodied a theory of socio-economic development expressed in terms of four 'stages': hunting, pasturage, agriculture, and commerce, each of which is based on a particular 'mode of subsistence'.[10] The discovery of a new set of *Lectures* has made it clear that this 'four-stage' theory occupied a more prominent place in Smith's mind than had formerly been supposed—so much so, that it has been claimed that the theory should now be recognized as 'the basic conceptual framework within which the major part of Smith's argument is set'.[11]

It is, of course, too early to make a considered assessment of this contention. Yet it is already apparent that the four-stage framework provides a convenient starting-point for a reappraisal of Smith's treatment of the mercantile system. For according to this theory the prevailing mode of subsistence in any society not only influences the predominant pattern of economic activity, but also the entire range of social life, including ideas and institutions of property and government, the state of manners and morals, the legal system, and the division of labour. While Smith did not

[9] Skinner (ed.), op. cit. 7.

[10] LJ (B) 149; Cannan, 107. Other members of the Scottish school also accepted this theory. Cf. Andrew Skinner, 'Natural History in the Age of Adam Smith', *Political Studies*, xv (1967), esp. 38–40; also his 'Economics and History: The Scottish Enlightenment', *Scottish Journal of Political Economy*, xii (1965), 1–22.

[11] Ronald L. Meek, 'Smith, Turgot, and the "Four Stages" Theory', *History of Political Economy*, iii (Spring 1971), 12; and his earlier essay, 'The Scottish Contribution to Marxist Sociology', reprinted in his *Economics and Ideology* (1967). Also T. D. Campbell, *Adam Smith's Science of Morals* (1971), 79–83.

adopt a rigidly deterministic view of the process of change, acknowledging 'the complex interrelationships of economic, military, political, religious, moral, and legal factors',[12] he seems to have regarded the economic factor as the most fundamental. However, as in Karl Marx's case, the relationship between the economic substructure and the cultural and institutional superstructure is by no means clear cut.

Curiously enough, despite his unmistakable hostility to the mercantile system and his deep-seated suspicions of the activities and intentions of merchants, Smith regarded the commercial stage as the highest, most civilized form of society, and portrayed its beneficial influence on European development in glowing terms:

commerce and manufactures gradually introduced order and good government, and with them, the liberty and security of individuals, among the inhabitants of the country, who had before lived almost in a continual state of war with their neighbours, and of servile dependency upon their superiors. This, though it has been the least observed, is by far the most important of their effects.[13]

As Joseph Cropsey has shown, Smith regarded commerce and civilization as inseparable, in the sense that:

commerce generates freedom and civilization, and at the same time free institutions are indispensable to the preservation of commerce. If the advantages of commerce can be sufficiently impressed upon the general mind, freedom and civilization will automatically follow in its train, and mankind will perhaps be disposed to defend civilization, not necessarily out of love for freedom but out of love for commerce and gain.[14]

At first sight, these passages may suggest that Smith's attack on the mercantile system was utterly inconsistent if that system was, in fact, merely a necessary concomitant of the highest, most civilized stage of social development. Moreover, if the commercial society was also 'natural', in the sense of being inevitable, there was surely no point in fulminating against it.

There is, in fact, some justification for both these contentions. Yet it

[12] Campbell, op. cit. 82. It is therefore impossible to accept Leo Rogin's contention that Smith provided a 'theory of natural economic development which he imposes as a norm upon the historical career of nations since their emergence from the feudal period': *The Meaning and Validity of Economic Theory* (1956), 76.

[13] WN III.iv.4. Although Smith occasionally used the terms 'mercantile' and 'commercial' as equivalents, and even described 'the mercantile system' as 'the system of commerce', he used the phrase 'the mercantile system' solely as a description of those economic ideas and policies which he regarded as a perversion of the 'system of natural liberty'. The precise nature of the relationship between the mercantile system and the 'commercial' stage of societal development will be considered more fully below. In this essay the term 'commercial' will be applied exclusively to that stage.

[14] Joseph Cropsey, *Polity and Economy, An Interpretation of the Principles of Adam Smith* (1957), 95.

would be presumptious to suppose that a writer of Smith's stature could be dismissed so lightly. His critique of mercantilism was not merely the crude polemic it is sometimes taken to be; it was more sophisticated than this, and it is consistent with his general view of history, which is itself quite complex. For present purposes, then, the central question is: what was Smith's precise conception of the relationship between the growth of commerce and the emergence of the 'mercantile system'? Before confronting this problem directly it is necessary to consider the meaning of certain key terms in his writing and to comment on the question of his consistency and his use of historical data.

Smith obviously viewed mercantilist regulations as a perversion of the ideal of natural liberty, a state of affairs most nearly attainable in the commercial stage of development. But his account of the 'natural' progress of society through successive stages was neither clear nor detailed enough to serve as a basis for confident assertions about the inevitability or persistence of the mercantile system or the political power basis on which it rested. Despite elements of ambiguity in his semantic practice, Smith did not use the term 'natural' as equivalent to 'inevitable'. Indeed, Book III of *The Wealth of Nations*, which treats 'Of the Different Progress of Opulence in Different Nations' is specifically designed to show how, in the unfolding of European history, the 'natural' course of events has repeatedly been perverted or checked by human interference.[15] And if the mercantile system is neither inevitable nor irresistible it may succumb to a powerful polemical assault. Smith himself maintained that theories of political economy 'have had considerable influence, not only upon the opinions of men of learning, but upon the public conduct of princes and sovereign states' (WN I.lix). Although the prevailing theories and practices of government fell far short of his ideal—which he realized was unattainable in

[15] As Cropsey puts it, 'man is naturally disposed to reverse the natural', ibid. 40. In accordance with contemporary usage, Smith sometimes used the term 'natural' as equivalent to normal—i.e. spontaneous and instinctive in human behaviour, or, in social and economic affairs, what normally occurs or would occur in the absence of some human, legal, or institutional impediment. However, the term 'natural, was also used to connote 'ideal', and as Cropsey stresses, there is an important tension between the 'natural' and 'moral' elements in Smith's work. For a helpful analysis see Campbell, op. cit. 53–60; see also the discussion of the relationship between the 'natural' and the 'supernatural' by H. J. Bitterman, in 'Adam Smith's Empiricism and the Law of Nature', *Journal of Political Economy*, xlviii (1940), 487–520 and 703–37 (esp. 729). Another incisive treatment of this element is Jacob Viner, *The Role of Providence in the Social Order, An Essay in Intellectual History* (American Philosophical Society, 1972), esp. 47, 53–4, 81. According to Andrew Skinner, some members of the Scottish School, notably Kames and Millar, appeared to believe that the successive stages were, in fact, inevitable. Cf. 'Natural History in the Age of Adam Smith', 44–5. In his editorial introduction to *The Wealth of Nations*, p. 40, he imputes this idea to Smith, but on p. 34 he notes that Smith did not consider that progress beyond the second stage was inevitable. As will be shown later, even if the *sequence* was in some sense inevitable, there was nevertheless scope for considerable variations *within each stage*.

practice (see below, pp. 225–6)—he certainly hoped that his *magnum opus* would contribute to the reform of present discontents.

With regard to the inconsistencies in Smith's writings, Professor Macfie has reminded us that 'consistency was never the central aim or virtue of eighteenth century writers, especially of the Scottish sociological school. It certainly was not then the ark of the covenant that it is for our analysis-ridden age' (op. cit. 126). Yet we need not go as far as Viner, who remarked that 'when there was a sharp conflict between his generalization and his data, [Smith] usually abandoned his generalization'.[16] Although he was sensitive to the problem of applying *general* principles to *particular* circumstances of time and place, he did not so readily discard his principles as Viner maintains.[17] In discussing the role of government, for example, he certainly recognized numerous exceptions to the general principle of *laissez-faire*, but without significantly diminishing the impact of his plea for economic freedom.

There is, unfortunately, no general rule or principle by which to explain precisely when and why Smith was prepared to admit particular exceptions to his general principles. A twentieth-century professional historian, trained to respect the evidence, may be tempted to assume that the exceptions were determined by an examination of the relevant facts; but this would be to completely misunderstand the conception of history familiar to Smith and his Scottish contemporaries. This conception is what is nowadays known as 'hypothetical' or 'conjectural' history, which is not designed as an accurate account of the historical past, but is intended to reveal the orderly unfolding of the process of change and, more often than not, also to point a moral.[18] As J. M. Clark observed many years ago, Smith's account of socio-economic development contains 'the germs of a

[16] Op. cit 230. Viner explained Smith's inconsistencies by referring to his polemical purpose (232), but this is clearly an unsatisfactory explanation. More recently Viner somewhat modified his interpretation. 'Smith worked from what he called systems and what today would be called models. He was aware that "systems" are incomplete in the factors they take into account. Had he been able to complete his total system, he would probably have demonstrated that the apparent inconsistencies were often not real ones, but were merely the consequences of deliberate shifts from one partial model to another'; 'Adam Smith', in *International Encyclopedia of the Social Sciences* (1968) xiv. 323.

[17] Cf. Viner's classic account of this subject, 'Adam Smith and Laissez Faire'. Smith probably accepted David Hume's view that: 'General principles, if just and sound must prevail in the course of things though they fall in particular cases, and it is the chief business of philosophers to regard the general course of things.' See his *Economic Writings*, ed. E. Rotwein (1955), 4.

[18] The term 'conjectural history' derives from Dugald Stewart, to whom it was not a derogatory expression as it was for Thorstein Veblen, who described it as being 'of the nature of harmless and graceful misinformation'. Smith was a generalizing or 'philosophical' historian. 'Narrative that is not an occasion for or does not lead to, or does not in some way reinforce or illuminate a generalization or insight in sociology or economics or the like seems to have little interest for him.' Cf. Louis Schneider, *The Scottish Moralists on Human Nature and Society* (1967), lxii. It would take at least another article, probably a monograph, to examine Smith's merits and limitations as a historian.

genetic treatment', but 'they are tributary and subordinate to the system of natural liberty'.[19] His historical passages are frequently abstract and simplified in content, for they were more often designed as support for a preconceived theory than as a source of data on which to base inductive generalizations. Nevertheless Smith's use of history must be taken seriously for, unlike some of his contemporaries, he frequently cited particular facts and events, and employed this kind of material very effectively in his critique of the mercantile system. It is therefore appropriate to review this part of his work in some detail before considering its relationship to his generalized conception of the commercial stage of development.

III

As already noted, Smith recognized that a state of society 'where things were left to follow their natural course, where there was perfect liberty', was an unattainable ideal. 'The policy of Europe', he complained, 'nowhere leaves things at perfect liberty'; and even in commercial affairs, to expect 'that the freedom of trade should ever be entirely restored in Great Britain is as absurd as to expect that an Oceana or Utopia should ever be fully established in it'.[20] Civil government was a necessary evil, an imperfect remedy for the deficiencies of human wisdom and virtue, and its imperfections stemmed directly from its failure to 'sufficiently guard against the mischiefs which human wickedness gives occasion to'.[21] Like Locke and Hobbes, Smith took it for granted that government would normally be dominated by men of property and conducted in their interest. 'All for ourselves and nothing for other people', he remarked, 'seems, in every age

[19] Cf. his 'Adam Smith and the Currents of History' in J. M. Clark *et al.*, *Adam Smith, 1776–1926* (1928), 73. Quoted in Gladys Bryson, *Man amd Society: The Scottish Inquiry of the Eighteenth Century* (1968), 86. Ch. IV of this work contains a valuable account of the Scottish approach to the past.

[20] WN I.x.a.1, IV.ii.43. However, it is important not to exaggerate the significance of the failure to attain the ideal. 'If a nation could not prosper without the enjoyment of perfect liberty and perfect justice, there is not in the world a nation which could ever have prospered. In the political body, however, the wisdom of nature has fortunately made ample provision for remedying many of the bad effects of the folly and injustice of man; in the same manner as it had done in the natural body, for remedying those of sloth and intemperance' (WN IV.ix.28).

[21] TMS IV.i.2.2. The most familiar passage on the duties of the sovereign under the system of natural liberty is the following: 'first, the duty of protecting the society from the violence and invasion of other independent societies; secondly, the duty of protecting, as far as possible, every member of the society from the injustice or oppression of every other member of it, or the duty of establishing an exact administration of justice; and, thirdly, the duty of erecting and maintaining certain public works and certain public institutions which it can never be for the interest of any individual, or small number of individuals, to erect and maintain' (WN IV.ix.51). Although most commentators concerned with economic affairs have concentrated on the third class of governmental functions it should be noted that the second category is also ill defined and flexible. Cf. Viner, op. cit. 237. Indeed, as will appear below, it is virtually impossible to assess Smith's attitude to economic policy without taking due account of the conduct of administration and justice.

of the world, to have been the vile maxim of the masters of mankind.'[22] Yet despite occasional outbursts of this kind he was essentially a moderate reformer. 'No government is quite perfect, but it is better to submit to some inconveniences than make attempts against it.'[23] Indeed, he specifically warned against the 'spirit of system' which leads men to embark upon far-reaching schemes of constitutional reconstruction which would entail alteration 'in some of its most essential parts that system of government under which the subjects of a great empire have enjoyed, perhaps, peace, security, and even glory, during the course of several centuries together' (TMS VI.ii.2.15).

It is by no means clear from Smith's account which section of the propertied classes would 'naturally' have the upper hand in a commercial society, or which form of government would 'naturally' prevail. At first sight the answer seems obvious enough. In a commercial society every man 'lives by exchanging, or becomes in some measure a merchant', a state of affairs approximated in Holland, where almost every citizen is a 'man of business', or is engaged in 'some sort of trade'.[24] Such a community would, presumably, be governed by merchants or businessmen whose viewpoint should be representative of the community as a whole; and in fact Smith praised the 'orderly, vigilant and parsimonious administration' of Amsterdam which, however, he described as an aristocracy.[25] Nevertheless, despite these observations, he was utterly opposed to the notion that society should be governed by merchants. He complained bitterly of 'the mean rapacity, the monopolizing spirit of merchants and manufacturers, who neither are, nor ought to be, the rulers of mankind', and described

[22] WN IV.iv.10. Elsewhere, he remarked: 'The rich, in particular, are necessarily interested to support that order of things which can alone secure them in the possession of their own advantages . . . Civil government, so far as it is instituted for the security of property, is in reality instituted for the defence of the rich against the poor, or of those who have some property against those who have none at all' (WN V.i.b.12). In this respect the mercantile regulations, which tended to favour the rich at the expense of the poor, were quite characteristic.

[23] LJ (B) 95; Cannan, 69; Cf. TMS VI.ii.2.16: 'The man whose public spirit is prompted altogether by humanity and benevolence, will respect the established powers and privileges even of individuals, and still more of those of the great orders and societies into which the state is divided. Though he should consider some of them as in some measure abusive, he will content himself with moderating, what he cannot annihilate without great violence . . . when he cannot establish the right he will not disdain to ameliorate the wrong; but like Solon, when he cannot establish the best system of laws, he will endeavour to establish the best that the people can bear.'

[24] WN I.iv.1; I.ix.20. Smith did not distinguish between a government of merchants *per se* and one that is dominated or unduly influenced by merchants. But since merchants and manufacturers were treated as knowing their own interests clearly and being especially effective in getting their own way, the distinction is not of practical importance.

[25] WN V.ii.a.4. Elsewhere he remarked that 'The republican form of government seems to be the principal support of the present grandeur of Holland', and warned that 'The parsimony which leads to accumulation has become almost as rare in republican as in monarchical governments' (WN V.ii.k.80, V.iii.3.).

merchants as 'an order of men whose interest is never the same with that of the public, who have generally an interest to deceive and even to oppress the public, and who accordingly have, upon many occasions, both deceived and oppressed it' (WN IV.iii.c.9, I.xi.p.10). Yet the situation would not be entirely satisfactory under a government dominated by landed proprietors, even though their interests were 'strictly and inseparably connected with the general interest of the society'. Although they 'never can mislead' the public into promoting 'the interest of their own particular order', they were too often unable to recognize that interest. Moreover, the 'indolence, which is the natural effect of the ease and security of their situation, renders them too often, not only ignorant, but incapable of that application of mind which is necessary in order to forsee and understand the consequences of any public regulation'.[26]

The only social group in which Smith displayed any confidence whatever was the so-called 'natural aristocracy', who were elsewhere described as men 'educated in the middle and inferior ranks of life, who have been carried forward by their own industry and abilities' into the highest offices 'in all governments . . . even in monarchies' (WN IV.vii.c.74; TMS I.iii.2.5). However, this was an amorphous and somewhat ill-fated category, and for want of a better alternative Smith seemed to be more concerned to ensure a balance of power between the various 'orders' of society—the sovereign, nobility, landed gentry, merchants and manufacturers, clergy, and labouring poor—than to advocate rule by any particular order. He recognized that statesmen, like other human beings, were necessarily imperfect, but considered that as such imperfections were unavoidable they were more tolerable than the evils wrought by merchants or any other vested interest group.[27] Generally speaking, Smith implied that historical processes had generated a balanced constitutional position in England, and that the mercantile classes represented both a source and a focus of pressure within the system, especially through the House of Commons.

[26] WN I.xi.p.8. Landlords, like farmers and graziers, were widely scattered and could not easily combine to promote their own interests, whereas merchants and manufacturers were already assembled in cities and could therefore put pressure on the government to give them special privileges. This helps to explain why the long-term tendency of mercantilist economic policy was in favour of towns at the expense of the countryside. In the matter of trading companies the advantages were even more concentrated than this, for in these organizations metropolitan merchants frequently gained at the expense of merchants in the 'outports'. In this connection Smith's violent attack on trading companies may reflect his long-standing association with Glasgow merchants. See below, p. 236.

[27] 'The capricious ambition of kings and ministers has not, during the present and preceding century, been more fatal to the repose of Europe than the impertinent jealousy of merchants and manufacturers. The violence and injustice of the rulers of mankind is an ancient evil, for which, I am afraid, the nature of human affairs can scarce admit of a remedy. But the mean rapacity, the monopolizing spirit of merchants and manufacturers, . . . though it cannot perhaps be corrected may easily be prevented from disturbing the tranquillity of anybody but themselves' (WN IV.iii.c.9.)

Nevertheless, to the modern student of social processes and pressure group politics Smith's analysis is inadequate for it does not explain why the mercantile classes are more effective politically in some respects and contexts than in others. For example, while recognizing the primacy of national interests in all systems of political economy, and the special importance of national animosities in the growth of mercantilist regulations, he did not always clearly specify the relationship between national and sectional interests behind legislation.[28]

IV

The precise nature of Smith's attack on the mercantile system can be seen more clearly against the background of his general ideas on society and government. As Britain approximated more closely to his ideal of natural liberty than any other country, his criticisms of British economic policy were a good deal less severe than some of his more rhetorical passages might lead us to expect. Indeed they directly conflicted with Smith's own description of *The Wealth of Nations* as 'a very violent attack . . . upon the whole commercial system of Great Britain',[29] especially when his much more severe indictment of the policies of other European powers is taken into account. 'In Britain', Smith declared, 'there is a happy mixture of all the different forms of government properly restrained, and a perfect security to liberty and property . . . the nation is quite secure in the management of the public revenue, and in this manner a rational system of liberty has been introduced.'[30]

Admittedly the nation had suffered from the 'profusion of government which had retarded her natural progress'. Yet despite this, and many other setbacks, such as the fire and plague of London, the disorders of the revolution, two rebellions, and a series of wars, the century or so since the restoration had been 'the happiest and most fortunate period in our history' (WN II.iii.35). Britain's economic policy was undoubtedly bad, but its

[28] This explains some, though by no means all, of the difficulties Professor Stigler encountered in his analysis of Smith's account of the legislative process. Cf. Professor Stigler's 'Smith's Travels on the Ship of State' and below, p. 233. For my comments on this see *History of Political Economy*, vol. vii (1975) 132–6.

[29] In a Letter (208) addressed to Andreas Holt, dated 26 Oct. 1780, quoted in Scott, op. cit. 283.

[30] LJ (B) 63; Cannan, 45 (sentence order reversed). Similar comments appear in *The Wealth of Nations*. According to Viner, 'All of the influential British eighteenth-century theologians and moral philosophers, whatever their philosophical or theological beliefs, were agreed that once the Restoration of 1660, or once the Glorious Revolution of 1689, had occurred, neither religion nor morality called for any substantial change in the political structure, or in the social structure of England, or of Scotland. With respect to matters of more direct economic interest also, there was widespread belief that no major changes in economic institutions, policies, or patterns of behaviour were urgently called for on religious or moral grounds' (*The Role of Providence*, 58). This suggests that Smith did not regard the mercantile system as sinful or immoral. But see ibid. 65.

deficiencies were more than 'counter-balanced by the general liberty and security of the people', whereas at the opposite end of the scale, the civil and ecclesiastical governments of Spain and Portugal were so pernicious as to 'perpetuate their present state of poverty, even though their regulations of commerce were as wise as the greater part of them are absurd and foolish'.[31] English law, Smith maintained, was more favourable to the interests of commerce and manufactures than that of any country of Europe, 'Holland itself not excepted'.[32] Moreover even agriculture, which generally suffered under the mercantile system, was in England favoured not only indirectly, but also 'by several direct encouragements' which, though fundamentally illusory, demonstrated the legislature's 'good intention' and produced the important result that 'the yeomanry of England are rendered as secure, as independent and as respectable as law can make them'. Indeed, 'those laws and customs so favourable to the yeomanry, have perhaps contributed more to the present grandeur of England than all their boasted regulations of commerce taken together' (WN III.iv.20, III.ii.14). In France, by contrast, there was no legal encouragement to agriculture. The prevalence of metayage, short leases, and the taille combined to produce a situation in which cultivation and improvement were markedly inferior to English standards (III.ii.13,18–20, III.iv.21).

Smith fully appreciated the interdependence of commerce, manufactures, and agriculture, and was especially conscious of the effects of bad taxes on output and incentives. Here, too, he was very critical of French practice. The personal taille was especially absurd and destructive since it constituted a tax on profits; the cruel, oppressive, and discriminatory assessment of the corvée constituted 'one of the principal instruments of tyranny' in the hands of local administrators; and after describing the farming of taxes on salt and tobacco, which had annually resulted in several hundred people being sent to the galleys, and a considerable number to the gibbet, he concluded that these levies could be approved only by 'those who consider the blood of the people nothing in comparison with the revenue of the prince' (WN V.ii.k.75). Here, too, the contrast between Britain and France was striking. But while the French were 'much more

[31] WN IV.v.b.45. The overwhelming importance of 'that security which the laws in Great Britain give to every man that he shall enjoy the fruits of his own labour' was stressed a little earlier. 'This security was perfected by the revolution' of 1688, thereby encouraging individual initiative and the desire for self-improvement. 'The natural effort of every individual to better his own condition, when suffered to exert itself with freedom and security, is so powerful a principle that it is alone, and without any assistance, not only capable of carrying on the society to wealth and prosperity, but of surmounting a hundred impertinent obstructions with which the folly of human laws too often incumbers its operations' (WN IV.v.b.43).

[32] Ibid. III.iv.20. In contrast to agricultural systems of political economy which advocated policies contrary to the ends they proposed, the mercantile system did 'really and in the end' encourage 'that species of industry which it means to promote', though in so doing it drew resources from other, more efficient, uses (IV.ix.49).

oppressed by taxes than the people of Great Britain', they fared better than the citizens of other countries, for they enjoyed 'the mildest and most indulgent government' of any great empire in Europe after that of Great Britain. We suffered less than most other states from the inconveniences of taxes on consumable commodities; and on the whole:

Our present system of taxation . . . has hitherto given so little embarrassment to industry that, during the course of even the most expensive wars, the frugality and good conduct of individuals seem to have been able, by saving and accumulation, to repair all the breaches which the waste and extravagance of government had made in the general capital of society.[33]

A similar emphasis is apparent in Smith's comments on Britain's colonial policy as in his discussion of domestic affairs. Although her treatment of the colonial trade had been

dictated by the same mercantile spirit as that of other nations, it has, however, upon the whole, been less illiberal and oppressive than that of any of them . . . [indeed] the government of the English colonies is perhaps the only one which, since the world began, could give perfect security to the inhabitants of so very distant a province.

(WN IV.vii.b.50,52)

There was, of course, a marked contrast 'between the genius of the British constitution which protects and governs North America, and that of the mercantile company which oppresses and domineers in the East Indies', for the latter was a prime example of that species of monopoly which 'seems to be the sole engine of the mercantile system' (WN I.viii.26, IV.vii.c.89). England's North American policy was better than that of any other European power, though only somewhat less illiberal and oppressive than the rest, and in his attitude to this area we encounter one of the difficulties of interpreting Smith's meaning. For despite the vigour of his polemics and his powerful analytical demonstration of the distortions of the allocation of resources resulting from our colonial policy, he made the important concession that 'the natural good effects of the colony trade, however, more than counterbalance to Great Britain the bad effects of the monopoly, so that, monopoly and all together, that trade, even as it is carried on at present, is not only advantageous, but greatly advantageous'.[34]

[33] Ibid. WN V.iii.58. See also LJ (B) 318; Cannan, 245: 'Upon the whole we may observe that the English are the best financiers in Europe, and their taxes are levied with more propriety than those of any country whatever.' Yet in fairness to the Dutch it should perhaps be noted that the 'load of taxes' in the singular countries of Zealand and Holland were largely due to the debt burdens incurred in fighting wars to acquire and to maintain their independence. Presumably Smith regarded these costs of freedom as legitimate. Cf. WN V.ii.k.80.

[34] Ibid. WN IV.vii.c.50. Among the 'natural good effects of the colony trade' was the fact that the colonies provided a 'vent-for-surplus' of home commodities. The relationship between the conception of the influence of foreign trade on home employment and Smith's

The grounds for this judgement were several. Despite some restraints, there was freedom to export, duty free, almost all kinds of products of domestic industry to almost any foreign country; there was also freedom of internal transport within Britain; but 'above all', was

> that equal and impartial administration of justice which renders the rights of the meanest British subject respectable to the greatest, and which, by securing to every man the fruits of his own industry, gives the greatest and most effectual encouragement to every sort of industry.
>
> (WN IV.vii.c.54)

After a lengthy analysis of the disadvantages of the monopoly of colonial trade, Smith concluded that owing to the heavy outlay on defence and the low level of taxation paid by the colonists, 'under the present system of management . . . Great Britain derives nothing but loss from the dominion which she assumes over her colonies'. The British colonists, however, enjoyed far greater advantages than the subjects of other colonial regimes. Admittedly, their interests were sacrificed to those of British merchants, but not consistently so; and although they were prevented from 'employing their stock and industry in the way that they judge most advantageous to themselves . . . [which was] a manifest violation of the most sacred rights of mankind', in practice such prohibitions had 'not hitherto been very hurtful to the colonies'. Indeed, owing to the 'plenty of good land, and liberty to manage their own affairs their own way . . . there are no colonies of which the progress has been more rapid than that of the English in North America' (WN IV.vii.b.15). By contrast, the ecclesiastical governments of France, Spain, and Portugal were extremely oppressive to their colonies, especially the last two, on whose cruel, violent and arbitrary policies Smith dilated at some length, while he accused the Dutch of governing by means of an exclusive monopoly, with the inevitable restrictive consequences. (WN IV.vii.b.12)

V

This abbreviated survey of Smith's account of the mercantile system reveals his ability to combine economic principles with historical examples; it also shows that the system is far less monolithic and harmful in practice than might have been presumed on theoretical grounds alone. Yet at the same time, Smith's awareness of the national variants of the mercantile system makes it correspondingly more difficult to assess the precise

more familiar efficiency (i.e. international division of labour) argument is examined in Hollander, *Economics of Adam Smith*, Ch. 9. His attempt to reconcile the two theoretical approaches is ingenious, but not wholly convincing. However, a thorough discussion of the issues would not be in accordance with the main theme of this paper. For other discussions of this matter see Charles E. Staley, 'Adam Smith's Version of the Vent for Surplus Model', *History of Political Economy*, v (1973), 438–48, and the article by A. I. Bloomfield in this volume.

relationship of the system to his broader conception of the commercial stage of development. This is largely because Smith, unlike some nineteenth-century German economists and historians, did not visualize his 'stages' of development in a narrow, deterministic fashion. The mercantile system obviously represented a perversion or distortion of the ideal of natural liberty, which is most nearly attainable in a fully commercial society. But are we to infer that all the European powers whose policies Smith condemned had reached the commercial stage; or should that designation be reserved for Britain and Holland? He certainly recognized that any given nation's laws and institutions would normally lag behind its economic development,[35] hence it may be assumed that the more illiberal, authoritarian, and oppressive features of the French, Spanish, and Portugese régimes merely reflected their failure to cast off these inherited characteristics. But what determines how closely any given commercial society will in practice approach the ideal of natural liberty? Admittedly all fall short; but, to coin a phrase, some fall shorter than others. How far does Smith's account enable us to explain their respective positions both now and in the future?

The task of answering these questions is complicated by the fact that Smith was enough of a historian to be wary of making firm forecasts, and his writings contain a number of statements from which partially contradictory prognostications can be inferred. Whatever doubts there may be concerning the inevitability of successive stages of development, there is no reason to doubt his fundamentally optimistic belief in progress.[36] In the earlier forms of society, Smith maintained, oppressive and unjust government was almost inevitable; whereas justice and probity were, to him, such central features of the value system of a commercial society, where they were reinforced by regular face-to-face contacts in market situations, that it is tempting to suggest that these virtues will necessarily permeate government circles and eventually influence the nation's laws and economic policies. Yet Smith would probably have objected to any such simplistic extrapolation of individual behavioural characteristics

[35] 'Laws frequently continue in force long after the circumstances which first gave occasion to them, and which could alone render them reasonable, are no more' (WN III.ii. 4). It may be helpful to note that although Smith described four 'stages' of development, he considered only two 'systems' of political economy: those of 'agriculture' and 'commerce', of which the latter was 'the modern system'. The agricultural system, Smith noted, had 'never been adopted by any nation, and it at present exists only in the speculation of a few men of great learning and ingenuity in France'. However, a few pages later he acknowledged the influence of the Economists on 'some measures of public administration in favour of agriculture'. Smith presumably considered that in the hunting and pasturage states, the institutions of government, policy ideas, and practices were too underdeveloped to be compatible with any system of political economy (IV.2; IV.ix.2, 38).

[36] This is not, of course, to deny the significance of the long-term falling trend of the rate of profit in a country which had acquired its full complement of riches. See also the essay by Heilbroner, in this volume.

from the micro- to the macro-sociological level. While at one point he spoke of the 'fated dissolution that awaits every state and constitution whatever',[37] there is no reason to suppose that this necessarily implied a prospective withering away of mercantilistic regulations. Indeed, Smith repeatedly emphasized the strength and persistence of those public prejudices which had in the past inspired so much unwise legislation, and he scorned the suggestion that any nation would ever voluntarily relinquish control of its colonies.[38] In home affairs, much would obviously depend on the shifting balance of power between the various categories of property owners, who formed the bulk of the governing classes; and while Smith was far from explicit about the forces determining this power struggle, he certainly had no faith in merchants, and he made no suggestion that society might some day be dominated by committed libertarians. Such persons would, in any case, have been examples of the 'men of system' whose influence on governments he so deeply suspected.

Smith had little faith in constitution-makers or in detailed blueprints for political and social reform; and in his review of European policies he described the preconditions of the good society in generalized abstract terms, such as liberty, justice and security.[39] This largely explains why his treatment of the forms and processes of government is so disappointingly sketchy and inconclusive. In *The Wealth of Nations*, the most explicitly economic of his works, the polemical driving force behind his attack on the mercantile system was his profound hostility to monopoly. The intensification of his attack in later editions may suggest that he viewed this as a growing menace, notwithstanding the comparative mildness and liberalism of the British system of government. While a trading monopoly might be justifiable for a small country, or as a temporary device for assisting the establishment of an especially remote and risky trade, he detested trading bodies like the East India Company, which had assumed functions that properly belonged to the sovereign, functions they were totally unsuited to perform (WN IV.vii.c.103). Since monopoly was, for Smith, a simple injustice, resulting from a combination of human selfishness, unequal distribution of economic power, and inadequate legal restraints, he may

[37] LJ (B) 46; Cannan, 32. On the mortality of Empires see WN V.ii.c.6. For this brief comment on the early stages see the so-called 'Early Draft of the Wealth of Nations' in Scott, 352.

[38] 'To propose that Great Britain should voluntarily give up all authority over her colonies, and leave them to elect their own magistrates, to enact their own laws, and to make peace and war as they might think proper, would be to propose such a measure as never was, and never will be adopted, by any nation in the world . . . The most visionary enthusiast would scarce be capable of proposing such a measure with any serious hopes at least of its ever being adopted' (WN IV.vii.c.66).

[39] Indeed, it has even been suggested that for Smith all the preconditions of economic order were reducible to one: namely, justice. Cf. Skinner, Editor's introduction to *The Wealth of Nations*, 28.

have assumed that no subtle or detailed social or political analysis was required. Alternatively, he may have intended to incorporate this in his projected, but unfinished 'history of law and government'.[40]

Smith traced the origins of monopoly back to the 'corporation spirit' which prevailed in medieval towns,[41] and doubtless regarded exclusive trading companies, like other state-supported monopolies, as a regrettable legacy of the past. Yet he gave no clear guidance as to the likely future trend of monopolistic activity. To a modern reader, urbanization and the growth of large-scale industry might be supposed to enhance potential monopoly powers, whereas improvements of transport and any other means of widening the market would presumably aid the forces of competition. Private monopolies gave Smith less grounds for concern than those backed by legislation, and he repeatedly warned his readers of the merchants' and manufacturers' skill in gaining government aid for their vested interests.

Nevertheless, in his treatment of the mercantile system, as elsewhere in his works, Smith was no crude advocate of *laissez-faire*. As is well known, he defended the Navigation Acts, which modern historians have generally regarded as the keystone of mercantilism, on the grounds that 'defence is of much more importance than opulence';[42] and the significance of this particular exception to the general principle of economic freedom is enhanced by his earlier acknowledgement of the fact that as societies become richer defence becomes more, not less, important, owing to the decline of the martial spirit (LJ (B) 331; Cannan, 257–8).

Certainly the most remarkable, though not necessarily the most realistic, prognostication of the future of the mercantile system—or, rather, that part of it now generally known as the old colonial system—is to be found in those passages where Smith advocated a complete union of Britain and Ireland and a scheme of Imperial Federation.

As the breach between Britain and her American colonies grew wider while Smith was completing his *magnum opus* he could hardly refrain from comment on the future of our transatlantic territories; and in view of his

[40] See Letter (248) addressed to Rochefoucauld, dated 1 Nov. 1785, quoted in Meek, *Economics and Ideology*, 35 n.

[41] WN IV.ii.21. As noted by Arthur H. Cole, Smith displayed a lower opinion of merchants in *The Wealth of Nations* than in the *Theory of Moral Sentiments*, where he remarked that they had been 'unjustly denigrated'. The earlier distaste for commercial activities, he complained, had persisted even in a refined society like England; and this 'mean and despicable idea of earlier days' had 'greatly obstructed the progress of commerce.' Cf. 'Puzzles of "The Wealth of Nations"', *Canadian Journal of Economics and Political Science*, xxiv (1958), 4.

[42] WN I. 429; cf. IV.ii.30. Elsewhere Smith acknowledges the wisdom of protecting certain manufactures required for purposes of defence (WN IV.v.a.27). As Hollander notes, the principle here is that the natural liberty of individuals should be restrained where it conflicts with the security of the whole society (*Economics of Adam Smith*, 256). Changing conceptions of the role of defence, and the interdependence of profit and power, would presumably influence government policy on this matter.

belief that our colonial management had been a total loss to the mother country he might have been expected to recommend their complete emancipation. However, he knew that the existing empire was unlikely to be relinquished voluntarily, and suggested imperial federation (union?) as a possible alternative solution—though the language in which he presented his proposal makes it difficult to decide whether it was to be taken seriously or merely treated as a *ballon d'essai*.[43] Smith conceded that it would not be easy to develop a complete political and economic union of the colonies and the home country, but the plan was worth considering 'in a speculative work of this kind . . . Such a speculation can at worst be regarded as a new Utopia, less amusing certainly, but not more useless and chimerical than the old'. Yet in view of his profound misgivings about the wisdom, honesty and efficiency of contemporary British government he was surprisingly untroubled by the difficulties of his proposal.[44]

As one of a group of intellectuals with a developed taste for *histoire raisonnée* Smith should perhaps be exempted from judgements of the historical validity of his attack on the mercantile system. Yet he specifically declared his interest in the system as it applied 'in our own country and in our own times' (WN IV.2), and it would be unwise to ignore this matter completely. In fact, Smith's general assessment of the contemporary situation is borne out by the leading modern authority on the subject, who has stated that

> Adam Smith's history may not have been impeccable, but there was some truth in his contention that 'the mercantile system'—that complex of rules by which the government intervened to promote a certain conception of trade—was the result of 'arguments addressed by merchants to Parliaments and the Counsels of Princes, to nobles and country gentlemen . . . Admittedly the arguments of *The Wealth of Nations* were the product of logic working upon material drawn from the observation of three relatively mature mercantile economies: those of England, France and Holland. They did not have the same appeal to those who were still concerned with the earlier stages of the transition from agrarian to mercantile economy, to whom the invisible hand seemed to manifest itself all to infrequently.[45]

Yet even in this respect Smith was probably more right than wrong, since

[43] These problems are discussed in David Stevens's paper, 'Adam Smith and the Colonial Disturbances', above, p. 202.

[44] Smith's views on this subject have been repeatedly discussed in recent years. See, for example, Richard Koebner, *Empire* (1961) esp. 220–36; Donald Winch, *Classical Political Economy and Colonies* (1965), Ch. 2; and R. N. Ghosh *Classical Macro-Economics and the Case for Colonies* (1967), Ch. I. A fascinating earlier elaboration of this theme can be found in J. S. Nicholson, *A Project of Empire* (1909).

[45] Charles Wilson, 'Trade, Society and the State', in *The Cambridge Economic History of Europe*, (1900), iv, ed. E. E. Rich and C. H. Wilson, 496, 574. This 68-page chapter is the best single survey of the historical context against which the historical validity of Smith's treatment of the mercantile system can be gauged.

'with all its imperfections, there was an element of system, of coherence, and rationality in the British mercantile economy which distinguished it markedly from the chaos of Spain or the Italian States, and rendered it superior to that of France, or Sweden, or even Holland'.[46] Thus even in the most polemical parts of his writings Smith's sense of historical reality did not desert him. His insight into the nature of a commercial society was probably influenced by his association with Glasgow merchants. This did not make him an uncritical admirer of the mercantile community. But it has been suggested that his enthusiasm for liberty of commerce, though originally derived from intellectual sources, was reinforced by his knowledge of the progress of Glasgow since the Treaty of Union in 1707 (Scott, 114). His violent denunciation of trading companies may also reflect his Scottish perspective, since merchants in the 'outports' had long suspected that their metropolitan counterparts were unduly favoured by the national legislature. Yet it would be a serious mistake to reduce Adam Smith, a universal man, to the status of a mere product of specific historical circumstances. He spoke not merely for his country but for all Europe. His protest was directed against a body of restrictive regulations which had long outgrown their usefulness in Britain; and it was backed by a powerful corpus of analysis, much of which has survived to this day. His treatment of the 'mercantile system' was addressed to his contemporaries; but, like his economic theory, with which it was inextricably linked, it has retained its interest for subsequent generations.

[46] Charles Wilson, 'Government Policy and Private Interest in Modern Economic History', in his *Economic History and the Historian, Collected Essays* (1969), 150. This is not, of course, to suggest that Smith was necessarily correct either in matters of historical fact or in the explanations he proposed.

XII

Smith's Travels on the Ship of State

GEORGE J. STIGLER*

THE *Wealth of Nations* is a stupendous palace erected upon the granite of self-interest. It was not a narrow foundation: 'though the principles of common prudence do not always govern the conduct of every individual, they always influence that of the majority of every class or order' (WN II.ii.36).[1] The immensely powerful force of self-interest guides resources to their most efficient uses, stimulates labourers to diligence and inventors to splendid new divisions of labour, in short, it orders and enriches the nation which gives it free rein. Indeed if self-interest is given even a loose rein, it will perform prodigies:

> The natural effort of every individual to better his own condition, when suffered to exert itself with freedom and security, is so powerful a principle, that it is alone, and without any assistance, not only capable of carrying on the society to wealth and prosperity, but of surmounting a hundred impertinent obstructions with which the folly of human laws too often incumbers its operations; though the effect of these obstructions is always more or less either to encroach upon its freedom, or to diminish its security.
>
> (WN IV.v.b.43)

This very quotation neatly summarizes the basic paradox which forms our subject.

The paradox is simply this: if self-interest dominates the majority of men in all commercial undertakings, why not also in all their political undertakings? Why should legislators erect 'a hundred impertinent obstructions' to the economic behaviour which creates the wealth of nations? Do men calculate in money with logic and purpose, but calculate in votes with confusion and romance?

To ask such a question is surely to answer it. A merchant who calculated closely the proper destination of every cargo, the proper duties of every agent, the proper bank to negotiate each loan—such a merchant would calculate also the effects of every tariff, every tax and subsidy, every statute governing the employment of labour. Indeed no clear distinction

* Professor of Economics at the University of Chicago.

[1] *The Wealth of Nations* ed. Cannan (1904, 5th ed. 1930).

can be drawn between commercial and political undertakings: the procuring of favourable legislation *is* a commercial undertaking.

The widely read, widely travelled, superlatively observant author of *The Wealth of Nations* need not be told so obvious a thing as that self-interest enters also political life. A list of instances in which legislation is explained by the interests of several economic groups is compiled in Table I. The list is incomplete in two respects. Some references have no doubt been overlooked, and none is included unless Smith explicitly mentioned the interests which were served. Often Smith did not cite the economic interests which supported a law because their identity was self-evident. When the Statute of Labourers fixed wage rates in order to deal with the 'insolence of servants', Smith does not even bother to mention the probable role of employers in obtaining the legislation, probably because it was self-evident.

Even an incomplete list, however, is sufficient to document the extensive role of self-interest in economic legislation. The merchants and manufacturers are singled out for the unusual combination of cupidity and competence which marks their legislative efforts. Few other economic groups are absent from the list: the great landowners jostle the parsimonious local county's magistrates and the debtors in the queue for favourable legislation, and even the sovereign is ardent in the pursuit of his private interests.

TABLE I

Economic Classes and Their Political Behaviour

Political Behaviour	*Beneficiary*	*Reference*
1. Debasement of currency	Sovereign: to reduce debts	I.v.11
2. Prohibition of combinations of workman	Employers	I.viii.13
3. Usury laws	Sovereign: to reduce debt service	I.ix.9
4. Exclusive privileges of corporations	Members of corporations (guilds)	I.x.c
5. Statute of apprenticeship	Members of corporations	I.x.c.8
6. Settlement law (Poor law)	Local communities	I.x.c.45
7. Wage-fixing laws	Employers	I.x.c.61
8. Opposition to turnpikes	Counties near London	I.xi.b.5
9. Prohibition on planting of new vineyards	Vineyard owners	I.xi.b.27
10. Restriction on planting of tobacco	Tobacco farmers	I.xi.b.3
11. Bounty on corn exports	Agricultural class	I.xi.g.10
12. Protection of woollen trade	Woollen trade	I.xi.m.8,9
13. Protection of hides	Leather trade	I.xi.m.11
14. Legal tender of paper money	Debtors	II.ii.100

Table 1 *continued*

Political Behaviour	*Beneficiary*	*Reference*
15. Primogeniture	Landowners	III.ii.3
16. Varieties of tariffs	Protected industries	IV.ii.1
17. Abolition of seigneurage	Bank of England	IV.vi.22
18. Colonial policy	Merchants	IV.vii.b.21–4
19. Selection of 'enumerated' commodities	Merchants and fishermen	IV.vii.b.35, 36
20. Free importation of raw materials	Manufacturers	IV.viii.4
21. Grants to regulated companies	Merchants	V.i.e.3,4
22. Defeat of Walpole's tax reforms	'Smuggling Merchants'	V.ii.k.28
23. Exemption of home brewing from tax	Rich consumers	V.ii.k.46–55
24. Use of debt to finance wars	To avoid Taxpayers revolt	V.iii.37
25. Raising value of currency	Debtors in Rome	V.iii.61
26. Abolition of slavery in Pennsylvania	Quakers (who had few slaves)	III.ii.10

A shorter list can be compiled of policies which have been obtained by economic classes under the mistaken understanding that they are beneficial. The main examples are:

(1) Attempts to increase the pay of curates have simply drawn more candidates into the clergy (WN I.x.c.34).

(2) The bounty on exports of corn, first passed in 1688, has not appreciably benefited the farmers or landowners because it raises money wages[2] (WN I.xi.g.10, IV.v.a.20–5).

(3) The practice of primogeniture has lost its onetime role of achieving security of property, and injures the landowner (WN III.ii.4–6).

(4) The institution of slavery is uneconomic, but panders to pride[3] (WN III.ii.9, 10).

(5) Laws against forestallers, engrossers, etc., serve only to appease popular prejudice (WN IV.v.b.7–26).

Even such mistaken uses of political power are testimony to the pursuit of self-interest in the formulation of public policy.

So far, however, we have established only two propositions in Smith's discussion of legislation:

A. Sometimes (often?) economic legislation is passed at the request of economic groups who hope to benefit by the legislation.

[2] There is a related argument on the taxation of necessaries (WN V.ii.k.9–14).

[3] Hence the institution serves self-interest, but not production.

B. On occasion a group is mistaken in the consequences of the legislation and receives no benefit or even positive harm from its legislative programme.

The first proposition is platitudinous. The second proposition is probably of wholly minor scope: some of Smith's examples are simply wrong (in particular, the corn export subsidy surely benefited landowners) and others (such as primogeniture) do not recieve a convincing explanation. In any event, men make mistakes in economic life—witness the South Sea Bubble—so why not occasionally also in political life?

A much stronger proposition, one would have thought, would come appropriately from the premier scholar of self-interest:

C. All legislation with important economic effects is the calculated achievement of interested economic classes.

Appropriate or not, Smith implicitly rejected the use of self-interest as a general explanation of legislation. The rejection manifested itself in various ways.

1. The most important evidence is that for most legislation no group is identified which could have fostered the law and would benefit from it. The most important area of this neglect is the discussion of taxation. Each tax is described, its incidence explained, and its merits and demerits assessed with hardly ever an explanation of why such a tax exists. As we shall see, this omission of consideration of the political bases of taxes had serious effects upon Smith's policy proposals.

2. Puzzles in legislation are posed where none would exist if Smith had considered systematically the role of self-interest in legislation. Consider the example of laws forbidding payment of wages in kind. Smith observes that 'Whenever the legislature attempts to regulate the differences between masters and their workmen, its counsellors are always the masters. When the regulation, therefore, is in favour of the workmen, it is always just and equitable; but it is sometimes otherwise when in favour of the masters' (WN I.x.c.61). Smith illustrates this conclusion by the just and equitable laws forbidding truck wages.

What a puzzling event! The legislature, creature of the masters, deprives the masters of the opportunity (which Smith says they sometimes exercised) to defraud their workmen with overpriced goods. Surely Smith's puzzle is connected with the fact that a legislature dominated by the agricultural class passed a law forbidding truck wages in certain non-agricultural industries (textiles, iron, apparel).[4]

[4] We need not explore the reason truck wages were preferred in some trades; George Hilton's explanation does not appear to be completely general: 'The British Truck Sysetm in the Nineteenth Century', *Journal of Political Economy* (June 1957).

Other examples are at hand. The laws forbidding the lower classes to wear fine textiles (WN I.xi.o.9–10) surely were not designed simply to keep them from wearing clothing that was 'much more expensive'; one is entitled to suspect the support of the manufacturers of cheaper raiment. The prohibition on banks of the issue of small bank notes was more likely calculated to discourage entry into banking than to keep bank notes in knowledgeable hands (WN II.ii.90–1). A much more sceptical eye would have been turned to arguments such as that absolute governments treat slaves more kindly than republican states (WN IV.vii.b.54).

3. Smith gave a larger role to emotion, prejudice, and ignorance in political life than he ever allowed in ordinary economic affairs. The mercantile policies directed to the improvement of the balance of trade with particular countries have their origin in 'national prejudice and animosity' (WN IV.iii.a.1). The legislation against corn traders is so perverse as to lead Smith to compare it to laws against witchcraft (WN IV.v.b.40); indeed 'the laws concerning corn may every where be compared to the laws concerning religion' (WN IV.v.b.40). In fact all unwise economic legislation from which no politically strong constituency drew benefits must be non-rational legislation.

The agricultural classes, the classes with preponderant political power in Smith's England, are singled out for their benevolence and stupidity:

When the public deliberates concerning any regulation of commerce or police, the proprietors of land never can mislead it, with a view to promote the interest of their own particular order; at least, if they have any tolerable knowledge of that interest. They are, indeed, too often defective in this tolerable knowledge. They are the only one of the three orders whose revenue costs them neither labour nor care, but comes to them, as it were, of its own accord, and independent of any plan or project of their own. That indolence, which is the natural effect of the ease and security of their situation, renders them too often, not only ignorant, but incapable of that application of mind which is necessary in order to foresee and understand the consequences of any public regulation[5] (WN I.xi.p.8, also IV.i.10).

Yet Smith notes often enough legislation which has been procured by the agricultural classes for their own interests[6] (WN III.ii.16, III.iv.20, IV.vii.b.33, V.ii.k.55,56).

Little attention is paid to the political process and that little is

[5] The labourers are no better: 'But though the interest of the labourer is strictly connected with that of society, he is incapable either of comprehending that interest, or of understanding its connexion with his own' (WN I.xi.p.9).

[6] In an interesting reversal of the argument, Smith argues that when tenants possess the vote, their landlords treat them better! (WN III.ii.14).

tantalizingly diverse. In some respects the sovereign is an incompetent manager. He cannot conduct a trading enterprise:

Princes, however, have frequently engaged in many other mercantile projects, and have been willing, like private persons, to mend their fortunes by becoming adventurers in the common branches of trade. They have scarce ever succeeded. The profusion with which the affairs of princes are always managed, renders it almost impossible that they should. The agents of a prince regard the wealth of their master as inexhaustible; are careless at what price they buy; are careless at what price they sell; are careless at what expense they transport his goods from one place to another.

(WN V.ii.a.6)

Again, 'the persons who have the administration of government [are] generally disposed to reward both themselves and their immediate dependents rather more than enough' (V.ii.k.7). Only the post office, Smith states in a rare moment of inverted clairvoyance, can be successfully managed by 'every sort of government'. In general, monarchies are conducted with 'slothful and negligent profusion' and democracies with 'thoughtless extravagance' but aristocracies such as Venice and Amsterdam have 'orderly, vigilant and parsimonious administration' (WN V.ii.a.4).

Yet on other occasions Smith views political behaviour in perfectly cold-blooded, rational terms. The discussion of the 'recent disturbances' which constituted the American revolution provides a striking example.

Men desire to have some share in the management of public affairs chiefly on account of the importance which it gives them. Upon the power which the greater part of the leading men, the natural aristocracy of every country, have of preserving or defending their respective importance, depends the stability and duration of every system of free government. In the attacks which these leading men are continually making upon the importance of one another, and in the defence of their own, consists the whole play of domestic faction and ambition. The leading men of America, like those of all other countries, desire to preserve their own importance. They feel, or imagine, that if their assemblies, which they are fond of calling parliaments, and of considering as equal in authority to the parliament of Great Britain, should be so far degraded as to become the humble ministers and executive officers of that parliament, the greater part of their own importance would be at an end. They have rejected, therefore, the proposal of being taxed by parliamentary requisition, and like other ambitious and high-spirited men, have rather chosen to draw the sword in defence of their own importance.

(WN IV.vii.c.74)

Smith shrewdly proposed to draw these leaders away from 'peddling for the little prizes' in the 'paltry raffle of colonial faction' by giving representation to the colonies in Parliament, where dazzling prizes might be won by ambitious colonists in the 'great state lottery of British politics'.[7]

In general, however, Smith's attitude toward political behaviour was not dissimilar to that of a parent toward a child: the child was often mistaken and sometimes perverse, but normally it would improve in conduct if properly instructed.

The canons of taxation illustrate both the attitude and the fundamental weakness of Smith's position. The maxims are:

1. The subjects of every state ought to contribute towards the support of government, as nearly as possible, in proportion to their respective abilities; . . . .
2. The tax which each individual is bound to pay ought to be certain, and not arbitrary.
3. Every tax ought to be levied at the time, or in the manner, in which it is most likely to be convenient for the contributor to pay; . . . .
4. Every tax ought to be so contrived as both to take out and to keep out of the pockets of the people as little as possible, over and above what it brings into the public treasury of the state (WN V.ii.b.1–6).

Many of the specific taxes Smith proceeds to examine fail to meet one or more of these criteria, and many reforms are accordingly proposed.

A Chancellor of the Exchequer would have found these rules most peculiar. If adopted, they would obtain for him at least the temporary admiration of the professors of moral philosophy but this is a slender and notably fickle constituency on which to build a party. The two basic canons of taxation are surely rather different:

1. The revenue system must not imperil the political support for the regime.
2. The revenue system must yield revenue.

Smith's maxims touch on aspects of a revenue system which are relevant to its productivity and acceptability, not always in the direction he wished, but they form a wholly inadequate basis for judging individual taxes.

One may—for generations economists have—give advice lavishly without taking account of the political forces which confine and direct policy. In the absence of knowledge of these political forces, however, the advice must often be bad and usually be unpersuasive. Why tell the sovereign that free trade is desirable, if one has no method of disarming the merchants and manufacturers who have obtained the protectionist measures? Why

[7] The retention of the unprofitable colonies by Great Britain is attributed to the interests of the administration-bureaucracy (WN IV.vii.c.66). For a lesser example of the explanation of political behaviour by interests of the sovereign, see WN V.i.d.17.

tell the French sovereign to abandon the taille and capitations and increase the vingtièmes, when only a revolution could dislodge the tax-favoured classes?[8] Why believe that better turnpikes await only the appointments of a better class of commissioners (WN V.i.d.9)?

The contrast between Smith's discussions of political reform and other reforms is instructive. The dons of Oxford, he says, grossly neglect their duties of instruction. Does he preach to each don a moral reform, seeking a pledge of diligence and good sense? Smith would have considered such a remedy to be silly: the teacher is intelligently pursuing his interest, which is 'to live as much at his ease as he can' because his income is independent of his efforts (WN V.i.f.4). A system of remuneration based upon effort and achievement, not a weekly sermon, would bring about the changes Smith wishes.

In the political scene no corresponding search is made for the effective principles of behaviour. Therefore reforms must be effected, if effected they can be, by moral suasion. At best this is an extraordinarily slow and uncertain method of changing policy; at worst it may lead to policies which endanger the society. Of course erroneous and undesirable public policies arise out of failures of comprehension as well as out of the efforts of self-serving groups, but there is little reason to accept Smith's implicit assumption that the main source of error is ignorance or 'prejudice'. Yet Smith's only remedy for erroneous policy is sound analysis, and that remedy is appropriate only to a minority of objectionable policies.

It may appear that Smith's failure to apply the organon of self-interest to political behaviour requires no explanation. Political science had been a normative literature for 2,300 years before Smith wrote and continues to remain normative to the present day. The great Bentham, who did apply a theory of utility-maximizing behaviour to political as well as other social phenomena, never stirred an inch beyond preaching, to see how well his theory actually explained legislation, and that is why his great organon remained sterile.

Yet it is uncomfortable to explain Smith's failure by the failure of everyone else, for he is a better man than everyone else. His ability to examine the most pompous and ceremonial of institutions and conduct with the jaundiced eye of a master economist—and the evident delight he took in such amusement—is one of the trademarks of his authorship. The 'uniform, constant, and uninterrupted effort of every man to better his condition' (WN II.iii.31), why was it interrupted when a man entered Parliament? The man whose spacious vision could see the Spanish war of 1739 as a bounty and who attributed the decline of feudalism to changes in consumption patterns, how could he have failed to see the self-interest written upon the faces of politicians and constituencies? The man who denied the state

[8] And Smith so recognized: (WN V.ii.k.77).

the capacity to conduct almost any business save the postal, how could he give to the sovereign the task of extirpating cowardice in the citizenry? How so, Professor Smith?

A NOTE ON FAILURES OF SELF-INTEREST

It is in the political arena that Smith implicitly locates the most numerous and consistent failures of self-interest in guiding people's behaviour, but this is not the only place where self-interest fails. Since the effective working of self-interest is so central to Smith's work, it may be useful to sketch the nature of the failure he described.

Every failure of a person to make decisions which serve his self-interest may be interpreted as an error in logic: means have been chosen which are inappropriate to the person's ends. Nevertheless it is useful to distinguish several categories of failure, all of which are found in *The Wealth of Nations*.

Class I: The individual knows the 'facts' but fails to anticipate the consequences of his actions. The occasional behaviour of the landlord is an example in Smith's book:

> Improvements, besides, are not always made by the stock of the landlord, but sometimes by that of the tenant. When the lease comes to be renewed, however, the landlord commonly demands the same augmentation of rent, as if they had been all made by his own.
>
> (I.xi.a.2, III.iii.13)

The landlord is short-sighted in his greed: he removes the incentive to the tenant to make improvements which would yield more to tenant and landlord than the going rate of return. Hence there exists a system of rents which would make both tenant and landlord better off. This superior form of tenancy does not require the co-operation of any third party—only clear reasoning and a little inventiveness in writing a lease are necessary. The failure of self-interest to be served arises out of a failure to reason correctly.

The following are additional examples of the failure of individuals to reason correctly:

i. The apprenticeship system does not give appropriate incentives to the apprentice to be diligent in his work (WN I.x.c.14).

ii. Only a landlord can work no-rent land because he demands a rent from others (WN I.xi.c.13).

iii. The crown lands would be more valuable if they were sold off (WN V.ii.a.18).

One important sub-class of failures due to imperfect knowledge involves the future: future gains are overestimated, or future costs underestimated. Examples are:

i. The possible gains are overestimated relative to the possible losses in risky ventures (WN I.x.b.22,33).
ii. Workers do not anticipate in seasons of plenty the higher prices of provisions in seasons of scarcity (WN I.viii.29).
iii. Workmen paid by piece are 'very apt to overwork themselves, and ruin their health and constitution in a few years' (WN I.viii.44).
iv. In the absence of usury laws, lenders will deal with 'prodigals and projectors' (who will be unable to repay the loans?) (WN II.iv.15).

Class II: In an important range of situations, the employer or master is unable to control his agents so they will act in his interest. Among the examples are:

i. Slaves are often managed by a 'negligent or careless overseer' (WN I.viii.41).
ii. Monopoly is the great enemy of good management (WN I.xi.b.5).
iii. The East India Companies employees trade only in their own interest (WN IV.vii.c.105, V.i.e.18).

Smith does not explain why *all* agents or employees do not display the same tendency to self-serving conduct, and it may be that this charge is made only against institutions which he objects to also on other grounds.

Class III: In the production of what is now called a public good, self-interest does not lead the individual to supply the correct amount of the good. Smith gives the example of the inadequate preparation by the individual citizen for war (WN V.i.a.12). This failure is not so much of self-interest as it is a failure of individual action.

The first class of (non-political) failures is much the most important in *The Wealth of Nations* if importance is measured by number and variety of examples. A good number of these failures are due to incomplete factual information, and it would only be anachronistic to lament Smith's failure to discuss the problem of the optimum investment of the individual in the acquisition of knowledge. The implicit charge of inadequate analysis of known facts, it should be observed, is made against all classes: the greedy landlord, the impetuous labourer, the negligent employer, the short-sighted lender. No principle is apparent by which one can distinguish these failures from the many decisions which effectively advance these various persons' self-interests: the decisions are not especially subtle or especially demanding of information. One could make a fair case. I believe, that every alleged failure was non-existent or of negligible magnitude. The high priest of self-interest, like all other high priests, had a strong demand for sinners.

XIII

Adam Smith's First Russian Followers

A. H. BROWN*

THE links between the Scottish and the Russian Enlightenment in the second half of the eighteenth century were stronger than is generally realized. The presence of a number of educated Russians in Scotland at that time, the much larger body of educated Scots in Russia, and the direct impact made by the published works of leading representatives of the Scottish Enlightenment are the three most obvious points of connection. The influence was almost entirely in one direction, and indeed it is hardly surprising that Russian eighteenth-century thought made no impact upon Scottish intellectual life. The first Russian university, the University of Moscow, was founded as late as 1755, and the achievements of the embryonic Russian intelligentsia in the eighteenth century were but a pale prelude to the magnificent achievements of Russian culture a century later. In Scotland, in contrast, there has never been a period before or since when her universities achieved such a position of intellectual pre-eminence as they enjoyed during the last two thirds of the eighteenth century[1] when probably only the Dutch universities could be regarded as serious rivals.

Among Russians in Scotland, the most important in terms of transmitting the ideas of the Scottish Enlightenment were Semyon Efimovich Desnitsky and Ivan Andreyevich Tret'yakov who studied in Glasgow University from 1761 until 1767. It is they, as will presently be made clear, who have overwhelmingly the best claim to be regarded as Adam Smith's first Russian followers. Also worthy of note was the presence of Princess

* Fellow of St. Antony's College, Oxford.

A full acknowledgement of the numerous academic debts I have incurred in the course of the research on which this essay is based must await the publication of a fuller account of my findings. I should, however, like to take this opportunity to thank those who facilitated my access to, and helped me locate, archival material in Glasgow and in Moscow. For their co-operation in Glasgow University, I am particularly grateful to Lady Edith Haden-Guest and to the late Clerk of Senate, Professor Christian J. Fordyce. For their help in the Soviet Union, I am greatly indebted to L. P. Dem'yanova of the Moscow University Foreign Department, to the late Professor S. F. Kechek'yan of Moscow University Law Faculty, and to Professor M. T. Belyavsky of Moscow University History Faculty.

[1] The late C. R. Fay suggested that the half-century of Adam Smith's adult life (1740–90) might fairly be regarded as Scotland's Augustan Age (Fay, *Adam Smith and the Scotland of his Day* (1956) 2). Any such periodization is, of course, a highly individual and controversial matter. Some would wish to extend the period backwards while others would include the first third of the nineteenth century.

Ekaterina Dashkova and her son in Edinburgh during the late 1770s when the young Dashkov studied in Edinburgh University[2] and his mother sought the company of his teachers and others of the *literati*. Doubtless Princess Dashkova was exaggerating somewhat when she tells us that 'the immortal Robertson, Blair, Smith and Ferguson came twice a week to spend the day with me', but there is no reason to doubt that she knew them well.[3]

In the large category of Scots in eighteenth-century Russia, there were a great many professional men, including doctors, soldiers, engineers, architects, and diplomats. It is a curious fact that three physicians in succession to the Empress of Russia (James Mounsey, Matthew Halliday, and John Rogerson) all came from the same Scottish county of Dumfriesshire. Independently of such personal contacts, an important link between the Scottish and Russian Enlightenment was provided by the published works of the leading Scottish thinkers, even if these, more often than not, were read in their French translations. In so far as the ideas of some of the Scottish theorists were transmitted, it was almost entirely the work of Semyon Desnitsky. This holds true, for example, of Francis Hutcheson, Lord Kames, and John Millar, though quite apart from the activities of Desnitsky, there was familiarity among the best-educated Russians with several of the works of William Robertson, David Hume, Adam Ferguson, and Adam Smith.

Desnitsky and, to a much lesser extent, his colleague, Ivan Tret'yakov, must, nevertheless, be regarded not only as vital links between Scottish and Russian intellectual life generally but as the first Russians to imbibe and propagate the ideas of Adam Smith. While it is possible to argue about whether the brothers, Alexander and Simon Vorontsov, Princess Dashkova, or the Count N. S. Mordvinov were the first Russians to be impressed by *The Wealth of Nations*, Smith's influence upon Desnitsky and Tret'yakov can be dated much earlier—to the period between 1761 and early 1764 when Smith gave up the Chair of Moral Philosophy at Glasgow University. Desnitsky was not only the first Russian to draw attention in print to the significance of Smith's *Theory of Moral Sentiments* which had been published in 1759 but, more significantly, he and Tret'yakov published in Russian before the end of the 1760s some of Smith's major ideas, including a number which Smith himself did not commit to print until the publication of *The Wealth of Nations* in 1776.[4]

[2] To show her gratitude, Princess Dashkova presented Edinburgh University with a Cabinet of Medals which the Principal, William Robertson, produced at a Senate meeting in 1779. They were handed over to Professor John Robison (who had spent some years in Russia) for translation of the inscriptions, and this was the last the University saw of them until Robison's death in 1805, by which time two of the medals had disappeared (Edinburgh University MSS., Da. 1.3017).

[3] *The Memoirs of Princess Dashkov*, translated and edited by Kyril Fitzlyon (1958), 147.

[4] Cf. Mikhail P. Alekseyev, 'Adam Smith and His Russian Admirers of the Eighteenth Century', Appendix VII to W. R. Scott's *Adam Smith as Student and Professor* (1937);

Since Desnitsky and Tret'yakov are little known outside the Soviet Union, it may be useful to provide a brief account of their lives and works before going on to pay particular attention to their period of study in Glasgow University, including their contact with Adam Smith, and to the ideas which they propagated upon their return to Russia. The exact year of Desnitsky's birth has so far eluded discovery, but his place of birth is known. He was born in Nezhin in the Ukraine, the second son of a *meshchanin*[5]. Tret'yakov, the son of an army officer,[6] was born in 1735 in Tver' (now Kalinin). He received his early education in the religious seminary in Tver' and then had a short spell in Moscow University. Desnitsky attended the seminary attached to the Troitsko-Sergievskoy monastery, then the 'gymnasium' attached to Moscow University which educated children of the *raznochintsy*,[7] from which he moved in 1760 into Moscow University itself.

During their short spell as students of Moscow University, the paths of Desnitsky and Tret'yakov crossed for the first time, and they were never after to be far apart. The Empress Elizabeth of Russia, like her father, Peter the Great, believed in picking out young Russians of exceptional talent and sending them abroad to complete their education. In 1761 Desnitsky and Tret'yakov were singled out in this way and the university chosen for them was Glasgow. Both Russian students spent six years at Glasgow University, returning to Russia in 1767. In 1768 they both became Professors of Law in Moscow University, the first Russians to hold Chairs of Law in Russia's first university. The majority of the university

G. Sacke, 'Die Moskauer Nachschrift der Vorlesungen von Adam Smith', *Zeitschrift für Nationalökonomie*, ix (1938); and Norman W. Taylor, 'Adam Smith's First Russian Disciple' (on Tret'yakov), *Slavonic and East European Review*, xlv, No. 105 (July 1967). Among the main Russian language works on Desnitsky and Tret'yakov should be mentioned: N. M. Korkunov, 'S. E. Desnitsky: Pervyy russkiy professor prava,' *Zhurnal ministerstva yustitsii* (1894–5, No. 2, Dec. 1894); M. T. Belyavsky, *M. V. Lomonosov i osnovanie Moskovskogo universiteta* (1955), 234–51; S. A. Pokrovsky, *Politicheskie i pravovye vzglyady S. E. Desnitskogo* (1955); P. S. Gratsiansky, 'S. E. Desnitsky o proiskhozhdenii gosudarstva, sem'i i chastnoy sobstvennosti', *Uchenye zapiski, Vsesoyuznyy institut yuridicheskikh nauk* (No. 17, 1963); M. M. Shtrange, *Demokraticheskaya intelligentsia v Rossii v XVIII veke* (1965), 193–204. The only book to be devoted entirely to Desnitsky is that by S. A. Pokrovsky. Unfortunately, it is replete with errors of fact and of interpretation. A more useful work under the editorship of Pokrovsky is *Yuridicheskie proizvedeniya progressivnykh russkikh mysliteley: vtoraya polovina XVIII veka* (1959), which reprints with annotations some of the works of Desnitsky, Tret'yakov, Kozel'sky, and Radishchev.

[5] A member of the petty bourgeoisie.

[6] Some nineteenth-century Russian writers suggested that Tret'yakov was the son of a priest, and Professor Norman Taylor (op. cit.) rebukes a Soviet historian of economic thought, the late Professor I. S. Bak, for claiming that Tret'yakov was in fact the son of an army officer. Though Bak made many other mistakes concerning Tret'yakov, on this point he was right and Taylor wrong. The evidence is to be found in W. Innes Addison (ed.), *The Matriculation Albums of the University of Glasgow from 1728 to 1858* (1913), 63.

[7] Those of non-noble birth. There was a separate gymnasium for the children of the nobility.

professors were Germans, and Desnitsky and Tret'yakov, like the other young Russian professors within the university, found themselves disagreeing with their German colleagues on political and scholastic as well as nationalistic grounds. The German scholars resisted the change from lecturing in Latin to lecturing in Russian, an innovation Desnitsky and Tret'yakov strongly supported, and they tended not to share the liberal, reformist, and anti-clerical attitudes which were common to Desnitsky and Tret'yakov. Both Tret'yakov and Desnitsky encountered difficulties with the secular and ecclesiastical authorities and both retired prematurely from the service of the university. Tret'yakov resigned in 1773 and died at an early age in 1776, the very year in which his former Glasgow teacher, Adam Smith, published his greatest work. Desnitsky remained a professor until 1787 and died in 1789, a year earlier than Adam Smith.

Most of the published works of Desnitsky and Tret'yakov are in the form of public lectures given on university open days. Desnitsky's most important single work is not, however, in that form. This is his *Proposal concerning the Establishment of Legislative, Judicial and Executive Authorities in the Russian Empire* which was addressed to Catherine II in 1768. Desnitsky, in addition to his published lectures, also translated a work on agriculture by the Englishman, Thomas Bowden, to which he wrote a long introduction full of praise for the British people and their institutions (and critical by implication of Russian social institutions), and, of greater consequence, he translated into Russian the first volume of Blackstone's *Commentaries on the Laws of England* which Novikov published in three volumes in Moscow between 1780 and 1782, with important annotations by Desnitsky added to Blackstone's text.[8]

Merely to mention the titles of a few of the principal published lectures of Desnitsky and Tret'yakov is to draw attention to the links of some of them with Adam Smith and the Scottish Enlightenment for anyone familiar with the concerns of the latter. They include: *A Discourse on the Origin and Foundation of State-Supported Universities in Europe* (a lecture delivered by Tret'yakov in 1768 and accordingly attributed to him, but which in fact was composed by Desnitsky[9]); *A Discourse on the Causes of Public Opulence and the Slow Enrichment of Ancient and Modern Nations* (Tret'yakov, 1772); *A Legal Discourse on the Beginning and Origin of Matrimony among the Earliest Peoples and on the Perfection to which it would appear to have been brought by Subsequent Enlightened Peoples* (Desnitsky, 1775); and *A Legal*

[8] Both Soviet and western scholars have usually and mistakenly stated that Desnitsky translated the first three volumes of Blackstone into Russian.

[9] The evidence for this is to be found among Desnitsky's annotations to the copy of the work in Glasgow University Library. I have discussed it in some detail in my article, 'S. E. Desnitsky i I. A. Tret'yakov v Glazgovskom universitete (1761–7)', *Vestnik Moskovskogo Universiteta* (*Istoriya*) No. 4 (1969), 75–88.

Discourse about the Different Ideas which People have concerning the Ownership of Property in Different Conditions of Society (Desnitsky, 1781).

More will be said later about the actual influence of Adam Smith upon the content of these lectures, but some attention must first be devoted to the six years which the future Moscow professors spent in their Scottish university. The choice of Glasgow was a fortunate one. Among the four Scottish universities, Edinburgh and Glasgow achieved the greatest distinction at this time, and between these two the predominance of Edinburgh has often been exaggerated.[10] Though, as a town, Edinburgh had the more brilliant intellectual society and more club life, predominance between the universities varied from subject to subject and from time to time. In the first half of the 1760s even Edinburgh University did not possess quite such a range of brilliant men as the university in which Desnitsky and Tret'yakov found themselves. Adam Smith had been a professor there since 1751 and he was to remain long enough to lecture to the Russian students before leaving early in 1764 to take up a much better-paid post than a Glasgow professorship—that of travelling tutor to the young Duke of Buccleuch. Smith was a popular lecturer, for he was completely absorbed in his work and was able to communicate his enthusiasm. If, however, Smith's genius as a scholar and his ability as a teacher earned him the respect of those who attended his lectures, how much a majority of his listeners understood of what they heard is a matter for debate. The students varied enormously in age. Some were adults in their late twenties, but many were boys in their early teens. A man as greatly talented in his own literary sphere as James Boswell, who studied at Glasgow the year before the arrival of Desnitsky and Tret'yakov, remembered only trivial details from Adam Smith's lectures—for example, the information that 'Milton never wore buckles but strings in his shoes'.[11] This titbit of information was imparted in Smith's course of lectures on rhetoric and belles-lettres which were attended also by the Russian students who apparently valued them less highly than the lectures on ethics and jurisprudence.[12] In a pamphlet published in Glasgow in 1761 called *Defects of a University Education*, the Rev. William Thom, quite an astute critic of the universities in general and of Glasgow in particular, refers clearly to Smith when he writes: '. . . whatever scheme the professor of morality contrives or embraces, he uses a long train of thin metaphysical reasoning to establish

[10] It is greatly exaggerated, for example, by David Daiches in his book, *The Paradox of Scottish Culture: the Eighteenth Century Experience* (Oxford University Press, 1964).

[11] *The Private Papers of James Boswell from Malahide Castle* (1937), i. 107.

[12] An incomplete set of students' notes of Smith's literary lectures was discovered as recently as 1958. The notes were taken in the academic session 1762–3, which is almost certainly the year in which Desnitsky and Tret'yakov heard them. See John M. Lothian (ed.), *Lectures on Rhetoric and Belles Lettres delivered in the University of Glasgow by Adam Smith* (1963).

it, and spends a great part of the year in laying down arguments for, and answering objections against, his system; arguments very pleasing, and perhaps intelligible to himself, as they are familiar to him, and he believes they will please and improve his pupils; but they are too subtle to be understood by them and leave little or no impression upon any of their minds'.[13] It is to Smith's lectures on Ethics rather than to his lectures on Jurisprudence that Thom is, of course, referring. Desnitsky and Tret'yakov made some use of the lectures on Ethics in their later work, but it was above all the Jurisprudence lectures which influenced them. Whatever the size of the group who understood the import of Smith's lectures, it is clear that Desnitsky and Tret'yakov belonged to it. Thom is perhaps excessively sceptical concerning the effects of Adam Smith's teaching and we can contrast with his opinion the view of Thomas Reid who, having moved from Aberdeen University to succeed Smith, wrote to a friend 'that there was a great spirit of enquiry abroad among the young people in Glasgow—the best testimony that could be rendered of the effect of Smith's teaching. It had taught the young people to think.'[14]

From a study of the internal evidence in Desnitsky's and Tret'yakov's published lectures, it has long been possible to infer that they attended the lectures of Adam Smith, but should any shadow of doubt remain, it is possible now to dispel it with documentary evidence. Two letters written by Desnitsky and one by Tret'yakov survive in the Glasgow University archives. They contain little in the way of significant new information, but one of them, written by Desnitsky to the Dean and Members of the Faculty of Glasgow University on 31 December 1765, is of some interest. It indicates that Desnitsky and Tret'yakov expected to be recalled to Russia at the end of the 1765–6 academic year and puts forward their request to be accepted as candidates for the degree of doctor of law. After offering 'our most grateful acknowledgements for the advantages we have enjoyed at this university', the Russian students continue:

At the same time, as we have the highest idea of those advantages, we cannot help wishing it were known, after we return to our Country, that we have not neglected to make use of them as far as we were able. We humbly request, therefor, that the Faculty would take into Consideration, whether our attendance on Dr. Smith's class of Ethicks and Jurisprudence and our attendance for three years on Mr Millar's classes of civil law may procure us a Liberty of offering ourselves Candidates for a Degree in Law, and of Submitting ourselves to the Trials, which are requisite in order to obtain it.[15]

[13] *The Works of the Rev. William Thom, late Minister of Govan* (1799), 267.

[14] John Rae, *Life of Adam Smith* (1895), 59. For evidence of Smith's great popularity as a teacher, see A. F. Tytler, *Memoirs of the Life and Writings of Lord Kames* (1814), i. 194–5.

[15] 'Petition of the two Russian Students to be admitted Candidates for a Doctor's degree in Law, 31 December, 1765', Glasgow University Archives.

So far as Millar's lectures are concerned, Desnitsky and Tret'yakov refer only to those on civil law, for Roman law was the most basic element in a legal education in Scotland at that time. But from the evidence in Desnitsky's later works, it is possible to be fairly certain that he also attended Millar's classes on Scottish law, as well as his pioneering 'lectures on government'. Desnitsky and Tret'yakov undoubtedly worked more closely with John Millar than with any other Glasgow professor and when the University agreed to their request to submit doctoral dissertations, it was Millar who was allocated the task of supervising them. Millar at this time was still a young man, scarcely any older than the Russian students themselves. He had been appointed to the Chair of Law, which he was to hold with great distinction for forty years, in 1761 at the early age of twenty-six. Millar is rightly regarded as one of the fathers of modern sociology, but he might equally well be regarded as a pioneer of political science. He developed a number of themes and ideas which had already been present in the lectures of Francis Hutcheson and of Adam Smith and gave the first full and systematic course of lectures on the government of different nations to be delivered in any British university.

On the small staff of the University during the years Desnitsky and Tret'yakov spent in Glasgow there was a remarkably large proportion of men whose names have stood the test of time. Apart from Adam Smith and John Millar, there was Smith's successor, Thomas Reid, the Common-Sense Philosopher, who held the Chair of Moral Philosophy from 1764 until 1796; Joseph Black, who was Professor of Medicine and lecturer in Chemistry until 1766, a brilliant scientific innovator who is remembered chiefly as the discoverer of latent heat; and James Watt who was mathematical instrument-maker to the University. Black was one of the Russian students' teachers,[16] and there is strong evidence to suggest that Desnitsky was personally acquainted with Watt, who had a workshop in the College grounds. Somewhat surprisingly, this evidence is to be found in Desnitsky's *Proposal concerning the Establishment of Legislative, Judicial and Executive Authorities in the Russian Empire* which he submitted to Catherine II in 1768. In the course of his discussion of reform of local administration in Russia, Desnitsky makes a number of technical suggestions in connection with fire-fighting (much-needed suggestions in view of the

[16] The Moscow University authorities on more than one occasion expressed concern that Desnitsky and Tret'yakov appeared to be studying a wide variety of unrelated subjects. They did not know that they were in fact following the typically broad course for the Scottish M.A. at that time and that it was by no means uncommon for a student to attend Joseph Black's lectures on chemistry as well as those of Adam Smith and John Millar. In 1765 Joseph Black had to confirm in writing that the Russian students had indeed attended his class for a year in which they had studied chemistry and even some medicine. See N. A. Penchko (ed.), *Dokumenty i materialy po istorii Moskovskogo Universiteta vtoroy poloviny XVIII veka*, ii, *1765–6* (1962), 253.

frequency with which Russian wooden buildings burned down) and adds:

. . . it would not be superfluous if there could be an order to send for one mechanic from Britain for the manufacture of the new copper fire pumps. Such a person is Mr. Watt, a man highly skilled in mechanics, mathematics and natural philosophy, who if he came with his own workers to Russia, could for the price of forty or fifty thousand roubles make in one year a sufficient number of the very best machines from state materials.[17]

Desnitsky's specification of an approximate sum of money required for the manufacture of steam engines in Russia suggests that he had discussed his proposal with Watt and it is highly probable that Watt would have been prepared to meet the challenge should his terms have been granted.[18]

It is clear from Desnitsky's writings that he carried back to Russia an overwhelmingly favourable impression of his Scottish university; and this despite the fact that his six years in Glasgow were not entirely free from major problems. From material available in various Russian archives[19] it is known that Desnitsky and Tret'yakov received their financial allowances from Russia irregularly and that they were more than once in serious financial difficulties. The first of these occasions was discussed in the Glasgow University Senate on 11 August 1762, when a meeting attended, among others, by the University Principal William Leechman, Adam Smith, John Millar, and Joseph Black decided to advance the Russian students a loan of £40. The Minute states:

The University meeting having taken into consideration the state of the two Russian gentlemen, sent to this University by the recommendation of Lord

[17] *Predstavlenie o uchrezhdenii zakonodatel'noy, suditel'noy i nakazatel'noy vlasti v rossiyskoy imperii* (in *Yuridicheskie proizvedeniya progressivnykh russkikh mysliteley: vtoraya polovina XVIII veka*, 115).

[18] None of the works on Watt mentions this proposal (which was not taken up by the Russian authorities), though they do refer to invitations which reached him from Russia during the 1770s. For instance, one of Watt's biographers writes: 'In 1773 he had received an invitation from his friend Robison to come to Russia "where he had recommended him to fill some station". But in the spring of 1775 an offer was made to him of employment in Russia, under the Imperial Government, which, at a somewhat earlier period, might probably have met with his thankful acceptance; for the salary promised was £1,000 per annum, and the duties required would have suited well his own inclinations and acquirements'. James P. Muirhead, *The Life of James Watt*, (1858), 262. By that time, however, Watt was beginning to advance in reputation and prosperity within Britain and he rejected the offer. (The first letter from Robison to Watt urging him to move to Russia was actually sent in Apr. 1771.)

[19] The three archives in Moscow containing material on Desnitsky and Tret'yakov are the Central State Archive of Ancient Documents (TsGADA), the Ministry of Foreign Affairs archive, and the Gorky Library of Moscow University. All relevant material in the last-named of these archives has been published in three volumes (1960–3) under the scholarly editorship of N. A. Penchko. Some of the TsGADA material has also been utilized by N. Penchko in her valuable article, 'Vydayushchiesya vospitanniki Moskovskogo universiteta v inostranikh universitetakh (1758–71 gg.)', *Istoricheskiy Arkhiv* (1956), No. 2.

Mansfield, communicated by the Earl of Errol, and having been informed that for some time past, probably on account of the confusions in which the Government of Russia has been involved,[20] they have been disappointed of their remittances which they had reason to expect from Russia, the meeting unanimously think it a duty incumbent upon them to advance money to these two gentlemen until their remittances shall arrive.[21]

Adam Smith was, in fact, the intermediary who handed over the loan to Desnitsky and Tret'yakov and who two months later received repayment from them. We read in the Senate Minutes of 27 October 1762 that 'Dr. Smith delivered from the two Russian gentlemen the sum of forty pounds sterling which had been advanced to them' and that a receipt 'was put into Dr. Smith's hands to be given up to them'.[22] As Smith was a professor who took a keen interest in his students, it is very probable that his direct acquaintanceship with Desnitsky and Tret'yakov went beyond this, but we lack concrete evidence of further personal contacts between them.

The names of Desnitsky and Tret'yakov do not appear again in the minutes of University meetings until 31 December 1765, when (astonishing as it seems today) a Faculty meeting took place. In the minutes of that meeting we read that 'a petition was given in from Simeon Desnitzkoy and John Tretjakoff both A.M., desiring to offer themselves candidate for the Degree of Doctor of Laws. Mr Millar is appointed to examine them privately and to report their qualifications to the next Faculty meeting.'[23] At the next meeting on 9 January 1766, 'Mr. Millar reported that he had examined Mr. Simeon Desnitzkoy and Mr. John Tretjakoff privately and had found them qualified to undergo a publick examination—a meeting is accordingly appointed to be held on Thursday next the 16th inst. at 3 o'clock . . .' (ibid. 143). On the appointed day, Desnitsky and Tret'yakov were examined publicly and 'being desired to withdraw, the meeting approved of the specimen they had given of their knowledge and Law and calling them in, acquainted them therewith and prescribed to Mr. John Tret'yakov the Title 4 of Book 2nd of the Pandects, "De in Jus vocando" as the subject of a thesis which he is to read and defend in public, and to Mr. Simeon Desnitzkoy, Title 1st of Book 28th of the Pandects, "De testamentis ordinariis" ' (ibid. 144).

The theses on these passages from Justinian's *Pandects* (or *Digest*), which do not appear to have survived, were not of present-day doctoral dimensions, for on 8 February 1766 the Russian students read them aloud to the Faculty. The Dean of Faculty George Muirhead and John Millar were appointed to examine the theses and to report on them to the next

[20] The 'confusions' referred to were, of course, the forced abdication and murder of Peter III in July 1762, and Catherine II's accession to the Russian throne.

[21] Glasgow University Archives/Senate Minutes, vol. 30, 162.

[22] Ibid. 204.

[23] Glasgow University Archives/Faculty Minutes, 1732–68, vol. 33, 141.

Faculty meeting. In the minutes of the meeting of 8 April it is reported that Muirhead and Millar had examined the theses 'and had not found anything in them improper to be published'. Desnitsky and Tret'yakov were accordingly given permission to publish them. Oddly, however, no more is heard of the dissertations in the university records of the remainder of that academic year, and an entire year later, Desnitsky and Tret'yakov had still not received their doctoral degrees. Why there was such a long delay in 1766 cannot be explained on available evidence, but the further delay after December of that year is more readily understandable.

The explanation is to be found in a violent clash which took place between Desnitsky and John Anderson, the Professor of Natural Philosophy, on 8 December 1766. Though Desnitsky acted unwisely, it is clear that Anderson was far from blameless. An able though eccentric individual, he could be extremely disagreeable and ill-tempered and later in his career he was seldom on speaking terms with his academic colleagues. Among his numerous accomplishments, however, was a knowledge of music and he was the conductor of the university choir (or the 'band', as it was then known) in the college chapel. It was in connection with Anderson's duties as conductor of the band that Desnitsky fell foul of him. Desnitsky, apparently, regarded himself as something of a singer, for the trouble arose out of his desire to sit in the choir seats in the chapel. Anderson refused him permission to do so (apparently rudely) and Desnitsky, taking this as an affront, sought the advice of one of his fellow students. The student, presumably one of Desnitsky's best Glasgow friends, was Alexander Fergusson, a descendant of Annie Laurie, later an advocate and laird of Craigdarroch, and a friend of Robert Burns. He is celebrated in Burns's poem, 'The Whistle', for his achievement in drinking two other famous drinkers, Sir Robert Lawrie and Robert Riddell, under the table, and is described there as

> Craigdarroch, so famous for wit, worth and law

Desnitsky apparently did not inform Fergusson of all the relevant facts in the dispute, and Fergusson advised him to insult the professor. Desnitsky accepted this advice and the Principal of the University informed the Senate on 9 December 'that one of the Students had affronted one of the Masters, going to his Class yesterday about eleven o'clock in the College Court'.[24] The minutes of the various university meetings which considered this event do not make clear the exact nature of the offence, but what in fact happened was that Desnitsky approached Anderson in the crowded College Court and pulled his wig off.[25] The University took a serious view

[24] Glasgow University Archives/Senate Minutes, vol. 31, 176.

[25] In the course of a legal dispute between Anderson and Glasgow University in 1787, the University in its evidence, referred to the incident with Desnitsky: 'In the year 1767

of this and the Lord Rector, the Earl of Selkirk, was called in to adjudicate. At a meeting on 6 January 1767 attended by the entire body of students and professors of the University of Glasgow, the Rector pronounced sentence, judging that

the Insult offered by Mr. Desnitzky to Mr. Anderson was a manifest Breach of all Order, and a Contempt of the Authority of the University, and therefore deserved no less a punishment than Expulsion. That he would accordingly have pronounced a Sentence of Expulsion against any native of Britain, or Foreign or whomsoever. But that in Commiseration to Mr. Desnitsky's peculiar circumstances, who might, by such a Sentence, be utterly ruined, he was willing to mitigate the Sentence which the offence deserved . . .'[26]

Most other foreign students at Glasgow University were sent there by their families. In noting that expulsion might 'utterly ruin' Desnitsky (as indeed it would have done), the Rector almost certainly had in mind the fact that Desnitsky, in contrast, had been sent by the state authorities of Imperial Russia. As an alternative punishment, he laid down the terms in which Desnitsky had to deliver apologies before the whole university to the University itself, to Anderson, and to Alexander Fergusson. In his apology to Fergusson, Desnitsky stated his awareness 'that the punishment due to my Offence on the 8th of December last has been greatly mitigated from various reasons of Compassion, and particularly from the strong incitement and instigation of some of my Companions: but being also now sensible that I acted extremely improperly in not informing some of them of all the exact Circumstances when I took their Advice; and in consequence of which Mr. Alexander Fergusson, student of law, both advised me to violent conduct, and also, by acknowledging his Advice, has involved himself in my Guilt. I therefore beg his Forgiveness . . .'[27] Fergusson (who had been a prominent political opponent of the Earl of Selkirk in the Rectorial election the previous year)[28] did not escape punishment. The

(sic) Mr. Desnitsky a Student from Russia, happening of a Sunday in the Publick Chapel to be, as he conceived affronted by the Pursuer (Anderson), he privately demanded some satisfaction or apology. This having been refused, he in the College area amidst a concourse of Students attacked the Pursuer and pulled off his wig.' *Anderson* v. *The College of Glasgow*. Court of Session Papers (Scottish Record Office, Edinburgh), Acts and Decreets, Dalrymple, 23 Nov. 1787. See also the Rev. William Thom, *The Trial of a Student at the College of Clutha in the Kingdom of Oceana* (Glasgow, 1768); reprinted in Thom, *Works*, 406–7.

[26] Glasgow University Archives/Senate Minutes, vol. 31, 193 (Minutes of meeting of Comitia).

[27] Ibid.

[28] There is even some interesting evidence that Desnitsky, as well as Fergusson, had taken an active part in the rectorial election and that the election formed part of the background to the dispute between Anderson and Desnitsky. The litigious Anderson had privately printed his side of the case against the University in the legal process referred to in note 25 above. 'Though Mr. Desnitzkey had received nothing but good usage from the Pursuer,' he wrote, 'he was made a tool at the election of a Rector, and he insulted the Pursuer, first in the College Chapel, and afterwards in the College Court. To this he was

Lord Rector granted that 'there were many favourable Circumstances in Mr. Fergusson's Case, and particularly that when Mr. Desnitsky asked his Advice about an Affront which he believed he had received from Mr. Anderson, Mr. Desnitsky had concealed from Mr. Fergusson, Mr. Anderson having apologised for it'.[29] But the Rector felt that the authority of the University and the 'due Subordination of the Students' must be seen to be maintained and he 'therefore ordered the said Mr. Alexander Fergusson to be conducted immediately to prison by the Bedal for a little time, not as a Mark of Ignominy but of due severity in Maintenance of the Discipline of the College. The said sentence was executed accordingly.'[30] While the unfortunate Fergusson was being taken off to prison, the Rector 'further declared it as his Opinion that Mr. Anderson or any other Master sitting along with and conducting the band of Singers, has in common sense a just Right to keep improper persons from entering the seats in the Chapel where the Band which leads the Congregation in singing sits'.[31]

Fergusson apparently bore no ill-will towards Desnitsky as a result of the case, and when he returned to Glasgow in 1768 as a young advocate in the role of junior counsel in the defence of David Woodburn, another student whom the University had put on trial, he defended himself in a spirited speech against aspersions cast upon him on the grounds that the University had previously imprisoned him. He retorted that

> this audience, or some of them, might go away with a belief that I was imprisoned for some immorality or crime; but I was imprisoned for espousing the cause of a friendless and innocent foreigner, who had been basely affronted, insulted, and oppressed, in this very place. And instead of being ashamed of it, I should rejoice to be every week imprisoned in such a cause. And I went to prison, for a few minutes, of my own accord; for if I had not consented to it, I knew well that this court had no right, and dared not imprison me or any man in their steeple.[32]

instigated by other persons, and particularly by one Student who had been very keen in the business of the election.' (*Anderson Against College, Taylor and Richardson, 1786–87*, Murray Collection, Glasgow University Library.) Fergusson had actually challenged the validity of the election of the Earl of Selkirk on the grounds 'that a number of persons who attend a Course of Experiments given by Mr. Anderson professor of Natural Philosophy . . . for one hour or two in the week, who neither do nor ever did attend any class in the University, matriculated and admitted to vote along with the Masters and Students in the general Comitia for choosing a Rector' (Glasgow University Archives/Senate Minutes, vol. 31, 178–9). John Millar was one of the professors who supported Fergusson in his claim that there had been improprieties in the election of Selkirk, whose opponent in the Rectorial was James Oswald, a friend of Adam Smith.

[29] The statement that Anderson apologized to Desnitsky conflicts with the University account of the affair (see note 25 above). Since the latter version was, however, written twenty years after the incident, some credence must presumably be given to Selkirk's statement at the time that Anderson (quite untypically) offered an apology of sorts to Desnitsky.

[30] As note 26. [31] Ibid. [32] Thom, *Works*, 422.

In choosing to punish Desnitsky in such a way that the Moscow University authorities would be unaware of his misdemeanour, it is possible that the Rector was influenced by the advice of John Millar, for Millar, who was the Russian students' academic supervisor, was a member of a committee of four which originally investigated the affair. He was also a professor who over the years earned a reputation for coming to the defence of students in trouble. The voice of Millar must also have been an influential one in the decision to grant the Russian students the degree of doctor of law. He was their principal examiner and would have a better idea than any other member of the university staff of the quality of their work. In a letter of 7 April 1767, in Tret'yakov's hand, the Russian students state that they have 'lately received orders to repair home with all convenient speed' and they therefore earnestly entreat the Faculty 'to allow them to undergo the remaining part of their tryals' for their law degree.[33] The University's reply is recorded in the Faculty Minutes of 20 April 1767, which state that 'in consequence of a petition from Messrs. Tretiakoff and Desnitsky representing that they have received orders to go home with all convenient speed, the Meeting dispenses with their defending their Theses in public as appointed in a former meeting, and being satisfied with the specimens given of their knowledge in the Civil Law, appoints the Degree of Doctor of Law to be conferred upon them by the Vice Chancellor when he shall judge it convenient.'[34]

When the Russian students returned to Moscow, they met with a difficult reception. There was a reluctance on the part of the Moscow University authorities to recognize their Glasgow qualifications and opposition to them from some of the German professors. They were forced to undergo oral examinations, and faced a demand that they sit an examination in mathematics since this was one of the subjects which they had *inter alia* studied in Glasgow. Desnitsky flatly refused to take the examination. Tret'yakov took it and failed abysmally. In their oral legal examination, however, both students (and Desnitsky in particular) distinguished themselves. They were both accorded teaching positions in Moscow University and Desnitsky especially very quickly achieved prominence as a scholar. He was not at first able to teach exactly what he wanted, but in the 1770s he extended his range, and by 1783 the syllabus of Moscow University shows Desnitsky to be giving a course of lectures on the History of Russian Law, a course of lectures on Justinian's *Pandects* from the compendium of Heineccius, and a comparison between the Roman and the Russian law. 'Professor Desnitsky, who reads these lectures,' the syllabus states, 'also teaches the English language from a Grammar compiled by himself: four

[33] 'Petition of Ivan Tret'yakov and Simeon Desnitzky, 7th April, 1767', Glasgow University Archives.

[34] Glasgow University Archives/Faculty Minutes, vol. 33, 163.

hours in the week.' Desnitsky was elected a founding member of the Russian Academy in 1783. He may have owed this honour both to a probable acquaintanceship with Princess Dashkova and to the fact that he had been chosen to be a major contributor to the projected *Dictionary of the Russian Academy* which was published in six very beautiful volumes between 1789 and 1794. Desnitsky contributed many of the legal and political terms to the dictionary and, in the words of the Soviet jurist who has produced the most scholarly study of Desnitsky, in the process 'exercised a well-known influence on the development of the study of the history of Russian law'.[35]

Among the discernible influences on the thought of Desnitsky are Lomonosov,[36] Montesquieu, and Blackstone, but the overwhelmingly predominant influences are those of Adam Smith and John Millar. A good many, though by no means all, of Desnitsky's economic views may be traced back to Smith, but so far as his socio-political and legal views are concerned, it would almost certainly be a fruitless task to attempt to unravel which ideas came from Smith and which from Millar, in view of the fact that Smith was such a major influence upon Millar himself, and since the Russian students attended the lectures of both Glasgow professors. It is probable that it was only after the departure of Smith from Glasgow that Millar began his course of 'lectures on government', for these lectures drew, to some extent, upon Smith's lectures on jurisprudence.

In any event, it is fair to say that a great many of the ideas of a theoretical nature in the lectures of Desnitsky and Tret'yakov, as well as numerous points of detail, can be traced back to the Glasgow lectures of Smith and Millar. (The process of comparison is facilitated by the survival of students' notes of the lectures of both Scots professors, though, sadly, the original lecture manuscripts were destroyed.) A clear distinction must, however, be drawn between the degree of originality of Desnitsky's contribution and that of his colleague, Tret'yakov. Whereas Tret'yakov has been accorded an inflated reputation by a number of Soviet scholars, his intellectual achievements do not really amount to much more than the translation of some of his Glasgow lecture notes into Russian. Desnitsky, in contrast, showed himself to be fully capable of independent thought, notwithstanding the fact that he too quoted at great length (sometimes with, more

[35] P. S. Gratsiansky, 'S. E. Desnitsky o proiskhozhdenii gosudarstva sem'i i chastnoy sobstvennosti', 172.

[36] In between his short period of study in Moscow University and his arrival in Glasgow, Desnitsky, by way of preparation for further study abroad, spent some months studying physics, philosophy and rhetoric at the Academy of Sciences in St. Petersburg where he must almost certainly have come into direct contact with Lomonosov. Evidence of Desnitsky's sojourn in Petersburg is to be found in a document entitled 'Skazka, kakova podana v Gerol'diyu o professore Desnitskom' (Story given to the Herald about Professor Desnitsky), 1781, in the Moscow archive, Tsentral'nyy gosudarstvennyy arkhiv drevnikh aktov (TsGADA, 1722–96), Fond 16, No. 168 (14), document 130, p. 540.

often without, acknowledgement) from Adam Smith and John Millar.[37] Rather more of Adam Smith's economic thought is to found in the work of Tret'yakov than in that of Desnitsky. On the whole Desnitsky showed a greater concern with political institutions, comparative law, and the analysis of social institutions, but in his earliest works he expressed interesting views on economic policy.

Full justice cannot be done to Desnitsky's own contribution to the history of Russian social thought within the confines of this essay, nor even to the scope and diversity of the influence of Smith and Millar upon him. The most that can be attempted is an indication of the significance of the influence of Smith and, to a lesser extent, Millar upon Desnitsky and Tret'yakov with the help of some particular examples, drawn mainly from their economic and sociological ideas.

Tret'yakov's main exposition of economic themes is contained in his public lecture delivered in Moscow University in 1772 entitled *A Discourse on the Causes of Public Opulence and the Slow Enrichment of Ancient and Modern Nations*[38] which so closely follows Smith's *Lectures on Jurisprudence* that to speak of Smith's 'influence 'upon it is an understatement. It becames abundantly clear from this and other public lectures of the Russian professors that they took back with them from Glasgow very good sets of students' notes. It was almost certainly in the academic session 1762–3 that Desnitsky and Tret'yakov heard Adam Smith's lectures[39], and it is unlikely, as the late George Sacke[40] observed, that their English would have been good enough at that point for them to take very full and accurate notes of Smith's lectures by themselves. Sacke may have been right in speculating that the future Moscow professors supplemented their own notes by purchasing one of the sets of student notes of Smith's lectures

[37] Desnitsky frequently acknowledged his debt to Smith's *Theory of Moral Sentiments*, though, not altogether surprisingly, he did not attribute to Smith or Millar material which he culled from their lectures.

[38] *Rassuzhdenie o prichinakh izobiliya i medlitel'nogo obogashcheniya gosudarstv kak u drevnikh, tak i u nyneshnikh narodov* (Imperial Moscow University Press, 1772); reprinted in slightly shortened version in *Yuridicheskie proizvedeniya progressivnikh russkikh mysliteley*.

[39] For two reasons it is highly improbable that the Russian students attended Smith's lectures in the academic year 1761–2. Firstly, it was very unusual for students to attend the Moral Philosophy class in their first year at Glasgow University. Secondly, Desnitsky and Tret'yakov had an extremely weak knowledge of English when they arrived in Glasgow in 1761, and they had to take private English lessons. However, in a letter already quoted in the text of this essay, they do mention the fact that they attended 'Dr Smith's class of Ethicks and Jurisprudence'. This would appear to imply that they heard complete courses of lectures from Smith and not merely the fragment of the lecture course which he was able to deliver in 1763–4 prior to his departure from Glasgow early in 1764. The possibility that the Russain students attended the Jurisprudence lectures of 1763–4 *in addition to* those of 1762–3 cannot, however, be ruled out, in view of the enormously favourable impression which Smith's lectures had made upon them and the likelihood that at first hearing they would miss (at the very least) some nuances because of the linguistic problem.

[40] 'Die Moskauer Nachschrift der Vorlesungen von Adam Smith'.

which were apparently in circulation at that time, though it seems equally plausible to suggest that they might have enlisted the help of Scottish student friends when they were writing out fair copies of their notes. Whatever the means by which such full notes were obtained, Tret'yakov's 1772 lecture contains such well-known points from Smith's lectures as the passages on the division of labour, scarcity and plenty (with the familiar examples of precious stones and of water), the weakness of government in primitive society and its inability to offer protection to its subjects (or to industriousness), Smith's observation that the wealth of a state does not primarily consist of its gold and silver (and hence bank failures are not so damaging to a country as is commonly thought), and his view that nations, like individuals, will be impoverished if they consume more than they produce. Even the famous pin-making illustration of the division of labour (not in itself original to Smith) is to be found in Tret'yakov, and in a form which may be a slightly more accurate rendering of Smith's remarks than that recorded by the anonymous student whose notes came to be edited by Edwin Cannan.[41] Apart from routine adulation of Catherine II, Tret'yakov's lecture contains nothing which is not to be found in the lectures of Adam Smith.[42] Yet it has earned him many tributes from Soviet historians of Russian economic thought,[43] some of whom have gone so far as to contrast certain of the ideas expressed in Tret'yakov's 1772 lecture with the views which they suppose Smith to have held.[44]

If the major interest in Tret'yakov's economic thought lies in the accuracy with which he recorded the views of Adam Smith, Desnitsky showed somewhat greater discrimination and independence. Even though

[41] *Lectures on Justice, Police, Revenue and Arms delivered in the University of Glasgow by Adam Smith, Reported by a Student in 1763*. In this edition of the lectures, it is stated that 'If all the parts of a pin were made by one man . . . it would take him a whole year to make one pin . . . If the labour is so divided that the wire is ready-made, he will not make above twenty a day . . .' (LJ (B) 213; Cannan 163). In Tret'yakov's version, if a workman had to conduct the whole process himself, he would 'scarcely be in a position to make in a year one watch, or in a day one pin . . .' (*Yuridicheskie proizvedeniya* . . . , 299). Smith, in *The Wealth of Nations*, writes that, in the absence of division of labour, a workman 'could scarcely perhaps, with his utmost industry, make one pin in a day, and certainly could not make twenty' (WN I.i.3).

[42] This point may readily be confirmed by reference to Norman W. Taylor's article, 'Adam Smith's First Russian Disciple'. Professor Taylor publishes a translation of Tret'yakov's *Discourse on the Causes of Public Opulence and the Slow Enrichment of Ancient and Modern Nations* side by side with the relevant passages from the Cannan text of Smith's lectures.

[43] See, e.g., I. S. Bak in A. I. Pashkov (ed.), *Istoriya russkoy ekonomicheskoy mysli*, vol. 1, IX–XVIII vv (1955), 558–70; and N. K. Karataev, *Ekonomicheskie nauki v Moskovskom universitete 1755–1955* (1956), 25–32.

[44] Smith would appear to have been less closely studied by Soviet scholars (with a few notable exceptions) than the esteem in which he was held by both Marx and Lenin might lead one to expect. When in 1966 I first referred to the copy of the *Lectures on Justice, Police, Revenue and Arms* held by the Lenin Library in Moscow, the pages of Divisions II and III of Part I of the book (published seventy years previously) were still uncut.

Desnitsky devoted comparatively little space in his works to economic affairs, what he did have to say was of considerable consequence. His economic ideas are to be found mainly in his *Proposal concerning the Establishment of Legislative, Judicial and Executive Authorities in the Russian empire*[45] (especially appendix four) and also in the *Discourse on the Origin and Foundation of State-Supported Universities in Europe*,[46] the public lecture which bears Tret'yakov's name but which was written by Desnitsky.[47] Since both these works were completed in 1768, a year or less after Desnitsky's departure from Glasgow, it would be surprising if there were not traces there of the influence of his years abroad. In fact, his suggestions for political reform (which form the main body of the text of the *Proposal*) bear the mark of English and Scottish ideas and of British constitutional practice. At the same time, his proposals are skilfully adapted to Russian circumstances and the work as a whole is both extremely able and, in many respects, original. His economic proposals were undoubtedly influenced by the views of Adam Smith, but they are not a slavish reproduction of them and, on certain issues, Desnitsky adopts a different attitude from that of Smith.

What makes the economic part of Desnitsky's *Proposal* doubly interesting is that a number of his proposals were incorporated by Catherine the Great in the Second Supplement to her *Nakaz* which she also completed in 1768. Not only Desnitsky, therefore, but, indirectly, Adam Smith exercised influence over this famous document of Catherine's which was published in French, German, and English as well as Russian several years prior to the publication of *The Wealth of Nations*. Some of Desnitsky's observations are taken over word for word by Catherine; others are somewhat altered; and some, of course, are ignored. But a sufficient number of entire sentences from Desnitsky's *Proposal* are adopted by Catherine to put her debt to him beyond doubt. This prompts the interesting reflection that if Desnitsky and Tret'yakov were Adam Smith's first two Russian followers, the Tsarina was the third person in the Russian Empire to be influenced by Smithian economic ideas, though doubtless she remained unaware of the fact.

The number of detailed suggestions from Desnitsky which Catherine follows faithfully is too great for them to be discussed fully here.[48] One or two examples must suffice. In her discussion of the preliminary questions

[45] *Predstavlenie o uchrezhdenii zakonodatel'noy, suditel'noy i nakazatel'noy vlasti v rossiyskoy imperii*, in *Yuridicheskie proizvedeniya*.

[46] *Slovo o proisshestvii i uchrezhdenii universitetov v Evrope na gosudarstvennykh izhdiveniyakh*, a public lecture delivered at the Imperial Moscow University by Ivan Tret'yakov on 22 Apr. 1768 (Moscow University Press, 1768).

[47] See note 9 above.

[48] For a fuller discussion of the complicated question of the influence of Desnitsky (and Smith) on Catherine, see A. H. Brown, 'S. E. Desnitsky, Adam Smith and the *Nakaz* of Catherine II', *Oxford Slavonic Papers*, N.S. vii (1974), 42–59.

to be asked prior to the imposition of taxes, Catherine (articles 582–6) follows Desnitsky precisely. Her formulation reads:

1. On what objects ought taxes to be imposed?
2. How to make them least burdensome for the people?
3. How to diminish the expenses of collecting taxes?
4. How to prevent frauds in the revenue?
5. How is the revenue to be administered?[49]

Several of these points made by both Desnitsky and Catherine bear a marked resemblance to Adam Smith's 'maxims with regard to taxes in general' (WN V.ii.b.3–6), but the influence of Smith on Desnitsky, and hence on Catherine, becomes more clearly evident when we examine some of Desnitsky's and Catherine's remarks under the second of these headings.

In Catherine's version (article 590) we have: 'But in order to make the imposts less sensitively felt by the subjects, it ought at the same time to be preserved as a general rule, that in all circumstances monopolies should be avoided, that is, a privilege should not be given to anyone, exclusive of all others, to trade in this or that commodity.'[50]

Desnitsky, after making a strong attack on the practice of tax-farming, sums up his discussion of this point thus: '. . . in order, as far as possible, to make the imposts made upon the subjects not sensitively felt, it is necessary to preserve as general rules: (1) in all circumstances to avoid monopolies; (2) not to impose internal duties on any kind of goods; (3) when tax-farmers are to be found, to exercise extremely rigorous supervision over them.'[51]

It is not only in Smith's celebrated hostility to monopoly that Desnitsky has followed his Glasgow teacher. All three of Desnitsky's 'general rules' were dear to Smith's heart. On the first of these points, the notes of Smith's lectures taken by a student contemporary of Desnitsky are sufficiently eloquent: '. . . monopolies . . . destroy public opulence . . . When only a certain person or persons have the liberty of importing a commodity, there is less of it imported than would otherwise be; the price of it is therefore higher, and fewer people supported by it . . . In monopolies, such as the Hudson's Bay and East India companies, the people engaged in them make the price what they please . . . exclusive privileges of corporations have the same effect. The butchers and bakers raise the price of their goods as they please, because none but their own corporation is allowed to sell in the market, and therefore their meat must be taken, whether good or not' (LJ (B) 231–2; Cannan, 179–80).

[49] *Nakaz Imperatritsy Ekateriny II* (ed. N. D. Chechulin, St. Petersburg, 1907), 154. Cf. Desnitsky, *Predstavlenie*, 138–41.

[50] *Nakaz*, 155.

[51] Desnitsky, *Predstavlenie*, 140.

On the question of internal duties, Smith commented in his lectures: 'In the method of levying our customs we have an advantage over the French. Our customs are all paid at once by the merchants, and goods, after their entry in the custom house books, may be carried by a permit through any part of the country without molestation and expense, except some trifles upon tolls, etc. In France a duty is paid at the end of almost every town they go into, equal if not greater, to what is paid by us at first; inland industry is embarrassed by theirs, and only foreign trade by ours.' (LJ (B) 317; Cannan, 244–5).

Smith follows these remarks immediately with some observations relevant to Desnitsky's suspicions of tax-farmers: 'We have another advantage in levying our taxes by commission, while theirs [France's] are levied by farm, by which means not one half of what they raise goes into the hands of the government . . . the rest goes for defraying the expense of levying it, and for the profit of the farmer.' (LJ (B) 317–18; Cannan, 245). In *The Wealth of Nations*, Smith writes: 'Even a bad sovereign feels more compassion for his people than can ever be expected from the farmers of his revenue. He knows that the permanent grandeur of his family depends upon the prosperity of his people, and he will never knowingly ruin that prosperity for the sake of any momentary interest of his own. It is otherwise with the farmers of his revenue, whose grandeur may frequently be the effect of the ruin, and not of the prosperity of his people' (WN V.ii.k.74).

Not all of Desnitsky's economic opinions, however, correspond with those of Adam Smith. In the main body of his *Proposal*, Desnitsky devotes a section to reform of local government, in the course of which he proposes that the civil authority in the towns be organized in six departments. To the second department he allocates the task of keeping an eye on

> the cheapness of foodstuffs to be sold in the particular city . . . that is, to observe a zealous supervision so that in all shops and in all markets the goods are sold at a known price and by weight and measure established by state decree. And in addition to that, the duty of the second department will be to stamp out profiteers and middlemen who, by increasing the price of things, cause the inhabitants unnecessary loss and make it difficult for them to maintain themselves.[52]

Adam Smith, in contrast, took a very poor view of attempts to fix prices, holding that the market forces, left to themselves, would do the job better. 'In ancient times', he wrote, 'it was usual to attempt to regulate the profits of merchants and other dealers, by rating the price both of provisions and other goods. The assize of bread is, so far as I know, the only remnant of this ancient usage. Where there is an exclusive corporation, it may perhaps be proper to regulate the price of the first necessary of life. But where there

[52] Ibid. 118.

is none, the competition will regulate it much better than any assize' (WN I.x.c.62). Smith was, of course, far from oblivious to the danger of traders acting in consort. In a famous passage, he writes: 'People of the same trade seldom meet together, even for merriment and diversion, but the conversation ends in a conspiracy against the public, or in some contrivance to raise prices' (WN I.x.c.27). The difference between his position and Desnitsky's was that he felt that to provide other traders with access to the market would be a more effective means of keeping prices down than state intervention. Though it was impossible to prevent meetings of traders 'by any law which either could be executed, or would be consistent with liberty and justice', the law 'ought to do nothing to facilitate such assemblies; much less to render them necessary' (WN ibid).

The views of Adam Smith and of Semyon Desnitsky on the best means of financing education also make an interesting contrast. The conclusions reached by each of them may be regarded as products of their distinctive experience. The greatest influence upon Smith's views on the economics of education was his personal experience of the universities of both Scotland and England (in particular, Glasgow and Oxford). In Glasgow professors could more than double their small salaries by the receipt of annual fees from the students who attended their lectures; the greater the number of students who attended their classes, the more they earned. Smith favoured a system where a university teacher 'still has some dependency upon the affection, gratitude, and favourable report of those who have attended upon his instructions', for he believed that 'these favourable sentiments he is likely to gain in no way as well as by deserving them, that is by the abilities and diligence with which he discharges every part of his duty' (WN V.i.f.6). If, however, the emoluments of members of a college or university come from either state or private endowments and a teacher derives the whole of his income from such sources, 'his interest is, in this case, set as directly in opposition to his duty as it is possible to set it' (WN V.i.f.7). As Smith goes on to make clear, this last sentiment was a product of his six years' sojourn at Balliol. In a sentence which shocked a number of his readers (not least James Boswell, whose attitude to English social institutions was generally sycophantic), Smith observes: 'In the university of Oxford, the greater part of the public professors have, for these many years, given up altogether even the pretence of teaching.'[53]

Matters were not improved if authority over, and the financial support of, university teachers lay not 'in the body corporate, the college, or university', but in an outside body, whether Church or State. Whereas in

[53] WN V.i.f.8. While a student at Balliol in 1740, Smith wrote that 'it will be his own fault if any one should endanger his health at Oxford by excessive study, our only business here being to go to prayers twice a day, and to lecture twice a week'. (Letter 1, addressed to William Smith, dated 24 Aug. 1740, Bannerman MSS. XII, Glasgow University Library.)

the former case the teachers in the college will be very indulgent towards one another and every man will consent 'that his neighbour may neglect his duty, provided he himself is allowed to neglect his own' (WN V.i.f.8), an 'extraneous jurisdiction . . . is liable to be excercised both ignorantly and capriciously' (WN V.i.f.9). For Smith, the administration of French universities served as a good example of the effects of 'an arbitrary and extraneous jurisdiction' (V.i.f.9).

Desnitsky, in contrast, in the *Discourse on the Origin and Foundation of State-Supported Universities in Europe*, argues very strongly in favour of such state support. He is full of praise for Peter the Great who 'before the arrival of sciences in Russia did not spare his treasure in the construction of places where they could be acquired' and who besides this travelled to Europe and 'summoning the sciences from there, gathered them in his embrace, and scattered them in different places' in the Russian empire.[54] Desnitsky also expresses his approval of the practice in Russia and elsewhere in Europe of the state providing the incomes of teachers and students.[55] This may readily be understood in the light of Desnitsky's own background. Though the majority of those who received a higher education in Russia were members of the nobility, an important minority of students of humbler social origin were enabled to study by means of state support. This was true, for example, of the greatest Russian scientist of his age, Mikhail Lomonosov, the son of a fisherman from a village close to Archangel, who was enabled to pursue his studies at the University of Marburg. It was likewise true of Semyon Desnitsky who, even as a pupil in the 'gymnasium' attached to Moscow University, was a state-supported scholar. His study in Glasgow for six years was at the expense of the Moscow University authorities and, ultimately, of the State. Desnitsky, the son of a *meschanin* (in all probability a small trader or craftsman) in the mercantile Ukrainian town of Nezhin could not, without state support, have received a university education at home and abroad and achieved the honour of becoming the first Russian professor of law.[56]

[54] *Slovo o proisshestvi i uchrezhdenii universitetov v Evrope na gosudarstvennykh izhdiveniyakh*, 9.

[55] Ibid. Though Adam Smith held different views on the question of state support for universities, the impression should not be given that he was a doctrinaire supporter of private education. In fact, he was a persuasive advocate of state support for the basic education of the common people, all of whom should be taught to 'read, write, and account'. 'For a very small expense', he argued, 'the public can facilitate, can encourage, and can even impose upon almost the whole body of the people, the necessity of acquiring those most essential parts of education' (WN V.i.f.54).

[56] In Scotland, though not in England, an unusually high proportion, by eighteenth-century standards, of boys of humble birth were able to attend university. This was partly a matter of cultural tradition and partly because it cost so little to do so. Referring to the period 1760–1832, the late Professor Pryde wrote: 'One of the best features of the universities was their retention of the policy of the 'open door' to the poor student, who, if he had the talent, could pass from burgh or parish school to his chosen college, frequently

The influence of Adam Smith upon Desnitsky's jurisprudential and socio-political thought is at least as great as his influence over Desnitsky's economic ideas. For example, in the long lecture on 'The Best Means of Teaching Jurisprudence'[57] (fifty-one pages in its original published version) which Desnitsky delivered at a public assembly in Moscow University on 30 June 1768, in honour of the sixth anniversary of the accession of Catherine the Great to the throne, there are a great many passages drawn verbatim from Smith's Glasgow lectures. In this work, Desnitsky, after paying tribute to the richness of the British philosophical tradition, writes:

From hence have appeared the renowned Hobbes, Cumberland, Mandeville, Locke, Berkeley, Bolingbroke, Sidney, Harrington, and the more recent Hutcheson, David Hume and Mr. Smith; and of the last two named one has published his metaphysics and the other his moral philosophy, to the great pleasure of the scholarly world. In my opinion, if I am not mistaken, the moral philosophy of Mr. Smith is more closely connected with natural jurisprudence than are all the other systems of this science'

In 1770, in a work entitled *A Discourse on the Reasons for the Death Penalty in Criminal Cases* which draws both upon Smith's Glasgow lectures and his *Theory of Moral Sentiments*, Desnitsky announced that he hoped soon to publish a translation of the *Moral Sentiments*.[58] For reasons which remain unclear,[59] this work never appeared, though Desnitsky continued

with the aid of a bursary, which, even if it were £10 a year or less was a great help, for living expenses were low' (George S. Pryde, *Scotland from 1603 to the present day* (1962), 166–7). It was quite normal for students at Edinburgh and Glasgow Universities to pay around £15 a year for their living and educational expenses, while students at St. Andrews and Aberdeen could make do on even less. By the standards of Scottish students, Desnitsky and Tret'yakov should have been extremely well-off during their years in Glasgow, for they were paid an allowance of £80 a year each. The irregularity with which they received these payments, however, rendered their situation much less comfortable than the size of their allowance would suggest.

[57] *Slovo o pryamom i blizhayshem sposobe k naucheniyu yurisprudentsii* (1768).

[58] *Slovo o prichinakh smertnykh kasney po delam kriminal'nym* (1770); reprinted in *Yuridicheskie proizvedeniya*, 193.

[59] It is possible that the translation of the *Moral Sentiments* was opposed by the ecclesiastical authorities in Moscow, for Desnitsky had already more than once fallen foul of them. Smiths views on religion are not free from ambiguity, but Desnitsky's propagation of some of Smith's opinions was part of the cause of his difficulties with the Orthodox Church hierarchy. There is much in the *Moral Sentiments* which could have caused them further offence. Smith's religious scepticism emerged still more clearly in private than when he was writing for publication. Thus, in a letter (163) to Alexander Wedderburn dated 14 Aug. 1776 he writes: 'Poor David Hume is dying very fast, but with great cheerfulness and good humour and with more real resignation to the necessary course of things, than any whining Christian ever dyed with pretended resignation to the will of God' (MS. Gen 510 (47), Glasgow University Library). *The Theory of Moral Sentiments* was not, in fact, published in the Russian language until 1868. The Russian translation of *The Wealth of Nations* appeared between 1802 and 1806. At various times prior to the revolution of 1917, Adam Smith proved to be too radical for the taste of Russian officialdom. During the reign of Alexander III (to be precise, on 5 Jan. 1884), both *The Wealth of Nations* and *The Theory of Moral Sentiments* appeared in a list of translated books to be

to incorporate passages from Smith's book in his own writings. Thus, for example, two years later in his *Legal Discourse concerning things Holy, Sacred, and Accepted as Pious, with Examples of the Laws by which they have been Defended by Various Nations*, Desnitsky makes extensive use of Smith's discussion from Chapter 1 of the *Moral Sentiments* on why we sympathize with the dead, in the text referring to his argument as 'the irrefutable demonstration of a great philosopher' and, in a footnote, giving the name of the 'great philosopher'.[60]

In his two most sociological works, *A Legal Discourse on the Beginning and Origin of Matrimony* (1775)[61] and *A Legal Discourse about the Different Ideas which People have concerning the Ownership of Property in Different Conditions of Society* (1781),[62] Desnitsky draws not only upon Smith, but, at least as much, on John Millar, though in the later of these two works (written fourteen years after his return from Glasgow to Moscow), he develops his argument more independently than in the earlier. A great many points to be found in Desnitsky's 1775 work are present in John Millar's *Observations Concerning the Distinction of Ranks in Society*[63] which was first published in 1771. The overlap is particularly great between Desnitsky's work and Millar's first two chapters ('Of the rank and condition of women in different ages' and 'Of the jurisdiction and authority of a father over his children'). Desnitsky's explanation of the improvement in the position of women in society in terms of their increasing usefulness in the domestic economy is a major theme with Millar. A great many of Desnitsky's particular examples and detailed citations may also be traced to Millar. Desnitsky at no point cites Millar's book and it is quite likely that he never read it. Millar's published works followed his lectures closely and it is possible that he also referred his students orally to the same sources which he cites himself. Apart from his frequent citation of Adam Smith's *Theory of Moral Sentiments*, Desnitsky quotes the works of such other leading figures in the Scottish Enlightenment as David Hume, William Robertson, and Lord Kames. It would be surprising if he were to make use of an actual book, as distinct from lectures notes, of his former Glasgow teacher, Millar, without acknowledging the fact. Indeed, it is known that

banned from all reading-rooms and public libraries in Russia. Among others who figured in this *Index* were Karl Marx and John Stuart Mill. See John F. Baddeley, *Russia in the Eighties* (1921), 206.

[60] *Yuridicheskoe razsuzhdenie o veshchakh svyashchennykh, svyatykh i prinyatykh v blagochestie, s pokazaniem prav, kakimi onyya u raznykh narodov zashchishchayutsya* (1772), 41.

[61] *Yuridicheskoe razsuzhdenie o nachale i proiskhozhdenii supruzhestva u pervonachal'nykh narodov i o sovershenstve, k kakomu onoe privedennym byt kazhetsya posledovavshimi narodami prosveshchenneyshimi* (1775).

[62] *Yuridicheskoe rassuzhdenie o raznykh ponyatiyakh, kakie imeyut narody o sobstvennosti imeniya v razlichnykh sostoyaniyakh obshchezhitel'stva* (1781).

[63] John Millar, *Observations Concerning the Distinction of Ranks in Society* (1771).

Desnitsky found it difficult to obtain books published in Britain after his return to Russia and it is clear that most of his books in English were purchased during his years in Glasgow in the 1760s.

In considering the significance of Adam Smith (and John Millar) in relation to Desnitsky, I have left the most important point to the end. It is not just the detailed borrowings of Desnitsky which are important, though the fact that he introduced a number of the specific economic, legal, and sociological ideas of his Glasgow teachers into Moscow University circles is not an inconsequential one. More essential is the fact that Desnitsky's entire concept of jurisprudence and of the study of man in society was shaped by his years of study in Scotland. Some of the ideas which he adopted were part of the common currency of the Enlightenment and it should be noted that Montesquieu was an important influence upon educated Russians, as he was on leading figures of the Scottish Enlightenment. There is, however, no doubt that in Desnitsky's case, it was from Smith and Millar that he acquired his particular way of approaching legal studies. Professor Macfie has remarked of Millar that his special talent was 'that of the comparative lawyer turned sociologist and reformer'.[64] The same might be said of his pupil Desnitsky, except that we should have to qualify this by adding that from the very beginning of his teaching career in Moscow University Desnitsky was a comparative lawyer, sociologist, and reformer.

Desnitsky is not only and rightly considered as 'the founder of Russian jurisprudence',[65] but as the founder of a particular school of jurisprudence whose approach can best be described as comparative-historical. Students of Adam Smith and of John Millar would probably agree that if any two words are adequate to describe the approach adopted by Smith in his lectures on jurisprudence and by Millar in his lectures on law and government, they would have to be 'comparative-historical'. That the postulated relationship is not simply an argument *post hoc, ergo propter hoc* is indicated by the numerous parallel passages in the works of Smith, Millar, and Desnitsky, and by the respectful tone, approaching veneration, which Desnitsky adopts when he refers by name to Adam Smith. In more specific terms, it may be said that Desnitsky's key tool of analysis (utilized most extensively in his work of 1775 on the development of marriage and of 1781 on ideas concerning the ownership of property) is the theory of the

[64] A. L. Macfie, 'John Millar: A Bridge between Adam Smith and Nineteenth Century Social Thinkers?', *The Individual in Society: Papers on Adam Smith* (1967), 149.

[65] In 1835 an article in the *Journal of the Ministry of Public Education* described Desnitsky as 'the pride of the university and the creator of the Russian study of jurisprudence'. A. V. Evrov, 'Istoriya metod nauky zakonovedeniya v XVIII veke', *Zhurnal ministerstva narodnago prosvescheniya* (1835, no. 6, issue 2). In 1955 Professor I. S. Bak noted: 'Desnitsky was the first professor to specialize in the field of Russian law. His lectures had a tremendous influence on those who heard them. Desnitsky is the founder of Russian legal science and his own school of jurisprudence, which attracted many students and followers' (in A. I. Pashkov (ed.), *Istoriya russkoy ekonomicheskoy mysli* (1955), 571).

stages of development of society, a theory which was common to both Smith and Millar and which became the conceptual basis of the comparative-historical approach of the Russian professor.

A number of Russian writers (both pre-Soviet and Soviet) have attributed to Desnitsky the distinction of first formulating the idea that there are the following four stages in the development of society: (1) the stage at which men are hunters and fishermen and live off the spontaneous fruits of the earth; (2) the stage at which they become shepherds—which means that they begin to acquire property in the form of animals; (3) the stage at which they become husbandmen—begin to cultivate the soil and so also start to acquire property in the form of land; and (4) the commercial stage—at which people begin to engage in mercantile activity. Though a number of different variants of the theory of stages of development were to be found among Scottish thinkers during the second half of the eighteenth century, the four stages outlined above were precisely those acknowledged by Smith and Millar, both of whom (though in a more fully explicit way, Millar) made much use of this conceptual framework in their Glasgow lectures as the most meaningful basis for comparison of different societies, institutions, and customs.[66]

Desnitsky refers to this mode of analysis as one discovered by 'the newest and most assiduous explorers of human nature',[67] though he suggests that Roman writers such as Julius Caesar, Tacitus, and Sallust also 'measured the successes' of their own and other peoples against the yardstick of 'such conditions of the human race' (ibid). The apparent contradiction between the simultaneous attribution of novelty and appeal to ancient precedent is no doubt to be explained by the much more systematic and explicit way in which the methodology began to be applied by eighteenth-century writers, among whom Smith and Turgot would appear to have been the earliest to take up and develop this mode of analysis.[68] Certainly, this methodology is the cornerstone of Desnitsky's comparative-historical

[66] In LJ (B) 149; Cannan 107, we find the cryptic statement: 'The four stages of society are hunting, pasturage, farming and commerce' (107). In Millar's 'Lectures on Government', a fuller delineation is provided. (See Lecture 3 in the sets of student notes of David Boyle and James Millar, MS. Murray 88, Glasgow University Library.) In the more recently discovered set of student notes of Smith's Lectures on Jurisprudence which is to be published as part of the Adam Smith bicentenary series of publications (notes much fuller in many respects than the Cannan version), the four stages of development figure prominently. Cf. Ronald L. Meek, 'Smith, Turgot, and the "Four Stages" Theory', *History of Political Economy*, iii, No. 1 (Spring 1971), 9–27.

[67] *Yuridicheskoe rassuzhdenie . . . o sobstvennosti, Yuridicheskie proizvedeniya progressivnykh russikikh mysliteley*, 244.

[68] See Meek, 'Smith, Turgot, and the "Four Stages" Theory'. It seems unlikely that such an analytical framework was ever consciously employed by any ancient writer. For two recent (and contrasting) accounts of ancient notions of 'progress', see Ludwig Edelstein, *The Idea of Progress in Classical Antiquity* (1967) and E. R. Dodds, *The Ancient Concept of Progress* (1973).

approach. Thus, for instance, after discussing the weakness of government among primitive peoples and how 'for their better subsistence and for common defence against their enemies' they unite into communities, discover agriculture, and learn how to build defensive walls, he goes on: 'Such an origin and development of human society is common to all the primitive peoples, and in accordance with these four conditions of peoples we must deduce their history, government, laws and customs and measure their various successes in sciences and arts.'[69]

Desnitsky was in many respects the most significant, as well as (in company with Tret'yakov) the earliest, of Adam Smith's eighteenth-century Russian followers. His work has received little attention from western scholars and those few who have expressed interest in it have tended to do so only for the light which it may throw upon the content of Adam Smith's lectures.[70] Desnitsky's lectures do provide further corroboration of the authenticity of the two sets of student notes on Smith's lectures which are being published as part of the bicentenary edition of Smith's *Works*,[71] but to regard them as little more than a third set of student notes would be to underestimate seriously Desnitsky's independence of mind. The relationship of Desnitsky's work to the thought of Adam Smith is, indeed, an important object of study, both for an understanding of Desnitsky and in connection with Smith's influence in Russia, but it by no means exhausts the significance of Desnitsky. This is not the place to attempt to present a rounded picture of Desnitsky's thought and of his influence as a jurist.[72] It must suffice to say that his contribution to Russian intellectual life from the late 1760s until the late 1780s amounted to very much *more* than introducing the ideas of Adam Smith into Moscow University circles (and to Catherine II). It would likewise be wrong to denigrate Desnitsky on account of his unacknowledged verbatim borrowings from his Scottish teachers. In an eighteenth-century context, this need not be regarded as either particularly unusual or especially reprehensible.[73] Desnitsky paid

[69] By 'arts' (*khudoshestvakh*) Desnitsky means handicrafts and manufactures. *Yuridicheskoe rassuzhdenie . . . o sobstvennosti*, 245.

[70] Cf. G. Sacke, 'Die Moskauer Nachschrift der Vorlesungen von Adam Smith', and W. R. Scott, 'Studies relating to Adam Smith during the last Fifty Years' *Proceedings of the British Academy*, xxvi (1940).

[71] There are, for instance, numerous passages in Desnitsky's lectures which are similar to (and sometimes verbatim renderings of) passages in the Smith lecture notes edited by Cannan and those discovered by Lothian. Prior to the discovery of the latter set of notes, the lectures of Desnitsky could, in principle, be used to fill out the summary version of some of Smith's points provided by Cannan's anonymous student, as Sacke first demonstrated. The lectures of Desnitsky (and Tret'yakov) are perhaps a particularly useful guide to the broad themes dealt with by Smith in his Glasgow lectures of the early 1760s. But any attempt to infer how Smith expressed himself in detail from Desnitsky's handling of the same points is extremely risky.

[72] This I hope to do at much greater length in another place.

[73] That Desnitsky felt no need to be apologetic about it is indicated both by the fact that he sent copies of two of his earliest works to Glasgow, and by the fact that he was a

his Glasgow professors the tribute of courageously upholding many of their major ideas in an environment which was often extremely hostile to such radical thoughts. Adam Smith himself, from whom so many of the ideas came, can indeed be cited in his support: 'To approve of another man's opinions is to adopt those opinions, and to adopt them is to approve of them' (TMS I.i.3.2).

party to a proposal by his colleague, Professor Erazmus, that his works should be translated into Latin so that they would be accessible to scholars abroad and in order that they might be sent to various European universities in exchange for foreign books. See Penchko (ed.), *Dokumenty i materialy po istorii Moskovskogo universiteta*, ii. 16 and 157–8. (The proposal was rejected by the Curator of the University, Adodurov.)

XIV

The Conflict between Montesquieu and Hume

A Study of the Origins of Adam Smith's Universalism

PAUL E. CHAMLEY*

INTRODUCTION

UNTIL about the middle of the eighteenth century, the pathway of classical universalism was not devoid of obstacles. Few people would have denied the basic unity of human nature. On this point, the Enlightenment upheld the teaching of traditional beliefs. However, this postulate did not necessarily lead to universalism in point of social organization. Geographical determinism was ruling. It made it possible to reconcile the universalist principle with the actual fact that nations differ from each other as well as their social systems. But at the same time it set narrow limits to the areas to be governed by economic liberalism as well as to the capacity for human nature to accommodate itself in accordance with the needs of trade.

In *L'Esprit des lois*, Montesquieu gave this long-standing doctrine a support which, though not entirely unequivocal, nevertheless carried considerable weight. In his view, different climates tend to divide humanity up into different and even conflicting types of organization. Out of these differences, inequalities will result, and unity will not be restored by peaceful means alone.

In his *Essays on National Characters*, Hume categorically rejects the theory of climatic determinism. This was in fact foreshadowed by his earlier philosophical works. In Hume's view, the character of a people is formed by custom, and collective customs arise and are altered by imitation. He emphasizes the role of the upper classes in setting the example, and the decisive action of political organization. Such a doctrine could easily be extended to relations between peoples. One consequence is that no natural determinism hinders the peaceful diffusion of the principles of good government, and that their dissemination is indeed made easier by the laws of human understanding. The result also is that far from setting rigid limitations, human nature lends itself to the division of labour. The *Essay*

* Professor in the Faculty of Economic Science in the University of Strasbourg.

on National Characters thus appears to be one of the preliminaries of Smith's teaching.[1]

The object of this study is to show the terms of the conflict between Montesquieu and Hume, to reconstruct its development, and to describe some of the consequences which immediately ensued.[2]

PART ONE—THE DOCTRINAL TERMS OF THE CONFLICT

Section 1. Montesquieu's theory of national characters

Montesquieu gave his theory of national characters a central position in *L'Esprit des lois*.[3] He attached so much importance to it that he had devoted a separate study to this subject: *l'Essai sur les causes qui peuvent affecter les esprits et les caractères*.[4] In this work he expresses the opinion that 'moral causes form the character of a people and determine its spiritual quality more than physical causes'. But he observes too that 'the complexity of the causes forming the character of a people is very great'.

This preparatory work does not do away with all the difficulties. For in *L'Esprit des lois*, Montesquieu must resolve himself to ruthless systematization: 'This subject is of vast dimensions. In this mass of ideas which arise in my mind, I propose to give more attention to the order of things than to the things themselves; I must clear away right and left, I must get through, I must see light' (19.1). In actual fact, he rather proceeds the opposite way. He sacrifices over-all coherence to clarity of detail. This is almost inevitable

[1] The following places in the works of Smith show a particularly clear imprint of Hume's views on the differentiation of individual and collective characters: TMS V.1, 2. LRBL 30.20f. Smith shows here that in the same country diverging tendencies can coexist, in accordance with a corresponding framework of collective customs. The example he quotes is entirely in the manner of Hume. LJ (B) 220–21; Cannan, 170. WN I. ii. 4.

[2] The author would like to express his thanks to the many people who helped him to carry out the researches for this study. At the beginning of his inquiry he had the advantage of having an interview with Dr. Robert Shackleton. Particularly valuable assistance was given by Mr. N. E. Evans of the Public Record Office, London; Mr. Robert Donaldson and Miss Ann Matheson, of the National Library of Scotland, Edinburgh; Mr. Bernard A. Bernier, Jr., Head, Reference Section, Serial Division, Library of Congress, and the staff of this section, as well as the staff of the Bibliothèque Nationale et Universitaire in Strasbourg, and the Service des Archives of the Quai d'Orsay. Professor E. C. Mossner kindly pointed to a mistake in the manuscript.

Of course, the author alone is responsible for the conclusions he draws from the data which were at his disposal.

The expense incurred in the work were mainly met by the research funds of the Faculté des Sciences Économiques de Strasbourg.

The translation was undertaken by Mrs. Elizabeth MacLennan and kindly revised by Mr. and Mrs. J. P. Wersinger. Passages from Montesquieu and from his correspondents were translated by the author. The final typescript was prepared by Mr. Skinner.

[3] The quotations from this work are taken from the original edition in two volumes, Geneva, 1748. The two numbers indicate volume and chapter.

[4] *Essay on the Causes which might affect the Minds and the Characters*. This work, written between 1736 and 1744, was first published in 1892; cf. R. Shackleton, *Montesquieu, A Critical Biography* (1961), 314, 406. It will be referred to hereinafter as *l'Essai sur les causes*.

with the fragmentary form which he chooses to give the book—more than six hundred chapters in a thousand pages. Since he cannot disentangle 'the complexity of the causes forming the character of a people', he cuts his way through by means of dogmatic statements, as in a brilliant conversation which delights in paradoxes, without paying too much attention to inconsistencies. These are numerous.[5] The most serious concern the actual meaning of Montesquieu's tenets relating to national characters.

First of all, we shall try to sum up the views expressed about this in *L'Esprit des lois*. The impact of this part of the work on Hume and his doctrine will be dealt with in a second section. This will give an opportunity for assessing the discrepancy between the real and the apparent meanings of Montesquieu's theory.

(a) *The main elements of the theory: from materialism to ethnic messianism*

In order to explain national characters, Montesquieu first takes physical causes into account. If we define them strictly, as does *l'Essai sur les causes*—and *L'Esprit des lois* agrees in principle—physical causes consist in the action of the climate upon thoughts and feelings, through a physiological process of which they are a continuation and a reflection. Since heat has the effect of distending muscular or cerebral 'fibres', this is proof that a hot climate will be sure to weaken minds and slacken characters. Montesquieu states that he found proofs of this kind when studying under the microscope the effects of heat and cold upon a section of sheep's tongue: 'I observed the external tissue of a sheep's tongue . . . I had half of that tongue frozen. . . .' For him, the human organism is a 'machine' (14.2; 14.12); a man reacts to physical causes with the precision of a thermometer:

> Go nearer southern countries, and you will feel as though you were drawing away from morality itself.
>
> (14.2)

> Go from the equator to our pole, you will see drunkenness increase with the degrees of latitude. Travel from the same equator to the opposite pole, you will find that drunkenness goes towards the south the same way it went towards the north.
>
> (14.10)

However, the unilateral doctrine often attributed to Montesquieu is obviously foreign to him: he sees the climate as only one of the factors

[5] The imperfections in this work are probably not entirely due to the complexity of the subject. The author's failing sight must have some bearing on the matter. There is something pathetic in the increasingly blind man keeping to his lordly manners, while struggling for light amidst the intricacies of his inquiry. Publication was delayed for a long time. It was already well advanced by 1742. Cf. Letter from Montesquieu to President Barbot dated 2 Feb. 1742.

contributing to the 'general spirit':[6] 'Several things govern mankind, climate, religion, the general maxims of government, the examples from things passed, habits, manners, out of which flows a general spirit which derives from them' (19.4). As time goes on, moral causes become more important; laws are perfected and extended, 'the examples from things passed' accumulate, society's spiritual heritage grows in many different ways. It would seem logical to conclude that the general spirit is formed more and more by an internal dialectic, and is less and less under the direct influence of the climate (cf. Shackleton, 318).

Moral causes themselves, however, are subject to physical causes, so much so that they aggravate their evil effects:

> In order to overcome the laziness due to the climate, it would be necessary for the laws to withdraw all the means of living without working; but in the south of Europe, they do just the opposite.
>
> (14.7)

> Foe, the Indian legislator, followed what he felt when he put men in an extremely passive condition; but his doctrine, born out of the laziness of the climate, and favouring it in its turn, has caused a thousand evils.
>
> (14.5)

Certain countries—for example, China and Ethiopia—show how a wise ruler can triumph over physical causes, but the opposite seems to be much more frequently the case: in Eastern countries, the permanent tyranny of the climate is 'the cause of the immutability of religion, habits, manners, and laws' (14.4). '. . . Asia is ruled by a spirit of servitude from which she never was relieved; and in all the histories of that country, you will never meet any single instance pointing to a free soul; you will never find there anything but heroism and servitude' (17.6). Several other passages have the same fatalistic ring about them.

However, in Montesquieu's view the most important question is not to know whether the main causes are physical or moral, but whether the combined action of physical and moral causes points the destiny of a nation in a good or bad direction. His point of view is rather more prescriptive than descriptive. He comes down on the side of reason, creative activity, and liberty, against superstitition, laziness, and slavery. But no prophecy can affect the course of events without itself resting upon the tendencies which are immanent in them. Montesquieu's idea on this point breaks through in two places. It seems legitimate to bring them together although they are a hundred pages apart: the work is badly constructed.

On the one hand, at least regarding European nations, Montesquieu

[6] In *L'Esprit des lois*, 'esprit général', 'esprit de la nation', 'caractère d'un peuple' are synonymous. In *L'Essai sur les causes*, Montesquieu talks of 'the general character of a people', 'the character of a nation'.

believes there is a natural convergence of physical and moral causes, in so far as the latter themselves derive from the climate. Physical causes predispose northern nations to action, and at the same time their physical environment increases their needs. The opposite is true of southern nations:

There is in Europe a kind of balance between the nations of the south and those of the north. The first have all sorts of conveniences of life, and few needs; the second have plenty of wants, and few conveniences of life. To the first, nature has given much, and they ask but few things from her; to the others, she has given but few things, and they ask much from her. The balance is maintained by the laziness she has given to the nations of the south, and by the industry and the activity she has given to those of the north. These are compelled to work hard, since otherwise they would lack everything, and would become barbarous. This is what made servitude natural among the people of the south, for, as they can easily do without wealth, they can do without liberty still easier. On the other hand, the people of the north need freedom, because freedom increases their means of satisfying all the needs nature has given them. Therefore, the people of the north are in a strained condition, as long as they are neither free nor barbarous; almost all the people of the south are, in some way, in a violent state, as long as they are not slaves.

(21.3)

On the other hand, although physical and moral causes concur to produce differences between the peoples of Europe and to fix their national characters, they do not guarantee any kind of stable equilibrium. The very character of northern peoples does not allow them merely to counterbalance those of the south:

I do not know if the famous *Rudbeck*, who praised so much Scandinavia in his Atlantic, has mentioned that great prerogative which must put its inhabitants so much above all the other nations of the world; viz. that they have been the resource of the liberty of Europe, that is, of almost all the liberty which exists today among men.

The Goth *Jornandez* has called the north of Europe the manufacture of mankind. I rather should call it the manufacture of the instruments which break the chains wrought in the south. This is the country where are born those gallant nations who leave their homes in order to destroy the tyrants and the slaves, and teach men that, nature having made them equals, reason could make them dependent only for their happiness.

(17.5)

In this way, Montesquieu's theory of national characters inserts itself in a general interpretation of history according to which history divides itself into three periods. In the beginning, all men are equal: 'Nature having made them equals' (17.5); '. . . all men are born equals' (15.7). Inequalities are caused by humanity being scattered into different climates, which have produced free nations and slave nations. Taken to its extreme, this principle of differentiation tends to re-establish universal equality. Simultaneously, humanity will be raised to a higher level of development thanks to the virtues and achievements of the liberating nations. Reason, immanent in history, does not proceed without violence.

Montesquieu was among the first adepts of speculative Freemasonry.[7] Perhaps masonic ideology inspired him in both his humanist prophetism and his Neoplatonist idea of the movement of history.[8]

(b) L'Esprit des lois *in its relation to the* Treatise *and the* Enquiry concerning Human Understanding

It is not certain whether Montesquieu had read the *Treatise of Human Nature* before writing *L'Esprit des lois*. At the very least we may doubt if he read it carefully. Where his ideas conflict with Hume's, this is probably not deliberate. None the less, the central part of *L'Esprit des lois* bears objectively the appearance of an attack on the *Treatise* and its author.

The disagreement relates essentially to the explanation of national characters and to questions of method. It is aggravated by some of Montesquieu's strictures on the English character.

1. Nearly ten years before the publication of *L'Esprit des lois*, Hume had shown that the principles of the *Treatise* give a very simple answer to the problem of national characters:

No quality of human nature is more remarkable, both in itself and in its consequences, than the propensity we have to sympathize with others, and to receive by communication their inclinations and sentiments, however different from, or even contrary to, our own. . . . To this principle we ought to ascribe the great uniformity we observe in the humours and turn of thinking of those of the same nation; and 'tis much more probable, that this resemblance arises from sympathy, than from any influence of the soil and climate, which, tho' they continue invariably the same, are not able to preserve the character of a nation for a century together.[9]

Another passage in the *Treatise* seems to detract from this argument, but this is simply one of the minor inconsistencies Hume sometimes lapses into when he changes the aims of his argument. This passage could suggest that the same kind of determinism rules solar or climatic phenomena and national characters: 'There is a general course of nature in human actions, as well as in the operations of the sun and the climate. There are also characters peculiar to different nations and particular persons, as well as common to mankind. . . .' (*Treatise*, 402f.).

[7] As early as 1730, Montesquieu was admitted as a freemason at Horn Tavern Lodge, Westminster. Cf. R. Shackleton, op. cit. 139ff., 172ff.

[8] For another example of this influence, in the writings of an admirer of Montesquieu, cf. P. Chamley, *Économie politique et philosophie chez Steuart et Hegel* (1963) 109ff.

[9] *A Treatise of Human Nature*, ed. L. A. Selby-Bigge (1967), 316f.

Hume probably realized later the ambiguity created by this juxtaposition. The *Enquiry concerning Human Understanding* removes all doubt and singles out two degrees of determinism pertaining to human nature, which is both universal and liable to being divided into national characters:

It is universally acknowledged that there is a great uniformity among the actions of men, in all nations and ages, and that human nature remains the same, in its principles and operations.[10]

We must not, however, expect that this uniformity of human actions should be carried to such a length as that all men, in the same circumstances, will always act precisely in the same manner, without making allowance for the diversity of characters, prejudices, and opinions. Such a uniformity in every particular, is found in no part of nature . . .

Are the manners of men different in different ages and countries? We learn thence the great force of custom and education, which mould the human mind from its infancy and form it into a fixed and established character.[11]

In these passages, the principles of classical universalism are being typified. However, it should be observed that national characters are now explained by custom[12] and no longer by sympathy.

L'Esprit des Lois contradicts Hume's propositions, however one interprets the work.

We have seen that Montesquieu's theory is a vaguely pluralistic one. Montesquieu comes to no general conclusion on the question of whether physical or moral causes have greater weight, or even, more simply, whether climate exercises a decisive influence. Hume's is the more one-sided theory. Reduced to its expression in the *Enquiry*, it is comprised in Montesquieu's, for *L'Esprit des lois* too gives custom and education a place among the causes of national characters. Moreover, Hume gives scarcely any proofs of his theory. Montesquieu develops and illustrates his copiously, however vague the object of it is.

Judging by appearances, things look simpler, for the two authors seem to oppose one another totally. Not content with giving a place to physical causes, Montesquieu appears to accord them a privileged role.

This impression is chiefly enhanced by his very confused vocabulary. To

[10] *An Enquiry concerning Human Understanding*, § 65. The quotation from this work, as well as from *An Enquiry concerning the Principles of Morals* are taken from the edition by L. A. Selby-Bigge (1966).

[11] Ibid. § 66. Hume explains the formation and consolidation of certain religious beliefs by means of similar principles. Cf. Ibid. § 97. This paragraph forms part of section x, 'Of Miracles', whose publication in this work is one of the main differences between it and the *Treatise*. It should be noted that §§ 65 and 66 of the *Enquiry concerning Human Understanding* are part of the three sections of Book II ('Of the Passions') of the *Treatise* which were transposed from it to the *Enquiry* as early as 1748. The major part of Book II was taken up again, in a much abbreviated form, in 1757 (*A Dissertation on the Passions*).

[12] 'Education' is likened to 'custom'. Cf. Ibid. § 162.

begin with, Montesquieu takes climate and physical causes in the strict sense as synonymous. He then attributes to the climate certain consequences—such as the challenge man faces in his natural environment—where physical causes strictly speaking do not have any influence at all. The expression 'physical causes' itself, which one would have thought unequivocal, is being given a wider meaning (17.6). On the other hand, in contrast to *L'Essai sur les causes*, *L'Esprit des lois* hardly refers to moral causes. They are only expressly mentioned once (14.6). They do not appear in any book or chapter heading, while climate and physical causes are repeatedly mentioned. Climate explains vice and virtue, industry and indolence, sobriety and drunkenness, 'monachism' and the British constitution.

Possibly Montesquieu did not intend to give such great weight to physical causes. He may have seen them simply as a basic natural fact,[13] whose power ought to be demonstrated so that mankind might be helped to overcome it. The overriding importance of the normative view would paradoxically explain the very small space given to moral causes. In addition, words are equivocal: 'moral' causes frequently yield immoral consequences. In the only case where Montesquieu refers to moral causes, they happen to fall in with the laws of morality. Clearly, he shuns speaking of moral causes because he is anxious to avoid ambiguities, but in doing so he induces his reader to believe that he underrates moral causes as against physical ones.

When Montesquieu, forgetting the conclusions reached in *L'Essai sur les causes*, draws the conclusion that 'the empire of climates is the first of all empires' (19.4), he sums up in this phrase both the ambiguity and the seeming tendency of his theory. It is not surprising that many of his readers (including his own contemporaries) remembered only this aspect of *L'Esprit des lois* (cf. Shackleton, 302). From the beginning, Montesquieu was taken for a systematic theorist on the influence of climate in the strict sense of the term. Even today, critics are at pains to correct this opinion (Shackleton, 313f.).

2. As far as method is concerned, Montesquieu is in agreement with the empiricism initiated by Locke and of which Hume is the main representative by that time. He borrows from the vocabulary of Locke and Hume, and also from Hume's atomistic ideas and analytical categories: '. . . imagination, taste, sense, liveliness depend upon an infinite number of small sensations' (14.2). In the same way as Hume (e.g. *Treatise*, 276), he speaks of '. . . the soul which has . . . received impressions' (14.4).

But while Locke and Hume took care not to give their philosophy a materialistic leaning, Montesquieu goes boldly ahead and leads empiricism

[13] The main developments relating to climatic influence precede the definition of the 'general spirit'. In this definition, climate is mentioned in the first place among the components of the 'general spirit'.

astray. Certainly Hume talks of 'anatomising' understanding, but from his point of view nothing could be more arbitrary than the double telescoping which allows Montesquieu to cancel all distance between anatomy proper and individual psychology, as well as between this and collective psychology. The *Treatise* shows how the Newtonian method can be generalized to the human sciences. *L'Esprit des lois* disregards one of the main rules expressing this: '. . . any hypothesis, that pretends to discover the ultimate original qualities of human nature, ought at first to be rejected as presumptuous and chimerical' (*Treatise*, XXI).

3. One of the longest chapters of *L'Esprit des lois* discusses the character of the British people. Montesquieu declares:

> But these proud men, since they live mostly alone with themselves, would often find themselves surrounded by unknown people; they would be shy, and one would mostly find in them an awkward blend of false shame and pride. The character of the nation would show itself chiefly in their writings, where they would appear as people inclined to meditation, and who would have thought quite alone. (19.27)

This description fitted the solitary author of the *Treatise of Human Nature*[14] better than any other. But Hume himself had rejected this character. After the failure of the *Treatise*, he had decided to become a man of the world and not to bore his readers any more. The only literary genre he attempted after this was the essay.

In fact the two large volumes of *L'Esprit des Lois* are much more like the *Treatise* than Hume's later works. Montesquieu, with his casual airs, shows himself to be prone to rash deductions. Still worse, he repeats in an aggravated form the fault in composition which disconcerts the reader of the *Treatise*. This work begins with a dogmatic expression of the theory of association; qualifications come later, but they do not suffice to correct the first impression.[15] From chapter fourteen on, which can be considered as the real beginning of *L'Esprit des lois*,[16] Montesquieu proceeds in exactly the same way, with the aggravation that his empiricism is pushed almost to a caricature.

Section 2. The Essay on National Characters

(a) *Hume's demonstration*[17]

Hume divides his *Essay* into two main parts. In the first, after defining the

[14] Cf. E. Mossner, *The Life of David Hume* (1954), 103. Mossner quotes the significant evidence given by Henry Mackenzie at the beginning of the story of Pasteur La Roche *The Mirror* (1779–80), no. 42.

[15] Cf. N. Kemp Smith, *The Philosophy of David Hume* (1965), 110ff., 387f.

[16] R. Shackleton, op. cit. 302, quotes the following judgement made by a contemporary critic: '. . . I read thirteen books of Montesquieu's *Spirit of Laws* without making the least discovery. But at length the fourteenth book rewarded all my toils.'

[17] The quotations from the *Essay of National Characters* are taken from the edition by T. H. Green and T. H. Grose: *The Philosophical Works of David Hume*, vol. 3 (1889). The figures in italics refer to the pages of that volume.

problem in detail, he resolves it analytically, beginning with general observations on the behaviour of men and animals. He verifies his conclusions in a second part, which is more extensive than the first, but calls for less in the way of commentary.

1. Hume begins by observing that at first sight human nature obviously shows itself to be flexible according to social groupings, and not to be under the constraint of physical causes as animals are. The difference springs from the fact that man has a social and imitative nature. Our propensity for social life and our disposition to enter into the feelings of others spring from the same basic source, which also makes our passions and inclinations contagious.

But while mankind harbours an infinite number of different tendencies, these are not all equally represented in the members of a new community. In any case it is not likely that the sample of tendencies would be the same among the rulers of different societies just being formed, since ruling classes are but small groups. Therefore there must be some tendencies which are dominant from the beginning, simply because they occur more frequently in society as a whole or at least in its more influential spheres. Through imitation, they gain increasing significance, till at last some tincture of them stains the character of all members of that society, though each preserves some originality.

At the end of his analysis, Hume points out its central principle: it is sympathy—'a sympathy or contagion of manners'.

We have seen that the *Treatise* explains national characters by sympathy, and the *Enquiry concerning Human Understanding* by education and custom. The *Essay* explicitly refers to the principle of sympathy, but in fact it shows that sympathy is linked to custom, which in turn can be reduced to the principle of association.

For society as for the individual, character is made up of habits acquired during childhood. These evolve out of accumulated impressions, which are all the stronger at that age for being new: 'Whatever it be that forms the manners of our generation, the next must imbibe a deeper tincture of the same dye; men being more susceptible of all impressions during infancy, and retaining these impressions as long as they remain in the world.' The difference between the individual and society, however, is that society is not endowed with any psychic consciousness by means of which the accumulated impressions could be tied together. This function is fulfilled by sympathy. Although there is nothing altruistic in it, sympathy between the individual selves establishes a network of mutual links which strengthens cumulatively[18] until it takes the appearance of a collective soul.

[18] Hume thinks that this kind of mechanism tends towards a state of equilibrium, because of the decreasing amplitude of the reactions. Cf. *Treatise*, 365.

This process derives its impetus from the mind's need to feel vivid impressions and to enliven them by their association with each other and with ideas (*Treatise*, 352f.). Building upon this fundamental tendency, chance decides for each nation to which degree more specific tendencies in human nature will develop. As the process goes on, both the cohesion of the individual self and that of society are reinforced:

. . . where, beside the general resemblance of our natures, there is any peculiar similarity in our manners, or character, or country, or language, it facilitates the sympathy. The stronger the relation is betwixt ourselves and any object, the more easily does the imagination make the transition, and convey to the related idea the vivacity of conception, with which we always form the idea of our own person.

(*Treatise*, 318; cf. 301)

Beyond the dialectics of the individual and society, the problem of national characters interests Hume in that it shows the universality of the principle of association and the affinities between it and the principle of attraction. An individual or collective character is an amalgam of tendencies strengthened by accumulation. It is like a physical body whose attraction is all the greater for having already grown at the expense of its environment. Speaking of the principle of association, Hume had said in the *Treatise*: 'Here is a kind of ATTRACTION, which in the mental world will be found to have as extraordinary effects as in the material, and shew itself in as many and as various forms' (*Treatise*, 12f.).

2. In the *Preface* to the same work, however, Hume notes that moral sciences do not offer the same facilities for experimentation as the others. He draws the following conclusion:

We must therefore glean up our experiments in this science from a cautious observation of human life, and take them as they appear in the common course of the world, by men's behaviour in company, in affairs, and in their pleasures. Where experiments of this kind are judiciously collected and compared, we may hope to establish on them a science which will not be inferior in certainty, and will be much superior in utility to any other of human comprehension.

(*Treatise*, xxxiii)

The second part of the *Essay on National Characters* is the best illustration of this method which Hume has given: 'If we run over the globe, or revolve the annals of history, we shall discover everywhere signs of a sympathy or contagion of manners, none of the influence of air or climate' (249).

In the course of the commentaries which Hume adds to the many instances he sets forth in this part of the *Essay*, the practical reach of his theory and the perspectives which it opens for liberalism become apparent.

Collective customs are flexible: 'The manners of a people change very considerably from one age to another, either by great alteration in their government, by the mixtures of new people, or by that inconstancy to which all human affairs are subject' (250). They are determined mainly by the ruling classes, as we have seen, and by the action of governments: 'The same national character commonly follows the authority of government to a precise boundary . . .' (249).

The increase in international trade tends to draw nations together: 'Where several neighbouring nations have a very close communication together, either by policy, commerce, or travelling, they acquire a similitude of manners proportioned to the communication' (251). Sympathy between nations cannot fail to follow. In its turn this sympathy will strengthen international society, for custom, morality and legislation tend to consolidate spontaneous sympathy.

(b) *The relationship between the* Essay on National Characters *and* L'Esprit des lois

In its very presentation the *Essay on National Characters* contrasts with *L'Esprit des lois* in a way which seems calculated; its conciseness, its clarity, its simple and scholarly construction, its precise reasoning, the ease of its style make it one of the most brilliant works Hume ever produced, and these good qualities tend to bring out the imperfections in the work done by Montesquieu on the same subject.

As a whole, the *Essay* is a *de facto* reply to *L'Esprit des lois*. While appearing to be nothing but an impersonal academic dissertation, it maintains and develops the doctrine of the *Treatise* in contrast to that of Montesquieu. A closer comparison of the two texts shows that in many places Hume's argument seems to echo that of Montesquieu. Hume begins by giving a clear definition of physical and moral causes. As we have seen, this is one of the least satisfactory points in Montesquieu's work. He then proceeds to develop general points, the main theme of which is the influence of profession on character. Here he puts in a long footnote to prove that all religions degrade the character of their ministers. This immoderate outburst is surprising and it was deeply resented by the British clergy (cf. Mossner, 260ff.). But far from making amends, Hume intensified his attack in a new edition.[19]

Doubtless Hume's animosity towards the clergy of his own country can explain the violence and fury of this aggression; three years previously, the Scottish Presbyterian hierarchy had wrecked Hume's academic ambitions. But the footnote on the ecclesiastical character is more readily understandable when set over against *L'Esprit des lois*. According to Montesquieu, climate tends to develop differences even in religions. Christianity is the best of all religions, but the climate in southern countries affects it adversely

[19] Smith, for his part, is concerned that his friend's ideas should achieve respectability. Hume's angry diatribe against priests as compared with soldiers is turned by Smith into a decent parallel between the clergyman's character and that of the officer. Cf. TMS V.2.

and makes it deviate towards 'monachism', with its vices, laziness and accumulation of wealth. So the theory of climates tends to justify Christianity and especially the Protestant confessions, to which belonged Hume's principal enemies. Against this, the *Essay* sets the counterpoise of its polemics.

Montesquieu disregards the phenomenalist principles of the experimental method. Hume discreetly draws attention to them: '. . . physical causes have no discernible operation on the mind' (249).[20]

According to Montesquieu, climate makes northern peoples free or barbarous, and therefore conquerors. Hume allows that most conquests have been made from north to south, but this tendency does not, he says, show greater courage and ferocity on the part of northern peoples rather than southern; it is explained by the poverty of the former and the opulence of the latter.

One of Montesquieu's themes is the challenge met by human faculties in various degrees in the physical world. This idea is in the *Treatise*, but is not related to the problem of national characters. The *Essay* in its turn establishes this relation.

The character of the English people is the only one Montesquieu finds it necessary to analyse in detail. Hume observes drily that what is most remarkable about this national character is that it is the least remarkable of all.[21]

By one of these balanced comparisons which he likes to establish between southern and northern nations, Montesquieu assigns to southern nations too great an inclination for 'passionate relations between the sexes', and in northern ones a tendency to drunkenness. Hume in his turn examines this argument too, but in terms appropriate for showing clearly the difference between his own manner of argument and Montesquieu's dogmatic reasonings. He does not reject outright the adverse arguments, and ends on a detached note, without giving in on the main issue.

PART TWO—THE HISTORY OF THE ESSAY ON NATIONAL CHARACTERS

The relations between Montesquieu and Hume have several odd aspects. The *Treatise* pre-dates *L'Esprit des lois* by a long time; however, it is probable that the reply given by the second to the first is unconscious. The *Essay on National Characters* gives such a pointed reply to *L'Esprit des lois* that it seems intentional, but the publication of *L'Esprit des lois* preceded that of the *Essay* by a very short time. Some authors even think the opposite

[20] In the last edition to appear during his lifetime, the one in 1770, Hume made this point more explicit by adding the following sentence: 'It is a maxim in all philosophy, that causes which do not appear, are to be considered as not existing.'

[21] Dogmatic judgements on the English character were to remain a source of annoyance to Hume. Cf. the reference to Galiani in *The Letters of David Hume*, ed. J. Y. T. Greig (1932), ii.205f. This work will be referred to hereinafter by the abbreviation *Letters*.

—that the *Essay* preceded *L'Esprit des lois*.[22] For, quite apart from the question raised by its relationship with *L'Esprit des lois* in point of doctrine, the circumstances in which the *Essay* was written and published have remained obscure. The coincidence of these two questions is hardly likely to be a chance one.

Section 1. The problem of the origins of the Essay

To begin with, we shall look at the terms of the problem. Then we shall examine the solutions (implicit and explicit) which have been put forward up to now.

1. On 16 February 1748 Hume sets out for the continent. For the second time he goes as secretary to his fellow countryman General St. Clair. This time the purpose is a mission to the combined army under the command of the King of Sardinia—the War of the Austrian Succession being under way. The combined forces of Austria and Sardinia, supported by the English fleet, are grappling with the Franco–Spanish army in the region of Nice and Genoa. Relations between Vienna and Turin are bad. The Austrians behave like occupiers in their ally's country and do not seem anxious to carry the war over to the enemy country. General St. Clair's task is to smooth out the difficulties and to make the coalition work. He stops at Vienna, but his destination is Turin, where he is to replace General Wentworth who died at his post in November 1747.

In a letter which he sent from London to his brother John Home on 9 February, Hume said: 'I leave here two works going on, a new edition of my *Essays*, all of which you have seen, except one, *Of the Protestant Succession*... The other work is the *Philosophical Essays*...' (*Letters*, i.111). On the other hand, on 13 February he wrote to Charles Erskine, Lord Tinwald, the father of one of his travelling companions:

> ... Andrew Millar is printing a new edition of certain Essays that have been ascribed to me; and as I threw out some that seemed frivolous and finical, I was resolved to supply their place by others that should be more instructive. One is against the original contract, the system of the Whigs, another against passive obedience, the system of the Tories, a third upon the protestant succession ...

Some of his friends advised him against printing the third of these essays, and so he leaves the decision to Lord Tinwald (*Letters*, i.112f.).

[22] At least one of them, Leslie Stephen, *History of English Thought in the Eighteenth Century* (1962, first published in 1876), ii.155, noted the connection between the two works. It puzzled him, because he puts the publication of the *Essay* six years before that of *L'Esprit des lois*. The connection he establishes is therefore all the more remarkable. G. Vlachos, *Essai sur la politique de Hume* (1955), 127, points to Stephen's error, but as the chronological data still worry him, he advanced the publication of *L'Esprit des lois* by a few months. The present study was undertaken independently of these two authors: they were encountered in the course of it.

Hume did not return to England until about the end of December of that year. The new essays were published in the mean time. They appeared in two forms: they were included in the third edition[23] of *Essays Moral and Political*, and they also were published separately in a little sixty-page volume, with the title *Three Essays, moral and political*, Never before published, which compleats the former Edition, in two Volumes . . . By David Hume, Esq. . . . M.DCC.XLVIII—up to the time of these two publications, Hume's works had been anonymous.[24]

The *Essay on the Protestant Succession* did not appear in these two volumes, but they contained a piece which was quite unexpected, the *Essay on National Characters*. In both publications, this one is put at the beginning of the new essays, so it does not really take the place of the *Essay on the Protestant Succession*.[25] The problem is to explain the appearance of the *Essay on National Characters*.

2. Most authors pay scant attention to the *Three Essays*,[26] but Greig adopts a different attitude.[27] After noting that Lord Tinwald apparently[28] decided to withdraw the *Essays on the Protestant Succession*, he makes the following statement:

David, however, had left in Millar's hand the manuscript of yet another essay, 'Of National Characters', with instructions that it should be used, if necessary, to complete the volume. And so it happened—David having gone abroad. Millar first of all issued the three new essays—'The Original Contract', 'Of Passive Obedience', and 'Of National Characters'—in a separate booklet. Then, some time in the autumn of 1748, he published what he incorrectly called the third edition of the Essays Moral and Political. This contained the three new essays. It was in the small booklet that David Hume's name first appeared upon a title-page. Thereafter he acknowledged everything he wrote in book form.

[23] There was in fact only a third edition for the series of essays published for the first time in 1741 and re-edited in 1742 at the same time as the publication of a volume of new essays. For these, the edition of 1748 was the second.

[24] The first publisher, A. Kincaid, did not respect this anonymity right to the end. In the *Edinburgh Evening Courant* of 5 July 1748, he published an announcement mentioning, among books available: 'Essays, moral and political, by David Hume, Esq., Philosophical Essays, by ditto'.

[25] On this point, the current presentation (cf. *Letters*, i.113; Mossner, op. cit. 180) is not quite correct.

[26] Before 1931 only Leslie Stephen seems to have noted the existence of the little volume devoted to the *Three Essays*. 'David Hume', in *Dictionary of National Biography* (1891), XXVII.225.

[27] J. Y. T. Greig, *David Hume* (1931), 170.

[28] In the account of E. C. Mossner, op. cit. 180, this slight but not unimportant shade gets lost; the biographer gives as an established fact the decision which Lord Tinwald might have taken.

This narrative was never afterwards put to doubt.[29] It is full of new details, which the publisher of Hume's correspondence gives with an air of quiet authority. If it were correct, the question of the causal relationship between *L'Esprit des lois* and the *Essay on National Characters* would be settled: without stating a precise date,[30] Greig suggests that the *Essay* was published well before *L'Esprit des lois* since this appeared in the autumn, as we shall see. According to him, the *Essay* was even written before Hume left for the continent. So we should have to admit that Hume quite unwittingly struck Montesquieu—and very pointedly—while aiming at other writers, such as Arbuthnot.[31]

Such a circumstantial recital would, however, call for proof and it does not include any. It is flatly given the lie by a notice which appeared in the London *Daily Advertiser* of 18 November 1748, in the following words:

This day is published, in one volume in twelve, price bound 3s. (Formerly printed at Edinburgh in two volumes). The third edition, corrected, with the addition of three more Essays never before printed, of *Essays, Moral and Political*. By David Hume, Esq.; Printed of A. Millar, opposite Katherine-Street in the Strand. Where may be had, the three additional Essays. Price sew'd one shilling.

Since the *Three Essays* also carry the words: 'Never before published', this little volume appeared on the same day as the third edition of the *Essays*. The publishers' intention is clear: the *Three Essays* were published separately so that the unsold copies of preceding editions would sell more easily[32] while at the same time making it possible for purchasers of the older work to acquire them. Moreover, if the *Three Essays* had appeared at an earlier date, they would not have gone unnoticed. But neither the *Daily Advertiser* nor the literary periodicals mention such a publication.[33] Keynes

[29] T. E. Jessop, *A Bibliography of David Hume and of Scottish Philosophy from Francis Hutcheson to Lord Balfour* (1838), 17, repeats Greig's assertion that Hume abandoned his anonymity for the first time with the publication of the *Three Essays*.

E. C. Mossner, op. cit. 180, 208, 260, is substantially in agreement with Greig: according to him, the *Three Essays* appeared shortly after Feb. 1748. Hume would have been preparing them since 1747, and the essay 'Of National Characters' first appeared in *Three Essays Moral and Political*.

[30] Jessop, loc. cit., implicitly adds one particular detail. He states that the *Three Essays* were the starting-point of Hume's collaboration with the publisher A. Millar. As the *Philosophical Essays*, which appeared on 24 Apr. 1748, were already published by Millar, it would follow that the *Three Essays* must have appeared before that date.

[31] It is strange that, although he quotes certain authors, Hume does not mention any of the main exponents of the theory of physical causes.

[32] During 1748, A. Millar and A. Kincaid continued to bring out advertisements referring to the previous editions of the *Essays Moral and Political*. Cf. *Daily Advertiser*, 25 Apr. 1748; *Edinburgh Evening Courant*, 5 July 1748.

[33] Taken by itself, Kincaid's advertisement in the *Edinburgh Evening Courant* could raise doubts. It mentions Hume's name, and his name figures on the *Three Essays*, but not on the first editions of *Essays Moral and Political*. Furthermore, all the other works contained in the same advertisement appeared in Apr. and May 1748. However, the terms of Millar's announcements in the *Daily Advertiser* of 25 Apr. and 18 Nov. 1748 leave no room for doubt. Kincaid's publicity, as indeed the title indicates, alludes to the old editions of the *Essays*, not to the *Three Essays*.

and Sraffa[34] had remarked on the casual way in which Greig treats the relations between Hume and Smith. It now appears that he does the same with the *Essay on National Characters* and so, voluntarily or not, with the relations between Montesquieu and Hume.

There remains, however, one further question: although Greig's false allegations about the publication date of the *Three Essays* discredit what he says about the composition date of the *Essays on National Characters*, this is not enough to prove him to be wrong on the last point. Was the *Essay* not already fit for publication when Hume left England?

Hume declares in his autobiography that he interrupted his 'studies' during the time he spent with General St. Clair. But this evidence is suspect; Hume contradicts it himself in his correspondence with Montesquieu (cf. Mossner, 218). His letters of February 1748 to his brother and to Lord Tinwald show that when he left he was not even considering publishing this *Essay*. Moreover, they give us to understand—especially the second one—that at the time this text did not exist. Had it existed, Hume could scarcely have hidden from Lord Tinwald that he had in his possession another possibility if his correspondent did reject the *Essay on the Protestant Succession*.

One of the peculiar aspects of the problem is the disappearance of all the correspondence relating to the *Essay on National Characters*. This is all the stranger since the question dealt with in this *Essay* occupied Hume for the whole of his life. The first of Hume's extant letters to his publisher Andrew Millar is dated 1755. Shortly before his death, Hume had some of his letters returned to him in order to burn them. Others were destroyed by his nephew (cf. *Letters*, i.xxi). Still others must have been lost. Only one letter of the Turin period has been preserved, probably on account of its subject-matter. It is the one accompanying the description of his travels which Hume sent to his brother, Henry Home. The rest have disappeared, in particular a letter to which the first refers. The fact that this first one has been preserved tends to show that the content of the various letters determined their fate. At least it is certain that Hume was in correspondence with England. On the other hand, it is hard to believe that he would not have kept an eye on his literary enterprises when he attached such great importance to them. Given these facts, it is difficult to admit that the new edition of the *Essays*, already in print at the beginning of February, could have been delayed until after mid-November if the *Essay on National Characters* had been ready in advance.

[34] *An Abstract of a Treatise of Human Nature*, 1740, A Pamphlet hitherto unknown, by David Hume, Reprinted with an Introduction by J. M. Keynes and P. Sraffa (1938), xvif. Among the circumstances of the present case, it should be mentioned that the *Daily Advertiser* for 1748 is not extant in any public library in Great Britain. It was somewhat unexpectedly found in the Library of Congress, the staff of which kindly located the announcements and supplied the texts.

All in all, it seems reasonable to conclude that the *Essay* had probably not been written when Hume left for the continent.

3. This being so, the next step is to envisage the supposition plainly suggested by the internal relationship between the two works: could Hume not have written his *Essay* after the publication of *L'Esprit des lois*? In April 1749, he himself declares to Montesquieu that he read this book 'last autumn in Italy'.[35] Upon examination, this supposition proves extremely doubtful.

Montesquieu's correspondence[36] gives us pretty exactly the publication date of *L'Esprit des lois*: a very limited folio edition, not paper-bound, was printed at the very end of October 1748. The quarto edition, for the public, was on sale in Geneva at the beginning of November. In his letter of April 1749 to Montesquieu, Hume refers to this latter edition.

As to the publication date of the *Essay on National Characters*, when we compare it to that of *L'Esprit des lois*, we must take account of the fact that England still kept the Julian Calendar at the time: according to it, 18 November 1748 would correspond to 29 November 1748 in the Gregorian Calendar. So the publication of *L'Esprit des lois*, therefore, preceded that of the *Essay on National Characters* by a month.

It must be noted first of all, that even if such an interval could have left Hume time to write, and have the *Essay on National Characters* published, we would still have to explain why the third edition of the *Essays* was delayed until the autumn. Apart from this difficulty, a month's interval seems too short for all that would have had to happen in the time. One has to imagine the following sequence of events: once printed, *L'Esprit des lois* is sent to Turin; it comes into Hume's hands; he reads it with care, pen in hand, as he tells Montesquieu later; he collects references and writes the *Essay*; he sends it to London to be printed as the first of the three new essays; a first draft is printed; the proofs are corrected; the final text is printed; the book is made up and put on sale. In addition to the time required for all these events to take place, allowance should be made for inevitable slack periods.

Transport delays alone could not have been less than a fortnight. From Geneva to Turin, the post took four days;[37] a parcel of large books could probably not have travelled so quickly. Messengers plying between Turin and Whitehall through Germany and Holland took more than two weeks, sometimes more than three. The end of hostilities re-established postal communications across France before the autumn,[38] but the

[35] G. Vlachos's thesis (op. cit.) is grounded on this statement.

[36] Letters addressed to Montesquieu by Jacob Vernet on 4 Nov. 1748 and by Madame de Tencin on 14 Nov. 1748.

[37] This is the time taken for the news of General Wentworth's death to reach Geneva.

[38] Public Record Office, State Papers, 92/56. All the details given in the text on the relations between Geneva and Turin, except where indicated, are taken from this source, in conjunction with the archives of the French Ministry of Foreign Affairs.

time taken for the journey could not have been less than ten or twelve days.

Hume spoke French so badly that he probably could not read the book very quickly[39] and he had a thousand pages to read. He worked very slowly. For him, to think was to dream: '. . . reading and sauntering and dozing, which I call thinking . . .' (*Letters*, ii.134). Some years later, he said to his publisher: 'My manner of composing is slow, and I have great difficulty to satisfy myself' (*Letters*, i.219).

In addition, Hume's circumstances might have helped on his studious reverie during the whole of the spring and summer, but they suddenly deteriorated in the autumn. No sooner had he arrived in Turin than General St. Clair saw the main object of his mission disappear, since peace negotiations had begun at Aix-la-Chapelle. They finished in October, but then a last flurry of diplomatic activity took place at Turin. The conclusion of the peace treaty awaited the agreement of the King of Sardinia. He believed that his interests had not been well looked after by his allies. The task of removing this obstacle rested with the English court representative in Turin and with General St. Clair. The message from Turin telling the English minister of the last episodes dates from 9 November. It is doubtful that up to that moment General St. Clair's secretary could have devoted himself to reading the two volumes recently published in Geneva, which must have arrived in Turin a few days before. He had enough time up to his departure to enable him to write down the reading-notes from which he took the observations he sent to Montesquieu five months later, but not to enable him to compose the *Essay on National Characters* and have it published.

Hume's nature was circumspect and phlegmatic. 'Easiness' is a rule of his conduct as well as of his system. It would be difficult to assume that he suddenly launched himself, along with his publisher, into the feverish activity which one has to imagine so as to render it at all conceivable that the composition of the *Essay* did not take place until after the publication of *L'Esprit des lois*. Furthermore, we should have to admit that, again for no known reason, the third edition of *Essays Moral and Political* would also have been deferred until that moment, as if Hume and his publisher had been waiting for Montesquieu's book.

What we know of Hume's character—even towards the end of his life he used intrigue to further his own interests[40]—does on the other hand agree with a different explanation, which is suggested by the documents.

[39] In Turin itself, in 1748, he states that French is not his strong point. Cf. Mossner, op. cit. 216.

[40] Cf. Hume's letters to John Crawford (*Letters*, ii.281, and *New Letters of David Hume*, ed. R. Klibansky and E. C. Mossner, 1969), 203, and the comment by F. H. Heinemann, *David Hume, The Man and his Science of Man, Containing some Unpublished Letters of Hume* (1940), 25ff.

Section 2. From L'Esprit des lois *to the* Essay on National Characters

(a) *The publication of* L'Esprit des lois

The circumstances of the printing and publishing of *L'Esprit des lois* have been recounted several times.[41] Montesquieu valued his anonymity very highly and this was to be the source of the troubles he had with the undertaking. He thought first of all of having his book published in Holland, but the chance came to have the work done in Geneva. Pierre Mussard, one of the Republic's Councillors of State, was in Paris in the summer of 1747 to negotiate a treaty with France, and Montesquieu confided the manuscript to him. Without revealing the author's name, as he himself said, Mussard showed it to some friends in Geneva, in particular to Jacob Vernet, a clergyman and literary man, who had met Montesquieu in Rome in 1727. Vernet guessed the name of the author, says Mussard, and willingly undertook to supervise the printing and correct the proofs. The printing was entrusted to Jacques Barillot.[42] Vernet served as a go-between between him and Montesquieu.

The work should have been finished in the summer of 1747, but it dragged on; Montesquieu was slow in sending the last part of his text, the printer took ill and died, Vernet took his task somewhat lightly. As for his anonymity, Montesquieu had been rather ingenuous if he thought that he could have it preserved, especially from so far away. Geneva was a small town. Everyone of any importance, and people from all parts, knew one another. News of such strong local and general interest could not be kept secret there for long. From October of 1747 (cf. Shackleton, 242) the book had been the subject of rumour and the word went from Geneva to Paris.

The giving away of the secret embarrassed those in whom it had been confided. They exculpated themselves as best they could to Montesquieu, Vernet as early as 13 November 1747, Mussard on 4 November 1748, once the work had appeared. Vernet's letter is of more consequence than he could have thought: it is in it that we find the clearest outside indication of an early link between *L'Esprit des lois* and the *Essay on National Characters*, but in such an indirect way that this evidence does not seem to have attracted attention. Vernet declares to Montesquieu:

> For sure, I didn't pronounce the name of the author, nor say anything that could reveal it. I know all too well up to which point discretion and faithfulness must be pushed in such matters. But I don't guarantee that everybody has been as reserved as myself. It is certain at least that three or four persons who had some knowledge of this printing have named the author, by hearsay or by conjecture,

[41] Cf. F. Gébelin, 'La publication de l'Esprit des Lois', *Revue des bibliothèques* (1924); R. Shackleton, op. cit. 240ff.

[42] The spelling of this name used here is that given in the original edition of *L'Esprit des lois* and is not the usual one.

upon which one has taken care to shut their mouths. M. de Champeaux is not ignorant of it. He talked about it to M. Mussard and to me as though the fact were well known. A secretary of M. de Villette's, chargé d'affaires of the English court at Turin, who passed here, came across a sheet at the printer's shop, guessed at once, either from the matter, or from the style, whose hand it was by, and told it to someone. But he departed, and it is no more talked about. I tell you, Monsieur, all that has been reported to me . . .

These details make it necessary to bring to light more of the historical background of Hume's stay and his thinking at Turin.

(b) *The connections between Geneva and Turin*

'M. de Villette' was actually Arthur Villettes, the English court representative in Turin. He had no secretary acknowledged as such, unlike his predecessor,[43] although when he happened to fall ill, it was an assistant who told London of the situation. This was Lewis Barbauld; probably a descendant of the French Huguenots, like Villettes,[44] and probably also like another English diplomat in the same region, count de Marsay, English court representative at Geneva. Born in 1679, settled in the Cantons since 1717, count de Marsay drafts in French the messages he sends to Whitehall, but his dispatches are very infrequent at this time. His age and his poor sight make it impossible for him to be very active. He spends some months in Paris towards the end of 1747 having a cataract operation[45] and he asks his son to replace him where necessary. He knows Pierre Mussard very well.[46]

At this time the Republic is threatened from several sides. Countries at war come to her in search of mercenaries. An officer from the King of Sardinia stays in Geneva to supervise recruitment. A Dutch diplomat is negotiating the enrolment of officers and soldiers in the different Cantons.[47] The French court representative, Pierre de Champeaux, declares that neutrality has been violated. Villettes is afraid that France will use these activities as a pretext for annexing the Canton of Geneva. The Republic asks him to intervene with the King of Sardinia. In these circumstances, nothing could be more likely than the presence of an agent of Villettes in

[43] D. B. Horn, *British Diplomatic Representatives 1689–1789* (1932), 124.

[44] Cf. *Dictionary of National Biography* (1899), LXVIII.311 (article Villettes, William Anne).

[45] To try to help Montesquieu when he was nearly blind, Charles Bonnet tells him in a letter dated 1 Apr. 1754 of 'M. le comte de Marsay . . . fort sujet aux fluxions des yeux . . .' who had a successful operation shortly before.

[46] In July 1748 count de Marsay transmits with warm support the letters addressed by Mussard to the King of England and to the Duke of Newcastle to urge the inclusion of the Republic of Geneva in the treaty of Aix-la-Chapelle.

[47] The *Essay on National Characters* refers to these practices: 'The Batavians were all soldiers of fortune, and hired themselves into the *Roman* armies. Their posterity make use of foreigners for the same purpose that the Romans did their ancestors' (250f.).

Geneva towards the end of 1747. The crisis-point is reached in the autumn of 1747 and the winter of 1748.

While the illness of count de Marsey obliges Villettes to extend his activities from Turin to Geneva, Pierre de Champeaux extends his from Geneva to Turin. He had been sent to Turin in 1745–6 to try to win the Kingdom of Sardinia over to the French alliance, and he keeps contacts in this country. At Geneva, his chief role is to direct French diplomatic and military espionage in Piedmont. He has agents at court, in the King's own circle, and among the high-ranking officers of the Piedmontese army in the field.

It is noteworthy that (according to Vernet) the printing of *L'Esprit des lois* at Geneva should have aroused the curiosity of the two agents sent to that region by the European powers for purposes of espionage. But the political interest in the event was probably accompanied by a more philosophical curiosity. Pierre de Champeaux had been a member of L'Entresol; he actively co-operated in the success of the venture (Shackleton, 243). In Turin, one of the most important statesmen was the Marquis de Breille. He and Montesquieu held each other in mutual esteem, of which their correspondence bears testimony. They met in Vienna where the Marquis represented the King of Sardinia when Montesquieu was staying in the city. The Marquis de Breille was also a close friend of Villettes.[48]

These are the facts. They fit together fairly well, even if they do leave a slight margin of uncertainty. It would seem that there is a choice of two suppositions.

The first is to accept Jacob Vernet's evidence as it stands. Villettes's secretary could have discovered the printing going on at Barillot's by chance when he came to Geneva on business. In this case chance was probably helped along by confidences which the visitor received thanks to his contacts in Geneva, among whom Councillor Mussard and the son of count de Marsay no doubt figured prominently. If he did visit Barillot, it was to find out more about the contents of Montesquieu's book. Besides, even if he made the discovery by himself,[49] it is hard to imagine a man educated enough to guess the name of the author not having the curiosity to get to know the text.[50]

[48] In a passage dated Mar. 1748, Villettes speaks of the Marquis de Breille '. . . with whom I have contracted a particular friendship'. Other messages confirm that Villettes and the Marquis had close links with each other.

[49] It is surprising to see how easily the author's name has been guessed; according to Mussard, Vernet guessed it, and according to Vernet, Villettes's secretary guessed it at first glance when he saw 'a sheet at the printer's shop'.

[50] Montesquieu reproaches Barillot for having divulged the secret of his anonymity. It must have been difficult for this family of artisans, stricken by the illness and the death of its head, to defend itself against the curiosity of the influential people who were interested in his work.

There might be another explanation. The main reason for Villettes's secretary being in the Canton of Geneva could have been coupled with a mission to gain information from Barillot for Villettes or the Marquis de Breille. The news of the printing of *L'Esprit des lois* could have spread from Geneva to Turin thanks to the links established between the two cities by English and French agents.[51] Or again the Marquis de Breille learned the news from Paris, where it was no longer a secret. His brother, count de Solar, also an admirer of Montesquieu, was the Sardinian ambassador there.[52]

In any case, the theme of *L'Esprit des lois*, something of its contents, and its imminent publication, had been known in Turin for six months when Hume arrived there. The news was known and must have aroused the keenest interest in the very circle which was to be Hume's until the autumn.

To what extent Hume had a prior knowledge of Montesquieu's work still remains an open question. However, at this point, the anecdotal findings may be supplemented by the conclusions derived from the comparative analysis of the two works. Since the *Essay* fits in exactly with the part of *L'Esprit des lois* dealing with the influence of climate on national characters, Hume's information must have gone at least as far as that.

In this way, starting from Vernet's testimony, both the internal relationship between the two works and the late publication of the third edition of *Essays Moral and Political* find their explanation.

A curious concatenation of circumstances would thus appear to have been at the origin of the *Essay on National Characters*. The two authors travel towards each other by widely different paths. Montesquieu sends his manuscript to Geneva by chance, and it takes a very long time for it to be printed. In the mean time, Hume arrives in Turin. At so short a distance, they are practically in contact with each other, owing to the close connections between the two cities and particularly between the circles to which Montesquieu's confidants and Hume belong. The link is established in advance by the French-speaking agents in the service of the British government. During his travels, Hume had observed with great interest the peculiarities of the peoples he visited (cf. *Letters*, i.114ff.). These impressions were fresh in his mind when he arrived in Turin, to find himself confronted on this theme with Montesquieu.[53]

[51] In Turin, no less than in Geneva, everything was known. 'Spies in every house. Here even the walls speak', notes Montesquieu when he passed through this city in 1728. He concluded: 'At any rate Turin in small and well-built: it is the most beautiful village in the world.'

[52] Villettes and the Marquis de Breille could have been informed by the Abbé Guasco, whom the Marquis at any rate knew, and with whom, at least since the end of 1746, Montesquieu discussed a translation of the work in progress.

[53] In the story of Pasteur La Roche, Henry Mackenzie tells (cf. *The Mirror*, no. 44) that 'le philosophe' visits the Pasteur on the occasion of a journey to Geneva. But the unfolding

PART THREE—SUBSEQUENT DEVELOPMENTS

After 1748, personal contact was established between Montesquieu and Hume. This did not prevent Hume from unilaterally and wilfully increasing the gap between their respective doctrines. These divergences will be pointed out in a first section.

But Hume found at least one question in *L'Esprit des lois* which caused him more embarrassment—that of inequality. In a second section we shall examine how Hume treats it and the way he takes into account Montesquieu's views on that issue.

Section 1. The divergences

Montesquieu took the initiative in the personal relations between himself and Hume. It seems that their mutual friend John Stuart the merchant had shown him the *Essays* which had just been published.[54] He sent a copy of *L'Esprit des lois* to their author. This was tantamount to underlining the relationship between the two works and to inviting Hume to pursue the discussion.

Hume replied by a long formal letter in French. But the French is obviously not from his own pen.[55] Nor is his reply quite straightforward. Not content with dodging the tacit questioning of Montesquieu, he makes a series of observations tending mainly, he says, to corroborate the 'system' of his correspondent.

It is in this letter that he says of *L'Esprit des lois* that he 'read it last autumn in Italy'. He is unaware that Montesquieu knows of the indiscretions committed in Geneva for Villettes's benefit. Has Montesquieu established a link between these, Hume's stay in Italy, and the appearance of the *Essays*? This is doubtful, since he was so absent-minded (cf. Shackleton, 77). In any case, Hume's letter seems to have puzzled him. He carefully notes the observations in it, but he draws Hume back to the heart of the matter:

of the story does not really need this last detail. The time when the journey would have taken place (towards 1740) does not agree with Hume's biography, but the fact itself is not impossible. In 1748 a long spell of inactivity, the fine weather, the nearness of Geneva, the neutrality of this territory, made such a trip easy for Hume, and his official role could give him a pretext for it. These circumstances, with the indication given us by Mackenzie, Hume's reticence about his stay in Turin and the gaps in his correspondence, make it difficult to do away entirely with the idea that he himself might have been among those visiting Barillot's printing shop.

[54] Letter from Montesquieu to Hume, 19 May 1749.

[55] The few words in French which Hume attempts in a letter in 1767 show how poor his French still is even after a lengthy stay in the most cultivated of Parisian society. Cf. *Letters*, ii.128. In 1769, talking of Crebillon, he writes: 'He sent me over his last work, with a very obliging letter; but as I must write him in French, I have never answered him' (*Letters*, ii.205).

I prefer to speak to you about a beautiful dissertation in which you are giving a much greater influence to moral causes than to physical causes, and it seemed to me—so far as I am able to give an opinion—that the subject is treated thoroughly, however difficult it is to treat it, and written from a master's hand, and full of new ideas and remarks.[56]

But Hume never engaged in a direct discussion with Montesquieu. Subsequently, in spite of their exchanges of civilities, the obstacles lying between them—the difference in age, Montesquieu's blindness,[57] Hume's reserve, their diverging ideas—kept them apart.

In 1751 the publication of the *Enquiry concerning the Principles of Morals* gave Hume an opportunity to take back the concession made to Montesquieu —privately and very superficially—about the justness of his 'system'. Hume begins by mentioning in a complimentary way what he finds correct in *L'Esprit des lois*:

The laws have, or ought to have a constant reference to the constitution of government, the manners, the climate, the religion, the commerce, the situation of each society. A late author of genius, as well as learning, has prosecuted the subject at large, and has established, from these principles, a system of political knowledge which abounds in ingenious and brilliant thoughts, and is not wanting in solidity.

(*Enquiry Concerning the Principles of Morals*, § 158)

At the end of this passage, Hume suggests that *L'Esprit des lois* is brilliant rather than solid. This cautious criticism is obviously aimed at the paradoxes in the theory of climates. In a letter to Hugh Blair, dated 1 April 1767 (*Letters*, ii.133), Hume expresses himself more openly, but without altering the substance of his criticism: 'It [*L'Esprit des lois*] has considerable merit, notwithstanding the glare of its pointed wit, and notwithstanding its false refinements and its rash and crude positions.' This is the most direct criticism Hume made of Montesquieu's theory of climates. He never attacked it openly, even after the appearance of *L'Esprit des lois*, as if the *Essay on National Characters* had placed him once and for all in a false position.

Still, in the *Enquiry concerning the Principles of Morals* the main point is a different one. Hume has in mind Montesquieu's over-all system. In a rather odd way, he relegates to a footnote the criticism he makes of it: 'This illustrious writer, however, sets out with a different theory, and supposes all right to be founded on certain *rapports* or relations; which is a

[56] Letter from Montesquieu to Hume, 19 May 1749.

[57] Montesquieu has read to him by John Stuart the *Essays* of Hume, since he cannot see the text. 'M. Stuart and I, he says, began also to read another work of yours, in which you abuse a little the ecclesiastical order.' What is this 'other work' if not the long diatribe against the clergy added in a footnote to the *Essay on National Characters*? This misunderstanding tells us a good deal, in more than one respect.

system that, in my opinion, will never be reconciled with true philosophy. . . .' According to Hume, Montesquieu's error is to reduce legislation to a rational construction which can be deduced from certain data, instead of recognizing that in the last analysis our moral decisions obey our sensitive perceptions, and that, as a result, moral conventions are founded on utility and laws on collective interest.

Going a little beyond the concepts used by Hume himself, it seems possible to make the following paraphrase of his criticism: like all dogmatism, Montesquieu's doctrine oscillates between two extremes. His general conception of 'relationships' is superficial and abstract—Hume calls it 'this abstract theory of morals'; his anthropology ends in gross materialism. Now the theory of understanding, as Hume conceives it, teaches us that in moral sciences we can achieve neither rational certainty nor complete knowledge of perceptible realities. The *Enquiry concerning the Principles of Morals* corrects Montesquieu's error in the first direction. The *Essay on National Characters* had redressed the one he committed in the second. This double correction is quite in keeping with Hume's manner. His aversion for dogmatism leads him to proceed by negating antinomic theses rather than by developing a positive system.[58]

However, his impulsive nature sometimes makes him push the argument too far.[59] Perhaps one of the advantages he found in cultivating the essay form was that it obliged him to restrain his impulses, and allowed him to pursue his line of thought in short stages. The *Essay on National Characters*, in its first form, is only a starting-point for Hume. Many of the changes he made in the original text show his anxiety to avoid formulations which were too absolute.[60] But improvements in detail were not enough to correct what was extreme in Hume's own theses. According to the *Essay on National Characters*, climate does not, even by means of moral causes, create any noticeable difference in behaviour among peoples of temperate climates. Only peoples living beyond the Arctic circle or in the tropics would be unable to attain higher forms of civilization; those of the north because of extremely unfavourable climatic conditions, those of the south for the opposite reason (252).

The *Essay on Commerce* (1752) revises this judgement. In a 'digression' inserted at the end of this essay, Hume extends the principles of geographic determinism to the different European nations. Economic activity, with all the consequences it brings with it, intensifies the more the climate stimulates it. To end with, he gives as a general application of this to all

[58] Cf. J. A. Passmore, *Hume's Intentions* (1952), *passim*. A remark in the same vein has already been made by S. Feilbogen, 'Smith und Hume', *Zeitschrift für die gesamte Staatswissenschaft*, xlvi (1890), 709ff.

[59] 'He argues beyond his brief', Passmore, op. cit. 15.

[60] In the present state of the editions, these variants can only be noticed by looking at the originals. In this regard, the edition of Green and Grose does not keep its promises.

mankind his former idea of the cultural sterility of tropical peoples (296ff.).

Although he had restricted himself to moral causes, Hume may have been afraid of having come too close to Montesquieu's ideas on the continuity of the relationship between latitude and the behaviour of peoples. A later edition of his essays[61] gives him the chance to point out a rift between the white race and the rest of mankind, in a lengthy footnote added to the *Essay on National Characters*. 'I am apt to suspect the negroes, and in general all the other species of men (for there are four or five different kinds) to be naturally inferior to the whites. There never was a civilized nation of any other complexion than white, nor even any individual eminent either in action or in speculation . . .' (252). So Hume falls in his turn into a sort of ethnic messianism, but on a wider scale than Montesquieu and by making use of a strictly racial criterion: 'Such a uniform and constant difference could not happen, in so many countries and ages, if nature had not made an original distinction betwixt these breeds of men' (ibid.).

Montesquieu had vehemently rejected these kinds of ideas, and had crushed them with sarcasm (cf. especially 15.5). Hume's cosmopolitanism thus shows its first limitation.

Section 2. The problem of inequality

The theme of national characters continues to occupy Hume during the next years. At the end of 1754, he includes it in the order of the day of the 'Select Society' in Edinburgh. Several times, up to 1758, this subject is put down for discussion by this learned society, among whose most eminent members were Lord Kames and Adam Smith (cf. Mossner, 218).

However, with the *Essay on Commerce*, the main interest attached to this problem has shifted. It is no longer a quarrel about physical and moral causes. Out of the discussion on the effects of climate, there emerges the problem of inequality. At this juncture, Hume's attitude to Montesquieu's ideas changes markedly. In dealing with the first question, his reaction was quick and vigorous; he built on his own system. In the second, which is directly concerned with the principles of liberalism—*L'Esprit des lois* places them in doubt on this occasion—Hume's manner is hesitant, and he finds it difficult to free himself from Montesquieu's hold.

To begin with, let us set forth the positions held by the two authors on this question before they met.

(a) *Montesquieu's and Hume's positions up to 1748*

1. In Montesquieu's view, the problem of inequality is perhaps the most important of all. It arises in the relations between nationals of the same state, and also in those of states among themselves. But Montesquieu simplifies its terms, at least as far as the first of the two fields is concerned.

[61] *Essays and Treatises on Several Subjects*, 4 vols., 1753–4.

For individuals only the extremes of slavery and liberty seem to be conceivable to him.[62]

As far as relations between nations are concerned, Montesquieu's ideas evolved. His first impulse is optimistic, and leads him to cosmopolitanism:

A prince thinks he grows mightier by the ruin of his neighbour. The opposite is true. Things are such in Europe that all States depend upon each other. France needs the opulence of Poland and Muscovy in the same way as Guyenne and Brittany need that of Anjou. Europe is a State made up of several provinces.[63]

Having taken into consideration the effects of climate, and having probably also been subjected to the influence of his friend Jean-Francois Melon,[64] Montesquieu presents quite a different doctrine in *L'Esprit des lois*. He still compares trading nations with parts of the same state, but in a much more limited way. The sole purpose of the comparison is now to show that international trade demands institutions common to all participating countries (21.17), and that funds should circulate readily from one country to another (20.21). But he no longer thinks that the interests of different states necessarily harmonize. Some states are in such a condition of inferiority that all they can do is withdraw from international commerce, since trading only aggravates the inequality. In actual fact, the role of the 'dominant nation' (19.27), is played by England. Even she applies certain restrictions to her trade in order to further increase the advantages she gets from it (20.11).

2. In Hume's work, reflection on inequality at first takes up relatively little space. The doctrine of sympathy makes it possible to minimize the issue. The *Treatise* (357ff., cf. *Enquiry*, § 201) develops the idea that the sight of others' riches and power evokes our spontaneous approval. This has nothing whatever to do with speculation on the advantage we might draw from taking part in others' prosperity. We participate in it in imagination, thanks to a spontaneous transfer of impressions.

In the same way, and in the same sense, the interest we take in the prosperity of a foreign nation is an impulse of sympathy. We sympathize

[62] Cf., for example, 20.4 to the end. Steuart, *An Inquiry into the Principles of Political Economy*, Book II, Ch. XIII, carefully distinguishes between different forms of dependence. The definitions he gives are clearly intended to correct Montesquieu, just as the *Essay on National Characters* corrects the terminology used in *L'Esprit des lois* as to physical and moral causes.

[63] *Pensées, Oeuvres complètes* (A. Masson, 1955), tome ii, 134 (no. 318). Cf. also, *Réflexions sur la monarchie universelle en Europe*, XVIII (ibid., tome iii, 362): 'Europe is no more than one nation made up of several ones. France and England need the opulence of Poland and Muscovy, in the same way as one of their provinces needs the other, and the State which believes it can increase its power through the ruin of its neighbour generally weakens itself together with him.'

[64] J. F. Melon, *Essai politique sur le commerce*, (1734), Ch. I, shows how 'l'île dominante' destroys the 'balance d'égalité'.

more easily with our fellow countrymen (*Treatise*, 318), but a free mind is a citizen of the world, 'a man of humanity'. In the course of his journey to Turin, Hume discovers with rapture the beauty and richness of the countries he passes through, and the good manners of their inhabitants. He is angry that chauvinistic propaganda has misled him. Having arrived at the Danube, he draws conclusions from this experience:

There are great advantages in travelling, and nothing serves more to remove prejudices. For I confess I had entertained no such advantageous idea of Germany. And it gives a man of humanity great pleasure to see that so considerable a part of mankind as the Germans are in so tolerable a condition.

(*Letters*, i.126)

We cannot completely trust our sympathetic impulses, but custom and experience educate them. Thanks to this education, sympathy is able to attend in all cases the often bewildering play of the social machine:

Judges take from a poor man to give to a rich; they bestow on the dissolute the labour of the industrious; and put into the hands of the vicious the means of harming both themselves and others. The whole scheme, however, of law and justice is advantageous to society; and 'twas with a view to this advantage, that men, by their voluntary conventions, establish'd it. After it is once establish'd by these conventions, it is *naturally* attended with a strong sentiment of morals; which can proceed from nothing but our sympathy with the interests of society.

(*Treatise*, 579f.)

Thus Hume starts with the same facile optimism and the same cosmopolitan prejudice as did Montesquieu. The subsequent history of his ideas on this topic is made up of his efforts to defend this position, largely with the help of arguments taken from *L'Esprit des lois*, against the doubts raised by the same work.

(b) *The impact of* L'Esprit des lois

The *Essay on National Characters* limits itself to recognizing the fact of the inequalities in development among peoples, in order to explain them, as we have seen, by moral causes.[65] In the *Political Discourses* (1752), Hume takes more detailed account of climatic influence, and as a consequence he abates much of his optimistic views on inequality.

The *Essay on Commerce* observes that social inequalities weaken the State. But they depend on the climate and on the quality of the soil. In England these natural factors are such that agriculture demands large-scale investments. Every farmer is a capitalist and it follows that the rewards of labour are high. On the other hand, the natural circumstances of more southern countries allow great inequalities to exist.

[65] The expression 'from their few necessities' which Hume uses (252) to explain the laziness of southern peoples, does not appear in the 1748 editions.

In this work Hume makes only a limited use of Montesquieu's observations. He transposes the principle of increasing inequalities to the relations between individuals in certain countries. He obviously hesitates to recognize the validity of this principle in international relations. While taking up and developing an idea which Montesquieu himself may have suggested to him (cf. 20.3), Hume disagrees with his conclusions. He thinks that economic progress and enrichment bring with them the penalty of a prohibitive rise in cost of production. In the long run the most advanced nation should isolate itself from the others in order to preserve the advantages it has acquired.

The *Essay on Money* explicitly generalizes the principle of growing inequalities to international relations (cf. 310f.), but it maintains that it would be more than compensated for by differences in costs. Thus it would have been wrong for Montesquieu to worry about the 'jealousy of commerce' (cf. 21.7, 21.10). Favourable circumstances would prevent the 'dominant nation' from achieving universal domination: 'There seems to be a happy concurrence of causes in human affairs, which checks the growth of trade and riches, and hinders them from being confined entirely to one people: as might naturally at first be dreaded from the advantages of an established commerce' (310). But this was conventional optimism. In reality, even if inequalities were not to increase indefinitely, imbalance could continue to exist, and with it domination.

Several years later, Hume thought he had found the answer to this problem. He presented it in the last of his economic essays, with a title borrowed from Montesquieu: *On the Jealousy of Trade* (1758). He had outlined the argument in a letter to Lord Kames dated 4 March 1758—just at the end of the time when the effects of climate were under discussion in the 'Select Society': 'We desire, and seem by our absurd politics to endeavour to repress trade in all our neighbours, and would be glad that all Europe were reduced to the same state of desolation as Turkey: the consequence of which would be, that we would have little more than domestic trade. . . .' (*Letters*, i.272). The *Essay* itself ends with the following statement:

> I shall therefore venture to acknowledge that, not only as a man, but as a British subject, I pray for the flourishing commerce of Germany, Spain, Italy, and even France itself. I am certain that Great Britain, and all those nations, would flourish more, did their sovereigns and ministers adopt such enlarged and benevolent sentiments towards each other.
>
> (348)

Hume may have believed that his spontaneous impulse of cosmopolitan sympathy had not deceived him. Moreover, his system of morality seemed to be confirmed by experience. His policy of benevolence between nations is at one with the principle of sympathy. It describes the same movement of egocentric reflection and also produces similar results, since it tends to strengthen international society while developing each of the members of it.

But Hume had probably found his argument in *L'Esprit des lois*, in the places where Montesquieu speaks of commercial Europe as a single state. Starting from this idea, we can suppose that he rediscovered unawares the idea which Montesquieu had written down earlier in the *Pensées* and in the *Réflexions sur la monarchie universelle en Europe*. This means that he was satisfied with an idea which Montesquieu had gone beyond. Apart from the fact that his thesis rests on too simple an economic reasoning, Hume seems to forget the link which he himself established in the *Essay on Commerce* between economic development and military power. The *Treatise* already notes that states owe each other less justice than individuals (*Treatise*, 568f.). How can one guarantee that nations now disadvantaged would not put their progress to good effect in order to acquire a dominant position in their turn, and derive all possible advantage from it? To get rid of this difficulty, Hume may again have had recourse to Montesquieu: 'The natural effect of commerce is to incline to peace. Two trading nations put one another in mutual dependence: while one has an interest to buy, the other has an interest to sell, and all unions are founded on mutual needs' (20.2). But Montesquieu surely envisages trade between nations of equal strength, whose exchanges are not falsified by fundamental inequalities.

It would seem as though the *Essay on the Jealousy of Trade* suggested that the statesman of the 'dominant nation' should take risks with the peaceful virtues of trade. Once again led on by his own argument, Hume ends up with a rather utopian system, 'too perfect for human nature' (*History*, vii.133).

This superficial construction also reveals a tendency in classical thinking to minimize the problems of distribution. In fact, it goes beyond Hume's own convictions, and his own deeper sympathy. Even in the enthusiastic correspondence of 1748 a doubt is already noticeable: 'Germany is undoubtedly a very fine country, full of industrious honest people, and were it united, it would be the greatest power that ever was in the world' (*Letters*, i.126).

Already before his glamorous stay in Paris, his idea of international society is not indiscriminate. He delights in a westernizing narcissism. To him, the French and the English are the most civilized peoples, heirs of the Greeks and the Romans. Right at the end of his life, according to John Home's testimony, his cosmopolitanism is replaced by a dichotomic or even Manichean view of the European political scene: 'He . . . laments that the most civilized nations, the English and the French, should be on the decline; and the Barbarians, the Goths and Vandals of Germany and Russia, should be rising in power and renown.'[66]

[66] *The Works of John Home* (1822), i.170.

At bottom, his thoughts are still more pessimistic, and his attachments more limited. England is the true refuge of civilization, not so much by herself but owing to the future power of the English-speaking colonies of America. This opinion was stated as early as 1767, among the scoldings he sends to Edward Gibbon, the historian, for having taken part in the publication of an English literary review written in French: 'Let the French . . . triumph in the present diffusion of their tongue. Our solid and increasing establishments in America, where we need less dread the inundation of Barbarians, promise a superior stability and duration to the English language' (*Letters*, ii.171).

Finally, then, Hume comes back to some of Montesquieu's ideas. He assigns a privileged role to the 'dominant nation'. He establishes a hierarchy among European nations[67] according to their geographical position—in the longitudinal sense, it is true. However, the pessimism which beclouds the end of his meditation on the destiny of nations shows the precariousness of the doctrine he bequeaths to his successors, in one respect at least.

As for Montesquieu, while entertaining no illusions about the attractiveness of his work, he still declares in his Preface, with his usual naivety: 'I do not think I totally lacked genius.' Considering the role which he played in this long debate, only intervening once, he may be pardoned for this. Even the opinion of Keynes, who saw in him the greatest of the French economists,[68] appears a little more readily acceptable.

[67] Concerning the relations between rich nations and 'poor and barbarous' ones, cf. Adam Smith, WN V.i.a.

[68] J. M. Keynes, *Théorie générale de l'emploi, de l'intérêt et de la Monnaie* (1959), 12 (Preface to the French translation).

PART II

Analytical Table of Contents of Part II

I

On the Role of Utility and Demand in *The Wealth of Nations*

S. Hollander*

THE interpretation offered by Paul H. Douglas in 1928 refers to Smith's rejection of utility as a 'determinant of value', and attributes to Smith the view that utility 'is not even a necessary prerequisite of exchange value'. The reason for the abandonment of utility as a determinant of value by Smith (and his successors) lies, it is suggested by Douglas, in the comparison of the total utilities yielded by varying types of objects rather than their marginal utilities. Smith's emphasis upon water as a *class* and diamonds as a *class* was the source of the error and represented a real challenge for the development of marginal analysis.[1]

In their well-known account, Professors Robertson and Taylor do not contend that Smith actually rejected utility as a determinant of value. But they seek to *explain* what they believe is the novel orientation of *The Wealth of Nations*. For while Francis Hutcheson—whose position is traced via Gershom Carmichael to Pufendorf and ultimately to the Scholastics and Aristotle—had placed the emphasis firmly 'on the two basic elements of usefulness and scarcity', Smith makes only the briefest *explicit* reference to utility (in the paragraph dealing with 'value-in-use and value-in-exchange') concluding the discussion of value with an analysis in terms of production costs and the introduction of a labour standard, 'utility or "value-in-use" having been dismissed from the scene'. And scarcity—both the term and the concept—is accorded little attention at the 'critical point' in the analysis.[2] In point of fact, a similar contrast is drawn between *The Wealth of Nations* and the *Lectures* with their 'perceptive connection and lucid linking together in a basic and fundamental explanation of utility, scarcity and demand'.[3] These contrasts indicate, it is suggested, 'a major turning point in the history of economic thought'.[4] For those who

* Professor of Economics at the University of Toronto.

[1] Douglas, 'Smith's Theory of Value and Distribution', in J. M. Clark *et al.*, *Adam Smith, 1776–1926* (1928), 78.

[2] H. M. Robertson and W. L. Taylor, 'Adam Smith's Approach to the Theory of Value', *Economic Journal* lxvii (June 1957), 181–4.

[3] Ibid. 187.

[4] Ibid. 185.

adopt the approach to economics which emphasizes the essential roles of scarcity and utility 'there can be only regret' for Smith's emphasis in *The Wealth of Nations*, 'which led on to at least a serious under-emphasis on, and, at times, to the almost complete eclipse of these ideas in British political economy for nearly a hundred years'.[5] In their own view Smith's position may be accounted for in terms of a concern with the long-run causes of variation in (*per capita*) real national income for which issue deep analysis of the nature of demand and its utility underpinning had little purpose.[6]

In our view these commentaries do not do justice to Smith's position. In the first place, while it is indeed essential to take into account the orientation of his predecessors, the general picture is *not* one of such overwhelming emphasis upon utility and scarcity as has been suggested, and accordingly it seems inappropriate to perceive as a 'problem' requiring a 'solution' Smith's deliberations regarding costs even if they were markedly 'one-sided' in their emphasis. The fact is that Aristotle, Aquinas, and subsequently the later Scholastics (such as Molina, Lugo, and Lessius) when considering the *determination* of price placed greater emphasis upon costs than upon utility and demand, although it is true that utility was frequently envisaged as a necessary *condition*, or even as the 'cause' or 'source', of value. But it is Pufendorf's contribution that must be noted with particular care in the light of his influence upon Francis Hutcheson. He defined the 'foundation' of price as the 'aptitude of a thing or action, by which it can either mediately or immediately contribute something to the necessity of human life, or to making it more advantageous and pleasant'. And the actual *determinant* of price is said to depend not only on 'the need for the article' but also on its scarcity.[7] This discussion, however, pertains to the state of 'nature' where exchange occurs between the parties by way of a bargaining process. In organized states the so-called 'natural price' is relevant, defined as a price set by those 'who are sufficiently acquainted with both the merchandise and the market' in light of the labour and the expenses 'commonly' incurred, with an allowance for a moderate 'profit'. A temporary market price was also recognized determined by relative scarcity. But no adequate account was provided of the precise relationship envisaged between the market and cost prices, an observation which may be applied equally to the scholastic literature. A fundamental hiatus thus remained and Hutcheson did not contribute to further elucidation of the issue. Finally, it must be added that in the discussions by the leading

[5] Ibid. 188. E. Kauder, 'Genesis of the Marginal Utility Theory', *Economic Journal*, lxiii (Sept. 1953), 650, takes the position that Smith 'made waste and rubbish out of the thinking of two thousand years'.

[6] 'Adam Smith's Approach to the Theory of Value', 191–3.

[7] 'On the Law of Nature and of Nations (1672)', *The Classics of International Law*, no. 17, vol. II (1934), 676f.

eighteenth-century 'lay' contributors, particularly Cantillon and Steuart (and previously Petty), the orientation is without question towards cost price, the means of reducing all cost elements to a common unit, and the nature of profit. And once again the precise process by which the long-run ('normal') cost price emerges left much to be desired.

It is, therefore, scarcely surprising that Smith showed great concern with the nature of cost price, and the processes whereby a tendency of price towards costs is assured in the long run. As for Smith's approach in the *Lectures*, there is at least as much concern with production costs and long-run price as there is with the market price. And we may there discern a preliminary attempt to combine the conceptions into a theory of allocation. But there is also no convincing evidence to indicate an unconcern with utility and demand in *The Wealth of Nations* relative to that reported in the *Lectures*. The source of the view to the contrary appears to lie in Smith's adoption of a labour-commanded index of 'real value'; his comments on 'value-in-use'; and the restriction of the analysis of long-run price in Book I.vii to constant-cost industries.

The choice of a labour-commanded index of 'real value', it will be recalled, had a twofold objective. On the one hand, it was intended to provide a measure of the *disutility* represented by the effort counterpart of the national income; on the other, it was intended as an indirect measure of purchasing power over commodities since 'every man is rich or poor according to the degree in which he can afford to enjoy the necessaries, conveniencies, and amusements of human life' (WN I.v.i). There can thus be no question of the ultimate 'subjective' orientation of Smith's argument and the choice of index is evidence thereof, not evidence to the contrary.

In Smith's unhappy contrast between 'value-in-use' and 'value-in-exchange', according to which 'the things which have the greatest value in use have frequently little or no value in exchange' while 'those which have the greatest value in exchange have frequently little or no value in use',[8] the term 'value-in-use' must be understood in the narrow sense of biological significance and not in the economist's broad sense of desirability. The proposition amounts to an insistence that physical properties of commodities are quite irrelevant in the determination of exchange value. It is solely this category of utility which Smith rejected as a value determinant and, indeed, as a necessary condition of exchange value. From his observations in this regard we can learn nothing of his position regarding the relationship between price and utility in the sense of desirability.[9]

[8] WN I.iv.13.

[9] Professor Douglas, 'Smith's Theory of Value and Distribution', 80, goes to some lengths to account for Smith's so-called rejection of utility 'as a possible cause of value' in terms of his 'moralistic sense'. Of course, Douglas remarks, 'as the moralists from Ruskin on have pointed out, economic values are not necessarily moral values'. But according to

There is, in fact, no evidence that Smith rejected utility in the latter sense as a necessary condition of exchange value. The contrary is without any question true, as is clear, for example, from the following extract which is quite unambiguous:

Unless a capital was employed in manufacturing that part of the rude produce which requires a good deal of preparation before it can be fit for use and consumption, it either would never be produced, because there could be no demand for it; or if it was produced spontaneously, it would be of no value in exchange, and could add nothing to the wealth of the society.

(WN II.v.5).

Similarly, we may refer to Smith's discussion of the causes of price variations over time in the case of the 'materials of cloathing and lodging', which evidently constitute a class possessing high 'value-in-use' (in a biological sense), yet whose 'usefulness' (per unit) in the sense of desirability varies with quantity:

In the one state [an early state of development] . . . there is always a superabundance of those materials, which are frequently, upon that account, of little or no value. In the other there is often a scarcity, which necessarily augments their value. In the one state a great part of them is thrown away as useless . . . In the other they are all made use of, and there is frequently a demand for more than can be had . . .'

(WN I.xi.c.3).

The role actually accorded utility in the broad sense is equally clear in the following discussion of the demand for precious metals, which is based on a wide variety of desirable characteristics, which happens to include their 'value in use'. Thus 'the demand for those metals arises partly from their utility, and partly from their beauty'; in fact, their '*principal merit* . . . arises from their beauty, which renders them peculiarly fit for the ornaments of dress and furniture' (WN I.xic.31; italics supplied). In addition some reference is made to the phenomenon of conspicuous consumption; 'The merit of their beauty is greatly enhanced by their scarcity. With the greater part of rich people, the chief enjoyment of riches consists in the parade of riches, which in their eye is never so complete as when they

our understanding of the discussion in *The Wealth of Nations*, this is precisely the point which *Smith* was making.

It may also be noted that, in Smith's view, a commodity might be of high use value because of its cultural properties, and not merely by dint of biology: 'By necessaries I understand, not only the commodities which are indispensably necessary for the support of life, but whatever the custom of the country renders it indecent for creditable people, even of the lowest order, to be without . . . Under necessaries therefore, I comprehend, not only those things which nature, but those things which the established rules of decency have rendered necessary to the lowest rank of people. All other things I call luxuries; without meaning by this appelation, to throw the smallest degree of reproach upon the temperate use of them' (WN V.ii.k.3).

appear to possess those decisive marks of opulence which nobody can possess but themselves.' To these determinants of general desirability Smith adds finally the *utilitarian* demand for the metals arising from their monetary function: 'That employment . . . by occasioning a new demand, and by diminishing the quantity which could be employed in any other way, may have . . . contributed to keep up or increase their value' (WN I.xi.c.31).

We may now draw together the elements which constitute Smith's position. The 'paradox of value' was not formulated as a *problem* requiring a *solution*; it was rather a statement of fact regarding the irrelevance for exchange value of the physical (biological or cultural) properties of commodities. Smith did not reject utility in the economist's sense of the term as a necessary condition of exchange value; on the contrary he accounted for the latter in terms of utility and scarcity in the traditional manner. Needless to say, the latter approach was not watertight because of the absence of an explicit incremental conception, but this 'deficiency' did not *preclude* an explanation of price in terms of relative scarcity.[10] Moreover, the explanation was not considered to be in conflict with the theory of price which runs in terms of production costs.[11]

The subsequent development of marginal utility certainly improved the treatment of price in terms of relative scarcity. We must, however, try to avoid an outlook narrowly constrained by the marginalist principles of 1871. There is a strong element of truth in the observation that the history of demand theory is not to be identified with the history of utility.[12] Despite the absence of a formal notion of marginal utility—the lack of which, from a modern perspective, may not be a deficiency at all—Smith made extensive use, in a variety of applied economic problems of a theory of *choice*.

[10] It was the view of Professor Schumpeter that while the paradox of value had long been resolved in terms of the concept of relative scarcity, Smith (by 'dismissing' value-in-use) barred 'for the next two or three generations, the door so auspiciously opened by his French and Italian predecessors', *History of Economic Analysis* (1954), 309. It is clear from our account that we cannot accept this view. But what must be noted is the following observation regarding Galiani, who is said to be the most proficient of Smith's predecessors: 'What separates Galiani from Jevons and Menger is, first, that he lacked the concept of marginal utility—though the concept of relative scarcity comes pretty near it—and, second, that he failed to apply his analysis to the problems of cost and distribution' (ibid. 301). In our view the first observation applies equally to Smith who made full use of the concept of relative scarcity and, in addition, made considerable progress towards the resolution of the second set of problems.

[11] Thus with regard to the preceding extract relating to conspicuous consumption Smith refers to the 'enhancement' of the 'merit' of a commodity 'by its scarcity, or by the great labour which it requires to collect any considerable quantity of it' (WN I.xi.c.31, 32). See also below (p. 321) for a further illustration. For a similar view, see also Andrew Skinner, 'Introduction', *The Wealth of Nations* (1970), 48–9.

[12] G. J. Stigler, 'The Development of Utility Theory', *Journal of Political Economy*, lxiii (Aug./Oct. 1950), reprinted in Stigler, *Essays in the History of Economics* (1965), 70.

Where a hierarchy of basic wants exists there is little scope for a theory of choice; the significance of demand theory is much diminished if substitution in consumption is 'technically' precluded. The presumption that at the time Smith wrote wage goods consisted of a few primary products has done much to establish the supposed negligibility of the role of demand in *The Wealth of Nations*. In point of fact Smith was thoroughly aware of the complexity even of the working-class budget, and the role of relative commodity prices in the choice of the basket is given great attention.

That the working-class budget was envisaged to be sophisticated is clear from Smith's analysis of changes in the 'cost of living'. While technical progress was reducing the prices of a number of consumer goods (potatoes, carrots, turnips, cabbages, apples, onions, coarser woollens and linens, coarser metals, furniture), increased taxes were having the opposite effect in other cases (soap, candles, salt, leather, liquor).[13] Now it is conceded by Smith that if certain prices rise and others fall 'it becomes a matter of more nicety to judge how far the rise in the one may be compensated by the fall in the other'. But it was his belief that in contemporary circumstances real labour incomes were rising, for the quantity of those relatively more expensive items 'which the labouring poor are under any necessity of consuming, is so very small, that the increase in their price does not compensate the diminution in that of so many other things' (WN I.viii.35; cf. I.xi.m.10). This observation does not refer to the small weight attached to certain items in an actual basket; it is rather a statement to the effect that consumers are in a position to *substitute* other goods in place of the relatively expensive items. The implications of the recognition of substitutability in consumption are of considerable importance. For it was Smith's view that only to the extent that workers devote their rising command over commodities towards specific categories would a population response be set in motion. In principle, the government might, by the judicious imposition of excise taxes, *direct* consumption away from 'luxuries' and towards these categories: 'The high price of such commodities ['luxuries'] does not necessarily diminish the ability of the inferior ranks of people to bring up families. Upon the sober and industrious poor, taxes upon such commodities act as sumptuary laws, and *dispose them either to moderate, or to refrain altogether from the use of superfluities which*

[13] WN I.viii.35. Smith also points out that the contemporary upward trend in the prices of a number of animal foods (poultry, fish, wild fowl, venison) was less important than the fall in the price of potatoes and maize for the working class. (Butcher's meat generally was no longer rising; and the current rise in corn prices although significant was abnormal and merely due to bad harvests.) 'They suffer more, perhaps, by the artificial rise which has been occasioned by taxes in the price of some manufactured commodities; as of salt, soap, leather, candles, malt, beer, and ale, &c.' (WN I.xi.n.11). We should also recall Smith's discussion of the choice in terms of relative price between coal and wood for domestic heating (ibid. I.xi.c.14–19).

they can no longer easily afford' (WN V.ii.k.7). It is, at the same time, noted that substitution is much limited in the case of certain lower-case consumers—'the dissolute and disorderly'—who 'might continue to indulge themselves in the use of such commodities after this rise in price in the same manner as before' (ibid; italics supplied). In effect, demand elasticity is here analysed in terms of the extent of substitutability in consumption; and alternative patterns of tastes are recognized for the 'typical' consumer in different social groupings. (It will also be recalled that Smith elsewhere gave a second rationalization for the degreee of elasticity which turned on the fraction of the budget absorbed by the commodity in question; the smaller the fraction, the less the price-consciousness of the consumer.)

As a second illustration of the role of substitution in consumption we note Smith's observation that the price of wood imposes a ceiling upon the price of coal, or in other words, that the demand for coal becomes perfectly elastic at a specific level because of the availability of an excellent alternative. (The observation, at the same time, illustrates admirably the significance of utility in the broad sense of 'desirability'; 'Coals are a less agreeable fewel than wood; they are said too to be less wholesome. The expence of coals, therefore, at the place where they are consumed, must generally be somewhat less than that of wood' (WN I.xi.c.15)).

The analyses of rationing over time provides a further significant illustration of the role accorded demand by Smith. The function of the corn dealer (or speculator) is to assure that corn stocks last from harvest to harvest:

It is the interest of the people that their daily, weekly, and monthly consumption, should be proportioned as exactly as possible to the supply of the season. The interest of the inland corn dealer is the same. By supplying them, as nearly as he can judge, in this proportion, he is likely to sell all his corn for the highest price, and with the greatest profit; and his knowledge of the state of the crop, and of his daily, weekly, and monthly sales, enable him to judge, with more or less accuracy, how far they really are supplied in this manner.

(WN IV.v.b.3).

It is by the judicious use of prices that the rationing process is undertaken by the dealer:

It is his interest to raise the price of his corn as high as the real scarcity of the season requires, and it can never be his interest to raise it higher. By raising the price he discourages the consumption, and puts every body more or less, but particularly the inferior ranks of people, upon thrift and good management. If, by raising it too high, he discourages the consumption so much that the supply of the season is likely to go beyond the consumption of the season, and to last for some time after the next crop begins to come in, he runs the hazard, not only of losing a considerable part of his corn by natural causes, but of being obliged to sell what remains of it for much less than what he might have had for it several

months before. If by not raising the price high enough he discourages the consumption so little, that the supply of the season is likely to fall short of the consumption of the season, he not only loses a part of the profit which he might otherwise have made, but he exposes the people to suffer before the end of the season, instead of the hardships of a dearth, the dreadful horrors of a famine.
(WN IV.v.b.3)

It is Smith's conclusion that government intervention in the corn trade was ruinous precisely because of its neglect of the effects of low price upon the rate of consumption (WN IV.v.b.7–8).

The tradition that Smith 'played down' demand analysis derives also from almost exclusive concentration upon the chapter 'Of the Natural and Market Price of Commodities' (I.vii) which utilizes the assumption that industries are characterized by constant-cost conditions. But this chapter was designed for a specific purpose, namely to elucidate the fundamental propositions regarding resource allocation. For this purpose the assumption of constant costs was adequate. It is quite clear, however, that it did not represent Smith's typical position regarding cost conditions. The issue can best be appreciated as an aspect of the 'dynamics of consumption'.

Smith categorized agricultural produce (other than corn) into broad classes according to the secular pattern of price movement. The first category includes all those items which are more or less fixed in supply—for example, rare birds, fishes, and game—and which face a demand which is continually increasing as (real) incomes rise: 'The quantity of such commodities, therefore, remaining the same, or nearly the same, while the competition to purchase them is continually increasing, their price may rise to any degree of extravagance, and seems not to be limited by any certain boundary' (WN I.xi.k.1). By contrast are instances of products amenable to increase in response to secularly rising demand. The analysis of these latter cases is eloquent testimony to Smith's full recognition of the economic significance of scarcity and at the same time illustrates the fact that the 'explanation' of price in terms of 'supply and demand' or 'relative scarcity' was not regarded as an 'alternative' to that in terms of costs. The scarcity approach was not, to rephrase our contention, restricted to the analysis of 'market price'. We refer to Smith's observation that in the course of economic development the extensions of tillage on the one hand, and consequent reductions in the supply of cattle hitherto available on the wilds as free goods (that is at zero cost), and rising demand on the other—related both to increasing population and real purchasing power per head—tend to force up cattle prices ultimately rendering the production of butcher's meat profitable, at which time some land areas, initially prepared for cereals, will be utilized for commercial cattle raising. A (long-run) price ceiling is, therefore, ultimately imposed as demand for butcher's meat continues to rise. A similar analysis is made of cattle rearing for dairy products:

The second sort of rude produce of which the price rises in the progress of improvement, is that which human industry can multiply in proportion to the demand. It consists in those useful plants and animals, which, in uncultivated countries, nature produces with such profuse abundance, that they are of little or no value, and which, as cultivation advances are therefore forced to give place to some more profitable produce. During a long period in the progress of improvement, the quantity of these is continually diminishing, while at the same time the demand for them is continually increasing. Their real value, therefore, the real quantity of labour which they will purchase or command, gradually rises, till at last it gets so high as to render them as profitable a produce as any thing else which human industry can raise upon the most fertile and best cultivated land. When it has got so high it cannot well go higher. If it did, more land and more industry would soon be employed to increase their quantity.

(WN I.xi.l.1; cf.I.xi.b.7–8, I.xi.n.3–4)

The third category includes all those cases where output variation in response to expanding demand is 'either limited or uncertain'. The category covers wool and hides (which are treated as joint products with the carcase). Even in an underdeveloped economy there is sufficient demand, emanating from the world market if not domestically, for wool and hides to assure commercial preparation. The secular increase in domestic real incomes, therefore, has a much smaller (relative) effect upon the total demand for such products than in the case of butcher's meat. But the supply of wool and hides will be affected along with that of butcher's meat as the latter is increased in response to expanding demand. (WN I.xi.m)

The category also includes commodities produced at increasing cost. The following statement relating to the fisheries contains a clear formulation of diminishing *average* returns as output increases in response to secularly rising demand:

But it will generally be impossible to supply the great and extended market without employing a quantity of labour greater than in proportion to what had been requisite for supplying the narrow and confined one. A market which, from requiring only one thousand, comes to require annually ten thousand ton of fish, can seldom be supplied without employing more than ten times the quantity of labour which had before been sufficient to supply it. The fish must generally be sought for at a greater distance, larger vessels must be employed, and more expensive machinery of every kind made use of. The real price of this commodity, therefore, naturally rises in the progress of improvement.

(WN I.xi.m.15)[14]

[14] Smith refers elsewhere to different processes available in the white herring fishing industry. Fishing can be undertaken by relatively large size 'busses or decked vessels' or by smaller boats. (A tonnage subsidy granted to the industry had in fact encouraged the use of the former method in Scotland.) But the economic choice, in the absence of the subsidy,

Contrasting with agricultural cost conditions are those of manufacturing industry. Smith predicted in the case of manufactured goods a *downward* secular trend in (real) costs. In light of the role accorded scale economies in *The Wealth of Nations* these instances take on particular importance. It follows that an increase in demand from an initial state of full industry equilibrium will cause an increase in price in the short run only, while the new long-run equilibrium price is below the initial level. This conclusion is clearly stated by Smith as follows: 'The increase of demand, besides, though in the beginning it may sometimes raise the price of goods, never fails to lower it in the long run. It encourages production, and thereby increases the competition of producers, who, in order to undersell one another, have recourse to new divisions of labour and new improvements of art, which might never otherwise have been thought of' (WN V.i.e.26).

Little purpose is served by *strict* conceptualization of the preceding observations in terms of the modern distinction between a change in the production function and a movement along a given production function to hitherto inappropriate areas. It would appear that Smith had in mind a combination of the two notions. For while he refers to the adoption of *newly* generated technology, the requisite development clearly is undertaken by large firms only and is visualized as an almost automatic consequence of size.[15] A second characteristic of the Smithian treatment is the absence of a true theory of the firm, and thus of the limits to the output of the firm. Smith simply takes for granted—without formal justification—that the size of the average productive unit will rise along with the expansion of the industry. Thirdly, the predictions regarding unit costs take into account alterations in input prices. It is Smith's contention, for which no analytical support is provided, that unit labour requirements will fall sufficiently to outweigh the effects of rising wage rates.

Yet whatever the conceptual difficulties involved in Smith's account

between the processes is explained in terms of the nature of the fisheries, or the scale at which it is undertaken, rather than the factor-price structure: 'the mode of fishing for which this tonnage bounty in the white herring fishery has been given (by busses or decked vessels from twenty to eighty tons burthen), seems not so well adapted to the situation of Scotland as to that of Holland; . . . Holland lies at a great distance from the seas to which herrings are known principally to resort; and can, therefore, carry on that fishery only in decked vessels, which can carry water and provisions sufficient for a voyage to a distant sea. But [the Scottish coastlines] are everywhere intersected by arms of the sea . . . A boat fishery, therefore, seems to be the mode of fishing best adapted to the peculiar situation of Scotland: the fishers carrying the herrings on shore, as fast as they are taken, to be either cured or consumed fresh' (WN IV.v.a.33). It is clear that Smith had in mind the resort to more expensive methods at large scale involving the use of busses.

[15] The view that cost-reducing methods—utilizing machinery for their embodiment—would be introduced by large firms appears to be an extension of the view that the use of machinery is dependent upon prior subdivision of labour, which in turn is dependent upon large-scale operations: 'As the operations of each workman are gradually reduced to a greater degree of simplicity, a variety of new machines come to be invented for facilitating and abridging those operations' (ibid. II.3).

there can be no question of the general principle, namely that 'the increase of demand' in manufacturing 'never fails to lower price in the long run'. It is apparent that the analysis of I.vii ('Of the Natural and Market Price of Commodities'), which is strictly limited to the case of constant long-run costs, is not representative of Smith's general position according to which demand plays a fundamental role in the long run as well as in the short run. Moreover, while Smith's conception of competition as entailing *rivalry* in a race to obtain or to discard supplies[16] appears more appropriate from the viewpoint of traders or dealers, the same notion also appears in the present treatment of cost-price determination which involves decisions regarding production on the part of resource owners; thus an increase in demand in the long run 'encourages production, and thereby increases the competition of producers, who, in order to under-sell one another, have recourse to new divisions of labour and new improvements of art'. Smith's concept was an all-embracing one.

[16] G. J. Stigler, 'Perfect Competition, Historically Considered', *Journal of Political Economy*, lxv (Feb. 1957), reprinted in Stigler, *Essays in the History of Economics*, 235.

II

Ricardo and Adam Smith

MAURICE DOBB*

ONE of the familiar anecdotes in the history of economic thought concerns Ricardo's first acquaintance with *The Wealth of Nations*: how his 'interest in political economy was first awakened by his taking up a copy of *The Wealth of Nations* by chance while on a visit to Bath in 1799'.[1] Over the following years this, together with current articles on political economy in the *Edinburgh Review* (from 1802), formed a frequent topic of conversation with his Stock Exchange friend Hutches Trower.[2] Manifestly Adam Smith was the inspiration and starting-point of Ricardo's general thinking on the subject; as was, of course, true of the thinking of others in those decades—although Ricardo had less the disciple attitude than had Malthus, for example, and on a number of quite crucial points was willing, as we shall see, to criticize or supplement and to go beyond. We now have Mr. Sraffa's persuasive hypothesis that the arrangement (sometimes criticized) of the *Principles* of 1817 is to be explained by the fact that it was patterned upon *The Wealth of Nations*, so far at least as the order of topics dealt with is concerned.[3] As is well known, Ricardo's *Principles* opens with a quotation from Smith. This and a further passage are cited approvingly; after which for several pages there follows critical comment on the familiar ambiguity of Chapter V of Book I of *The Wealth of Nations* concerning the 'measure of value', with its reference to 'labour commanded', or the amount of labour purchasable in the market, as the standard measure.[4] Towards the

* Fellow of Trinity College, Cambridge, and Fellow of the British Academy.

[1] *Works and Correspondence of David Ricardo*, ed. P. Sraffa, vol. x, *Biographical Miscellany* (1955), 35. Hereinafter referred to as *Works*.

[2] Ibid. vii.246 (letter of Ricardo to Trower, 26 Jan. 1818): 'I remember well the pleasure I felt, when I first discovered that you, as well as myself, were a great admirer of the work of Adam Smith, and of the early articles on Political Economy which had appeared in the Edinburgh Review. Meeting as we did every day, these afforded us often an agreeable subject for half an hour's chat.'

[3] Although Ricardo 'wrote according to the sequence of his own ideas . . . within each of the first two parts [of the *Principles*] the order of the chapters coincides closely with the order in which the topics are treated in *The Wealth of Nations*, as comparison of the chapter-headings shows' (Ibid. i.xxii–xxiii, and cf. table of chapter-headings, xxiv–xxv). Mr. Sraffa adds that 'the only important difference is in the place given to Rent' (which immediately follows Value and comes before Wages and Profits).

[4] Sometimes he [Smith] speaks of corn, at other times of labour, as a standard measure; not the quantity of labour bestowed on the production of any object, but the quantity which it can command in the market: as if these were two equivalent expressions' (ibid. 14).

end of the *Principles* Chapters XX to XXVIII are all critical discussions of particular opinions or doctrines of Smith, which (together with that of Malthus on Rent)[5] formed the group of chapters referred to in correspondence between Ricardo and James Mill as 'the appendix'. In a letter to Mill while writing his book, Ricardo said that 'in reading Adam Smith, again, I find many opinions to question, all I believe founded on his original error respecting value'.[6] It is in this group of chapters that his criticism of these opinions is set down; and we shall have something more to say about them later.

Already in his topical pamphlet of 1815, the *Essay on Profits*, Ricardo showed himself aware of a corollary of Smith's doctrine that stood in conflict with his own ideas and with the general case he was mounting against the Corn Laws. This was, no doubt, the source of his reference to Smith's 'original error regarding value', if it was not what he had immediately in mind. The fact that Malthus inclined towards Smith's position on this issue must have enhanced its importance for Ricardo and confirmed him in thinking that herein lay a crucial parting of the ways for economic theory.

It will be remembered that the corner-stone of Ricardo's thesis in the 1815 *Essay* is a theory of profits couched initially in simplified product-terms, i.e. in terms of corn. In agriculture corn appears as both input (in the shape of 'feed' to labourers) and output; and profit as the difference between the two is accordingly made to depend on the level of corn-wages and the corn-productivity of labour. In face of diminishing returns, productivity of labour will tend to fall, and hence the ratio of product to corn-wages, with extension of the margin of cultivation (i.e. the internal margin of the application of capital to land and/or the external margin as additional land is brought under the plough). Thus, at the same time as rent is increased, the rate of profit tends to fall. Since there cannot (in the long term) be divergent rates of profit in different lines of production, what was true of agriculture must be true of profits in manufacture as well. The only effective way of countering this tendency (apart from agricultural improvement) was to allow free import of corn. This, by keeping down the price of corn, would be favourable to farmers and manufacturers, but equivalently unfavourable to the interest of the landowning class as rent-receivers.

As Ricardo expressed the gist of his argument:

Profits of stock fall only, because land equally well adapted to produce food cannot be procured; and the degree of the fall of profits, and the rise of rents, depends wholly on the increased expense of production. If, therefore, in the progress of countries in wealth and population, new portions of fertile land

[5] The chapter 'On Machinery' was added to the 3rd edition and does not appear in editions 1 and 2.

[6] Letter to Mill of 2 Dec. 1816, ibid. vii.100.

could be added to such countries, with every increase of capital, profits would never fall, nor rents rise.

(*Works*, iv.18)

Two pages later he concludes: 'The sole effect then of the progress of wealth on prices, independently of all improvements, either in agriculture or manufactures, appears to be to raise the price of raw produce and of labour, leaving all other commodities at their original prices, and to lower general profits in consequence of the general rise of wages.'[7]

In this way Ricardo supplemented or completed the Smithian doctrine of the tendency for profits to fall as capital accumulates, which Smith had explained in terms merely of supply and demand and competition by generalizing what tends to happen in one trade or industry to the economy as a whole.[8] But in doing this Ricardo found himself in conflict with another precept of Smith, which if accepted would have severely upset his own theory. What if prices of manufactures rose when corn prices and wages rose: in that case, surely, profits in manufacture would not fall? On the next page to the sentence that we have just quoted from the *Essay* there appears a footnote which reads as follows:

It has been thought that the price of corn regulates the prices of all other things. This appears to me a mistake. If the price of corn is affected by the rise or fall of the value of the precious metals themselves, then indeed will the price of commodities be also affected, but they vary, because the value of money varies, not because the value of corn is altered. Commodities, I think, cannot materially rise or fall, whilst money and commodities continue in the same proportions, or rather whilst the cost of production of both estimated in corn continues the same.

(*Works*, iv.21)

The view that is rejected in this footnote is, of course, that of Smith, to the effect that, since corn is the wage-good *par excellence*, a rise in its price, communicating itself to the price of labour, will tend to raise prices generally: hence the price of corn ultimately regulates the prices of all other commodities. In the Chapter 'On Bounties on Exportation' in the *Principles* Ricardo was to expand the argument of the footnote and to quote extensively the passages from Adam Smith where 'the common error which has misled Dr. Smith' (as he calls it) is set forth. Malthus, in their correspondence of

[7] Ibid. 20. Ricardo was always careful to state this tendency with the qualification regarding 'improvements'. Although there were some at the time who argued that agricultural improvement would overbear any such tendency, (as Cannan observed) 'there is no doubt whatever that Ricardo, like West and Malthus, believed that the returns to agricultural industry do actually diminish in the course of history in spite of all improvements' (E. Cannan, *History of the Theories of Production and Distribution* (2nd ed., 1903), 166).

[8] Adam Smith, *The Wealth of Nations*, 'When the stocks of many rich merchants are turned into the same trade, their mutual competition naturally tends to lower its profit; and when there is a like increase of stock in all the different trades carried on in the same society, the same competition must produce the same effect in them all' (I.ix.2).

1814, had adopted another version of an essentially Smithian position (i.e. as regards value) when he argued that, contrary to profits in trade and industry adapting themselves to the profit–wage ratio in agriculture, profits in the former may be raised from the side of demand when new markets are opened and exports are increased (*Works*, vi.104). In this case profits in agriculture are likely to be raised by withdrawal of capital from agriculture and its transfer to the more profitable trade.

It was evidently the need to provide an answer to this type of objection that helped to direct Ricardo's thoughts in the direction which was to lead to the famous first chapter in the *Principles*, 'On Value', and to the restating of his argument about profits, which formed the nub of his theory of distribution, in terms of labour in place of corn (*Works*, i.xxxi–xxxiii). In the *Essay* the nearest he was to come to such a general statement was this:

> The exchangeable value of all commodities, rises as the difficulties of their production increase. If then new difficulties occur in the production of corn, from more labour being necessary, whilst no more labour is required to produce gold, silver, cloth, linen etc. the exchangeable value of corn will necessarily rise, as compared with those things. On the contrary, facilities in the production of corn, or of any other commodity of whatever kind, which shall afford the same produce with less labour, will lower its exchangeable value.
>
> (*Works*, iv.19)

A fairly common view in textbooks on the history of economic thought is (or used to be) that as regards the theory of value there is a fairly direct and unbroken tradition running through Smith to Ricardo and thence (with some accretions from Senior's 'abstinence') through J. S. Mill to Marshall; this tradition emphasizing cost of production and conditions of supply as determinants of what Smith called 'natural value' (by contrast with market price, or what Marshall was to term 'short-period price'). This 'classical' type of theory was depicted as standing in contrast with the search for basic determinants on the demand side, namely in utility, *ophelimité*, or consumers' preferences, which had been anticipated by J. B. Say, and then explicitly championed and developed by Jevons and the Austrians. The reality is, however, less simple than this, and, I believe, in some important respects quite different from what is implied in the usual view.

For a developed industrial society (after 'the accumulation of stock and the appropriation of land') Adam Smith advanced an expenses-of-production, or 'components', theory of value, in which the 'natural price' of a commodity was arrived at by a *summation* of the three 'component parts of price', wages, profits, and rent—components which varied in their relative importance in different lines of production. This is what Mr. Sraffa has called the 'Adding-up Theory' (*Works*, i.xxv).

In every society the price of every commodity finally resolves itself into some one or other, or all of those three parts; and in every improved society, all the three enter more or less as component parts into the price of the far greater part of commodities. . . . Wages, profit and rent are the three original sources of all revenue as well as of all exchangeable value.

(WN I.vi.10,17)

As for these component revenues themselves, these were determined by conditions of supply and demand prevailing respectively in the market for labour, for capital, and for land. Such was the fountainhead of the cost of production, or expenses of production, theory as this was to prevail as orthodoxy throughout most of the nineteenth century and to be defended by Marshall.

It might seem (and apparently did seem) a plausible corollary of this theory that, if for any reason one of these components were to rise, this rise would result in a rise (if an unequal one) in general prices. It seemed plausible, at least, until Ricardo posed the question: in terms of *what* will prices rise; and if in terms of money that is itself a commodity, how is this possible—unless the cost of production and the value of the money-commodity have themselves fallen? If only because it yielded a corollary of this kind, such a theory seemed to Ricardo unsatisfactory. More fundamentally it was for him unsatisfactory because it yielded no determination of the ratio of profit to wages—a relationship that in his system was crucial. Be it noted that it was this that Ricardo had in mind when he dismissed 'supply–demand' explanations as superficial or inadequate. This was *not* because he was blind to the fact that supply–demand relationships were operative forces in every market situation, and the proximate causes of any change in market price:[9] it was because *per se* they provided insufficient determination, at any rate as employed in the 'components of price' theory.

In this context Ricardo opposed his own notion of the 'rule' or 'cause' of value to Adam Smith; applying it always to the question of what happens to prices (and to profits) when wages *change*. He did so by discarding the conceptual barrier which Smith had erected (or at least the rigidity of that distinction) between 'the early and rude society' preceding 'accumulation of stock and the appropriation of land' and modern (capitalist) society, and accordingly asserting the relevance of Smith's initial value-principle to the latter as well as to the former type of society—a relevance which Smith

[9] Schumpeter, for example, criticizes Ricardo for depicting the issue as being his own theory of 'labour quantity *versus* supply and demand', and holds that this 'implies, of course, that Ricardo was completely blind to the nature, and the logical place in economic theory, of the supply-and-demand apparatus . . . This reflects little credit on him as a theorist. For it should be clear that his own theorem on equilibrium values is only tenable . . . by virtue of the interplay of supply and demand' (*History of Economic Analysis* (1954), 600–1).

had denied. Ricardo did so primarily because such a value-principle (in terms of labour expended) provided a determination of profit once the level of wages was given: it enabled one to express profits as depending on the 'proportion of the annual labour of the country (which) is devoted to the support of the labourers' (*Works*, i.49), or as it had been expressed in an early version of the theory, on 'the proportion of production to the consumption necessary to such production' (*Works*, i.xxxii; vi.117–18).

It might seem that in doing this Ricardo was taking a step backwards by failing to see that diversity of proportions of the 'components of price' in different industries would affect the relative prices of different products: the consideration that was no doubt uppermost in Smith's mind when he advanced his adding-up-the-components-of-price theory as the appropriate one for a society other than the primitive. But this would, again, be a misunderstanding—a misunderstanding not unconnected with (as well as explained by) the particular perspective from which Ricardo approached the problem. In his preoccupation with the profit–wage ratio, Ricardo, as we have said, saw the problem as consisting in the effect of a change in wages upon profits and prices. Although the primary emphasis of his theory was that a rise in wages would reduce profits equivalently (and conversely for a fall in wages), he was by no means blind to its differential effect on prices. On the contrary, in the course of writing the *Principles* he emphasized, in a letter to James Mill, the 'curious effect' of a rise of wages upon prices: namely that, contrary to raising prices generally, as the Smithian corollary supposed, it would cause the prices of commodities 'which are chiefly obtained by the aid of machinery and fixed capital' to *fall*.[10] This he treated not only as his own discovery but as a powerful reinforcement of his case against Smith and against what he conceived to be the erroneous implications of his 'adding-up-components' theory. It caused him to say that 'Adam Smith has no where analysed the effects of the accumulation of capital, and the appropriation of land, on relative value'.[11] Instead of the principle of quantity of labour as the foundation of value being displaced by the accumulation of capital and the appropriation of land, its operation was merely 'modified or altered'.

Thus there were essentially *two* lines of tradition, or separate branches of classical theory, so far as value and distribution were concerned; both of them deriving from Adam Smith, but one of them limited by him to an outmoded socio-historical context, and accordingly left undeveloped and

[10] Actually, in the first edition the stated conclusion was that no commodities rose in price, while those produced with fixed capital fell. But Mr. Sraffa has pointed out that this was because Ricardo's standard in which prices were measured was produced by 'unassisted labour'. In later editions, however, Ricardo shifted the definition of the standard to something produced under conditions representing a 'mean', and in terms of this some things rose in price while others fell, with the average remaining unchanged.

[11] *Principles of Political Economy and Taxation* (1st ed., 1817), 16; *Works*, i.22–3.

unutilized by him. That there were two such contrasting traditions has been obscured by the fact that the so-called 'Jevonian revolution', in its revolt against all 'cost' theories in favour of demand-determination by utility, identified the two distinct versions of the former and depicted Ricardo as the main propagator of the rejected doctrine. A further reason may well have been that the Ricardian version of the two classical traditions was adopted, as well as being carried further, by Marx, and virtually ended there by reason of the sharp polemics that it was to arouse in its specifically Marxian form. Marshall, be it noted, habitually referred to Ricardo when he had in mind 'cost of production' in the tradition of Smith (adding-up-components) and Mill, and indeed interpreted Ricardo in this sense. (To Marshall's eyes Marx had simply 'misunderstood Ricardo', and mischievously so.)

A significant feature of the Ricardian approach to distribution seems also to have been overlooked—something that has significance not only within the context of the 'natural' versus 'institutional', 'supra-historical' versus 'historico-relative' debate concerning economic 'laws', but for the boundaries of the subject. When Ricardo laid emphasis on distribution and 'the laws which regulate' it as 'the principal problem in Political Economy', this was presumably not only because of the importance of distribution for its own sake, but also because he saw it as the key to the determination of prices. According to his approach, a theory of distribution came *prior* to a theory of prices, or of Smithian 'natural value'—the direct opposite to the Mengerian order of determination from 'goods of first order' to 'goods of higher order'. But this meant that a theory of distribution could not be constructed entirely within the sphere of exchange or the market, and be explained in terms of market forces. A social, or institutional, historico-relative *datum* had to be introduced at the very base of the structure of explanation—introduced, as it were, from outside the sphere of market-relations, to which it has become customary nowadays for economic analysis and explanation to be confined. This social *datum* consists of some postulate about the way in which the level of real wages is determined (or what Marx was to call 'the value of labour-*power*')—something which must be essentially historico-relative in the sense of being dependent upon the socio-economic institutions (e.g. property-ownership and its distribution) of any given time and place.

It was, indeed, the comparatively unknown (until quite recently) Russian mathematical economist V. K. Dmitriev who, at the close of the century, belatedly afforded a neat answer to misunderstanding and criticism of Ricardo's theory.[12] The answer was epitomized in a single equation (for

[12] He quotes specifically Walras's criticism about using 'one equation to determine two unknowns'—which Walras attributed to 'the English School' (*Elements of Pure Economics*, English ed., trans. W. Jaffé (1954), 425).

a two-product case, where one product served as input into itself and the other), and amounted to saying that once the real wage and the productivity of labour in the two industries are given, as well as the time over which in each industry the labour is 'advanced', prices as well as profit are immediately determined.[13] But if only by reason of the language-barrier, his interpretation has remained unknown, and Marshall's interpretation and defence of the so-called Smith–Ricardo–Mill line as a cost of production theory has obscured the real nature of Ricardo's theory for most West European and American economists.

Those chapters towards the end of *The Principles of Political Economy and Taxation* that we mentioned earlier, referring to more particular points in *The Wealth of Nations*, are related directly or indirectly to the same general issue about value. While they do not add anything substantial to Ricardo's theory, which is fully stated in the first five or six chapters,[14] they add something at least by way of dotting *i*'s and crossing *t*'s, and for this reason deserve mention in the present context.

Regarding the 'Effects of Accumulation on Profits and Interest', Ricardo remarks that 'Adam Smith, however, uniformly ascribes the fall of profits to accumulation of capital, and to the competition which will result from it, without ever adverting to the increasing difficulty of providing food for the additional number of labourers which the additional capital will employ' (*Works*, i.289). The latter is, of course, a direct reference to his own theory that, given real wages, profit depends on the productivity of labour in the wage-goods industry (providing food). Whether increased production (he goes on) 'and the consequent demand' occasioned thereby 'shall or shall not lower profits, depends solely on the rise of wages, and the rise of wages, excepting for a limited period, on the facility of producing the food and necessaries of the labourer'. There later comes an explanatory paragraph which was added in the second edition and was lacking in the first.

It follows then from these admissions [of Smith] that there is no limit to demand—no limit to the employment of capital while it yields any profit, and that however abundant capital may become, there is no other adequate reason for a fall of profit but a rise of wages, and further it may be added, that the only adequate and permanent cause for a rise of wages is the increasing difficulty of providing food and necessaries for the increasing number of workmen.[15]

[13] V. K. Dmitriev, *Essais économiques* (1968; translated from the Russian edition of 1904 by Bernard Joly), 38. The essay on Ricardo, which forms the first part of the work, was published in 1898.

[14] Marx, indeed, commented that the essence of Ricardo's theory was 'contained exclusively in the first six chapters', while referring to the 'faulty architectonics' of the work as a whole (*Theories of Surplus Value*, Part II (1968 and 1969), 166–7).

[15] *Works*, i.296. The 'admissions' referred to in this passage are those cited by Ricardo in the two preceding paragraphs (295–6).

The next chapter is on export bounties, where he is concerned once more with the Smithian view that corn prices regulate all other prices. The chapter opens with the sentence: 'A bounty on the exportation of corn tends to lower its price to the foreign consumer, but it has no permanent effect on its price in the home market.'[16] Smith on the contrary had supposed that the bounty would lay a tax upon the home consumer by raising the price in the home market. Not only this, but by raising the price of corn it would tend to raise the price of 'all other home-made commodities'. On both counts Ricardo disagrees. If the 'natural price' of corn is unchanged, corn prices can be raised no more than temporarily; and even if they are raised, and this should result in a rise of money wages, the effect of this will be on profits and not on the general level of prices. This latter view Ricardo contrasts with that of 'Dr. Smith and . . . most other writers on this subject': namely, 'because the price of corn ultimately regulates wages, that therefore it will regulate the price of all other commodities'.

In the Chapter 'On the Doctrine of Adam Smith concerning the Rent of Land', Ricardo confronts the well-known ambiguities (if not inconsistencies) in Smith's account of rent as a component part of price with his own theory as expounded in Chapter II. He starts by expressing agreement with certain passages where Smith declares that if the produce of certain land is insufficient to replace 'the stock which must be employed . . . together with its ordinary profit', this land can yield no rent to the landlord; also with Smith's account of the rent of mines. Regarding the latter 'the whole principle of rent is here admirably and perspicuously explained, but every word is as applicable to land as it is to mines; yet he affirms that "it is otherwise in estates above ground. The proportion [value] both of their produce and of their rent, is in proportion to their absolute, and not to their relative fertility."' Ricardo's chief objection is, of course, to the statement that 'rent forms one of the component parts of the price of raw produce'. This is contrasted with Ricardo's proposition that 'price is every where regulated by the return obtained by [the] last portion of capital, for which no rent whatever is paid' (*Works*, i.329).

Two incidental points are, perhaps, worth mentioning in this chapter of the *Principles*. Firstly, Ricardo makes it quite clear that his own theory can be stated in terms of the internal margin of application of capital to a *given* area of land as well as in terms of an external margin of resort to inferior land, and that his position is by no means dependent on the actual existence of 'no-rent land'. On the second page of this chapter he writes:

[16] It may be noted that he is here accepting Adam Smith's assumption in his chapter on bounties (WN IV.v), that exportation is at the expense of home consumption but does not act as a stimulus to increased production. Smith's view had been that the effect of the bounty would be to raise only the 'nominal price' of corn and not its 'real price'; accordingly it would give no encouragement to the farmer to employ more labour and to grow more corn.

But if it were true that England had so far advanced in cultivation, that at this time there were no lands remaining which did not afford a rent, . . . whether there be or not, is of no importance to this question, for it is the same thing if there be any capital employed in Great Britain on land which yields only the return of stock with its ordinary profits, whether it be employed on old or on new land.

(*Works*, i.328)

Secondly, Ricardo makes the further complaint that

Adam Smith never makes any distinction between a low value of money, and a high value of corn, and therefore infers, that the interest of the landlord is not opposed to that of the rest of the community. In the first case, money is low relatively to all commodities; in the other, corn is high relatively to all. In the first, corn and commodities continue at the same relative values; in the second, corn is high relatively to commodities as well as money.

(*Works*, i.336)

In the chapter 'On Colonial Trade' Ricardo's disagreement is somewhat different in kind and comparatively minor. On the whole he approves, and applauds, Smith's demonstration of 'the advantage of a free trade and the injustices suffered by colonies' under a régime of regulated trade. His disagreement is only as to whether the 'mother country may not sometimes be benefited by the restraints to which she subjects her colonial possessions': 'a measure which may be greatly hurtful to a colony may be partially beneficial to the mother country' (*Works*, i.339,340). To this he adds that, while he agrees that 'the monopoly of the colony trade will change and often prejudicially, the direction of capital', in his opinion (and in disagreement with Smith) it would not affect the rate of profit: even if it did, 'it would not occasion the least alteration in prices; prices being regulated neither by wages nor profits' (*Works*, i.344–6).

In the chapter 'On Gross and Net Revenue' Ricardo's difference from Smith has little directly to do with their respective theories of value; but it is connected nevertheless with Ricardo's general attitude towards distribution, in particular to profits (along with rent) as some kind of surplus.[17] The chapter opens with the well-known statement: 'Adam Smith constantly magnifies the advantages which a country derives from a large gross, rather than a large net income' (*Works*, i.347). The difference of emphasis has continued down to the present day in varying contexts and has had some modern echoes. 'What would be the advantage', he asks, 'resulting to a country from the employment of a great quantity of productive labour, if,

[17] It is not without interest in this connection to note that Marx considered Ricardo as having a 'theory of surplus-value, which of course exists in his work, although he does not define surplus-value as distinct from its particular forms, profit, rent, interest' (*Theories of Surplus Value*, Part II, 169). He had also treated Adam Smith's 'deduction' theory as a concept of surplus-value in embryo (ibid., Part I (no date), 83–6).

whether it employed that quantity or a smaller, its net rent and profits together would be the same?' The answer is given that it is from rent and profits only that 'any deductions can be made for taxes, or for savings' (*Works*, i.347–8). Thus Ricardo's emphasis seems to have constituted a recognition that surplus was the criterion of 'productive' as applied to labour and its maximization a prime objective of economic activity.

The chapter 'On the Comparative Value of Gold, Corn and Labour in Rich and Poor Countries' is in part a comment on Smith's habit of treating corn and labour as a measure of value of other commodities (and hence the values of corn and labour as constant), and partly an assertion of his own theoretical principle that both will tend to rise (owing to diminishing returns) with rising population as against Smith's statement that 'gold and silver will naturally exchange for a greater quantity of subsistence in a rich than a poor country, in a country which abounds with subsistence than in one which is but indifferently supplied with it' (this latter statement appearing in one of the more discursive and prolix chapters of *The Wealth of Nations*).[18] Ricardo advances his own, and directly contrary, opinion that 'the value of gold, estimated in corn' will tend to be 'low in rich countries, and high in poor countries'. To this he attaches a denial that gold (relative to corn) will 'necessarily be lower in those countries which are in possession of the mines, though this is a proposition maintained by Adam Smith' (*Works*, i.377). Ricardo may well have considered this chapter of *The Wealth of Nations* an example of misleading use of general supply–demand reasoning to the neglect of the rooting of 'natural value' in conditions of production (it must be remembered that the chapter in question was concerned with long-run tendencies to which long-run and not short-run influences were presumably relevant).

To this issue of his own approach versus the supply–demand type of reasoning he returns in his quite short Chapter XXX, 'On the Influence of Demand and Supply on Prices', in which he is concerned with certain statements of Buchanan, Say, and Lauderdale, and no longer directly with *The Wealth of Nations* (although it seems likely that general reference to the latter was not altogether out of mind). The chapter opens by reaffirming that

> it is the cost of production which must ultimately regulate the price of commodities, and not, as has been often said, the proportion between the supply and demand: the proportion between supply and demand may, indeed, for a time, affect the market value of a commodity, until it is supplied in greater or less abundance, according as the demand may have increased or diminished, but this effect will be only of temporary duration.
>
> (*Works*, i.382)

[18] *The Wealth of Nations*, I.xi.e.34. Smith himself refers in the 'conclusion' to 'this very long chapter' (I.xi.p.1).

To this he adds: 'The opinion that the price of commodities depends solely on the proportion of supply and demand, or demand to supply, has become almost an axiom in political economy, and has been the source of much error in that science.' The statement by Buchanan which he cites in illustration of this is that money wages will not be altered by a change in the price of provisions, or by a tax on wages, since this 'would not alter the proportion of the demand of labourers to the supply'.[19] From Say he cites the statement that cost of production determines merely the *lowest price* to which a thing can fall for any length of time; and from Lauderdale that changes in the proportions between amounts supplied and demanded 'are the sole causes of alteration of value'. It is not without interest that Ricardo should have concluded: 'This is true of monopolized commodities, and indeed of the market-price of all other commodities for a limited period . . . Commodities which are monopolized, either by an individual, or by a company, vary according to the law which Lord Lauderdale has laid down' (*Works*, i.384–5). It is a commonplace that Ricardo shared with Smith the characteristic of being *par excellence* a theorist of perfect competition.

[19] *Works*, i.382. He had earlier referred to the argument of Buchanan as 'a great mixture of truth and error' (217).

III

Compensating Wage Differentials

ALBERT REES*

THE GENERAL CONCEPT

OF the many ideas of Adam Smith that have stood the test of time, few have weathered better or are still more relevant than the idea of compensating wage differentials.[1] This idea is set forth in Book I, Chapter X of *The Wealth of Nations*, 'Of Wages and Profit in the Different Employments of Labour and Stock', and particularly in Part I of the chapter.

The basic idea of compensating differentials follows from the first two sentences of chapter X:

> The whole of the advantages and disadvantages of the different employments of labour and stock must, in the same neighbourhood, be either perfectly equal or continually tending to equality. If in the same neighbourhood, there was any employment evidently either more or less advantageous than the rest, so many people would crowd into it in the one case, and so many would desert it in the other, that its advantages would soon return to the level of other employments. (WN I.x.a.1).

If the non-pecuniary advantages of different employments are unequal, then the pecuniary rewards must be unequal in the opposite direction to preserve the equality of total advantages. These offsetting pay differentials are now called 'compensating differentials', or 'equalizing differentials', terms that were not used by Smith. The distinguishing characteristic of a true compensating differential is that it will not be eroded by perfect mobility of labour—it will exist even in long-run competitive equilibrium.

The shift in the focus of economists' attention away from the whole of the advantages and disadvantages of an employment to the money wage, and to the reflection in this wage of the non-pecuniary aspects of the job, arises first from recent concern with systematic measurement of economic magnitudes, and second from the development of the concept of supply curves of labour, which plot employment against money wages. Non-pecuniary advantages or disadvantages can be highly varied, and have no common denominator other than their reflection in the wage rate. However, recent changes in terminology and analytical technique do not

* Professor of Economics at Princeton University.

[1] I am indebted to my colleagues Daniel S. Hammermesh and A. P. Thirlwall for helpful comments on an earlier version of this paper.

diminish the importance of the original concept, which is still with us in a slightly different guise.

The examples given in *The Wealth of Nations* all refer to earnings in different occupations and to the choice of occupation by workers. It should, of course, be clear that the concept of compensating differentials has much broader applicability. It can be used to explain differences in wages within an occupation between employers, between industries, and between geographic locations.

It is sometimes thought that the reasoning behind the concept of compensating differentials is circular or tautological. Thus a well-known contemporary author writes:

When confronted by the awkward fact that people do not always seek the better paid job, even when they know it is there, the economist has always resorted to the argument that we do not maximize money, but net satisfactions . . . Once the assumption that man maximizes money is replaced by the assumption that he maximizes net satisfactions *which are not specified*, no predictions of his market behaviour can be made.[2]

To the extent that this passage is directed against Smith, it can be faulted in two aspects. First, the concept of net advantage or net satisfactions did not arise as a way of covering up deficiencies in the predictive power of a theory of monetary maximization. On the contrary, the concept of net advantage is the original one, and lapses into a theory of monetary maximization came later, as a result of the difficulties of measuring non-monetary factors. Second, whatever the deficiencies of neo-classical economists in failing to specify the components of net advantage, these deficiencies cannot be blamed on Smith. He specified in detail the five factors that in his view constituted the non-monetary advantages and disadvantages of employment, and we shall turn to these in a moment.[3]

Nevertheless, Walker's passage gives rise to an important caution. The concept of net advantage does not in itself constitute a testable or refutable hypothesis. Rather it is a framework that leads to the formulation of testable hypotheses, which are of the form of 'x or y or z is a net disadvantage or advantage of employment'. These specific hypotheses are of more or less value depending first on how well they stand up against the evidence and second on how general they are—how broadly they are applicable across time and space. One would not expect the components of net advantage to be exactly the same in 1976 as in 1776. What is remarkable,

[2] Kenneth F. Walker, 'The Psychological Assumptions of Economics', *The Economic Record*, xii (June 1946), 72–3. Italics in the original.

[3] For an extensive discussion of the methodological issues arising from classical wage theory, see Simon Rottenberg, 'On Choice in Labour Markets', *Industrial and Labour Relations Review*, ix (Jan. 1956), 183–99; 'Comment' by Robert J. Lampman, ibid. (July 1956), 629–36; and the 'Reply' by Rottenberg, ibid. 636–41.

however, is the extent to which Adam Smith's original list is still relevant.

It is well known that Smith's argument in Chapter X was to some extent suggested by Chapters 7 and 8 of Richard Cantillon's *Essai sur la nature du commerce en general*, which had been published in 1755.[4] However, too much stress should not be put on Smith's indebtedness. Cantillon's chapters are very short (one page each). The principal arguments of Chapter X of *The Wealth of Nations* are present, but only in an embryonic form. Smith both develops them in much more detail and links them together in a far more systematic way.

We now proceed to the discussion of the components of net advantage identified by Smith.

AGREEABLENESS AND DISAGREEABLENESS

Agreeableness and disagreeableness are Smith's terms for the first of the five factors that together account for 'Inequalities arising from the Nature of the Employments themselves', which is the title of Part I of Chapter X. The other set of factors is discussed in Part II under the rubric 'Inequalities occasioned by the Policy of Europe', and consists of legal barriers to mobility and grants of monopoly.

The terms 'agreeableness and disagreeableness' include 'the ease or hardship, the cleanliness or dirtiness, the honourableness or dishonourableness of the employment', and these attributes are illustrated by examples such as the following: 'A journeyman blacksmith, though an artificer, seldom earns so much in twelve hours as a collier, who is only a labourer, does in eight. His work is not quite so dirty, is less dangerous, and is carried on in day-light, and above ground'' (WN I.x.b.2).

One can no longer make exactly the same comparison for lack of wage data for blacksmiths. However, in March 1972 average hourly earnings in coalmining in the United States were $5·22 and in fabricated metal products $3·92, and the work of a coalminer is still dark, dirty, and more dangerous than that of most other occupations. The miner is now a more skilled worker, and some part of his earnings are attributable to the special strength of the mineworkers' union, but there is no doubt still a compensating differential involved.[5]

There are many other cases, however, in which one now finds workers doing dirty, dangerous, or disagreeable work at very low wages. I believe these cases to be the result of two sets of forces that Smith did not consider because they were not present in the Britain or France of his day.

[4] See footnote to Chapter X in the Edwin Cannan edition of *The Wealth of Nations* (1930) and also Joseph J. Spengler, 'Richard Cantillon: First of the Moderns', *Journal of Political Economy*, lxii (Oct. 1954), 423.

[5] I am informed by Professor Laurence Hunter of Glasgow University that as of 1970 there was no differential in hourly earnings between mining and metal manufactures in the United Kingdom.

The first is demand-deficiency unemployment, the second is racial discrimination in employment.

Smith, of course, considers seasonal and casual unemployment as the third of his five factors creating inequalities in wages. However, he could not have known involuntary unemployment of the kind that is present in modern industrial countries with market economies both at the trough of the trade cycle and during government attempts to restrain inflation by curbing aggregate demand. The earliest recorded trade cycle in Great Britain has its trough in 1793, and we cannot be certain that there was cyclical unemployment before then.[6] During recent business recessions, the downward rigidity of money wages has prevented the unemployed from securing good jobs by offering to do them for less than the going wage. In such circumstances there may be workers who have been unemployed for long periods who will accept disagreeable work at low wages rather than have no work at all, and this makes compensating differentials unnecessary. The higher the level of liquid assets of the unemployed and the stronger the system of unemployment insurance or other forms of income maintenance, the weaker the tendency for the unemployed to take disagreeable jobs at low wages. However, it should still be true that compensating differentials will be best observed in periods of full employment.[7]

The second basic reason why compensating differentials may not appear for disagreeable work is racial discrimination in employment. In many multiracial societies, including the United States, almost all employment is controlled by the dominant race (whites). There are employer stereotypes of what constitutes 'white work' and 'black work', which may be closely correlated with the agreeableness of the job. To the extent that blacks are excluded from the agreeable jobs, they increase the supply of labour to the disagreeable jobs and keep down the wages in them. One would therefore expect the rigorous enforcement of legislation against racial discrimination in employment to result in the emergence of larger wage premiums for disagreeable jobs.

There is one important respect in which Smith's theory about the agreeableness of jobs now seems to be incomplete. He writes throughout as though all workers had identical tastes—as if what is disagreeable to one is disagreeable to all. If this were true, the supply curve of labour to any

[6] See Arthur F. Burns, 'Business Cycles: General', *International Encyclopedia of the Social Sciences* (1968), ii.230.

[7] It follows from the argument in the text that one should not attempt to preserve the wage structure that emerges in a depression during a subsequent period of very full employment. For example, in the Buffalo, New York area during 1944 there was a critical manpower shortage in foundries. This was aggravated by the fact that unskilled wages in foundries for hot, heavy, dirty work were lower than those in air-frame plants for light, clean work. Nevertheless stabilization authorities were reluctant to alter relative wages and instead relied entirely and unsuccessfully on direct manpower controls. See Leonard P. Adams, *Wartime Manpower Mobilization* (1951), especially, 72.

occupation would be perfectly elastic at a wage rate just enough above or below that of other occupations to reflect the uniform assessment of their non-pecuniary attributes. In this case, relative wages are determined entirely by supply conditions and are invariant in the long run to shifts in the demand for labour among occupations.

Smith lived in a society which by present American or even present British standards was culturally quite homogeneous. In such a society the assumption of uniform tastes is quite natural. Thus when Smith writes, 'The trade of a butcher is a brutal and an odious business; but it is in most places more profitable than the greater part of common trades' (WN I.x.b.2), the strength of the language reflects not only the author's tastes, but no doubt that of most others.[8] In a more diverse culture, this assumption of naturally uniform tastes may be less relevant. For example, suppose that 1 per cent of workers do not find being a butcher 'brutal' or 'odious', but on the contrary enjoy it. If the employment of butchers is less than 1 per cent of employment in all trades taken together, it would then clearly be possible to fill all the positions for butchers without any compensating wage differential.

More generally, if tastes differ, we can form a supply curve of labour to an occupation by arranging all of the people who might enter it from left to right along the horizontal axis in order of decreasing preference for this kind of work or, (what is the same thing) increasing supply prices. Thus arranged, they form an upward sloping supply curve of labour to the occupation. A permanent increase in the demand for labour in this occupation relative to others will now cause a rise in its relative wage in long-run equilibrium.

THE DIFFICULTY AND EXPENSE OF LEARNING THE BUSINESS

The idea that wages vary with the difficulty and expense of learning an occupation has been an extraordinarily fruitful one, not only for the study of wages but in the broader contexts of capital theory and the theory of economic growth. Smith's initial statement of the theory of human capital could hardly be improved upon in so short a passage:

> When any expensive machine is erected, the extraordinary work to be performed by it before it is worn out, it must be expected, will replace the capital laid out upon it, with at least the ordinary profits. A man educated at the expence of much labour and time to any of those employments which require extraordinary dexterity and skill, may be compared to one of those expensive machines. The

[8] For further evidence of Smith's view that approbation or disapproval of a social or occupational role are universal and natural, see *The Theory of Moral Sentiments* (6th ed. 1790) I.iii.2.1: 'The man of distinction, on the contrary, is observed by all the world. Everybody is eager to look at him . . .' The words 'all' and 'everybody' recur later in the passage. I am grateful to Mr. A. S. Skinner for calling this passage to my attention.

work which he learns to perform, it must be expected, over and above the usual wages of common labour will replace to him the whole expence of his education, with at least the ordinary profits of an equally valuable capital. It must do this too in a reasonable time, regard being had to the very uncertain duration of human life, in the same manner as to the more certain duration of the machine.

(WN I.x.b.6)

It is in this passage and the rest of the section in which it is included that Smith's debt to Cantillon is greatest. However, Cantillon merely suggests that the labour of an artisan or craftsman will be 'dear in proportion to the time in learning the trade and the cost and risk incurred in becoming proficient'.[9] He does not make the separation that Smith does between the repayment of the capital outlay and the return on it.

The revival of interest in the idea of human capital during the 1960s, led by T. W. Schultz and Gary Becker, has provided the impetus for the most important developments in labour economics in the past fifteen years.[10] One may ask how Smith's treatment differs from the much more extensive recent work. A large part of the answer is that much of the recent work is concerned with making precise estimates of the rate of return on different kinds of investment in human capital, or of the present value of such investments, while Smith merely considered general orders of magnitude or directions of wage differences. A second difference is that Smith considers only formal programmes of schooling or apprenticeship as investment in human capital, while the recent treatments also include less formal kinds of on-the-job training and learning from experience.

It is one of the strengths of Smith's treatment that he distinguishes implicitly between the time needed to learn an occupation, which would create wage differentials in a state of 'perfect liberty', and the time that may be institutionally required. If the latter exceeds the former, as in the case of overlong apprenticeships, the resulting wage differentials are 'too large' in the sense that they will include an element of monopoly rent in addition to a normal return on investment.

Judging by the attention given to them in Part II of Chapter X, overlong apprenticeships were the chief way of restricting entry to trades in the late eighteenth century. However, Smith also refers to the refusal of masters to take apprentices and to limits on the number of apprentices to be trained by any one master. Another restrictive device not mentioned by Smith has sometimes been used by craft unions in the United States, which is to fix the wages of apprentices 'too high' relative to the wage of journeymen—that is, higher than the ratio of their productivities. This device operates by reducing the willingness of employers to take apprentices.

[9] Cantillon, op. cit., translated by Henry Higgs (1931), 19.

[10] See, in particular, T. W. Schultz, 'Investment in Human Capital', *American Economic Review*, li (Mar. 1961), 1–17, and Gary S. Becker, *Human Capital* (1964).

Smith recognizes clearly that only outlays on training made by workers and their families will be reflected in wage differentials. If training for any occupation is subsidized, the supply of those trained will increase and the private return to the training will be lowered accordingly. It is for this reason that Smith complains of the scholarships and bursaries that draw people into the clergy. The complaint implies that the number of people in an occupation should be entirely determined by the tastes and resources of future workers and by the market demands of individual consumers; it should not be influenced by public policy. This is a view that would find little support today, and least of all among university students and their teachers. A training subsidy is now generally considered justified to the extent that trained people do not receive their whole social product, as may be true for example of research scientists.

THE CONSTANCY OF EMPLOYMENT

The observation that hourly or daily wages vary with the constancy of employment has somewhat narrower applicability than the other sources of compensating differentials. Smith states the case as follows:

> In the greater part of manufactures, a journeyman may be pretty sure of employment almost every day in the year that he is able to work. A mason or bricklayer, on the contrary, can work neither in hard frost nor in foul weather, and his employment at all other times depends upon the occasional calls of his customers. He is liable in consequence to be frequently without any. What he earns, therefore, while he is employed, must not only maintain him while he is idle, but make him some compensation for those anxious and desponding moments which the thought of so precarious a situation must sometimes occasion.
>
> (WN I.x.b.12)

The last sentence quoted suggests that not only must the daily wage of a mason or bricklayer be higher than that of a journeyman in manufacturing, but that the annual earnings must also be somewhat higher as a kind of risk premium.

Smith's argument is still valid and it is still applied to exactly the same trades. I have heard it made many times by Mr. Thomas Murphy, the General President of the Bricklayers, Masons, and Plasterers International Union, though Mr. Murphy tells me that he has never read *The Wealth of Nations*. Smith's observation that the daily wages of a mason are generally higher than those of a carpenter would be true today in most places in the United States, though not in all. On 1 July 1969 the average union wage rate for bricklayers was $6·06 and for carpenters $5·77 an hour; the rate for bricklayers was higher in fifteen of the twenty-one largest cities.

As with other kinds of compensating differentials, however, that for inconstancy of employment may disappear when there is less than full employment or discrimination against racial or ethnic minorities. Migratory farm workers who harvest fruits and vegetables in the United States get low daily rates despite the inconstancy of their employment; the great majority of these workers are black or Spanish-speaking.

THE TRUST TO BE REPOSED

Smith's principle that wages vary with the trust to be reposed in the workman is not of the same sort as the other factors discussed in Chapter X. The general nature of these is to compensate the workman for some disadvantage of the job or for the expense of learning it. The fact that a goldsmith makes more than other workers of equal skill, however, is probably not needed to compensate him because he dislikes being entrusted with precious materials. It is true that some workers may dislike taking responsibility, but it is also true that others enjoy it. Rather the need for a wage premium must arise from a shortage of workmen worthy of such trust.

Paul H. Douglas has interpreted Smith as meaning that the higher wage of those entrusted with valuables is needed to reduce their temptation to be dishonest.[11] It may be doubted whether the wage premiums are generally high enough to accomplish much in this direction, though bank employees were doubtless relatively better paid in the eighteenth century than they are now. In any event, the premium even on this interpretation still is not one that compensates the worker for disutility; it arises on the demand rather than the supply side of the labour market.

If the scarcity of trustworthy workers is the correct interpretation of this factor, then it is only one of a much larger class of rents to scarce or rare talents, including those of 'players, opera-singers, opera-dancers, etc.', whom Smith discusses under a different rubric. He attributes some of the rewards of the latter group to the opprobrium attached to exercising such talents for gain (WN I.x.b.25). Such opprobrium no longer exists, but the pecuniary rewards for exceptional talents of these kinds are still very high.

The principle of trustworthiness is not discussed at much length in *The Wealth of Nations*; it is the only case in which the treatment is not clearly superior to Cantillon's. Perhaps Smith himself sensed that this principle was not congruent with the other four.

THE PROBABILITY OF SUCCESS

Smith's argument that wages vary with the probability of success is the hardest to follow of the discussions of the five main factors (WN I.x.b.21). It begins with the observation that someone trained in one of the mechanic trades is almost certain to succeed in practising it, but someone trained in a liberal profession is not. In the latter case fairness would require that the

[11] Paul H. Douglas, 'Smith's Theory of Value and Distribution', in *Adam Smith, 1776–1926* (1928), 84.

gains of the successful few be large enough to repay with interest the training costs of all. Cannan's interpretation of the argument in the footnotes to his edition of *The Wealth of Nations* seems to be correct; *average* wages vary inversely with the riskiness of the calling because new entrants have an 'over-weening conceit of their abilities' (WN I.x.b.26) and overrate their chances of winning one of the few large prizes. It follows that the prizes are not large or numerous enough to create a perfectly fair lottery, and the rate of return on all training for their professions is below that for the mechanic trades.

The portion of the argument that makes it consistent with the first three factors is the portion relating to the public admiration of genius or talent. The receipt of psychic income from fame and distinction is part of the total reward of a successful poet or philosopher, and hence justifies a lower monetary reward.

Smith's main example of people crowding into a profession because of a few large prizes is the law, an example that might still serve. More striking current examples might be the stage or cinema, with hundreds of aspiring actors, actresses, and directors willing to work for little or nothing in summer stock in the hope that their work will lead to discovery and success. The unionization of Broadway and Hollywood prevents this ready supply from bidding down the wages of bit players in the main centres of the entertainment industry.

Smith finds it necessary to distinguish his argument about risk in this section from his earlier discussion of hazardous trades and the constancy of employment. In the earlier sections, workers were risk-averse; bricklayers and masons had to be compensated for the desponding moments in which they considered the risk of unemployment. In this section young workers making occupational choices are risk-lovers. The distinction is attempted between risks that are entirely external and those that interact with personal qualities. In concluding his discussion of the low wages of sailors, who underrate the dangers of the sea, Smith writes:

> The distant prospect of hazards, from which we can hope to extricate ourselves by courage and address, is not disagreeable to us, and does not raise the wages of labour in any employment. It is otherwise with those in which courage and address can be of no avail. In trades which are known to be very unwholesome, the wages of labour are always remarkably high.
>
> (WN I.x.b.32)

A better reconciliation might have been reached by considering not whether wages are raised at all by risk, but whether they are raised enough. If coalminers overrate their luck, wages in mining may still be higher than in other trades, but by less than enough to compensate for the true risks of death and injury.

Both in the discussion of agreeableness and disagreeableness and in the discussion of the probability of success, Smith discusses occupational hazards as though they were inherent in an occupation and could not be reduced by any deliberate action of the employer. This is, of course, only partially true. No account of precaution can make mining coal as safe an occupation as banking, but proper equipment and procedures can reduce the accident rate in mining below what it would otherwise be.

We assume that accidents can only be prevented at a cost, and that after some point there are diminishing returns to successive increments of expenditure on accident prevention. The optimal expenditure is one just large enough so that the expected cost of preventing an additional accident exceeds the probable full cost of such an accident if it occurred. A compensating wage differential based on full knowledge of the risks by workers and the full reflection of these risks in wages would give employers the optimal incentive to make expenditures on health and safety, and it is this situation that by Smith's reasoning would prevail in the 'unwholesome' trades. On the other hand, where workers believe that they can extricate themselves from danger 'by courage and address', the profit-maximizing employer has insufficient incentive to invest in accident prevention. In such a case the optimal incentives to employers would have to be provided by requiring them to carry workmen's compensation insurance (or to self-insure) under a system in which *all* costs of accidents are covered by benefits and premiums are directly related to employer experience. Present American workmen's compensation laws fail this test because workers cannot recover their full losses in most cases.

SOME EXTENSIONS

So far we have been following very closely the particular factors listed by Smith in defining the causes of inequalities in wages. It is now time to look into the application of his framework to new areas.

One of the most obvious extensions is to differences in the conditions of employment between different employers in the same occupation. Some occupations, such as those of typists or janitors, are found in a wide variety of industries, and there may be non-pecuniary advantages or disadvantages connected with the industry in which the worker is employed. Thus a typist might prefer to be employed by an insurance company than by a steel mill or an oil refinery. Strictly speaking, this preference has to do with the location of the job rather than the industry of the employer, since presumably there would be no objection to being employed by the headquarters office of an oil or steel company if the office is located in a central business district rather than at the mill or refinery.

A more general kind of locational preference, especially important for female employees, is the preference of an employer who is located near where the employee lives. To work for such an employer saves the worker the time and direct costs of commuting over long distances. For this reason one would expect employers located in residential neighbourhoods to pay lower wages than those located in industrial areas or central business districts. In a recent study of the Chicago labour market it was found that employers of female clerical workers located in residential areas paid on average 12 cents an hour less than those located elsewhere. This coefficient is about 6 per cent of the mean wage and comes from multiple regressions in which a number of other factors, including age, experience, and education, were controlled.[12]

It is well known that in the United States large establishments pay higher wages on average than small establishments in the same industry.[13] This pattern becomes much weaker when one controls for other factors such as occupational mix and city size that may be correlated with establishment size. Nevertheless, it may still be present.[14]

It is not clear whether size-of-establishment differentials where they exist are compensating differentials in a pure sense. It could be that other things being equal workers in general prefer small establishments and dislike the formal rules, long chains of command, and more impersonal management that are characteristic of large establishments.[15] On the other hand, establishment size could still be acting as a proxy for some other factors not adequately controlled in existing studies. For example, other things being equal a large establishment will have to draw its work force from a wider geographical area than a small one, and must therefore at the margin offer workers a larger premium to cover the costs of getting to work.

A very clear example of compensating differences in wages between employers is present in the market for university teachers in the United States, where individual universities are free to set their own salary scales. Persistently over many years the universities with the highest prestige have offered the lowest starting salaries for new Ph.D.s, and despite this have generally succeeded in recruiting many of the ablest new entrants to the market. This may be true in part because the employers have a rather clearly defined prestige ranking and this prestige enters directly into the utility function of the teacher. Perhaps more important is that a new faculty

[12] See A. Rees and G. P. Shultz, *Workers and Wages in an Urban Labour Market* (1970), Table 7.1.

[13] See, for example, Richard A. Lester, 'Pay Differentials by Size of Establishment', *Industrial Relations*, vii (Oct. 1967).

[14] See Rees and Shultz, op. cit. 184–9.

[15] For two quotations that express worker preferences for small plants because they facilitate good interpersonal relations and friendliness, see Lloyd G. Reynolds and Joseph Shister, *Job Horizons* (1949), 16. It is, of course, hard to know how representative such examples are.

member will learn more at a university where much research is going on in his field and where the senior faculty members are known for the quality of their research. This on-the-job training will improve his future productivity and perhaps his earnings in future jobs. The negative salary differential could then be viewed as a kind of payment for greater post-doctoral investment in human capital.

Recent work on racial discrimination in labour markets also makes use of the concept of compensating differentials. Three cases are generally distinguished: (a) where the employer discriminates against black employees; (b) where white employees discriminate against black colleagues; and (c) where white customers discriminate against services performed by black workers. In the second of these cases, it is argued that employers of integrated workforces will have to offer white employees or all employees a wage premium above the wage paid by employers of whites only to offset the dislikes of white workers for working with blacks.[16] However, I am not aware of a case in which a wage premium for integrated as compared with all-white work forces has been identified in wage data.

The desire for a wage premium to compensate for the race of one's colleagues is not inherently rational like the desire to be compensated for danger, noise, dirt, or other adverse physical working conditions. There is therefore no reason to assume that such tastes cannot be changed by education, legislation, or similar measures.

As the preceding discussion suggests, the notion of compensating differentials can be applied among the employees of a single employer, and other examples are not hard to find. Where a factory or other establishment works shifts, it is customary to pay a premium for the second or third shift relative to the day shift, particularly if workers are not rotated among shifts. The premiums compensate shift workers for such costs as having different schedules from their families.

The case of compensation within the work force of a single employer is of particular interest because it involves a different kind of evidence to determine if a differential is of the appropriate size. Where a differential is paid to all the workers in an establishment, or all those in an occupation, a differential that is too small should result in unfilled vacancies persisting over considerable periods or in a poorly qualified work-force, while one that is too large would result in an excess supply of qualified applicants even in periods of full employment. The evidence of appropriate internal differentials would consist in a peculiar distribution of the work force. For example, if workers are permitted to choose shifts on the basis of seniority, too small a differential would result in almost all senior workers choosing the day shift, while too large a differential would lead almost all senior

[16] See, for example, Kenneth Arrow, 'The Theory of Discrimination', in O. Ashenfelter, and A. Rees, eds., *Discrimination in Labour Markets* (1973).

workers to choose the night shift. On this kind of evidence most shift differentials in the United States would be judged too small, and the usual overtime premium of 50 per cent generally too large.

Where wage premiums for working under disagreeable or dangerous conditions are established by collective bargaining rather than by market forces, it becomes very difficult to determine whether they are of appropriate size. The trade unions in the construction industry in the United States have obtained many such premiums, and these will differ substantially from place to place both in nature and amount. Premiums are established for working on high structures, for working with unpleasant substances such as creosote, or even for working directly under a helicopter. On the whole, these premiums seem more likely to be too large than too small.

The argument of Part I of Chapter X does not deal with geographical differences in wages because these had already been covered in Chapter VIII, 'Of the Wages of Labour'. One might expect the principle of compensating differentials to operate among places as well as among occupations, so that real wages would be lower in a place with an agreeable climate than in one whose climate is harsh and unpleasant. Smith, however, observed that money wages varied much more than the price of consumer goods, and not in a way that fitted a theory of compensating differentials. This leads him to the conclusion that labour is rather immobile geographically; 'it appears evidently from experience that a man is of all sorts of luggage the most difficult to be transported' (WN I.viii.31).

It is still probably true that geographical mobility is too small to establish a pattern of real wage differentials consistent with a theory of compensating differentials. Improvements in transportation have greatly lowered the monetary costs of moving long distances, but not the psychic costs. The net flows may be toward the places that combine high real wages and pleasant surroundings, but the flows are not large enough to create the equilibrium that would bring them to an end.[17]

This observation suggests that we should look at the dynamics of Smith's model. He speaks of the whole of the advantages and disadvantages of different employments being either *perfectly equal* or *continually tending to equality*. The first case is one of equilibrium; the second is one in which equilibrium has been disturbed and is in the process of being restored. The disturbance was no doubt an event that caused a change in the demand for labour in an employment, since the model of Chapter X is one of constant long-run supply prices. The distinction between this case and the case of geographical mobility may in fact not be that occupational mobility

[17] The mere existence of net flows in the right direction is insufficient to support the wage predictions of classical theory. The failure to realize this is a defect of Rottenberg's 'On Choice in Labour Markets'.

exceeds geographical mobility—it may lie in the nature of the forces that produce the disequilibrium. If a system that reacts in the right direction to a disequilibrating force is disturbed by a single shock, it will eventually attain a new equilibrium (not necessarily the same as the old one). However, if the disequilibrating force acts continuously, whether or not the system reaches a new equilibrium depends not only on the direction of the response but also on its strength. In the case of geographical wage differences, one of the causal factors is often a high rate of natural increase of population in the low-wage area. Substantial net out-migration may be needed merely to offset this, and can occur without making any contribution toward equalizing real wages.

CONCLUSION

The concept of compensating wage differentials has been a hardy device for generating fruitful hypotheses about wage structure. Clearly, not all hypotheses growing out of the concept will be supported by the evidence, nor will all of them apply at all places and at all times. Yet it would be hard to imagine a theory of relative wages that did not make some use of this concept.

It has recently been fashionable to try to explain wages entirely on institutional grounds, to rest almost all of wage structures on differences in bargaining power, and to minimize the importance of labour markets. There is, of course, some basis for the recent view. Many of the institutions now central to wage determinations, such as the trade union, were unknown in Smith's time, and their growth has meant that the influence of market forces on wage structure is less direct and perhaps less sure than it was in his day. This does not mean that this influence is not present, or even important. A full understanding of wage structure involves both markets and non-market institutions, and to ignore either one will result in incomplete explanations.

IV

Adam Smith on Competition and Increasing Returns

G. B. Richardson*

ADAM Smith regarded competition as both a desirable and a natural state of affairs. Despite what he considered to be 'the mean rapacity, the monopolising spirit of merchants and manufacturers', he took the view that neither monopoly nor restrictive agreements would prove effective unless given state backing such as might be afforded, for example, by legal incorporation. In this connection he observes, 'In a free trade an effectual combination cannot be established but by the unanimous consent of every single trader and it cannot last longer than every single trader continues of the same mind. The majority of a corporation can enact a by-law with proper penalties which will limit competition more effectually and more durably than any voluntary combination whatever'. It would seem therefore that Smith did not wish the state to adopt an active anti-trust policy; it was necessary only that it should not support the restriction of competition save in exceptional cases, such as the granting of a patent on a new machine, a royalty to an author, or exclusive rights to merchants who 'undertake, at their own risk and expense, to establish a new trade with some remote and barbarous nation'.[1]

Smith's view of competition, in so far as public policy is concerned, can thus be stated quite succinctly. Needless to say, he is writing about the conditions of his time and it is idle to ask whether he would have approved of international commodity agreements or the co-ordination of investments in steel-making capacity. It is more rewarding to examine, as we shall now do, the theoretical arguments upon which his case for free competition is based.

Let us observe at the outset that competition features within *The Wealth of Nations* in two distinct contexts; first, in the account given of the balancing of supply and demand in particular markets, and, secondly, in

* Fellow of St. John's College, Oxford.

[1] It is interesting to note that Smith associates the 'wretched spirit of monopoly' chiefly with businessmen. 'Landlords, farmers and labourers', he says, 'have commonly neither inclination nor fitness to enter into combinations' but are persuaded 'by the clamour and sophistry of merchants and manufacturers' to tolerate combination between those who buy their labour or sell them goods (*The Wealth of Nations*, ed. Cannan (1930), I.x.c.25).

the explanation of structural and technological development. Smith offers us in effect both a theory of economic equilibrium and a theory of economic evolution; and in each of these competition has a key role to play. Within *The Wealth of Nations* no obvious tension exists between the two theories, partly no doubt because they are sketched out in a manner loose enough to make it difficult to establish inconsistency. Later writers, however, in striving for greater analytical rigour, developed the theory of equilibrium in terms of a model of reality that is clearly very different indeed from that implicit in Smith's theory of evolution. The question of compatibility between Smith's two lines of thought—or at any rate between the ways in which they have since been extended—thus now poses itself more sharply. Before turning to examine it, however, let us recall what Smith had to say.

We find in *The Wealth of Nations* an account of the balancing function of competitive markets that clearly anticipates our modern doctrine. The essence of it is contained in the Chapter entitled 'Of the Natural and Market Price of Commodities' which describes how actual prices tend to gravitate to their 'natural' or cost-determined levels. Competition is shown to be necessary to this process, it being pointed out that monopoly, by raising prices and reducing supply, would 'derange more or less the natural distribution of the stock of society'. Smith therefore both identifies the tendency towards equilibrium and implies (albeit imprecisely) that the allocation of resources thereby produced is optimal from society's point of view. It may therefore seem reasonable to regard later theories of competitive equilibrium as providing a formalization of Smith's vision with its several deficiencies made good. In this way, intellectual continuity seems to be preserved; what Smith could see in a glass, darkly, it took Walras, with his more refined technique, to bring fully into light. But this view of the matter seems to be mistaken. It appears plausible only so long as Smith's theory of economic evolution is left wholly out of account.[2]

Whereas Smith's theory of equilibrium is set out in Chapter VII of the first book of *The Wealth of Nations*, his view of economic evolution is expounded even earlier, in the opening three chapters. He there discusses the division of labour and what he has to say about it has become so familiar that one might expect all the implications long since to have been drawn. Perhaps therefore we need only remind ourselves that Smith is advancing here a disequilibrium theory in the sense that he views the economy as in a state of constant and internally generated change. Perpetual motion results from the fact that the division of labour is at once a cause and an effect of economic progress. In Chapter I we are told how the division of labour

[2] This paper was already in draft before the publication of Professor Kaldor's article 'The Irrelevance of Equilibrium Economics' in the *Economic Journal*, lxxxii (Dec. 1972) and I did not try to adapt it to take account of what he said. The arguments I put forward here are similar in important respects to those of Professor Kaldor.

increases wealth and in Chapter III how a widening of the market, which increased wealth would bring about, enables the division of labour to be carried further forward. 'That the division of labour is limited by the extent of the market—the title of this latter chapter—is a principle the full range and force of which may have been partially concealed by the fact that Smith discusses market extension in terms of transport improvement. Writing in the second half of the eighteenth century, it was natural for him to stress this aspect of the matter; but unless one recognizes that the extent of the market also depends on wealth, which is in turn created by the division of labour, the dynamic character of the interaction may not fully be realized. Yet what we have here are the essentials of a theory of self-sustaining economic growth, essentials that were to be more fully developed much later in Allyn Young's justly celebrated article entitled 'Increasing Returns and Economic Progress'.[3]

Let us recall two of Smith's observations. He points out that the division of labour, where expanding markets permit, leads to the establishment of new trades. Thus in the Highlands of Scotland, 'every farmer must be butcher, baker and brewer for his own family' whereas in towns these trades acquire separate identities (WN I.iii.2). Smith also implies that technological change is partly endogenous; it is the division of labour, by enabling men to concentrate on particular operations, that leads to improvement in machinery and technique. Smith recognized, however, that although 'many improvements have been made by the ingenuity of the maker of the machines, when to make them became the business of a particular trade', yet others were made by 'those whose trade it is not to do anything but to observe everything; and who, upon that account, are often capable of combining together the powers of the most distinct and dissimilar objects'. We are also told that speculation is itself promoted by the division of labour, it being 'sub-divided into a great number of different branches, each of which affords occupation to a particular tribe or class of philosophers' (WN I.i.9).[4]

Smith therefore provides an account of the process of innovation, sketched out in a couple of paragraphs, that is strikingly close to modern formulations. What is lacking, I suppose, is explicit analysis of innovation in terms of an investment decision in which costs are set against prospective receipts, the magnitude of which is dependent on the demand for the relevant commodity and thereby on the size of the market within which it sells. But this is a matter of presentation; what concerns us now is to note that technological progress for Smith is not an extraneous circumstance affecting economic growth but integral to his theory of economic develop-

[3] *Economic Journal*, xxxviii (Dec. 1928).

[4] Development of Smith's ideas and empirical support for them is to be found in J. Schmookler, *Invention and Economic Growth* (1966).

ment. Fundamental technical advance is not in fact needed to drive Smith's engine of economic growth: it is necessary only that the growth of output should bring into being new activities and processes which would have been introduced earlier had markets been larger and which, once introduced, bring about a further augmentation of output. Smith, however, did not choose to separate the further exploitation of technology from its improvement; for although the two things are conceptually distinct, he realized (as the inventors of 'learning by doing' have since rediscovered) that the one leads to the other.

In *The Wealth of Nations*, therefore, competition is given more to do than equate demands and supplies within the context of a given industrial structure and a given technology; the invisible hand has also to adapt both structure and technology to the fresh opportunities created by expanding markets. In our modern micro-economic theory, on the other hand, it is the equilibrating and allocative functions of competition that obtain all but exclusive attention; technical progress is made exogenous and structural evolution largely ignored. The theorist has come to attend to the things he can most easily handle and in this way our perception of reality has adapted to the development of our mental machinery. Marshall, it must be said, stands apart; unwilling to push aside the analytically inconvenient, and fully aware of Smith's two lines of thought, he reminded us that 'economic problems are imperfectly presented when they are treated as problems of statical equilibrium and not of organic growth'. Indeed he went so far as to say that the limitations of equilibrium theory 'are so constantly overlooked, especially by those who approach it from an abstract point of view, that there is a danger in throwing it into definite form at all' (*Principles of Economics* (8th ed. 1930), 461). Later economists have had fewer inhibitions.

In order to present our equilibrium analysis we now normally take a particular organization of industry as given; and that normally presumed, perfect competition, might reasonably be regarded as a denial of Smith's central principle erected into a system of political economy. For whereas for Smith the division of labour was at any point of time limited by the extent of the market, under perfect competition all the gains from the division of labour are assumed already to have been exhausted. Should the demand for a good rise then, under perfect competition, supply will increase through the entry of more firms into the industry; in the new equilibrium there will be more producers of this good and fewer of others, the structure of industry remaining otherwise unaltered. The price of the good will either stay the same or, if higher rewards have to be paid to attract additional factors, it will rise. Smith presumed, on the other hand, that a sustained increase in the demand for a good would generally permit a realization of hitherto unexploited scale economies and thereby lower its price. Thus he explicitly states that an increase in demand 'though in the beginning it may sometimes raise the price of goods, never fails to lower it in the long run. It encourages production, and thereby increases the competition of the producers, who, in order to undersell one another, have recourse to new divisions of labour and new improvements of art, which might never otherwise have been thought of' (WN V.i.e.25).

It is therefore abundantly clear that Smith had a conception of the working of the economic system very different from that implicit in the formal models employed by modern equilibrium analysis. He appears to have held that the economies of scale and specialization were never exhausted in that an extension of the market would always permit a finer division of labour and a consequent reduction in costs. In this sense, his theory of economic evolution presumes the general prevalence of increasing returns. Nowadays, on the other hand, economists employ a model—perfect competition—which postulates universally diminishing returns to scale, it being presumed that increasing returns must tend to concentration and eventual monopoly. Whether increasing returns can be reconciled with competitive conditions is, it need scarcely be said, a much discussed (and perhaps as yet unsettled) question. Let us now consider it once again in the light of Smith's account of structural evolution.

Adam Smith did not appear himself to be in the least troubled by the thought that competition and increasing returns might not be able to coexist; it was competition indeed that provided the force that drove merchants and manufacturers to seek out, develop, and exploit the inexhaustible opportunities provided by the economies of scale and specialization. It may therefore be that incompatibility between competition and increasing returns is made to appear ineluctable to the modern theorist by the nature of the model of economic reality in terms of which he habitually thinks. We typically start with a fixed list or set of products. A firm employs factors of production to make one of these products and we consider how unit costs vary with the scale of the operation. Increasing returns are said to prevail so long as the firm can increase the output of the product, given time for adjustment, with a less than proportionate increase in total cost. If we then consider a group of firms making identical products for the same market, then it is clear that, so long as any of them experiences increasing returns, competition must produce concentration and, in the end, monopoly.

Let us note first that this conclusion is altered if we relax one of the simplifications of the model and assume that firms are no longer compelled to make one specified good out of the fixed list but can differentiate their product to meet the demands of some particular group of customers. In this situation, as Chamberlin showed, an equilibrium can be reached where each producer operates under increasing returns, with marginal cost below average cost, but is nevertheless subject to competition from rivals offering goods similar but not identical to his own. And the same situation is to be found where each producer has a limited regional market but is in active competition with others on its frontier. To this extent at any rate there is agreement that competition can coexist with increasing returns.

Chamberlin's theory of monopolistic competition does presume an inter-firm division of labour the extent of which is limited by the size of the market; to that extent it corresponds much more closely to Smith's vision than does the perfectly competitive model. Nevertheless, it retains a static character foreign to Smith; preferences and production possibilities are given and the equilibrium appropriate to them represents a configuration of production that will remain the same so long as they do not change. We can come closer to Smith's thinking—and closer also to economic reality—by departing more radically from the framework of assumption underlying our standard competitive models. Chamberlin in effect abandoned the assumption that final output consisted of a fixed list of goods and allowed firms by means of product differentiation to practise a horizontal division of labour. Let us now consider the implications of giving firms the freedom to practise a vertical division of labour by assuming—what is in fact the case—that the production of any one commodity is undertaken not by any one firm but by very many firms each of which specializes in a particular phase or stage of the process. It will for this purpose be convenient to regard firms as undertaking *activities* rather than making and selling products, these activities having to do with the discovery and estimation of future wants, with research, development, and design, with the execution and co-ordination of processes of physical transformation, with the marketing of goods, and so on.[5] We must then recognize that activities have to be carried out by organizations with appropriate *capabilities*, that is to say with appropriate knowledge, experience, and skills. The capability of an organization may derive, for example, from command of some technology, such as electronics, or some technique of marketing. Activities that require the same capability for their undertaking I shall call *similar* activities. Where activities represent different phases of a process of production that have in one way or another to be co-ordinated, I shall call them *complementary*. An example may make the use of these terms clearer. Clutch linings are complementary to clutches and to cars but, in that they are made by firms with a capability in asbestos fabrication, they are similar to drain-pipes and heat-proof suits.

Let us now make use of these notions to re-examine the relationship between competition and increasing returns. Whereas previously we assumed a number of competing firms to be making the same product, we must now envisage them as undertaking the same set of activities. If of

[5] The following analysis of production in terms of activities is set out more fully in my article 'The Organisation of Industry', *Economic Journal*, lxxxii (1972).

course these activities are strictly inseparable, in the sense that the firm has no option save to expand or contract the complete set, then the situation is as it was; increasing returns, if they operate, will apply to the scale of the complete set and concentration remains inevitable so long as the competitors are selling in the same market. But strict inseparability will be unusual; firms will normally be able to expand or acquire some activities and to contract or abandon others. The activities within the set, moreover, may each individually exhibit increasing returns (though in different degrees), and although complementary, they will in general not be similar. Given these conditions, firms will usually seek a selective rather than a uniform expansion, tending to specialize in a more closely similar group of activities and coming to rely, to an increasing extent, on sales to or purchases from other businesses. Whether or not increasing returns operate with respect to the activity set as a whole may therefore be irrelevant; it will not shape the developing industrial structure so long as firms can find it appropriate to expand selectively the activities in which, relative to competitors, they have a comparative advantage.

As a general rule, therefore, increasing returns would lead to specialization and interdependence rather than to straightforward concentration. But for this to happen, as Smith pointed out, the market has to be large enough. Specialization may offer significant advantages only if accompanied by investment in appropriate equipment (which may have a minimum economic scale) and given the sustained attention of a technical and managerial team. The market for a firm seeking to specialize in a particular activity will be provided by firms which originally undertook it themselves but gave it up (and therewith any attendant advantages from self-sufficiency) when an outside supplier offered a sufficient cost saving. Some of these firms may be in the same industry as the company now embarked on specialization, but others may operate in widely different fields. In examining the relationship between competition and increasing returns we first focused on a single group of competitors and the changes that would be produced within it, but these changes will interact with structural changes in industry generally so that the extent of the division of labour, as Smith said, will depend upon the size of the market as a whole.

Structural mutation of this kind is described by Smith in terms of characteristically simple examples. At one stage of a country's economic growth, the market may be large enough to support the trade of a carpenter, but only as markets further expand would this trade come to be further differentiated into those of joiner, cabinet-maker, wheelwright, ploughwright, cart-maker, and the like. That the same tendency is still at work is evidenced by the emergence of the many component makers supplying the automobile industry or by the fact that management can now turn to an increasingly wide range of consultants specializing not only in such broad fields as business organization, advertising, and market research, but also in particular technologies such as lighting, ventilation, or paper-making. But it is perhaps important to keep in mind that increasing returns *need* not produce vertical disintegration any more than they *need* produce straightforward market concentration. There may be important technical advantages in undertaking linked activities in the same place; thus the manufacture of glucose is conveniently carried out in conjunction with the wet milling of starch and paper-making in conjunction with the production of wood pulp. The consolidation of complementary activities within a single enterprise will in any case enable their co-ordination to be planned in respect of both quantities and specifications. What we must not forget are the strong forces that pull the other way, forces owing their existence both to the fact that complementary activities are in general dissimilar and to the fact that each of them may individually offer increasing returns to scale. And where these forces come to dominate, the co-ordination of complementary activities will be secured, not through administration within a firm, but through the market mechanism or by co-operation between firms. It should not be imagined, however, that this outcome need favour small-scale enterprise. Having developed a particular capability, a firm will seek to exploit it through expansion into similar activities. Thus Dupont could move from a base in nitro-cellulose explosives into cellulose lacquers, plastics, rayon, and cellophane; and Marks and Spencers, having acquired marketing and organizational techniques in relation to clothing, were led to apply them to food. In this manner, firms may become very large and concentration may rise in relation to the economy as a whole even although it remains unchanged in relation to particular markets.

I have suggested that increasing returns may lead not to market concentration but to specialization and interdependence. But is it not the case, one might argue, that the tendency to monopoly will in the long run again reassert itself, if not in relation to complete sets of activities, then in relation to the component activities themselves? Will we not find, at the end of the road, precisely that state of monopolistic competition described by Chamberlin, the only difference being that differentiation takes place in the vertical as well as the horizontal dimension?

One answer to this question, and the most fundamental, is that the end of the road may never be reached. And this indeed is the implication of Smith's evolutionary theory. For just as one set of activities was separable into a number of components, so may each of these in turn become the field for a further division of labour. Any movement to concentration and monopoly, in respect of any one activity, may therefore be set aside in the same way as was the tendency towards monopolization of the set from which it came. Whether monopoly does in fact result is of course partly a matter of words; the smaller the degree of differentiation we make the ground for recognizing a distinct activity, the greater will be the apparent prevalence of monopoly but the keener the competition to which monopolists are subject. But monopoly power is likely to be weakened not only by the presence of substitutes and the threat of entry as ordinarily understood. Established positions are constantly under pressure not merely because of autonomous changes in taste and technique but also by virtue of the fact that at any point of time there will exist unexploited opportunities for the division of labour and the consequent regrouping of activities. For according to Smith's theory of economic development, industrial structures will be in constant need of adaptation; the very process of adaptation, by increasing productivity and therefore market size, ensures that the adaptation is no longer appropriate to the opportunities it has itself created.[6]

Increasing returns, it has been argued, may lead firms to expand selectively into similar activities rather than to push for ever larger market shares. The logic of this strategy is further strengthened, moreover, when we turn from the side of costs to that of demand. It may be easier to outflank a competitor than to take him head on, and easier to expand into new markets than painfully to edge competitors out of old ones. By the time that a firm has gained a substantial share in one market, it may be time to start looking for others; nothing stands still and there is little point in finally gaining a monopoly when demand for the product starts to turn down. With the benefit of hindsight, one may wonder whether Kreuger's famous attempt to establish a world match monopoly made much financial sense.

We have been considering whether monopoly would necessarily be produced (as our equilibrium theory might make us suppose) by increasing returns. It may be instructive, in conclusion, to ask why monopoly should not emerge in any case simply because firms choose to come together. On the face of it, they would gain from doing so. Even if the merger of all the firms in an industry was expected to leave total profits no higher than before, at least the firms would be relieved of uncertainty about the likely size of their share. And if there were any scale economies unexploited, any scope for rationalization of production or of distribution or any possibility of monopolistic exaction, then profits could be increased and everyone made better off than they would have been in competitive conditions.

[6] Such a theory of unending development might seem to be implied by what Smith has to say about widening markets, technical progress, and the division of labour. Nevertheless, in WN I.ix he envisages a country 'which had acquired that full complement of riches which the nature of its soil and climate, and its situation with respect to other countries, allowed it to acquire'. And in such a country 'which could therefore advance no further', 'both the wages of labour and the profits of stock would probably be very low'. It is perhaps not easy to reconcile these pessimistic prognostications with Smith's stress on the prevalence of increasing returns (at any rate in manufacturing) and with the fact that technical progress is mainly endogenous to his system. The reader seeking an explanation of these matters is recommended to consult the article by Mr. Eltis, entitled 'Adam Smith's Theory of Economic Growth', which is contained in this volume.

Certainly, therefore, there are forces that put firms together; what are the forces that keep them apart?

Adam Smith thought of competition in terms of activity rather than structure and refers, characteristically, to 'a competition' taking place between suppliers.[7] By concentrating on numbers, cross elasticities, and the like, it is easy for us to lose sight of essential characteristics of business competition, characteristics that it shares with competition in the boxing ring or the race track. Surely it is of the essence of competition that the participants hold uncertain and divergent beliefs about their chances of success; yet, despite this, theorists commonly choose to couple competition with the assumption of perfect foresight. As a result, a false assessment may be made of the circumstances upon which the preservation of competition are likely to depend. Let us suppose that a number of rival firms are aware that, should they combine, their aggregate profits would be enhanced. An appropriate sharing of these monopoly profits would therefore make it possible for each firm to be made better off than it would have been had competition continued. On the face of it combination would seem, to the outsider, to be the rational course to adopt. But it would not in fact be adopted unless each firm considered that its share of the joint profits would be greater than the profits *that it itself believed it could earn* in the competitive struggle. If the firms hold sanguine—and conflicting—views about their prospects, this condition might well not be fulfilled both because the expected monopoly profits were not high enough and because agreement might not be reached about their division. Joint profit maximization appears to be the inevitable outcome of oligopoly only when we fail to recognize that rivals will in general hold inconsistent views of their competitive chances. Vanity, pride, pugnacity, nationalism, and the spirit of adventure also work to prevent competitors from coming to terms, but the more fundamental obstacle is surely that division and uncertainty of belief which, however difficult to accommodate within our theoretical schema, is likely to prove an enduring feature of the real world.

Whether the obstacles to combination are sufficient to check the forces

[7] Professor Kornai, in his book *Anti-Equilibrium* (1971), 392–5, argues that genuine competition takes place within a market only in conditions of 'pressure' or 'suction', that is, approximately, of excess supply or excess demand. Given excess supply, sellers are compelled to endeavour to wrest custom from each other; given excess demand, buyers are caught up in the same kind of struggle. 'The concept of competitive equilibrium', he maintains, is therefore 'a complete paradox'.

Adam Smith, it is interesting to observe, appears to have taken the same view, in observing that: 'When the quantity of any commodity which is brought to the market falls short of the effectual demand, all those who are willing to pay the whole of the rent, wages and profit, which must be paid in order to bring it thither, cannot be supplied with the quantity they want. Rather than want it altogether, some of them will be willing to give more. A competition will immediately begin among them, and the market price will rise more or less above the natural price . . .' (WN I.vii.9). Thus Smith seems to imply that competitive activity is taking place only when the equilibrium of a market is disturbed.

working towards it will depend of course on the particular circumstances of time and place. It seems to me that governments may have a more positive part to play here than Smith, writing two centuries ago, seemed disposed to allow them; perhaps even nowadays, however, there is some substance in his view—at any rate if we think in terms of the world market as a whole—that competition is the natural state of affairs. Adam Smith was no model-builder; less than most economists does he seem to make some things clearer by bundling others out of sight. But although his focus may lack sharpness, it was unusually wide.

V

Some Aspects of the Treatment of Capital in *The Wealth of Nations*

MARIAN BOWLEY*

I

IN the introduction to his edition of *The Wealth of Nations* Edwin Cannan argued that neither the theory of distribution introduced into Book I nor the theory of capital of Book II was necessary to the argument of *The Wealth of Nations*. He went so far as to state that 'if Book II were altogether omitted the other Books could stand perfectly well by themselves'.[1] This view of so authoritative a commentator has encouraged the habit which has become widespread, of considering *The Wealth of Nations* in a somewhat piecemeal fashion, as a quarry for building stones rather than as a building. Professor Hollander has put forward an opposing view, treating *The Wealth of Nations* as a systematic study of an automatic equilibrating system and its relation to growth and hence to policy.[2] I myself agree with Professor Hollander. Thus in this essay I intend to consider Adam Smith's treatment of capital in the actual order in which it occurs in *The Wealth of Nations* in order to show how the role of capital came to dominate it, and as it seems to me, to replace the division of labour as the major influence on growth. The essay will also be concerned with the importance that Adam Smith appeared to attach to the role of capital in relation to resource allocation.

It is fairly obvious that in the work of Adam Smith's successors the technical characteristics of the division of labour were taken for granted and that the problems of capital accumulation (and for a time of course population) dominated discussions of growth. The process of this 'take-over' occurred in two stages in *The Wealth of Nations*. The first is associated with the intrusion of profits and the Physiocratic theory of 'advances' into the analysis of the components of price, the price mechanism, and distribution and resource allocation in Book I. The second stage is embodied in Book II. It involved recognition of the direct productivity of capital, the

* Professor Emeritus of Political Economy at University College London.

[1] *The Wealth of Nations*, ed. Cannan (1930), vol. i., p. xxx. All references are to this edition.

[2] *The Economics of Adam Smith* (1972), 19 ff. See also the article by Adolph Lowe, which is reprinted in this volume.

discussion of accumulation and of the possible conflict between the conclusions of the price mechanism analysis and Smith's belief that some sectors of the economy were inherently more productive than others.

II

In the lectures given at Glasgow in the early 1760s Adam Smith claimed that the increase in wealth depended on the development of the division of labour. He concerned himself *inter alia* with the necessity of exchange and of a price system for its development and considered also the conditions limiting the division of labour, such as the size of the market (LJ (B) 211; ed. Cannan, 161). There is, however, no mention of profits and rent in the analysis of the price system. Moreover, in the sections of the lectures dealing with the division of labour stock is completely ignored, though much later on, in the section dealing with the 'causes of the slow progress of opulence', it is explained that the accumulation of stock is necessary to the division of labour, in order to carry producers over the period between the commencement of specialized work and its completion (LJ (B), 285–99; ed. Cannan, 223–31). The basic conditions determining the wealth of nations are also stated in *The Wealth of Nations* itself in a way which leads directly to the division of labour thesis, and the plan of the book is determined by this. Adam Smith's conviction about the division of labour apparently had not changed, but the universe that Adam Smith set out to examine in *The Wealth of Nations* was much more complex than that dealt with in his Glasgow lectures. In the universe of *The Wealth of Nations* he included profit and rent in the component parts of price, examined what determined their levels and set out some sort of theory of capital. Whatever reasons had led Adam Smith to deal only with a simpler universe in his lectures, it is clear that in writing a major work he realized that it was necessary to use a more complex model. Not only were there available various theories of profits, such as Cantillon's and Sir James Steuart's but also the Physiocratic treatment of 'advances of stock' had already demonstrated the importance of capital.[3] Nevertheless it seems clear that the fact that profit and capital theory were introduced into his analysis after Adam Smith had decided that the division of labour was the prime technical means of increasing productivity, and had worked this out in his lectures, must have influenced his treatment of capital in *The Wealth of Nations*.

The 'Introduction and Plan of the Work' with which *The Wealth of Nations* begins is, I think, worth looking at very carefully for the light it throws on Adam Smith's approach to capital. As everyone will remember (when reminded) the Introduction opens with a statement of the circumstances that determine the wealth per head of a nation. The proportion of

[3] See Hollander, op. cit., Ch. 3, and my *Studies in the History of Economic Theory before 1870* (1973), 121–2.

the annual output to population, Adam Smith says, 'must in every nation be regulated by two different circumstances; first, by the skill, dexterity, and judgement with which its labour is generally applied; and, secondly, by the proportion between the number of those who are employed in useful labour, and that of those who are not so employed'. (WN I.3). It must be emphasized that the distinction between those employed in useful labour and those not so employed (as Smith makes clear) is simply a distinction between those who work and those who do not work, the latter being those who are either too young or too old, and those who will not, or need not, work. This is not the distinction between productive and unproductive labour which appears later.

Adam Smith goes on to point out that the first circumstance, the skill, dexterity, etc. with which labour is applied, seems to have much more influence on the wealth of nations than the proportion between workers and non-workers. He has observed that in advanced nations a great number of people do not work at all and many of them consume individually the product of a large number of labourers, 'yet the produce of the whole labour of the society is so great, that all are often abundantly supplied, and a workman, even of the lowest and poorest order, if he is frugal and industrious, may enjoy a greater share of the necessaries and conveniencies of life than it is possible for any savage to acquire' (WN I.4). The first book, Adam Smith states, will be devoted to explaining the causes of the improvements in the skill, dexterity, and judgement in the use of labour which increases the productive powers of labour, and the way in which 'its produce is naturally distributed among the different ranks and conditions of men in the society' (WN I.5). It will be noticed that no reference has so far been made to stock or capital.

It might have been expected that the second book would be concerned with the second factor, the proportion of those employed in 'useful labour'. This factor, however, is now qualified. Adam Smith says that 'it will hereafter appear' that 'the number of *useful and productive labourers* . . . is every where in proportion to the quantity of *capital stock* which is employed in setting them to work, and to *the particular way in which it is so employed*' (WN I.6, italics supplied). No further explanation of 'useful and productive labour' is given, 'unproductive labour' is not mentioned, nor is 'capital stock' defined.[4] It will be noticed that the question of the way in which

[4] Cannan suggests in his comment on this passage that the word productive has been slipped in as an 'unimportant synonym of "useful" but subsequently ousts "useful" altogether and is explained in such a way that unproductive labour may be useful' (WN i.2, n.4). This seems to me a misunderstanding of the purpose of Adam Smith's distinctions. Adam Smith starts by contrasting useful labour with idle, non-labouring persons, and further subdivides useful labour into productive and unproductive. In later passages where he refers to *idle* it is not usually necessary to repeat that both productive and unproductive labour are useful though it is emphasized when he defines 'unproductive' labour (WN II.iii.1). The distinction between idlers and others receives a good deal of

capital is employed is also introduced for the first time. He goes on to set out the actual order of explanation which will be followed in Book II, viz. the nature of capital stock, the way in which it is gradually accumulated, and 'the different quantities of labour which it puts into motion, according to the different ways in which it is employed' (WN I.6). Although he does not mention 'productive labour' in this scheme, it will be remembered that the heading of Book II Chapter III is 'Of the accumulation of capital, or of productive and unproductive labour'. So anyone reading the Introduction can discover easily that accumulation of capital and productive and unproductive labour are regarded as the same topic. One of the advantages of reading the Introduction is that it makes it evident that the problems of the proportion of useful and productive labour and the way it is employed necessitates the study of the nature and accumulation of capital. I do not think this is accidental. It seems to me that Adam Smith was quite clear that the elaborate study of capital was not necessary to an understanding of the division of labour, but that it was necessary if the causes of difference in levels of wealth and growth rates were to be fully understood together with their consequences for policy. I shall show presently why I think this so.

The third and fourth books of course deal with the historical development of policies of the 'conduct or direction' of labour and the theories arising from them. It is here that the critique of the mercantilists and physiocrats appears, and it is natural that these critiques, or the intention of including them, also greatly influence the arrangements of content of Book II.

III

In the chapters dealing with the division of labour as such, i.e. the explanation of 'the greatest improvement in the productive powers of labour' (Chapters I, II, and III of Book I) no reference whatever is made to stock or capital. Nor is there any reference in Chapter IV 'Of the Origin and Use of Money' or in Chapter V 'Of the Real and Nominal price of Commodities'. It is only when Adam Smith gets to 'The Component Parts of Price', Chapter VI, that stock is mentioned at all. In the more complex world dealt with in *The Wealth of Nations* it was necessary, as I have argued already, to deal with profits and rent in relation to prices and distribution. Once introduced, the importance assumed by stock and profits on stock in the analysis grows dramatically. This is in sharp contrast to the treatment in the lectures. In the chapter 'Of the Component Parts of Price' stock is treated in an offhand way. It is introduced as having accumulated in the

attention when he is discussing the types of cities and societies which encourage idleness, and he does of course make it clear that those nominally occupied in menial services are frequently idle, e.g. WN II.iii.12,13.

hands of particular persons with no explanation of why, and it then turns out that people with stock in excess of that which they need for their own employment provide the demand for labour. Adam Smith goes on to argue that people with this excess of stock will naturally wish to employ it in setting to work industrious persons. It is made clear that the stock consists of materials and subsistence. The existence of profits is explained very simply by the argument that unless the value of the produce is sufficient to pay profits to the employer on 'the whole stock of materials and wages which he advanced' he will have no motive to employ the labour (WN I.vi.5). There is still no explanation of why people need stock for their own employment, or why advances have to be made to people without stock.

But Adam Smith goes on to state that profits and incidentally rent are also incomes that arise *independently* of the separation of ownership of stock or land from the labourer. For profits, rent, and wages are described as 'three different sorts of revenue' which when they belong 'to different persons, . . . are readily distinguished; but when they belong to the same they are sometimes confounded with one another'. In illustrating this in the case of the independent craftsman Adam Smith quite casually remarked that an independent artisan 'who has stock enough both to purchase materials, and to maintain himself till he can carry his work to market', gains both profit and wages (WN I.vi.22).

Thus here for the first time we are told, quite incidentally, that stock is necessary to carry the worker through the period of production. It seems evident that Adam Smith must have assumed that this view was generally accepted and needed no emphasis.

The fundamental character of the income distributive system is established by showing that wages, profits, and rent make up and are paid from the price of a commodity, and the resource allocative function of the market/natural price relationship is set out in the next chapter, Chapter VII. It is, however, in Chapter VIII on wages that the whole Physiocratic concept of advances takes over as it were and transforms the elementary idea of the necessity of stock to enable the labourer to maintain himself during the production period. This is elaborated in Chapter IX on profits and embellished of course in Chapter X dealing with profits and wages in different occupations respectively.

The overwhelming importance of the advances made by the entrepreneur is demonstrated by the transformation of the earlier simple statement that people with surplus stock will employ labour as a result of the introduction of the concept of the wage fund. Adam Smith concludes that the whole demand for labour is a function of the ability and willingness of those with surplus stock and revenue (revenue is introduced here for the first time as part of the demand for labour) to use it employing labour. It is the employer who decides in what ways labour will be employed, and it is by means of the advances to support the labourer that the resources are actually allocated to different uses. This realization that the Physiocratic elaboration of the concept of advances was relevant to the universe of *The Wealth of Nations* was of the greatest importance to Adam Smith's development of capital theory.

It must be remembered that hitherto there has been no analysis of a relation between stock and growth, and that there has been no analysis of the productivity of stock. That is, the treatment has been essentially static as far as stock is concerned. Stock has been shown to provide the means of allocating resources between different uses because it provides the advances to labour. It is perhaps this treatment that has led to the view held by some people that Adam Smith did not regard capital as productive. However, the wage fund theorem introduces growth in relation to stock, for, in explaining that the demand for labour depends on the funds destined for the employment of labour, Adam Smith argued (a) that this demand cannot grow unless the fund grows, and (b) that the fund can grow only if stock and revenue grow—that is, by definition, if the wealth of the country grows. This of course leads to the theory dealing with wages and profits in advancing, stationary, and declining states.

We are not concerned with pursuing wage theory, but we must refer to the relation of the rate of profit to saving which emerged in Book I in connection with the advancing, stationary, and declining states. The main features can be summarized: The stationary state was characterized by a rate of profit at which there would be neither net saving nor net dis-saving so that the rate of net accumulation would be zero. This rate of profit is described in Chapter IX as follows: 'The lowest ordinary rate of profit must always be something more than what is sufficient to compensate the occasional losses to which every employment of stock is exposed' (WN I.ix.18). If the rate is above this there will be net saving, but Adam Smith considered the rate of this saving was determined by the wealth of the society and sociological and psychological influences and would not be profit-rate elastic. Similarly in the declining state Adam Smith treated the rate of capital consumption as independent of the rate of profit which would actually become higher than the rate in the stationary state. Capital consumption would depend on the sociological and psychological character of the society.[5] Finally it must be remembered that Adam Smith, like many of his contemporaries, believed that the rate of profit tended to fall with the continued accumulation of stock. The full explanation of the tendency of the rate of profits to fall is not in fact contained in the chapter on profits. The explanation of how the competition of capitals in particular occupations reduces profits (at the same time as wages tend to rise) does

[5] See on this G. S. L. Tucker, *Progress and Profits in British Economic Thought 1650–1850* (1960), Ch. 3, and Bowley op. cit. 193–6.

not really emerge until the end of Book II Chapter V, in the discussion of different employments of capital.[6]

So far then in Book I Adam Smith has considered the technical causes of improvements of the productive powers of labour by means of the division of labour. He has set out his theory of the price mechanism and its functions of resource and income allocation. He has also elaborated the ways in which divergences between market and natural prices of goods and factors may occur, and he has attacked policies obstructing the free movement of resources and the realization of equality between market and natural prices. In this book also he has put forward his theory of the way in which macro-forces determine the distribution of income between factors by determining the *natural* prices of factors. In this Book I Adam Smith has also claimed that advances of stock are necessary to sustain labour during the production period, and shown that advances of stock are of overwhelming importance as the means of resource allocation. He has not, however, indicated the reasons for, or even the existence of, increases in the productivity of labour with increases in the use of stock. Hence he has made no attempt to show that capital is productive although he has discussed the progressive state. Nevertheless stock (and profits) have intruded into the analytical schemes in the vital matter of advances and resource allocation. Thus starting out, as in his lectures, with the thesis that the division of labour was *the* cause of increases in the productivity of labour on which the growth of wealth depended, Adam Smith finished up Book I with the conclusion that a necessary condition of growth was the use and accumulation of capital.

IV

The conclusion as to the importance of capital reached in Book I obviously necessitated the investigation of the nature of capital, and its accumulation. This in any case was necessary before the questions could be answered as to whether or not the ways in which capital was employed affected the growth of wealth and the proportion of useful labour employed—these questions had been formulated, it will be remembered, in the Introduction (WN I.6). Thus it followed that the study of capital was necessary to the formulation of critiques of various theories of economic policy. It is perhaps natural, therefore, that Book II 'Of the Nature, Accumulation and Employment of Stock' should be introduced by considering whether the employment of capital increases the productivity of labour as distinct from merely making the division of labour possible and providing the means of allocating labour between uses. This seems to me to be the explanation of the fact that (apart from a repetition of the order of the discussion to be followed) the Introduction to Book II is entirely devoted to a discussion of the ways in which

[6] See Bowley op. cit. 220–2 and Section V below, n. 9.

the use of capital increases the productivity of labour. The second, third and fourth paragraphs of the Introduction set out for the first time 'the effects of the increase of stock upon industry [i.e. labour] and its productive powers' (WN II.2–4).

In this passage Smith also introduces for the first time the importance of stock in relation to the acquisition of machinery (for although in Book I he had pointed out that machinery facilitated and abridged labour, he did not refer to the need for stock). In Book II, Smith sets out in some detail the reasons why the proportion of stock devoted to different purposes, i.e. provisions, machinery, materials and tools and wages, will change. Provisions, he points out, will become a smaller proportion as each labourer is supported by more capital invested in materials, machinery, and tools. He argues that the ability of the employer to 'make among his workmen the most proper distribution of employment, and to furnish them with the best machines which he can either invent or afford to purchase' is increased 'in proportion to the extent of his stock, or to the number of the work-people whom it can employ'. Hence not only the quantity of industry 'increases with the increase of stock which employs it, but in consequence of that increase, the same quantity of industry produces a much greater quantity of work' (ibid.). Here then is an unambiguous recognition of the existence of a positive marginal product of capital, but it is stated in terms of increases in the productivity of labour. Similar statements appear later in other places, for instance in Book II Chapter II 'Of Money'. Here Adam Smith says that the purpose of fixed capital is to increase the productive powers of labour, that is to enable the same number of labourers to produce more (WN II.ii.7). It follows that capital is not only an essential means of allocating and advancing subsistence and materials to labour, but that capital is also regarded by Adam Smith as productive in a direct manner. I am delighted to find myself in agreement with Professor Hollander on this point.[7]

Chapter I of Book II is intended by Adam Smith to explain the nature of capital stock. In doing this he introduces the very important distinction between stock and capital stock. The latter is defined as the portion of stock devoted to the employment of those labourers who are useful *and* productive. This distinction is generally recognized as crucial to Adam Smith's theory of accumulation and to his analysis of the advantages of the different employments of capital.

The division of stock into that reserved for consumption in the hands of the consumers (including durable consumer goods) and capital stock is familiar to everyone. It will be remembered that the characteristic which distinguishes capital stock, circulating of fixed, from other stock is that it is used with the intention of obtaining a revenue from it. It will be remembered that circulating capital consists of four parts, money, provisions *not*

[7] Hollander, op. cit. 150–6.

in the hands of the consumer, materials and work in progress, and finished work *not* in the hands of the final consumers. The circulating capital circulates over varying periods of time according to its nature, 'either annually, or in a longer or shorter period'. It is 'regularly withdrawn from it, and placed either in the fixed capital or in the stock reserved for immediate consumption' (WN II.i.23).

The significance of the divisions of capital is further elaborated in the second chapter of Book II 'On Money' where Adam Smith shows the relation between money and capital. He describes money as 'the great wheel of circulation, the great instrument of commerce' which 'though it makes a part and a very valuable part of the capital, makes no part of the revenue of the society to which it belongs' (WN II.ii.23). This concept was not invented by Adam Smith and he notes that a number of estimates have been made of the quantity of money required to carry out the function of circulation. The general argument of the chapter concerns the demonstration of the distinction between money and the goods it circulates, the economies made possible by banking, and dangers of over-issue of paper money. It leads naturally to the views put forward in Book II Chapter IV 'On Interest'. Although these topics are outside the scope of this paper attention needs to be drawn to two matters. First and most obvious, the argument of this chapter and of that on interest are necessary to Adam Smith's full critique of the mercantile system. These chapters could not have been omitted as Cannan suggested without weakening Adam Smith's policy analysis. Second, it seems to me of some relevance to the later discussion of the different employments of capital, to notice the importance Adam Smith attaches to the function of money as a means of circulation. Capital had first appeared in Book I in relation to the need for the circulation of stock from 'the haves' to 'the have-nots' in the form of advances, and the function of the wage fund as a resource allocator became clear before the end of the book. Here in Book II emphasis is laid on the importance of the circulating function of money as the means of transferring real resources, or control of them, from one use or one person to another.

We must turn now to the third chapter of Book II which contains Adam Smith's theory of saving and capital accumulation. The chapter opens with Adam Smith's own definition of productive labour, clearly adopting from the Physiocrats the idea that a distinction was relevant to accumulation and growth. Like the Physiocrats he defined productive labour as labour which 'adds to the value of the subject upon which it is bestowed' while unproductive labour 'adds to the value of nothing' (WN II.iii.1). But Adam Smith's definition of productive had to be consistent with his original thesis that the development of the division of labour was the main influence increasing the productivity of labour *and* with the new thesis of the productivity of capital. The Physiocrats' limitation of productive labour to that employed in agriculture had to be abandoned. Adam Smith argued that the relevant distinction was in fact between those who produced material goods and those who produced immaterial goods, services. The contrast was between the manufacturers and agriculturists on the one side and the menial servant on the other. The distinction between useful and productive is now clear. Goods and services equally are required because they are deemed useful; therefore all labour producing goods and services is useful and has value if they are in demand. However, only that labour that produces material goods is both useful *and* productive. Not content to class labour producing services as simply useful Adam Smith emphasized the contrast by labelling them unproductive. In the effort to clarify the distinction in effect Adam Smith explained it as follows:

> But the labour of the manufacturer fixes and realises itself in some particular subject or vendible commodity, which lasts for some time at least after that labour is past. It is, as it were, a certain quantity of labour stocked and stored up to be employed, if necessary, upon some other occasion. That subject, or what is the same thing, the price of that subject, can afterwards, if necessary, put into motion a quantity of labour equal to that which had originally produced it. The labour of the menial servant, on the contrary, does not fix or realise itself in any particular subject or vendible commodity. His services generally perish in the very instant of their performance, and seldom leave any trace or value behind them, for which an equal quantity of service could afterwards be procured.
>
> (WN II.iii.1)

Although the labour of productive labour produces stock, which may or may not be consumed or saved, it is obvious that unless productive labour adds sufficient value to the materials to enable the value of the final product to repay the cost of materials and wages, replacement of and wear and tear of tools and fixed capital and yield a profit on the whole lot, the productive labour will not be employed. Hence Adam Smith feels safe in claiming that in general the employment of productive labour, unlike that of unproductive labour, will add a net value to the product over and above the value of material and wages.

Adam Smith concludes that the smaller or the greater the proportion of the annual produce of the country used to maintain unproductive labour, so the greater or less will remain for productive labour. Hence the means of production for the following year and therefore the next year's product will depend on this proportion. Thus any stock a man intends to employ as capital will be used only to employ productive labour, for only by these means will his capital be returned to him. Any stock intended to employ unproductive labour is necessarily 'withdrawn from his capital, and placed in his stock reserved for immediate consumption' (WN II.iii.6).[8]

[8] Adam Smith's successors differed among themselves as to the validity of the distinction between productive and unproductive labour. For a brief account see Cannan, *A History of*

One of the conclusions which it was stated in the Introduction would emerge from Book II was that 'the number of useful *and productive*' labourers is in 'proportion to the quantity of capital stock' used to employ them. Since this conclusion is the result of choice of definitions for productive and unproductive labour it is not very remarkable, and its interest lies in the reason of why he chose to approach the theory of accumulation in this way. A reason that suggests itself is that the distinction between productive and unproductive provided at least a distinction more likely, *pace* the Physiocrats, to provide a lead to a theory of the relation of savings to accumulation, than his original distinction between the idle and the industrious.

This brings us to the famous theory of the dependence of saving on parsimony. Capitals he said 'are increased by parsimony', they are diminished 'by prodigality and misconduct'. Capital can only be increased by saving from revenue, it is not increased by industry, for the product of industry may be either saved or consumed by its owner. The advances principle and Adam Smith's analysis of circulating capital lead directly then to the statement that parsimony would increase the fund 'destined for the maintenance of productive hands', so that what had been saved would be employed in setting productive labour to work. Parisimony would tend therefore to increase 'the exchangeable value of the annual produce of the land and labour of the country', for it promotes additional industry 'which gives an additional value to the annual produce'. This leads Adam Smith to his famous statement so important to the classical economists: 'What is annually saved is as regularly consumed as what is annually spent, and nearly in the same time too; but it is consumed by a different set of people' (WN II.iii.18).

Everything saved is invested and is transferred from the consumption of the saver, or his friends or menial servants, to the use of productive labour. In short, here is a statement of the theorem that saving is another method of allocating resources between different uses. It has, however, a different significance from the transfer of resources from one occupation to another in response to profitability, which merely alters the composition of the national income in response to demand, etc., e.g. for shoes instead of cloth. The direction of transfers of resources between consumption and saving determines whether the national income is decreased or increased. Further, the transfers of resources between shoes and cloth are stimulated by the tendency to equalize profits in the attempt to maximize profits. The decision to save or consume, however, cannot be dependent on attempts to maximize profits. It has been pointed out that provided the rate of profit is above some crucial minimum, the decision to save or consume and how

the Theories of Production and Distribution in English Classical Political Economy from 1776 to 1848 (1894), 25ff.

much to save will depend on income and on psychological and sociological influences. Profit maximization as a resource allocator only comes in at the micro-level in determining *how* the savings are invested, and there it is apparently the sole determining factor. Moreover, it seems that the decision to save *should* be for eternity, and that no time preference *should* lead to decisions to consume capital. This is made clear in the remarkable passage describing parsimony as an almost sacred act. The frugal man by saving, Adam Smith declared, not only provides for the maintenance of an additional number of productive labourers 'for that or the ensuing year, but, like the founder of a public workhouse, he establishes as it were a perpetual fund for the maintenance of an equal number in all times to come'. It is guarded by a very powerful principle, 'the plain and evident interest' of its owners, for 'no part of it can ever afterwards be employed to maintain any but productive hands, without an evident loss to the person who thus *perverts it from its proper destination*' (my italics) The idea of consuming capital by treating as revenue that which his forefathers 'had, as it were, consecrated to the maintenance of industry' seemed to Adam Smith antisocial. Every prodigal diminished the fund for the maintenance of productive labour and consequently the annual produce of the whole country, the real wealth and revenue of its inhabitants. The prodigal by 'feeding the idle with the bread of the industrious, tends not only to beggar himself, but to impoverish his country' (WN II.iii.20).

In short, Adam Smith argued that 'the annual produce of the land and labour of any nation' can only be increased 'in its value' by increasing the number of productive labourers or their productivity. No significant increase of either sort can be made, he declared, without an increase of capital, either to provide the advances for the additional productive labourers, or to improve or increase the machines available, or to provide for a more effective division of labour (WN II.iii.32). Thus by the end of the chapter 'On Accumulation' (Book II Chapter III) Adam Smith had concluded that all significant increases in output depended on capital investment. After dealing with interest in Chapter IV he was ready, in Chapter V, to take up the outstanding question of whether employment of capital in one of the main sectors of the economy was superior to another from the point of view of the size or growth of annual income.

V

In the *Lectures* Adam Smith had already stated that agriculture was 'of all other arts the most beneficent to society' (LJ (B) 289; ed. Cannan, 224). As everyone knows he had not changed this opinion when he came to write *The Wealth of Nations*. Possibly indeed acquaintance with the Physiocrats had strengthened his belief. Since he disagreed, however, with the extreme claims on behalf of agriculture of the Physiocrats on the one hand and the mercantilist extreme views about trade on the other, he had to investigate the problem.

He was faced with the question of whether the attempts of entrepreneurs to maximize their profit in a free market led to faster growth than could be obtained by encouragement of special sectors. This question, of such importance for the development of classical economics, makes Book II Chapter V 'Of the different Employments of Capitals' of particular interest. The chapter also shows the importance that I think Adam Smith attached to the resource allocation role of capital developed in Book I, for it seems to me that it includes an attempt to measure in some way the benefits of this allocative function.

In order to compare the advantage of different ways of employing capital, Adam Smith needed some means of measuring the productivity of a given amount of capital in different sectors of the economy. He regarded this productivity as identical with the net product of, or 'value added' by the capital to, the annual produce, i.e. the total of wages, rents, and profits after replacing the materials and instruments used up and maintaining the fixed capital.

He had already concluded that the only way of increasing the annual value of the national income was to increase the number of productive labourers employed, or to increase their productivity. Productive labour only being employed by capital, it is easy to slip over to the conclusion that the number of productive labourers employed by £x of capital provides a test of the addition to the annual wealth of the community by that £x of capital. It is in this sort of way I suggest that he was led to taking the numbers of productive labourers employed by £x of capital as the measure of the net product of that investment in a particular employment. In brief, instead of doing what the Census of Production commonly does, working out the net product of an industry and then dividing it by the numbers employed and calling this the net product per head of labour, he tried to discover the net product per £x invested. It is evident that these sort of considerations could lead him to ignore the great difficulty of defining capital so as to be able to make valid comparisons of the sort that he wanted.

A further reason can be suggested. In all his discussion of capital and the productivity of capital he never allocated the product between labour and capital in terms of their *relative productive contributions*, to use Say's terminology. He always referred to the productivity of labour being increased by the use of capital, i.e. he thought in terms of the gross product of labour and capital together. Hence it was easy for him to forget that part of the net output of an investment of £x will be due to the use of capital invested in materials, tools, etc., and output will not therefore increase in proportion to the number of productive labourers employed. Indeed it is easy to show the reverse may be the case. Thus the larger the proportion of the capital used in advancing wages, the less is available for providing materials and other aids to labour, and the productivity of his individual labourer will decline on Adam Smith's own principles expounded in many places in *The Wealth of Nations*. However, as he included wages both in circulating capital *and* in the annual income, Adam Smith (perhaps naturally in a pioneering study) seems to have overlooked this.

It is easy to show the failure of Adam Smith's attempt to use the number of productive labourers employed as the measure of the net contribution of, the value added by, £*x* of capital employed in different ways.[9] The failure concerns this essay relatively little. What is relevant here is that Adam Smith tried to make a measurement and that he himself believed that he had been successful. Hence he believed that he had shown that the net product of £*x* of capital employed was greater in agriculture than in industry, in industry than in wholesale trade, and greater in wholesale than in retail trade. His discussion of various types of trade is particularly interesting. For instance he stressed the importance of the function of the retailer's capital which he said 'replaces, together with its profits, that of the merchant from whom he purchases goods, and thereby enables him to continue in business'. Similarly the capital of the wholesaler is shown to replace, with a profit, the capitals of the farmers and manufacturers whose goods he purchases and whom he thus enables to continue in operation. Adam Smith adds 'it is by this service chiefly that he [the merchant] contributes indirectly to support the productive labour of the society, and to increase the value of its annual produce' (WN II.v.10). Here is another illustration of the importance that Adam Smith attached to the resource allocation function of capital which appeared in Book I. It is the conviction of this importance, it seems to me, that provides at least part of the explanation of his attempt to assess the relative contributions to production (i.e. the relative desirability) of different types of trade. This is why the capital engaged in the internal trade, which Adam Smith argues enables the capitals of two sets of home producers to be replaced with their profits, is regarded by him as generally able to give 'encouragement and support to a greater quantity of productive labour in that country, and increase the value of its annual produce more than an equal capital employed in the foreign trade of consumption' (WN II.v.31).

Adam Smith's measurement confirmed his own belief in the intrinsic superiority of agriculture. It also confirmed his conviction that supporters of the mercantile system were mistaken in their predilection for foreign trade. The negative conclusion that the less productive sectors should not be specially encouraged presented no difficulties. It was not so evident that

[9] e.g. Hollander, op. cit. 198–9. The whole of the section on the structure of capital (188–99) and Ch. 10 throw much light on the problem of identifying the issues with which Adam Smith was concerned.

the particularly productive sectors, e.g. agriculture, should not be encouraged. Adam Smith had the authority of the Physiocrats, however, for the view that any type of sectoral encouragement was wrong and that free internal and external trade with competitive markets would allocate resources so as to maximize growth. He sets out their argument with obvious approval in his critique of their system which he describes in this connection as 'liberal and generous' (WN IV.ix.24).

Adam Smith did not rely on the authority of the Physiocrats, however. He introduced the influence of demand on value to provide a conclusive argument against intervention. Thus he argued:

> When the produce of any particular branch of industry exceeds what the demand of the country requires, the surplus must be sent abroad, and exchanged for something for which there is a demand at home. Without such exportation, a part of the productive labour of the country must cease, and the value of its annual produce diminish.
>
> (WN II.v.33)

He justifies this argument by the example of Great Britain as a country with a limited range of productive endowments, which would produce more corn, woollens, and hardware than the demand of the home market required, therefore 'the surplus . . . must be sent abroad, and exchanged for something for which there is a demand at home. It is only by means of such exportation, that this surplus can acquire a value sufficient to compensate the labour and expenses of producing it' (WN II.v.33). When the foreign goods bought with the exports 'exceed the demand of the home market', they must be re-exported in exchange for 'something more in demand at home'. Adam Smith concludes that 'the most roundabout foreign trade of consumption, therefore, may, upon some occasions, be as necessary for supporting the productive labour of the country, and the value of its produce, as the most direct'. Ultimately, when the stock of the country becomes so great that it cannot all be 'employed in supplying the consumption, and supporting the productive labour', the suplus will flow into the carrying trade and perform these services for other countries, benefiting itself presumably only by the receipt of profits (WN II.v.35).

This argument, it will be noticed, helps to complete the fragmentary discussion of the tendency of the rate of profits to fall in Book I, Chapter IX.[10] The main significance of the argument directly relevant to this essay is not this, however. It is that the passage rejects additions to physical output as the criterion of productivity. It recognizes that demand is necessary to give value to goods, that the demand for any one good can be satiated and that it is variety which is important in maintaining aggregate demand. This is consistent with both the rejection of the physical input

[10] On the falling rate of profit see Tucker, op. cit. Ch. IV, Hollander, op. cit. 179ff., and Bowley, op. cit. 220–2.

(labour) theory of value and the discussions of the nature of wants in Book I. The conclusions depend on the previous analysis of value and prices. Thus decreases in the prices of individual products with increases of capital employed in their production indicate absolute or relative surpluses; the falling profits lead to shifts in investment in the attempt to earn better profits. Hence the maximization of profit motive leads to resource allocation in response to demand, irrespective of the superior productivity of different employments of capital assessed by a physical measure, the numbers of productive labourers employed. Even if Adam Smith's physical measure of productivity had been adequate and had led to the same conclusion, it is clear that it would have been rejected in the same way by taking into account the influence of demand on value. The case for non-intervention and reliance on the price mechanism is automatically demonstrated in Adam Smith's opinion. Nevertheless the importance of different physical net products of different employments of capital is not wholly abandoned; Adam Smith uses it to help explain the differences in rates of growth that may be expected in countries at different stages of development.

The conclusion about the different employments of capital were reached independently of the division of labour, and the whole discussion of capital in Book II appears to treat capital accumulation as the more fundamental factor in relation to growth. The 'take over' of the dominant role by capital was completed. Nevertheless the way in which Adam Smith had introduced capital into his analytical system, via the applications of the concept of advances to the division of labour, did, I think, affect his treatment of capital significantly. It seems to account for his emphasis on the resource allocation function of the use of capital, illustrated for instance by this method of separating capital stock from stock by which capital investment was defined as a particular way of using stock. It can also explain the attraction to him of the distinction between productive and unproductive labour. This made it easy to argue that parsimony (and therefore capital accumulation) essentially merely involved a transfer of resources between uses, the use of labour in one way rather than in another. However unsatisfactory his definitions must be considered, they had the consequence of introducing capital as involving a particular method of using resources, as a process. There is a strong resemblance between this concept of a process and the later developments of the theory of the capitalistic process of production by Bohm-Bawerk. One aspect of Adam Smith's approach led to much difficulty to later economists and seems to have confused Adam Smith himself. This was his continuation of the custom of writing in terms of changes in the productivity of labour when he really meant the productivity of labour and capital combined, it was, however, a natural consequence of approaching the theory of capital via the division of labour.

VI

Adam Smith on Profits—Paradox Lost and Regained

NATHAN ROSENBERG*

ADAM Smith's treatment of the business community in general and the entrepreneur in particular is an especially interesting subject.[1] It seemed therefore to be both useful and rewarding to ferret out and to examine Smith's treatment of the role of the entrepreneur in *The Wealth of Nations*.[2] After all, in a book which has been regarded as the *locus classicus* of the *laissez-faire* ideology for 200 years, a book which shook the world by recommending a maximum degree of freedom for business enterprise—in such a book surely the entrepreneur would play a major role. Although this originally seemed like a reasonable expectation, it was not fulfilled. As I should certainly have realized, Smith's analytical distinctions here were inevitably limited by the modest state of capitalist development itself, and the relatively small degree of specialization of function which still prevailed in the middle of the eighteenth century. Indeed, Smith had made a significant contribution to analytical economics merely by his forceful recognition of profit on capital as constituting a separate and distinct income category.[3]

I have not, I am happy to report, returned from this brief excursion into intellectual history completely empty-handed. Instead of the story which I had hoped to tell, I want to report upon a rather unexpected paradox which

* Professor of Economics, Stanford University.

[1] See Nathan Rosenberg, 'Some Institutional Aspects of *The Wealth of Nations*', *Journal of Political Economy* (December 1960), 557–70.

[2] Adam Smith, *The Wealth of Nations*, ed. Cannan (1937).

[3] On this subject, see the perceptive article by Ronald Meek, 'Adam Smith and the Classical Concept of Profit', *Scottish Journal of Political Economy* (June 1954). Meek states (138–9) that: 'Many of Smith's predecessors had recognized, of course, that those who employed stock in mercantile pursuits generally received a net reward which was proportioned not to the effort, if any, which they expended, but rather to the value of the stock employed. In Smith's new model it was recognized that net gains similar in this respect to mercantile profit were now also being earned on capital employed in other economic pursuits, such as agriculture and manufacture. But, even more important, it was also recognized that the *origin* of these net gains was now very different from what it had formerly been. To Smith's predecessors, generally speaking, profit had appeared as "profit upon alienation"—i.e., as the gain from buying things cheap and selling them dear. To Smith, on the other hand, profit began to appear as an income uniquely associated with the use of capital in the employment of wage-labour . . .'

I encountered. I would like, moreover, to try to unravel this paradox. My determination to do so is not confined to a certain taste for intellectual history—although that would be justification enough—but also because the paradox is one which goes to the heart of Adam Smith's *Weltanschauung*.

Stated in somewhat oversimplified terms, my paradox lies in the fact that Adam Smith treated high wages as being unqualifiedly a Good Thing, and high profits as being unqualifiedly a Bad Thing. Why should so eloquent a spokesman for capitalism and *laissez-faire* regard high profits with such a jaundiced eye? Indeed, he closes his chapter on profits with the following devastating barrage:

> Our merchants and master-manufacturers complain much of the bad effects of high wages in raising the price and thereby lessening the sale of their goods both at home and abroad. They say nothing concerning the bad effects of high profits. They are silent with regard to the pernicious effects of their own gains. They complain only of those of other people.
>
> (WN I.ix.24)

So fervently did Smith believe these sentiments that the statement actually appears, substantially unchanged, in two different places in *The Wealth of Nations*.[4]

The question of whether high wages were desirable had such an obviously affirmative answer to Smith that he did not even undertake to justify it but rather asserted it with a rhetorical flourish.

> Is this improvement in the circumstances of the lower ranks of the people to be regarded as an advantage or as an inconveniency to the society? The answer seems at first sight abundantly plain. Servants, labourers and workmen of different kinds make up the far greater part of every great political society. But what improves the circumstances of the greater part can never be regarded as an inconveniency to the whole. No society can surely be flourishing and happy, of which the far greater part of the members are poor and miserable.
>
> (WN I.viii.36)

If Adam Smith's views here do not strike our egalitarian sensibilities as particularly startling, that is partly because of a drastic shift in attitudes which Smith himself played some role in bringing about. For earlier in the eighteenth century the dominant view was of the social utility of poverty. Smith's predecessors were very much exercised—indeed, some were absolutely obsessed—over the socially undesirable consequences of high or

[4] 'Our merchants frequently complain of the high wages of British labour as the cause of their manufactures being undersold in foreign markets; but they are silent about the high profits of stock. They complain of the extravagant gain of other people; but they say nothing of their own. The high profits of British stock, however, may contribute towards raising the price of British manufactures in many cases as much, and in some perhaps more, than the high wages of British labour' (WN IV.vii.c.29). This statement appeared in the first edition of the book, whereas the one in the text above made its appearance in the second edition.

rising wages. It had been a firmly accepted part of the conventional wisdom that high wages would reduce effort, that the working class response to higher wages could be described—in the jargon of a later day—in the form of a backward-sloping labour supply curve. The dominant view was well expressed by Arthur Young, that repository of conventional wisdom, who wrote in his *Farmer's Tour Through the East of England* in 1771 that 'Every one but an idiot knows that the lower classes must be kept poor or they will never be industrious; I do not mean, that the poor of England are to be kept like the poor of France, but, the state of the country considered, they must (like all mankind) be in poverty or they will not work.'[5] Similarly, Sir William Temple, in his *Vindication of Commerce and the Arts*, says categorically of labourers that '. . . the only way to make them temperate and industrious, is to lay them under the necessity of labouring all the time they can spare from meals and sleep, in order to procure the necessaries of life'.[6] Such were the dominant views of Smith's time.[7]

In such a context, Smith's views were both enlightened and advanced. Moreover, they were novel in a respect which needs to be made quite explicit. Not only did Smith believe that high wages were intrinsically desirable because they improved the standard of living of the mass of the population. He also believed—and here he clashed head-on with the prevailing view—that the working class supply of effort was positively sloped, that higher wages called forth greater effort and not less.

The liberal reward of labour . . . increases the industry of the common people. The wages of labour are the encouragement of industry, which, like every other human quality, improves in proportion to the encouragement it receives. A plentiful subsistence increases the bodily strength of the labourer, and the comfortable hope of bettering his condition, and of ending his days perhaps in ease and plenty, animates him to exert that strength to the utmost. Where wages are high, accordingly, we shall always find the workmen more active, diligent, and expeditious, than where they are low.

(WN I.viii.44)

[5] Arthur Young, *Farmer's Tour Through the East of England* (1771), iv. 361.

[6] Sir William Temple, *Vindication of Commerce and the Arts* (1786), 534. First published in 1758.

[7] For an excellent scholarly presentation of the mercantilists' attitude toward labour, see Edgar S. Furniss, *The Position of the Labourer in a System of Nationalism* (1957). For a careful study of the transition from the old set of views to the later ones, see A. W. Coats, 'Changing Attitudes to Labour in the Mid-eighteenth Century', *Economic History Review* (1958), 35–51. Coats states (46) that: 'Apart from a few isolated advocates of a "high wage economy", most British economists before 1750 regarded low wages as an essential pre-condition of the maintenance of a high volume of exports, although the plea that the British workman should enjoy a higher standard of living than that of his continental counterpart represented a tacit admission that successful competition in foreign markets did not require that home wage levels should be equal to or lower than foreign wage levels. By contrast, in the third quarter of the century there was growing support for the view that high wages and rising living standards were not merely compatible with, but were even a necessary concomitant of the prosperity of our domestic and exported manufactures.'

Although Smith concedes that higher wages are likely to induce some workers to reduce the number of hours worked, he is insistent that such workers constitute only a minority of the labour force. Indeed, Smith appears to be genuinely concerned over the opposite possibility, that a system of incentive wages will cause many workers to suffer the deleterious effects of *overwork*. In this respect he is the first economist of whom I am aware for whom this was a major concern.

Some workmen, indeed, when they can earn in four days what will maintain them through the week, will be idle the other three. This, however, is by no means the case with the greater part. Workmen, on the contrary, when they are liberally paid by the piece, are very apt to over-work themselves, and to ruin their health and constitution in a few years. A carpenter in London, and in some other places, is not supposed to last in his utmost vigour above eight years. Something of the same kind happens, in many other trades, in which the workmen are paid by the piece, as they generally are in manufactures, and even in country labour, whenever wages are higher than ordinary.

(WN I.viii.44)

Where workers do, in fact, avail themselves of long intervals of leisure, Smith finds the cause, not in laziness or deficiency of character, but in deeply-rooted physiological causes.

Excessive application during four days of the week, is frequently the real cause of the idleness of the other three, so much and so loudly complained of. Great labour, either of mind or body, continued for several days together, is in most men naturally followed by a great desire of relaxation, which, if not restrained by force or by some strong necessity, is almost irresistible. It is the call of nature, which requires to be relieved by some indulgence, sometimes of ease only, but sometimes too of dissipation and diversion. If it is not complied with, the consequences are often dangerous, and sometimes fatal, and such as almost always, sooner or later, bring on the peculiar infirmity of the trade. If masters would always listen to the dictates of reason and humanity, they have frequently occasion rather to moderate, than to animate the application of many of their workmen.

(WN I.viii.44)

When Smith turns from the examination of the economic behaviour of the capitalist, his attitude shifts from that of compassion and understanding to one of compulsive and cantankerous criticism and suspicion. The long-term interests of capitalists, to begin with, do not coincide with those of society.

the . . . rate of profit does not, like rent and wages, rise with the prosperity, and fall with the declension, of the society. On the contrary, it is naturally low in rich, and high in poor countries, and it is always highest in the countries which are going fastest to ruin. The interest of this third order [i.e. capitalists], therefore, has not the same connexion with the general interest of the society as that of the other two [i.e. landlord and worker].

(WN I.xi.p.10)

As a result, capitalists as a class are simply not to be trusted.

The proposal of any new law or regulation of commerce which comes from this order, ought always to be listened to with great precaution, and ought never to be adopted till after having been long and carefully examined, not only with the most scrupulous, but with the most suspicious attention. It comes from an order of men, whose interest is never exactly the same with that of the public, who have generally an interest to deceive and even to oppress the public and who accordingly have, upon many occasions, both deceived and oppressed it.

(WN I.xi.p.10)

A businessman who had been taught to regard Adam Smith as a capitalist apologist might well be excused for wondering what sort of strange capitalist apologetics this is, and if this is what we are likely to get from our friends, just what may we expect from our enemies? Part of the answer may be stated briefly. High profits which persist are often the result of those private conspiracies against which Smith so eloquently inveighed, or of government dispensations of exclusive privileges.[8] In both cases the result is an impediment to resource mobility upon which the effective functioning of a market economy must be predicated. The alacrity with which businessmen have entered into such arrangements in the past and their persistence and ingenuity in subverting the disciplining effects of the market is the main reason that the text of *The Wealth of Nations* abounds in phraseology extremely critical of the business community: 'the sneaking arts of underling tradesmen'; the 'mean and malignant expedients' of merchants and manufacturers; the 'clamour and sophistry of merchants and manufacturers'; the 'interested sophistry of merchants and manufacturers', 'the mean rapacity, the monopolizing spirit of merchants and manufacturers', traders who argue with 'all the passionate confidence of interested falsehood'.

Smith's criticisms of mercantilism, which take up a large portion of his book, also issue from the same cause. Smith sees mercantilism as the successful attempt of rapacious businessmen to exploit the machinery of government for their own self-aggrandizement. Such efforts really had their historical origin in the exclusive corporative spirit of privileged groups which grew up in medieval towns and cities.

[8] Profits must also remain relatively high in some areas to compensate for additional risk or for a disagreeable activity. For example: 'The keeper of an inn or tavern, who is never master of his own house and who is exposed to the brutality of every drunkard, exercises neither a very agreeable nor a very creditable business. But there is scarce any common trade in which a small stock yields so great a profit' (WN I.x.b.4).

Country gentlemen and farmers, dispersed in different parts of the country, cannot so easily combine as merchants and manufacturers, who being collected into towns, and accustomed to that exclusive corporation spirit which prevails in them, naturally endeavour to obtain against all their countrymen, the same exclusive privilege which they generally possess against the inhabitants of their respective towns.

(WN IV.ii.21)

The violence of Smith's polemic against mercantilism lay in the fact that it enabled merchants to better their condition in a manner which did not contribute to the nation's economic welfare. As a result of the dispensation of monopoly grants, of the arbitrary bestowal of 'extraordinary privileges' and 'extraordinary restraints' upon different sectors of industry by the government, the individual merchant was provided with innumerable opportunities to enrich himself without enriching the nation. Even when legislation is passed with an ostensibly legitimate social purpose in view, the opportunities for profit-making are likely to be restructured in such a way as to lead to private enrichment and not social enrichment. Thus, with respect to the herring bounty, Smith sardonically observes: '. . . the bounty to the white herring fishery is a tonnage bounty; and is proportioned to the burden of the ship, not to her diligence or success in the fishery; and it has, I am afraid, been too common for vessels to fit out for the sole purpose of catching, not the fish, but the bounty.'[9]

The more interesting part of the answer to my question, however, lies not in monopolistic barriers or other impediments to the achievement of static efficiency with respect to resource use. Rather, it involves the realm of dynamic change over time, and broader influences shaping human behaviour. For the growth of trade and commerce and, in their wake, manufactures, are of course associated historically with the rise of the capitalist class. This class gradually displaces the landlord class which had previously dominated the European economy and polity, and had squandered society's social surplus by maintaining a large army of retainers and by what Smith calls 'rustic hospitality'. The new goods made available by expanding commerce bring in their wake drastic social and political changes.

But what all the violence of the feudal institutions could never have effected, the silent and insensible operation of foreign commerce and manufactures gradually brought about. These gradually furnished the great proprietors with something for which they could exchange the whole surplus produce of their lands, and which they could consume themselves without sharing it either with tenants or

[9] WN IV.v.a.32. Smith adds the following extraordinary bit of accounting: 'In the year 1759, when the bounty was at fifty shillings the ton, the whole buss fishery of Scotland brought in only four barrels of sea sticks. In that year each barrel of sea sticks cost government in bounties alone £113 15s; each barrel of merchantable herrings £159 7s 6d' (ibid.).

retainers. All for ourselves, and nothing for other people, seems, in every age of the world, to have been the vile maxim of the masters of mankind. As soon, therefore, as they could find a method of consuming the whole value of their rents themselves, they had no disposition to share them with any other persons. For a pair of diamond buckles perhaps, or for something as frivolous and useless, they exchanged the maintenance, or what is the same thing, the price of the maintenance of a thousand men for a year, and with it the whole weight and authority which it could give them. The buckles, however, were to be all their own, and no other human creature was to have any share of them; whereas in the more ancient method of expence they must have shared with at least a thousand people. With the judges that were to determine the preference, this difference was perfectly decisive; and thus, for the gratification of the most childish, the meanest and the most sordid of all vanities, they gradually bartered their whole power and authority.[10]

The growth of the commercial sector and the increasing control over income flows by the capitalist class are a critical element in Smith's version of economic growth because, whereas the landlord directed society's surplus resources into frivolous, unproductive activities, the capitalist now directs these resources into productive channels. As Smith puts it, 'It is the stock that is employed for the sake of profit, which puts into motion the greater part of the useful labour of every society.'[11]

Smith's sociological analysis of the rise of capitalism—primarily in Book III of *The Wealth of Nations*—has been strangely neglected, and will, unfortunately, also be neglected here, since it would require a separate paper to treat adequately. A couple of things, however, need to be asserted. By providing a ready market for agricultural products, the growth of commercial and manufacturing towns provides powerful new incentives to the attainment of efficient resource use in agriculture. Furthermore, and for Smith most important, the growth of commerce, by dissolving feudal ties and obligations, makes good government possible for the first time.

[10] WN III.iv.10; see also III.iv.5. For further discussion, see Nathan Rosenberg, 'Adam Smith, Consumer Tastes, and Economic Growth', *Journal of Political Economy* (May/June 1968), 361–74.

[11] WN I.xi.p.10. The structure of feudal society effectively suppressed the possibility of capital accumulation from all classes—albeit in different ways: 'Under the feudal constitution there could be very little accumulation of stock, which will appear from considering the situation of those three orders of men, which made up the whole body of the people: the peasants, the landlords, and the merchants. The peasants had leases which depended upon the caprice of their masters; they could never increase in wealth, because the landlord was ready to squeeze it all from them, and therefore they had no motive to acquire it. As little could the landlords increase their wealth, as they lived so indolent a life, and were involved in perpetual wars. The merchants again were oppressed by all ranks, and were not able to secure the produce of their industry from rapine and violence. Thus there could be little accumulation of wealth at all; but after the fall of the feudal government these obstacles to industry were removed, and the stock of commodities began gradually to increase.' LJ (B) 282–3 ed. Cannan, 220.

. . . (C)ommerce and manufactures gradually introduced order and good government, and with them, the liberty and security of individuals, among the inhabitants of the country, who had before lived almost in a continual state of war with their neighbours, and of servile dependency upon their superiors. This, though it has been the least observed, is by far the most important of their effects. (WN III.iv.4)

This good government includes the reduction of crime, which Smith associates with the elimination of the personal ties of dependency of feudalism. He asserts in his *Lectures* that 'Nothing tends so much to corrupt mankind as dependency, while independency still increases the honesty of the people'. And he concludes that 'The establishment of commerce and manufactures, which brings about this independency, is the best police for preventing crimes' (LJ (B), 204–205; ed. Cannan, 155).

Finally, as suggested earlier, the rise of a capitalist class brings an increasing proportion of society's resources—including agriculture itself—under the control of a more efficient class of decision-makers.[12] But it is the dynamic aspect of this point which requires emphasis. The growth of commerce is instrumental in shaping character, in altering tastes, and in providing new and more powerful incentives. The growth of commerce, by increasing the importance of the capitalist class as compared to large landowners, increases the proportion of those in society devoted to parsimony and frugality, 'those who are naturally the most disposed to accumulate' (WN IV.vii.c.61), as compared to those who live lives of indolence and prodigality.[13] Commerce inculcates habits of orderliness, reliability, pre-

[12] Smith succinctly lays out the differences in attitude and mentality between the merchant and landowner: 'The wealth acquired by the inhabitants of cities was frequently employed in purchasing such lands as were to be sold, of which a great part would frequently be uncultivated. Merchants are commonly ambitious of becoming country gentlemen, and when they do, they are generally the best of all improvers. A merchant is accustomed to employ his money chiefly in profitable projects, whereas a mere country gentleman is accustomed to employ it chiefly in expence. The one often sees his money go from him and return to him again with a profit: the other, when once he parts with it, very seldom expects to see any more of it. Those different habits naturally affect their temper and disposition in every sort of business. A merchant is commonly a bold; a country gentleman, a timid undertaker. The one is not afraid to lay out at once a large capital upon the improvement of his land, when he has a probable prospect of raising the value of it in proportion to the expence. The other, if he has any capital, which is not always the case, seldom ventures to employ it in this manner. If he improves at all, it is commonly not with a capital, but with what he can save out of his annual revenue' (WN III.iv.3).

[13] Adam Smith's close friend, David Hume, had said: '. . . (A)s the spending of a settled revenue is a way of life entirely without occupation, men have so much need of somewhat to fix and engage them, that pleasures, such as they are, will be the pursuit of the greater part of the landholders, and the prodigals among them will always be more numerous than the misers. In a state, therefore, where there is nothing but a landed interest, as there is little frugality, the borrowers must be very numerous, and the rate of interest must hold proportion to it. The difference depends not on the quantity of money, but on the habits and manners which prevail'. David Hume, *Writings on Economics*, ed. Eugene Rotwein (1955), 50.

cision, and painstaking attention to detail. Participation in business enterprise inevitably inculcates certain behaviour patterns—in particular, those of 'order, oeconomy and attention' (WN III.iv.3) Commerce introduces probity and punctuality. But it is important to note that Smith's argument makes these qualities emerge and spread *as a direct response to personal self-interest.*

Whenever commerce is introduced into any country probity and punctuality always accompany it. These virtues in a rude and barbarous country are almost unknown. Of all the nations in Europe, the Dutch, the most commercial, are the most faithful to their word. The English are more so than the Scotch, but much inferior to the Dutch, and in the remote parts of this country they are far less so than in the commercial parts of it. This is not at all to be imputed to national character, as some pretend; there is no reason why an Englishman or a Scotchman should not be as punctual in performing agreements as a Dutchman. It is far more reducible to self-interest, that general principle which regulates the actions of every man, and which leads men to act in a certain manner from views of advantage, and is as deeply implanted in an Englishman as a Dutchman. A dealer is afraid of losing his character, and is scrupulous in observing every engagement. When a person makes perhaps twenty contracts in a day, he cannot gain so much by endeavouring to impose on his neighbours, as the very appearance of a cheat would make him lose. When people seldom deal with one another, we find that they are somewhat disposed to cheat, because they can gain more by a smart trick than they can lose by the injury which it does their character. . . . Wherever dealings are frequent, a man does not expect to gain so much by any one contract, as by probity and punctuality in the whole, and a prudent dealer, who is sensible of his real interest, would rather choose to lose what he has a right to, than give any ground for suspicion. Everything of this kind is odious as it is rare. When the greater part of people are merchants, they always bring probity and punctuality into fashion, and these, therefore, are the principal virtues of a commercial nation.

This discussion of the character-forming aspects of a commercial society now provides the basis for our confrontation with the 'paradox of high profits', with which this paper is concerned. A commercial society needs to be perceived as a set of institutions which, although at one level it may be treated as a collection of legally free individuals engaging in free contractual agreements, at another level is an intensely coercive system. By this I mean that, in order to succeed under a system of competitive capitalism, one needs to develop certain characteristics—the characteristics of order, economy, attention, and probity, with which Smith is concerned and which are the qualities essential for success under the unique pressures imposed upon individual participants in the business arena by capitalist institutions. The capitalist is haunted by the spectre of bankruptcy. 'Bankruptcy is

[14] LJ (B), 326–28, ed. Cannan, 253–5. For Smith's characterization of the 'inconveniences' of a commercial society, see also 328–33, ed. Cannan, 255–59.

perhaps the greatest and most humiliating calamity which can befal an innocent man. The greater part of men, therefore, are sufficiently careful to avoid it. Some, indeed, do not avoid it; as some do not avoid the gallows' (WN II.iii.29). These characteristics, it should be clear, do not come naturally to man. Man does not by nature prefer the active and energetic life to the life of indolence and repose. Indeed, Smith asserts that 'It is the interest of every man to live as much at his ease as he can' (WN V.i.f.7). As a consequence, Smith regards it as axiomatic that 'In every profession, the exertion of the greater part of those who exercise it, is always in proportion to the necessity they are under of making that exertion' (WN V.i.f.4). Landlords '. . . are the only one of the three orders whose revenue costs them neither labour nor care, but comes to them, as it were, of its own accord, and independent of any plan or project of their own' (WN I.xi.p.8). Their characteristic indolence, therefore, is viewed by Smith as '. . . the natural effect of the ease and security of their situation'.[15]

But, while the landed classes live a life of indolence, self-indulgence, and ostentation, they are merely doing what other classes would do if they had the opportunity. For 'A man of a large revenue, *whatever may be his profession*, thinks he ought to live like other men of large revenues; and to spend a great part of his time in festivity, in vanity, and in dissipation.'[16] The great virtue of competitive capitalism, from this point of view, is that the intense pressures of the market place render such behaviour extremely difficult or impossible on the part of the capitalist class. So long as profits are difficult to earn, and so long as competitive pressures keep the rate of profit low, the system itself may be relied upon to force the capitalist to display the traditional virtues of his class. However, high rates of profit, when they persist, constitute evidence that the competitive mechanism is, for whatever reason, not functioning properly. While it is obvious that this has undesirable consequences in terms of resource allocation (WN IV.viii.

[15] WN I.xi.p.8. In speaking of large landed proprietors, Smith remarks: 'To improve land with profit, like all other commercial projects, requires an exact attention to small savings and small gains, of which a man born to a great fortune, even though naturally frugal, is very seldom capable. The situation of such a person naturally disposes him to attend rather to ornament which pleases his fancy, than to profit for which he has so little occasion. The elegance of his dress, of his equipage, of his house, and household furniture, are objects which from his infancy he has been accustomed to have some anxiety about. The turn of mind which this habit naturally forms, follows him when he comes to think of the improvement of land. He embellishes perhaps four or five hundred acres in the neighbourhood of his house, at ten times the expence which the land is worth after all his improvements; and finds that if he was to improve his whole estate in the same manner, and he has little taste for any other, he would be a bankrupt before he had finished the tenth part of it' (WN III.ii.7).

[16] WN V.i.g.42, italics supplied. Similarly, although Smith's statement about landlords who 'love to reap where they never sowed' is frequently cited, it is usually cited minus a critical qualification which Smith attaches. 'As soon as the land of any country has all become private property, the landlords, *like all other men*, love to reap where they never sowed, and demand a rent even for its natural produce' (WN I.vi.8. italics supplied).

c.25), it has not been commonly noticed that such easily earned profits had other undesirable consequences, to which Smith attached enormous importance. For:

> . . . besides all the bad effects to the country in general, which have already been mentioned as necessarily resulting from a high rate of profit; there is one more fatal, perhaps, than all these put together, but which, if we may judge from experience, is inseparably connected with it. The high rate of profit seems every where to destroy that parsimony which in other circumstances is natural to the character of the merchant. When profits are high, that sober virtue seems to be superfluous, and expensive luxury to suit better the affluence of his situation. But the owners of the great mercantile capitals are necessarily the leaders and conductors of the whole industry of every nation, and their example has a much greater influence upon the manners of the whole industrious part of it than that of any other order of men. If his employer is attentive and parsimonious, the workman is very likely to be so too; but if the master is dissolute and disorderly, the servant who shapes his work according to the pattern which his master prescribes to him, will shape his life too according to the example which he sets him. Accumulation is thus prevented in the hands of all those who are naturally the most disposed to accumulate; and the funds destined for the maintenance of productive labour receive no augmentation from the revenue of those who ought naturally to augment them the most. The capital of the country, instead of increasing, gradually dwindles away, and the quantity of productive labour maintained in it grows every day less and less. Have the exorbitant profits of the merchants of Cadiz and Lisbon augmented the capital of Spain and Portugal? Have they alleviated the poverty, have they promoted the industry of those two beggarly countries? Such has been the tone of mercantile expence in those two trading cities, that those exorbitant profits, far from augmenting the general capital of the country, seem scarce to have been sufficient to keep up the capitals upon which they were made. . . . Compare the mercantile manners of Cadiz and Lisbon with those of Amsterdam, and you will be sensible how differently the conduct and character of merchants are affected by the high and by the low profits of stock. . . . Light come light go, says the proverb; and the ordinary tone of expence seems every where to be regulated, not so much according to the real ability of spending as to the supposed facility of getting money to spend.
>
> (WN IV.vii.c.61)

It is only the force of competition, apparently, which can be relied upon to keep the capitalist from behaving like an extravagant landowner. This is so because a major determinant of economic behaviour is the ease or difficulty involved in the earning of income. While it may be going too far to suggest that, although Smith did not subscribe to a backward sloping supply curve for labour, he *did* subscribe to it for the capitalist, he does believe that a rise in the rate of profit will reduce the quality, if not the supply, of capitalist effort.

It is true that the barbs which Smith directed at the wealthy usually have large landowners as their target. But there is a good historical reason for this. When Smith wrote, in the middle of the eighteenth century, the land-owning classes still thoroughly dominated English society and provided far more conspicuous targets for his attack on great wealth than did the rising class of merchants and manufacturers. But it should be abundantly clear from what has preceded that Smith's sharp invective against the 'indolence and vanity of the rich' (WN V.i.d.5) is not, in principle or intention, confined to any single class in society. Rather, these are characteristics which are attached to the possessors of wealth, from whatever source that wealth is derived, because such possession conditions its owners in highly predictable ways.[17]

This brings me to what is both my final point and perhaps a new paradox to replace the one which I have attempted to resolve. I have argued that Smith's hostility to high profits is rooted in his belief that such profits dull the edges of capitalist performance—as in Cadiz and Lisbon—both by dulling his incentive and capacities as an *earner* of income and by destroying his frugality in *disposing* of that income. The trouble—and the paradox—of high profits is that the *attainment* of wealth corrupts the forces leading to the *generation* of wealth—as is obviously the case with the large landowner. Therefore a recurring theme of the book bearing the title *An Inquiry into the Nature and Causes of the Wealth of Nations* is that, at least on the individual level, the easy attainment of great wealth is likely to destroy the individual's capacity to contribute to the wealth of nations.[18] In this respect, the supreme and essential virtue of competition is that, while it permits the attainment of modest wealth, it places the easy amassing of great wealth virtually beyond reach. It may fairly be said, therefore, that although Adam Smith certainly does not celebrate the social role of the individual capitalist, he does indeed celebrate the role of the capitalist system—or, more precisely, the role of competitive capitalism.

Yet, with all of Smith's preoccupation with the wealth of nations, he also believes that the pursuit of wealth does not take place for the direct gratification or utilitarian purposes provided by an abundance of worldly goods, but rather because the possession of such goods brings their owner the high esteem and approbation of his fellow man.[19] That paradox—and

[17] See Nathan Rosenberg, 'Some Institutional Aspects of *The Wealth of Nations*'.

[18] Smith also noted the inverse correlation between income level and human fertility. 'A half-starved Highland woman frequently bears more than twenty children, while a pampered fine lady is often incapable of bearing any, and is generally exhausted by two or three. Barrenness, so frequent among women of fashion, is very rare among those of inferior station. Luxury in the fair sex, while it inflames perhaps the passion for enjoyment, seems always to weaken, and frequently to destroy altogether, the powers of generation' (WN I.viii.37). It is curious that Malthus never examined the important implications of this statement for his theory of population.

[19] '... (W)hat are the advantages which we propose by the great purpose of human life which we call bettering our condition? To be observed, to be attended to, to be taken notice

surely the insistence upon the relative unimportance of the wealth of nations by the author of *The Wealth of Nations* deserves to be called a paradox—has to be pursued through Smith's earlier work, *The Theory of Moral Sentiments*. But that is another story.

of with sympathy, complacency, and approbation, are all the advantages which we can propose to derive from it. It is the vanity, not the ease or the pleasure, which interests us. But vanity is always founded upon the belief of our being the object of attention and approbation. The rich man glories in his riches, because he feels that they naturally draw upon him the attention of the world, and that mankind are disposed to go along with him in all those agreeable emotions with which the advantages of his situation so readily inspire him. At the thought of this, his heart seems to swell and dilate itself within him, and he is fonder of his wealth upon this account, than for all the other advantages it procures him' (TMS I.iii.2.1). Smith makes this point almost aphoristically in *The Wealth of Nations* when he asserts that 'With the greater part of rich people, the chief enjoyment of riches consists in the parade of riches ' . .' (WN I.xi.c.31). See also Nathan Rosenberg, 'Adam Smith, Consumer Tastes, and Economic Growth', especially 364–7.

VII

Adam Smith and Society's Decision-makers[1]

JOSEPH SPENGLER*

What are the causes that make communities change from generation to generation . . . ? . . . The difference is due to the accumulated influence of individuals, of their examples, their initiatives, and their decisions.

William James

MY general concern in this essay is with the positive and negative roles played, in Smith's account, by those in whom considerable power of decision was vested. My particular concern is Smith's implicit estimate of the sources of change in the economy of his day, of the degree to which change originated with creative individuals as compared to the degree to which it originated in the system and the subsystem embracing those with the power of decision. Worthy of concern but herein neglected is the degree to which progress in specialization and the division of labour, notable in Smith's lifetime, was affecting the number and character of these creative individuals.

The kinds of decisions and change under analysis are those bearing directly or indirectly upon the 'progress of opulence'. For Smith, who early began his search for the causes of the slowness with which 'opulence' progressed (LJ (B) 285–307; Cannan, 223–36), in his *The Wealth of Nations* centred his inquiry upon the nature and the causes of increase in the annual produce—in the annual flow of 'necessaries and conveniences'—of the economies of nations (WN I.2). His concern was not so much aggregate output as average output, not so much output as such as growth of the stream of 'revenue or subsistence for the people' and 'revenue sufficient for the public services' (WN IV.1). The circumstances immediately regulating this flow were 'first, . . . the skill, dexterity, and judge-

* Professor of Economics at the Duke University, North Carolina.

[1] References in the text are to the Modern Library edition of *The Wealth of Nations*, ed. Cannan (1937). On Smith on policy see Lionel Robbins, *The Theory of Economic Policy* (1951), and W. J. Samuels, *The Classical Theory of Economic Policy* (1966); W. D. Grampp, *Economic Liberalism* (1965). On the role of system in Smith's philosophical and analytical approach, neglected in his *Lectures on Rhetoric and Belles Lettres*, ed. J. M. Lothian (1963) but developed in his philosophical essays (Astronomy, IV.19,75–6; Ancient Physics, 1–2) see A. S. Skinner, 'Adam Smith: Philosophy and Science', *Scottish Journal of Political Economy*, xix (1972), 307–19; H. F. Thompson, 'Adam Smith's Philosophy of Science', *Quarterly Journal of Economics*, lxxix (1965), 212–33; T. D. Campbell, *Adam Smith's Science of Morals* (1971).

ment with which [a nation's] labour is generally applied; and secondly, . . . the proportion between the number of those who are employed in useful labour, and that of those not so employed' (WN I.3). At issue, then, is the comparative degree to which, in Smith's opinion, improvement in these circumstances was achievable over time by decision-makers and the degree to which improvement might call for change in the regnant politico-economic system.

Since, in a sense, every individual is an economic decision-maker, a distinction needs to be made between those who are essentially passive and hence describable as decision-takers and those who are properly describable as decision-makers. In the former category may be placed those (e.g. consumers and working men) who, with few options and subject to narrow budgetary constraints, were without capacity, as individuals, significantly to influence the economic situation or behaviour of others. In the second category, by contrast, may be placed strategic, critical, and substantially other-affecting decision-makers.

Smith's discussion of decision-makers is confined in the main to his *The Wealth of Nations*, but not entirely. While he did not identify entrepreneurs as such in his *Moral Sentiments*, he did imply that members of 'middling and inferior' ranks were most likely to succeed in enterprise even as they were most suited to fill administrative posts, and he noted that the road to reasonable fortune was open to persons who were prudent and of some ability (TMS I.iii.2.5; I.iii.3.5). He observed also that, as a rule, greater rewards were enjoyed by the industrious, and that those who engaged 'in an enterprize with forethought and all necessary preparation' tended to prevail 'over such as oppose them without any' (TMS III.i.5.10).

Inasmuch as Smith, together with the decision-makers of whom he wrote, was subject to influences[2] originating in his empirical and ideational settings, these settings may be examined. Of especial importance are the physical and other constraints to which, in Smith's opinion, decision-makers were subject, along with mechanisms of socio-economic change and the connections that bound men together in communities and affected relations between public and private interests.

Smith himself was aware of the influence which the environments of men may exercise upon their thinking, having observed in his early essays the dependence of inquiry upon the presence of established 'law, order, and security' (Astronomy, III; IV.21); he also noted the dangers arising from factionalism (TMS II.ii.3; VI.ii.2.7–10). Plans embodying support of particular sorts of industry 'were, perhaps, first introduced by the private interests and prejudices of particular orders of men, without any regard to, or foresight of, their consequences upon the general welfare of society; yet

[2] e.g. see J. M. A. Gee, 'Adam Smith's Social Welfare Function', *Scottish Journal of Political Economy*, xv (1968), 283–97, esp. 296–9; also Grampp, op. cit., *passim*.

they have given occasion to very different theories of political economy . . . Those theories have had a considerable influence, not only upon the opinions of men of learning, but upon the public conduct of princes and sovereign states' (WN I.8).

I THE EMPIRICAL SETTING

Smith's century, the eighteenth, was congenial on both economico-political and ideational grounds to the development and acceptance of that philosophy which permeated *The Wealth of Nations*. Many of the conditions hindering the natural progress of opulence had been removed (WN III–IV). Moreover, as Wesley Clair Mitchell and others have observed, individual initiative had become a mass phenomenon in Britain. Law, order, and security obtained, making it possible, Smith believed, for individual enterprise to flourish and even for curiosity to foster innovation (Astronomy, III). The great and growing scope for the exercise of individual initiative was conducive in turn to that spontaneous co-operation to which economists were later continually to call attention.[3] Public discussion was playing an ever larger role in government, especially at the local level, and thus was facilitating political experimentation as well as increasing the need for economic and political information and analysis. There was plenty of room, therefore, for the play of man's desire to better his condition and even for individuals to recover from economic misfortune.[4] There were grounds for economic optimism as well. Industrial development, specialization, and enterprise were flourishing. England's economy had been expanding, at least since 1740, so much so that by the early 1770s it seems to have been launched on the path of sustained growth, destined to undergo revolutionary transformation already by the time of Smith's death.[5] Moreover, developments in the world external to England, especially the discovery of America and a sea passage to the East Indies, had enlarged the scope for division of labour and the exploitation of economic opportunity (WN I.xi.g.25, IV.i.33, IV.vii.c.80–5).

Smith himself inferred that man's material lot, which (he believed) had been slow to improve before his time, was advancing at a more rapid pace (WN I.xi.6, II.iii.35–6, III.iv.20). This inference was in keeping, of course,

[3] e.g. see F. M. Taylor, *Principles of Economics* (1925), Chs. 2–3; G. A. Elliott, 'The Impersonal Market', *Canadian Journal of Economics and Political Science*, xxiv (1958), 453–64.

[4] See Mitchell, *Lecture Notes on Types of Economic Theory* (1949), Chs. 6–8. On eighteenth-century England and Scotland see also T. S. Ashton, *An Economic History of England* (1955); Dorothy Marshall, *English People in the Eighteenth Century* (1956); Asa Briggs, *The Age of Improvement* (1959), Chs. 1–2; Phyllis Deane, *The First Industrial Revolution* (1965), Ch. I; Eli Ginzberg, *The House of Adam Smith* (1934).

[5] According to Phyllis Deane and W. A. Cole, average real output rose at least one-fifth between 1700 and 1760, or about 7–24 per cent per year. *British Economic Growth 1688–1959* (1962), 78. See also their essay in H. J. Habakkuk and M. Poston, eds., *The Cambridge Economic History of Europe*, VI, Part I (1966). Cf. Ashton, op. cit. 125.

with the sanguine expectations of Scottish writers, among them the belief that man's institutional structure would improve and press economic man to behave compatibly with the national welfare.[6]

As we show more fully later, Smith was able to infer, on empirical[7] as well as on philosophical grounds, that economic phenomena were interrelated. This enabled him, as Viner states, to give 'to economics for the first time a definite trend toward a logically consistent synthesis of economic relationships',[8] and helped him as well to identify the main economic decision-makers operating within the economy of his day. Smith's insight into the interdependence of the components of an economy not only made him aware of its necessarily evolving character, given change in any component, but also helped him to appreciate the almost omnipresent potential of Britain's growing specialization and division of labour and the corollary importance of its developing transportation facilities and what B. Ohlin later called good 'transfer relations'.[9]

Smith's conceptualization and description of the British economy suggest that he inferred it to be performing all five of what today we consider the essential functions of an economy, some better than others, of course. These functions have been described by Knight and Friedman[10] as follows:

(1) Standards must be set, together with a social scale of values, so it becomes possible to 'decide what is to be done, that is what goods and services are to be produced, and in what proportions'.

(2) Production must be organized by so allocating 'the available productive forces and materials among the various lines of industry' as to get done the things settled upon as most worth doing.

(3) A society's output needs to be apportioned among members of society, preferably in such way as to make a person's share vary with his product and thus provide incentive to efficiency.

[6] See Gladys Bryson, *Man and Society* (1945); A. L. Macfie, *The Individual in Society* (1967), esp. Chs. 1–2; A. S. Skinner, 'Economics and History—The Scottish Enlightenment', *Scottish Journal of Political Economy*, xii (1965), 1–22; Nathan Rosenberg, 'Some Institutional Aspects of *The Wealth of Nations*', *Journal of Political Economy*, lxviii (1960), 557–70; H. M. Robertson, *The Adam Smith Tradition*, Inaugural Lecture, University of Cape Town (1950).

[7] See H. J. Bitterman, 'Adam Smith's Empiricism and the Law of Nature', *Journal of Political Economy*, xlviii (1940), 487–520, 703–4; also Macfie, op. cit. 44.

[8] Jacob Viner, 'Adam Smith and Laissez Faire', J. M. Clark, *et al.*, *Adam Smith, 1776–1926* (1928), 116. See also A. W. Coats, 'Adam Smith: The Modern Re-Appraisal', *Renaissance and Modern Studies*, vi (1962), 25–48.

[9] *Interregional And International Trade* (1933), 176n. See also Jacob Viner's comments on division of labour on pp. 103–9 of his *Guide to John Rae's Life of Adam Smith* bound with the reprinted edition of Rae's work (1965). On changes under way see Ashton, op. cit. On transport and trade see ibid., Chs. 3, 5; C. R. Fay, *The World of Adam Smith* (1960), Ch. 3; WN I.iii.3–7, I.xi.b.5, I.xi.g.28, III.iii.13, V.i.d.1–15.

[10] F. H. Knight, *The Economic Organization* (1933; 1951), 7–15; Milton Friedman, *Price Theory* (1962), 9–11.

(4) Provision needs to be made for economic maintenance and progress, for the accumulation of personal and material capital and improvements in technical progresses and business organization, at rates and in forms compatible with the distribution of the burdens and benefits of the progress resulting.

(5) Since production cannot be adjusted quickly whereas consumption is susceptible of rapid change, consumption must be kept adjusted to production in the short run whereas over the longer run production gradually gets accommodated to changes in consumption. Within this organization three fundamental functions are performed by the price system, namely, transmitting information effectively and efficiently and, by so doing, guiding consumers and stimulating producers to behave optimally.

II IDEATIONAL SETTING

Conceptualization played an important role in Smith's mode of analytical inquiry into the nature of science and its development (Astronomy, II.12), into the organization of society and the nature of man and his response to the socio-economic environment encasing him (TMS I.iii.2–3; VI.ii.2; VII.iii.1), and into the structure of economies and the response of individuals to differences in economic structure (WN *passim*). His mode of conceptualization must therefore have reflected both the contemporary environment of ideas and his view of human behaviour, a view conditioned by his observations and his historical study. His consciousness of the impact of system, theoretical as well as empirical, thus made him always sensible of the macro-economic framework within which man's propensities and micro-economic behavioural tendencies found expression.

When Smith was developing his views, a set of concepts in common vogue was conducing to a systematic approach in inquiry. He lived in a century very sensible of Isaac Newton's revolutionary impact, at a time when what Joseph Glanvill (1636–80) called the 'Climate of Opinion' had for a century or more made for the visualization of the 'hidden processes of Nature' and the revelation of 'an Invisible Hand in all things'—of that 'harmonious system' which, James Thompson wrote, Newton's 'deep searching saw at last', and which Fontenelle pictured in terms of the hidden 'Machines of the Theatre' utilized in French opera.[11] This system, Leibniz had asserted, was the best to be had, subject, as Euler had made explicit, to behaviour in keeping with the principles of minimum, maximum, and optimization.[12]

[11] For citations from Glanvill and Fontenelle see Basil Willey, *The Seventeenth Century Background* (1953), Ch. 9, esp. 188–9. Compare Smith's use of 'machine' (Astronomy, IV.19,30; Language, 41). The lines cited are from James Thompson's poem, 'To the Memory of Sir Isaac Newton' (1727), lines 28, 65; this was in Smith's library as were Fontenelle's *Oeuvres*. On Smith's treatment of 'system' see J. F. Becker, 'Adam Smith's Theory of Social Science', *Southern Economic Journal*, xxvii (1961), 13–21. On Newton's influence on Smith see Skinner, 'Adam Smith', Thompson, op. cit.; Campbell, op. cit.

[12] D. J. Wilde and C. S. Beighter, *Foundations of Optimization* (1967), 4–6. See also Jacob Viner, *The Role of Providence in the Social Order* (1972).

Smith himself noted both the presence of order where chaos seemed to rule and philosophy's role in discovering 'the invisible chains which bind together . . . disjointed objects' and its 'endeavours to introduce order into this chaos of jarring and discordant appearances' (Astronomy, II.12, III.3; WN V.i.f.25). Moreover, he sometimes conceptualized society as a great machine. Essentially a realist, however, he could not accept a 'mechanistic' description in much more than a metaphorical sense (TMS II.ii.3, IV.i.1.10–11, VII.iii.1.1–3).[13]

Furthermore, though he remarked a tendency for good results to be produced even when not expected, as if 'by an invisible hand' (IV.i.1.10; WN IV.ii.9), he noted that the agents seemingly co-ordinated by this unseen hand were not automata but individuals animated by a variety of motives, among them man's universal desire to better his condition (WN I.viii.44, II.iii.28,31,36, IV.v.b.31; TMS VII.iii.1.1–3).

This desire played a dynamic part in both of his main works. Smith found evidence of this desire in man's behaviour and in his economic history, for Smith as for Hume a laboratory, which enabled him to abstract an economic system in operation and to see decision-makers and decision-takers at work in this system, subject to constraints flowing from it and its environment. In the *Moral Sentiments* the object of man's desire to better his condition was defined not only in explicit material terms (I.iii.2) but also in terms of ambition and vanity based upon public approbation and status, usually a concomitant of wealth (I.iii.2–3, IV.i.1, VII.iv.24). Smith added, however, that 'power and riches' merely produced 'a few trifling conveniences to the body' (TMS IV.i.1.8) and that man's moral sentiments tended to be corrupted by admiration of the rich coupled with neglect of the poor (I.iii.3, IV.i.1.8). Yet he did not condemn commercial society, saying that regular commercial relations made for good manners, liberty, and security (LJ (B) 326–7; ed. Cannan, 252–4; WN III.iv.4) and that 'the road to virtue and that to fortune . . . are . . . in most cases very nearly the same' (TMS I.iii.3.5). Moreover, since man was a being of discretion and the one most fit to look after himself, legislatures were incapable of making his behaviour conform to a system of Utopian prescriptions supposedly conducive to man's welfare and happiness (TMS II.ii.2.1, II.ii.3, IV.i.1.11, VI.ii.1.1, VI.ii.2.17–18, VII.ii.3.16, VII.iii.1.2). Smith did, however, find in a system of laws 'that the people can bear' what amounts to a second best (VI.ii.2.17–18; cf. WN IV.v.b.53 on the laws of Solon).

Smith recognized that if generally beneficial results were to flow from man's desire to better himself, there might be need for more guidance of

[13] On alternative interpretations of the meaning of the 'mechanistic' viewpoint of classical science developed in the seventeenth century see E. J. Dijksterhuis's epilogue in his *The Mechanization of the World Picture* (1961). On Smith's views see Macfie, op. cit. 68–71, 112–13, also 40; Campbell, op. cit. Chs. 3, 10.

his efforts than an 'unseen hand' was providing.[14] The ill effects to which 'misrepresentations of self-love' might give rise could be and usually were restrained by the 'general rules of morality' which bore upon what was fit and proper—rules which experience in society had produced and habit supported (TMS I.iii.3.5, II.ii.3, III.4–5, VI.iii, VII.iv.36–7). The state, too, when undergirded by 'justice' (which was more important than efficiency), could keep the factions composing a society in balance (II.ii.3, VI.ii.2) and thus reinforce rules of morality. By contrast, in *The Wealth of Nations*, concerned mainly with economic behaviour and its optimization, Smith counted upon competition—a process barely noted in his earlier work (TMS II.ii.2.1, III.3.6)—to restrain adverse effects associated with man's way of trying to better himself.

> In every profession, the exertion of the greater part of those who exercise it, is always in proportion to the necessity they are under of making that exertion. This necessity is greatest with those to whom the emoluments of their profession are the only source from which they expect their income, or even their ordinary revenue and subsistence . . . where competition is free, the rivalship of competitors . . . obliges every man to endeavour to execute his work with a certain degree of exactness . . . Rivalship and emulation render excellency, even in mean professions, an object of ambition, and frequently occasion the very greatest exertions.
>
> (WN V.i.f.4)

Our review of Smith's writings up to this point raises a fundamental question regarding his conception of the manipulable sources of change. On the one hand, he holds in effect that the impetus to individually beneficial behaviour flows from the propensities inherent in individuals, from the inclination of man to truck and barter and from the desire of each to better his condition. On the other hand, how effective and how generally salutary are the results flowing immediately and ultimately from pursuit of this desire depends upon the nature of the socio-economic system within which the pursuit is carried on. Moreover, Smith implied, systems varied in greater measure than did the desire of the representative individual to better himself. One found only a very moderate capacity for dynamic change in individuals, since they differed little from one another, given similar environments, and, when acting as individuals and in their functional capacities, lacked the power to produce much economic change. Change must therefore originate mainly within the system, in modification of parameters of the system in such a way as to give full play to man's desire to better himself. Such change proved compatible with the general welfare in proportion as the system and subsystem within which the individuals conducted their affairs embodied rules that appropriately canalized their

[14] Cf. Macfie, op. cit. Chs. 4, 6.

behaviour, especially that of entrepreneurial decision-makers. Full compatibility between individual pursuit of self-interest and the general welfare was unlikely, however, Smith's argument suggests, because private interests were too strong (WN V.i.e.28–40). In so far as this argument is valid, Smith turns out to be not only an advocate of individual freedom but also a proponent of suitable, in place of perverted, institutions. Accordingly, a country would grow in wealth and power if the rules of political economy were observed (WN I.i, III.i). Earlier he had observed that while a fair exchange and distributive mechanism could not always make man's command over non-necessities (TMS I.iii.2–3) match his aspirations after rank and station, it did tend to make life's necessities available to each and all (I.iii.2.1, II.ii.3.3, IV.i.1.10).

III DECISION-MAKERS, ENTREPRENEURS, CONSTRAINTS

Smith assumed in effect that a nation's annual produce depended upon how its decision-makers employed the inputs at their disposal, and that the behaviour of these decision-makers was conditioned by the socio-economic environment within which they carried on their affairs. Accordingly, as already remarked, while his decision-makers were dynamic agents, their performance was curbed by the constraints to which they were subject and which influenced other elements in the all-embracing socio-economic system. Moreover, while some constraints and elements were incident upon most decision-makers, other elements affected some more than others, e.g. farmers or landlords more than manufacturers, merchants, or government officials. The constraints Smith implicitly divided into those which are physical and natural, those which are governmental in origin, and those, some of long standing, which are institutional in character. In this section we deal at a general level with propensities of entrepreneurs, together with constraints and systemic influences; in Section IV we deal with types of entrepreneurs.

While Smith does not explicitly define an entrepreneur and his functions, his decision-maker differs from Schumpeter's dynamic change-producing entrepreneur as well as from Cantillon's and Say's. Indeed, it remained for J. B. Say, with his interest in micro-economic connections, to develop the concept and functions of the entrepreneur while Smith's Ricardian successors, interested mainly in macro-economic connections, continued to neglect the role of entrepreneur as such.[15]

Smith's neglect of Cantillon's treatment of the entrepreneur is somewhat surprising in that Cantillon indirectly touched upon determinants of the rate of growth of output per head, attributed by Smith to the relative

[15] G. Koolman, 'Say's Conception of the Role of the Entrepreneur', *Economica*, xxxviii (1971), 269–87. While Smith mentions 'innovation' once in *Moral Sentiments*, he is referring to political innovation (VI.ii.2.12).

number of persons employable who were actually 'employed in useful labour' and to the skill of those so engaged (WN I.3). Cantillon stated[16] that 'the Fancies, the Fashions, and the Modes of Living of the Prince, and especially of the Landowners, determine the use to which Land is put in a State', and that 'the Circulation and Exchange of Goods and Merchandise as well as their Production are carried on in Europe by Undertakers'. In so doing he put his finger upon the two agencies by which economic growth had been in the main immediately determined. For whereas the former group controlled most of that part of the national income which was disposable and investible in economic development in a predominantly agricultural society, the undertakers determined how effectively inputs were used outside agriculture and also accounted for some savings. Cantillon was thus in a position, had he elected to do so, to explain why there had been so little economic growth over the centuries and how the bourgeoisification of society had served to accelerate economic development. After all, had enough of the national income been devoted to *productive* investment in the future to increase average income something like 1–4 per cent per year, it would have been at least 6 times as high in Cantillon's day as in the year 1000 when the medieval upsurge was just beginning.

While Smith noted that decision-makers faced risk and uncertainty in varying degree (WN III.i.3), his conception of the role of undertaker made Cantillon's distinction between uncertain and certain incomes of little use; it ran in essentially routine terms. While he makes the amount of an undertaker's 'profit' depend on the 'value of the stock employed', he suggests that differential hazard and skill may affect this amount somewhat as may the trouble of employing borrowed funds (WN I.vi.6,18; I.ix.16). An investment entailing less risk and uncertainty was more attractive under otherwise similar conditions than one with which greater risk and uncertainty were associated; hence investment in home trade was preferred to that in foreign trade, and investment in agricultural land to that in home trade (WN IV.ii.6).[17] Presumably, what an undertaker accomplished, though not free of effects of aleatory elements, depended, as did his accomplishment in other activities, upon the exertion he put forward in the face of competition. For risk apparently was not very great, other than in a few hazardous trades that attracted the over-optimistic (WN II.iii.29).

[16] *Essai sur la nature du commerce*, ed. Henry Higgs (1931), Part I, Chs. 13–14. On views expressed before Cantillon wrote see B. F. Hoselitz, 'The Early History of Entrepreneurial Theory', *Explorations in Entrepreneurial History*, iii (15 Apr. 1951), 193–200, reprinted in J. J. Spengler and W. R. Allen, eds., *Essays in Economic Thought: Aristotle to Marshall* (1960), 234–47.

[17] On Smith's notions of profit see R. L. Meek, 'Adam Smith and the Classical Concept of Profit', *Scottish Journal of Political Economy*, i (1954), 138–53; also Koolman, op. cit. See also my 'Adam Smith's Theory of Economic Growth', *Southern Economic Journal*, xxv (1959), 397–415; xxvi (1959), 1–12.

Freedom from constraint within a system assuring security[18] was essential if nations were to initiate growth processes and eventually escape poverty and indigence (LJ (B) 285–7,293–4; ed. Cannan 222–3,227); for then parsimony would result, together with efficient allocation of capital and hence growth of industry and division of labour. 'Every individual is continually exerting himself to find out the most advantageous employment for whatever capital he can command. It is his own advantage, indeed, and not that of society, which he has in view. But the study of his own advantage naturally, or rather necessarily leads him to prefer that employment which is most advantageous to the society' (WN IV.ii.4,9). He was alert to the advantage of pursuing manufacturing in towns and in the vicinity of an abundance of provisions conducive to low living costs (WN III.iii.20). There was no need to protect infant industry (WN V.i.e.30, IV.ii.13, IV.ix.22). 'Gain is the end of all improvement', in industry as in agriculture (WN I.xi.n.14). It is not from the 'benevolence' of tradesmen 'that we expect our dinner, but from their regard to their own interest. We address ourselves, not to their humanity but to their self-love,' to their 'advantages' (WN I.ii.2). Where 'competition is free, the rivalship of competitors, who are all endeavouring to justle one another out of employment, obliges every man to endeavour to execute his work with a certain degree of exactness . . . Great objects, however, are evidently not necessary in order to occasion the greatest exertion' (WN V.i.f.4).

In the absence of the discipline of competition, entrepreneurial freedom could result in sub-optimal use of resources. Competition tended to be effective when there was a multiplicity of decision-makers in the form of vendors acting as individuals, good transport facilities that enlarged the market open to consumers (I.xi.b.5, II.v.7, also I.iii.3,4, I.xi.g.28, III.iii.20) and freedom on the part of any vendor to 'change his trade as often as he pleases' and to specialize in so far as he finds it economically feasible to do so (WN I.vii.6, IV.v.b.15). One could infer the absence of effective competition when price deviated from its 'natural' level (WN I.vii.9), imports were restricted (IV.ii.21,22), profits were excessive (I.ix.24), 'management' was not 'good', the best interests of consumer and producer (I.xi.b.5) were not served, wages were held down by masters acting in combination (I.viii.13), capital was undersupplied and uneconomically used (II.iii.19–21, IV.vii.c.88–97), corporate privilege and prolonged apprenticeship conduced to misallocation of resources, and other adverse results were manifest (I.x.c, IV.v.b).

[18] 'The natural effort of every individual to better his own condition, when suffered to exert itself with freedom and security, is so powerful a principle, that it is alone and without assistance, not only capable of carrying on the society to wealth and prosperity, but of surmounting a hundred pertinent obstructions with which the folly of human laws too often incumbers its operations' (WN IV.v.b.43).

Representative of the behaviour of decision-makers in the absence of effective competition was that of manufacturers and merchants. Manufacturers opposed freedom of trade and 'every law that is likely to increase the number of their rivals in the home market'—so much so that 'like an overgrown standing army, they have become formidable to the government and upon many occasions intimidate the legislature' (WN IV.ii.43). Merchants too, though answering most closely to the modern description of the entrepreneur, were not likely to behave in full conformity with the general welfare if free of effective competition.

> Merchants and master manufacturers are, in this order, the two classes of people who commonly employ the largest capitals, and who by their wealth draw to themselves the greatest share of public consideration. As during their whole lives they are engaged in plans and projects, they have frequently more acuteness of understanding than the greater part of country gentlemen. As their thoughts, however, are commonly exercised rather about the interest of their own particular branch of business, than about that of society, their judgment, even when given with the greatest candour (which it has not been on every occasion), is much more to be depended upon with regard to the former of these two objects, than with regard to the latter . . . The interest of the dealers . . . in any particular branch of trade or manufactures, is always in some respects different from, and even opposite to, that of the public. To widen the market and to narrow the competition, is always the interest of the dealers . . . The proposal of any new law or regulation of commerce which comes from this order . . . comes from an order of men, whose interest is never exactly the same with that of the public, who have generally an interest to deceive and even to oppress the public.
> (WN I.xi.p.10)

Smith did not play up the innovator; indeed, in his description of the origin of division of labour, together with his emphasis upon a system of natural liberty and justice-assuring rules, he implies that *continued pursuit* of self-interest by each and all rather than activity on the part of trail-breaking entrepreneurs was the main source of economic progress. His view thus resembles the evolutionary theory later put forward by Menger. For, while division of labour manifested man's nature and was supported by his 'prudence' and his desire to promote his 'private interest', it was not the effect of utility-seeking human wisdom and foresight, but 'the necessary, though very slow and gradual, consequence . . . [of man's] propensity to . . . exchange' (WN I.ii.1,3; V.i.a.14). In Smith's view division of labour was the major source not only of *per capita* income growth but also presumably of his continued optimism (TMS II.ii.3,5; IV.i.1.10) respecting economic growth. 'It is the great multiplication of the productions of all the different arts, in consequence of division of labour, which occasions, in a well-governed society, that universal opulence which extends itself to the lowest ranks of the people' (WN I.i.10, I.ii). The development of division of labour was conditioned, however, by that of complementary, supporting processes. For subordinate to division of labour though determinative of its scope were expansion of transport, the regnant system of rewards and penalties, absence of monopolistic constraints, freedom of each individual to respond to incentives and give expression to his desire to better his condition, and a price and information system that made known the alternatives available to individuals and thus enabled them to choose the more profitable courses of action.[19]

Having described the motives which, according to Smith, animate decision-makers and the forces which drive them, we turn to the universe of undesirable constraints within which they operate, usually to the disadvantage of consumers and their 'consumption' which is 'the sole end . . . of all production' (WN IV.viii.49). These constraints may be grouped according to their sources, man's natural environment, his institutions, and government policy.

Within the first category may be included constraints which are physical or social-structural in character. Purely physical constraints encumbered growth processes in general and, as a result, restricted the options open to entrepreneurs as when physical constraints gave rise to uncertainty and increasing costs, e.g. in fishing, mining, forestry, and branches of agriculture (WN I.xi.c.1–17, I.xi.m.14–21, I.xi.n.10). Of primary concern to Smith, however, was whether, under existing institutional or governmental conditions, undertakers in primary industry (e.g. fisheries, mining, agriculture) were unduly handicapped in their efforts to surmount uncertainty and natural constraints (WN I.xi.c.1–17, I.xi.n.14–21, III.i, IV.v.a.33–4). Of especial concern therefore was a country's transport potential and the degree to which it was being developed, since upon its development depended not only extension of division of labour but also capacity for escape from local relative scarcity of suitable land and natural resources (WN I.iii.3–4, I.xi.b.5, I.xi.g.28, III.iii.13, III.iv.20, V.i.d).

Certain general politico-cultural conditions noted by Smith bore rather widely upon a society and its economy and hence hampered undertakers (WN III.iv.20). Most important was the degree of security (WN III.iii.12, V.i.b.2) and the quality of administration of justice (WN V.iii.7), and quite important were the prevailing attitudes toward business and idleness (WN I.ix.20, II.iii.12,13, III.i.5, IV.ix.40) and the destructive impact of

[19] On division of labour see my 'Adam Smith on Population', *Population Studies*, xxiv (1970), 377–88, esp. 378–82; also N. Rosenberg, 'Adam Smith on the Division of Labour: Two Views or One', *Economica*, xxxii (1965), 127–39; E. G. West, 'Adam Smith's Two Views on the Division of Labour', *Economica*, xxxi (1964), 23–62 and below, 540. On the fundamental importance of capital in the process of economic evolution, see Haim Barkai, 'A Formal Outline of a Smithian Growth Model', *Quarterly Journal of Economics*, lxxxiii (1969), 396–414. On institutional evolution see Carl Menger, *Principles of Economics* (1950), Ch. 8.

progressive division of labour upon intellectual, social, and martial virtues in the absence of adequate countervailing action by the government—i.e. action in the form of appropriate public education for the common people who, unlike the well-to-do, cannot so well look after their interests (WN V.i.f.52–61). Of minor importance was the disesteem in which certain occupations were held, since higher rates of pay served to overcome this disesteem (WN I.x.b.1–32).

A variety of institutions were unfavourable to enterprise, serving, in general, as did governmental policies, to discourage capital formation and the optimal distribution of capital, labour, and other resources among uses. Since most of these constraints were customary or governmental in origin and in effect reinforced by the state, any distinction between constraints of institutional or governmental origin is somewhat arbitrary. This presented no major problem to Smith since he did not need to distinguish sharply inasmuch as the state could give up its own adverse policies as well as abolish those for which it was not immediately responsible; indeed, Smith implies that uneconomic institutions such as slavery tended to succumb to change in self-interest as the burden of their adverse impact grew (WN III.ii.10–16, III.iv.10–15).[20]

Outstanding among the institutions that hampered enterprise were those associated with feudalism and control of disorder in the past (WN I.xi.n.1, III.ii, V.i.g.22) and some of those continuing into the modern period—e.g. primogeniture and entail, which prevented the subdivision of great estates and the alienation of land (WN III.ii.1–7, III.iv.19, IV.vii.b.19), and thus checked increase in the number of smaller and more efficient proprietors. For as a result, social mobility, characteristic of more industrialized society, was slowed (WN III.iv.16), as was the conversion of tenants into small proprietors and the reduction of the exposure of tenants to rackrenting. Somewhat parallel were effects associated with corporations and the apprenticeship system, arrangements originating with the emergence of towns in the time of feudalism; these conferred exclusive trading privileges upon corporation members and limited access of non-members to trades and employments, thereby curbing competition to the disadvantage of the underlying population (WN I.x.c.1–32,44). The rules of apprenticeship, as developed and administered in Britain and France, accentuated the shortage of persons engaged in particular trades and obstructed the circulation of labour from one employment to another (WN I.x.b.8, I.x.c.1–18,41–54). Smith stated that the privileges of corporations and the statutes of apprenticeship should be abolished, along with English laws restricting the settlement of the poor and thereby violating their natural liberty (WN I.x.c.45–59, IV.ii.42). He also condemned combination of

[20] See Viner on the possible reason for Smith's not coming out strongly against colliers' serfdom in Scotland, *Guide to John Rae's Life of Adam Smith*, 109–16, esp. 116.

masters designed to hold down wages and constraints on the right of an entrepreneur to change his business (WN IV.v.b.16).

Governmental policy tended to be unfavourable to a great deal of private enterprise because it held down the formation of capital, made for uneconomic use of capital, and, by conferring favours or protection upon favoured interests, freed them of the salutary discipline of competition. Governments also deprived entrepreneurs of opportunity by attempting to carry on enterprises which they were incapable of running effectively (see WN IV.vii.9, IV.vii.b.22, IV.vii.c.102, V.i.d, V.ii.a.4). By its various policies government thus favoured producer interests at the expense of consumers (WN IV.viii.53).

Smith was particularly concerned at government waste because of the critical importance of capital and hence of parsimony (see generally WN II.iii) in augmenting employment and extending the division of labour. In fact, unless aggregate frugality exceeded public and private prodigality and production exceeded consumption, a country's economy tended to contract.[21] That it did not contract was only because private parsimony tended to outweigh prodigality and to enable capital to accumulate despite governmental waste—'kings and ministers . . . are themselves always and without exception, the greatest spendthrifts in the society' (WN II.iii.36).[22]

Governmental decisions led to misallocation of capital in two ways.

(1) Capital was shunted from more into less productive uses. 'Every injudicious and unsuccessful project in agriculture, mines, fisheries, trade, or manufactures' diminishes funds 'destined for the maintenance of productive labour' (WN II.iii.26). To such misuse government contributed notably inasmuch as 'the whole, or almost the whole public revenue, is in most countries employed in maintaining unproductive hands' (WN II.iii.30). Smith noted, however, that expenditure upon durable goods, even when they were not the most useful, was preferable to that on non-durable goods and services, in so far as durables of the wealthy tended to pass into the hands of 'the inferior and middling ranks of people' (WN II.iii.39,42).

[21] 'Capitals are increased by parsimony, and diminished by prodigality . . . Parsimony and not industry, is the immediate cause of the increase of capital. Industry, indeed, provides the subject which parsimony accumulates. But whatever industry might acquire, if parsimony did not save and store up, the capital would never be the greater' (WN II.iii.14,16).

[22] 'In the midst of all the exactions of government, . . . capital has been silently and gradually accumulated by the private frugality and good conduct of individuals, by their universal, continual, and uninterrupted effort to better their condition. It is this effort, protected by law and allowed by liberty to exert itself in the manner that is most advantageous, which has maintained the progress of England towards opulence and improvement in almost all former times, and which, it is to be hoped, will do so in all future times' (WN II.iii.36). The 'common people' were not given to the 'vices of levity' found among 'people of fashion' (WN V.i.g.10).

(2) Capital was shunted away from segments of the private sector where natural liberty prevailed (I.x–xi) and the wants of the population were economically served, and diverted to sectors in which monopoly and privilege were lodged. At most, he noted, only a temporary patent or trade monopoly was justifiable (WN V.i.e.30; LJ (B) 174–5; Cannan, 129–30). Smith pointed in particular to mercantilism as a system; to restrictions upon entrepreneurial freedom associated with grants of privilege to companies (WN IV.vii.c.9,19,63; and generally V.i.e), to the sanctioning of long time monopoly, so unfavourable to good management (WN I.vii.27–8, I.xi.b.5); to indefensible trade restriction (WN IV.ii, IV.ix.25); to restrictions upon colonial trade (see especially IV.vii.c) and recourse to a system of bounties (WN IV.v.a) that ought to be abolished; and to restrictions upon the export of skills (WN IV.viii.43–8). He observed also that protective policies had even accentuated famine and dearth (WN IV.v.b) and that monopolistic protection tended to make plodders of businessmen and to reduce their drive (WN IV.ix.3).

Smith's discussion of financial needs bore upon enterprise in two ways, in that government was not suited to conduct business for profit (WN V.ii.a) and in that the state could injure business by improper taxation. He pointed to distortion of resource use by discriminatory taxes and tithes (WN V.ii.d.1–3, V.ii.g.8) and by local duties which restrained interior commerce (WN V.ii.k.70–5). These distortions resembled those occasioned by restraints and encouragements of particular activities. Accordingly, he lay down maxims designed to minimize as much as feasible the discouragement occasioned by taxation to agricultural and and other forms of enterprise (e.g. see WN V.ii sections d–g, h, i, and k). Smith was generally opposed to what he considered inequitable distribution of the tax burden. Therefore, he recommended that Britain rid herself of the cost of colonies in peace and war by converting them into components of a federated empire to whose support all would be required to contribute (WN V.iii.88–92).[23]

IV CATEGORIES OF DECISION-MAKERS

Having examined the restraints and other conditions bearing upon decision-makers in general, we may inquire into Smith's assessment of the character and environment of each of the main categories into which his undertakers fall, namely, agricultural, manufacturing, and commercial.

[23] 'If any of the provinces of the British empire cannot be made to contribute towards the support of the whole empire, it is surely time that Great Britain should free herself from the expence of defending these provinces in time of war, and of supporting any part of their civil or military establishments in time of peace, and endeavour to accommodate her future views and designs to the real mediocrity of her circumstances' (WN V.iii.92). Concerning a memorial allegedly prepared by Smith (in 1788) for Lord North, see G. H. Guttridge 'Adam Smith on the American Revolution: An Unpublished Memoir', *American Historical Review*, xxxviii (1933), 714–20.

Decisions respecting agriculture, Smith suggests, were being made by farmers, landlords, and recent investors in agriculture. These decisions were important because of the importance of agriculture's economic role[24] and the dependence of national and urban growth upon the capacity of agriculturalists to produce a surplus. Of immediate concern was under-investment in agriculture, together with constraints on agricultural efficiency flowing from unfavourable governmental policies, defective land-tenure systems, and imperfect management on the part of owners and cultivators of land.

Progress in agriculture called for sufficient investment as well as for 'much more skill and experience than the greater part of mechanic trades' (WN I.x.c.24), skill likely to be forthcoming and appropriately applied when prices warranted (I.xi.1.12). It also called for close attention to the business of cultivation, a condition most likely to be met when farmers and country gentlemen carried on agriculture since they were not given to monopolistic behaviour and instead promoted 'the cultivation and improvement of their neighbours farms and estates' (WN IV.ii.21).

Agriculture was drawing too little investment despite the attractiveness of investment in agriculture.[25] The 'profits of agriculture', often overstated by 'projectors', were insufficient to attract as much capital as it could absorb; for these profits, even if on a par with those in manufacturing and commerce, seldom if ever gave rise to 'splendid fortunes' (WN II.v.37), at least outside America (WN II.v.21, III.iv.19, V.ii.c.51). In the past the flow of capital and management into agriculture had been slowed by advantages conferred by the state upon non-agricultural undertakings as well as by feudal institutions and class structures, systems of land tenure inimical to incentive on the part of cultivators, and insecurity of property (WN III.iv). Some of these adverse conditions had disappeared as 'gradual improvements of arts, manufactures, and commerce' made available products for which landowners had surrendered control of their lands to tenants in the form of long-term leases which made the latter independent (WN V.i.g.25, III.iv.10–19).[26] Even so England's pattern of landownership

[24] Agricultural output was around two-fifths of the total output when Smith was writing, Deane and Cole suggest; op. cit. 78–79, see also Ashton, op. cit. Ch. 2.

[25] 'Upon equal, or nearly equal profits, most men will choose to employ their capitals rather in the improvement and cultivation of land, than either in manufactures or in foreign trade' which are more liable to accident, uncertainty, and insecurity of capital and which do not 'afford the pleasure of a country life' and 'the tranquility of mind which it promises' (WN III.i.3). Of relevance here may be B. A. Holderness, 'Landlord's Capital Formation in East Anglia, 1750–1870', *Economic History Review*, xxv (1972), 434–47.

[26] As C. R. Fay put it, 'the lords of feudalism' abandoned 'their retinues of land pirates' perhaps for 'a pair of diamond buckles', prompted to do so 'by an Invisible Jade'. See C. R. Fay, 'Adam Smith and the Dynamic State', *Economic Journal*, xl (1930) 25–35, esp. 27–8. Smith found in this process an instance of the working of salutary historical forces, 'a revolution of the greatest importance to the public happiness', one unintended by its authors but exemplifying a dynamic, opulence-increasing force fundamental to his theory of

remained defective. Land was insufficiently subdivided and much of it continued to be uncultivated; a system of small-scale and efficient land-cultivating proprietorship of the sort found in the North American colonies had not developed (WN III.iv.19). In Smith's day, therefore, resources continued to be diverted from agriculture by idlers who consumed a great part of the product of the 'industrious' (WN I.vi.24). Among these idlers Smith must have included 'landlords' who, 'like all other men, love to reap where they never sowed' (WN I.vi.8) and leave to a tenant no more than that with which 'he can content himself without being a loser' (WN I.xi.a.1), a practice which presumably reduced a tenant's incentive and ability to cultivate and thereby diminished output (WN V.ii.c.13,14). Idleness on the part of potential workers in agriculture was associated with deficiency of investment, he implies elsewhere (WN II.iii.12).

Although Smith believed that the interests of the landlords as receivers of rent coincided with the general interest of society, he indicated that they were seldom improvers or effective cultivators of land (WN IV.ii.7), being much inferior in this respect to farmers and merchants with investments in agriculture. Underlying the poor performance of landlords was 'that indolence which is the natural effect of the ease and security of their situation' (WN I.xi.p.8) and the systems of land tenure under which they and their tenants and bailiffs operated and shared in the output. For these systems gave no one great incentive to improve, and even when the landlord was inclined to improve his property he might be discouraged as well as made less able to do so by the incidence of heavy taxes and other burdens upon agriculture (WN V.ii.c). Although agricultural progress and profit depended upon modes of cultivation and types of crops (WN I.xi.b.27, I.xi.1.3, III.ii.14), conditions of tenure, inherited from the past and still manifest in primogeniture and entail, disinclined landlords to invest in agricultural progress and left tenants without the means or the incentive to do so.

The efficiency with which land property was used turned on its size, the conditions under which it was held and cultivated, and the availability of funds for investment in agricultural progress. 'A small proprietor . . . who knows every part of his little territory, who views it all with the affection which property, especially small property, naturally inspires, and who upon that account takes pleasure not only in cultivating but in adorning it, is generally of all improvers the most industrious, the most intelligent, and the most successful' (WN III.iv.19). 'After small proprietors, however, rich and great farmers are, in every country, the principal improvers. There

economic development, namely, the emergence of new commodities and resulting changes in the composition of demand and the behaviour of households and individuals. See Nathan Rosenberg, 'Adam Smith, Consumer Tastes and Economic Growth', *Journal of Political Economy*, lxxvi (1968), 361–74.

are more such perhaps in England than in any other European monarchy,' or country except Holland and Berne (WN III.ii.20).

Merchants, because of their experience, temper, outlook, and disposable funds, were 'the best of all improvers' of land. A merchant is accustomed to employ his money chiefly in profitable projects; whereas a mere country gentleman is accustomed to employ it chiefly in expense. The one often sees his money go from him and return to him with a profit: the other, when he parts with it very seldom expected to see any more of it. Those different habits naturally affect their temper and disposition in every sort of business. A merchant is commonly a bold; a country gentleman, a timid undertaker. The one is not afraid to lay out at once a large capital upon the improvement of his land, when he has a probable prospect of raising the value of it in proportion to the expense. The other, if he has any capital, which is not always the case, seldom ventures to employ it in this manner. If he improves at all, it is commonly not with a capital, but with what he can save out of his annual revenue . . . much more spirited [are] the operations of merchants . . . than those of mere country gentlemen. The habits, besides, of order, economy and attention, to which mercantile business forms a merchant, render him much better to execute, with profit and success, any project of improvement (WN III.iv.3).[27]

Smith notes that while the level of investment in agriculture in a country like America turned on how profitable it was to invest in intensive exploitation (WN I.xi.1.4), investment in English agriculture was held down by the class structure. Small farmers were handicapped by lack of funds for investment even when they operated land on a lease of sufficiently long term to permit recovery of investment with large profit. It was true that under English law and custom—laws that 'perhaps contributed more to the present grandeur of England, than all their boasted regulations of commerce taken together' (WN III.ii.14), the 'security of the tenant is equal to that of the proprietor'. Even so, little capital flowed into agriculture. Not only were 'the yeomanry . . . regarded as an inferior rank of people', whose status was not high enough for men to aspire to; they were also unable, on the small holdings they cultivated, to net enough to invest heavily and enlarge their holdings (WN III.ii.20).

Turning now to trade and manufacturing we find that Smith takes it for granted that one engaged in these lines knows his business much better than one not so engaged and that differences in luck as well as in skill affect their earnings. He points out that a 'frugal and thriving man' will increase his stock and amount of profit faster than one who is not frugal. Indeed, 'it seldom happens, however, that great fortunes are made even in great towns

[27] On the importance of merchant houses in financing the textile industry see S. D. Chapman, 'Fixed Capital Formation in the British Cotton Industry, 1770–1815', *Economic History Review*, xxiii (1970), 235–66.

by any one regular, established, and well-known branch of business, but in consequence of a long life of industry, frugality, and attention.' 'Sudden fortunes' arise mostly from speculation, among merchants who continually change trades, shifting into whatever 'is likely to be more than commonly profitable' and quitting it when they foresee 'that its profits are likely to return to the level of other trades' (WN I.x.b.38). Both traders and manufacturers were inclined to manoeuvre governments into swelling their profits. 'The interested sophistry of merchants and manufacturers' had confounded 'the common sense of mankind', giving currency to 'political' and governmental 'maxims' that affect nations adversely (WN IV.iii.c.10).

Smith dealt with professional people when examining the degree to which risk and uncertainty affected their incomes. Professional people seldom became engaged in activities in the guise of undertakers unless their business was of the sort pursued by (say) apothecaries (WN I.x.b.35), though their incomes were affected by overestimation of chances of success and underestimation of chances of failure. Very few professional people amassed pecuniary fortunes (as merchants and manufacturers might) and most, because of the degree to which professions were overcrowded, realized incomes that were low, given their outlay in time and money upon preparation for their careers. Responsible for overcrowding and low pay in some professions was subsidization (WN I.x.c.34–40) of entry into these professions (e.g. clergy, teachers, men of letters) and the impact of exaggerated expectations respecting others (e.g. lawyers, physicians, poets, philosophers). The excessive fortune hoped for in some professions was associated with the 'desire of the reputation which attends upon superior excellence in any of them', and with the 'overweening-conceit' or 'natural confidence which every man has more or less, not only in his own abilities, but in his own good fortune'. In the end, therefore, a degree of 'public admiration' entered into the reward of members of approved professions. In contrast, a pecuniary offset to public discredit entered into the reward of members of professions (e.g. players, opera singers) whose exercise was considered 'as a sort of public prostitution'. In general, Smith inferred, wages or salaries in professions and comparable undertakings in which an individual's probability of success varied tended to be relatively low because those entering these activities overvalued the chance of gain and undervalued the chance of failure or loss (WN I.x.b.21–32).

Smith allowed little scope to the assumption of entrepreneurial functions by agents of the state. Sovereigns were not suited to carry on business for profit (WN V.ii.a). Basing reward on performance produced the best results in the public as in the private sector. Yet it was difficult to mobilize in support of the general welfare such regard as agents of the state had to their own interests. 'Public services are never better performed than when their reward comes only in consequence of their being performed, and is proportioned to the dilligence employed in performing them.' Since this often was not the case, users of public services were in danger of being overcharged.[28]

In essence, Smith reserved to the state two sets of undertakings, those in which costs and benefits did not tend to coincide and those which only the state could carry out effectively. Essential institutions and works needed to be erected and maintained by the sovereign when costs and benefits could not be internalized—those of 'such a nature that the profit could never repay the expence of any individual or small number of individuals, and which it therefore cannot be expected that any individual or small number of individuals should erect or maintain' (WN V.i.c.1). The undertakings in question, besides defence and the administration of justice, included certain works for facilitating commerce e.g. transport facilities not suited to private operation (WN V.i.c) and promoting education (WN V.i.f) in so far as the support of these works and activities could not be made adequately incident upon beneficiaries and hence suited to private operations.

Smith's critique extended to essentially private entrepreneurial collectivities that had been established with the help of the state and, in some instances, had been appointed to govern colonies. An exclusive company constituted the 'worst of all governments', a barrier to colonial development and a nuisance 'in every respect' (WN IV.vii.b.22, IV.vii.c.108, V.ii.a.7). 'Regulated companies' were monopolies on a par with 'corporations of trades' (WN I.x.c) and as 'useless' even when not also 'oppressive' (WN V.i.e.5–11). Joint stock companies seldom succeeded except when enjoying exclusive privilege, and then tended to waste and mismanagement; they were unable 'to carry on successfully any branch of foreign trade, when private adventurers' could 'come into any sort of open and fair competition with them' (WN V.i.e.18,26–32). Indeed, only four trades could be carried on by a company with no exclusive privilege, namely, banking, insurance, canals, and water works; for each of these trades involved operations that were routine and subject to strict rules, required a larger capital than a private copartnery could collect, and yielded great and general utility. In no other instance was the internal management of a joint stock company likely to establish 'that natural proportion which would otherwise establish itself between judicious industry and profit, and which, to the general industry of the country, is of all encouragements the greatest and the most effectual' (WN V.i.c.40).

Smith believed, it may be inferred, that costs and benefits tended to be

[28] Smith reports how, 'in order to increase their payment, the attorneys and clerks [in legal proceedings] have contrived to multiply words beyond all necessity, to the corruption of the law language of, I believe, every court of justice in Europe' (WN V.i.b.22).

internalized so long as a firm or an entrepreneur operated under conditions of free competition. It was essential, therefore, that nearly all economic activity be carried on competitively, within the private sector, and that unduly short-run views of the economy be avoided.[29] When an undertaking did not fit nicely into the private sector, it was essential none the less that it be carried on as nearly as possible in keeping with the rules operative in the private sector.

Of the functions properly reserved to the state, preservation of justice was essential not only to the conservation of security, individual liberty, and an orderly economy (WN V.i.b), but also to the continuity of a society (TMS II.ii.3,4,6; VII.ii.3,16) and presumably to the appropriate circumscription of self-love (TMS III.4, III.5,6,9; VII.iv.8); Without civil government, property and essential subordination could not endure, nor could the system of natural liberty.[30]

While Smith stressed the need for the state to provide essential education for the common people (WN V.i.g.52–61), he opposed subsidization of the education of better-to-do youth, believing, as noted earlier, that 'rivalship', 'emulation', and dependence upon performance for reward produce the 'greatest exertions'. Such education had best be supplied under competitive private auspices. 'Those parts of education, it is to be observed, for the teaching of which there are no public institutions, are generally the best taught' (WN V.i.f.16). 'The improvements which, in modern times, have been made in several different branches of philosophy, have not, the greater part of them, been made in universities.' 'In general, the richest and best endowed universities have been the slowest in adopting . . . improvements' (WN V.i.f.34). 'Were there no public institutions for education, no system, no science would be taught for which there was not some demand, or which the circumstances of the times did not render it either necessary, or convenient, or at least fashionable, to learn' (WN V.i.f.36). Since there were 'no public institutions for the education of women', there was 'nothing useless, absurd, or fantastical in the common course of their education . . . In every part of her life a woman feels some conveniency or advantage from every part of her education. It seldom happens that a man, in any part of his life, derives any conveniency or advantage from some of the most laborious and troublesome parts of his education' (WN V.i.g.47). Smith suggested also that while 'the expence of the institutions for education and

[29] 'To relieve the present exigency is always the object which principally interests those immediately concerned in the administration of public affairs. The future liberation of the public revenue, they leave to the care of posterity' (WN V.iii.26).

[30] 'Avarice and ambition in the rich, in the poor hatred of labour and the love of present ease and enjoyment, are the passions which prompt to invade property, passions much more steady in their operation, and much more universal in their influence. Wherever there is great property, there is great inequality. For one very rich man, there must be at least five hundred poor, and the affluence of the few supposes the indigence of the many' (WN V.i.b.2).

religious instruction' could be 'defrayed by the general contribution of the whole society', it 'might perhaps with equal propriety, and even with some advantage, be defrayed altogether by those who receive the immediate benefit of such education and instruction, or by the voluntary contribution of those who think they have occasion for either the one or the other' (WN V.i.i.5).

V FINAL IMPRESSIONS

It is evident that Smith believed that inputs would be most economically transformed into marketable output so long as transformation and marketing were carried out by private entrepreneurs subject mainly to unlimited competition. It was desirable, therefore, that of a nation's aggregate output of goods and services there be produced in the public and semi-public sectors only that small share which could not be equitably and economically supplied by private enterprise.

Turning now to Smith's conception of the private entrepreneur upon whom rested the major burden of operating a dynamic economy, we find less than clear the genesis both of Smith's conception of entrepreneur and of the system within which he might carry on his activities near optimally. That he drew inferences from what he saw and read is evident, but not whether he had in mind particular entrepreneurs.[31] Smith's conception of an entrepreneur and his functions was more in keeping with Britain's economy of the first two-thirds of the eighteenth century than with that emerging in the last third. Smith's conception did not correspond closely to Cantillon's, nor did it anticipate Schumpeter's; neither did it resemble Say's closely, though his undertaker did in effect perform functions which Say later identified, albeit routinely and subject to the constraints flowing from the socio-economic structure within which Smith lived. Essential to being a good undertaker was hard work prompted by man's inborn desire to better himself, together with knowledge born of specialized experience and little related to natural talent.[32] Essential to an economic decision-maker's behaving compatibly with the general welfare was his being subject to a system of pressures originating mainly in a free market though subject to rules of justice and propriety imposed by custom or enforced by the state.

[31] Smith had helped James Watt, 'principal parent' of an Industrial Revolution based on machine power (Fay, *The World of Adam Smith*, 81), but he could not have approved Watt's later monopolistic behaviour. Ashton, op. cit. 107.

[32] Smith held, as did many eighteenth-century philosophers, that 'the difference of natural talents in different men is, in reality, much less than we are aware of . . . The difference between the most dissimilar characters . . . seems to arise not so much from nature, as from habit, custom, education. When they came into the world, . . . they were, perhaps, very much alike (WN I.ii.4–5).

While most individuals exercised economic choice and hence were economic decision-makers, only a minority, acting *as individuals*,[33] had enough power to guide or influence large undertakings and hence to influence the market. Of these many would be destined to fail if not sheltered against the competition of smaller firms; for they could not meet the survivor test, having taken on functions which could be better performed by smaller firms, together with the market, than within the large firms in question.[34] Survival depended also upon the nature of the firms and industry under consideration, according to Smith's assessment of the survival power of non-exclusive companies. However, under a regime of free competition, most economic decision-makers in a firm of a size freeing them of the need to enter protective monopolistic arrangements, tended to perform their functions effectively, compatibly with the general welfare, and at a sufficient profit.

The force that drove the individual to exert himself, to save, and to maintain natural progress was man's inborn desire of bettering his condition, especially under conditions of 'freedom and security' (WN II.iii.28,31,36). This force was not, however, necessarily self-limiting; it could, as has been indicated, lead to one man's exploiting or taking advantage of another. Accordingly, whether or not entrepreneurial drive gave rise to the public welfare turned on the kind of system in which the decision-maker found himself. It was necessary, therefore, that this drive should be under sufficient control not only to facilitate exchange but also to insure compatibility between the well-being of the individual and that of society—a compatibility highly probable in the absence of (what today economists call) market imperfections.[35] Presumably, contractual relations formed in the absence of perfect competition and of rules assuring justice and equity could not alone result in exchange productive of adequate co-operation and mutual aid, together with compatibility between the welfare of the public and that of decision-makers. What else was necessary?

Smith proceeded upon the assumption that man, though not a 'man of system', was a social animal living within a societal system and under a set of rules (TMS III.4–5, VI.ii.2.15–18). His nature had fitted him to 'subsist only in society', and his generic 'sympathy' or 'fellow-feeling' tended somewhat to counter his self-love and self-centredness (TMS I.i.1.1;

[33] An aggregate of individuals could exercise influence as when a trader's 'customers' subjected him to 'real and effectual discipline' (WN I.x.c.31). While the 'inferior ranks' constituted the main market in a country, each consumed very little (V.ii.k.43); they presumably could not therefore easily organize and influence a trader.

[34] On the 'survivor principle' see G. J. Stigler, *The Organization of Industry* (1968), 72–4. On intra-firm versus extra-firm organization of activities see R. H. Coase, 'The Nature of the Firm', *Economica*, iv (1937), 386–405.

[35] The ultimate method for achieving Adam Smith's ideal could only be the removal of imperfections of the market.' So writes S. Moos, 'Is Adam Smith Out of Date?', *Oxford Economic Papers*, ii (1951), 200.

II.ii.2.1; II.ii.3.1–2,6; IV.2.1).[36] Accordingly, while there was need for 'justice' (TMS II.ii.3.4), Smith argued in substance that so long as the state did not lend support to special interests, or undergird institutions having such effect, market imperfections would be minor, and private and public economic interests would tend to be compatible.

All systems either of preference or of restraint, therefore, being thus completely taken away, the obvious and simple system of natural liberty establishes itself of its own accord. Every man, as long as he does not violate the laws of justice, is left perfectly free to pursue his own interest his own way, and to bring both his industry and capital into competition with those of any other man, or order of men. The sovereign is completely discharged from a duty, in the attempting to perform which he must always be exposed to innumerable delusions, and for the proper performance of which no human wisdom or knowledge could ever be sufficient; the duty of superintending the industry of private people, and of directing it towards the employments most suitable to the interest of the society. According to the system of natural liberty, the sovereign has only three duties to attend to; three duties of great importance, indeed, but plain and intelligible to common understandings: first, the duty of protecting the society from the violence and invasion of other independent societies; secondly, the duty of protecting, as far as possible, every member of the society from the injustice or oppression of every other member of it, or the duty of establishing an exact administration of justice; and thirdly, the duty of erecting and maintaining certain public works and certain public institutions, which it can never be for the interest of any individual, or small number of individuals, to erect and maintain; . . .

(WN IV.ix.51)

Smith expected that his ideals were much more likely to be realized in America than in Britain, which was not realizing her potential, based upon her fertile soil and excellent 'transfer relations',[37] as was and would America (WN I.viii.23, III.iv.19, and generally, IV.vii.c). Smith viewed America, observes Fay, as a 'refuge' from a failing or not very dynamic Europe and Asia and from 'the restraints which encumber life as it is', as a 'land of hope in which a new start could be made'. There 'liberty' and the economic principles expounded in *The Wealth of Nations* could flourish, give rise to opulence in keeping with the country's potential, and serve as exemplar to non-dynamic lands. Perhaps, as Fay suggests, Smith anticipated the passage of the torch from England to America when the 'theory of dynamic growth' which he took over 'from the panoply of force' became fully applied there to increasing man's 'well-being' and exemplifying the validity of Smith's

[36] F. H. Giddings built his sociology upon the concept of 'consciousness of kind' which resembled in some degree Smith's sympathy. See *The Principles of Sociology* (1896), preface, 17ff.

[37] See note 9 above.

principles.[38] Smith, of course, reckoned without the Industrial Revolution, on the horizon if not already in process at the time he was writing. At the same time he did not look forward explicitly to a day when western countries might become as populous as China and Bengal were sometimes represented as being, though he did describe all empires as living on borrowed time.[39]

[38] See Fay, 'Adam Smith and the Dynamic State', 25–8, and 'Adam Smith, America and the Doctrinal Defeat of the Mercantile System', *Quarterly Journal of Economics*, xlviii (1934), 204–16. See also C. R. Fay, *Imperial Economy* (1934).

[39] Smith remarked that 'empires, like all other works of men, have hitherto proved mortal' and hence advised that constitutions intended to be 'permanent' should be suited 'not to those circumstances which are transitory, occasional, or accidental, but to those which are necessary and therefore always the same' (WN V.ii.c.6). On Bengal and China see WN I.viii.24–5, I.ix.14–15.

VIII

Adam Smith's System of Equilibrium Growth

ADOLPH LOWE*

I EMERGENCE OF A THEORETICAL 'SYSTEM'

IN tracing the historical development of a science one expects to encounter a more or less steady progress from initial fragmentary insights to an ever more comprehensive body of knowledge in which, first, empirical regularities, then explanatory laws and more inclusive theories, and, finally, a grand synthesis of all the special theories are established. The very contrary is true of the modern history of economics. At its beginning stand the grandiose designs of classical economics, marked by an expanse of substance and a stringency of deductive reasoning that during the subsequent development was achieved again only by the classical heretic Marx. Thereafter theoretical development presents itself under the curious aspect of a progressive erosion of the original system, to be partially reversed only during the present generation.

It is significant that, in the course of this process, the meaning of 'theory' itself has changed. The change was described as early as 1885 in Alfred Marshall's Inaugural Lecture as the difference between a 'body of concrete truth' and an 'engine for the discovery of concrete truth'. The same idea can be expressed as the contrast between the 'magnificent dynamics' (W. J. Baumol) characterizing the work of the classical economists and the 'box of tools' (Joan Robinson) forged and assembled by their neo-classical successors. It was the conviction of the former that the empirical market systems possessed a unique structure and underwent a unique evolution the essential features of which could be depicted in a *theoretical system*, permitting unconditional predictions of short-term and long-term motion.

As a consequence, these constructs bear a deterministic character so radical that it is difficult to find an analogy for them anywhere in the realm of the natural sciences. There Laplace's vision has come true: they are the product of an 'intelligence' which claims to be able to 'comprehend all the forces by which nature [read 'society'] is animated and the respective positions of the entities which compose it . . . nothing would be uncertain for it, and the future, like the past, would be present for its eyes.'[1]

In this paper I propose to illustrate this extreme version of a deterministic

* Emeritus Professor of Economics at the New School for Social Research, New York.

[1] See Pierre Simon, Marquis de Laplace, *Traité de probabilité* (1886), vi–vii.

system by examining the treatise that has opened the era of scientific economics: Adam Smith's *The Wealth of Nations*. In doing so we shall discover that, in the nature of the case, such a 'system' not only embraces the micro- and macro-motions of the economic process proper, but it includes as well the political and social processes of civil society at large, and even proclaims certain value judgements as to the desirable course of social evolution.

II THE ENVIRONMENTAL 'CONSTANTS' IN SMITH'S SYSTEM AND THE STATIONARY FEEDBACK MECHANISM

Some constructive effort is required if one tries to distil the essence of an analytical model from the mixture of theoretical propositions, empirical descriptions, historical discourses, and political recommendations with which Smith's *magnum opus* presents itself to the uninitiated reader. The student interested in basic doctrine is compelled to gather the building blocks from widely scattered passages. Moreover, he will quite frequently have to unearth implicit assumptions in order to impart meaning to explicit statements, and conjectural interpretation cannot always be avoided. But since there is practical agreement on the individual premises and theorems among the experts, the risk of misconstruction is minimal.[2]

We must begin with describing the ultimate 'data' on which Smith builds his model. In the typical constructs of social—and for that matter, of physical—analysis these data can be divided into constants and independent variables. Thus in the example of the thermostat, the furnace, the pipes, and the 'actuator' fall in the categories of constants, whereas the temperature affecting the actuator and the quantity of fuel in the storage tank belong to the independent variables. It is the singular feature of Smith's model that—with one exception—it does not contain any independent variables. In particular, all extra-systemic factors influencing the stability and growth of the system are governed by intra-systemic processes, so that the very distinction between extra- and intra-systemic motion loses its meaning.

The precise manner in which such reciprocal causation is achieved will occupy us presently. But we must first enumerate the real data, namely those natural, psychological, and institutional factors which affect the processes to be analysed without themselves being affected by them. Their essential characteristic is that, though the result of a long evolution from an original 'rude state of society', they are supposed to have attained their final shape in the competitive organization of the modern Western 'system

[2] The strategic passages in *The Wealth of Nations* are found in Chs. II, III, VIII, and IX of Book I and Chs. III, IV, and V of Book II, not to forget the brief but enlightening Conclusion to Book I, Ch. XI. For further details see my 'The Classical Theory of Economic Growth', *Social Research*, xxi (1954), 127–58, and Joseph Spengler, 'Adam Smith's Theory of Economic Growth', *Southern Economic Journal*, xxvi (1959), 397–415, and xxvii (1959), 1–12.

of natural liberty' (WN IV.ix.51). Being neither influenced by the ongoing core process nor subject to further historical development, these factors can be treated as genuine 'constants' of the analysis.

Starting out with the institutional constants, we find a competitive market-place under the protection of a constitutional government whose main duties consist in the preservation of law and order. Among the laws themselves, those assuring personal freedom and freedom of contract are, under the aspect of market transactions, the most important, in addition to those which safeguard private property. Smith is fully aware of the unequal distribution of such property—of the class character of society—as an essential condition for the operation of the economic mechanism as he describes it (WN V.i.b.2–7). Social mobility of the factors of production is explicitly postulated (WN I.vii.30,31; I.x.a.1); technical mobility, namely smallness and non-specificity of the basic combination of factors, is implicitly assumed, as we shall have occasion to observe. Finally, division of labour and free exchange are the organizational principles on which the competitive system builds.

These principles are themselves only the institutional crystallization of certain innate human propensities: the 'propensity to truck, barter, and exchange' (WN I.ii.1) and the 'desire of bettering our conditions' (WN I.iii.28) which, together with the urge to procreate, form the psychological items in the list of constants. To complete this list we must add the assumption of constant returns on natural resources, that is, an optimistic view of nature's bounty which, for all practical purposes, permits the output of agriculture and of the extractive industries to adjust itself to rising demand without any check on real output and income—at least, until a dimly perceived but long-distant point of resource exhaustion is reached.

On these foundations—active forces emanating from specific human propensities, and particular natural and social constraints—Smith establishes a 'law of motion', which describes the intra-systemic adjustments to changes in the initial conditions, especially to changes in taste. This law, subsequently defined as the law of supply and demand,[3] sets forth what, in modern terms, can be interpreted as a negative feedback mechanism that is to assure long-run equality of quantities demand and supplied at the lowest level of prices compatible with the technical conditions of production. Thus this mechanism serves the maintenance of equilibrium *within the economic core process* by reallocating a given stock of resources, and can be defined as *stationary feedback mechanism*. It has been incorporated into all versions of classical and neo-classical theory[4] and, notwith-

[3] Though Smith never formulated the law explicitly, it is fully implied in his discussion 'Of the Natural and Market Price of Commodities' (WN I.vii).

[4] See my *On Economic Knowledge* (1965 and 1970), Ch. 4.

standing the work of some forerunners such as Cantillon, is not the least of Smith's achievements on which his repute as 'father of economics' rests.

III THE DYNAMIC FEEDBACK MECHANISM

However, Smith derives from the same set of constants a second feedback mechanism, which has by no means been generally accepted or even widely recognized. There essential *extra-systemic* forces are integrated with the motion of the core process. This transforms the stationary setting of the latter into a dynamics of 'balanced growth', which extends the range of determinacy far beyond intra-systemic motion.

It is the interaction of two circular mechanisms that regulates in Smith's system the stimuli which impinge on that motion in so far as they are connected with changes in the aggregate of the factors of production. What, then, is the precise manner in which the 'constants' of the system influence these variables of growth, namely, the supply of labour, natural resources, and capital, and also technology or the order in which the productive factors are combined?

In the nature of the economic core process the productive factors are continuously drained off the market by being transformed into outputs, and they must be steadily replenished if the economic circuit is to be maintained, not to say expanded. Now, it is Smith's contention that three fundamental laws of long-term motion determine the course in which these agents, while producing output, are themselves reproduced on an increasing scale by such output.

(1) There is, first of all, a law which governs the *supply of labour*. It is based on two complementary hypotheses. On the one hand, competitive forces are at work that tend, over the long run, to reduce the level of real wages to the subsistence level. The causal nexus is the same which later became known as the 'iron law of wages'. What is meant is that changes in the real wages offered evoke compensatory changes in the size of the working population because 'demand for men, like that for any other commodity, necessarily regulates the production of men' (WN I.viii.40).

On the other hand, real wages can and do rise so long as the natural and technical conditions of a country permit a steady increase in its real product. Even then the link between real wages and the size of population is not cut. Only in such a society can demand for labour, as expressed in 'the funds which are destined for the payment of wages' (WN I.viii.18), run ahead of supply. And though Smith also in this case expects that an increase in population will occur—infant mortality is likely to fall when real wages rise (WN I.viii.40) and procreation is stimulated since children are an asset in a seller's market for labour (WN I.viii.23)—a rising wage fund can keep wages above subsistence for an indefinite period.

Thus at any moment the supply of labour is governed by two balancing forces: the propensity to procreate, which itself is a composite of a biological urge and a calculation about the 'value of children', and the available wage fund. The former is, as we saw, a constant, but one which by itself would cause the system to 'run down' to a stationary level of labour supply and thus of output. This tendency can be counteracted only by the latter force—the wage fund—which is a variable. How is it determined?

(2) This leads us to a law of *accumulation*. The funds which govern the demand for labour result from saving, which is the outward expression of another psychological constant: the desire of bettering our conditions. Of course, it is not by saving as such but by the use people make of their savings that conditions can be bettered. Accumulation, which for Smith and all classical writers includes both saving and investment, 'is the most likely way of augmenting their fortune' (WN II.iii.28), provided that a 'neat or clear profit' (WN I.ix.18) can be earned.

The level of profit and interest, however, is as precarious as the level of wages, because competition among manufacturers and lenders increases with the rise of a country's capital stock (WN I.ix.2; II.iv.8). Once more the system would 'run down' if the tendency of profits to level out were not counteracted by another variable element. As is the case with wages, 'it is not the actual greatness of national wealth, but its continuous increase' (WN I.viii.22) that favours profits. Such a rise of 'national wealth' (synonymous with what today we call national income) can be stimulated only by a rise in productivity.

(3) In the concept of *productivity* we encounter the strategic variable of the whole system. Productivity depends, first of all, on a country's geographic position and its supply of natural resources. The latter, as we have already seen, is treated as a constant over the practically relevant time span. Therefore the true source of a rise in productivity is technical progress. We must not, however, equate Smith's notions of technical progress with the large-scale innovations which characterize a fully developed industrial system. What he has in mind he defines as progressive 'division of labour', so impressively described in the first three chapters of the work. It comprises the economics of specialization, and also the use of such machinery as serves to 'facilitate and abridge labour' (WN I.i.5).

Now, it is essential for the understanding of the dynamic mechanism to realize that in this conception technology, and in particular the introduction of machinery, is regarded as a complement of, rather than a substitute for, labour. In other words, far from displacing labour and thus exerting a potential pressure on employment and wages—the major variable in Marxian dynamics—division of labour in this inclusive sense is itself conditional on a prior increase in labour supply. 'The number of workmen in every branch of business generally increases with the division of labour in that branch, or rather it is the increase in their number which enables them to class and subdivide themselves in this manner' (WN II.3).

Strange as these ideas may sound to a modern reader, they make good sense as soon as we remember that *The Wealth of Nations* appeared in the early years of the Industrial Revolution and, in fact, describes the conditions of the small-scale manufacturing system that preceded full-scale industrialization. But this identification of technical progress with labour-attracting forms of specialization has far-reaching consequences for the entire model. Rises in productivity on which, as we saw, a satisfactory level of both wages and profits depends cannot take place spontaneously. They are conditional on a prior increase of aggregate demand since, as the title of the famous Chapter III of Book I puts it: division of labour is limited by the extent of the market. Far from being treated as an independent variable, technical progress for Smith can only develop 'in proportion to the riches and populousness' (WN I.iii.4) of the country in question and in proportion to its trade with other countries. Therefore, and this is Smith's third law of dynamic motion, it is the rate of increase in aggregate demand that governs the rate of increase in productivity.

Smith is quite outspoken as to the principal source of such steady increase in demand. Though he is renowned as the proponent of international division of labour, 'according to the natural course of things . . . the greater part of the capital of every growing society is first directed to agriculture, afterwards to manufactures, and last of all to foreign commerce' (WN III.i.8). Thus pride of place belongs to the domestic market, that is, to a steady increase in population equipped with sufficient 'effectual demand'—our argument has turned a full circle.

It may be helpful to retrace the sequence of this circular or rather spiral process and to emphasize once more the strategic spots where the constants exert their recurring influence. We should remember that we contemplate a process in motion. In order to follow up the sequence of events we must break into the chain of interdependent links artificially at some point. The most opportune place to do so is the point where a prior increase in aggregate employment, stemming from the preceding 'turn of the spiral', has raised aggregate demand, thus providing new investment opportunities for further division of labour. These opportunities raise profit expectations and thus demand for savings, in this manner keeping the level of the rate of interest above the minimum and, considering the propensity for 'betterment', stimulating the supply of savings. Such savings offered for investment represent demand for additional labour and maintain real wages above the subsistence level. Under the influence of the propensity to procreate, labour supply responds, even if with a time lag, to the wage stimulus so that the original investment opportunities can be realized through rising employment. This raises payrolls and market demand above the level expected when the spiral under observation first began to turn, creating new investment opportunities and the opportunity for another turn.[5]

It should be emphasized that the long-term feedback mechanism, which underlies this spiral process, is 'positive', that is, self-enforcing rather than compensatory. But the 'coupling' is such as to preclude any 'runaway', the bio-sociological period of human maturation setting an upper limit to the rate of change of the system.

IV STATIONARY AND DYNAMIC FEEDBACKS IN JOINT OPERATION

In order to comprehend the structure of Smith's model in its entirety, we must now relate the stationary feedback, which maintains taste-adequate equilibrium of goods production for a fixed aggregate of inputs and outputs, with the dynamic feedback which governs the expansion of this aggregate. In this all-inclusive construct the following characteristics stand out.

We note first of all, that the sectoral adjustments of supply to demand, which sustains the equilibrium of the market, are only minor oscillations in a steady process of aggregate expansion. Owing to the mechanism of specialization, reproduction of inputs and outputs coincides with their increase. Therefore—and this distinguishes all classical systems from the models of neo-classical theory—the equilibrium of the aggregate is never truly stationary, but always dynamic, making growth the frame of reference for all sectoral movements. Only in the distant future, when a country has 'acquired that full complement of riches which the nature of its soil and climate, and its situation with regard to other countries, allowed it to acquire' (WN I.ix.14), will nature's latent stinginess manifest itself and the system tend toward a stationary state.

No less important than growth as such is its steady nature. Distortions are excluded from the system by the stationary as well as by the dynamic feedback mechanism. The former assures the prompt adjustment of the qualitative order of supply to the one independent variable in the system, consumers' tastes. The latter, by continuously 'transforming' commodity output into factor input and thus into new commodity ouptut, keeps the spiral of expansion closed and at the same time reduces the rate of expansion to the slow growth rate of population. The crucial factor in all this is technology, namely, the small-scale organization of production, the adaptation of machinery to labour rather than the converse, and the unlimited possibilities of rising productivity rooted in progressive division of labour. Without such technical progress the system would run down to a stationary level long before nature itself sets a limit to expansion. But ultimately it is

[5] A lucid exposition of the model has been given in W. O. Thweatt, 'A Diagrammatic Presentation of Adam Smith's Growth Model', *Social Research*, xxiv (1957), 227–30.

the labour-attracting character of the postulated technology which assures dynamic equilibrium. There can never be any discrepancy between factor demand and factor supply. Rising productivity by inducing rising employment and income creates its own demand.

It should now be clear why, with the exception of consumers' tastes, Smith's system does not contain any independent variables. Once the dynamic process is set in motion, the linkage of the variables with the natural, psychological, and institutional constants creates a reciprocity of cause and effect—though at any given moment cause and effect are clearly distinguishable—which excludes any influence from outside the mechanism. This, together with the slow rate of growth, bestows on the system, and thus on the analysis of its movements, a degree of determinacy which in other fields is attained only under strictly circumscribed laboratory conditions. The postulate 'other things remaining equal', conventionally taken as a methodological rule, here gains empirical significance: it describes the actual state of affairs as controlled by a double feedback mechanism. Only changes in taste fall outside their 'loops' but the bipolar nature of these changes evokes a compensatory motion of its own. All other changes are channelled through circular mechanisms and are as such strictly calculable.

Still another feature of the model is worth mentioning. The major stimuli strictly controlled, there is no room left for 'uncertainty of expectations'. Moreover, prevailing expectations, based on the past and present experience of equilibrium, cannot be other than equilibrating. Consequently the scientific observer can disregard expectations altogether, as Smith and the other classical writers in fact did.

What cannot, of course, be disregarded is the nature of the prevailing action directive. It stands outside the circular mechanisms, but is no less determinate: it forms an essential part of the system's constants. Actually it is the fundamental force which impels and unifies the motions of the socio-economic process. In applying the principle of receipt maximization not only to the commodity market but also to the factor markets and, above all, to the 'production' of men, Smith raises the pecuniary motive which rules the market to the universal motive power in society at large. On empirical as well as philosophical grounds we may have good reasons for repudiating an interpretation of social relations in the image of market relations. But we must realize that only by an all-encompassing hypothesis in which economic relations are presumed to govern the wider social process—a truly materialistic conception of history—did Smith succeed in making the economic process truly 'circular' and thus fully determinate.

V NORMATIVE ROOTS OF SMITH'S PREMISES

The constants of Smith's model are the data from which the unbreakable spiral of the steady process of growth is derived. But data and resulting process are related in still another and more subtle manner about which a word must be said in conclusion.

Though the growth process once it is set in motion pursues its course with the inexorability of a law of nature, Smith is interested not only in the reciprocal 'causes' of the growing 'wealth of nations' but also in its 'nature'. More precisely, he by no means accepts the outcome of the secular process of production with indifference. Rather he singles out two specific goals as the 'distinct objects' of a 'political economy', understood as 'a branch of the science of a statesman or legislator'. These goals are 'first, to provide a plentiful revenue or subsistence for the people . . . and, secondly, to supply the state or commonwealth with a revenue sufficient for the public services' (WN IV.1). In other words, the effectiveness of the growth process, in terms both of aggregate output and of its distribution among the social strata involved in its production, is subject to a value judgement, the criterion of which is the welfare goal just stated.

Now, and this is the miracle performed by the 'invisible hand', the spiral of unplanned economic growth, which the initial set of natural, psychological, and institutional constants releases, propels society toward this very goal: maximum wealth through the steady increase of the annual produce of land and labour, benefiting equally those who live by rent and wages.[6] Thus the dynamic laws which map out the path of economic evolution are themselves the vehicles which carry society toward what for Smith is the 'good life'.

But this coincidence between that which 'inevitably occurs' and that which is 'good' is not assured by just any set of data. It is clearly restricted to the framework of constants as outlined above. True, some of these constants, namely the natural and psychological ones, are regarded by Smith as unalterable, describing the external and internal endowment of man. But this is by no means the case with the institutional constants which are summarized by him in the concept of a 'system of natural liberty' (WN IV.ix.51). Outside this form of political organization even the psychological propensities remain *dormant*, and the force symbolized in the pecuniary incentive, which alone can steer the process of development in the proper channels, will be frustrated. Inexorable as is the process of growth, the political and social conditions from which alone it can take off and by which it is sustained are not themselves preordained. They are the product of history, but of a history in which human choices in the form of political decisions play a decisive role.

How central this idea is for Smith can be gauged from the fact that one-third of the book is devoted to a description and critique of the possible

[6] It should be noted, however, that Smith has considerable doubts as to the possibility of harmony between the 'general interest' of society and the sectional interests of 'those who live by profits'.

alternatives to the institutional order of natural liberty. Mercantilism, and the ancient and modern systems devoted to the one-sided furthering of agriculture are denounced because each is 'subversive of the great purpose which it means to promote' (WN IV.ix.50). Only the co-operation of free men left to themselves in pursuing their interests under a government protecting law and order will succeed in promoting that purpose: steady increase in wealth and welfare.

In speculating about the origin of the spatio-mathematical order of the universe, the metaphysicians of the seventeenth and eighteenth centuries came up with an engineering model which helps to elucidate the synthesis of 'determinism and freedom' in Smith's doctrine. Once the world machine has been constructed its motions are found to be fully determined by the laws of Mechanics, and to proceed in full autonomy. But the divine engineer or heavenly clockmaker who established the initial conditions and gave the system the initial push was a free agent, not himself subject to mechanical laws. By the same logic the determinist motion of Smith's model presupposes a prior free decision on the part of the political sovereign in favour of one rather then another set of institutions.

But what is the criterion for his choice? In deciding against the arbitrary 'preferences' and 'restraints' which dominated the political systems of the past in favour of a system of natural liberty the sovereign adopts the macro-goal of maximizing welfare by maximizing wealth. The reason why a system of natural liberty is the suitable means for the attainment of that socio-economic end is its consequences for individual economic behaviour. It activates the dormant force of receipt maximization for the motion of economic growth through which alone the welfare goal can be approximated.

Thus we arrive at the important conclusion that Smith's theoretical construct rests on a normative foundation. Steady progress toward maximization of wealth benefiting all major strata of economic society is postulated as the macro-goal to the attainment of which the productive effort is directed. The spiralling path of growth, the laws of behaviour which impel its pursuit, the pecuniary incentive which shapes such behaviour, and last but not least, the institutional environment in which alone such behaviour and motivation can assert itself, all these events and underlying forces are more than just factual occurrences. They are at the same time the means to an end, an end which the philosopher Smith prescribes to the economist Smith as the *terminus ad quem* for his inquiry, and which the economist Smith enjoins the 'statesman or legislator' to adopt, as maxims for his political decisions.[7]

[7] It need hardly be mentioned that the source upon which the philosopher Smith draws is the Natural Law doctrine in the peculiar synthesis of Stoic and Epicurean elements, which is achieved in his *Theory of Moral Sentiments* (1759).

But when all this has been said, it must be stated with equal emphasis that nowhere in Smith's model do normative arguments penetrate into the chain of economic reasoning itself. Once he presides over a regime of natural liberty, Smith's sovereign is reduced to a guardian of law and order. Again like the divine engineer, he stands aloof from his creation and is 'completely discharged from . . . the duty of superintending the industry of private people' (WN IV.ix.51). To build the 'economic machine' required for the attainment of the postulated social goal is an act of political will. Once it operates it obeys, as does the Newtonian cosmos, nothing but the laws of a deterministic order.

IX

Adam Smith's Theory of Economic Growth

W. A. Eltis*

Adam Smith's theory of growth has provided better predictions of the course that economic development was to follow in the nineteenth and twentieth centuries than the theories of his great successors, Malthus, Ricardo, and Marx, who predicted at best constant living standards for the great mass of the population. In Smith's account, increasing returns and 'learning by doing' (as growth theorists now call it) in industry play a central role, and in an economical and well-governed society these can be expected to continually increase the *manufactured* goods that workers can afford to buy. Right at the start of *The Wealth of Nations* he pointed out that as a result of the division of labour, an 'industrious and frugal peasant' enjoyed, as well as enough food for subsistence, a woollen coat, a coarse linen shirt, shoes, a kitchen grate, knives and forks and kitchen utensils, earthenware or pewter plates, and glass windows with the result that his 'accommodation' greatly exceeded that of an African King.[1] Workers, like peasants, gained from the division of labour which produced these benefits, and Smith certainly did not believe that the maximum possible advantages from this had been obtained by 1776.

The compatibility of Smith's theory of growth with what has happened since is not, however, its principal claim to modern attention. It is possible that this rests on a most persuasive line of argument it contains which modern theory has almost wholly lost sight of. In twentieth-century growth theory, the rate of investment generally has no effect at all on an economy's long-term rate of growth of output and living standards. This is true of almost all neoclassical growth theory, and of some Keynesian growth theory in addition.[2] In Smith's theory, however, capital accumulation leads to increased population and employment, and provided that the market for manufactured goods is widened by this, an increased division of labour will follow which will have favourable effects on labour productivity. If competition is sufficient, and an increase in capital will generally increase

* Fellow of Exeter College, Oxford.

I am grateful to Professor B. J. Gordon and Dr. K. Hennings for very helpful comments on an earlier draft of this paper.

[1] Adam Smith, *An Inquiry into the Nature and Causes of the Wealth of Nations*, ed. Cannan (1930), I.i.11. All subsequent references are to this edition.

[2] See F. H. Hahn and R. C. O. Matthews, 'The Theory of Economic Growth: A Survey', *Economic Journal*, lxxiv (Dec. 1964).

competition, the prices of manufactured goods will then fall with unit labour costs with the result that the quantity and range of manufactured goods that workers can afford to purchase will increase. It follows therefore that in Smith's account of growth, faster capital accumulation is associated with a faster rate of growth of employment and output, and faster growth in living standards. In modern growth theory, Arrow comes nearest to Smith's results with his 'learning by doing' model where the rate of growth of labour productivity and wages per head depend on the rate of growth of employment opportunities provided by new machines.[3] Very few other modern theorists have arrived at Smith's results. Thus, if a strong inter-connection between investment and growth is central to the development process, Smith's theory of growth must stand high, for it is one of the very few where investment has highly favourable long-term effects.

A number of problems are naturally involved in any attempt to present Smith's theory of growth in modern terms. *The Wealth of Nations* was not written with the rigour of modern growth theory, or indeed that of Ricardo's *Principles of Political Economy and Taxation.* It is most unlikely that Smith's book would have had the vast influence it achieved if the argument had been presented in the form of a logical derivation of conclusions from carefully stated premises, with each term precisely defined. Because the book was written to persuade and to carry any literate reader along, definitions and assumptions often need to be inferred from the general argument, and as this deals with much more than growth and development, some of the propositions that relate to growth must be obtained from other parts of the argument.

In the present paper, an attempt will be made to present an account of Smith's theory of growth and development in modern terms, but before this is done, something must be said about Smith's basic assumptions, for these involve a number of problems of interpretation which must be resolved before a theory that can genuinely pretend to be his can be outlined. Part I of this paper, 'Adam Smith's Assumptions', will be concerned with these problems, and the various propositions that are to be found in *The Wealth of Nations* about returns to scale in industry and agriculture, the distinction between productive and unproductive employment and its relevance to the rate of capital accumulation, the effect of accumulation on wages, and so on, are discussed there with the object of arriving at the appropriate assumptions for a modern restatement of Smith's theory of growth. In Part II, 'A *Wealth of Nations* Growth Model', the theory that follows from the assumptions arrived at in Part I will be set out and discussed, and finally, in Part III, 'The Results of the Model and some of Adam Smith's Conclusions', the results arrived at in Part II will be

[3] See Kenneth J. Arrow, 'The Economic Implications of Learning by Doing', *Review of Economic Studies*, xxix (June 1962).

compared with various propositions and predictions about growth and development that are to be found in *The Wealth of Nations*. Smith does not merely predict continuing progress based on industry, for he clearly believed that growth would eventually cease when a country's potential for development was fully realized, the development then achieved depending in part on a society's laws and institutions. He expected the rate of profit to fall as full development was approached, and this means that a model that predicted an indefinite continuation of growth would not be Smith's.[4] In addition, it is clear that Smith thought that agriculture provided a more useful foundation for growth than industry, even though industry offered greater potential benefits from the division of labour. This apparent paradox must be explained by any model that claims to be Smith's. The model outlined in this paper passes these tests (and others) and it will be argued that the results it produces correspond to those in *The Wealth of Nations*.

I ADAM SMITH'S ASSUMPTIONS

In this part of the paper, Smith's basic assumptions about four of the factors that influence the development of economies will be discussed, namely his assumptions about returns to scale in the different sectors of the economy; about the relationship between the ratio of productive to unproductive employment and the rate of capital accumulation; about how requirements for fixed and circulating capital vary with growth; and about how growth and income distribution interact. His assumptions about returns to scale in industry and agriculture will be considered first.

Chapter I of Book I of *The Wealth of Nations* opens with an account of the advantages to be derived from the division of labour, and after illustrations including the famous pin factory, Smith writes:

> This great increase of the quantity of work which, in consequence of the division of labour, the same number of men are capable of performing, is owing to three different circumstances; first to the increase of dexterity in every particular workman; secondly, to the saving of the time which is commonly lost in passing from one species of work to another; and lastly, to the invention of a great number of machines which facilitate and abridge labour, and enable one man to do the work of many.
>
> (WN I.i.5)

The first two of these are now very familiar, but the third is less so, and it will be seen that it is important. It is obviously relevant to the correspondence between Smith's argument and Arrow's 'learning by doing' growth model that has been remarked upon.

[4] The dichotomy between Smith's arguments that point to indefinite progress as a result of increasing returns, and those that point to an eventual stationary state, is very clearly brought out in an unpublished paper by Dr. R. N. Ghosh.

The extent to which it is possible to take advantage of the division of labour depends on the number of workers who can be concentrated to manufacture a good at a single place, and this will depend on the market for the good. Smith points out that it takes 50 to 100 families to buy the product of a shoemaker working on his own, or an artisan in a single trade (WN IV.ix.45), and many more where the division of labour is pushed far, so a workshop with 100 workers will produce for far more than 5,000–10,000 families. Such a workshop can only exist if transport facilities are available to distribute products widely, and as water transport was by far the cheapest form of transport until the nineteenth century, there is much in *The Wealth of Nations* about the influence of the Mediterranean and navigable rivers on the location of the areas of the world able to exploit the potential advantages inherent in the division of labour.[5] Provided that the extent of the market is sufficient (and that the division of labour depends on the extent of the market is one of the best-known propositions in *The Wealth of Nations*) industrial output can be expanded more than proportionately with the labour employed in industry. Each increase in employment will lead to a further subdivision of tasks, which will lead to higher labour productivity:

> What takes place among the labourers in a particular workhouse, takes place, for the same reason, among those of a great society. The greater their number, the more they naturally divide themselves into different classes and subdivisions of employment. More heads are occupied in inventing the most proper machinery for executing the work of each, and it is, therefore, more likely to be invented.
>
> (WN I.viii.57; see also II.3–4)

Thus with tasks further subdivided, new machines will be invented, and once they are, labour productivity will rise to the level appropriate to that degree of division of labour. A further increase in labour productivity will be achieved when tasks can be still more subdivided, and this will be possible when there is a further increase in employment.[6]

Thus, if employment per firm rises with total industrial employment, the economy will move up a line like AB in Fig. 1 on p. 430 which shows the productivity level that is reached in the long run with each successively higher level of employment. The same diagram follows from Arrow's model, but there the horizontal axis would show successively produced machines, each worked by one worker, instead of aggregate industrial employment. However, the effect of these is the same, and in each case productivity advances at a rate depending on the rate at which the economy

[5] Joseph J. Spengler has emphasized the importance of this in 'Adam Smith's Theory of Economic Growth', *Southern Economic Journal*, xxv–xxvi (Apr. and July 1959), an article which gives a comprehensive account of the many different factors that influence growth in Smith's argument.

[6] See Samuel Hollander, *The Economics of Adam Smith* (1973), 208–12, for a similar account of the relationship between employment and technical progress in *The Wealth of Nations*.

expands its industrial labour force and capital stock. An account of Smith's lectures delivered in the early 1760s in Glasgow suggests that he may have thought that AB rose very steeply, for the following statement has been attributed to him: 'For twenty millions in a society, in the same manner as a company of manufacturers, will produce 100 times more goods to be exchanged than a poorer and less numerous one of 2 mill.'[7] This implies that each 1 per cent rise in employment might be associated with an increase in labour productivity of 1 per cent,[8] which suggests exceedingly favourable production conditions wherever the division of labour can be usefully extended, and it was certainly Smith's view that it could be much further extended in industry.

Agriculture was, however, of considerably greater importance than

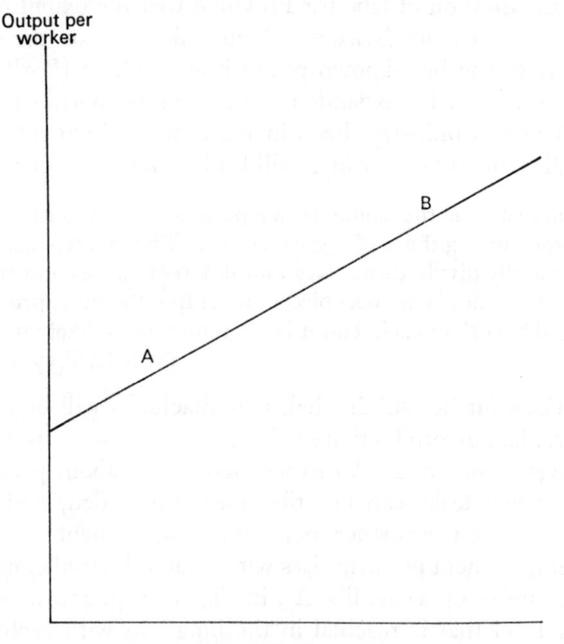

FIG. 1 *Employment in Industry*

[7] LJ (A), vi.166. A student who took lecture notes in a different year attributed a still more favourable statement to him, 'Twenty millions of people perhaps in a great society, working as it were to one anothers hands, from the nature of the division of labour before explained, would produce a thousand times more goods than another society consisting only of two or three millions' (LJ (B), 265; Cannan, 206). This student may well have added a nought to make a 'hundred' a 'thousand'.

[8] This also implies that a 1 per cent increase in output might be associated with an increase in labour productivity of $\frac{1}{2}$ per cent, implying what would now be called a Verdoorn coefficient of 0·50 in the long run. It is interesting to note that this is very close to the Verdoorn coefficient N. Kaldor found for the industry of developed economies in the period 1954–64 (*Causes of the Slow Rate of Growth of the United Kingdom* (1966)).

industry in an eighteenth-century economy, and here two to four families can consume the output of a farm worker (WN IV.ix.45), and:

> The nature of agriculture, indeed, does not admit of so many subdivisions of labour, nor of so complete a separation of one business from another, as manufactures. It is impossible to separate so entirely, the business of the grazier from that of the corn-farmer, as the trade of the carpenter is commonly separated from that of the smith. The spinner is almost always a distinct person from the weaver; but the ploughman, the harrower, the sower of the seed, and the reaper of the corn, are often the same. The occasions for those different sorts of labour returning with the different seasons of the year, it is impossible that one man should be constantly employed in any one of them.
>
> (WN I.i.4)

The fact that a farm of maximum attainable efficiency requires few workers to work together, and few consumers to provide a market, means that the potential from the division of labour will be fully exploited in agriculture in most countries at most times. There will then be no reason to expect increasing returns in food production. Some foodstuffs will have the same real labour costs, however rapidly productivity advances elsewhere, for instance, corn:

> In every different stage of improvement, besides, the raising of equal quantities of corn in the same soil and climate, will, at an average, require nearly equal quantities of labour; or what comes to the same thing, the price of nearly equal quantities; the continual increase of the productive powers of labour in an improving state of cultivation being more or less counterbalanced by the continually increasing price of cattle, the principal instruments of agriculture. Upon all these accounts, therefore, we may rest assured, that equal quantities of corn will, in every state of society, in every stage of improvement, more nearly represent, or be equivalent to, equal quantities of labour, than equal quantities of any other part of the rude produce of land.
>
> (WN I.xi.e.28)

Over much of the remainder of agriculture and mining, however, diminishing returns are to be expected: 'If you except corn and such other vegetables as are raised altogether by human industry, that all other sorts of rude produce, cattle, poultry, game of all kinds, the useful fossils and minerals of the earth, &c. naturally grow dearer as the society advances in wealth and improvement, I have endeavoured to show already' (WN I.xi.i.3). These all grow dearer in terms of both labour and corn. The exceptions in raw produce are vegetable foods, which fall in price relatively to corn because they are a cheap by-product of improved methods of cultivation; and other by-products, for instance hides, which may fall in price because their supply is increased relative to demand because of a faster increase in the number of cattle than in the demand for leather.

It then turns out that Smith assumes increasing returns throughout industry, and with the exception of vegetable foods and hides, etc., that unit costs will be constant, or that they will rise as employment increases in agriculture and mining where there is much less scope for the division of labour. It follows that whether the demand for manufactured goods grows as capital and employment rises will have a very great effect on the course that development follows. This is indeed the case, and it will turn out that the taste of the rich for manufactured goods, and potential export markets for these have a very great effect on the growth of economies.

If there is increased employment, and increased demand for manufactured goods, productivity in industry will rise, and the next step in the argument is to discover what, according to Smith, determines the rate of growth of employment. This depends on the rate of growth of capital, for an increase in aggregate employment will only be possible if there is an increase in the capital stock, since more wage goods and raw materials will be needed in advance of production if more workers are to be employed, and more fixed capital will be needed as well: 'As the accumulation of stock must, in the nature of things, be previous to the division of labour, so labour can be more and more subdivided in proportion only as stock is previously more and more accumulated' (WN II.3). Clearly the rate of growth of capital is crucial, and here one comes to the line of argument in *The Wealth of Nations* which is furthest from modern economics. The best starting-point to an understanding of Smith's approach to the determination of the rate of capital accumulation is perhaps the following passage:

> In all countries where there is tolerable security, every man of common understanding will endeavour to employ whatever stock he can command, in procuring either present enjoyment or future profit. If it is employed in procuring present enjoyment, it is a stock reserved for immediate consumption. If it is employed in procuring future profit, it must procure this profit either by staying with him, or by going from him. In the one case it is a fixed, in the other it is a circulating capital. A man must be perfectly crazy who, where there is tolerable security, does not employ all the stock which he commands, whether it be his own or borrowed of other people, in some one or other of those three ways.
>
> (WN II.i.30)

This immediately disposes of the possibility that part of a country's capital stock will not be fully utilized (provided that the institutions of a country maintain 'tolerable security' for creditors), and this proposition is a vital component of Say's law. Whatever goods are available that are not immediately consumed by their owners must either be used to make a profit, or sold (or lent) to those who expect to be able to make a profit. No one (if the above proposition is accepted) will allow goods to stand idly in warehouses, for this would be 'crazy'.[9]

[9] It may not be possible to use *fixed* capital at a profit at any reasonable set of factor prices if demand is insufficient, but this difficulty which is one of those that make Keynesian

Now, so far as circulating capital is concerned, and attention will be focused on this for the moment, a profit is made by getting more goods back at the end of a period than went out at the beginning, for instance, by feeding corn or its equivalent to farm workers who will then grow more corn than the cost of their wages and the necessary seed corn. Thus, that part of *circulating* capital that is not consumed by its owners must increase from period to period wherever profits are earned. However, circulating capital as a whole need not grow, because part of it is consumed (directly, or indirectly through the employment of unproductive workers, for instance servants) by its owners each year. If the owners consume $\frac{1}{4}$ of circulating capital each year, and then receive back $\frac{4}{3}$ times the $\frac{3}{4}$ they employ productively, the capital stock will neither rise nor fall from period to period. If they consume $\frac{1}{3}$, and receive back $\frac{4}{3}$ times the remaining $\frac{2}{3}$, the capital stock will fall by $\frac{1}{9}$ in each period; while it will grow by $\frac{1}{9}$ if they consume only $\frac{1}{6}$ and receive back $\frac{4}{3}$ times the remaining $\frac{5}{6}$. Thus, whether the capital stock grows or declines depends on the proportion that is used productively, and on how productive this is.

Both productive and unproductive labourers, and those who do not labour at all, are all equally maintained by the annual produce of the land and labour of the country. This produce, how great soever, can never be infinite, but must have certain limits. According, therefore, as a smaller or greater proportion of it is in any one year employed in maintaining unproductive hands, the more in the one case and the less in the other will remain for the productive, and the next year's produce will be greater or smaller accordingly; the whole annual produce, if we except the spontaneous productions of the earth, being the effect of productive labour.

(WN II.iii.3)

Something must obviously be said about Smith's distinction between productive and unproductive labour, which has disappeared from modern economics. This distinction is clearly crucial to Smith's argument, and he says the following about it:

There is one sort of labour which adds to the value of the subject upon which it is bestowed: there is another which has no such effect. The former, as it produces a value, may be called productive; the latter, unproductive labour. Thus the labour of a manufacturer adds, generally, to the value of the materials which he works upon, that of his own maintenance, and of his master's profit. The labour of a menial servant, on the contrary, adds to the value of nothing . . . A man grows rich by employing a multitude of manufacturers: he grows poor, by maintaining a multitude of menial servants . . . the labour of the manufacturer fixes and realizes itself in some particular subject or vendible commodity, which lasts for

unemployment possible was not noticed by Smith, and it may well have had little importance in the eighteenth century.

some time at least after that labour is past . . . [the menial servant's] services generally perish in the very instant of their performance, and seldom leave any trace or value behind them, for which an equal quantity of service could afterwards be procured.

(WN II.iii.1)

Here, there are three criteria for the distinction between productive and unproductive labour: (i) whether employment produces a profit, (ii) whether employment produces something storable, and (iii) whether a particular kind of employment can be continued indefinitely without new infusions of capital. Some activities, for instance agriculture and manufacturing, are productive according to all three criteria, while others, for instance, domestic service are unproductive according to all three, while there are activities, for instance teaching or building an extension to a palace, which satisfy some and not others. There are obviously difficult borderline cases (as there are in the modern distinction between investment and consumption) and the distinction has lapsed, but it may have force in distinguishing activities which contribute to growth from those that do not. As Smith continues:

The labour of some of the most respectable orders in the society is, like that of menial servants, unproductive of any value, and does not fix or realize itself in any permanent subject, or vendible commodity, which endures after that labour is past, and for which an equal quantity of labour could afterwards be procured. The sovereign, for example, with all the officers both of justice and war who serve under him, the whole army and navy, are unproductive labourers. They are the servants of the public, and are maintained by a part of the annual produce of the industry of other people. Their service, how honourable, how useful, or how necessary soever, produces nothing for which an equal quantity of service can afterwards be procured. The protection, security, and defence of the commonwealth, the effect of their labour this year, will not purchase its protection, security, and defence for the year to come. In the same class must be ranked, some both of the gravest and most important, and some of the most frivolous professions: churchmen, lawyers, physicians, men of letters of all kinds; players, buffoons, musicians, opera-singers, opera-dancers, &c.

(WN II.iii.2)

The labour of all these professions is included in modern National Income statistics, but few could doubt that if two developing countries had equal National Incomes, and one employed one-third of its labour in the above ways and the other one-tenth, the latter would find growth easier to achieve.

In Smith's growth argument, the real distinction is between labour that produces and makes available goods *that can be used as capital* and labour that does not. Thus, as Smith points out, 'artificers, manufacturers and merchants' (WN IV.ix.29) and for the same reason those concerned with transport, etc. are productive. The above distinction will suffice for the argument that follows, so long as workers do not consume services.[10]

The distinction between productive and unproductive labour is one feature of Smith's account of growth that has become obsolete. Another that is equally unfamiliar is the proposition that, so long as investment in fixed capital (which was a small fraction of the National Product in 1776) is ignored, the entire National Income is consumed in each period:

What is annually saved is as regularly consumed as what is annually spent, and nearly in the same time too; but it is consumed by a different set of people. That portion of his revenue which a rich man annually spends, is in most cases consumed by idle guests, and menial servants, who leave nothing behind them in return for their consumption. That portion which he annually saves, as for the sake of the profit it is immediately employed as a capital, is consumed in the same manner, and nearly in the same time too, but by a different set of people, by labourers, manufacturers, and artificers, who reproduce with a profit the value of their annual consumption.

(WN II.iii.18)

Thus, while part of the income of the rich is saved, the entire National Income is also consumed—saving by the rich amounting to the employment of productive rather than unproductive workers. This terminology confused Malthus, but not Ricardo as the following note on a passage in Malthus's *Principles of Political Economy* shows:[11]

Malthus. Parsimony, or the conversion of revenue into capital, may take place without any diminution of consumption, if the revenue increases first.
Ricardo. I say it always take place without any diminution of consumption. Mr. Malthus clogs the proposition with a condition 'if the revenue increases first'. I do not understand what Mr. M. means:—if the revenue increases first. Before what?

Malthus clearly saw saving as 'that part of income which is not consumed', while Ricardo appreciated that all the goods (with the exception of fixed capital) that are produced in one period are consumed in the next, either productively or unproductively.[12] If those who own the capital stock are

[10] The sole echo of Smith's distinction in modern theory is in Piero Sraffa's classically based *Production of Commodities by Means of Commodities* (1960) where goods (and presumably services) that are used as factors of production and those that are bought by workers influence the prices of other goods, the wage, the rate of profit, etc., while goods (and presumably services) that are solely consumed by non-workers do not.

[11] *The Works and Correspondence of David Ricardo*, ed. P. Sraffa (1951), ii.326.

[12] It is clear from the 6th chapter of *Commerce Defended* (1808) that James Mill also thoroughly understood Smith's argument (before he met Ricardo). Thus, 'We perceive, therefore, that there are two species of consumption; which are so far from being the same, that the one is more properly the very reverse of the other. The one is an absolute destruction of property, and is consumption properly so called; the other is a consumption for the sake of reproduction . . .' (69).

frugal, and governments are modest in their expenditure, most of the capital stock is consumed by productive workers with the result that it grows from period to period. If those who own capital, and, most important of all, governments, are extravagant, unproductive employment will predominate with the result that the capital stock will decline:[13] and in both cases the nation's circulating capital (apart from money) will be consumed each year.

That is Smith's theory of accumulation, and it has lapsed, presumably because of the difficulties in drawing a sharp borderline between productive and unproductive employment, and because of the growth in the ratio of fixed to circulating capital that has occurred since 1776.[14]

There is, of course, fixed capital in *The Wealth of Nations*, and it will be seen that this plays an important role in the argument, but it plays no part in the passages that deal with consumption and thrift that have just been discussed.[15] Fixed capital is part of the gross product of productive labour, and once this is allowed for, the entire product of productive labour in one period is not used up in the next, and with growth, fixed capital per worker must evidently rise:

> The quantity of materials which the same number of people can work up, increases in a great proportion as labour comes to be more and more subdivided; and as the operations of each workman are gradually reduced to a greater degree of simplicity, a variety of new machines come to be invented for facilitating and abridging those operations. As the division of labour advances, therefore, in order to give constant employment to an equal number of workmen, an equal stock of provisions, and a greater stock of materials and tools than what would have been necessary in a ruder state of things, must be accumulated beforehand. (WN II.3)

Thus growth in industrial production will be accompanied by growth in both raw materials (in volume, and relative price also in the case of some minerals) and in fixed capital per worker.[16] The same is true in agriculture where there is an increase in cattle and sheep per worker as development continues, and in addition, as was noted earlier, the price of cattle will rise relative to the cost of labour.

[13] 'Great nations are never impoverished by private, though they sometimes are by public prodigality and misconduct. The whole, or almost the whole public revenue, is in most countries employed in maintaining unproductive hands.' (WN II.iii.30).

[14] How difficult it is to return to Smith's assumptions is illustrated by Haim Barkai whose stimulating modern restatement of Smith's theory of growth ('A Formal Outline of a Smithian Growth Model', *Quarterly Journal of Economics*, lxxxiii (Aug. 1969)) has distinct saving and investment functions, where planned investment depends on the rate of profit and planned saving on thriftiness conditions. In consequence he believes that Smith needs an 'extreme' version of Say's law to achieve $I = S$.

[15] See Hollander, op. cit. 188–204, for a possible explanation of this.

[16] Spengler (op. cit. 7) has noted the importance of this line of argument in *The Wealth of Nations*.

Now because raw materials and fixed capital requirements per head grow as capital accumulates, employment will not increase as quickly as the capital stock. Smith has Malthus-type arguments, though it will turn out that there are important differences, to show that population will expand with the demand for labour: '. . . the demand for men, like that for any other commodity, necessarily regulates the production of men; quickens it when it goes on too slowly, and stops it when it advances too fast' (WN I.viii.40). However, increased raw material and fixed capital costs per worker will act as a leakage which prevents population and employment from growing *pari passu* with the capital stock. Moreover, if wages also rise as capital accumulates, there will be a further 'leakage' of circulating capital—to the payment of higher wages per worker—which would reduce the rate of growth of employment still further in relation to the rate of growth of capital. Whether wages rise with the rate of growth of the capital stock is therefore a matter of some importance.

At first sight, it appears in contradiction to what was said at the start of the paper that wages will not rise continuously as capital accumulates, for as Hollander points out, it is apparently the *level* and not the rate of growth of wages that depends on the rate of capital accumulation.[17] Thus:

> It is not the actual greatness of national wealth, but its continual increase, which occasions a rise in the wages of labour. It is not, accordingly, in the richest countries, but in the most thriving, or in those which are growing rich the fastest, that the wages of labour are highest. England is certainly, in the present times, a much richer country than any part of North America. The wages of labour, however, are much higher in North America than in any part of England.
>
> (WN I.viii.22)

> . . . it is in the progressive state, while the society is advancing to the further acquisition, rather than when it has acquired its full complement of riches, that the condition of the labouring poor, of the great body of the people, seems to be the happiest and the most comfortable. It is hard in the stationary, and miserable in the declining state.
>
> (WN I.viii.43)

These passages, and others like them, suggest that Smith's theory of wages corresponds to that illustrated in Fig. 2 where the wage at different rates of growth of circulating capital is shown by the schedule WW. Where there is no growth of capital, the wage is $0W_s$, Malthus's 'natural' or 'subsistence' wage, and it will exceed this if capital is growing as in England, or better still, North America, and fall short of it if capital is declining as in Bengal.

If this were Smith's theory, a country with a faster rate of accumulation than another would need to pay higher wages, but once the wage in each country reached that shown in Fig. 2, no further increase in wages would

[17] See Hollander, op. cit. 157–8.

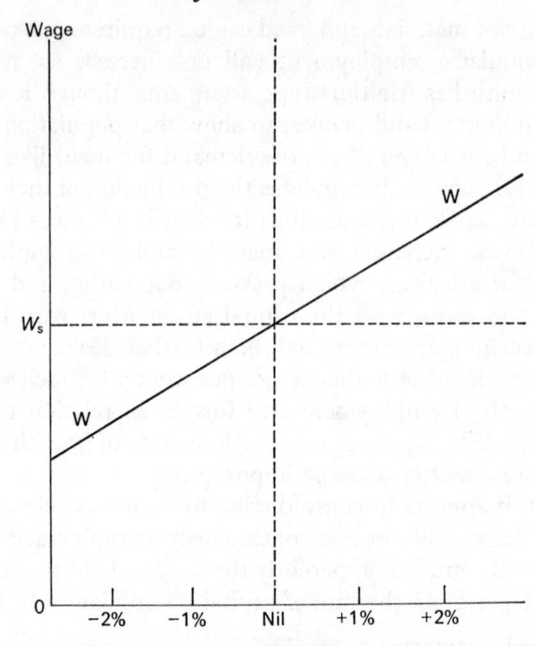

FIG. 2 *Rate of Growth of Capital*

be needed to produce the appropriate rate of population growth. Thus, if the rate of accumulation increased in any country, there would be a leakage into higher wages at first as part of the extra capital stock had to be diverted to the payment of higher wages per head, but this would cease once wages had risen sufficiently to produce the new rate of population growth. After this only extra fixed capital and raw materials per head would prevent employment from rising as fast as the capital stock.

However, the view that wages will reach the *level* appropriate to the rate of accumulation and then rise no further is only correct if two important qualifications are made. First, it must be possible for employment and population to grow fast enough to prevent a continuous rise in wages. This is evidently not always possible: 'Notwithstanding the great increase [in population] occasioned by such early marriages, there is a continual complaint of the scarcity of hands in North America. The demand for labourers, the funds destined for maintaining them, increase, it seems, still faster than they can find labourers to employ' (WN I.viii.23). Wages must obviously go on rising so long as this situation persists—and similar conditions have applied to many countries since 1776.[18] The second

[18] M. Blaug points out that wages may rise continuously in Smith's argument where the demand for labour grows faster than the supply in *Economic Theory in Retrospect* (1962), 46–7.

qualification is that, as Smith points out, the argument represented in Fig. 2 applies precisely to the wage measured in corn:

> ... the money price of labour, which must always be such as to enable the labourer to purchase a quantity of corn sufficient to maintain him and his family either in the liberal, moderate, or scanty manner in which the advancing, stationary or declining circumstances of the society oblige his employers to maintain him. (WN IV.v.a.12)

Hence, Fig. 2 corresponds to Smith's theory of wages if the vertical axis shows wages measured in corn. Now, as capital accumulates and employment grows, the prices of most manufactured goods will fall continuously in relation to the price of corn as labour is more and more subdivided in the manufacture of each good.[19] This means that the wage will rise when it is measured in manufactured goods, and this is precisely the line of argument that was presented at the start of the paper as the great feature that distinguishes *The Wealth of Nations* from later classical writing.

To sum up Smith's theory of wages: measured in corn, only the level of wages will vary with the rate of growth of capital, but measured in manufactured goods, the rate of change of wages will also vary with this so the manufactured goods a worker can buy will rise continuously with capital accumulation—as goods become cheaper relative to corn and labour. Measured in cattle or poultry, wages fall as capital accumulates because these become continuously dearer in relation to corn, but measured in vegetables, wages rise, and in Smith's opinion cheaper vegetables will matter more than dearer meat to most poorer workers (WN I.xi.m.10). Thus as the wealth and population of a country grow, workers may come to eat a little better or worse (depending on their relative expenditure on vegetables and meat), but they will enjoy a continuous growth in purchasing power in terms of manufactured goods, and as only a small fraction of the labour force is so poorly paid that most of its income must go on food, the great majority of workers will gain substantially. Thus, as capital accumulates, most workers will become better off, and they will continue to become better off for so long as accumulation is able to continue. This means that as a society advances, employment will grow less quickly than the capital stock, both because of the need to increase fixed capital and raw materials per worker, and because wages per worker will rise—if these are thought of as a weighted average of corn, meat, and manufactures.

The above argument suggests that Smith's theory of wages differs in several important respects from the 'iron law of wages' to which it is often

[19] It might be thought that the increased subdivision of labour would reduce the relative prices of all manufactured goods, but in a 'few' cases the unfavourable effects of rising raw material costs outweigh the favourable effects of increasing returns in the manufacturing process (see WN I.xi.o.2).

supposed that the classical economists all subscribed. This should not appear surprising. Malthus certainly thought that he had discovered something new in 1798, and he would have rejected the view that his theory of population and wages was all in Smith. There are, moreover, optimistic passages about the effect of economic development on living standards in *The Wealth of Nations* which have no parallel in the work of Malthus and Ricardo. It should not therefore be taken for granted as it often is that Smith's theory of wages was the same as that of his successors.

To turn now to profits, these are determined by two main considerations in *The Wealth of Nations*. On the one hand, capital accumulation reduces profits:

> The increase of stock, which raises wages, tends to lower profit. When the stocks of many rich merchants are turned into the same trade, their mutual competition naturally tends to lower its profit; and when there is a like increase of stock in all the different trades carried on in the same society, the same competition must produce the same effect in them all.
>
> (WN I.ix.2)

However, new investment opportunities raise the rate of return:

> The acquisition of new territory, or of new branches of trade, may sometimes raise the profits of stock, and with them the interest of money, even in a country which is fast advancing in the acquisition of riches . . . Part of what had before been employed in other trades, is necessarily withdrawn from them, and turned into some of the new and more profitable ones. In all those old trades, therefore, the competition comes to be less than before.
>
> (WN I.ix.12)

Perhaps the crucial factor is stock in relation to the business that is transacted, or in modern terms, the ratio of capital to output:

> In a country fully stocked in proportion to all the business it had to transact, as great a quantity of stock would be employed in every particular branch as the nature and extent of the trade would admit. The competition, therefore, would every-where be as great, and consequently the ordinary profit as low as possible.
>
> (WN I.ix.14)

This suggests that the rate of profit may rise or fall in the course of development, and that it should certainly tend to fall where the rate of capital accumulation much exceeds the rate of growth of output.

This completes the consideration of *The Wealth of Nations* that enables us to state the assumptions about returns to scale, capital accumulation, fixed capital requirements, and wages that are appropriate to a modern restatement of Smith's theory of growth. The essential assumptions that must be carried forward to Part II are that there will be increasing returns to scale in industry until a country's full potential for development is realized, and constant or diminishing returns in agriculture and mining; that the ability to exploit the inherent potential for growth that follows from increasing returns depends on capital accumulation which is a function of the ratio of productive to unproductive employment and the profitability of productive employment; and that fixed capital, raw materials, and wages per head (as a weighted average of manufactures and food) will all rise as the economy grows, while whether there is upward or downward pressure on profits should depend largely on the relative growth rates of capital and output. There is no production function where the substitution of capital for labour depends on relative factor prices in *The Wealth of Nations*.

II A WEALTH OF NATIONS GROWTH MODEL

In this section of the paper, the growth model that follows from the assumptions arrived at in Part I will be presented in two stages. A very simple version of the model will be presented first, and in this the complicating effects of fixed capital will be ignored. It will emerge that it is possible to arrive at most of Smith's results with a very simple circulating capital model. However, fixed capital plays an important role in *The Wealth of Nations*, and it will be brought into the second stage of the argument to produce a richer and more general model, though one that is a little more complex than the circulating capital model that is presented first.

It emerged in Part I that returns to scale play a crucial role in *The Wealth of Nations*, and that they depend on the extent to which the tasks performed by labour can be subdivided. A function which shows the effect of this is:

$$Y = \lambda . L_p^Z \qquad (1)$$

where Y is the output achieved in the very long run at each level of productive employment, L_p, while λ is a constant, and Z shows whether returns to scale are increasing, constant, or diminishing. If there are constant returns, Z will equal 1 and doubling L_p will then double Y. If there are increasing returns, Z will exceed 1, causing Y to vary more than proportionately with L_p, while it will vary less than proportionately if Z is less than 1.[20] In the example from Smith's lectures that was quoted in Part I, a ten-times increase in L_p raised Y a hundred times in industry, and this result would be produced by a Z of 2.

It follows from (1) that:

$$g = Z . n_p \qquad (2)$$

[20] Equation (1) can be written as $(Y/L_p) = \lambda . L_p^{Z-1}$, and this produces the schedule, AB, of Fig. 1, i.e. a rising straight line (on a double log scale) with a slope of $(Z-1)$.

where g is the long-term rate of growth of output $(1/Y.dY/dt)$, while n_p is the rate of growth of productive employment $(1/L_p.dL_p/dt)$, so the long-term rate of growth of output is Z times the rate of growth of productive employment.

Of course, employment cannot be increased without capital accumulation, and two equations are relevant to the relationship between the rate of growth of employment and the rate of capital accumulation. First, there is the population supply equation, where the rate of growth of population and the labour force (and these will be assumed to grow at the same rate) depend on the rate of capital accumulation. This equation can be written as:

$$n = A.k_c \tag{3}$$

where n is the rate of growth of the total labour force $(1/L.dL/dt)$, k_c is the rate of growth of circulating capital $(1/K_c.dK_c/dt)$, and A is a constant. In a purely Malthusian model, A would be 1, but it will be less than 1 in a *Wealth of Nations* growth model because raw material[21] and possibly also wage costs per head[22] rise with capital accumulation. It is to be noted that the proposition that A is less than 1 (which will prove to be of crucial importance) does not rest solely on the argument that wages rise with capital accumulation. An increase in raw material costs per worker as capital accumulates is quite sufficient to make A less than 1, even if wages are entirely unaffected by the rate of capital accumulation.

The second equation that relates the rate of growth of employment to the rate of capital accumulation is the 'wages fund' equation that follows from the proposition that circulating capital is used to provide wages and raw materials prior to production. If the proportion of the labour force that is employed productively is q, it can be assumed, following Smith, that a fraction, q, of circulating capital, i.e. $q.K_c$ is used to provide wages and raw materials for L_p productive workers, and if the cost of providing wages and raw materials for each productive worker is W:

$$q.K_c = L_p.W. \tag{4}$$

Then, if q, the proportion of the labour force that is employed productively, is constant, the rate of growth of circulating capital will equal the rate of growth of productive employment *plus* the rate of increase in the cost of employing a worker, i.e.

$$k_c = n_p + w \tag{5}$$

where k_c and n_p are the rates of growth of circulating capital and productive

[21] See p. 436 above. [22] See p. 439 above.

employment as before, while w is the rate of increase in the wage and raw material costs of employing a worker ($1/W.dW/dt$).

If q is constant, $n_p = n$, and (2), (3), and (5) will then allow the long-term rates of growth of output, employment, and the wage and raw material costs of employing a worker to be expressed as multiples of the rate of growth of circulating capital. Thus:

$$g = A.Z.k_c \tag{6}$$

$$n = n_p = A.k_c \tag{7}$$

$$w = (1-A).k_c. \tag{8}$$

Then the rate of growth of circulating capital determines the rates of growth of output, population, and wage and raw material costs per head, and a faster rate of capital accumulation will produce faster long-term rates of growth of each of these. Output may grow faster or more slowly than the capital stock, but population and wage and raw material costs per head must both grow more slowly than capital, since A must be less than 1.

To complete the model, what determines k_c, the rate of growth of circulating capital, must be set out. This has been worked out for a circulating capital model of the kind outlined here by Sir John Hicks, and his equation can be arrived at as follows.[23] Y_t, the output of productive workers in period t, can be regarded as the economy's circulating capital in period $(t+1)$, so $K_{c,t+1} = Y_t$. An expression for $K_{c,t}$ can be obtained from (4), i.e.

$$K_{c,t} = \frac{1}{q}(L_{p,t}.W_t),$$

with the result that

$$\frac{K_{c,t+1}}{K_{c,t}} = q\left(\frac{Y_t/L_{p,t}}{W_t}\right).$$

Then:

$$\frac{K_{c,t+1}-K_{c,t}}{K_{c,t}} = q.\left(\frac{Y_t/L_{p,t}}{W_t}\right)-1. \tag{9}$$

Now $(K_{c,t+1}-K_{c,t})/K_{c,t}$ is the rate of growth of circulating capital per period. Up to now, k_c has been written for this, and these are equivalent, but the correct form of the accumulation equation is necessarily a period one since one year's output is the next year's capital. (9) shows that the rate of growth of circulating capital depends on q, the proportion of the labour force employed productively, and on the ratio of output per productive worker, Y/L_p, to W, the cost of employing a worker, and this clearly corresponds to Smith's own argument. Thus, if for instance two economies

[23] See J. R. Hicks, *Capital and Growth* (1965), Ch. 4.

have equal technical opportunities for growth, and one has less unproductive employment than the other, i.e. a higher q, that economy will also have a faster rate of capital accumulation (from (9)), and therefore faster growth rates of output, population and wages per head (from (6), (7), and (8)).

The next step in the argument is to consider the question of whether the rate of capital accumulation will rise or fall through time. If q is given for various economies as is being assumed, the rate of capital accumulation will grow if $(Y/L_p)/W$ grows, i.e. if Y grows at a faster rate than $L_p . W$, and vice versa. The rate of growth of Y is g which equals $A.Z.k_c$ (from (6)), while the rate of growth of $L_p . W$ is $(n_p + w)$ which equals k_c (from (7) and (8)), so the rate of capital accumulation will rise through time if $A.Z.k_c$ exceeds k_c, and fall if $A.Z.k_c$ is less than k_c. This leads to the very simple condition:

$$\text{Rate of change of } k_c \gtrless 0 \quad \text{where } Z \gtrless 1/A. \qquad (10)$$

Then, whether an economy will enjoy a rising or a falling rate of capital accumulation will depend simply on whether Z, the returns-to-scale variable, is greater or less than $1/A$, and $1/A$ must exceed 1 since A must be less than 1. Then accumulation can only continue at an increasing or constant rate in conditions where increasing returns predominate, and these must be sufficient to hold Z at or above $1/A$. Thus, it is to be noted that the mere existence of increasing returns will not be sufficient to produce indefinite progress.

It turns out that the relationship between Z and $1/A$ does not merely determine whether the rate of capital accumulation will rise or fall through time. It is evident from (6) that g will exceed k_c, i.e. that an economy will enjoy a rising output-capital ratio, if Z exceeds $1/A$, and vice versa.[24] Moreover, as 'profits and rent' are the excess of output over wage and raw material costs, the share of 'profits and rent' in output will grow where $(Y/L_p)/W$ grows, and decline where this declines, so this too will depend on the relationship between Z and $1/A$. Where Z exceeds $1/A$, the share of 'profits and rent' in output will grow, and it will decline where Z is less than $1/A$. Furthermore, as (output/capital) rises where Z exceeds $1/A$, and (profits and rent)/output also rises,

$$\left(\frac{\text{output}}{\text{capital}}\right) \times \left(\frac{\text{profits and rent}}{\text{output}}\right) \text{ which equals } \left(\frac{\text{profits and rent}}{\text{capital}}\right)$$

must rise, and as profits are likely to gain in relation to rent where output

[24] In Irma Adelman's interesting restatement of Smith's theory of growth (*Theories of Economic Growth and Development* (1962)), Ch. 3, increasing returns together with capital accumulation always produce a falling marginal capital–output ratio. She arrives at this result because she does not allow for the need for increasing raw materials per worker, etc., as capital accumulates.

grows faster than capital, it is particularly clear that (profits/capital) or the rate of return on capital will rise through time where Z exceeds $1/A$.

Three possible development paths for growing economies can then be distinguished:

1. Where Z exceeds $1/A$, the rate of capital accumulation will increase from period to period, while the capital–output ratio will fall and the rate of profit on capital and the share of 'profits and rent' in output will rise.
2. Where Z equals $1/A$, the rate of capital accumulation, the capital–output ratio, the rate of profit, and the share of 'profits and rent' will be constant.
3. Where Z is less than $1/A$, the rate of capital accumulation, the rate of profit, and the 'share of profits and rent' will fall continuously, while the capital–output ratio will rise continuously, until capital accumulation ceases, and once capital accumulation ceases, there will be no further change in the capital–output ratio, the rate of profit, etc.

Thus, whether Z is greater or less than $1/A$ is a matter of the utmost importance. It is no wonder that there are numerous passages in *The Wealth of Nations* (which will be mentioned in Part III of this paper) where attention is drawn to the favourable effects on the long-term growth opportunities of the economy of growing demand for industrial goods at home and abroad (as a result of the full exploitation of trading opportunities), for these will increase the over-all Z of the economy since industry has a high Z.

The economy's Z will be high where the proportion of the labour force employed in industry is high, and the opportunities to benefit from a further subdivision of labour are still considerable. If a point is reached where further subdivision produces diminishing benefits, Z will fall from period to period, and it must then eventually become less than $1/A$, however high its original starting point. The rate of capital accumulation will slow down as soon as Z becomes less than $1/A$, and the capital–output ratio will start to rise, while the rate of profit on capital and the share of 'profits and rent' in output will both start to fall—until a point is reached eventually where accumulation ceases altogether, and a society will then have realized its full potential for development, given its ratio of unproductive employment, etc.

These are the principal results that follow from the circulating capital model that has been considered so far. It is now time to introduce fixed capital into the argument, and this can be done in the following way. Up to now, it has been supposed that the employment of L workers will merely require a circulating capital of $W.L$, and it can be assumed from this point onwards that a fixed capital of $\Phi.L^B$ will also be needed, where Φ is a constant, and B exceeds 1. With $B > 1$, fixed capital requirements will grow more than proportionately with population and employment as Smith assumed. Writing K for total capital, K_c for circulating capital, and K_f for fixed capital, it is being assumed that:

$$K = K_f + K_c = \Phi . L^B + W . L. \tag{11}$$

The introduction of fixed capital will not alter the basic returns-to-scale equation which led to (2): more capital is now needed to provide employment for a given labour force, but its output can still be written as $\lambda . L^Z$.[25] Moreover, fixed capital will not affect the population supply equation or the wages fund equation ((3) and (5)), so (6), (7), and (8) will be unaltered. It is only (9), the capital accumulation equation, that will be altered, and this will be affected in the following way. It was assumed earlier that the entire output of period t became the circulating capital of period $(t+1)$ so that $Y_t = K_{c,t+1}$, but part of the output of period t will now need to consist of additions to fixed capital. Provided that Y_t is the output of period t *net* of the depreciation of fixed capital, Y_t will become the circulating capital of period $(t+1)$ *plus* the addition to fixed capital between periods t and $t+1$. Thus:

$$Y_t = K_{c,t+1} + (K_{f,t+1} - K_{f,t}).$$

Now $K_{c,t}$ will equal $1/q . L_{p,t} . W_t$ as before so that:

$$\frac{K_{c,t+1} - K_{c,t}}{K_{c,t}} = q\left(\frac{Y_t/L_{p,t}}{W_t}\right) - 1 - \frac{K_{f,t+1} - K_{f,t}}{K_{c,t}}.$$

As

$$A . B . K_{f,t}\left(\frac{K_{c,t+1} - K_{c,t}}{K_{c,t}}\right)$$

can be written for $(K_{f,t+1} - K_{f,t})$:[26]

$$\frac{K_{c,t+1} - K_{c,t}}{K_{c,t}} = \frac{q\left(\frac{Y_t/L_{p,t}}{W_t}\right) - 1}{1 + A . B . (K_{f,t}/K_{c,t})}. \tag{12}$$

Now a comparison between (9), the capital accumulation equation in the earlier circulating capital model, and the present capital accumulation equation shows that the rate of growth of capital in the earlier equation now has to be divided by $[1 + A . B . (K_f/K_c)]$. Thus the rate of growth of capital will always be lower (*cet. par.*) in the present fixed capital model.

[25] It is to be noted that Z will exceed 1 to a greater extent than before if increasing returns are stronger in a fixed capital model (and fixed capital certainly plays a substantial part in Smith's account of increasing returns in industry), but a higher Z would have no effect on the basic form of (2).

[26] $K_{f,t+1} - K_{f,t} = \phi . L^B{}_{t+1} - \phi . L^B{}_t = \phi . L^B{}_t((1+n)^B - 1) = n . B . \phi . L^B{}_t$ since n will be small in a single period. Now $K_{f,t}$ can be written for $\phi . L^B{}_t$, and $A . (K_{c,t+1} - K_{c,t})/K_{c,t}$ for n (from (7) using the period form of this equation which is legitimate where n is small).

This is because the provision of fixed capital for extra workers is an additional factor in the capital cost of growth, so more resources will be needed, for instance a higher ratio of productive employment, to produce any given growth rate.

It was shown above that the critical condition for a constant rate of growth in the circulating capital model was that Z should equal $1/A$. Clearly, if Z equalled $1/A$ in (12), $(Y/L_p)/W$ would be constant, but the growth rate would still fall continuously if K_f/K_c was rising, and rise if this was falling. Thus, if the ratio of fixed to circulating capital rose through time, the need to invest in fixed capital as employment grew would act as an increasing brake on accumulation, while it would act as a brake of diminishing intensity if the ratio of fixed to circulating capital was falling. Whether this ratio rises or falls through time is therefore important.

The ratio of fixed to circulating capital will rise if k_f, the rate of growth of fixed capital, exceeds k_c, the rate of growth of circulating capital, and vice versa. k_f is the rate of growth of K_f, i.e. the rate of growth of $\Phi . L^B$, and this is $B.n$, or $A.B.k_c$ (from (7)) so that:

$$k_f/k_c = A.B. \tag{13}$$

Then the ratio of fixed to circulating capital will be constant if $A.B = 1$, i.e. if $B = 1/A$: and it will rise through time if B exceeds $1/A$, and fall if B is less than $1/A$. Hence, the need to provide fixed capital for a growing labour force will act as an increasing brake on growth if $B > 1/A$, and a diminishing brake if $B < 1/A$.

In the earlier circulating capital model, the rate of capital accumulation and the economy's other major variables were constant through time when Z equalled $1/A$, and this proposition will not be disturbed if the ratio of fixed to circulating capital is also constant, i.e. if B also equals $1/A$. Then the condition for a constant rate of growth, a constant rate of profit, a constant capital–output ratio, and constant distribution is that $B = Z = 1/A$.

Clearly the development of the economy through time will depend on how high B and Z are in relation to $1/A$. The simplest way of analysing the effect of values of B or Z that are inappropriate for a constant rate of growth is to assume in each case that the value of the other is appropriate, i.e. that $Z = 1/A$ where the value of B is inappropriate, and that $B = 1/A$ where Z is inappropriate. These possibilities will be considered in turn.

1. The effect of an inappropriate B

If B exceeds $1/A$ (and Z), the ratio of fixed to circulating capital will rise continuously, and this will reduce the rate of capital accumulation from period to period. Moreover, the capital–output ratio will rise continuously. Equality between Z and $1/A$ will ensure that the ratio of circulating capital to output is constant (from (6)), but as fixed capital rises continuously in relation to circulating capital, the over-all capital–output ratio must rise from period to period. Equality between Z and $1/A$ keeps the share of 'profits and rent' in output constant, but if a rising capital–output ratio acts against profits relative to rent, then the share of profits will fall and the share of rents rise. A rising capital–output ratio will reduce the rate of profit on capital, even if the share of profits is constant, and if this falls, the rate of profit will be doubly reduced. Hence a higher B than Z and $1/A$ will produce a declining rate of growth, a declining rate of profit, a rising capital–output ratio, and possibly a declining share of profits also. A lower B will produce the opposite effects.

2. *The effect of an inappropriate* Z

If Z exceeds B and $1/A$ where these are equal, the ratio of fixed to circulating capital will be constant, so the model will behave exactly as the circulating capital model that was analysed earlier, i.e. a higher Z will produce accelerating growth, a rising rate of profit, a rising share of profits, a falling capital–output ratio, etc. A lower Z will produce the opposite effects.

It appears then that the effects on the economy of a high B and a low Z are rather similar. The analysis has, of course, been simplified by focusing attention on one variable at a time. Smith may well have envisaged a growing ratio of fixed to circulating capital, especially in view of what he said about cattle, i.e. a B that exceeded $1/A$, and strong increasing returns for a time if a country could so arrange its affairs (through trading opportunities and so on) that it could take advantage of the potential gains from increasing returns in industry over a considerable range of its output: this being followed by a period where increasing returns became less important as the advantages from further subdivisions of labour diminished. Here Z would start high and then fall. If this was his view, then the present model would produce the result of either accelerating or declining growth while B and Z both exceeded $1/A$: the high Z would act as a stimulus and the high B as a brake, and either could exercise the dominant influence, though obviously a high enough Z would be bound to do so. Once Z fell, however, the high B and low Z (in relation to $1/A$ which must always exceed 1) would both act as an increasing brake on growth. Moreover, the high B and low Z would both reduce the rate of profit from period to period, etc. More will be said about the relationship between Smith's predictions in *The Wealth of Nations* and the predictions of the model in Part III, the concluding section of this paper.

However, before the present account of the model is completed, it may be worthwhile to relax one further assumption. Up to now, in the account that has been given, the various sectors of the economy have been considered together, so that Z has been a kind of weighted average of returns to scale in industry and agriculture, etc. Suppose instead that the various sectors are considered separately, starting with corn where it is clear Smith thought that Z was 1 (since he assumed constant costs), and that $1/A$ and B exceeded 1 because of the need to increase fixed capital (i.e. cattle) and raw materials per worker. With these assumptions, the rate of growth, the rate of profit, and the share of 'profits and rent' would all decline (at a rate depending on the extent to which B and $1/A$ exceeded Z), and the capital–output ratio would rise continuously, when these were all measured in corn. Then a declining rate of profit in agriculture would be the only possible result of the model, and assuming that profit rates are equalized between sectors, manufactured goods would have to be so priced that a declining rate of profit was also earned on the manufacture of these, with the result that the entire benefits from increasing returns would be more than reflected in lower prices. Real wages (measured in manufactured goods) would then benefit substantially. The agricultural part of this argument has perhaps a little too much of Ricardo in it, and it may well be more sensible to think of Smith's as a 'weighted average' model with each sector playing a part, rather than one where production conditions in the corn sector determine the rate of profit in the other sectors of the economy. However, Smith's chapter on corn bounties has a lot of Ricardo in it (though there may be some special pleading in this chapter), and the possibility that he had an underlying corn model of the kind considered in this paragraph in mind cannot be excluded. Both this model and the 'weighted average of sectors' model can be set out with the help of the basic relationships that have been outlined.

III THE RESULTS OF THE MODEL AND SOME OF ADAM SMITH'S CONCLUSIONS

The model, like *The Wealth of Nations*, attributes overwhelming importance to the rate of capital accumulation. Without this, population and the labour force would not grow, industry would not expand so the potential gains in productivity that could follow from increased subdivisions of labour could not be exploited, and the manufactured goods that workers could buy would not increase. The rate of capital accumulation itself depends on the proportion of the labour force that is employed productively, and on the efficiency of productive workers. The first three paragraphs of *The Wealth of Nations* bring out that these are, in Smith's view, the key factors, so the central features of the model certainly correspond to Smith's own view of what is crucial.

This preliminary correspondence is not surprising, because an account of *The Wealth of Nations* could hardly be produced which failed to attribute overwhelming importance to accumulation and what causes it, and the virtues of thrift, '. . . every prodigal appears to be a public enemy, and every frugal man a public benefactor' (WN II.iii.25), and of economies in public expenditure. These were among Smith's main legacies to the nineteenth century.

A second central feature of the argument of the model is the role of increasing returns, and Smith devoted the first three chapters of *The Wealth of Nations* to the division of labour, so a modern account of his argument must allow these to play an equally crucial role. In the model that has just been outlined, the relationships between Z, the returns-to-scale variable, and A and B are crucial, and Z is perhaps best thought of as a weighted average of returns to scale in industry and agriculture. Hence, if Smith's view was similar, there should be a number of passages in *The Wealth of Nations* which speak of the crucial effect on the rate of development of an economy of the size of the industrial sector of the economy in relation to the agricultural. Perhaps two quotations will suffice to demonstrate the importance of building up a manufacturing sector:

A small quantity of manufactured produce purchases a great quantity of rude produce. A trading and manufacturing country, therefore, naturally purchases with a small part of its manufactured produce a great part of the rude produce of other countries; while, on the contrary, a country without trade and manufactures is generally obliged to purchase, at the expence of a great part of its rude produce, a very small part of the manufactured produce of other countries. The one exports what can subsist and accommodate but a very few, and imports the subsistence and accommodation of a great number. The other exports the subsistence and accommodation of a great number, and imports that of a very few only. The inhabitants of the one must always enjoy a much greater quantity of subsistence than what their own lands, in the actual state of their cultivation, could afford.

(WN IV.ix.37)

And two pages later:

Without an extensive foreign market, [manufactures] could not well flourish, either in countries so moderately extensive as to afford but a narrow home market; or in countries where the communication between one province and another was so difficult, as to render it impossible for the goods of any particular place to enjoy the whole of that home market which the country could afford. The perfection of manufacturing industry, it must be remembered, depends altogether upon the division of labour; and the degree to which the division of labour can be introduced into any manufacture, is necessarily regulated, it has already been shown, by the extent of the market.

(WN IV.ix.41)

There are also passages which speak of the benefits derived by European industry from the colonization of America (WN IV.vii.c.7), and of the advantages that are derived where the rich buy manufactures instead of employing servants, and these refer to other advantages of a demand for manufactures (WN II.iii.38–42).

Clearly capital accumulation and increasing returns play a central role in *The Wealth of Nations*, but there are other propositions in the book which do not at first sight fit the view that a thrifty society will enjoy indefinite progress as a result of increasing returns, provided that the market for manufactures grows. There are two types of proposition in *The Wealth of Nations* that do not correspond with this first approximation to Smith's argument, and these must be explained in any attempt to provide a modern reconstruction.

First, Smith argued that a given employment of capital in agriculture would provide a larger surplus for reinvestment (and therefore more growth of employment) than an equivalent investment of capital in industry —which apparently contradicts the view that growth is a function of the ratio of industrial to agricultural output. Thus:

> When the capital of any country is not sufficient for all . . . purposes, in proportion as a greater share of it is employed in agriculture, the greater will be the quantity of productive labour which it puts into motion within the country; as will likewise be the value which its employment adds to the annual produce of the land and labour of the society. After agriculture, the capital employed in manufactures puts into motion the greatest quantity of productive labour, and adds the greatest value to the annual produce.
>
> (WN II.v.19)

For

> The labourers and labouring cattle, therefore, employed in agriculture, not only occasion, like the workmen in manufactures, the reproduction of a value equal to their own consumption, or to the capital which employs them, together with its owners' profits; but of a much greater value. Over and above the capital of the farmer and all its profits, they regularly occasion the reproduction of the rent of the landlord.
>
> (WN II.v.12)

And, Smith adds:

> It has been the principal cause of the rapid progress of our American colonies towards wealth and greatness, that almost their whole capitals have hitherto been employed in agriculture . . . Were the Americans, either by combination or by any other sort of violence, to stop the importation of European manufactures, and, by thus giving a monopoly to such of their own countrymen as could manufacture the like goods, divert any considerable part of their capital into this employment, they would retard instead of accelerating the further increase in the value of their annual produce, and would obstruct instead of promoting the progress of their country towards real wealth and greatness.
>
> (WN II.v.21)

Now these statements, which superficially contradict what has been said so far, follow directly from the model that was outlined in Part II. There, the rate of capital accumulation which determines the growth of employment depends very substantially on q, the ratio of productive employment, and on $(Y/L_p)/W$, the ratio of output per worker to the cost of employing a worker, and any increase in $(Y/L_p)/W$ will more than proportionately raise the rate of capital accumulation. Now, $(Y/L_p)/W$ is clearly highest in agriculture for the reasons that Smith gives, and it is even proper to include rent in Y/L_p for the purposes of this accumulation equation if there are constant costs in agriculture. However, the argument appeared incorrect to Smith's successors, for instance Ricardo,[27] but it follows directly from the re-statement of Smith's theory in this paper. The unimpeded use of resources in agriculture is central to the achievement of an adequate rate of capital accumulation, because the ratio of output per worker to the cost of employ-ing a worker is highest in agriculture. However, the *effects* of accumulation as distinct from what causes this depend upon Z, and the effect of a Z greater than 1 will be more favourable, the higher the ratio of industrial output in total output. There is thus a trade-off between agriculture which favours the *rate* of accumulation, and industry which favours the *effects* of accumulation. Smith was fully aware of both propositions, but in the context of a world where some countries achieved no accumulation at all, while Great Britain and most other European countries had taken five hundred years to double the population they could support, (WN I.viii.23) the first priority could reasonably be the achievement of accumulation: and to obstruct this through *artificial* policies to raise Z by helping industry *at the expense* of agriculture was misguided, and these policies are criticized throughout Book III of *The Wealth of Nations*. In the case of North America, accumulation was so rapid that it was continuously raising wages even in terms of corn, and there was nothing to be gained by slowing down the rate of accumulation.

A second set of passages in *The Wealth of Nations* which stand in the way of the simple interpretation that accumulation and increasing returns will lead to unlimited progress are the passages which speak of the eventual completion of the accumulation process, after which wages and profits would both become low, for instance:

In a country which had acquired that full complement of riches which the nature of its soil and climate, and its situation with respect to other countries, allowed

[27] See Ricardo, *Principles* (*Works and Correspondence*, i), Ch. 26. Hollander, op. cit. 195, 280–7, has also suggested that this part of Smith's argument is 'unsound'. He has, however, seen the argument as the purely static one that the employment of capital in agriculture produces an *immediately* higher *level* of employment, and this only follows if capital costs per worker are lower in agriculture, which is not clear. He does not mention Smith's dynamic argument that agriculture produces a faster *rate of growth* of employment, as in North America, and therefore a level of employment that rapidly becomes higher.

it to acquire; which could, therefore, advance no further, and which was not going backwards, both the wages of labour and the profits of stock would probably be very low.

(WN I.ix.14)

Here, there are low wages, low profits, and zero growth, even though thriftiness conditions, etc., may be very favourable. The implication of 'full complement of riches' is, however, that gains from the division of labour are no longer possible. Once increasing returns cease in the model outlined in this paper, Z falls to 1 or below, and this leads to a declining rate of growth, a declining rate and share of profits, and a rising capital–output ratio, etc. Now, as the rate of capital accumulation falls, the wage (measured in corn) will fall which will restore profitability for a time, but the low Z will always set profits on a downward path again until, as Smith says, the wage (in corn) has become appropriate to a stationary state, and profits will also have fallen very low when this is reached. Thus, passages of the kind just quoted are fully in line with the predictions of the model if it is assumed that the benefits from the division of labour have upper limits.[28]

In the stationary state that has just been described, the wage is, of course, high in terms of manufactured goods, since the division of labour has reached an upper limit, and Smith did not mention this, though it follows from his argument where there are many passages which explain that the relative prices of most manufactured goods must fall as a society progresses, and there is no suggestion that this trend is ever reversed. He spelt out the details of the stationary state no more than Keynes bothered to provide a detailed description of the ultimate destination of a Keynesian economy with the rentier 'euthanised', and the rate of profit reduced to negligible proportions. Such propositions were not relevant to the main work of Smith and Keynes, which was to provide an account of the working of the economies that they lived in.

Smith was arguably as successful as Keynes in this great task. His was recognized as an accurate and plausible account of the way in which eighteenth-century economies worked by most of his contemporaries, and his influence on public policy was as great as that of Keynes, and, it may turn out, longer lasting, for the central policy propositions of *The Wealth of Nations* dominated British economic policy and legislation for over a century.

[28] William O. Thweatt in 'A Diagrammatic Representation of Adam Smith's Growth Model', *Social Research*, xxiv, no. 2 (1957), shows a continuous increase in the rate of profit as capital accumulates, and following Schumpeter, he describes Smith's growth model as a 'hitchless' one. His diagrammatic representation clearly fails to take the factors which produce a declining rate of profit in *The Wealth of Nations* into account. A. Lowe mentions one of these in 'The Classical Theory of Growth', *Social Research*, xxi, no. 2 (1954), the article on which Thweatt's lucid diagram is based, but he says that a Smithian economy will move forward in 'dynamic equilibrium' in the absence of 'disturbances from without'. See also the article by Lowe in this volume.

Smith did not, however, write out an account of his theory of growth and development that had the impact that it should have had on the thought of professional economists. Something like the model in this paper is needed to integrate increasing returns and the accumulation equation with his propositions about increasing raw material costs, etc., and while Smith may well have understood the full complexities of his argument—a great thinker will hardly arrive at consistent results by chance—he only published (and he may only have put on paper) what could be understood by all. Because of this, increasing returns in industry played virtually no part in the thought of his successors; their books omitted anything equivalent to Smith's first three chapters, and without this, a crucial element in classical economics was lost.[29]

[29] Cf. N. Kaldor, 'The Irrelevance of Equilibrium Economics', *Economic Journal*, lxxxii (Dec. 1972).

X

Adam Smith and the Theory of International Trade

ARTHUR I. BLOOMFIELD*

INTRODUCTION

ADAM Smith is justly famous in the history of international-trade doctrines for his vigorous attack on mercantilism and for his spirited espousal of free trade. For his day and beyond, this accomplishment alone would compel attention. In this area, as in others, his profound insights and subsequent influence assure him a lasting place in the history of economics.

By contrast, there has been a tendency to slight Smith's contributions to the pure theory of international trade. Various writers, while acknowledging his undeniable importance and influence as an economist, have referred to shortcomings, oversimplifications, and even inconsistencies in his theorizing on foreign trade. Others have questioned the originality of his free-trade ideas.

Bastable, for example, notes that 'we cannot say that there is any special contribution to the theory of foreign trade in *The Wealth of Nations.* [Smith's] views on the real advantage of such trade are somewhat doubtfully expressed, while his explanation of the division of gain between two trading countries is plainly erroneous. Nor has he grasped the condition governing the international distribution of the precious metals.'[1] Robbins speaks of Smith's foreign-trade doctrines as having 'very little analytical edge' and as being 'mixed up with doctrines which take a good deal of charitable interpretation to make sense at all in this context'.[2] Viner, in reviewing the earlier English economic literature, argues that 'all the important elements in Smith's free-trade doctrine had been presented prior to *The Wealth of Nations*', although he expresses doubt that these earlier expositions had much influence on Smith (or Hume).[3]

* Professor of Economics, University of Pennsylvania. The author is indebted to his colleagues Professors Wilfred J. Ethier, Irving B. Kravis, and Sidney Weintraub for helpful comments, and to Mr. David A. Gart for valuable assistance in checking references and in handling other library chores.

[1] C. F. Bastable, *The Theory of International Trade* (1903), 168–9.

[2] L. Robbins, *Money, Trade, and International Relations* (1971), 191.

[3] J. Viner, *Studies in the Theory of International Trade* (1937), 108–9. Viner also cautions that there has been great exaggeration of the extent to which free-trade views already prevailed in the English literature before Smith (ibid. 91–2).

Other historians of trade theory likewise give Smith only passing notice.[4] Contemporary trade theorists who have enough antiquarian interest to refer to the classical economists usually confine their respects to Ricardo and Mill and, with a few notable exceptions, tend to disregard Smith altogether. Even Smith's critique of mercantilism, it is said, was marred by undue polemics and by the fact that he himself was not completely free of the misconceptions and prejudices that he was attacking.

Such explicit and implicit assessments of Smith's position in the evolution of trade theory seem to be unduly slighting. Admittedly, his trade theory does not match that of Ricardo or Mill. But it stands up very well in relation to that of the more eminent of his contemporaries and predecessors. His analysis of foreign trade was much more detailed than that of Hume—on whom he undoubtedly drew to some extent—and in various respects went much beyond it. His performance in this area was clearly superior to that of the Physiocrats,[5] Steuart, and even Cantillon. Apart from his debt to Hume, moreover, most of his trade doctrines seem to have been worked out more or less independently. Even if he *had* drawn on the scattered elements of free-trade doctrine available in the literature before Hume, he would still deserve credit, in this field as in others, for an admirable job of synthesis, systematization, and elaboration.

Smith, moreover, made a number of important contributions to trade theory, most notably in his analysis of the growth-stimulating effects of foreign trade through widening the extent of the market. That analysis, which was well ahead of its time, was subsequently neglected in the mainstream of classical and neo-classical trade theory, only to be 'rediscovered' years later. He saw more clearly than any one before him—to cite but a few examples—the importance of differences in relative factor endowments and of transport costs in influencing the course of trade. He posed, and set the pattern of approach to, a number of important issues in trade theory which later classical economists were to develop in greater detail.

For these reasons, therefore, Smith's foreign-trade doctrines—which were spread over a very substantial part of *The Wealth of Nations*[6]—would seem to merit systematic re-examination in a commemorative volume such as this. Admittedly, Smith was not a great trade theorist, but

[4] J. W. Angell, *The Theory of International Prices* (1926), 33–7; and C. Y. Wu, *An Outline of International Price Theories* (1939), 82–4. See also E. F. Heckscher, *Mercantilism*, revised edition (1935), ii. 332: 'Adam Smith's achievement . . . was not particularly important in the pure theory of foreign trade, but of all the more importance in the practical policy of free trade.'

[5] A. I. Bloomfield, 'The Foreign-Trade Doctrines of the Physiocrats', *American Economic Review* (Dec. 1938), 716–35 (reprinted in *Essays in Economic Thought*, ed. J. J. Spengler and W. R. Allen (1960)).

[6] Little attention will be given here to Smith's earlier *Lectures on Justice, Police, Revenue and Arms*, ed. E. Cannan (1896). On the subject of foreign trade, that book contains little that was not incorporated in much more detailed form in *The Wealth of Nations.*

he comes up, on the whole, with a performance that deserves respectful consideration.

THE BASIS OF TRADE

Smith finds the fundamental basis for foreign trade, viewed statically, in what has since been called absolute advantage.[7] Under free trade all goods will tend to be produced in those countries where their absolute real costs of production are lowest. Countries will tend to export those goods that can be produced at lower real costs at home than abroad, and to import those goods that can be produced at lower real costs abroad than at home. Smith does not clearly or directly link up this proposition with an international adjustment mechanism translating real costs into money costs and money prices. Nowhere does he see that it could pay a country to import some goods even though the goods in question could be produced at lower real costs at home than abroad—which was of course the major contribution of the theory of comparative costs.[8] Almost at the beginning of his book he does make a statement that could have been developed into a theory of comparative costs, but fails to follow through: 'The most opulent nations . . . generally excel all their neighbours in agriculture as well as in manufactures; but they are commonly more distinguished by their superiority in the latter than in the former' (WN I.i.4). Unlike Ricardo, he does not explicitly see the relation between the terms of trade and cost ratios in the trading countries; and, like Ricardo, he has no adequate explanation of how the terms of trade are determined.[9] It is also of interest to note that, while clearly aware of the mutual benefits of international specialization based on absolute differences in real costs (and of specialization between regions of a country[10]), he does not list these in his introductory chapters on the division of labour, an omission that Cannan was to regard as 'rather curious'.[11] Indeed, throughout his book he focuses mainly on the economies of scale associated with the division of labour,

[7] Adam Smith, *The Wealth of Nations*, ed. E. Cannan, The Modern Library (1937), IV.ii.11–15.

[8] Nor does Smith recognize the case described by Taussig as 'equal differences in costs'. F. W. Taussig, *International Trade* (1927), 19–22. I can find no textual basis for Blaug's statement: 'Even Adam Smith knew that no foreign trade could arise when the cost ratios for two goods between two countries were equal.' M. Blaug, *Economic Theory in Retrospect*, (1968), 126.

[9] See F. D. Graham, *The Theory of International Values* (1948), 8: 'For very good reasons, no doubt, Smith said nothing about international, as contrasted with domestic, values, and we may perhaps assume that for international values he would offer no explanation other than higgling.'

[10] In discussing trade between 'town' and 'country', for example, Smith writes: 'The gains of both are mutual and reciprocal, and the division of labour is in this, as in all other cases, advantageous to all the different persons employed' (WN III.i.1).

[11] E. Cannan, *History of the Theories of Production and Distribution*, 3rd edition (1924), 47.

wherever the specialization might take place, rather than on geographical specialization as such.[12]

Viner leaves the clear impression that Smith, while basing his theory of international specialization on absolute differences in real cost, did not state the more general proposition advanced by several earlier writers to the effect that a country would find it advantageous to import commodities whenever they could be obtained in exchange for exports at a smaller real cost than their production at home would entail (the so-called 'eighteenth century rule').[13] As it happens, Smith does state that proposition explicitly when discussing the advantages of trade between 'town' and 'country' and in a context where it is clear that he would have applied it equally to foreign trade. He writes: 'The inhabitants of the country purchase of the town a greater quantity of manufactured goods, with the produce of a much smaller quantity of their own labour, than they must have employed had they attempted to prepare them themselves' (WN III.i.1).[14]

The reason for absolute differences in real costs of production, according to Smith, lies mainly in differences in climate, qualities of soil, and other natural or acquired advantages. For example, in referring to differences in various countries in 'soil, climate, and situation', he notes that the 'silks of France are better and cheaper than those of England, because the silk manufacture, at least under the present high duties upon the importation of raw silk, does not so well suit the climate of England as that of France' (WN I.i.4). His famous illustration about the difficulties of growing grapes in Scotland is prefaced by the remark that the 'natural advantages which one country has over another in producing particular commodities are sometimes so great, that it is acknowledged by all the world to be in vain to struggle with them'; and it is followed by the observation: 'Whether the advantages which one country has over another, be natural or acquired, is in this respect of no consequence' (WN IV.ii.15).[15] In letter (201) addressed to Henry Dundas dated 1 November 1779, he dismisses fears that English and Scottish manufacturers will be unable to compete with the pauper labour of Ireland, if free importation were granted to that country, in the following words:

[12] J. S. Chipman, 'A Survey of the Theory of International Trade: Part 2, The Neo-Classical Theory', *Econometrica* (Oct. 1965), 737.

[13] Viner, *Studies*, 440–1 and 104–6. Viner goes on to argue that the doctrine of comparative costs is 'but a statement of some of the implications of this rule, and adds nothing to it as a guide for policy' (ibid. 440). He added that: 'Its chief service was to correct the previously prevalent error that all commodities would necessarily tend to be produced in the locations where their real costs of production were lowest' (ibid. 441).

[14] The same proposition is also stated explicitly in a later discussion of foreign trade, but is expressed in terms of commodities, rather than real resources, saved (WN IV.ii.12).

[15] (WN IV.ii.15). Elsewhere he speaks of 'countries which, either from excessive heat or cold, produce no grapes, and where wine consequently is dear and a rarity' (WN IV.iii.c.8, see also I.vii.24).

Ireland has neither the skill nor the stock which would enable Her to rival England . . . though both may be acquired in time . . . Ireland has neither coal or wood; the former seems to be denied to her by nature; and though her Soil and Climate are perfectly suited for raising the latter, yet to raise it to the same degree as in England would require more than a Century.[16]

Smith carries these ideas farther by showing an awareness of the fact that the basis and commodity composition of trade are also related to differences in the relative abundance and hence in the relative prices of the various productive factors in various countries. Although he thinks of these differences as resulting in absolute rather than comparative differences in costs, yet he lays down with remarkable clarity the elements of the proposition later to be made famous by Heckscher and Ohlin:

Land is still so cheap, and, consequently, labour so dear among them [the American colonies] that they can import from the mother country, almost all the more refined or more advanced manufactures cheaper than they can make them for themselves. Though they had not, therefore, been prohibited from establishing such manufactures, yet in their present state of improvement, a regard to their own interest would, probably, have prevented them from doing so.

(WN IV.vii.b.44)

Agriculture is the proper business of all new colonies; a business which the cheapness of land renders more advantageous than any other. They abound, therefore, in the rude produce of land, and instead of importing it from other countries, they have generally a large surplus to export . . . The greater part of the manufactures . . . they find it cheaper to purchase of other countries than to make for themselves.

(WN IV.vii.c.51)

In our North American colonies, where uncultivated land is still to be had upon easy terms, no manufactures for distant sale have ever yet been established in any of their towns.

(WN III.i.5)

In countries which are fast advancing to riches, the low rate of profit may, in the price of many commodities, compensate the high wages of labour, and enable those countries to sell as cheap as their less thriving neighbours, among whom the wages of labour may be lower.[17]

[16] This letter is reproduced in full in John Rae, *Life of Adam Smith* (1895), 353–5. Smith expresses similar views in Letter 202 addressed to the Earl of Carlisle, dated 8 Nov. 1779 (ibid. 350–2). The role of differences in natural conditions in influencing the pattern of international specialization—frequently interpreted as an act of God to promote foreign commerce—is an old one. See J. Viner, *The Role of Providence in the Social Order* (1972), 27–54. Smith himself never formulated this idea in providential terms, but it is implicit in his writings. See also Viner, *Studies*, 100–3.

[17] WN I.ix.23; see also I.ix.24 and IV.vii.c.29. Attention has also been drawn to these various passages by S. Hollander, 'Some Implications of Adam Smith's Analysis of Investment Priorities', *History of Political Economy* (Fall 1971), 245–8. See also Viner, *Studies*, 503–7, where he cites from Smith and other classical writers in challenging Ohlin's

Throughout *The Wealth of Nations*, Smith continually refers to foreign trade (and trade between 'town' and 'country') as an exchange of 'surpluses' of particular commodities above their domestic consumption or requirements, thus leaving the impression that a 'basis', or at least a condition, of trade is the existence of such surpluses.[18] Indeed, he even states that the extent of a country's foreign trade is necessarily limited 'by the value of the surplus produce of the whole country and of what can be purchased with it' (WN II.v.36). Elsewhere he writes that 'the foreign trade of every country naturally increases in proportion to its wealth, its surplus produce in proportion to its whole produce' (WN IV.vii.c.22). It is conceivable that Smith is merely stating a tautology, with exports of individual commodities necessarily consisting of the excess of their domestic production over their domestic absorption—and moving in accord with absolute differences in real cost. But, as will be discussed in the next section, it seems clear that he means more than this.

Unlike Ricardo and later classical economists, Smith does not differentiate foreign and domestic trade on the basis of different assumptions as to the mobility of productive factors internationally and domestically. He assumes neither perfect mobility internally nor perfect immobility externally for purposes of his trade theory. It is not in fact entirely clear whether in practice he even assumes markedly differing degrees of mobility in the two cases.

Under competitive conditions, Smith does imply that there would be perfect factor mobility internally, conceived mainly in the occupational sense. This comes out most clearly in his analysis of the mechanism set into play when there exist temporary divergences between the 'market' and 'natural' prices of individual commodities and thus between the 'market' and 'natural' rewards to individual factors of production in the industries concerned. These divergences will tend to be eliminated by the transfer of factors into or out of these industries until equilibrium is restored (WN I.vii.12–16). Perfect internal factor mobility is also implicit in Smith's later analysis of differences in money wages and in rates of profit in the various employments of labour and capital. Here he argues that in competitive equilibrium any such differences will tend to correspond exactly to differences in the disutilities or 'net advantages' associated with such employ-

assertion that the significance of differences among countries in the relative abundance of the various productive factors for the course of trade was first touched on, not by the English classical school, but in French works. It might be noted that Hume, while aware of differences in natural conditions and skills as a cause of trade, had not explicitly recognized the role of differences in the relative abundance and prices of the various productive factors.

[18] It is not suggested that this notion was confined to Smith. Other writers such as Hume, Steuart, and some of the Physiocrats, had also on occasion referred to the exchange of surpluses or 'superfluities' involved in trade. But no writer had ever stressed the role of 'surpluses' in trade as much as Smith did.

ments (WN I.x.b). This clearly implies that there is perfect mobility of labour and of capital among different employments of each.

In actual fact, of course, perfect competition in the factor markets did not exist. As Smith notes, the exclusive privileges and monopoly power of corporations had the effect of restricting the free movement of capital among different industries and firms, while the statutes of apprenticeship, the laws of settlement, and other legislation and business practices served to obstruct the free transfer of labour among different occupations and places within a country. As a result, there existed differences, often for lengthy periods of time, between market and natural rates of factor returns in individual industries, as well as differences between money wages and between rates of profit in different employments of labour and capital in excess of those attributable to the differences in the disutilities associated with each.[19] On several occasions Smith refers to the comparative ease with which labour *could* be transferred between occupations were it not for the legislative barriers that tended to obstruct such transfer, but at times he speaks of a high degree of labour mobility in actual fact (WN I.x.c.42–3; IV.ii.42). Elsewhere, in commenting on the considerable differences in the wages of common labour in a great town and its neighbourhood, he makes the remark—clearly referring in this case to geographical rather than occupational mobility—that 'it appears evidently from experience that a man is of all sorts of luggage the most difficult to be transported' (WN I.viii.31).

With regard to international factor mobility, Smith has almost nothing to say about labour migration except for what is implicit in his discussion on colonies. On the other hand, he does refer explicitly in a number of isolated passages to international capital movements, properly defined (and in a few cases to *stocks* of foreign investments).

For example, he refers to the 'great sums' that the Dutch lend to private persons in countries where the rate of interest is higher than in their own, and to the importance of Dutch holdings of the French and English public debt (WN I.ix.10); to transfers of capital from England to France where the rate of profit is higher (WN I.ix.9); to the 'considerable share' held by the Dutch and several other foreign nations in the British public debt (WN V.iii.52); to Dutch capital 'continually overflowing, sometimes into the public funds of foreign countries, sometimes into loans to private traders and adventurers of foreign countries' (WN IV.vii.c.96); and to the American colonists 'borrowing upon bond' from rich people in the mother country (WN IV.vii.c.38). In a few places he specifically mentions the

[19] WN I.vii.20–31, and generally, I.x.c. Smith also notes: 'Whatever obstructs the free circulation of labour from one employment to another, obstructs that of stock likewise; the quantity of stock which can be employed in any branch of business depending very much upon that of the labour which can be employed in it' (WN I.x.c.44).

trade credits granted by British merchants to merchants abroad (WN IV.vii.c.38; V.iii.83; III.i.3). And in several passages he speaks of individuals transferring their capital from one country to another because of 'a very trifling disgust' (WN III.iv.24), a 'public calamity' (WN V.ii.k.80) 'a vexatious inquisition, in order to be assessed to a burdensome tax' (WN V.ii. f.6) or 'the mortifying and vexatious visits of the tax-gatherers' (WN V.iii.55). These passages, indeed, suggest a high degree of international capital mobility.

There are many passages in *The Wealth of Nations* where Smith only *implies* capital movements, and then of a specialized kind. These passages occur in connection with his many discussions of the employment of domestic capital in the 'home-trade', the 'foreign trade of consumption' (trade between the home country and foreign countries), and the 'carrying trade' between foreign countries (WN II.v.24ff.). The capital employed in each of these three cases is that of the wholesale merchant, who buys stocks of goods at one price in expectation of their sale at a higher price.[20] The last two employments of capital are presumably embodied at any moment of time both in stocks of goods and in net claims on foreigners (trade credits) arising out of the trading activities. 'Movements of capital' into and out of the 'foreign trade of consumption' and the 'carrying trade' would involve international capital movements, properly defined, only to the extent that they involve changes in the amount of net claims on foreigners. When Smith speaks, as he often does, of changes in the amount of domestic capital engaged in these two trades, because, for example, of a diversion of capital to these 'more distant employments'[21]—or when he speaks of the tendency towards an equalization of the rate of profit in the colonial trade and all other branches of British trade (WN IV.vii.c.19, 48–9) because of the attraction or 'revulsion' of capital—his language sometimes suggests an equivalent amount of capital movements, properly defined. But capital movements would be involved only to the extent that there are changes in the amount of net claims on foreigners, and then only of the kind associated with the financing of international trade.

Smith implies a relative disinclination to export capital when he makes the following remarks:

> . . . upon equal or nearly equal profits, every wholesale merchant naturally prefers the home-trade to the foreign trade of consumption, and the foreign trade of consumption to the carrying trade. In the home-trade his capital is never so long out of his sight as it frequently is in the foreign trade of consumption. He can know better the character and situation of the persons whom he trusts, and if he should happen to be deceived, he knows better the laws of the country from which he

[20] See, e.g., WN II.v.14: 'The capital of a wholesale merchant . . . may wander about from place to place, according as it can either buy cheap or sell dear.'

[21] As in his chapter on colonies.

must seek redress. In the carrying trade, the capital of the merchant is, as it were, divided between the two foreign countries, and no part of it is ever necessarily brought home, or placed under his own immediate view and command.

(WN IV.ii.6; cf. IV.vii.c.86)

By this passage Smith presumably means no more than that a merchant prefers, because of the greater risk attached to foreign trade, to deal with domestic rather than foreign merchants and to have the stock of goods comprising his 'mercantile capital' move within his home country rather than across national boundaries. To the extent that capital movements are implied, they are again of the kind associated with financing foreign trade. To be sure, the reasons given by Smith could be used to justify an argument that people have a relative aversion to export capital in a broader sense—including direct and portfolio investment—but this is not what he has in mind. Nicholson praised Smith for his recognition, in this and related passages dealing with foreign trade, of the international mobility of capital, in contrast to the assumption of the later classical economists in their trade theory of external capital immobility. In fact, he regards this recognition as one of Smith's significant 'lost ideas'.[22]

If Smith does not differentiate foreign and domestic trade on the basis of clearly differing assumptions as to factor mobility externally and internally, on what basis then does he do so? The main basis of differentiation is that a given amount of capital invested in the home trade allegedly 'puts into motion' a greater quantity of productive labour at home (and thus adds a greater value to a country's annual produce) than an equal domestic capital employed in the 'foreign trade of consumption'; and that the latter in turn has a greater impact in this respect than an equal domestic capital employed in the 'carrying trade'.[23]

These assertions are based on two sets of assumptions. First, while these three uses of mercantile capital are supposed in each case to 'replace two capitals', the first replaces two domestic capitals, the second only one (and one foreign capital), and the third no domestic capitals at all (but two foreign ones). Secondly, the 'frequency of returns' on capital—the turnover rate—is alleged to be greatest in the case of the home trade and least in the case of the 'carrying trade'. Smith further argues, but on the basis of different assumptions, that capital employed in agriculture provides a greater stimulus to the employment of productive labour than that in

[22] J. S. Nicholson, *A Project of Empire* (1909), xiii and *passim*; and C. Iversen, *Aspects of the Theory of International Capital Movements* (1935), 95–6.

[23] Within the category of the 'foreign trade of consumption', Smith also distinguishes a 'direct' and a 'roundabout' trade (the latter consisting of foreign goods purchased for home consumption, not with domestic products, but with other foreign goods), as well as trade with neighbouring countries and with more distant countries. In each of these two sub-categories, the former is alleged to 'put into motion' a greater quantity of productive labour at home than the latter (WN II.v.24–30).

manufactures, and the latter in turn to that in the various categories of trade (WN II.v.12–19). All these various uses of a nation's capital, despite their differing employment-generating effects, are described as advantageous and necessary. But none should be artificially encouraged, since in 'the natural course of things' capital will in fact tend to flow, 'upon equal or nearly equal profits', into each of these uses in the order of their social advantage as measured by the criterion of the amount of employment of domestic productive labour (WN III.i.3–9; IV.vii.c.86, and IV.ii.6).

It is not necessary here to examine the validity of these distinctions between the differing employment-generating effects of different employments of capital, or their compatibility with other aspects of Smith's theoretical system. These distinctions have been criticized over the years—and in a few cases defended—by various commentators on *The Wealth of Nations*, or they have been passed over by others in puzzlement or embarrassed silence. McCulloch, who closely followed Smith in so many other respects,[24] objected to these arguments,[25] as did Ricardo.[26] The whole subject, and especially the compatibility between Smith's 'employment-generating' criterion of social advantage and the 'equalization-of-profits' criterion which he uses elsewhere, has recently been examined in some detail by Hollander.[27]

What is of interest here is the emphasis laid by Smith on the 'frequency of returns' on capital as a key factor influencing the differing effects of the home trade and the various categories of foreign trade. That in turn is predominantly a function of the distance, and thus of the time, involved in shipping goods in the two cases.[28] Smith takes it for granted that the distance factor is greater in foreign trade than in home trade, and the frequency of returns less. In this respect he also lays great stress on the advantages of trade with neighbouring countries over trade with the more distant America, and of direct over roundabout trade. Even here, however, his distinction between home and foreign trade on the basis of distance is not absolute. For he admits that in trade between the southern coast of England and the northern and north-western coasts of France, the distance

[24] D. P. O'Brien, *J. R. McCulloch: A Study in Classical Economics* (1970).

[25] See McCulloch's edition of *The Wealth of Nations* (1859), 159–60n, 162n, 164–5n. E. G. Wakefield, who claimed to have drawn inspiration from Smith for some of his ideas, stated bluntly, with regard to Smith's distinctions, that 'there is no reason for supposing that any one mode of employing capital is, in any way, more advantageous than any other'. See Wakefield's edition of *The Wealth of Nations* (1835–9), vol. ii. 473n.

[26] D. Ricardo, *The Works and Correspondence of David Ricardo*, ed. P. Sraffa (1951–5), i. 347–51.

[27] Hollander, *op. cit.*

[28] Smith admits that 'peculiar circumstances' may sometimes also influence the frequency of returns. He cites as one such factor the tendency for the American and West Indian colonies to borrow as much as possible from the mother country, mainly in the form of running in arrears with their British suppliers. This reduced still further the frequency of returns on British capital engaged in the colonial trade (WN IV.vii.c.38).

is no greater, and thus the frequency of returns is no less, than in the British home trade. (WN IV.iii.c.12).

Smith's interest in the distance factor is also reflected in his many references to transportation costs as an important influence on the pattern of foreign trade. The following are examples:

The commodities most proper for being transported to distant countries . . . seem to be the finer and more improved manufactures; such as contain a great value in a small bulk and can, therefore, be exported to a great distance at little expence. (WN IV.i.29, 30)

Manufactures, those of the finer kind especially, are more easily transported from one country to another than corn or cattle. It is in the fetching and carrying manufactures, accordingly, that foreign trade is chiefly employed. In manufactures, a very small advantage will enable foreigners to undersell our own workmen, even in the home market. It will require a very great one to enable them to do so in the rude produce of the soil.[29]

Manufactures, as in a small bulk they frequently contain a great value, and can upon that account be transported at less expence from one country to another than most parts of raw produce, are, in almost all countries, the principal support of foreign trade.

(WN IV.ix.41)

The materials of lodging cannot always be transported to so great a distance as those of cloathing, and do not so readily become an object of foreign commerce. (WN I.xi.c.5)

In a number of passages dealing with trade between 'town' and 'country', he reaches similar conclusions regarding the influence of transport costs on home trade (WN III.i.1; III.iii.20). He frequently emphasizes also that gold and silver move most readily into international trade because of their small bulk and great value (WN I.xi.c.21, II.v.29, IV.i.12,14).

It is clear from the foregoing that Smith recognizes the importance of transport costs in determining the commodity composition and volume of a country's trade, both foreign and domestic. He sees that these costs bear more heavily on primary products and coarse manufactures than on the finer manufactures. He recognizes the greater degree of 'natural protection' from foreign competition afforded by transport costs to the former as compared with the latter. He closely approximates the proposition, later stated explicitly by Mill,[30] that some goods may not enter into international trade at all because their transport costs more than outweigh the differences in their production costs in the trading countries. In a number of passages,

[29] WN IV.ii.16. Smith goes on to discuss the limited effect that a removal or relaxation of import restrictions would have on the import of cattle, salt provisions, or corn because of their bulkiness and high transport costs. In many passages, however, he admits that primary produce does in fact move into international trade on a large scale.

[30] J. S. Mill, *Principles of Political Economy*, ed. by W. J. Ashley (1923), 588–90.

moreover, he stresses the importance of the availability and quality of transport facilities, not only in widening the extent of the market, but also in influencing the location of industries. (WN I.iii.3–8, I.xi.b.5, III.iii.20, III.iv.20).

In his emphasis on distance and transport costs as factors affecting trade, Smith showed insights that were not followed through by the great majority of later trade theorists who have generally abstracted from these elements in their analysis. It is only in comparatively recent years that the distance factor in trade has begun to be systematically explored by trade (and location) theorists and also to be incorporated into econometric analyses of trade.[31]

THE GAINS FROM TRADE

Despite the low ranking given to foreign trade in his hierarchy of employments of capital, Smith is of course aware of the enormous benefits conferred by trade, and especially by free trade. Several kinds of gains can be distinguished in *The Wealth of Nations*, altough Smith himself does not always make the distinctions clearly.

First, there are the allocative efficiency gains arising from international specialization based on absolute differences in costs. Trade enables a country to buy goods from abroad at a lower real cost than that at which they can be produced at home. In arguing the case against trade restrictions, for example, Smith writes:

> If a foreign country can supply us with a commodity cheaper than we ourselves can make it, better buy it of them with some part of the produce of our own industry, employed in a way in which we have some advantage. The general industry of the country . . . is certainly not employed to the greatest advantage, when it is thus directed towards an object which it can buy cheaper than it can make . . . [and which] could, therefore, have been purchased with a part only of the commodities . . . which the industry employed by an equal capital would have produced at home, had it been left to follow its natural course. The industry of the country, therefore, is thus turned away from a more, to a less advantageous employment, and the exchangeable value of its annual produce, instead of being increased . . . must necessarily be diminished.
>
> (WN IV.ii.12)

Here the emphasis is on more efficient resource allocation and on the possibility of minimizing through trade the aggregate real costs at which a given amount of real income can be obtained. Elsewhere, however, in somewhat contradictory fashion, he stresses the desirability of importing

[31] For a discussion of some of the recent theoretical literature in this field, see Chipman, *Econometrica* (July 1965), 511–13. For an econometric analysis of trade incorporating distance and transport costs, see H. Linnemann, *An Econometric Analysis of International Trade Flows* (1966).

goods such as materials, tools, and provisions, for the employment and maintenance of industrious people, 'who re-produce, with a profit, the value of their annual consumption', as contrasted with goods, such as wines and foreign silks, which are 'likely to be be consumed by idle people who produce nothing' (WN II.ii.33, IV.v.a.19). He comforts himself with the knowledge that most imports are in fact of the former kind.

Secondly, Smith touches in a few passages on the subjective consumers' gains from trade in the form of increased 'enjoyments'. Not only does trade make possible a greater abundance of goods, but it also involves the exchange of a country's 'superfluities', for which there is no demand, 'for something else, which may satisfy a part of [its] wants and increase its enjoyments'.[32] The increased enjoyments are at times regarded also in the sense mainly of a greater *variety* of goods: 'The surplus produce of America, imported into Europe, furnishes the inhabitants of this great continent with a variety of commodities which they could not otherwise have possessed, some for conveniency and use, some for pleasure, and some for ornament, and thereby contributes to increase their enjoyments'.[33] But this is about as far as Smith goes in discussing the consumption side of the gains from trade.

For more important to Smith, in keeping with the developmental orientation of *The Wealth of Nations*, is the stimulus to economic growth provided by foreign trade through widening the extent of the market. He speaks with enthusiasm of the 'new and inexhaustible market to all the commodities of Europe', and the resulting 'new divisions of labour and improvements of art', opened up by the discovery of America (WN IV.i.32); of the new market for European commodities, and the consequent increase in their annual production, stemming from the opening of trade with the East Indies (WN IV.i.33); and of the general stimulus to European 'industry' (and of the increased 'enjoyments') provided by trade with the colonies (WN. IV.vii.c.1–9). There are also countless references to the market for 'surplus produce' afforded by foreign trade and to the resulting incentive to increase these surpluses continually. Smith's interest in the size of markets is further evident in a passage where he discusses the benefits that would accrue from a larger trade between Britain and France. Trade between these two countries, if it were not restricted, would be more mutually beneficial than their trade with any other country, not only

[32] WN IV.i.31; and IV.vii.c.4–9, 80. See also LJ (B), 261; Cannan, 204: 'The very intention of commerce is to exchange your own commodities for others which you think will be more convenient for you . . . Our very desire to purchase them shows that we have more use for them than . . . the commodities which we give for them.'

[33] WN IV.vii.c.5. In speaking of the trade benefits brought about by the discovery of America, Smith also refers to the fact that the 'commodities of Europe were almost all new to America, and many of those of America were new to Europe. A new set of exchanges, therefore, began to take place which had never been thought of before' (WN IV.i.32).

because of their closer proximity—which would make the 'frequency of returns' greater—but also because of the larger market for each other's goods resulting from their greater wealth and population (WN IV.iii.c.12, LJ (B); 264–5 ed. Cannan 206).

Smith summarizes these particular mutual benefits of foreign trade to any two trading countries in the following words:

> It carries out that surplus part of the produce of their land and labour for which there is no demand among them, and brings back in return for it something else for which there is a demand. It gives a value to their superfluities, by exchanging them for something else, which may satisfy a part of their wants, and increase their enjoyments. By means of it, the narrowness of the home market does not hinder the division of labour in any particular branch of art or manufacture from being carried to the highest perfection. By opening a more extensive market for whatever part of the produce of their labour may exceed the home consumption, it encourages them to improve its productive powers, and to augment its annual produce to the utmost, and thereby to increase the real revenue and wealth of the society.
>
> (WN IV.i.31)

Apart from the reference to increased 'enjoyments', already commented upon, there are two main ideas in this passage. First, foreign trade, by widening the extent on the market, improves the division of labour and thereby raises productivity within each of the trading countries. Second, foreign trade provides an outlet for surpluses of particular goods above domestic requirements. Myint refers to these as the 'productivity' theory and the 'vent for surplus' theory, respectively.[34] John Stuart Mill regarded the first as an indirect benefit of foreign trade 'of a high order',[35] but rejected the second as a 'surviving relic of the Mercantile Theory'.[36] Ricardo likewise rejected the second, finding it 'at variance with all [Smith's] general doctrines on this subject'.[37] McCulloch followed Smith on both,[38] and even Bastable, whose unfavourable comments on Smith's trade doctrines were noted at the beginning of this paper, showed some sympathy with his 'vent for surplus' argument.[39] Haberler, in commenting on Myint's distinction, has questioned the need to distinguish a separate 'vent for surplus' theory, arguing that, if not itself part and parcel of the

[34] H. Myint, 'The "Classical Theory" of International Trade and the Underdeveloped Countries', *Readings in International Economics*, ed. R. E. Caves and H. G. Johnson (1968), especially 319–23. The vent for surplus theory has been recently analysed by S. Hollander, *The Economics of Adam Smith* (1973), 268–76, and C. E. Staley, 'A Note on Adam Smith's Version of the Vent for Surplus Model', *History of Political Economy* (Fall 1973), 438–48.

[35] Mill, *Principles*, 581. [36] Ibid. 579.

[37] Ricardo, *Works*, i. 294–5, 291n. [38] O'Brien, op. cit. 197ff.

[39] Bastable, op. cit. 20–1.

'productivity' theory, it is simply an extreme case of comparative costs.[40] But whether there is here one idea or two, both are related to the widening of the market through foreign trade; and it is clear that herein lies the main benefit of foreign trade according to Smith.

Of interest is the fact that in this passage Smith does not include among the benefits of trade the more efficient allocation of resources through international specialization on which he elaborates elsewhere. The reason for this omission seems to be that here he is stressing the 'dynamic' benefits of trade in the form of wider markets, not the 'static' gains in the form of greater allocative efficiency which were to be stressed by later classical economists. These two types of gains are not inconsistent but stem simply from two different levels of analysis, an approach used by Smith in other areas of his book.

There can surely be no dispute with the 'productivity' theory. Widening the extent of the market, through foreign trade or in other ways, leads, as Smith had already argued in the opening chapters of his book, to increased skill and dexterity on the part of workers, improved and more specialized processes of production, the stimulation of technological advance, and, more generally, increasing returns and economic growth.[41] Indeed, Young, in exploring the implications of Smith's famous theorem that the division of labour is limited by the extent of the market, described it as 'one of the most illuminating and fruitful generalisations which can be found anywhere in the whole literature of economics'.[42] And Kaldor has recently reminded economists once again of the importance of this theorem and called attention to the consequences of its frequent neglect in the mainstream of 'equilibrium economics'.[43]

It is much more difficult to determine exactly what Smith had in mind by his 'vent for surplus' argument, if it is indeed a separate idea. A clue as to its meaning is provided by the following remark:

When the produce of any particular branch of industry exceeds what the demand of the country requires, the surplus must be sent abroad, and exchanged for something for which there is a demand at home. *Without such exportation, a part*

[40] G. Haberler, *International Trade and Economic Development* (1959), 9n.

[41] WN I.i–iii; see also I.xi.o.1. There seems to be no explicit recognition in *The Wealth of Nations* of the converse proposition, namely that increasing returns are a *cause* of trade, as was later to be stressed by B. Ohlin, *Inter-regional and International Trade* (1935), 54–8, 106–11. On the other hand, one distinguished observer has stated: 'Stretching matters a bit, I might include him [Smith] as a precursor of Bertil Ohlin's emphasis upon increasing returns to scale as a cause of interregional and international trade.' P. A. Samuelson, 'The Way of an Economist', *International Economic Relations*, ed. P. A. Samuelson (1969), 4.

[42] A. A. Young, 'Increasing Returns and Economic Progress', *Readings in Welfare Economics*, ed. K. J. Arrow and T. Scitovsky (1969), 230. See also G. J. Stigler, 'The Division of Labor is Limited by the Extent of the Market', *Journal of Political Economy* (June 1951), 185–93.

[43] N. Kaldor, 'The Irrelevance of Equilibrium Economics', *Economic Journal* (Dec. 1972), 1237–56.

of the productive labour of the country must cease, and the value of its annual produce diminish. The land and labour of Great Britain produce generally more corn, woollens, and hard ware, than the demand of the home-market requires. The surplus part of them, therefore, must be sent abroad, and exchanged for something for which there is a demand at home. It is only by means of such exportation, that this surplus can acquire a value sufficient to compensate the labour and expence of producing it.[44]

The implication of this passage is that, for reasons unexplained, a country tends to produce surpluses of particular commodities above domestic demand, and that in the absence of foreign markets the production of these surpluses would cease, the productive factors involved would go into unemployment, and the national income would fall. The existence of foreign markets would enable the continued production of these surpluses and the consequent absorption into employment of factors that would otherwise be idle. Indeed, foreign markets would stimulate the country to increase the production of these surpluses (WN IV.vii.c.7,8,48)—presumably by drawing on growing labour and capital supplies, and perhaps on the pool of 'unproductive labour' engaged in services.

But why do these surpluses tend to be produced in the first place? And why, if foreign markets for them are not available, are the resources involved not transferred, as Ricardo and Mill were to ask, to the production of other goods at home for which there *is* a demand, and especially goods of a kind imported from abroad? Indeed, as noted earlier, Smith speaks often of the internal mobility of factors, even though it was to some degree restrained by legislation and business practices. Nor does the problem, at least in the case of Great Britain, seem to arise from any serious lack of employment opportunities at home. For example, Smith speak of the comparative ease with which over 100,000 demobilized British soldiers and seamen after the Seven Years War were absorbed in other occupations, with 'no great convulsion . . . [and] no sensible disorder' (WN IV.ii.42). To be sure, this is not a large number, even in relation to Britain's comparatively small population at that time, but this remark is suggestive. There appears to have been no serious deficiency of aggregate demand in Britain at the time that Smith wrote, and there is little in *The Wealth of Nations* to suggest otherwise.[45] On the contrary, Smith insists that employ-

[44] WN II.v.33 (italics supplied). This is followed by a somewhat more involved illustration (WN II.v.34) to the effect that if the amount of tobacco annually imported into Britain happens to exceed the home demand, the excess must be re-exported. If that is not possible, the excess amount of tobacco would cease to be imported 'and with it the productive labour of all those inhabitants of Great Britain, who are at present employed in preparing the goods' with which the excess tobacco is annually purchased. See also WN II.v.16,17 where the same idea is again stated.

[45] See, e.g., A. W. Coats, 'Adam Smith: the Modern Re-Appraisal', *Renaissance and Modern Studies*, vi (1962), 36–8; and Hollander, *History of Political Economy* (Fall 1971), 239,247n.

ment opportunities at home are adequate to absorb the growing labour force and supply of capital.

Myint has interpreted Smith's 'vent for surplus' argument to apply to a previously isolated country about to enter into international trade which possesses 'surplus productive capacity' in one form or another because of 'an inelastic demand for the exportable commodity and/or a considerable degree of internal immobility and specificness of resources' bound up with underdeveloped economic organization.[46] Kindleberger suggests that Smith may have presupposed a 'highly skewed resource base' leading to concentrated trade of a sort often found in relatively underdeveloped countries—in part because of a lack of complementary factors to produce other commodities for which the natural resources exist.[47] Cannan argues that Smith may have supposed that 'the country has certain physical characteristics which compel its inhabitants to produce certain particular commodities' (WN II.v.33n).

Myint's interpretation, if valid, would seem most readily to fit the case of the underdeveloped colonial possessions of which Smith speaks. Foreign trade would indeed in such cases create a demand for the output of resources that would otherwise remain unexploited—surplus land and other natural resources in the Americas and surplus labour in the East Indies. But one of the difficulties here is that Smith applies his surplus-produce notion more generally. He writes: '*In every period, indeed, of every society*, the surplus part of the rude and manufactured produce, or that for which there is no demand at home, must be sent abroad in order to be exchanged for something for which there is some demand at home' (WN III.i.7; italics supplied).

Such an interpretation, would seem, therefore, for the reasons already noted, not to apply as readily to Great Britain (and perhaps other more 'developed' countries of Western Europe) as to the colonies. Even the British 'corn, woollens, and hard ware' cited by Smith as examples of 'surplus produce' would not appear to have been commodities to the production of which factors were specific, or products of a 'highly skewed resource base'.[48] And even if the home demand for these commodities were inelastic, it would seem that most of the productive factors involved could, at least in the condition of Britain described by Smith, have found other home employment.

On the other hand, Smith does point out, although not in connection

[46] Myint, op. cit. 323, 325. This interpretation is accepted by D. Winch, *Classical Political Economy and the Colonies* (1965), 7–8. The activation of dormant resources through foreign trade is in fact an integral part of the trade-and-growth models of Myint himself, W. A. Lewis, H. A. Innis, D. C. North, and others. See R. E. Caves '"Vent for Surplus" Models of Trade and Growth', in *Trade, Growth, and the Balance of Payments, Essays in Honour of Gottfried Haberler* (1965), 99–115. See also R. Nurkse, *Equilibrium and Growth in the World Economy* (1961), 283–90, 304–5.

[47] C. P. Kindleberger, *Foreign Trade and the National Economy* (1962), 30.

[48] Even with regard to corn, Smith speaks frequently of the multiplicity of uses of land.

with his discussion of foreign trade, that in 'all the great countries of Europe [presumably including Britain] . . . much good land still remains uncultivated' and that agriculture 'is almost every-where capable of absorbing a much greater capital than has ever yet been employed in it' (WN II.v.37). It is possible, then— further pursuing Myint's line of reasoning—that, even in the case of European countries, Smith may have implied that foreign trade would enable the utilization of some of this uncultivated land, in addition to drawing into agricultural production for export part of the growing labour and capital supplies and of the pool of 'unproductive labour' engaged in services. But Smith does not explicitly say this. Even if he did imply it, it would still not take account of the surpluses of manufactured goods of which he speaks. Conceivably Smith could also imply the existence in Britain of a large body of *underemployed* agricultural labour that could be activated by foreign trade. But again he does not say so.

In the light of these considerations, therefore, one must conclude that there still remains something of a mystery as to the exact meaning of Smith's 'surplus-produce' argument, at least when applied to Britain and other more 'developed' countries of Europe. It is probable that more may have been read into this argument than Smith in fact intended.

In scattered passages Smith also recognizes other stimulating effects of foreign trade on domestic growth. In his historical chapters in Book III, he notes that foreign trade introduced into trading cities 'the improved manufactures and expensive luxuries of richer countries [and] afforded some food to the vanity of the great proprietors, who eagerly purchased them with great quantities of the rude produce of their own lands' (WN III.iii.15). When the 'taste for the finer and more improved manufactures [so introduced] became so general as to occasion a considerable demand, the merchants . . . naturally endeavoured to establish some manufactures of the same kind in their own country . . . in imitation' (WN III.iii.16, 19). It gave proprietors in countries hitherto without foreign trade something to exchange against the surplus of their lands, previously consumed in 'rustic hospitality at home' and on the maintenance of a large body of retainers and dependents ('unproductive labour'), and so provided an incentive to improve the cultivation of their lands and the size of their agricultural surpluses.[49] Thus foreign trade contributed indirectly to domestic growth by the demonstration and imitation effects that it prompted.[50]

[49] WN III.iv.5ff. See also N. Rosenberg, 'Adam Smith, Consumers Tastes, and Economic Growth', *Journal of Political Economy* (May-June 1968), 361–74.

[50] These ideas may have come to Smith from Hume. See D. Hume, *David Hume: Writings on Economics*, ed. E. Rotwein (1970), 10–14, 78–9. They were also standard themes in the writings of later classical economists, such as Malthus, McCulloch, and J. S. Mill. Modern writers on the less developed countries have tended rather to stress the adverse impact on growth of the demonstration effect through a lowering of the savings ratio.

Foreign trade also transmits technology. Smith speaks of 'that mutual communication of knowledge and of all sorts of improvements which an extensive commerce from all countries to all countries naturally, or rather necessarily, carries along with it' (WN IV.vii.c.80). Elsewhere he argues that if China permitted a larger foreign trade, and especially carried a considerable part of it in its own ships, it would greatly increase its manufacturing industry because 'the Chinese would naturally learn the art of using and constructing themselves all the different machines made use of in other countries, as well as the other improvements of art and industry which are practised in all the different parts of the world' (WN IV.ix.41).

It is clear, to sum up the foregoing, that Smith plainly sees the great stimulus to growth afforded by foreign trade through widening the extent of the market. It promotes economies of scale, activates resources that would otherwise (at least in the case of underdeveloped primary-producing countries) be idle, stimulates 'industry', raises the level of economic incentives, and transmits technology. His analysis in this respect goes well beyond that of Hume and represents a dynamic approach to the gains from trade that was to be neglected by the later classical economists.

Smith is much more interested in emphasizing the mutual benefits of foreign trade, both dynamic and static, than in examining how these benefits are *divided* among the trading countries in any given case. At one point, however, he does explicitly address himself to this problem (WN IV.iii.c. 4–6), arguing that free trade may not be *equally* advantageous to any two partners. Utilizing his earlier thesis that a direct 'foreign trade of consumption' is always of more benefit than a roundabout one, in terms of its employment-generating effects, [51] he contends that if the balance of trade between two countries is equal, and if the exchange consists entirely of native commodities (a 'direct' trade), both countries will gain equally. If, on the other hand, one country exports to the other only native commodities, whereas the latter exports to the former only foreign commodities (a 'roundabout' trade), the greater benefit from trade is derived by the former. Since almost all countries exchange with one another partly native and partly foreign goods, that country 'in whose cargoes there is the greatest proportion of native, and the least of foreign goods [presumably for any given equal exchange of goods] will always be the principal gainer.' The whole argument, in which the international division of gains is interpreted in terms of relative effects on home employment, seems strangely reminiscent of the mercantilist 'balance-of-employment' argument.[52]

Later economists were to examine the problem of the international division of the gains from trade in terms of the relation between the trading countries' terms of trade and their comparative cost ratios. Although Smith is aware that it is to a nation's advantage in foreign trade 'to buy as cheap and

[51] See above, n. 23. [52] As described in Viner, *Studies*, 51–5.

to sell as dear as possible' (WN IV.ii.30), he seems to have no clear understanding of the forces determining the terms of trade, least of all their relation to cost ratios in the trading countries. He also seems to misunderstand the relation between the terms of trade and tariffs, arguing at one point that the high import duties imposed by Britain have the effect of turning the terms of trade *against* it.[53] His few other references to the terms of trade are marked by some ambiguity (WN IV.vii.c.27; IV.ix.37, V.ii.k.63).

TRADE POLICY

Among the most famous passages in *The Wealth of Nations* are those given over to a denunciation of mercantilist restrictions on trade. Smith argues that the 'mean and malignant expedients of the mercantile system', including prohibitions and high duties on imports, the 'exclusive monopoly of the colony trade', and bounties on exports, have the effect in each case of forcing the capital or trade of a country into channels to him much less socially advantageous than those into which they would have 'naturally' gone on their own accord. Self-interest based on the profit motive and on individual preferences for the various employments of capital is a much more efficient method of allocating a nation's resources than the acts of 'any statesman or lawgiver' (WN IV.ii.9, 10). Trade restrictions involve a misuse of resources and narrow the extent of the market.

Smith, however, is not an unqualified supporter of free trade, any more than he is of *laissez-faire* in general. He favours restrictions on foreigners that encourage industries necessary for national defence because 'defence . . . is of much more importance than opulence'. On this ground he supports the Navigation Act, in view of its stimulus to British shipping (WN IV.ii.24–30), as well as bounties on the exports of British made sail-cloth and gunpowder (WN IV.v.a.36). He refers to circumstances under which it may be desirable, for a 'sort of reasons of state', to restrain the export of corn, although he contends that this would be an act 'which ought to be exercised only . . . in cases of the most urgent necessity' (WN IV.v.b.39). He approves of the imposition of a tax on the export of British wool because it would yield a very considerable revenue to the government and afford an advantage to British manufacturers over foreign competitors (WN IV.viii.29–32). And he favours moderate import duties on foreign manufactures, mainly for revenue purposes (WN V.ii.k.32).

Smith approves of some retaliatory import duties when there is the possibility that they will procure the repeal of high duties or prohibitions by foreign countries on the import of some British manufactures: 'The

[53] '. . . if foreigners, either by prohibitions or high duties, are hindered from coming to sell, they cannot always afford to come to buy . . . By diminishing the number of sellers, therefore, we necessarily diminish that of buyers, and are thus likely not only to buy foreign goods dearer, but to sell our own cheaper, than if there was a more perfect freedom of trade' (WN IV.ii.30).

recovery of a great foreign market [again the stress on foreign markets!] will generally more than compensate the transitory inconveniency of paying dearer during a short time for some sorts of goods.' But when there is no possibility of such repeal, 'it seems a bad method of compensating the injury done to certain classes of our people, to do another injury ourselves, not only to those classes, but to almost all other classes of them'.[54] He is aware of the infant-industry argument for tariffs, but he is not impressed by it.[55] He does not recognize the terms-of-trade argument for tariffs. He very sensibly argues that when a tax is imposed at home on the produce of some domestic industry, an equal import duty should be imposed on like foreign products so as to leave competition between domestic and foreign industry on the same footing as before. By the same reasoning, he justifies drawbacks on exports of domestic goods subject to excise or inland duties (WN IV.iv). The implicit assumption underlying these justifications for 'border-tax' adjustments is that the indirect taxes referred to are fully shifted forward to the consumer.

In his discussion of the effects of high import duties and prohibitions, Smith recognizes that the price of the goods in question will rise on the domestic market and that the output of the protected industries will be stimulated. But he seems to deny that these restrictions will increase aggregate employment or the level of economic activity in the tariff-imposing country: 'No regulation of commerce can increase the quantity of industry in any society beyond what its capital can maintain. It can only divert a part of it into a direction into which it would not otherwise have gone . . . [and] the immediate effect of every such regulation is to diminish [the country's] revenue.'[56] Note here the implicit assumption of full employment, not of a 'surplus productive capacity' that might be activated.

In similar vein, Smith argues that the effect of bounties on the export of domestic goods (except when they are really drawbacks) 'can only be to force the trade of a country into a channel much less advantageous than that in which it would naturally run of its own accord'.[57] He also recognizes

[54] Compare this with the more sophisticated argument of Torrens to the effect that retaliation against foreign tariffs would be beneficial to England, even if it did not lead to a reduction of those tariffs, in view of its impact upon the terms of trade. See L. Robbins, *Robert Torrens and the Evolution of Classical Economics* (1958), 187ff.

[55] 'By means of such regulations [high duties] . . . a particular manufacture may sometimes be acquired sooner than it could have been otherwise, and after a certain time may be made at home as cheap or cheaper than in the foreign country. But . . . it will by no means follow that the sum total, either of its [a society's] industry, or of its revenue, can ever be augmented by any such regulation' (WN IV.ii.13).

[56] WN IV.ii.3,13. Smith also argues for gradualness in reducing tariffs in the case of industries employing 'a great multitude of hands' and in opening the colony trade to foreign nations (WN IV.ii.40, IV.vii.c.44).

[57] WN IV.v.a.3. Indeed, trade is forced into a channel 'that is actually disadvantageous; the trade which cannot be carried on but by means of a bounty being necessarily a losing trade' (WN IV.v.a.24).

with insight that the effect of an export bounty will be to make the price of the subsidized commodity somewhat higher in the home market, and somewhat lower in the foreign, than it would otherwise be.[58] An export bounty thus 'imposes two different taxes upon the people: first, the tax which they are obliged to contribute, in order to pay the bounty; and secondly, the tax which arises from the advanced price of the commodity in the home market'(WN IV.v.a.8). He argues that, in the case of corn, the higher home price, by raising money wages and other elements of cost proportionately,[59] would not even stimulate corn production.

In this chapter on colonies, which Schumpeter describes as 'great and justly celebrated . . . a masterpiece not only of pleading but of analysis',[60] Smith relentlessly pursues his attack on mercantilist trade policies.[61] The opening of trade with the Americas and the East Indies conferred great benefits on the mother countries, for reasons already noted, and in similar fashion on the colonies themselves and on third countries. But the *monopoly* of the colonial trade by the mother country makes these benefits much less than they would otherwise have been, especially in the case of the colonies (WN IV.vii.c.9).

By rendering the colony produce dearer in all other countries, it lessens its consumption, and thereby cramps the industry of the colonies, and both the enjoyments and industry of all other countries, which both enjoy less when they pay more for what they enjoy, and produce less when they get less for what they produce. By rendering the produce of all other countries dearer in the colonies, it cramps, in the same manner, the industry of all other countries, and both the enjoyments and the industry of the colonies.

(WN IV.vii.c.9)

The mother country itself would have derived greater benefits from the colonial trade had there been no exclusive privileges. Not only does it

[58] WN IV.v.a.20. It would of course be possible, with the appropriate assumptions as to elasticities, for the home price to remain constant or even to fall, with the foreign price falling in each case sufficiently to create a price differential equal to the amount of the bounty (abstracting from transport costs and foreign tariffs). If the home price falls, we would have a 'perverse' case analogous to that which could arise as a result of the imposition of a tariff, as described by L. A. Metzler, 'Tariffs, the Terms of Trade, and the Distribution of National Income', *Journal of Political Economy* (Feb. 1949), 1–29.

[59] This and other aspects of Smith's treatment of export bounties were criticized by Ricardo, *Works*, i. 301–20. Indeed, Ricardo notes: 'Perhaps in no part of Adam Smith's justly celebrated work, are his conclusions more liable to objection, than in the chapter on bounties' (ibid. 304).

[60] J. A. Schumpeter, *History of Economic Analysis* (1954), 187.

[61] The colonial theories of Smith and of his successors have been extensively examined. See, e. g., K. E. Knorr, *British Colonial Theories, 1570–1850* (1944); Winch, op. cit.; B. Semmel, *The Rise of Free Trade Imperialism* (1970); R. N. Ghosh, *Classical Macroeconomics and the Case for Colonies* (1967); and E. M. Winslow, *The Pattern of Imperialism* (1948).

sacrifice part of the advantage which it, along with all other countries, would have derived from the colonial trade, but it subjects itself to a disadvantage in almost every *other* branch of trade.

Smith's main argument against the British monopoly of its colonial trade is that it diverts capital into that trade from other, and to him socially more advantageous, channels (WN IV.vii.c.19–55; 86–100). The artificial rise in the rate of profit in the colonial trade—resulting from the exclusion of foreign capital from it—attracts British capital formerly employed in other branches of trade, 'as well as withholding from them a great deal more which would otherwise have gone to them' (WN IV.vii.c.22). In so doing, it keeps the rate of profit in these other trades higher than it would otherwise be.[62]

Using as his criterion of social advantage the quantity of productive labour 'put into motion' by a given capital, Smith thus argues that the monopoly of the colonial trade diverts British capital 'from a foreign trade of consumption with a neighbouring, into one with a more distant, country; in many cases, from a direct foreign trade of consumption, into a round-about one; and in some cases, from all foreign trade of consumption, into a carrying trade. It has in all cases, therefore, turned it, from a direction in which it would have maintained a greater quantity of productive labour, into one, in which it can maintain a much smaller quantity'.[63] Smith's recognition of the distinction between 'trade creation' and 'trade diversion' is summed up in this statement: 'In consequence of the monopoly, the increase of the colony trade has not so much occasioned an addition to the trade which Britain had before, as a total change in its direction' (WN IV.vii.c.23).

The foregoing argument, it will be observed, runs in terms of full employment of British resources (or at least of capital) and of their diversion from other employments into the colonial trade. But, in somewhat inconsistent fashion, Smith, when turning to a discussion of the colonial trade in its 'natural and free state' as contrasted with its monopolization, reverts to his 'vent for surplus' argument with its implication, in the absence of such trade, of some idle British resources. A new market is opened up for British 'surplus produce', Britain is encouraged to increase those surpluses, and the new market will 'draw nothing from the old one' (WN IV.vii.c.48).

In his chapter on colonies Smith explicitly discusses, for the only time in his book, the effect of trade restrictions upon factor income shares. His

[62] This in turn, according to Smith, keeps British prices higher than they would otherwise be and thereby enables foreign merchants to undersell Britain on foreign markets and all those branches of trade in which it does not have a monopoly (WN IV.vii.c.28,29). Ricardo denied that the monopoly of the colonial trade would raise the rate of profit or prices at home (*Works*, i.344–6).

[63] WN IV.vii.c.46. It is surprising that Smith does not explicitly state that mercantile capital is also diverted from *home* trade as a result of the colonial monopoly.

argument runs entirely in terms of absolute rather than relative shares. The monopoly of the colonial trade, he tells us, keeps aggregate profits, aggregate wages, and aggregate rent in the mother country below the levels to which they would in each case have otherwise risen (WN IV.vii.c.57–60). So far as profits are concerned, the *rate* of profit is increased, but the colonial monopoly obstructs the natural increase of capital by restraining the growth of income and thus of saving. As a result, aggregate profits are held down because a small [rate of] profit upon a great capital generally afford[s] a greater revenue than a great profit upon a small one (WN IV.vii.c.59).

INTERNATIONAL MONETARY MECHANISM

Smith devotes comparatively little attention to the working of the international monetary mechanism. Indeed, his performance in this area has customarily been regarded as inferior to that of Hume.

Viner found it a 'mystery' that Smith, although acquainted with Hume and his writings, should have made no reference in *The Wealth of Nations* to the self-regulating adjustment mechanism in terms of price levels and the trade balance—as he had, approvingly, in his *Lectures*—and should have contented himself with an exposition of international specie distribution in the obsolete terms of the requirement by each country, without reference to its relative price level, of a definite amount of money to circulate its trade.[64] When a country's money supply exceeds that amount, as Smith notes in a number of passages, the excess will directly 'overflow', in the form of specie, through increased purchases of imports or other 'profitable employment abroad' (WN II.ii.30,48; II.iii.23).

Viner's statement has recently been challenged on two fronts. One writer, while accepting his assertion that Smith made no reference to the price-specie-flow mechanism in *The Wealth of Nations*, denies that it is a 'mystery' on the alleged ground that acceptance by Smith of the Hume doctrine would have conflicted with other aspects of his sytem.[65] Of more interest here is the assertion by Eagly that Smith did indeed state the price-specie-flow mechanism in his book.[66] He cites as evidence the following passage:

> . . . no commodities regulate themselves more easily or more exactly according to . . . effectual demand than gold and silver; because, on account of the small bulk and great value of those metals, no commodities can be more easily trans-

[64] Viner, *Studies*, 87. A similar view had been expressed much earlier by J. Hollander, 'The Development of the Theory of Money from Adam Smith to David Ricardo', *Quarterly Journal of Economics* (May 1911), 437–9.

[65] F. Petrella, 'Adam Smith's Rejection of Hume's Price-Specie-Flow Mechanism: A Minor Mystery Resolved', *Southern Economic Journal* (Jan. 1968), 365–74.

[66] R. V. Eagly, 'Adam Smith and the Specie-Flow Doctrine', *Scottish Journal of Political Economy* (Feb. 1970), 61–8.

ported from one place to another, from the places where they are cheap, to those where they are dear, from the places where they exceed, to those where they fall short of this effectual demand . . . When the quantity of gold and silver imported into any country exceeds the effectual demand, no vigilance of government can prevent their exportation . . . The continual importations [into Spain and Portugal] exceed the effectual demand of those countries, and sink the price of those metals there below that in the neighbouring countries. If, on the contrary, in any particular country their quantity fell short of the effectual demand, so as to raise their price above that of the neighbouring countries, the government would have no occasion to take any pains to import them.

(WN IV.i.12,13)

If it is recalled that by cheapness or dearness of the precious metals Smith means a high or low general price level,[67] then what he seems to be saying here is that changes in a country's price level relative to that prevailing abroad will cause specie flows—bringing price levels into line—because of the ease with which specie can be moved. This would still leave unexplained the intermediary link between price level differences and specie movements, namely, changes in the trade balance. But this link is provided in a later passage (in the chapter on export bounties) where, in the course of repeating his argument, Smith makes it clear that a change in relative price levels at home and abroad will indeed affect the trade balance.[68] Smith's exposition, as Eagly indicates, focuses on the specie market and the commodity price of specie rather than on the commodity market and the specie price of commodities. But all of the elements of the Hume doctrine are there. The treatment, however, remains inconsistent with Smith's other explanation of international specie distribution noted above.

How little importance Smith attaches to the price-specie-flow mechanism is evident in his treatment of the 'transfer problem' coming just a few pages after the passage cited above. In discussing the heavy payments that Britain had to make abroad during the Seven Years War, he states that these had to be made chiefly by exports of British goods because of an insufficiency of gold and silver at home. The 'mechanism' whereby this was achieved was, not by a change in relative price levels brought about by initial specie flows, but as follows: when the government contracted with merchants for remittances to foreign countries, the merchants 'naturally'

[67] e.g.: 'The cheapness of gold and silver, or what is the same thing, the dearness of all commodities . . .' (WN IV.v.a.19).

[68] e.g.: '. . . that degradation in the value of silver which, being the effect either of the peculiar situation, or of the political institutions of a particular country, takes place only in that country, is a matter of very great consequence . . . The rise in the money price of all commodities, which is in this case peculiar to that country, tends . . . to enable foreign nations, by furnishing almost all sorts of goods for a smaller quantity of silver than its own workman can afford to do, to undersell them, not only in the foreign, but even in the home market' (WN IV.v.a.17; see also IV.v.a.19–20, IV.v.b.32).

exerted their 'invention' to find a way to meet the payments to foreign correspondents by the export of commodities rather than specie because of the much greater profit to be made on the former than on the latter.[69]

On the other hand, Smith's alternative explanation of the mechanism of specie flows in terms of money requirements and money expenditures without reference to relative price levels—the one criticized by Viner—deserves more consideration than Viner gave it. Far from being 'obsolete' as he claimed, it could be regarded as being more 'modern' in spirit than the price-specie-flow explanation. By arguing that the quantity of money needed by a country bears a certain proportion to the value of its annual produce, and that any excess supply of money will be drained abroad in the form of specie as individuals adjust to their excess holdings of cash balances by increasing their foreign expenditures, Smith can be said to have anticipated, however crudely, the modern 'monetary approach' to balance-of-payments theory and adjustment.[70]

Smith is aware, as was Hume, of the equilibrating role of fluctuations in exchange rates within the specie points on the balance of trade. In criticizing a mercantilist argument that the high price of foreign exchange would necessarily increase England's trade deficit, he correctly argues: 'The high price of exchange . . . must necessarily have operated as a tax, in raising the price of foreign goods, and thereby diminishing their consumption. It would tend, therefore, not to increase, but to diminish, what they called, the unfavourable balance of trade, and consequently the exportation of gold and silver' (WN IV.i.9). But he does not use symmetrical reasoning on the export side, arguing simply that the high price of exchange will 'naturally dispose the merchants to endeavour to make their exports more nearly balance their imports, in order that they might have this high exchange to pay upon as small a sum as possible'.

CONCLUSION

It is easy to fault a man retrospectively, even a great man such as Adam Smith, for inability to perceive what his successors could. Admittedly, Smith did not come up with comparative costs, reciprocal demand, or others of the concepts and tools that were to be developed by later classical

[69] WN IV.i.26,27. Taussig commented on these passages as follows: 'Smith's explanation was hardly satisfactory in his day, much less in ours' (op. cit. 275). On the other hand, Einzig has stated: 'A contribution of importance was [Smith's] analysis of international transfers associated with major wars abroad.' P. Einzig, *The History of Foreign Exchange* (1962), 152.

[70] For the 'monetary theory' of the balance of payments, see R. A. Mundell, *International Economics* (1968), Ch. 8; H. G. Johnson, 'The Monetary Approach to Balance-of-Payments Theory', *Journal of Financial and Quantitative Analysis* (Mar. 1972), 1555–72; A. Collery, *International Adjustment, Open Economies, and the Quantity Theory of Money*, Princeton Studies in International Finance No. 28 (1971); and R. E. Caves and R. W. Jones, *World Trade and Payments* (1973), 322–7.

writers on international trade. That there were limitations in his trade theorizing cannot be denied. But his over-all performance in the analysis of international trade, while not backed by a striking core of theory, deserves respectful attention.

Smith showed profound insights as to the underlying basis and gains of trade. He analysed in greater detail than any of his predecessors the nature and benefits of international specialization and the factors affecting them. He saw more clearly than any one before him the importance of differences in relative factor endowments and of transport costs in shaping the pattern of international trade. He made an especially notable contribution in his analysis of the growth-stimulating effects of foreign trade. He may be said to have been a precursor of the modern 'monetary approach' to balance-of-payments theory and adjustment. He raised a large number of other important issues in trade theory that were to be developed by later classical writers on the basis of the pattern of approach that he set and the central ideas that he launched. And his analysis of the noxious effects of mercantilist trade practices and of the case for freedom of trade was, as has been widely recognized, an achievement of great significance for his time and beyond.

XI

Adam Smith and the Status of the Theory of Money

DOUGLAS VICKERS*

I

In the hundred years preceding the appearance of *The Wealth of Nations* considerable development had occurred, and a high degree of analytical sophistication had been reached, in the theory of money. The status to which the theory had attained and the structure of monetary thought in the eighteenth century determine the theoretical vantage-point from which our assessment of the monetary theory in Adam Smith's classic work must be considered.[1] *The Wealth of Nations*, it can be said without danger of controversion, is a great book, the product of a great mind, acute observation, and deep human sympathies. But it will not be our objective in this essay to establish what is already incontrovertible. Many of the central constructions of the work will be invoked to illumine our discussion of the theory of money. But our main task, eschewing even many of the more detailed monetary observations, will be the erection of adequate perspectives from which the sophistication and the viability of the theory of money can be evaluated. Our concern will be with the *status* of the theory of money within the context of the work as a whole, and as it was accorded a place of greater or lesser significance in Smith's total economic argument.

Our interpretative task, therefore, requires us to examine initially the principal achievements of monetary theory on the pre-classical side of the 1776 divide. Then against the perspectives thus established a more detailed evaluation can be made of Smith's place in the history of this important part of our subject. Smith, it will be argued at some length, did not embrace the perspectives or develop further the monetary dynamics of the more prominent of his predecessors, Cantillon, Hume, and Steuart, for example, and many of the potentially fruitful theorems which were extant before his time unfortunately languished. The theory of money did not receive a

* Professor of Economics, the University of Western Australia.

[1] Adam Smith, *The Wealth of Nations*, ed. Edwin Cannan (1937).

A more extensive examination of the pre-classical theory is contained in Douglas Vickers, *Studies in the Theory of Money, 1690–1776* (1959), and 'The Works . . . of Sir James Steuart: A Review Article', *The Journal of Economic Literature* (Dec. 1970).

'definitive exposition' in Adam Smith.[2] On the contrary, in *The Wealth of Nations* the theory of money lives a much more subordinate, even subdued, existence, and our discussion of it will need to account for the enigma of Adam Smith's view of the relative unimportance of money in the explanation of the monetary economy; relative unimportance, that is, in comparison with the respects in which monetary analysis had occupied the centre of the stage in earlier years, and in the perspective of the 'real' analysis in which Smith's considerable achievements lay.[3] It was not that money of some suitable form was not seen to be necessary for the effective functioning of the exchange economy. The early chapter 'Of the origin and use of Money' in Book I of *The Wealth of Nations*, following as it does the discussion of the limitation of division of labour by the extent of the market, puts that question beyond doubt. But money for Smith meant usually metallic money, and his 'real' analysis occupied him repeatedly with the labour cost of obtaining it and the notion that its exchange value was embedded, in the last analysis, in the intrinsic value it possessed. It was not that Smith had no notion of bank money, money substitutes, and paper money circulation. His important discussion of banking and his clear and articulate anticipation of the real-bills doctrine put this question beyond doubt also. But for him the principal utility and the significance of banking lay in its money-moving rather than its money-creating function, and in what has to be seen as its relevance for the velocity of circulation of money.[4]

The essence of the issues, in short, is implied in a relatively small number of observations. The 'sole use of money', Smith concludes, resides in its functioning as a medium of exchange.[5] Interest centres on hard metallic money, and the maximum maintainable circulation of paper money is determined simply by the amount of gold and silver money whose use can be economized because paper can be used to replace it (WN II.ii.58). The sustainable size of the money supply is determined by the level of real

[2] See Jacob H. Hollander, 'The Development of the Theory of Money from Adam Smith to David Ricardo', *Quarterly Journal of Economics* (1911), 432.

[3] We shall examine below the respects in which Smith's primary concern for longer-run 'real' dynamics and economic growth pushed a more detailed monetary analysis into a subordinate position.

[4] In connection with the mainstream of theoretical history we are here adumbrating note might be taken of Schumpeter's summary statement: 'The history of economic analysis in the period [preceding 1790] . . . ends with a victory of Real Analysis that was so complete as to put Monetary Analysis practically out of court for well over a century.' Joseph A. Schumpeter, *History of Economic Analysis* (1954), 282. As to Smith's profound significance for the Real Analysis which we have recognized in the text, Schumpeter further observes that 'Even if . . . monetary analysis . . . and the modern development of it is an improvement upon the real analysis of the nineteenth century, . . . the latter was not less superior to the monetary analysis of the eighteenth' (ibid. 288). Schumpeter here speaks of 'spirals of advance' in the development of economic theory.

[5] WN II.iii.23. The measure of value function is discussed, however, and in his *Lectures* Smith explicitly considers 'money, first as the measure of value and then as the medium or permutation of exchange' (LJ (B) 235; Cannan, 182).

activity and the needs of trade. If an excess of money supply above this level were issued it would return to the issuing bank for redemption, and in the absence of investment opportunities at home the money metals would be sent abroad (WN II.iii.27). Here is the doctrine of money reflux, the other half of the consistent real-bills argument. But in developing it, Smith fails to examine in any consistent fashion either the potential price-level effects or the interest-rate effects of excessive monetary circulation. It is in this, and its logical implication for the non-integrability of a thoroughgoing monetary and real analysis, as well as in his savings-investment argument, that we see Smith's real analysis triumphant. The logical hiatus on the last-mentioned level, critically important for the subsequent development of monetary macro-theory, lay, of course, in the failure to recognize that damaging interruptions may in fact occur in the savings-investment process, and that it may not be true that the portion of his income 'which a rich man . . . annually saves . . . is *immediately* employed as a capital'.[6] Hoarding of money, and consequent variations in the rates of flows of expenditures, could and did occur, with damaging economic repercussions.

But while none of this should detract from the greatness of Smith's achievement, our argument is that in the matter of the theory of money *The Wealth of Nations* does not deserve very high praise. In *The Wealth of Nations* the theory of money resides at a relative nadir in the swings of its long historical development. Deeper analysis and more extended argument occurred on both sides of the 1776 divide. The understanding of Smith's substantive position in the theory of money is benefited, moreover, by an appreciation of the structural dichotomies, one might say the methodological tensions, which inform *The Wealth of Nations*. Interlaced by parallel arguments and frequent reasoning by analogy, the work moves around the foci provided by three sets of opposing, but interrelated and never completely distinctive ideas.[7] First, the notion of the self-interest of economic entities and the invisible hand that guides their actions to socially beneficent outcomes is set against the considerable, and even, on a careful reading of the work, pervasive, argument for an appropriate institutional structure or framework of economic society. The latter, it is clearly envisaged, provides a societal context without which individuals' economic action could not be expected to cohere. Second, the argument regarding tendencies to market

[6] WN II.iii.18, italics supplied. See also T. W. Hutchison, *A Review of Economic Doctrines 1870–1929* (1953), 348.

[7] The level on which this statement is made is that of the potentially most fruitful standpoint from which to unravel and evaluate Smith's actual achievement in the theory of money, and our ensuing discussion will clarify more fully the relationships between the interpretative foci here referred to. The problem of the unity of Smith's work, for example the consistency of *The Wealth of Nations* and the *Theory of Moral Sentiments*, has been widely discussed, and valuable aspects of this and related questions of consistency appear in Jacob Viner's 'Adam Smith and Laissez Faire' referred to below, and in G. S. L. Tucker, *Progress and Profits in British Economic Thought, 1650–1850* (1960), Ch. IV.

equilibria, resource allocation and mobility, and the distribution of incomes is set against the discussion of the causes and the character of economic growth and development. Third, the argument that money is a veil beyond which the real problems of resource use, distribution, and development are resolved is set against the tendency, never in any context quite triumphant, to argue that money and monetary circulation can themselves have independent effects on the actual economic posture. In short, in *The Wealth of Nations* the argument revolves around three separate sets of relations: first, that of self-interest, the invisible hand, and the institutional framework of the economy; second, the statics of market equilibrium and the dynamics of economic growth; and third, the veil of money and the transmission of independent monetary influences. On each of these levels, and inherent in their respective analytical dichotomies, implications reside for the adequate interpretation of the Smithian theory of money.

II

We consider firstly the question of the status of monetary theory as it had developed on the pre-classical side of the Smithian divide. From the foundations laid by the philosopher-economist Locke and his contemporaries the theory of money advanced to achieve, in the decades preceding *The Wealth of Nations*, a relative maturity in the work of Cantillon, Hume, and Steuart.[8] The history of monetary analysis in this period is one of successive attempts at fashioning a body of theory which was empirically relevant, logically consistent, and in large degree the unifying element in the literature of economic affairs and policy. The developments achieved in monetary thought before its mainstream was submerged again by the different predilections of the classical theoretical system derived clearly from the preoccupation with the relevance of money (and the possibility of monetary disorders) for the healthy functioning of the economic system. This orientation consistently raised questions about the determination of the level and the stability of economic activity and employment. 'The money of the nation', John Locke had said at the beginning of the period, 'may lie dead, and thereby prejudice trade' (op. cit. 226). He pointed out that given the possibility of damaging interruptions to the flow of money it would conceivably be necessary to 'encourage lending' in order to maintain the level of monetary circulation. Money, Locke went to some lengths to

[8] See John Locke, *Consequences of the lowering of interest, and raising the value of money* (1691), and *Further considerations concerning raising the value of money* (1696), published together with J. R. McCulloch's, *Principles of Political Economy* (1870), 220–360; Richard Cantillon, *Essai sur la nature du Commerce en general*, Royal Economic Society edition, translated by Henry Higgs (1931); David Hume, *Essays, Moral Political and Literary*, Part II, Essays I to IX (1752; 1817); Sir James Steuart, *An Inquiry into the Principles of Political Oeconomy* (2 vols., 1767). See also my *Studies in the Theory of Money, 1690–1776* (1959) for further references and critical discussions.

establish, must be understood as having a 'price' as well as a 'value' (ibid. 238–9). It was at this point, in fact, that the theory of money as it developed during the eighteenth century was integrable with the general body of economic analysis. Because money attracted a price, the rate of interest, in the money markets, it was possible to demonstrate that comparable price conditions existed in what might be called the financial and the goods sectors of the economy. It could be shown that the conditions of equilibrium in each of these sectors were, in various ways, interdependent. The structure of the demand for money in the financial sector, and the nature of payments habits, which led to a consideration of 'the quickness of circulation' (ibid. 234) in the commodity sector, influenced the working of the monetary system. Money, its supply and its circulation, had an operative and variable significance for the determination of the level of activity and the level of prices in the commodity sector of the economy, and for the level of the rate of interest in the financial sector.

Throughout the eighteenth century, moreover, the question raised with increasing clarity was *how* a given level of economic activity and employment was related to the fact and the level of monetary circulation. From the equational-static, definitional propositions of Locke the analysis matured to consider explicitly, in Cantillon and Hume for example, the dynamics of the money flow process. 'Mr Locke has clearly seen', Cantillon acknowledged, 'that the abundance of money makes everything dear, but he has not considered *how* it does so. The great difficulty of this question consists in knowing *in what way* and *in what proportion* the increase of money raises prices' (op. cit. 161, italics supplied). And Cantillon, recasting the analysis from an equational-static to a causal-dynamic mould, went on to argue that the varying proportions in which prices would rise in the various 'channels of circulation', and the altered structure of prices which would result from a rise in the level of monetary circulation, would depend on the point at which the injection of new money entered the economic system and on the different consumption habits and dispositions to spend of the successive income recipients. The possibilities envisaged at this point, together with the varying elasticities of supply of commodities, determined the alternative shapes of the time-paths which the economy may follow from one equilibrium conjuncture to another (op. cit. 179). Indeed Cantillon, acutely aware of the probability that variations in the level and the rates of flow of money would induce cyclical disturbances of activity, argued for the temporary sterilization of a part of any excessive acquisition of new money supplies, to preserve the conditions of prosperity and avert the ensuing recession. The proposal was one for cutting off the excesses of the boom in order to avoid the distresses of the slump (ibid. 185).

David Hume likewise, in a comparably dynamic analysis, argued for the variable effects on price and activity levels of a change in the supply of money in circulation. He was aware explicitly, moreover, of the advanced theoretical notion of the time-lags inherent in the adjustment of economic quantities following the disturbance envisaged and the differential impact on incomes and prices which would result (op. cit. 283–6).

'The high price of commodities . . . follows not immediately . . . but some time is required before the money circulates through the whole state, and makes its effect be felt on all ranks of people . . . by degrees the price rises, first of one commodity, then of another; till the whole at last reaches a just proportion with the new quantity of specie . . .'[9]

There emerges, to adopt a phrase from Keynes, a new 'plurality of price levels'.[10] But of course it is true, as we shall note again, that while Hume was very much concerned with the 'interval or intermediate situation, between the acquisition of money and a rise of prices . . . because . . . that . . . keeps alive a spirit of industry in the nation, and increases the state of labour in which consists all real power and riches', he did emphasize also the importance of the equilibrium position to which, at any time and in a given situation, the economy could be understood to be tending. But Keynes's summary observation is undoubtedly correct, that Hume's place in the history of thought should turn on the fact that while he 'had a foot and a half in the classical world . . . he was still enough of a mercantilist not to overlook the fact that it is in the transition that we actually have our being'.[11] In Hume as in Cantillon, that is, a conscious attempt was made to construct the theory of the short-run dynamics of monetary economic behaviour.

Locke, of course, like Cantillon, Harris, and Hume after him, was a metallist. On the other side of the debate regarding the *form* of money, the antimetallists or 'cartalists' included Potter, Barbon, Berkeley, Law, and Steuart.[12] As the monetary thought of the eighteenth century matured the discussion focused increasingly on the priority of the *function* of money, and considerations as to the form of money were subordinated increasingly to those of functional efficacy. Barbon, taking as he did the opposite side to Locke in the currency controversies of the 1690s, systematized the cartalist notions of 'extrinsic' money, and he stands as the foremost of the early expositors of the conception that the thing that made money money, and the thing on which its value as an exchange medium depended, was the

[9] Op. cit. 283. The dependence of the substantive content of Hume's economic essays on his own methodological prolegomenon has been discussed in my *Studies in the Theory of Money* referred to earlier, and a recognition of this important fact and the significance of it for the interpretation of Hume's rightful place in the history of the theory of money is contained in George Horwich, *Money, Capital, and Prices* (1964), 431n.

[10] J. M. Keynes, *Treatise on Money* (1933), i.93.

[11] Keynes, *General Theory of Employment, Interest and Money* (1936), 343n.

[12] See William Potter, *The Key of Wealth* (1650); Nicholas Barbon, *A Discourse of Trade* (1690; ed. Hollander, 1905); George Berkeley, *Querist* (1735, 1736, and 1737); John Law, *Money and Trade Considered* (1720); and Sir James Steuart, op. cit.

simple fact that people were prepared to take it and hold it as suitable evidence of the discharge of indebtedness. There is in his work the logic of escape from the restrictive metallist assumptions which Locke had held, and Barbon stands as the logical anticipator of the monetary inflationists of the following century. There is a sense in which his argument that the thing that made money money was its 'currancy', was potentially one of the most fruitful propositions in the period under review.

John Law, one of the prominent inflationists of the early eighteenth century, is celebrated for his arguments directed to the establishment of note-issuing banks, his financial adventures in Europe, including his appointment in 1720 as the Controller-General of Finances for the Kingdom of France, and for his anticipation of the 'needs of trade' doctrine of banking. This latter was further developed in subsequent times, not only in Smith's banking theory but in the important banking school–currency school debate of the nineteenth century. John Law deserves recognition also for his notion of the variable elasticities of supply of produceable commodities following an increase in the rates of flow of money in the economy. Recognizing at the same time the price-forming function and the activity-forming function of the flow of money, he took care of the price-stability problem, at least on the level of theoretical analysis, by this important and implicit assumption of the price elasticities of supply (op. cit. 51, 52). But significantly, his argument involved, in turn, a further conclusion. If, in Law's theoretical system, an increase in the money supply could be expected, via the elasticity argument, to increase production and exports and improve rather than worsen the external balance of payments, then no outward flow of gold would occur and the old problem of protecting the international currency reserves would not arise. Furthermore, given the fact that permanently circulating money-substitutes were as effective as metallic money in achieving the desired end of healthier economic activity, there was no good reason why the level of internal monetary circulation should be made to depend, as in the earlier mercantilist fashion, on a favourable balance of trade and an inflow of bullion. Here is the logic of cartalism triumphant. The effective direction of causation as to money supply and the trade balance could well be reversed. There were, it was clear, easier and better ways of increasing the supply of money and of achieving desired economic objectives.

The significance of Law's arguments lies partly in his influence on Sir James Steuart, whose *Principles* of 1767 marks a distinct turning-point in the history of the theory of money. It gathers up the main threads of discussion and submits a unified statement of the theoretical and policy issues in monetary affairs. The *Principles* is in many respects a synthesis of earlier theoretical advances and in Steuart the movement toward a *theory* of money is relatively complete. He binds together in a coherent system the several strands of thought that had already appeared—the notion of policy action to maintain demand at a high-employment level, the conception of a dynamic analysis of the money-flow process, and the meaning and significance of extrinsic money supplies (see note 1, above). It is in connection with the last-mentioned point that Steuart's dependence on Law is clearly seen. Recognizing, and being anxious to preserve, the theoretical validities of Law's position at the same time as he avoided his policy errors and excesses, Steuart was concerned with the stability-of-value problem associated with Law's note-issuing schemes. Significantly, Adam Smith's arguments on the needs-of-trade banking doctrine were also concerned to avoid the disruptive instabilities which could conceivably arise from the same source. Law's problem stemmed from the other half of the banking doctrine, which reappeared explicitly and prominently in Smith's scheme of things, namely the argument that when sufficient money substitutes had been issued to satisfy the needs of trade any surplus which might appear in circulation would automatically be returned to the issuing source. It was the unsupportable doctrine of money reflux. For Law's proposal also (based as his money supply was on the value of land against which notes were issued) begged the question of the stability of the value of the land itself.[13] Quite apart from changes in real asset values which may derive from growth or variations in their intrinsic income-producing potential, the money value of the assets could change as did the availability of the notes of issue themselves. The theoretical possibility existed of an unlimited expansion of the note issue, *pari passu* with an induced and cumulative upward movement in the money values of the assets which were eligible as security.

The strands of argument we have sketched in the foregoing suggest that a twofold path issued from the theoretical developments of the eighteenth century. One led directly to the economics of value, distribution, and long-run macro-dynamics with which the English classicists became preoccupied. The other, whose construction was the peculiar achievement of the earlier eighteenth-century authors, led to the positive analysis of the level of economic activity and employment. It is in this latter direction that Steuart's *Principles*, soon to be eclipsed by *The Wealth of Nations*, clearly moved. His successors chose, in general, the other path. But in summing up the developments in the theory of money in the pre-classical period, four principal characteristics can now be observed. First, the *theory of the value of money* had been transformed from the static-equational form in which Locke at the beginning of the period had stated it. The value of money was determined by the conjunction of money *flows* and commodity *flows* in the several markets of the economy. Taking account of the new concept of elastic money supplies, moreover, the flow of money was dependent in

[13] Cf. the discussion of a similar point in Lloyd W. Mints, *A History of Banking Theory* (1945), 30ff.

some degree on the total demand for money to finance a desired level of trade and economic activity. Here, in other words, is the beginning of the income approach to the theory of money and money values and the notion, important in much, more modern, analysis, of the endogeneity of the economy's money supply. Second, the theory of the relation between the flow of money and the *level of activity and employment* had been examined at length and with increasing refinement. This phase of analysis had come to occupy the centre of discussion, and the remaining objectives of analysis were seen to be logically subordinate to it. Money was significant because it was money that unified and sustained the operations of the economic system. Third, the problems of the *reform of the coinage*, which in the earlier part of the period gave rise to some significant concepts, relating, for example, to the theory of money values, the economics of debtor–creditor relations, and the question of the deflation or otherwise which would be involved in recoinage at certain metallic standards, had lost the centre of attention to the theories of money-substitutes, banking, bank-money, and elastic credit supplies. Finally, the theory of the *rate of interest* had been broadened, not only to take account of the forces which determined the conditions of demand for and supply of loan money, but to exhibit also the interdependence which existed between the structure and level of activity in general and the conditions of equilibrium in the loan markets of the economy.

III

These propositions, however, and the fuller analysis to which the preceding discussion has pointed, summarize simply some of the more prominent features and conclusions of the monetary theory on the pre-classical side of the 1776 divide. It is germane to our objectives to ask what were the principal elements of the pre-classical analysis to which the theorists of the following century paid most attention, and which more than others informed the following developments of thought. An important linkage, of course, is established by the substantive content of *The Wealth of Nations*, and a review of the main points of Smith's preoccupations and achievements will assist our further evaluation of the status and relevance of the theory of money at that time.

For this purpose it is appropriate to move directly to the second of what we referred to earlier as the foci, or levels of methodological tension, the appreciation of which will best determine our understanding of the classic work before us. This has to do with the significance of money for general market equilibrium determination on the one hand and for economic growth on the other. It is here that we come to the heart of Smith's explicit theory of money. Of the necessary interpretative stance on this point there can be no doubt. Smith's main concern was economic growth. It may be that 'Adam Smith's "invisible hand" is a poetic expression of the most fundamental of economic balance relations . . .' and that 'Smith was a creator of general equilibrium theory',[14] but the issue before us relates to the primary and the conceptually ordered thrust of his work. Sir James Steuart, in line with the characteristic constructions of the earlier eighteenth century had taken an opposite analytical perspective and he built, as a result, a theory of short-run dynamic changes in the aggregate economy, which *The Wealth of Nations* substantially neglected. 'I think it absurd', Steuart said, 'to wish for new inhabitants without first knowing how to employ the old . . . I shall then begin by supposing that inhabitants require rather to be well employed than increased in numbers' (op. cit. i.59–60). And he produced, as a result, a theory of short-run employment and economic activity levels. For Smith, however, the problems of short-run allocation of resources, their employment, incomes, and economic mobility, became a subsidiary theme;[15] and this notwithstanding his vastly important analysis of market equilibrium forces, factor rewards, and income distribution in Book I of *The Wealth of Nations*. The key to Smith, and certainly the single most important standpoint from which his attitude to money is to be seen, has to do with capital accumulation, the long-run expansive trend of the system, and the increase in 'productive labour' which results.

> Wherever capital predominates, industry prevails . . . Every increase or diminution of capital, therefore, naturally tends to increase or diminish the real quantity of industry, the number of productive hands, and consequently the exchangeable value of the annual produce of the land and labour of the country, the real wealth and revenue of all its inhabitants.
>
> (WN II.iii.13)

'Capitals', of course, 'are increased by parsimony', and it is in this context that 'parsimony, and not industry' is the true mainspring of the economic advance. 'Parsimony, by increasing the fund which is destined for the maintenance of productive hands . . . puts into motion an additional quantity of industry . . .', and it is here that the critical, but, we have seen, analytically defective, assumption enters: 'What is annually saved is as regularly consumed as what is annually spent, and nearly in the same time too' (WN II.iii.18). It follows for Smith that 'every prodigal appears to be a public enemy, and every frugal man a public benefactor' (WN II.iii.25). Admittedly this interpretative orientation in our reading of *The Wealth of Nations* may call in question the cogency of much of the commentary on the

[14] K. H. Arrow, *International Encyclopedia of the Social Sciences* (1968), iv.376.

[15] See the important discussion in Hla Myint, 'The Classical View of the Economic Problem', *Economica* (May 1946) reprinted in Spengler and Allen, *Essays in Economic Thought* (1960).

classical economic literature and the supposed analytical priority of the value and distribution theory.[16] But in the Smithian position at least, the structure of the argument is clear. The increase of savings out of incomes increases the wage fund, providing an increase in circulating capital, leading to an increase in the employment of productive labour, and thence inducing an increase in population and, in the long run, causing again a depression of the real wage back towards the subsistence level from which the increase in the wage fund and the upswing of the secular advance had earlier raised it. There is in Smith, we may say, a double dynamics, having to do with the fluctuation of market prices around 'natural' prices and the attendant migration of factor resources on the one hand, and with the secular expansive trends on the other. We have argued, for purposes of establishing an interpretative perspective on *The Wealth of Nations*, for the logical priority of the latter.[17] And the important fact for the monetary thought of *The Wealth of Nations* is that it is precisely in the context of Smith's discussion of this larger dynamics that his definitive discussion of money appears. Money, along with, significantly, monetary circulation, is important because of the interpretation of it as a part of the circulating capital of the economy. Definitions, of course, had been laid down early in the work, definitions having to do with the forms and functions of money, market prices, and real and nominal values, including, to bring to the fore the finally and irreparably damaging assumption of the monetary theory, the intrinsic value of the money metals. It is in Book II, however, that the analysis as opposed to the definitions appears, including, as we shall observe below, the important discussion of banking.

In short, four propositions, taken together, constitute the heart of Smith's monetary theory at this point. They have to do, first, with the function of money as a circulating medium; second, with the meaning and determinative significance of its intrinsic value; third, with its assumed continual circulation and the absence of possible money hoarding; and fourth, with the determination of the maintainable volume of money in circulation by the stage of real development which the economy had attained. The important question of the rate of interest, which is not in Smith a monetary phenomenon, is taken up, and we shall find the argu-

[16] Note might be taken in this connection of William Baumol's discussion of the 'Magnificent Dynamics' of the classical period in his *Economic Dynamics* (1959), Ch. 2. Hla Myint, op. cit. 422, refers to 'a fundamental inconsistency in the currently accepted opinions concerning the classical economists . . . [the] belief that their main concern is to show that the equilibrium process of the free market will lead to a more efficient allocation of resources among different industries than state interference . . . [and the conception of] the economic problem as the struggle of man to transform resources given by nature into material wealth'.

[17] Cf. *The Wealth of Nations*, Book I, Ch. VII 'Of the Natural and Market Prices of Commodities' and Ch. X 'Of Wages and Profits in the Different Employments of Labour and Stock'.

ment in what follows inevitably overlapping also with the final question of money as a veil over the underlying real forces of the system.

In the context of the growth analysis Smith squarely summarizes the significance of money. Quite simply, 'the quantity of money, therefore, which can be annually employed in any country, must be determined by the value of the consumable goods annually circulated within it.' And 'the sole use of money is to circulate consumable goods' (WN II.iii.23). 'Money', he had said, is 'the great wheel of circulation' (WN II.ii.14), but he meant by this, consistently, hard or metallic money.[18] Moreover, given that the stock of money was interpreted as part of the circulating capital of the economy, and focusing, in the manner of numerous of his eighteenth-century predecessors, on the notion of monetary circulation as distinct from that of the money stock as such, Smith envisages a 'saving in the expense of collecting and supporting . . . money' as an improvement of the effectiveness of the money supply in circulation (WN II.ii.24). The notion envisaged is that of the velocity of circulation of money, and it is in this connection that banking operations and bank note issues are seen to have their effectiveness. 'The substitution of paper in the room of gold and silver money . . . [provides] a new wheel [of circulation]' (WN II.ii.26). Or explicitly, looking at the question of velocity from the point of view of its inverse, the required size of the money stock, 'the proportion which the circulating money . . . bears to the whole value of the annual produce circulated by means of it' is clearly reduced 'by the substitution of paper' and 'it must make a very considerable addition to the quantity of that industry, and, consequently, to the value of the annual produce of land and labour' (WN II.ii.40). Apparent activity and income-creating effects follow from the increased velocity of circulation, which is the manner of interpreting the effects of replacing by paper money-substitutes the hard money which would otherwise lie stagnant as 'dead stock'. 'The judicious operations of banking . . . convert(s) this dead stock into active and productive stock' (WN II.ii.86). But as we have seen, some care is required in the interpretation of this Smithian argument. For when all is said and done, 'the whole paper money of every kind which can easily circulate in any country never can exceed the

[18] David Hume had suggested earlier that 'money . . . is none of the wheels of trade: It is the oil which renders the motion of the wheels more smooth and easy' (op. cit. 279). The implication of this statement is that Hume is here anticipating again one of the principal aspects of the Smithian argument. Hume considered that in the long run the wealth of the nation depended not upon the supply of money in and of itself, but upon 'our people and our industry' (ibid. 309, cf. 324–5). Moreover, 'I should as soon dread, that all our springs and rivers should be exhausted, as that money should abandon a kingdom where there are people and industry. Let us carefully preserve these latter advantages, and we need never be apprehensive of losing the former' (ibid. 308). Hume significantly argues also, however, in line with his inflation thesis, that paper money could have the same effects as metallic money in that it 'gives encouragement to industry, during the intervals between the increase of money and the rise of prices' (ibid. 315).

value of the gold and silver, of which it supplies the place, or which (the commerce being supposed the same) would circulate there, if there was no paper money' (WN II.ii.48).

Here, plainly, is an unfortunate ambivalence which requires us to interpret Smith's argument finally as concentrating on the velocity-increasing, or the money-moving function of banking, rather than the money-creating function. The ambivalence, and Smith's repeated haste to return to the shelter of the hard-money concept, turned on his overriding concern for the labour cost or intrinsic value of the money metals. Indeed, in laying down the definitional foundation of his work Smith had summed up quite clearly: '... the price of goods comes ... to be adjusted, not to the quantity of pure gold or silver which the coin ought to contain, but to that which, upon an average, it is found by experience it actually does contain. By the money price of goods ... I understand always the quantity of pure gold or silver for which they are sold ...' (WN I.v.41–2). Yet in the same way as in his 'accumulation of capital' argument his clear functional view of money required him to regard bank notes as money because they 'serve all the purposes of money' (WN II.ii.27), he argued in his later 'Digression concerning Banks of Deposit' that 'a shilling fresh from the mint will buy no more goods in the market than one of our common worn shillings' (WN IV.iii.b.5). We observe, therefore, unfortunate criss-crossing ambivalences which mar what might have been, at critical points, analyses leading to more genuinely robust levels of monetary theory. And lest the consistent theoretical anchorage of the work be lost from sight, Smith cautions the reader that 'labour, it must always be remembered ... is the real measure of the value both of silver and of all other commodities' (WN I.xi.e.26).

It is this proposition, that 'labour ... is the only universal, as well as the only accurate measure of value' (WN I.v.17), underlying the discussion in Book I of real (or labour) and nominal (or money) prices of commodities, that actually causes an analytical breakdown in the discussion of the function of money, and enforces the conclusion that Smith did not in fact possess a viable theory of commodity prices at all. 'From century to century, corn is a better measure than silver ... from year to year, on the contrary, silver is a better measure than corn' of the relative values of different commodities (WN I.v.17). And of course, if the conclusion cannot be avoided that *The Wealth of Nations* contains no secure anchorage for a theory of money values, the proposition is similarly in jeopardy that it contains a sustainable theory of distribution. But the theory of value, beyond its monetary relevance and the ambiguities we have observed within it, must remain for further and subsequent examination.

Money was relevant to the processes of growth, finally, so far as it facilitated the transfer of savings from income earners to investors and in the course of doing so measured the rate of interest, and as it served also as the measure of the rates of profits actually realized on investment commitments. The question of interest is interdependent in *The Wealth of Nations* with that of the rate of profits, and the latter is measurable historically by observing the movements in the rate of interest. For 'what can commonly be given for the use of money ... [is] necessarily regulated by what can commonly be made by the use of it' (WN II.iv.11). But interest, we have observed, was not for Smith a monetary phenomenon.

> The quantity of stock ... of money which can be lent at interest in any country, is ... regulated by ... the value of that part of the annual produce which ... is destined not only for replacing a capital, but such a capital as the owner does not care to be at the trouble of employing himself ... Such capitals are commonly lent out and paid back in money, ... [but] money is ... but the deed of assignment ... it is itself altogether different from what is assigned by it.
> (WN II.iv.5,6).

Underlying the monetary phenomena in the loan markets were the real forces which generated a supply of savings out of incomes not consumed or required for self-employment, and a demand for investable funds depending on profit opportunities. Nicholas Barbon had emphasized a similar argument much earlier,[19] and Sir Dudley North had also concentrated on the notion that the supply side of the loan market was dependent on the availability of savings out of incomes after necessary or desired consumption expenditures. It was not so much, North argued, that 'low interest makes trade' as that 'trade makes interest low'. That is, 'trade increasing the stock of the nation makes interest low'.[20] The analysis, like that of Hume, was in a sense one of prodigality and thrift, rather than productivity and thrift, emphasizing as it did the preponderance on the demand side of the loan market of consumption borrowers. But for Hume also, in clear anticipation of Smith,

> low interest and low profits ... mutually forward each other, and are both originally derived from that extensive commerce, which produces opulent merchants, and renders the money interest considerable ... When commerce has become extensive, and employs large stocks, there must arise rivalships among the merchants, which diminish the profits of trade, at the same time as they increase the trade itself. The low profits of merchandise induce the merchants to accept more willingly of a low interest ...[21]

As for the associated theory of profits in *The Wealth of Nations*, two propositions should be noted. First, the thrust for expanded activity,

[19] Barbon, *Discourse of Trade* (1690), 20: 'Interest is the rent of stock ...'

[20] North, *Discourses upon Trade* (1691), 18.

[21] Hume, op. cit. 301; cf. 296–8, 300. I have examined the fuller course of the theory of interest in the eighteenth century elsewhere (see my *Studies in the Theory of Money, 1690–1776*), and avoiding further discussion of Smith's position at present it might be pointed out that his criticism of Locke in *The Wealth of Nations* at II.iv.9ff. does not appear sustainable.

secular growth, and higher *per capita* real incomes rested partly on the technological advances which the widening division of labour facilitated, and fundamentally on the increase in the annual size of the wage fund which saving made possible. But 'as the quantity of stock to be lent at interest increases . . . the profits which can be made by employing them necessarily diminish' (WN II.iv.8). The notion of the diminishing productivity of money capital is explicit, in substance if not in name, and is bolstered by the notion of diminishing investment opportunities at the margin of capital outlay. 'It becomes gradually more and more difficult to find within the country a profitable method of employing any *new* capital' (WN II.iv.8; italics supplied). And second, the diminution of the rate of profit is understood to derive from a pincer movement of diminishing income opportunities on the one side and increasing costs of production on the other.

> The owner . . . must not only sell what he deals in somewhat cheaper, but in order to get it to sell, he must sometimes too buy it dearer . . . The demand for productive labour, by the increase of the funds which are destined for maintaining it, grows every day greater . . . competition raises the wages of labour, and sinks the profits of stock . . . profits . . . are in this manner diminished, as it were, at both ends.
>
> (WN II.iv.8)

But the final problem in Smith's long-run real dynamics can be noted by observing that *The Wealth of Nations* does not possess an adequate theoretical linkage between the sustainability of monetary expenditure flows in the short run and the growth of incomes and activity levels in the long run. Smith, quite simply, 'failed to reckon with the contingency of hoarding out of saved income'.[22] Thus there was solidified in English economic thought what Schumpeter has called 'the Turgot–Smith theory of saving and investment' (op. cit. 324). This point, moreover, is relevant again to Smith's inescapable supposition that the value of money, even its exchange value in the final analysis, was embedded in the real cost of producing it, and it was impossible as a result to make a complete analysis of both the price-forming and the activity-forming effects of an increase in the level of the money supply. His short-run dynamics were simply not robust enough to handle the point, and a line of increasingly sophisticated analysis which we have seen to develop in the preceding decades was allowed to languish. We can note, in fact, what might be called a differential dynamic analysis, in which Smith compares the effects of an increase in 'the quantity of silver' with those of an 'increase in the quantity of commodities annually circulated within the country' (WN II.iv.11–12). Vastly different effects follow, depending on whether the forces pressing to market disequilibria emanate from the one side or the other. But no linkages are envisaged which permit an interpretation of the money flow as exerting independent causal

[22] Leo Rogin, *The Meaning and Validity of Economic Theory* (1956), 105.

influences on the levels of production and commodity market supplies. 'Any increase in the quantity of silver, while that of the commodities circulated by means of it remained the same, could have no other effect than to diminish the value of that metal.' But an 'increase of the quantity of commodities . . . would, on the contrary, produce many other important effects, besides that of raising the value of money. The capital of the country . . . would really[23] be augmented . . . the quantity of productive labour which it could maintain and employ would be increased . . . wages would naturally rise . . . the profits of stock would be diminished . . .' (WN II.iv.12) and so on. Immediately, consistent with the main preoccupation of *The Wealth of Nations*, the secular real dynamics has assumed the centre of the stage and what might have been an opportunity to develop a more satisfying monetary dynamics is lost.

Our thesis envisaged, finally, the tension in *The Wealth of Nations* between money as a veil beyond which the real transactions and developments of the economy occurred, and money as exerting potentially an independent economic influence. Interlaced as Smith's arguments are on the various levels on which we have considered them, we have in effect confronted this final point already. In his first introduction of the concept of money in the early chapters of Book I, before he moved to the importance of the *form* of money and embedded his argument irretrievably in intrinsic metallic values, Smith did emphasize the importance of 'the function of money' (WN I.iv.6). Money was important because it was 'the universal instrument of commerce . . .' (WN I.iv.11), and the circulation and widespread acceptance of it widened the area of exchange, extended the commodity markets, and facilitated the division of labour, with all that that meant for technological change, economic expansion, and secular growth in real incomes *per capita*. Money, it seemed, clearly performed a critically important role in the generalized market and competitive economy. But it is not necessary to reopen old discussions to caution against too ready a deductive and evaluative conclusion based on such a line of analysis. When Smith turns later in the work to conclude definitively on the significance of the money supply we find him espousing a position we have cause to regard as typical in *The Wealth of Nations*.

> In the course of a century or two, it is possible that new mines may be discovered . . . and . . . the most fertile mine that was then known may be . . . barren . . . Whether the one or the other of those two events may happen . . . is of very little importance to the real wealth and prosperity of the world, to the real value of the annual produce . . . Its nominal value . . . would, no doubt, be very different; but its real value, the real quantity of labour which it could purchase or command, would be precisely the same.
>
> (WN I.xi.m.21).

[23] Here the word 'really' is set in juxtaposition in Smith's context with 'nominally'.

Here again the real secular dynamics has pushed to the centre of attention, and not only is the question avoided of a possible dependence of the shape of the long-run growth path on the shorter-run activity variations conceivably attributable to monetary phenomena, but money is very much a veil over the ultimately determinative forces in the system. Definitively, 'the increase of the quantity of gold and silver . . . and the increase of . . . manufactures and agriculture, are two events which, though they have happened nearly about the same time, yet have arisen from very different causes, and have scarce any natural connection with one another' (WN I.xi.n.1).

For the short-run dynamic effects of variations in the money supply and the possibility that, in the manner of Smith's predecessors in monetary thought, simultaneous disturbances might be observed on both price levels and activity levels, one must turn to a full examination of the discussion of banking. The main conclusion of the work at this point, leaving aside a wealth of procedural and operating detail which deserves the closest study, has again been noted in the preceding analysis. Banking was important, we have said, for its money-moving rather than its money-creating function. 'It is not by augmenting the capital of the country, but by rendering a greater part of that capital active and productive than would otherwise be so, that the most judicious operations of banking can increase the industry of the country' (WN II.ii.86). And tying the issue down firmly to the precise monetary phenomena involved, Smith continues: 'That part of his capital which a dealer is obliged to keep by him unemployed, and in ready money for answering occasional demands, is so much dead stock, which, so long as it remains in this situation, produces nothing . . . The judicious operations of banking enable him to convert this dead stock into active and productive stock' (WN II.ii.86). But if it were to be argued, therefore, that 'the increase of paper money . . . necessarily augments the money price of commodities', such a conclusion would founder on the pervasive intrinsic metallism of the Smithian argument. In actual fact, 'as the quantity of gold and silver, which is taken from the currency, is always equal to the quantity of paper which is added to it, paper money does not necessarily increase the quantity of the whole currency' (WN II.ii.96).

But in the entire banking discussion Smith moves ambivalently around the questions we have just referred to, and he comes very near to the recognition of the activity-forming function of variable monetary circulation. Our conclusion, however, has emphasized the heart of the matter, to the neglect of numerous tangential arguments. Locked in, as Smith is, to the notion that paper money merely changes the form rather than the total of the money supply, and neglecting to follow through to the larger and more diversified effects of the implied increase in the velocity of circulation, the conclusion repeatedly enters at various stages of the argument, that the 'annual produce cannot be immediately augmented by . . . operations of banking' (WN II.ii.30). A possible mediate, as distinct from immediate, effect follows from the conceivable increase in the level of international trade which could result from the export of the gold and silver metals induced by an excessively high paper money circulation; excessively high, that is, compared with what the sustainable level of real activity and employment and the stage of real economic development of the country required. Here, precisely, is the point at which, we mentioned in a different context, Smith failed to integrate the theory of money and monetary circulation into a genuine analysis of aggregate economic equilibrium.

IV

An interpretative evaluation of the theory of money in the period we are examining must turn, we have said, on an appreciation of the status which the subject had achieved in the pre-Smithian decades and on the nature of the developments which occurred after 1776. The linkage between the earlier theory and the mainstream of the classical constructions is best described in terms of two central considerations. The first is methodological, the second substantive. Together they point *away from* what had been the main preoccupation of the nascent macro-analysis of the eighteenth century; namely the fear, which clearly stemmed from observation and experience, that if left to itself the economy would settle at a level of activity which involved a less than full utilization of its productive resources, implying in particular an underemployment of labour. In the first place, there passed over from the earlier eighteenth century the analytical device of emphasizing in any disequilibrium analysis the position at which the economy or economic forces could be envisaged to come to rest. This recalls the static-equational theorems which were examined in the earlier part of the period, Cantillon's conception that at the end of the dynamic chain of cause and effect a new equilibrium of forces could be envisaged, and what can be observed as the timeless-equilibrium theorems of David Hume.[24]

Second, the substantive point had to do with certain assumptions about the flow, in some contexts the maintainable flow, of money in the economy. It expressed itself partly in terms of the notion of the excess or redundancy of money supplies, partly in terms of the failure to recognize the importance of this latter point for the theory of interest, and partly in terms of an assumption that the supply and circulation of money would continue, in any given situation, to be such as to support a given and presumably satisfactory level of activity. In the theory of interest, for example, it is true

[24] See note 9 above regarding Hume's methodology, and Keynes's comment, in his *General Theory*, 343n, that 'Hume began the practice among economists of stressing the importance of the equilibrium position . . .'

that by the third quarter of the eighteenth century a more complete analysis had been made of the forces determining the demand for and supply of loan money. But the thing that had been insufficiently examined was the problem of redundant money supplies and the likelihood of their not finding profitable employment on the money-capital markets. Sir James Steuart had seen the problem. But he had answered it by assuming that funds which could not find employment at home would migrate in search of investment opportunities abroad. The problem of a widespread non-utilization of money was not faced in a consistent sense. From the insufficiently analysed redundancy theorems of the eighteenth century, and from the earlier theories of international price equilibrium, the classicists developed a rigorous theory of an international self-balancing mechanism which reflected both price variations and capital movements and, unfortunately, in fact if not always in theory, fluctuations in the internal level of production and trade.

Part, of course, of the way in which the corresponding classical theorems came to expression had to do with familiar notions regarding the impossibility of a general overproduction of goods. We have seen this expressed also in the Smithian doctrine of the automatic transmutation of savings into investment and the social beneficence, as a result, of frugality or parsimony. It is of historical and analytical interest, however, to observe the roots of this theorem in the earlier literature of the eighteenth century. The notion that the expenditure of the rich provided employment opportunities for the poor was widely argued at that time. Berkeley's *Querist* and Mandeville's *Fable of the Bees* have become well known in this connection.[25] But the concept, particularly in the form in which Mandeville had stated it, was not without its critics. George Blewitt, for example, while acknowledging that 'the grand maxim on which this treatise [Mandeville's] of luxury is founded is, that consumption breeds riches . . .', unfortunately refers also to 'the absurdity of supposing that frugality should enrich every single family, and impoverish a number of those families joined together in society'.[26] The fallacy of composition seems always to have been a trap for economic analysts. Or again, Josiah Tucker had anticipated the classical theorem in his negative answer to the question 'whether it is possible in the nature of things for all trades and professions to be overstocked?'[27] He had asked in reply, 'If a particular trade is at any time overstocked, will not the disease cure itself?' And he gave the kind of answer that was the more usual province of the next century of economic analysis. Considerations of

[25] See for example Berkeley, op. cit., Part 2, Query 243; and Bernard de Mandeville, *The Fable of the Bees, or Private Vices, Publick Benefits* (1714).

[26] George Blewitt, *An Inquiry whether a General Practice of Virtue Tends to Wealth or Poverty* . . . (1725), 50 and contents page.

[27] Josiah Tucker, *Reflections on the Expediency of a Law for the Naturalization of Foreign Protestants* (1751–2), Part II, 13.

frictional unprofitability would adjust the use of resources to demands in particular markets and there was no reason why factors in general need remain permanently unemployed. And the same point was made by Hutcheson in reply to Mandeville. Money not spent in one way would be spent in another.[28] Thus, to put the historical relationship in another form, the purely analytical assumption of an adequacy of monetary flows, which Cantillon and Hume had made for purposes of demonstrating the dynamics of the money flows process, passed over into the classical economics as the pervasive empirical postulate that all the money supply continued in circulation, in one place or another, in one form or another. What was subject to change was simply the direction of expenditure. The message of the theoretico-empirical analysis of Law, Berkeley, and in particular Steuart, on the other hand, was avoided.[29]

Against this perspective Smith, we have seen, stands with the new and what became the firmly embedded classical tradition.[30] An important question to which Smith was unable to give an answer was quite simply: 'How much money ought a country to have and what are the symptoms and measure of excess or deficiency?'[31] In Smith we find the same approach to the money reflux and redundancy theorem as we have observed in some of his predecessors, particularly in relation to the question of bank note reflux and the needs-of-trade doctrine of banking. For Smith, we can say, the relevant proposition is twofold: the amount of money, hard money or bank notes, which can be permanently maintained in circulation was dependent simply on the stage of development of real economic activity; and hard money (metals, not notes) in excess of this maintainable amount would be exported in search of investment income opportunities. Smith espoused to the end, and he was unable to allow the logic of his money-substitute analysis to rescue him from his proposition regarding the final determinative

[28] Frances Hutcheson, *Remarks upon the Fable of the Bees* (1750), 63–5.

[29] It was not the case, of course, that no significant dissent occurred at that time from the Smithian–classical savings-investment orthodoxy. See, for example, the important position of Jeremy Bentham, *Works*, ed. Stark (1952), and Terence Hutchison's perceptive analysis in 'Bentham as an Economist', *Economic Journal* (June 1956). 'For my own part', Bentham says, 'I never was able to obtain what to me appeared a clear insight into this part of the subject from the instructions of Adam Smith. Metaphors taken from wheels and water seemed to take the place too often of definition and exemplification' (op. cit. ii.342n).

[30] We must unfortunately leave unexamined a number of issues which bear in important ways on our main concern. First, a full analysis of the method and the achievements in the theory of money after Adam Smith, even avoiding the anachronism of casting our comparisons ahead to the rapidly industrialized decades of the nineteenth century, would require consideration of the arguments surrounding the Bank Restriction of 1797, the celebrated bullionist controversy, and the work of a large number of pamphleteer-economists, John Wheatley for example, as well as the leading performers from Thorton and Ricardo onwards. This ground has fortunately been thoroughly surveyed in Jacob Viner's masterly *Studies in the Theory of International Trade* (1937), Chs. iii, iv, and v, in Hollander, op. cit., and in Schumpeter, op. cit. 688ff.

[31] Hollander, op. cit. 436.

significance of the real labour cost of producing money (metals), and therefore its intrinsic value. It was this proposition, the pervasively important assumption regarding the intrinsic value of money, which destroyed the possibility at many points of a more satisfactory analysis. But for the questions now at issue, the adequacy of the money supply, paper money substitutes, and the notion of money reflux, Smith's doctrinal stance inhibited any adequate treatment of either the possible price-level effects or the interest-rate effects of an increased, or temporarily excessive, monetary circulation.[32]

The view, finally, which should properly be taken of the place of *The Wealth of Nations* in the history of monetary thought, as of other parts of our subject, depends also on the first of the interpretative foci we raised at the beginning. Fortunately, the masterly work again of Jacob Viner, as well as Lord Robbins and others, makes any extended discussion unnecessary. But it is of prime importance to realize that Smith in no sense argued in *The Wealth of Nations* for some kind of uninhibited *laissez-faire* in the economic and social order of things. The psychological, anthropological, and socio-cultural propositions in Smith which justify this statement deserve the fullest examination, but it must suffice to refer to three very important discussions bearing on this point.[33] Smith did, it is clear, speak repeatedly of the 'uniform, constant, and uninterrupted effort of every man to better his condition',[34] and though he frequently rests his case for the ready mobility of labour and resources on such an assumption, his view of human nature and its inherent proclivities is generally pessimistic, outside, that is, the institutional framework of law and justice necessary to contain them. 'Such, it seems, is the natural insolence of man, that he almost always disdains to use the good instrument, except when he cannot or dare not use the bad one' (WN V.i.g.19). More directly relevant to the framework of monetary transactions, and given the need, inevitably, for a carefully structured institutional framework within which the competitive enterprise economy could operate, Smith called for a definite set of banking regulations in the interests of financial stability. The point had to do with prohibitions

[32] Lloyd Mints, in his *History of Banking Theory,* already cited, concludes that 'Adam Smith . . . tacitly assumed that the aggregate circulating medium of the community, no matter how defined, had no influence upon the price level' (op. cit. 99); and 'Smith . . . ignored the price level and held that even in a closed economy no excess of [bank] issues could be maintained' (ibid. 143).

[33] See Jacob Viner, 'Adam Smith and *Laissez Faire*', in *Adam Smith, 1776–1926* (1928); Lionel Robbins, *The Theory of Economic Policy in English Classical Political Economy* (1952), especially Chs. I–III; and Nathan Rosenberg, 'Some Institutional Aspects of the *Wealth of Nations*', *Journal of Political Economy* (Dec. 1960).

[34] WN II.iii.31, cf. I.viii.41, II.iii.28. The same notion of an innate impulse or the 'desire of bettering our condition so strongly implanted in the human breast' appears also in Malthus's *Principles of Political Economy* (1836, London School of Economics reprint, 1936), 434; see a discussion at this point in B. A. Corry, *Money, Saving and Investment in English Economics 1800–1850* (1962), 128.

against the excessive issue of small denomination notes. 'Such regulations', Smith acknowledged, designed 'to restrain private people . . . may, no doubt, be considered . . . a violation of natural liberty' (WN II.ii.94). But by analogy, 'the obligation of building party walls, in order to prevent the communication of fire, is a violation of natural liberty, exactly of the same kind with the regulations of the banking trade which are here proposed' (ibid.).

Much could be made also, in the context of his discussion of human proclivities, of Smith's significant argument regarding risk and risk-bearing and their significance for realized rates of return on capital investment commitments. Recognizing the need for a risk premium in anticipated rates of return on investment outlays (WN I.ix.18,19, II.ii.64, and II.iv.14,15), he observed that the functioning of the money capital market is such that actual and realized rates of return may not in fact compensate for risk. The point at issue here has to do, in part, with the implication of psychological phenomena for equilibrium conditions in the money capital markets. 'The ordinary rate of profit', it is recognized, 'varies more or less with the certainty or uncertainty of the returns.' But while 'the ordinary rate of profit always rises more or less with the risk. It does not . . . rise in proportion to it, or so as to compensate it completely.' The problem, the thing that tended to increase the supply of high-risk capital and depress ex-post profit rates below reasonable ex-ante risk-premium expectations, was that 'the presumptuous hope of success seems . . . to entice so many adventurers into those hazardous trades, that their competition reduces the profit below what is sufficient to compensate the risk'.[35]

But the important issues of the institutional, socio-cultural, and philosophic milieu, vital though they are for the final evaluative stance it is necessary to adopt, all too quickly take our arguments beyond the more modest limits we set at the beginning. Of the greatness of the work we have examined there can be, as we have said, no danger of controversion. But it would be a work of supererogation even to consider in the context of our present objectives the distinguished place of *The Wealth of Nations* in the economic discipline at large. In the light of the kind and the content of monetary analysis in the decades on either side of 1776, however, *The Wealth of Nations* must be accorded a less illustrious place in the history of this branch of our subject than it commands in other and more general respects.

[35] WN I.x.b.33. The point has been spelled out in the text in cognizance of the very active modern interest in risk-return trade-offs and generalized capital market equilibrium.

XII

Adam Smith and the Bankers

S. G. CHECKLAND*

I

SOME attention has been given to Adam Smith's views on monetary questions at the level of high theory. But Smith also commented at length on the operation of banking systems both actual and ideal. It is necessary, of course, to relate these two levels of discussion to one another. In so doing there appears the classic dichotomy of outlook between the intellectual and the practising banker. This has been present at least since William Paterson and John Law and is today as lively as ever.

Smith's treatment is very largely based upon the Scottish banks,[1] as had been that of Sir James Steuart.[2] This, of course, is not surprising, for it was Smith's native system and had been largely formed in his lifetime. Moreover, it could fairly be claimed to be the most advanced pattern of banking in Europe, and presumably the world.

II

To establish a perspective on Smith's ideas about banking it is necessary to take account of the institutional evolution of the Scottish system. Great changes took place in it during his creative lifetime, beginning shortly after the 1745 Rebellion, when Smith was in the last two years of his tenure of the Snell Exhibition that had carried him from Glasgow College to Balliol, and continuing through his period in the Glasgow chair (1751–63), the famous continental tour (1764–6), and the years in which he wrote *The Wealth of Nations*, first in Kirkcaldy (1767–73) and then London (1773–6). Those parts of the book which dealt with banking underwent only the minor revisions after the first edition; nor did Smith take up the subject again in any other form.

At the time of the 'Forty-five' there were two 'public' banks in Scotland: the Bank of Scotland (founded in 1695) and the Royal Bank of Scotland (founded in 1727). These were the only institutions strictly entitled to be called banks. As public banks they enjoyed the status of limited liability, by

* Professor of Economic History in the University of Glasgow.

[1] The principal treatment of the Scottish banks is in WN II.ii.41–78.

[2] *Sir James Steuart, An Inquiry into the Principles of Political Oeconomy* (1767; ed. Andrew S. Skinner, 1966), Book IV, Ch. iii to xxii.

virtue of being state creations, the one by Act of the Scottish Parliament and the other by Royal Charter. Scotland had thus two such public banks while England had only one. This was to mean that neither of the Scottish banks could claim the central position enjoyed by the Bank of England to the south. After a period of open warfare the two banks had established a kind of truce. Each was wary of the other, keeping substantial holdings of its rival's notes in case it might be necessary to take either aggressive or defensive action. The Bank of Scotland had considerable Jacobite leanings; the Royal Bank had the opposing sympathy, having been the creation of a Whig clique led by Campbell, Duke of Argyll, part of the programme of Walpole's government for the pacification of Scotland.

There were also the private bankers, mostly based in Edinburgh. They inevitably became powerful in the parlours of the public banks, using the purchase of shares as a means of entering the bank directorates, and in varying degrees dominating them. The financing of the tobacco trade was not without its significance in this connection.[3] The bills of exchange drawn by the French Farmers-General provided a very important element of liquidity in Scottish banking, passing through the hands of the private bankers. Perhaps the greatest of these merchant bankers was William Alexander: he was the first merchant member both of the directorate of the Royal Bank and of the Edinburgh Town Council (Price, i.608). The private bankers did not issue notes, but used those of the public banks, made available to them through credits. A third order of banking institution had appeared in 1747–50 when in Aberdeen and Glasgow local groups of merchants set up provincial banking companies.

The two public banks composed their differences, entering into a pact of mutual support in 1752; they then set about the attempt to destroy the new provincial banking companies. The immediate incentive to do this was the issuing of notes by such companies; the public banks believed this to be lawfully their monopoly. The note issue was the basis of the business of the public banks, the private bankers having accepted the role of the public banks in this regard. The public banks succeeded in their destructive tactics in the case of Aberdeen, but the two Glasgow companies, the Ship Bank and the Arms Bank, fought off their attackers. Meanwhile the private bankers had further flourished.

Thus, when Sir James Steuart was setting out his views on banking in his *Inquiry into the Principles of Political Oeconomy*, between 1763 and 1767, the Scottish system had a kind of classic unity, with two tiers of institutions. The public banks were at its centre. They issued notes to borrowers on the basis of heritable (real) property, and on personal property. They were not

[3] Jacob Price, *France and the Chesapeake, a History of the French Tobacco Monopoly, 1674–1791 and of Its Relationship to the British and American Tobacco Trades* (1973), i. 539.

discounters of inland trade bills, and so had no direct connection with commerce; to these banks alone Steuart argued should be entrusted 'the great national circulation' (*Principles*, 485). They provided the credits and the bank notes on which the 'exchangers' (Steuart's name for the private bankers) could operate. The exchangers in turn performed the function of bill discounters, of course charging interest on their discounts, plus a commission of ½ per cent or more. They were the risk-bearers of the system, the link between the publicly created banks and the world of commerce. 'This set of men', said Steuart, 'are exposed to risks and losses, which they bear without complaint because of their great profits' (*Principles*, 484). Steuart envisaged that the private bankers could be controlled and when necessary sustained by the public banks. In any case casualties among the exchangers could never be serious for the system as a whole: 'These exchangers break from time to time; and no essential hurt is thereby occasioned to national credits.' Steuart, while delineating the respective functions of public banks and private bankers, took no account of the fact that the latter were more than bankers, being typically merchants and commission agents as well, using public bank resources in their own transactions, often speculatively. Steuart does not discuss the provincial banking companies.

But though Steuart, in one sense, conceived of a kind of ideal system based upon division of function, he could criticize the way these functions were performed, especially by the public banks. In his discussion of the long and difficult exchange crisis in the 1760s, when Scotland was drained of the precious metals, and bills on London rose to a high premium, Steuart condemned the public banks for their attempt to right the situation by reducing their credits. Their correct course, Steuart believed, would have been to maintain credit and incomes, by means of vigorous borrowing abroad (*Principles*, 507). Steuart presumably did not know that the public banks had indeed sought foreign credits in Holland, but had found the cost prohibitive.[4]

Steuart's discussion of banking went beyond the structure of Scottish institutions and the way they had behaved in the recent past. He envisaged a general system of public responsibility for the money supply, discharged through a public office, in the light of criteria derived from the economy as a whole: the tax system should be used to reinforce the policies that lay behind monetary action. 'The statesman', wrote Steuart, 'ought at all times to maintain a just proportion between the produce of industry and the quantity of circulating equivalent in the hands of his subjects for the purchase of it' (*Principles*, 323). Should the circulating medium be inadequate

[4] Bank of Scotland (hereinafter BS) *Minutes*, 20 March 1764; BS *Out Letter Book*, 6 July 1764. Bank of Scotland, Edinburgh, National Register of Archives (Scotland), Survey 945, 1/1/5.

the public office should 'supply the deficiency of the metals by such a proportion of paper credit as may abundantly supply the deficiency'. Presumably in Steuart's eyes the Scottish public banks had some such responsibility, though they were owned by shareholders and enjoyed no special position created by the state other than the limitation of their liability. Indeed he urged that the two banks should merge 'in order to form a really national bank' (*Principles*, 513).

Scarcely had Steuart committed his two-part scheme of Scottish banking to paper, a reasonable enough description of the roles of public banks and private bankers, when it began to lose its coherence. The public banks, having long desisted from discounting inland (i.e. Scottish) bills, re-entered upon that practice from 1761.[5] Already certain of the private bankers had pulled ahead of the rest, creating dominating positions both in the Scottish money market and within the public banks. The Glasgow banking companies, and those formed in Dundee and Ayr in 1763, and in Perth, Aberdeen, and Dumfries (all in 1766), did not trade on the basis of Steuart's division of function, but sought to operate as autonomously as possible, offering a full range of banking services, and relying heavily on their own note issues. Finally the situation was further complicated by the taking in of deposits by the public banks on a new scale after 1766, when the promissory note replaced the old Treasurer's bond; all Scottish banking institutions then became rivals for deposits.[6] The tidy rationale of Sir James Steuart of the mid-1760s was destroyed by the growth of the economy and the banking responses these provoked, especially in the provincial towns. There was now a three-part distinction of scale and function between public banks, private bankers, and provincial banking companies.

Steuart had had too little time on his return to Scotland to acquaint himself directly with the on-going developments in Scottish banking; by contrast his writings of 1777 on the working of the corn laws show that he had been able to inform himself in depth in practical terms of the real anatomy of the situation.[7] It is also probable that because the view Steuart took of banking fitted with his general economic philosophy, it cut him off from complex and changing realities.

In the 1760s there had been a good deal of public debate in Scotland about banking: it culminated in the Act of 1765. This banking statute and its preliminaries were of fundamental importance to Scottish practice. There were three principal questions. Should entry to banking be free? Should the use of paper substitutes for specie continue to be permitted without regard to the smallness of the units in which it was issued? Was

[5] BS *Minutes*, 27 Mar. 1761; Royal Bank of Scotland (hereinafter RBS) *Minutes*, 25 June 1761.

[6] BS, Balances taken from ledgers.

[7] 'Memorial on the Corn Laws', 14 Oct. 1777, in Skinner, ed., 737–8.

the use of the optional clause a legitimate banking practice? (The public banks and the Glasgow banking companies had taken to inserting in their notes a clause which, if activated by endorsement to the note, allowed the issuing bank to postpone redemption in specie for a period of six months, interest being payable at 5 per cent in the interval; WN II.ii.98.)

All three questions centred upon the note issue. One of the responses to the attempts by the public banks to curtail credit during the long exchange crisis was the issuing of petty notes by a great many parties, who thus entered upon quasi-banking activities. The small-notes mania of the 1750s and 1760s produced promises to pay for 10 shillings, 5 shillings, and even 1 shilling. It was easy to put such notes into circulation because of the chronic shortage of silver coin, making people willing to receive payment, especially of wages, in whatever medium was available. The two public banks had made no real effort to supply this need, though the Bank of Scotland issued notes for 10 shillings from 1760[8] and the British Linen Company had paid its cottage spinners and weavers this way. How far the private bankers joined in this kind of issue is not clear, though Mansfield & Co., one of the largest, appears to have issued 10 shilling notes. There was, of course, no legal restriction whatever on the issue or the size of notes in Scotland.

It was this great facility in issuing notes that made Scotland the most striking example of free entry into banking. Nothing whatever was required by way of capital provision or any other safeguard. To this the public banks took great exception, for they claimed with some justice that it was impossible to conduct any sort of reasonable monetary policy under such conditions. They desired, if banking companies could not be put down entirely, that they should be made to desist from issuing notes, acting as Sir James Steuart had envisaged his second tier of banking institutions, accepting the 'leadership' of the public banks and using their notes only.

The size of notes that should be permissible related to two questions: how was a convenient hand-to-hand currency to be provided in an economy in which the precious metals had already been replaced by paper money to a unique degree, and how far should the loss of specie be allowed to go as paper money displaced it ever lower down the scale of transactions?

The optional clause of course represented the fundamental question, how far was it permissible for the state to allow banking concerns, by 'agreement' with their note-holders, to depart from the principle of convertibility of notes on demand into specie? The clause had first come into being as a device necessary when there was bank war: a concern threatened by a rival with a run had only to decline, under the clause, to pay specie. But the optional clause could have a further, far-reaching effect: it could permit the bankers greatly to economize on their specie holdings, at the same time

[8] BS *Minutes*, 25 June 1760.

yet further reducing the precious metal element in the economy. Moreover, it was soon also discovered that the clause could be used by bankers in times of monetary stringency temporarily to exempt themselves from pressure and so to continue fairly generous credits. In this way short-term influences on the monetary situation could be cushioned, and in larger crises the bankers could liquidate their position in a more orderly manner. Conversely, the freedom to do such things freed the bankers from the strict discipline of the gold standard.

In 1764 the government in London became aware of the need to intervene in the banking situation in Scotland. It did so through the Privy Council. The Lord Privy Seal was a Scot. He had received correspondence from Provost Ingram of Glasgow on behalf of the local banking companies there, the Ship, the Arms and the Thistle Banks. The Provost enclosed a memorial, together with 'thoughts', to both of which documents Sir James Steuart had appended lengthy and penetrating notes.[9] James Oswald, Adam Smith's boyhood friend, was a member of the Council, together with another prominent Scot and friend of Smith, Gilbert Elliott.[10]

The knowledge that official action was pending caused the two public banks to make a joint approach to the government. They proposed that they should have 'an exclusive privilege of banking and of issuing printed notes'.[11] If pressed, their delegates were to offer to pay an agreed annual sum to be added to the developmental funds available to the Trustees for Improving Fisheries and Manufactures in Scotland. In so doing the Scottish public banks were asking for a position stronger even that that of the Bank of England, for though the Bank had a monopoly in the sense of a prohibition of other banking companies with more than six partners, at no time had the Bank had a sole right of note issue of the kind the Scottish banks were now seeking. If awarded such a monopoly the public banks were prepared to abandon the optional clause. Alternatively, the public banks proposed that a man or partnership might not issue notes without having ready to produce £10,000 in land or in the funds. The committee of the Privy Council that dealt with the delegates of the Scottish public banks was led by Oswald and Elliott. Adam Smith may well have been in London at this time (January 1764) for it was at the end of January that he and Henry, Duke of Buccleuch, met there preparatory to their departure for France. It is an intriguing conjecture whether Smith was consulted. In any case the answer given to the delegates was thoroughly Smithian. 'The right of banking', pronounced the Committee in the grand Enlightenment manner,

[9] Partners in the Glasgow banking companies, *Memorial, with notes by Sir James Steuart of Coltness*, 4 Feb. 1763; *Thoughts concerning banks and the paper currency of Scotland, with Notes by Sir James Steuart*, 1764. Both in *Mure of Caldwell. Selections of the family papers preserved at Caldwell*, Maitland Club part 2, vol. i (1883).

[10] BS *Minutes*, 1 Feb. 1764.

[11] Ibid., 6 Jan. 1764.

'is a matter not of Publick favour but of Right to every Subject in Common.'[12] The delegates were further informed that should the two public banks proceed at law in an attempt to put down the banking companies, the government itself would introduce new legislation to make such companies explicitly legal. The delegates were also told that the optional clause must go. Finally, it was proposed that not only should the 'small notes' cease, but that Scotland should have no notes under £5. This of course was the view held by Adam Smith.

The public banks were thus rebuffed. The only thing saved from the wreckage was the £1 and the guinea notes, for the government did not persist with the idea of a £5 minimum for Scotland. In England notes under £1 were made illegal in 1775 and those under £5 were banned in 1777.

But the ending of the optional clause did not mean that the Scottish banking system was one that rested upon the instant convertibility, in full, of notes into specie on demand. The Scottish bankers had developed other devices for minimizing such a requirement, plain though it was in law. They used the award of credits against clients to oblige them to be very moderate in their specie demands; a banker typically required borrowers to draw only his notes, and, if possible, to pay in only the notes of others. In this way the Scottish system was one of more or less continuous partial suspension of cash payments. In any case businessmen operating on any scale knew that in times of crisis the outcome depended not on the meagre specie supply in Scotland, but the availability of London credits.

Meanwhile the exchange crisis continued. In 1764 the two public banks had sought to sustain the Edinburgh–London exchange by loans from the Bank of England and from Amsterdam. Neither effort succeeded. The Bank of Scotland favoured an all-out war by the two public banks against other issuers, but the Royal Bank would not agree, partly because its protégé, the British Linen Company, was a vigorous issuer of notes.[13] As the Scottish specie supply reached dangerously low levels both banks bought silver in England and carted it by wagon to Edinburgh. This was very costly. In the course of 1762 the Bank of Scotland had brought from London upwards of £100,000 at a cost of about £4·10*s*. per cent, £3.4*s*. per cent being paid for exchange and £1.6*s*. per cent for carriage.[14] Between 1764 and 1769 the Royal Bank spent over £20,000 in this way, equal to the profits of a note circulation of £80,000.[15] The public banks also moved against 'English riders', that is men who collected specie for export; moreover they adopted strong sanctions against anyone who aided such activities.[16] By mid-summer 1769 the public banks had brought about

[12] Ibid., 1 Feb. 1764.
[13] Ibid., 5 Dec. 1764, 2 Jan., 5, 16 June 1766; RBS *Minutes*, 22 May 1765.
[14] *Select Committee on Banks of Issue* (1841), 303.
[15] RBS *Minutes*, 4 Dec. 1771. Also WN I.286.
[16] BS *Minutes*, 13 Mar. 1764; RBS *Minutes*, 18 December 1767.

a considerable credit reduction; the exchange crisis was a good deal relieved.

In this situation and in this year the firm of Douglas, Heron and Co., popularly known as the Ayr Bank, was formed, with powerful backing from the landed nobility of the south-west of Scotland, including Adam Smith's protégé, the Duke of Buccleuch. It at once began to isssue notes on a large scale by making available easy credits. The two public banks knew that they could not put down the Ayr Bank by their own efforts. Nor could they expect any help from the government in disciplining the system. They were also aware by this time that they themselves were under-capitalized. Retreat was the only tactic: they greatly reduced their lending and note issue, leaving the field very largely to the Ayr Bank. By December 1771 the issue of the Royal Bank had been brought down to £22,753.[17]

Between 1769 and 1772 the Scottish banking system consisted of the two public banks, the British Linen Company, the Ayr Bank, about twenty private bankers (all general merchant houses, among which two, Sir William Forbes and Co. and Mansfield and Co., greatly outdid the rest), and four banking companies operating as partnerships in Glasgow together with five others in different towns. There were initiatives afoot for further provincial banking companies. Moreover, at all levels banks and bankers had or sought London connections, either with the Bank of England as in the case of the public banks or with London bankers. All had learned the importance of London-held assets or London credits. The situation was thus a fairly complex one.

The Ayr Bank ran its hectic course, collapsing in June 1772. All but four private banking houses went with it. The shareholders of the Ayr Bank were confronted with an appalling deficit. The only way to prevent legal proceedings against them, and the sale of large parts of their landed estates, was to find a means of borrowing at long term in London. This was done through the sale of annuities, authorized by Act of Parliament. In this painful matter Adam Smith was of service to the Duke of Buccleuch and others. 'My attention', he wrote, 'has been a good deal occupied about the most proper method of extricating them.'[18] The annuities were a very expensive way of raising the necessary funds, but there appeared to be no alternative.

By the end of 1772 Scottish banking had been through ten extraordinary years, involving a prolonged exchange crisis, a major banking statute, a proliferation of new provincial banking companies, a purging of the private bankers, and the brief life cycle of a venture of extraordinary size, daring, and ineptitude.

There followed important new developments in Scottish banking, which

[17] RBS *Minutes*, 4 Dec. 1771.

[18] Letter of 5 Sept. 1772, in John Rae, *Life of Adam Smith* (1895), 253.

bring the story down to *The Wealth of Nations* in 1776. Under the influence of the Bank of Scotland the note exchange, briefly begun not long before the Ayr Bank failure, was revived and extended so that by 1774 the Scottish note exchange in Edinburgh unified the system: by weekly and later twice-weekly exchanges the argument, so often used in theoretical debate, that no bank could force into 'the Circle' more notes than the public would willingly hold, was given greater reality.[19] The bank of Scotland now embarked upon a branch system: by 1780 it had seven branches and by 1790 eighteen. The Royal Bank, though it did not open branches except in Glasgow in 1783, became Edinburgh agent for a number of provincial banking companies, providing them with credits. Both public banks set about strengthening their capital position. These developments, taken together, signified a new and more constructive approach on the part of the two public banks to their role within the system.

But Scottish banking at the level of the public banks continued to be highly political. There were rumours in 1774 that the Bank of Scotland, through one of the private banks (probably Mansfield and Co.) was trying to secure influence on the Court of the Royal Bank. The private bankers, especially the important ones, had large holdings of the stock of both public banks: this was both a good investment and a means of exercising control through the election of directors. A proposal for the union of the two public banks, as Steuart had suggested, came to nothing.[20] But one intrigue did succeed. Henry Dundas, in 1776, was in the early stages of building up his political control of Scotland. One path to doing so lay through the Royal Bank. Dundas persuaded William Ramsay and Patrick Miller, senior partners in Mansfield and Co., to sell a considerable part of their holding of Royal Bank stock in order to bring in new shareholders, and through them new directors. As a result of this tactic Sir Lawrence Dundas was ousted as Governor, and the Duke of Buccleuch, so lately involved in the Ayr Bank débâcle, put in his place.[21]

It is against this background, extending over Adam Smith's years from the age of twenty-two to the age of fifty-three, that his treatment of banking must be placed.

III

The creation of a successful banking sector requires that there be at least some degree of comprehension of the system by legislators together with reasonably adequate rules of conduct for its participants. The statesman

[19] BS *Minutes*, 8 July, 9 Dec. 1771, BS *Out Letter Book*, 19, 25 June, 8, 10, 17 July 1771; 29 June 1774.

[20] Anon., *A Letter to the Proprietors of the Bank of Scotland* (1777).

[21] William Ramsay to the Duke of Buccleuch, 22 July, Apr. 1790. Scottish Record Office, GD 113/283/8.

and the theorist start their reasoning from the needs of the economy; the banker typically starts from the conditions of profitability and safety of his own business, given its demand liabilities and the soundness of the local and regional trading with which his principal assets in the form of advances lie.

At the theoretical level it is necessary to identify the elements of which the system consists and the relationship of those elements to one another and, in interaction, their links with the economy as a whole. In the years in which *The Wealth of Nations* was forming, the fundamental theoretical problem could be expressed in the terms: how were the proper limits to the creation of bank notes, to replace or supplement the coin provided by the state, to be determined? The other elements of monetary debate, including the terms of entry into banking, related directly to this. In seeking an answer theorists had to define the role of money in the economy. Was its supply governed by automatic principles so that the issue of paper money had only a displacement effect? Did paper simply push specie out of circulation, without altering the size of the total money supply from what it would 'naturally' have been, namely such as was required by the level of trade and incomes, and without inducing further effects? Or was the money supply capable of being positively changed upward and downward by the action of the bankers or a public authority, through expansion or contraction of lending, with far-reaching repercussions upon employment, incomes and stability? Scotland had already been through this argument, some seventy years before *The Wealth of Nations*, when the protagonists had been William Paterson and John Law,[22] the former favouring a system of convertibility of notes into specie on demand, the latter advocating a policy of state manipulation of the money supply.

The banker seldom tried to answer such questions. His mind was rooted in his business. This was true over the miscellaneous range of public banker, private banker, and provincial banker. The basic question for all, in the state of banking in Smith's time, was: how much of one's own note issue could be got into the circle and kept there? This gave the banker his interest-free loan from the public, typically some multiple of the capital he had provided. But his note issue depended to a significant degree upon the terms upon which he was prepared to make advances in discounts or any other form. A weak banking concern or one trying to make a beginning would be tempted to accept the riskier kind of borrower, or to extend further in the upswing, thus exposing itself to losses. Under the simplified system envisaged by Sir James Steuart the public banks would act in the public interest, and would have some degree of control over other banking houses. But with the refusal by government to limit free banking in any

[22] John Law, *Money and Trade Considered: with a Proposal for Supplying the Nation with Money* (1705, 1750); William Paterson, *The Occasion of Scotland's Decay in Trade* (1705).

way, at a time when a number of new banking enterprises were coming into being, this ability was much weakened, if not destroyed.

IV

At the general theoretical level Adam Smith took the natural or equilibristic view of the money supply.[23] It could not properly be varied by bank or state action, except perhaps within very narrow limits. Certainly it should not be used as a tool of public policy.

Smith was, of course, very much aware of the temptation to use the state in monetary matters. The situation in various of the British colonies had attracted his attention, especially in America where certain colonial governments had not only issued their own notes, but had made them payable not on demand but several years after issue; to get such instruments into circulation, and keep them there, they were made legal tender and receivable in payment of taxes. Such action could only add to inflationary pressure; Smith cordially approved of the Act of the British Parliament in 1764 forcing colonial legislatures to stop such actions (WN II.ii.100–103). But simple abdication by the state in monetary matters was not enough. Though the state was not itself to be a direct participant, it had a responsibility to provide an appropriate legislative environment for banking, as indeed for every economic activity.

In Smith's thinking two sets of rules were thus required: one for the state, for the furtherance of an automatic monetary system, and one for the bankers, so that they might behave in a way appropriate to their own interests and yet promote an optimal banking situation.

The principles the state must maintain were, in Adam Smith's view, of two kinds. One asserted the rightness of free banking, but the other imposed certain constraints on banking action. The state should assume no supervision over entry into the banking business. But it should encourage the erection of as many banking enterprises as possible, and it should give monopolies to none (WN II.ii.106). Thus no banking concern should be in a position dominant over others, much less empowered to control their conduct. For with a multiplicity of modest banking concerns the consequences of the errors or speculations of a few, resulting in their ruin, would be dispersed throughout the system so that no serious damage could result. Free entry and vigorous competition were thus the formulae.

This view of Smith's is difficult to reconcile with the real situation in Scotland, with the two public banks very much larger and more powerful than any other part of the system, and bound by a pact of mutual assistance. It is perhaps surprising that the extraordinary tale of the Ayr Bank, which

[23] See Robert V. Eagly, 'Adam Smith and the Specie Flow Doctrine', *Scottish Journal of Political Economy*, vol. xvii. 1970.

conducted operations on a major scale with a naïveté passing into knavery, involving Smith's own patron and others of his friends in heavy losses, did not cause him to amend his simplistic atomistic view of the Scottish banking structure.

The competitive system, as envisaged by Smith, could have the further beneficent effect that the banks, in mutal competition, would press their note issues as far as they would go in terms of acceptability to the community, thus economizing on sterile specie holdings. Paper money could thus be an acceptable substitute for metallic currency because it replaced the more expensive instrument of commerce (gold and silver) with the less expensive (paper) (WN II.ii.26). Smith therefore approved of Scotland's abandonment of a high proportion of its stock of coin, for when necessary, 'goods will always bring in money'.

Yet certain constraints imposed by the state were necessary. There were three of these. The first had to do with the size of notes. Smith was a strong opponent of the Scottish small notes, and would, indeed, have restricted the size of notes to a minimum of £5. This he justified on the ground that in this matter of petty notes the natural liberty of a few 'beggarly bankers', which might endanger the security of the whole society, 'ought to be restrained by all governments' (WN II.ii.92–4). Such notes, by penetrating the pockets of 'many poor people' were a threat to such humble folk through the frequent bankruptcy of their issuers. Smith does not discuss the problem of shortage of the means of payment, in small denominations, which gave rise to such note issues.

But there was another reason for condemning notes under £5. The general principle was held by Smith that the smaller the size of the notes in circulation the further went the displacement of the precious metals by paper. Such petty notes might cause an almost total loss of specie, forcing it out of its final repositories, tills, and pockets. At this point Smith echoed the fears of Hume for a country that had almost none of the metals, its commerce and industry 'suspended upon the Daedalian wings of paper money'.[24] Indeed it is hard to see how a system of convertibility could be operated at all under such conditions. Smith believed that the Act of 1765 had had a good effect, in relieving the dangerous scarcity of gold and silver in Scotland (WN II.ii.92).

Smith, indeed, would have stopped the displacement of specie by notes at the level of 'dealers' (i.e. merchants and wholesalers), and not let it reach the level of consumers (WN II.ii.89–90). Smith saw the money supply as being different in kind at the levels of wholesale dealing versus retail. But to have implemented such a view in Scotland after 1765, confining notes to a minimum size of £5, would also have acted as a severe restraint on entry

[24] (WN II.ii.86); David Hume, *Writings on Economics*, ed. Eugene Rotwein (1955), 69. RBS *Minutes*, 12 May 1773.

to the banking business, for the £1 notes were an essential element in the profitability of the proliferating provincial banking companies.

The second infraction of natural liberty advocated by Smith in connection with banking had to do with the optional clause. For Smith, the Act of 1765 was right in denying the liberty to offer or accept a bank note, the convertibility of which was optional on the issuer. This remained true even though the acceptor was willing. For to some degree the optional clause had become yet another means of minimizing gold and silver holdings, contributing to the specie denudation of Scotland beyond the point of legitimacy. Moreover, it had also been used as a means of disciplining borrowers: those who insisted on gold instead of notes would have it hinted to them that if they did not abate their demands the clause would be operated against them.[25] Nor should any banking concern have the 'liberty' of such self-defence against factitious attack. Smith, indeed, had nothing to say about the legitimacy or effects of bank war through the collection of a rival's notes followed by a sudden demand for payment, a not infrequent Scottish occurence.

There were two arguments that might have been expected to make Smith sympathetic to the optional clause. The banks, by having available such a means of gaining time against sudden demands, would thereby be able to reduce the amount of sterile coin held in the system. But of course Smith thought in terms of an only partial displacement: the optional clause, like the small notes, might well cause it to be carried too far. Secondly, by using the clause the banks might be able to bring about a smoother contraction in times of difficulty. But this argument had no real weight against the view held by Smith that full and instant convertibility was necessary as an essential and continuous control on over-issue.

Smith's policy views on the money supply, then, rested on the belief that it was good to replace much of the sterile gold and silver in the system, exporting it and receiving real goods in exchange. But though the total money consisting of notes and specie together was to be left to natural forces, the encroachment of paper upon specie was to be controlled. This was to be done by the state prescribing a minimal size of note and forbidding the optional clause. By such means the optimal (or at least a better) relation between paper and specie would be achieved, with the former used for large transactions and the latter for small ones. Specie would therefore be available in the system at two principal levels: as reserves in the banks, uneconomized by the optional clause, and among retailers and wage payers, undisplaced by notes under £5. There was enough of the mercantilist in Smith to make him uneasy about an economy which did not have at least this much specie about.

The third monetary constraint approved by Smith was that of a state

[25] RBS *Minutes*, 12 May 1773.

imposed maximum on interest rates (WN II.iv.14). The case for a ceiling rate had two elements. It would prevent extortion through usury. But of much more general interest was Smith's belief that it was right to fix a maximum rate by law so that 'prodigals and projectors' would not be able to bid rates to high levels, being those 'who alone would be willing to give this high interest', so that 'sober people', who would bid for the use of money in terms of its probable returns in productive use, would be deprived. This would result in a great part of a country's capital passing out of productive into wasteful hands. But this ceiling rate should be somewhat above the price which is commonly paid for the use of money by sound borrowers; no law could hold the rate below this level. Smith thought the existing legal limit to be 'perhaps, as proper as any'. He thus approved a system in which the rationing of money by price was subject to a cut-off point of 5 per cent. Robert Scott-Moncrieff, agent of the Royal Bank in its Glasgow office from 1783, probably the biggest discounting concern in Britain outside London, described the effect of an interest ceiling on the banker: 'Every other trader', he wrote to head office, 'when his article is on demand can raise the price, but a poor banker has no such means of lessening the demand or profiting by it—every customer thinks he has a right to badger him and tear it from him.'[26] Steuart, in a perhaps paradoxical reversal of roles relative to Smith, condemned 'the absurdity of fixing the rate of interest by law among trading men in a trading nation'.[27]

In spite of the self-equilibrating character of the circulating medium as assumed by Smith, the total money supply had somehow got too big in the 1760s, giving rise to a sustained exchange crisis. How was the 'automatic' thesis to be reconciled with this? Smith's account of the behaviour of the banks has to be pieced together. The story begins, presumably about 1762, with the banks having 'over-traded a little' (WN II.ii.65). Businessmen had then demanded more. The banks and bankers declined to accommodate them. The projectors then had recourse to accommodation bills, drawing and redrawing upon one another and upon London, a practice called 'raising money by circulation' (WN II.ii.66–7). At this point, in Smith's account, the banks re-enter the picture. 'The bills which A in Edinburgh drew upon B in London, he regularly discounted two months before they were due with some bank or banker in Edinburgh; and the bills which B in London redrew upon A in Edinburgh, he as regularly discounted either with the bank of England, or with some other bankers in London' (WN II.ii.69). Smith in using the phrase 'some bank or banker in Edinburgh' makes no distinction between the two public banks and the private bankers. At this time, in the early 1760s, it would probably be the private bankers in Edinburgh who were making the advances in the form of

[26] Scott-Moncrieff Letters, RBS, 9 Oct. 1801.
[27] Note to *Thoughts Concerning Banking*, *Caldwell Papers* (Maitland Club) i. 212.

discounts, but going to the public banks in their turn for credits, in the manner envisaged by Steuart. Presumably it was the public banks which made the principal effort to limit credit in the first phase described by Smith, but then found themselves in the second phase unable to resist the pressure of the private bankers who were themselves in trouble. The Scottish banks and bankers are thus presented as having tried to restrain credit, and then acting as discounters of a flood of accommodation paper. In the end, instead of standing firm, the public banks had yielded to the importunities of the business world, when they ought to have brought the whole expansion up short. Though Smith does not say so, the Ayr Bank was one of the worst offenders because its borrowers used its notes to speculate in the London exchanges, buying London bills with them and thus causing them to be returned quickly on the Bank. The banks and bankers had between them augmented the money supply above what was 'natural': 'The greater part of this paper', wrote Smith, 'was, consequently, over and above the value of the gold and silver that would have circulated in the country, had there been no paper money.' The result had been adverse exchanges and a drain of specie.

Smith does not avail himself of the view that the exchange crises from 1762 were due to other, non-banking factors, as Steuart had argued (*Principles*, 506), including poor harvest and capital movements in the form of the withdrawal of English funds, but insists upon the responsibility of the projectors backed by the bankers. Smith does not take proper account of the efforts by the public banks to control the situation, which in turn created the conditions out of which further new banking companies, enjoying free entry, came. Instead, in describing the behaviour of the public banks when confronted in 1769 with the Ayr Bank, he implies that they had been following a highly inflationary policy, and welcomed the willingness of the Ayr Bank to take on bad borrowers as providing them an escape from an impossibly over-extended situation. In this way 'they were enabled to get very easily out of that fatal circle, from which they could not otherwise have disengaged themselves without incurring a considerable degree of loss, and perhaps some degree of discredit' (WN II.ii.74).

This indictment of the banks and bankers as capable of creating inflationary conditions on such a scale is never explicitly assimilated to Smith's general monetary theory. It may be that he regarded such inflation as of short term and subject to self-correction through specie loss abroad. But Scotland lived under such conditions more or less continuously for some ten years from 1762. Nor does Smith consider whether in that period inflation contributed to growth of output.

The fact was established, however that not only had 'the circulation . . . been overstocked with paper money', but it had been increased beyond its natural level as defined by the specie that would have been present on a specie system only. The ability of the bankers to create such a situation, and their actual behaviour in doing so arose because the banks as entities had lacked both an understanding of their situation and a code of conduct to guide them. Trouble had arisen because 'every particular banking company has not always understood or attended to its own particular interest' (WN II.ii.53). Note that at this point Smith seems to place the blame on 'banking companies'. It followed from this that a code of sound practice derived not from generalized monetary theory, but from the immediate and multiple transactions of the banks, would ensure the correctness of the money supply.

Smith believed that the practice 'of the banking trade . . . is capable of being reduced to strict rules' (WN V.i.e.32). Indeed the availability of such rules made banking one of the few activities capable of being treated in terms of standard practice to such a degree that it could safely be entrusted to joint-stock companies. Smith's code contained four elements. If these were continuously adhered to two consequences would follow. Every banking enterprise would be sound, and the total money supply would vary strictly with the needs of the economy—it would be continuously correct.

First, there was the real bills doctrine: bankers should discount only those bills that represented the financing of the movement of real goods at short term (WN II.ii.59). Each bill would thus be self-liquidating, for the delivery of the corresponding goods would provide for its discharge and for the reflux of the bank notes that had been advanced. Secondly, bankers in their cash credit advances (a form of overdraft) should insist that the account be frequently 'turned over', with repayments and new borrowing (WN II.ii.61). The banker would then be able to control his total advances at any given time by curtailment of renewals. Thirdly, the general principal of short-term lending only, embodied in the first two rules, was reasserted: only where repayment was certain within three or at most eight months should a loan be made (WN II.ii.60). Finally, a banker should relate a loan not to the total resources of a borrower, but only to that part of his capital which he would otherwise be 'obliged to keep by him unemployed and in ready money for answering occasional demands' (WN II.ii.59–63,86,93). That is to say, the banker should go no further than relieving a borrower of the need to keep a cash float. These rules were not of course original with Smith: all but the fourth were the standard canons of Scottish banking, though not of course always or necessarily the practice.

Was this code capable, as Smith suggested. of promoting an optimal money supply over time? Was it true that if each bank followed 'correct' practice the money supply would look after itself? Only two of the rules, the first and the last, had anything to say about how much should be loaned. The first was the more realistic, for it could be related to bills of lading and other documents. But it did not take account of changes in the prices of commodities during the lifetime of a bill; a fall would mean that the sums entered in the bill of exchange would be less than the value of the goods when sold. The fourth rule, related to the cash float, would be difficult to apply, for such a concept is hard to define and measure. There was, of course, one element of clarity in it: that the banker should certainly not finance fixed capital, and only a small proportion of variable capital, certainly not, for example, the wages bill. Rules two and three had to do with the length of life of loans: they merely asserted that they should be short in order that the banker could continuously review his situation. In general, no attempt was made to build a bridge between the money supply created under these rules and that which would, in aggregate, yield full employment. It was assumed that the 'natural' money supply that would be called for on a pure specie basis (e.g. that appropriate to the needs of the economy) would be forthcoming under the operation of these rules. It would seem highly likely however, that should the bankers have confined their lending to Smith's austere programme the economy might well not have had the money supply necessary to promote full employment.

How would the matter look from the banker's point of view? For them the critical questions always were: when should credit contraction be brought about, what means should be used (e.g. refusal of renewal of discounts *versus* reduction of advances on cash accounts or on other bases), who should be subjected to pressure (e.g. which borrowers should be made to repay), and how much, in aggregate, was it necessary to draw back?

Of course it could be argued that if Smith's four canons of bank lending were followed there would be no upswing, but merely a steady progression. Unfortunately Smith does not discuss the causes of the trade cycle, presumably finding them to lie in departures from his rules.

The implication in Smith is that if every lending transaction were in the terms prescribed the system would be stable at full employment. But from the point of view of the public banks, with their experience of crises, brought about or at least aggravated by other bankers who were competing for note issue via loans, it was necessary to bring in an element of generalized control. It was no good elaborating a system of ideal internal rules; loans did get made on other terms than those set out by Smith and it was necessary to be able to cope with the resulting situation when it arose. Hence the public banks' constant recurrence to the note issue as the most important condition of entry to banking.

V

There were a number of further loose ends in Smith's thinking about banking.

One had to do with the collective, imitative, and mutually exciting activities of bankers. Smith lays down the general proposition that 'though the principles of common prudence do not always govern the conduct of every individual, they always influence that of the majority of every class or order' (WN II.ii.36). This statement is of course a fundamental element of the liberal creed: the assertion of the free-standing individual, capable of rational choice within the parameters in which he finds himself. Yet Smith in his treatment of the inflation of the 1760s and early 1770s describes the bankers as collectively supporting inflation by discounting a flood of accommodation paper. 'The Scotch banks, no doubt', wrote Smith, 'paid all of them very dearly for their own imprudence and inattention' (WN II.ii.56).

Adam Smith does not directly discuss the question of the right of the public to insist upon disclosure by note issuers of their situation. His four canons for bankers were all domestic and interior: the bankers should be left to apply the rules to themselves, without state or public scrutiny. Steuart believed otherwise, at least so far as non-public banks, with no legal identity and no permanently committed capital, were concerned. All note issuers not trading with public authority, said Steuart, 'ought to be obliged to keep books open to inspection by the public'.[28] Such an insistence upon democratic scrutiny might be thought a fitting part of the system of natural liberty, improving the data upon which an individual could base his transactions with such bankers. An individual who did not like the behaviour of a banker as revealed in his books could then decline to accept his notes or otherwise trade with him, turning to another whose procedures were preferred. But at this point a difficulty arises. Would not such scrutiny by the public lead directly to state intervention? For a person aggrieved by the behaviour of a banker, judging him to be behaving dangerously, or of having so behaved, might well invoke the law. It would then be necessary for the judges to be provided with a set of principles. This would involve the state in laying down canons of sound banking. The outcome, therefore, of disclosure, could well be a state-enforced code of banking, a thing that would on general grounds be abhorrent to Smith. So stood the dilemma of disclosure. Steuart, for his part, does not enter into the difficulties of enforcing the opening of the books of bankers. Especially in a note-issuing situation such a requirement could make every banker vulnerable to attack by his rivals or his enemies, and might well unsteady public confidence in times of monetary disturbance. The view implied by Smith, of course, prevailed: Scottish and English banking companies proceeded on the basis of no required public disclosure down to the Companies Acts of the mid-nineteenth century, and with the legal minimum thereafter. With the affairs of the note-issuing bankers inviolate from public scrutiny there could be no question of requiring other business concerns not providing money

[28] Ibid., 226.

substitutes to disclose their position: the veil of secrecy was cast over business in general in the interest of the system of natural liberty.

The bankers were related to the state in yet another way. This too Smith passes over. It had to do with the remitting from Edinburgh to London of the public revenues. The right to hold public balances and transmit them was highly valuable, for it increased the disposable resources of bankers to the extent of the average holding of such monies. It was also important from the point of view of note issue, for taxes were paid in bank notes, so that the remitting bank received large sums of the notes of other banks and was accordingly in a position to substitute its own notes in the Circle and indeed, if so inclined, to harass its rivals. The Bank of Scotland, lacking political favour, had no standing with regard to the revenue: holding and remittance of the public funds was shared between the Royal Bank and the private bankers Sir William Forbes and Co., both highly acceptable to the ruling party. The Royal Bank had the account of the Receiver General of the Customs, while Forbes and Co. enjoyed the Excise Account. Forbes and Co. had inherited their preferred position from the firm out of which they had come, namely Coutts and Co. of Edinburgh, who had remitted the excise since 1742. Though the state had no business to dispense in Scotland in terms of issuing and managing the public debt, so profitable to the Bank of England, it did have the revenue to dispose of, and did so in terms of the patronage system. In this important sense the state was involved in Scottish banking, operating not by principle but by favour.[29]

Finally, there is the question of Smith's estimate of the Scottish money supply in the 1770s. His view was that 'in the present times the whole circulation of Scotland cannot be estimated at less than two millions, of which that part which consists in gold and silver, most probably, does not amount to half a million' (WN II.ii.43). This means that at least £1,500,000 must be accounted for in terms of bank notes. But calculations would put Scottish notes in the hands of the public at some £900,000. Any possible margin of error or variation could hardly bring this above a million. It seems probable that Smith, if he inquired about the size of note issue of the various banks, was given a figure representing those notes signed by directors and paid to the cashier. But the Scottish banks always held very large sums in their tills. It is this till money that would seem to have entered Smith's figure of issue to the public.

VI

Smith did not confront Steuart's views on banking; in this as in all other aspects of the economy he studiously ignored Steuart. Had he done so,

[29] William Ramsay to Duke of Buccleuch, 26 May 1790, Scottish Record Office, GD 113/283/7.

taking account of the non-homogeneity of Scottish banking institutions, his treatment might have gained in realism.

It has frequently been said that a good many aspects of Smith's thought were not rigorous in the integrative sense; that his mixture of theory and institutional treatment yield a picture that is highly elliptical. This is certainly true of banking. It was necessary, of course, that his views on the subject be consistent with his general approach to the economy, resting as it did on the market mechanism operated by men who enjoyed free entry and minimal supervision. The banking expression of Smith's system of natural liberty was a set of institutions composed of many enterprises, none capable of monopolistic power or even leadership, each guided by prudential rules, and all trading within an environment of law provided by the state. Acting in aggregate they would, Smith implied, provide an optimal money supply or an effective approximation to it. But in the light of banking conditions in the Scotland of Adam Smith's time, not to speak of the years to follow when matters approximated even less to his assumption, his view of banking omitted important aspects of reality which, if properly attended to, might have damaged his view of economic processes. Both Steuart and Smith can be accused of allowing the demands of their general systems of thought to affect their presentation of banking. Both left some important theoretical issues unbroached and both left some unresolved. But taken together they provide a most illuminating dichotomy, perhaps the best theoretical starting-point for a consideration of pre-industrial banking, and not without relevance for later times.

XIII

The Paradox of Progress: Decline and Decay in *The Wealth of Nations*

ROBERT L. HEILBRONER*

I

TWO centuries of examination under a magnifying glass have left few aspects of *The Wealth of Nations* exempt from meticulous study. Yet I believe that a central issue with respect to Smith's philosophic and historic 'vision' has failed to receive the attention it merits. This is the profound pessimism concealed within Smith's economic and social scheme of evolution. To be sure, many writers have noted that Smith's grand trajectory of economic development terminates in a stagnant as well as stationary state, and recently attention has been focused on Smith's recognition of 'alienation' as an integral part of commercial society.[1] To the best of my knowledge, however, these two strands of Smith's exposition have not been tied together to yield the conclusion that Smith's economic and social philosophies are ultimately indefensible in terms of one another. For the disturbing import of *The Wealth of Nations*, taken in its entirety, is that it espouses a socio-economic system that can find its justification neither in the promise of continuous economic betterment nor in the prospect of general social betterment. Instead we are faced with the disconcerting prognosis of an evolutionary trend in which both decline and decay attend—material decline awaiting at the terminus of the economic journey, moral decay suffered by society in the course of its journeying.

It is this insufficiently examined dark side of Smith's thought that I wish to explore in this essay. The task will lead to a discussion in three stages. First, I shall present as succinctly as possible the basic schemata of historical progress and economic growth, in order to set the stage for an analysis of

* Norman Thomas, Professor of Economics, Graduate Faculty, New School for Social Research, New York. I would like to thank Adolph Lowe, Andrew Skinner, and Frank Roosevelt for helpful comments on an earlier draft of this paper.

[1] A complete citation would be impossible. Let me merely note Paul H. Douglas, 'Smith's Theory of Value and Distribution', *Adam Smith 1776–1926* (1928, 1966); Jos. Spengler, 'Adam Smith's Theory of Economic Growth', *Southern Economic Journal* (1959), for discussions of Smith's 'Malthusianism'; see E. G. West, 'The Political Economy of Alienation', *Oxford Economic Papers* (Mar. 1969) together with the article by the same author in this volume; N. Rosenberg, 'Adam Smith on the Division of Labor: Two Views or One?', *Economica* (May 1965), for treatments of Smith's concern with alienation.

the central issues to follow. Next, we must look into the causes of moral decay and economic decline, as these are made explicit in *The Wealth of Nations* and in Smith's other works. Finally we must inquire into the roots of the problem which, I trust, will by then have clearly emerged. What we seek in the end is an explanation for this 'paradox' both within the framework of Smith's own assumptions and within the larger setting of the Enlightenment itself.

II

Smith was a founder of what we may call 'philosophical history'—a type of historical inquiry that sought to divine within the sequence of historical facts an underlying pattern explicable by reference to 'human nature', that *primum mobile* of the eighteenth century. We know from the *Lectures on Justice, Police, Revenue and Arms* that Smith had already in his late twenties envisaged society as passing through four stages: 'hunting, pasturage, farming, and commerce'.[2] In the *Lectures*, however, this stages-of-history sequence is introduced merely to lead to a discussion of property, whereas in *The Wealth of Nations* the scheme is reiterated with much greater historical detail and is utilized to suggest a proto-Marxian coincidence of civil institutions with the changing underpinnings of the material mode of production.[3]

Hence in *The Wealth of Nations* we meet a sequence of four different organizational modes through which society will tend naturally to pass, provided that it does not meet insuperable obstacles of nature or human misunderstanding. The sequence begins with 'the lowest and rudest state of society, such as we find it among the native tribes of North America', and terminates in a fourth stage, of which *The Wealth of Nations* virtually in its entirety must be the reference, characterized by a commercialization of agriculture, an encouragement to manufactures, and above all, by the pervasive presence and influence of the division of labour with its associated benefits of increased productivity.

We shall return to this scheme of historical evolution in our next section, but before we pass to the subject of economic growth proper it is necessary to underscore the prescriptive as well as the descriptive role played by the historical schema. There is a 'natural progress of things toward improvement', and although Smith makes it plain that deficiencies of nature or the

[2] LJ (B) 149; ed. Cannan 107.

[3] *The Wealth of Nations*, ed. Cannan (1937), esp. V.i.a and b. This 'materialist' conception of history is perhaps most explicitly stated by William Robertson: 'In every inquiry concerning the operations of men when united together in society, the first object of attention should be their mode of subsistence. Accordingly as that varies, their laws and policy must be different.' Quoted in Skinner's 'Introduction' to *The Wealth of Nations* (1970), 31, and above, p. 175.

follies of men can inhibit or even prevent progress, he leaves no doubt that in favourable circumstances society both *will* and *should* pass through these stages in sequence. It *will* pass through them because the underlying human impetus toward 'improvement' and social rank gives rise to a 'uniform, constant, and uninterrupted effort of every man to better his condition'.[4] This drive for self-betterment, Smith makes plain, is 'so powerful a principle, that it is alone, and without any assistance, not only capable of carrying on the society to wealth and prosperity, but of surmounting a hundred impertinent obstructions with which the folly of human laws too often incumbers its operations' (WN IV.v.b.43). And it *should* pass through them, first, because 'No society can surely be flourishing and happy, of which the far greater part of the members are poor and miserable' (WN I.viii.36); and second, because it is only through the agency of the system of perfect liberty, brought to its fullest effectiveness in commercial society, that this improvement can take place.

Thus the normative implications are plain enough. Commercial society resounds to the happiness and comfort of the 'great body of the people'. It remains only to indicate precisely how this comes about.

This question leads us to consider the interaction of drives, institutional forms, and feedback mechanisms—in short, the 'growth model'—that correspond with the social stage of commercial society. Here I shall follow the model originally proposed by Lowe.[5] The model describes a continuous growth process into which we break, for purposes of explication, at the moment at which the manufacturer (seeking to better his condition) responds to a growing effectual demand by enlarging his scale of production.

Thereafter, growth of output, stemming from the all-important division of labour, comes about as the natural consequence of the drive of increase profits by catering on an enlarged scale to a growing market. It remains only to be noted that the technological processes of manufacture are explicitly labour-attracting, rather than labour-displacing, an essential element in the smooth unrolling of the growth sequence.

There is, however, a problem with regard to the process. It lies in the fact that an increase in the demand for labour should lead, *ceteris paribus*, to a rise in the wages of labour; and this rise would then threaten the profits from which subsequent accumulations could be financed: 'High wages of labour and high profits of stock . . . are things, perhaps, which scarce ever go together, except in the peculiar circumstances of new colonies', writes Smith (WN I.ix.11). Thus the growth process is in danger of being retarded and eventually halted through the inability of the manufacturer to accumu-

[4] LJ (B) 205–11; ed. Cannan 157–61 for the desire for 'improvement'; TMS IV.i.1 for ambition; WN I.iii.8 for blockages of nature, and II.iii.31 and especially IV.v.b.43 for 'self-betterment'.

[5] A. Lowe, 'The Classical Theory of Economic Growth', *Social Research*, xxi (1954) and above, p. 415; also Spengler, op. cit.

late that stock which, as we have seen, must 'in the nature of things, be previous to the division of labour'.

But now enters the crucial feedback mechanism. The rise in wages induces an increase in the supply of labour, for 'the demand for men, like that for any other commodity, necessarily regulates the production of men' (WN I.viii.40). Smith does not explicitly spell out this part of the process (indeed, the parts of the growth model itself lie scattered throughout the chapters of *The Wealth of Nations*, so that the logic of the mechanism is no doubt clearer to us than it was to Smith himself), but there is no mistaking the means by which smooth and steady growth is assured. The critical linkage is a decrease in child mortality brought about by rising wages—a very important part of the growth model to which we shall subsequently return. But at this juncture it is enough to note that the rise in the supply of labour now acts as a counter-force against the rise in demand, both demand and supply curves shifting to the right. As a result, wage rates are prevented from rising to such an extent as to choke off further accumulations.[6] The accumulation process, therefore, proceeds, building up the wage-and-capital fund necessary for the next improvement in the division of labour.

It is understandable that Schumpeter should have termed such a beautifully co-ordinated growth process 'hitchless',[7] for evidently nothing stands in the way of a continuous increase in the productivity of labour. Yet, as we have noted, evidently the process cannot be 'hitchless', since it ends in decline. For at the end of the long rising gradient, we are suddenly confronted with the spectacle of a nation which has attained 'that full complement of riches which the nature of its soil and climate, and its situation with respect to other countries, allow(s) it to acquire', and we discover to our consternation that in such a nation 'the wages of labour and the profits of stock would probably be very low' (WN I.ix.14). Thus, 'hitchless' growth has somehow terminated in general poverty, a fact that suggests that there are, after all, some very important hitches concealed in the dynamics of *The Wealth of Nations*.

We shall examine the nature of these difficulties in the next section of this essay. But first it is necessary to document a critical fact that we shall need when we consider the problems of decline. This is the incontrovertible evidence that Smith saw the growth process as resulting for a long period in rising real wages. Dealing with the long-run trend, Smith makes this conclusion unmistakably clear:

The real recompense of labour, the real quantity of the necessaries and conveniences of life which it [the natural price or wage of labour] can procure to the labourer has, during the course of the present century, increased in a still perhaps

[6] W. O. Thweatt, 'A Diagrammatic Presentation of Adam Smith's Growth Model', *Social Research*, xxiv (1957).

[7] J. Schumpeter, *History of Economic Analysis* (1954), 572, 640.

greater proportion than its money price. The common complaint that luxury extends itself even to the lowest ranks of the people, and that the labouring poor will not now be contented with the same food, cloathing, and lodging which satisfied them in the past, may convince us that it is not the money price of labour only, but its real recompense, which has augmented.

(WN I.viii.35)

We shall shortly return to certain conclusions of this key paragraph when we investigate the problems of long-term decline. But it is clear that Smith is prescribing as well as describing a historical sequence whose present and immediate future is characterized by a significant improvement in the material well-being of the 'labouring poor'. Thus real long-term growth, hitchless or not, is unquestionably the great theme of *The Wealth of Nations*, providing the justification for the system of perfect liberty toward which the evolution of society has been proceeding.

III

We turn now to the 'darker side' of *The Wealth of Nations* and to consider how Smith's normative sequence of historical evolution leads, paradoxically, to both moral and material decline. In this section we must therefore establish that this grim finale is indeed explicitly present in *The Wealth of Nations*, postponing for our last section an inquiry into the causes and significance of this perverse state of affairs.

Let us begin by continuing our examination of the growth process whose smooth, self-sustaining upward path we have been examining. As we have already noted, this path must somewhere turn into a trajectory that descends to a final stage in which both wages and profits of stock must be very low. The reason is that:

In a country fully peopled in proportion to what either its territory could maintain or its stock employ, the competition for employment would necessarily be so great as to reduce the wages of labour to what was barely sufficient to keep up the number of labourers, and, the country being already fully peopled, that number could never be augmented. In a country fully stocked in proportion to all the business it had to transact, as great a quantity of stock would be employed in every branch of trade as the nature and extent of the trade would admit. The competition, therefore, would every-where be great, and consequently, the ordinary profit as low as possible.

(WN I.ix.14)

Finally, in such a country,

the usual market rate of interest . . . would be so low as to render it impossible for any but the very wealthiest people to live upon the interest of their money. All people of small or middling fortunes would be obliged to superintend themselves the employment of their stocks. It would be necessary that almost every man should be a man of business, or engage in some sort of trade.

(WN I.ix.20)

Thus what we see at the terminus is a society in which the long-term accumulation of capital has brought very odd results. The condition of the working class has been reduced to a Malthusian precariousness. The employer of moderate means ekes out a modest livelihood; a few men of great wealth live from their interest. The position of the landlords, prefiguring the conclusion of Ricardo, is presumably of all classes the most improved, owing to the pressure of population against the soil and the consequent high price of goods.[8]

To what can we attribute this Malthusian–Ricardian prospect? Nowhere does Smith actually explain the mechanism that leads him to the conclusions so unequivocally spelled out, but within the clear-cut statement of his premises, there is only one behavioural force that Smith must have reckoned on to produce this result. This is a rate of population growth that continues to be positive throughout the various stages of real *per capita* well-being implied in the long trajectory of economic growth and decline. In this regard, it is interesting (and as we shall subsequently see, important) to note that Smith divides the reproductive capabilities of the nation into two sharply differentiated demographic groups, corresponding to two sharply differentiated social classes: the poor whose breeding tendencies are high and the rich whose fecundity is markedly less:

Poverty, though it no doubt discourages, does not always prevent marriage. It seems even to be favourable to generation. A half-starved Highland woman frequently bears more than twenty children, while a pampered fine lady is often incapable of bearing any, and is generally exhausted by two or three. Barrenness, so frequent among women of fashion, is very rare among those of inferior station. Luxury in the fair sex, while it inflames the passion for enjoyment, seems always to weaken, and frequently to destroy altogether, the power of generation.

(Wn I.viii.37)

A thought that no doubt strikes the modern reader is whether this sharp differential in fertility might not narrow, as the real income of the working classes rose. This could then lead to a stationary state *à la* Mill, where birth and death rates reached equality short of the point of physiological minima. (That is, we might speculate that among those articles of 'luxury' to be acquired by a rising working class would be the means or arts of birth control practised by the upper classes.) But no hint of such a thing appears in Smith. Hence we must assume that the increase of population proceeds relentlessly until it reaches a point at which the increase in productivity

[8] In speaking of the possibility of substituting potatoes for grain, Smith concludes, 'Population would increase, and rents rise much above what they are at present' (WN I.xi.b.39).

stemming from the continuing division of labour is finally overwhelmed by the decreasing productivity of the land and resources available to the nation. At this point, real wages decline, working-class mortality rate rises, and eventually we reach the condition of 'dull' stationariness described above.[9]

IV

So much for the mechanics of the unhappy long-term outcome of the economic process proper. Now let us turn to the sociological side of the argument with evidence that the system of perfect liberty leads to a human condition that is inferior, rather than superior, to that of the preceding stages of the historical process. The passages in which Smith makes this invidious comparison are justly famous:

In the progress of the division of labour, the employment of the far greater part of those who live by labour, that is of the great body of the people, comes to be confined to a few very simple operations, frequently to one or two. But the understandings of the greater part of men are necessarily formed by their ordinary employments. The man whose whole life is spent in performing a few simple operations, of which the effects too are, perhaps, always the same or very nearly the same, has no occasion to exert his understanding, or to exercise his invention in finding expedients for removing difficulties which never occur. He naturally loses, therefore, the habit of such exertion, and generally becomes as stupid and ignorant as it is possible for a human creature to become. The torpor of his mind renders him, not only incapable of relishing or bearing a part in any rational conversation, but of conceiving any general, noble, or tender sentiment, and consequently of forming any just judgment concerning many even of the ordinary duties of private life . . .

(WN V.ii.f.50)[10]

Smith goes on to deplore as well the worker's loss of the attributes of courage and even physical vigour, concluding (WN V.ii.f.50) that 'his dexterity at his own particular trade seems, in this manner, to be acquired at the expense of his intellectual, social and martial virtues'. But what is more telling is his frank contrast of commercial society with the condition of life in previous stages of the historical sequence:

It is otherwise in the barbarous societies, as they are commonly called of hunters, of shepherds, and even of husbandmen in that rude state of husbandry that precedes the improvement of manufactures, and the extension of foreign commerce. In such societies, the varied occupations of every man oblige every man to exert his capacity, and to invent expedients for removing difficulties that are

[9] For a second, more problematical 'hitch' see my article on Smith in *The Journal of the History of Ideas*, xxxiv, no. 2 (Apr.–June 1973), 250–2.

[10] Cf. Ferguson, *An Essay on the History of Civil Society* (1767) Part IV, Sec. 1: 'Manufactures . . . prosper most, where the mind is least consulted, and where the workshop may, without any great effort of the imagination, be considered as an engine, the parts of which are men.'

continually recurring. Invention is kept alive and the mind is not suffered to fall into that drowsy stupidity, which, in a civilized society seems to benumb the understanding of almost all the inferior ranks of people. In those barbarous societies, as they are called, every man, it has already been observed, is a warrior. Every man too is in some measure a statesman and can form a tolerable judgment concerning the interest of the society, and the conduct of those who govern it.

(WN V.ii.f.51)

To be sure, as Smith explains, there is a price to be paid for this generally shared competence. It is that 'no man can acquire that improved and refined understanding, which a few men sometimes possess in a more civilized state' (ibid.). On the other hand, Smith frankly concedes that the few who possess this refinement of understanding contribute little to the general good of society unless they 'happen to be placed in some very particular situations' (ibid.). Hence the final judgement passed on the quality of life in commercial society is devastating: 'Notwithstanding the great abilities of those few, all the nobler parts of the human character may be, in great measure, obliterated and extinguished in the great body of the people' (ibid.).

These sentiments are by no means only a reflection of Smith's later views, for we find them spelled out in very nearly identical terms in the *Lectures* in which the scheme of philosophical history is first mentioned. There he reports on three 'inconveniences . . . arising from a commercial spirit':

The first we shall mention is that it confines the views of men. Where the division of labour is brought to perfection, every man has only a simple operation to perform; to this his whole attention is confined, and few ideas pass in his mind but what have an immediate connection with it . . . It is remarkable that in every commercial nation the low people are exceedingly stupid . . . Another inconvenience attending commerce [he continues] is that education is greatly neglected. In rich and commercial nations the division of labour, having reduced all trades to very simple operations, affords an opportunity of employing children very young. In this country [Scotland], indeed, where the division of labour is not very far advanced, even the meanest porter can read and write, because the price of education is cheap, and a parent can employ his child no other way at six or seven years of age. This, however, is not the case in the commercial parts of England. A boy of six or seven years of age in Birmingham can gain his threepence or sixpence a day, and parents find it in their interest to set them to work; thus their education is neglected.

(LJ (B) 328–30; Cannan, 255–6)

The want of education, Smith goes on to say, is 'certainly one of their greatest misfortunes', but in addition 'another great loss . . . attends the putting boys too soon to work'. It is that 'when he grows up he has no ideas with which to amuse himself. When he is away from work he must therefore betake himself to drunkenness and riot . . . So it may be very justly said that the people who clothe the whole world are in rags themselves.'

Finally, Smith laments in the *Lectures* that 'Another bad effect of commerce is that it sinks the courage of mankind and tends to extinguish the martial spirit' (LJ (B) 330–1; ed. Cannan 257). He concludes: 'These are the disadvantages of a commercial spirit. The minds of men are contracted, and rendered incapable of elevation. Education is despised, or at least neglected, and heroic spirit is almost utterly extinguished.' (LJ (B) 333; Cannan 259).

I have quoted extensively to focus our attention on passages that establish without doubt the fact that Smith relegated the moral quality of a system of perfect liberty to a position inferior to that of a 'ruder' but more wholesome epoch. This strain of Smith's thought has been analysed both with regard to its relation to the Marxian concept of alienation[11] and in terms of the problems it presents with regard to Smith's general advocacy of capitalism.[12] Yet, to my knowledge, no one has sufficiently stressed the fact that the deterioration of the human condition cannot be rationalized in terms of the very purpose for which the system of perfect liberty is espoused —namely, the material betterment of mankind that is supposed to flow from its workings.

V

Heretofore we have been concerned with presenting the textual foundation on which is based the dilemma to which we have addressed ourselves—a dilemma of economic progress accompanied by moral decay, and of moral decay coupled, in the end, with economic stagnation. Now we must turn to the larger questions that this 'contradiction' poses—not seeking to resolve them, for there is no resolution possible within the terms of Smith's premises, but attempting better to understand their causes and implications.

No doubt the initial clarification we must seek is an answer to why the problem occurs in the first place—that is, why the marvellously integrated scheme of philosophy, history, psychology, and economics ends, upon examination, in such a dismaying failure, in its own terms. There are, I believe, two answers to this question. The first is simple. It is Smith's inability to imagine conscious intervention in one all-important element of the process of historic change: population growth. When we reflect on the difference between Smith's terminus and that of J. S. Mill, it is this single element that makes all the difference, reinforced of course by the re-distributive philosophy that Mill boldly introduced. But quite without redistributive measures, a stationary state, brought into being before

[11] West, op. cit. and below, p. 540.

[12] Cf. Jos. Cropsey, *Polity and Economy* (1957) and above, p. 132. We shall return to Cropsey's argument in Part V of this article.

sharply decreasing returns to land had enforced a return to bare subsistence for the labouring class, would have afforded a prospect entirely different from that which Smith presents.

The second answer is perhaps of greater interest in terms of 'philosophical history'. It is the inadequacy of Smith's motive of 'self-betterment' as the basic explanatory principle of historical evolution. The simple drive for improvement or for rank does not decree, for example, that nomadism (pasturage) should be an indispensable stage, for there is no reason why a society of huntsmen could not leap directly into farming. Much more to the point, *it offers no hint of what organization of society might lie beyond the stage of commercial society.*[13]

What lacks, in other words, is an element—a logic—in the historical scheme capable of transcending or transforming the fate to which Smith's system eventually falls victim. Two such logics suggest themselves. One would be a greater reliance on an evolutionary idea of technological development, capable of overcoming, or of indefinitely postponing, the Malthusian finale.[14] The second might be a historical formulation in terms of a dialectic or class struggle along the lines that Marx was to introduce with *The Communist Manifesto*. The weaknesses of such a dialectical design are well known, and as we shall note, the very conception of a class struggle was absent from the historical paradigm within which Smith and his fellow *philosophes* laboured. But from our late vantage-point in history, when we seek to account for the inconsistency of Smith's partisanship for a system that led to both moral and economic decline, the absence of such a saving technological or dialectical driving force in place of the frail instrument of 'self-betterment' must certainly be placed in the forefront of our considerations.

This leads to a second major question: Would Smith himself have been disconcerted, had we pointed out to him the 'contradiction' of a model of progress that led to both social and economic failure? Two defences would surely have occurred to him. In the first place, the conception of history as a cyclical process, or as a vast drama ending in tragedy, would by no means have struck him, as an eighteenth-century thinker, with the same unpleasant force as it does ourselves, who still tend to conceive of history in the linear terms of the late nineteenth century. The theme of 'rise and fall',

[13] It is interesting to note that the Marxian schema, like the Smithian, is weakest in describing the 'inexorable' sequence of pre-commercial and post-capitalist institutions; and that the Smithian scheme, like the Marxian, is best at describing how the commercial system evolved from the feudal: 'what all the violence of the feudal institutions could never have effected, the silent and insensible operation of foreign commerce and manufactures gradually brought about' (WN III.iv.10).

[14] Nathan Rosenberg has pointed out (op. cit. 129f.) that in *The Wealth of Nations* there is indeed an explicit sequence in the *capacity* to invent that parallels the stages of socio-economic organization. But this changing capacity follows from, rather than initiates, the evolutionary movement itself.

of civilizations whose life histories resembled that of individuals, was very much a part of the intellectual currency of his times.[15]

Secondly, Smith would have protested that the dismal economic end he foresaw lay only at the horizon of historical sight when a nation's full complement of capital had been amassed. Indeed, he was careful to state that 'perhaps no country has ever yet arrived at that degree of opulence' (WN I.ix.15). In this defence he would have been perfectly justified, in that the Malthusian contribution to economic thought was not the discovery of the 'principle of population', but rather its placement in the immediate rather than the distant future.[16]

None the less, the defence has a certain element of evasiveness. For evidence of an inner uncertainty on Smith's part speaks to us from within *The Wealth of Nations*, despite the assurance that dominates the work as a whole. It lies in the constant ambivalence that Smith displays toward the attribute of human nature on which the entire historic and economic sequence depends—the acquisitive impulse through which 'self-betterment' expresses itself, at least in the commercial stage of society. Smith's disdain for the manners, the conspiratorial proclivities, the selfishness, and vanity of merchants is too well known to require documentation here (see for example, WN I.ix.24, I.xi.p.10). Equally familiar is his contempt for the activity of wealth-seeking as an end in itself: 'Power and riches', he writes in the *Theory of Moral Sentiments*, '. . . are enormous and operose machines contrived to produce a few trifling conveniences to the body; . . . immense fabrics which it requires the labour of a life to raise, which threaten every moment to overwhelm the person who dwells in them . . .' (IV.i.1.8). It is just because of this express disdain both for riches and for the quest for them that so much comment has been visited upon the Invisible Hand as the mechanism by which less-than-admirable actors, impelled by less-than-admirable motives, are brought in the end to serve as the agents of social improvement.

Indeed, it is just because of the curious implications of this argument that another interpretation has been suggested as the ultimate 'defence' of Smith's intention. It is that the motives and institutions of *The Wealth of Nations* form a system whose ultimate justification is to be sought not in terms of its economic or social, but its political and spiritual results. This is the conclusion of Joseph Cropsey, who writes:

. . . Smith's position may be interpreted to mean that commerce generates freedom and civilization, and at the same time free institutions are indispensable to

[15] Cf. e.g. Adam Ferguson, *An Essay on the History of Civil Society*, Part V, 'On the Decline of Nations'. (It should be noted, however, that Ferguson saw the possibility of decline stemming from corruption and loss of virtue, not as an inevitable consequence of economic processes.)

[16] Jacob Hollander, 'The Founder of a School', in *Adam Smith 1776–1926* (1966), 43.

the preservation of commerce. If the advantages of commerce can be sufficiently impressed upon the general mind, freedom and civilization will automatically follow in its train, and mankind will perhaps even be disposed to defend civilization, not necessarily out of love for freedom but out of love for commerce and gain.

'I wish to suggest,' Cropsey concludes, 'that Smith may be understood as a writer who advocated capitalism for the sake of freedom, civil and ecclesiastical.'[17] Thus Cropsey suggests that the Invisible Hand ultimately serves not merely to guide men on their proper economic stations, but conducts them to the battlements from which freedom is defended—in the name of property.

The suggestion is an ingenious one, but I fear it reads more of an 'intention' into Smith than the evidence permits. Freedom is an elusive concept at best, but if we use the word here, as I believe that Cropsey intends it to be used, as a synonym for political (and religious) liberty, it is difficult to square Cropsey's defence of Smith's system with the incapacity for self-government that Smith so clearly imputes to the lower orders. This incapacity, Smith makes clear, is the inherent defect not of the labouring man, but of the social condition into which he is forced by the system of 'perfect liberty' itself.

> Although the interest of the labourer is strictly connected with that of society [Smith writes], he is incapable either of comprehending that interest, or of understanding its connexion with his own. His condition leaves him no time to receive the necessary information, and his education and habits are commonly such as to render him unfit to judge even though he was fully informed.
>
> (WN I.x.p.9)

These are surely weak soldiers to whom to entrust the defence of liberty. Yet, unless liberty is to be protected by the labouring man himself, it will be nothing more than a cloak for exploitation. To be sure, there is the possibility that the spirit and understanding of the labourer might be fortified if he was systematically educated to an appreciation of higher things. But as Cropsey himself pointedly emphasizes, Smith can bring himself to say no more as to the herculean efforts that such an educational programme would require than that it would 'deserve the most serious attention of government'.[18] This 'serious attention', however, upon closer examination consists exclusively in recommendations for the establishment of trade schools in which the acquisition of an elementary education in 'geometry and mechanics' is to be encouraged by 'giving little premiums, and little badges of distinction, to the children of the common people who excel in them' (WN V.ii.f.56).

[17] Cropsey, op. cit. 95.

[18] Cropsey, op. cit. 90, cf. WN V.i.f.60.

Thus the defence of Smith's system in terms of political freedom seems to me to fall to the ground, and my objection is not merely a matter of textual exegesis. It follows, rather, from what I believe is both implicit and explicit in *The Wealth of Nations*—that the advocacy of a genuine *political* education as a necessary condition of freedom or liberty would have been not only uncongenial to, but even incompatible with, Smith's conception of the social order itself. But this leads us to a final consideration of the significance of the paradox of decline and decay in Smith's thought.

VI

I think it may be useful to begin this last stage of our inquiry by asking a question that had doubtless occurred to the reader. It is whether the paradox itself is ultimately a major importance, or whether the coincidence of moral decay and economic decline is not merely one more example of the endless anomalies and perplexities with which *The Wealth of Nations* abounds.[19] The question is of all the greater importance in view of the evident fact that on the surface *The Wealth of Nations* radiates a sense of confidence and promise that far outweighs those lurking difficulties on which this paper has been built. Thus it may seem merely pedantic or simply wrong to elevate the 'dark' side of Smith over the bright, particularly in so far as the final paradox of his argument was never recognized by Smith himself.

Nevertheless the paradox is there; and buried though it be, is in my view a problem of central importance. Indeed, I believe it is the buried paradox which, more than any other aspect of *The Wealth of Nations*, enables us to place Smith's masterpiece in its proper historical context, not merely as a pioneering effort in the social sciences, but as a paradigmatic exposition of the economic and sociological thought of its time.

Let me defend this position first by pointing out how remarkable it is that Smith, whose eye for sociological reality is so sharp, does not comment on the consequences of reducing the condition of the labouring man from the modest affluence to which *The Wealth of Nations* initially raises him, to the miserable subsistence to which he is finally condemned. Having taken note of the fact that life in the progressive state is 'cheerful' and 'happy' and that in a stationary one it is 'dull' and 'hard' (WN I.viii.43), Smith passes over without comment the enormous social strains that might be expected to ensue from a descent from one state to the other. This is all the more curious in that he has himself remarked that '*the labouring poor will not now be satisfied with the same food, cloathing, and lodging that satisfied them in*

[19] A. H. Cole, 'Puzzles of the Wealth of Nations', *Canadian Journal of Economics and Political Science* (Feb. 1958); and Jacob Viner, 'Adam Smith and Laissez Faire', reprinted in *Adam Smith, 1776–1926*.

former times' (WN I.viii.35). Yet, as to the wrenching dislocation implicit in the full decline to the final Malthusian terminus, he is silent.[20]

The omission particularly strikes us in view of Smith's open sympathies with the lot of the 'great body of the people'. With all the more force, then, does this failure of Smith's social imagination bring home to us the essentially 'class-bound' nature of his social vision. *The Wealth of Nations* is, by comparison with anything that had preceded it, by far the most 'dynamic' systematic treatise on social change that had yet been written, but what must now be brought to the fore is the narrow range within which those dynamics were contained. For when all is said and done, it is a social dynamics from which any possibility of a fundamental change in socio-economic structure has been removed.

Nowhere is this constriction of social vision more clearly revealed than in Smith's disregard of the implications of his own argument with regard to the source of value itself. In the original rude state of nature, as we all know, Smith maintained that 'the whole produce of labour belonged to the labourer', but under the commercial system, the labourer 'must in most cases share it with the owner of the stock who employs him' (WN I.viii.7). Smith is also clear that the share going to the owner is not his 'wages of management', but a return stemming from the power relations inherent in private property itself. Landlords 'demand' their rents only after land has become 'property'; and in all labour disputes, power runs to the property-holder because 'the masters can hold out much longer . . . In the long run the workman may be as necessary to his master as his master is to him, but the necessity is not so immediate' (WN I.viii.12).

Yet there is no suggestion in *The Wealth of Nations* that this unequal distribution of power might be open to social correction. Rather, as Paul Douglas has put it:[21]

this interpretation seems never to have entered Smith's mind. Landlords and men of industrial and commercial property were dominant in the society in which he wrote and he accepted them as part of the order of nature. With his hard-headed Scotch way of accepting the *status quo* he never thought of inquiring whether it would be possible to create an economic society in which profits and interest would disappear so that thus, as in his suppositious primitive society, the

[20] I might add that there has been a general failure of economists to explore the implications of 'subsistence' as a rising and irreversible parameter. Although the idea has been introduced into macro-economics in Duesenberry's 'rachet effect', the only effort of which I am aware to incorporate it into a larger model is to be found in Paolo Leon, *Structural Change and Growth in Capitalism* (1967). Leon writes, 'I postulate the existence, at each moment of time of a consumption level higher than the biological minimum, which is the minimum in a psychological sense' (23). This insight is confirmed by M. Hershkovitz, who writes, 'There is nothing more difficult to accept than a lowered standard of living' (quoted in Niels Roling, 'Adaptations in Development', *Economic Development and Cultural Change* (Oct. 1970), 73).

[21] Douglas, op. cit.; *Adam Smith 1776–1926*, 98.

workers should enjoy the full produce of their labour. The doors of Eden had been irrevocably closed to man, and there was no possibility of his ever re-entering them.

Thus in the end, the terrible dilemma of *The Wealth of Nations*—moral deterioration suffered on account of economic growth, and economic growth terminating finally in economic misery—reflects the inadequacies of a historical imagination bounded by an enlightened but only partially 'liberated' age. As Peter Gay has written: 'The question of the lower orders is the great unexamined political question of the Enlightenment'. As Gay makes clear, the motives behind this disregard are mixed; there is missing 'a serious attempt at working out the logic implicit in the philosophes' view of the Enlightenment', and there is also something else: 'a sense of despair at the general wretchedness, illiteracy, and brutishness of the poor, which appeared by and large incurable'.[22] Norman Hampson emphasizes the same theme in his overview of the age:

> Most of the men of letters of the period drew a sharp distinction between their own educated public and the illiterate rabble. Even radicals such as Helvetius and d'Holbach, who viewed much of the social order with anger and contempt, were pessimistic about the possibility of improving it . . . 'Progress', if it was possible at all, could only take the form of a movement toward a superior form of static society based on known and immutable values.[23]

In a word, the Enlightenment could conceive of radical notions of equality, justice, liberty, but it could not quite bring itself to apply these notions not only against the pretensions of aristocrats and churchmen, but of bourgeois society itself. In this ultimately fatal restriction of the imagination, Smith himself is finally caught.[24] Seeing the system of perfect liberty as a terminus rather than a wayfaring station for mankind, he is led unwittingly to describe a historical process whose destination becomes a betrayal of its purposes, and whose possible remedy—the political education of the labouring poor—would have been regarded as utter folly.

Here the work of the economist comes to an end and that of the social historian takes over. What I have sought to bring to the fore is, after all, no more than that Smith, albeit a major shaping intellectual force, was inevitably also a product of his time, sharing with it the limitations that seem to our age so patent and so crippling. But perhaps we can conclude with a reflection that redeems a great deal. It is true that Smith was hobbled by a class-bound social vision. None the less, he has something of great value to teach our age, where imagination no longer knows any bounds.

[22] Peter Gay, *The Enlightenment* (1966), ii.517.

[23] Norman Hampson, *The Enlightenment* (1969), 110.

[24] See J. M. A. Gee, 'Adam Smith's Social Welfare Function', *Scottish Journal of Political Economy*, xv (1968), for a discussion of the class orientation of Smith's concept of welfare.

This is the example of his unflinching honesty in appraising the very social institutions for which he was so eloquent a partisan; his saving scepticism in the face of heady ideas; and not least, the omnipresent sense of humanity that makes *The Wealth of Nations*, for all its partially blocked vision, a charter document of compassion and concern in the development of the social sciences.

XIV

Adam Smith and Alienation

Wealth Increases, Men Decay?

E. G. West*

It has often been pointed out that Adam Smith acknowledged that serious cultural and human hazards were entailed in the application of the principle of the division of labour in society. Yet, ironically, the division of labour was the basic principle upon which, in his economic analysis, the material wealth of nations primarily depended. Wealth certainly increased with growing specialization, Smith assured us; but he was disturbed that with daily life reduced progressively to a dull routine and with the growing monotony associated with repetitive factory work, men themselves might stagnate and become 'stupidified'.

Views differ as to the precise perspective in which Smith saw this 'flaw in the very pillar of his economic scheme'. Some indeed go so far as to see his recognition of it as inspiration for the Marxist–socialist critique of capitalist institutions.[1] We shall show in this article that Smith was far from letting the idea run away with him. Certainly he recognized that 'alienation' was an important social cost of capitalism needing serious consideration; but in the end capitalism itself could provide the answer. The 'blemish' or 'imperfection' could be counteracted by suitably devised antidotes such as publicly subsidized education. The subsidies could be provided from revenue obtained from taxes on the very capitalist production that was the source of the complaint.

* Professor of Economics, Carleton University, Ottawa.

[1] Nathan Rosenberg argues that Smith's remarks on the degrading effects of the division of labour 'constitute a major source of inspiration for the socialist critique of capitalist institutions as Marx himself acknowledged'. See 'Adam Smith on the Division of Labour: Two Views or One?' *Economica* (May 1965). Jacob Viner, in his introduction to John Rae's *The Life of Adam Smith* (1965), 35, associated Smith, Ferguson, and Wallace as writers on alienation in the general Marxian sense. Similarly, Duncan Forbes observes that 'it appears to have been Adam Smith who first broached the potentially explosive topic of the [Marxian alienation] effects of the division of labour', *Edinburgh in the Age of Reason* (1967), 47. George Elder Davie describes Smith as 'lucidly pointing forwards to the industrial society with its problems of "alienation" and "atomization" ', *Edinburgh in the Age of Reason* (1967), 24. The idea that Smith saw the division of labour as 'an important flaw in the very pillar of his economic scheme' is stressed by W. F. Campbell, *American Economic Review*, lvii, no. 2 (1966), 577. For a general argument to the effect that Marx was an heir to Adam Smith's sociology see R. L. Meek, *Economics and Ideology and Other Essays* (1967), 34–50.

The severity of any observer's reaction to 'alienation' relates to his own particular interpretation of it. If a writer knows what he means by being 'alienated' he should presumably know also what he means by being 'unalienated'. Concepts of alienation in fact differ according to each author's separate vision of the state of being 'unalienated'. This vision usually contains each writer's idea of man's 'true' state or his state of self-fulfilment. In Adam Smith's case the man who is *unalienated* (in the self-fulfilment sense of the term) is simply the one who finds a Hellenic type of happiness. Happiness is found not in isolation but in the society of one's fellows and only in a dynamic, creative, and forward-looking environment wherein the individual is absorbed in the pursuit of new excellence, new knowledge, and new invention (or to use Smith's terms: Wonder, Surprise, and Admiration).

The modern term 'alienation' is mainly a sociological one. Invariably work-oriented, it carries with it the assumption that the dignity of the worker cannot be maintained unless the work process allows autonomy, responsibility, and self-fulfilment. It will be helpful to specify two or three special dimensions of the term according to its modern usage.[2] Involving a complex of sentiments and attitudes, alienation from work includes especially the feelings of powerlessness, isolation, and self-estrangement. The concept will be examined under each of these three headings.

POWERLESSNESS

Modern sociology sees 'alienation from powerlessness' as a consequence of (i) the separation from ownership of the means of production, (ii) the inability to influence general managerial policies, (iii) the lack of control over the conditions of employment, and (iv) the lack of control over the immediate work process (Blauner, op. cit. 16). The most dramatic picture in these terms is that drawn by Marx. The historical process in his reasoning is presented in terms of inevitability; the worker finds himself caught up with inexorable 'laws of motion' inherent in capitalism. The division of labour in the broad sense of the phrase already characterized the pre-capitalist or feudal societies wherein the dominant class secured hierarchical privileges in an expediently engineered legal framework. The subsequent and inevitable development of capitalism, however, brought the division of labour into full fruition and thereby into much sharper focus. Marx emphasized that whereas previously the peasant workers had at least shared some minimum of property, with the coming of industrial capitalism there grew a new class of workers, the 'detail workers', who became completely separated from the means of production. From their previous abode in

[2] The three aspects here discussed are taken from R. Blauner, *Alienation and Freedom* (1964), Ch. 2. Blauner also includes a fourth heading: 'Meaninglessness'. For the purpose of application to our two authors this is best subsumed under 'Self-estrangement'. Blauner derives his groupings in turn from M. Seeman, 'On the Meaning of Alienation', *American Sociological Review* (1959), 783–96.

dispersed society, such individuals were eventually made to come together under a common supervision and under the common roof of the factory. The previous 'petty mode of production' attained its full classical form '. . . only where the labourer is the private owner of the means of labour which he uses; the peasant of the land which he cultivates, the artisan of the tool which he handles as a virtuoso. This mode of production presupposes parcelling out of the soil, and of the other means of production.'[3] With the rise of capitalism the 'fetters' of the feudal social organization were burst asunder:

Its annihilation, the transformation of the individualized and scattered means of production into socially concentrated ones, of the pigmy property of the many into the huge property of the few, the expropriation of the great mass of the people from the soil, from the means of subsistence, and from the means of labour, this fearful and painful expropriation of the mass of the people forms the prelude to the history of the capital.

(Ibid.)

ISOLATION

The alienated man is one who is isolated from real humanity, from himself, from his fellows, and from nature. Those writers who view the unalienated state as one where man is a social animal needing fellowship as much as food see the opposite in a system that forces him to be separate, lonely, and detached. This again is strongly represented in Marx who sees capitalism to be such a system. 'Only in association with others has each individual the means of cultivating his talents in all directions. Only in a community, therefore, is personal freedom possible.'[4] The traditional social communities, according to Marx, had a 'forced' or 'class based' character; even the family was 'unnatural' in this sense. Under the wide social division of labour each person belonged as a member of a 'mechanical' or functional group; he was not a spontaneous, free, and human individual.

SELF-ESTRANGEMENT

The third aspect of alienation is self-estrangement. In terms of modern sociology, it means that a worker becomes alienated from his 'inner self', and experiences 'a kind of depersonalized detachment rather than an immediate involvement or engrossment in the job tasks' (Blauner, op. cit. 26). Translated into Marxian terms the establishment of capitalism causes the work process to lose any semblance of individually purposeful activity. Workers become 'dehumanized'. Labour 'sustains their life only while stunting it'; work becomes an *external* experience; the fruits of work become

[3] *Capital*, i (1867), 801.

[4] *Marx–Engels Gesamtausgabe*, i.63–4. Quoted in Bottomore and Rubel, *Karl Marx, Selected Writings in Sociology and Social Philosophy* (1961), 247–8.

an *externalized* mass, 'outside themselves', and constantly growing in dominance over them.

ADAM SMITH ON ALIENATION

We shall argue that out of the three aspects of alienation so far outlined only the third (self-estrangement) could have possibly been intended in Smith's writings. We shall first discuss his economics and moral philosophy from the standpoint of the first two types of alienation: powerlessness and isolation.

1 *Powerlessness*

The division of labour was seen by Smith neither as an instrument of economic bondage nor as an institution the growth of which was inevitable. On the contrary, he saw it as an available means of man's economic 'liberation' from nature's niggardly environment. Indeed he feared that unless more writers would champion its cause foolish government policies would thwart its full development. Smith's picture of the state of affairs prior to the adoption of the division of labour was generally one of desperate struggle to survive. The material ungenerosity of nature was mankind's prominent and unhappy inheritance. Before men had managed seriously to conquer the scarcity problem, they had, in Smith's opinion, little prospect of cultural self-fulfilment. The capitalist division of labour which in Smith's treatment is used interchangeably with the word 'commerce', is a necessary condition for such progress. 'Opulence and Commerce commonly precede the improvement of arts and refinement of every sort. I do not mean that the improvement of arts and refinements of manners are the necessary consequences of commerce . . . only that it is a necessary requisite' (LRBL 23.3; Lothian, 132). Most of Smith's references to 'civilized' societies denote societies which have secured the benefits of a freely developed commerce and division of labour; his examples of societies that have not reached this stage are invariably described by him as 'barbarous', 'rude', and 'savage'.

Smith, of course, did not approach history with Marxist preconceptions of a dialectical process. He did not, for instance, have any clear convictions concerning the 'inevitability' of the exploitation of one 'class' by another. Smith's 'vision' of economic history was in fact quite different. Whereas Marx asserted that: 'The only moving forces which political economy recognizes are the *lust for gain* and the *war between seekers after gain*, competition . . .', Smith's whole emphasis was upon the claim that the emerging free-market economy provided a means for *mutual* gain; the vastly improved productivity of the division of labour was to the benefit of all classes; the effect was not to destabilize, but to 'cordialize' society.

It is common knowledge that Smith's statement that capital is 'a certain command over all the produce of labour' was misinterpreted by Marx. Smith, of course, was using labour as a measure of value, not as the exclusive source of it. Smith's failure to distinguish adequately for his readers between these two fundamental concepts was, as is well known, the source of this classic confusion. If he had simply pointed out that, conceptually, one could equally have reversed the analysis and spoken of labour 'commanding' capital, the Marxian interpretation would have been deprived of its basis. Nevertheless, in Smith's defence, any ordinary reading of *The Wealth of Nations* does not encourage any literal interpretation of the idea of the 'command', that is the idea of *personal power* of the owner of one factor over the owner of another. The division of labour provided *mutual* benefits to the scarce factors (of which labour was one). The market in the proper sense also provided *mutual* command. All factors received incomes. These would be spent upon (command), or be measured in, labour, corn, or capital. 'It is the great multiplication of the production of all the different arts, in consequence of the division of labour, which occasions, in a well-governed society, that universal opulence which *extends itself to the lowest ranks of the people*.'[5] Each worker supplies his fellows with 'what they have occasion for' and in turn 'they accommodate him as amply with what he has occasion for', and a general plenty diffuses itself *through all the different ranks of society* (WN I.i.10, italics provided).

In Smith's system therefore the worker does not suffer 'powerlessness' alienation, at least not in an acute sense of feeling himself to be at the mercy of a wage-exploiting employer. If one can speak of any subordination in Smith's economic system it is not to any one social group but to the consumer. There is no complaint in Smith that such subordination is undignified, unnatural, or alienating; for all individuals, even the humblest, are consumers, and in the absence of monopoly (and monopoly was conquerable) consumers are kings. Smith explains (in his second chapter) that the capitalist division of labour arises naturally from a propensity in human nature (whatever the class) to truck, barter, and exchange. This is in turn linked, it is true, to self-interest; but this is not the self-interest of one factor or class exclusively. Smith's conclusions concerning the long-run trend of wages under capitalism did not support the view that workers were 'powerlessly' facing 'inevitable' exploitation either in the quantitative or the qualitative (unhappiness) sense. So long as the national income was increasing, as it would be if the division of labour was being encouraged,

[5] *The Wealth of Nations,* Cannan edition, 1950, I.i.10. All further references will be to this edition. In the early draft of *The Wealth of Nations* the equivalent of this sentence contains the additional phrase '. . . notwithstanding the great inequalities of property . . .' It is also followed by an additional sentence: 'So great a quantity of every thing is produced, that there is enough both to gratify the slothful and oppressive profusion of the great, and at the same time abundantly to supply the wants of the citizen and peasant.' W. R. Scott, *Adam Smith as Student and Professor* (1937), 331.

the possibility of the decline or even the stagnation of wages was unlikely:

It deserves to be remarked, perhaps, that it is in the progressive state, while the society is advancing to the further acquisition, . . . that the condition of the labouring poor, of the great body of the people, *seems to be the happiest and the most comfortable* . . . The progressive state is in reality *the cheerful and hearty state to all the different orders of the society.*

(WN I.viii.43, italics supplied)

Certainly Smith indicated the *possibility* of (quantitative) wage exploitation. But this was exploitation in the sense of J. B. Clark and A. C. Pigou—the use of *relative* bargaining power superiority by the employers. Even this possibility, however, was remote. When the economy was growing, 'proper' wage levels were constantly being reached because of competitive bidding up of wages: 'The scarcity of hands occasions a competition among masters, who bid against one another, in order to get workmen, and thus voluntarily break through the natural combination not to raise wages' (WN I.viii.17). Smith supported his analysis with numerous pieces of evidence to show that wages had been rising 'in the course of the present century'.

Not only is there abundant evidence to show how Smith believed that labour 'commanded' capital no less than vice versa, that the factors 'are mutually the servants of one another' (WN III.i.4), he also clearly shows that 'skilled', as distinct from 'common', labourers were in a sense 'capitalists' in that they owned human capital.[6] Marxian writing, of course, is resistant to such a notion. To Marx the important class division between capital and non-capital was between the hiring and non-hiring propensities of the factors.[7] Smith's general emphasis upon the idea of private property in labour-skill seems nevertheless indicative that in his view 'powerlessness' at least in the sense of quantitative exploitation was not an inevitable feature of capitalism. Smith believed in a legal framework wherein all forms of private property could enter the market for private gain. Labour, whether skilled or unskilled, was one form of private property. 'The patrimony of a poor man lies in the strength and dexterity of his hands; and to hinder him from employing this strength and dexterity in what manner he thinks proper without injury to his neighbour is a plain violation of this most sacred property' (WN I.x.c.12).

[6] 'When an expensive machine is erected, the extraordinary work to be performed by it before it is worn out, it must be expected, will replace the capital laid out upon it, with at least the ordinary profits. A man educated at the expense of much labour and time in any of those employments which require extraordinary dexterity and skill, may be compared to one of those machines. The work which he learns to perform, it must be expected, over and above the usual wages of common labour, will replace to him the whole expense of his education; with *at least* the ordinary profits of an equally valuable capital' (WN I.x.b.6, italics supplied).

[7] In any case in Marxian analysis the mass of workers would become unskilled as capitalism progressed.

2 *Isolation*

There is no evidence to show that Smith believed that the 'detail workers' of capitalism felt isolated. Smith's *Theory of Moral Sentiments*, published in 1759, certainly emphasized that man was a social animal; the companionship of his fellows acting as 'impartial spectators' provided the central and natural guide to his personal conduct and moral development. But the propensity to barter and exchange, leading as it did to the division of labour under one roof, worked towards, not against, the direction of social intercourse. Such communion provided men with the 'impartial spectators' which they needed as a 'mirror' of their actions. The whole process was thus a coherent, positive, and constructive social process which led not into but out of a condition of isolation.

The view that the division of labour is a socially and culturally disintegrating force seems to have had the predominant attention of the twentieth-century scholars. It is perhaps too easily forgotten that alternative assessments were made in the eighteenth century. Joseph Priestley, James Harris, and John Maxwell for instance all argued that the division of labour promoted social cohesion. Adam Smith seems to have had much in common with these writers despite the views of some of his Scottish contemporaries such as Ferguson to the contrary.[8]

3 *Self-estrangement*

So far our examination of Smith has revealed not blame but enthusiastic praise for the market and the division of labour. We now come to his one complaint, and one which we think can only be fitted (if at all) under the heading of self-estrangement alienation. In Book V of *The Wealth of Nations* Smith reviews the proper obligation of the Sovereign. One of these duties, he argues, is to subsidize the education of the people. Ordinary people, he claims, cannot be expected to spend enough on education because the division of labour prevents them from being sufficiently appreciative of its benefits. Education is the necessary antidote to the culturally unpromising environment of the division of labour. The psychological environment is described by Smith in one outstanding passage which we shall refer to as the 'alienation passage'.

In the progress of the division of labour, the employment of the far greater part of those who live by labour, that is, of the great body of the people, comes to be confined to a few very simple operations, frequently to one or two. But the understandings of the greater part of men are necessarily formed by their employments. The man whose life is spent in performing a few simple operations, of

[8] See Milton M. Myers, 'Division of Labour as a Principle of Social Cohesion', *Canadian Journal of Economics and Political Science*, xxxiii, no. 3 (Aug. 1967), 432. Myers includes Smith among the eighteenth-century writers, who maintained that the division of labour created mutual need and therefore social cohesion.

which the effects too are perhaps always the same, or very nearly the same, has no occasion to exert his understanding or to exercise his invention in finding out expedients for removing difficulties which never occur. He naturally loses, therefore, the habit of such exertion and generally becomes as stupid and ignorant as it is possible for a human creature to become. The torpor of his mind renders him not only incapable of relishing or bearing a part in any rational conversation, but of conceiving any generous, noble or tender sentiment, and consequently of forming any just judgement concerning many even of the ordinary duties of private life.

(WN V.i.f.50)

This is almost the only reference to an alienation-type process in the whole of *The Wealth of Nations* and it is the one which Marx quotes in *Capital*. Before we try to assess it it will be necessary to look at the passage in the perspective of Smith's total writing.

There are in other parts of *The Wealth of Nations* isolated references to the psychological and cultural consequences of the division of labour that do not seem to sit comfortably with the alienation passage. Thus in Book I he argues that workers become 'slothful and lazy' *without* the division of labour; compare this with his claim in the alienation passage that they become 'stupid and ignorant' with it. Again, whereas in the very opening sentence of *The Wealth of Nations* Smith maintains that 'The greatest improvement in the productive powers of labour, and the greater part of the skill, dexterity and judgement with which it is anywhere directed, or applied, seem to have the effects of the division of labour', in the alienation passage he contends that the division of labour causes the worker to become 'torpid'. It is not impossible, of course, to conceive of persons who are men of energy, dexterity, and judgement at their trade but display slothfulness, stupidity, and ignorance elsewhere. The picture, however, seems to be an uneasy one.

Again, in Book I Smith asserts that the effect of the division of labour in encouraging exclusive concentration on one object makes workers 'much more likely to discover easier and readier methods of attaining that object'; whereas in Book V he argues that when a man in the division of labour performs only a few operations he has not occasion 'to exercise his invention in finding out expedients'. It is true that Smith argued that with the progress of the division of labour invention would itself become specialized; the 'quantity of science' would be increased when those employed in philosophy or 'speculation' became specialist inventors. His writing does not, however, give us the clear impression (as does that of Marx) that he meant that *all* invention would become thus compartmentalized to the exclusion of any inventive improvement by workers. All that Smith states is that some philosophers were already inventing and that philosophy would eventually become subdivided. Smith's approach was at all times pragmatic. His views on invention would seem to be best represented by the statement in his Glasgow lectures: 'We have not, nor cannot have, any complete history of the invention of machines, because most of them are at first imperfect and receive gradual improvements and increase of powers from those who use them' (LJ (B) 217; Cannan, 167).[9]

In *The Wealth of Nations,* the main encouragement for the division of labour was the typical disposition of men 'to truck, barter, and exchange'. Throughout his *Theory of Moral Sentiments* Smith reveals clearly his beliefs not only that the proper destiny of man was to be civilized, reasonable, independent, and dignified, but also that the growth of specialization and exchange was consistent with such human development in that it conformed with the important human virtue of prudence. There was no question here of being self-estranged. The propensity to exchange was in turn probably 'a necessary consequence of the faculties of reason and speech'. 'It is common to all men, and to be found in no other race of animals which seem to know neither this nor any other species of contracts' (WN I.ii.2).

In *The Wealth of Nations* the ultimate source of man's disposition to exchange, however, is his self-love; reason and speech are intermediate aids. It has been a common error of many of Smith's critics to equate 'self-love' with 'selfishness' and it is this false equation which has led many to conclude that this book is in opposition to the *Moral Sentiments*. In fact the self-love of both books consistently implies not a hostile antisocial trait but a simple, constructive, and common-sense prudence; it is not the vice of greed but the virtue of economy. Smith's division of labour which is the eventual corollary and servant of this basic human motivation needs to be seen in this same perspective.

In the progress of society the increasing ability of its poorest members to exchange and to overcome poverty by participating in the division of labour enabled them to improve their stature and to move away from an animal-like existence. From this point of view the process led to greater *potential* dignity, and certainly not to greater humility; self-love, with the aid of developing reason and speech, implies growing *self-respect*. When an animal wants to obtain something either of a man or another animal,

> . . . it has no other means of persuasion but to gain the favour of those whose service it requires. A puppy fawns upon its dam, and a spaniel endeavours by a thousand attractions to engage the attention of its master who is at dinner, when

[9] For further analysis of Smith's 'contradictory' views on the division of labour see E. G. West: 'Adam Smith's Two Views on the Division of Labour', *Economica* (Feb. 1964). For a later and different interpretation see N. Rosenberg, 'Adam Smith on the Division of Labour: Two Views or One?' Our brief comments above are in reply to Rosenberg's main point which is that Smith had a 'Marxist-type' view of an ultimately clear demarcation between an inventing class and the rest of society. For a more detailed reply see E. G. West, 'Adam Smith and Alienation: A Rejoinder', *Oxford Economic Papers* (June 1975).

it wants to be fed by him. Man sometimes uses the same arts with his brethren, and when he has no other means of engaging them to act according to his inclinations, endeavours by every servile and fawning attention to obtain their goodwill. In civilized society he stands at all times in need of the co-operation and assistance of great multitudes . . .

(WN I.ii.2)

Smith goes on to explain that a worker secures this assistance of his fellows in such civilized society from the vantage-point of independence, not from a position of servility. There is no protest, as there is in Marx, that work is *forced* labour. The offer of the best value of one's work in exchange for another's services was made willingly in an atmosphere of independent self-respect and prudent exchange.

Give me that which I want, and you shall have this which you want, is the meaning of every such offer; and it is in this manner that we obtain from one another those good offices we stand in need of . . . It is not from the benevolence of the butcher, the brewer, or the baker that we expect our dinner . . . *Nobody but a beggar chooses to depend chiefly upon the benevolence of his fellow-citizens.*

(WN I.ii.2, italics supplied)

It may be objected that these remarks of Smith referred to what Marx called the 'petty mode of production' and did not take full cognizance of the effects of the division of labour in its new, more mature, nineteenth-century setting—the factory system. However, Smith's remarks (see the last three quotations), which come from his second chapter, follow immediately upon his enthusiastic example of the pin factory (in chapter 1).

Smith's alienation passage has also to be set side by side with his contention that in 'the progressive state', by which he meant the state in which there is growth via the development of the division of labour, the condition 'of the labouring poor, of the great body of people, seems to be the happiest . . .' The 'progressive state' was the 'cheerful and hearty state to all the different orders of society'.

Smith, the eighteenth-century man of letters, approached the task of writing his book from several directions, and from different disciplines. Generous tolerance is usually awarded to such broad and inductive work provided that, on the whole, it provides, as *The Wealth of Nations* does indeed provide, over-all stimulus and illuminating insight. Although Smith may have been the first British writer to observe that the division of labour could degrade labour this was in fact a very popular eighteenth-century proposition which was also discussed by contemporaries such as Ferguson, Millar, and Wallace. Smith, moreover, would have been well acquainted with the French developments of the Lockean belief that 'environment makes the man' in the fashionable intellectual salons of Paris during his continental tour in the 1760s. His personal acquaintance with Helvetius might especially have demonstrated the prominence of this line of reasoning among the influential intelligentsia of the day. How far the incorporation of such striking views, or the psychological effects of the factory environment, into his major work was seen by him as no more than a contemporary and perhaps modish piece of authorship and how far he attached different weights to his economic compared with his sociological approach to the subject of the division of labour must remain open to question.

Obviously, there are very important differences between Smith's and Marx's treatment of alienation. Smith gives no evidence that he thinks his worker *feels*, or will one day awaken to the feeling of, estrangement or misery. The separation from the ownership of the means of production does not appear as a serious problem. Neither does Smith show that the worker is worried because of an inability to influence general managerial policies. The workers themselves, according to him, are happy and enjoying increased opulence in the progressive division of labour society (see again WN I.viii.43, quoted above p. 233). In his 'alienation passage' Smith seems in fact to be giving us no more than his own impressionistic view of what the workers are like in the factories together with his own personal view of what they 'ought' to be like.[10]

One further important point substantially excludes Smith from the use of a Marxian-type alienation concept. To Marx, self-estrangement stemmed largely from the fact that the capitalist division of labour forced the worker into activities which were not in accordance with his 'natural gifts'; in Marx's case the worker was transformed into a 'monster', a 'cripple' because he was 'rendered incapable of following his natural bent'. Smith, on the other hand, did not think that there was much in the notion of 'natural bents'. Displaying the eighteenth-century belief in the influence of nurture over nature he argued:

The difference of natural talents in different men is, in reality, much less than we are aware of; and the very different genius which appears to distinguish men of different professions, when grown up to maturity, is not upon many occasions so much the cause, as the effect of the division of labour. The difference between the most dissimilar characters, between a philosopher and a common street porter, for example, seems to arise not so much from nature, as from habit, custom, and education.

(WN I.ii.4)

Smith would thus not have favoured the Marxian-type argument that there were, for example, street porters who, because 'nature' had intended them

[10] It is noteworthy that in the 1828 edition of *The Wealth of Nations* the editor, McCulloch (see p. 211), is indignant at Smith's snap judgement about factory workers. He challenges the master's 'alienation' passage by maintaining an opposite view, i.e. that the division of labour has mentally and culturally *stimulating* effects upon factory employees and contrasts non-factory (country) workers unfavourably with them.

to be, for example, philosophers, were consciously or subconsciously frustrated or 'self-estranged'.

Our final judgement of the 'alienation' passage starts with the observation that Smith's alienation refers only to the workers—those whose employment is 'confined to a very few simple operations'. There is no argument, as there is in Marx, that the capitalists are also alienated and that humanity 'as a whole' suffers injury. Marx's alienation is universal, all-embracing, and uncompromising. It is present in the very beginnings of the market system, in the existence of property, and in the process of barter and exchange. Smith's alienation on the contrary does not have its seeds in the market system, in private property, or in competition. It is confined to one manifestation of capitalism—the factory system—and to one type of participant—the worker. The latter was involved in only one of the several categories of the division of labour that Smith outlined in the first three chapters of *The Wealth of Nations*. Smith's division of labour embraces not only process and occupational specialization within an enterprise but also specialization between firms and areas. It seems clear that his 'cultural' objection to it was only a matter of degree. Agriculture was experiencing the growing application of the division of labour but since it was not possible to split it into so many parts as in manufacturing there was, Smith tells us, no similar cultural threat.

One of the products of Smith's division of labour, 'the philosophers or men of speculation, whose trade it is not to do anything but to observe every thing; and who upon that account, are often capable of combining together the powers of the most distant and dissimilar objects', seems to have met with his fullest approval on all counts, cultural as well as economic. The professional inventors or philosophers, indeed, reached unprecedented bounds of human fulfilment since they enjoyed to the full all the stimulus of Wonder, Surprise, and Admiration. If these individuals could be placed in positions of some special responsibility, human character throughout the rest of society could be strengthened and safeguarded. Smith concedes that in the 'rude society' each person has such varied occupations that his attention is constantly maintained and 'drowsy stupidity' avoided; every man indeed was a warrior and a statesman capable of forming 'a tolerable judgement concerning the interest of the society'. But in the rude society, and here comes one of the key points in Smith's final judgement: '*no man* can well acquire that improved and refined understanding, which a few sometimes possess in a more civilized state' (WN V.i.f.51, italics supplied). This statement is pivoted upon what seems to have been a subsequently neglected cautionary observation in Smith. This observation can be described as a theory of compensating variety: 'Though in a rude society there is a good deal of variety in the occupations of every individual, *there is not a great deal in those of the whole society*. Every man does, or is capable of doing, almost everything which any other man does, or is capable of doing. Every man has a considerable degree of knowledge, ingenuity, and invention; *but scarce any man has a great degree*' (ibid., italics supplied). Smith continues with the observation that while in primitive societies this little but commonly possessed degree of knowledge is 'generally sufficient for conducting the whole simple business of society',

In a civilised state, on the contrary, though there is little variety in the occupations of the greater part of individuals, there is an almost infinite variety in those of the whole society. These varied occupations present an almost infinite variety of objects to the contemplation of those few, who, being attached to no particular occupation themselves have leisure and inclination to examine the occupations of other people. The contemplation of so great a variety of objects necessarily exercises their minds in endless comparisons and combinations, and renders their understandings, in an extraordinary degree, both acute and comprehensive (Ibid.)

Smith seems to have been cautiously hopeful about the prospects of such 'philosophers' communicating their new knowledge and excitement to others through the medium of specially devised institutions. Provided that the intellectual delight of contemplation could be shared throughout society, order, contentment, fulfilment, and the pursuit of excellence would be ensured for all. The special curriculum of the state-aided education that Smith actually proposes is fully consistent with these scientific and intellectual aspirations. Besides the three R's he advocated 'the elementary parts of geometry and mechanics' (WN V.i.f.55), and would therefore 'gradually exercise and improve the common people in those principles, the necessary introduction to the most sublime as well as to the most useful sciences' (ibid.). Smith's reformed or unalienated state therefore is both utilitarian (in the setting of 'trades') and 'sublime'. Smith's man sees his hopes of human fulfilment in the future; he is exhilarated by 'modern' scientific curiosity and therefore must constantly be fed with new knowledge; such knowledge meanwhile is more likely to pour forth in the dynamic world of commerce and competition. Wealth was hardly enjoyed as a thing in itself; it was often no more than the by-product of the restless energy which man was destined to satisfy.

Man was made for action, and to promote by the exertion of his faculties such changes in the external circumstances both of himself and others, as may seem most favourable to the happiness of all. He must not be satisfied with indolent benevolence, nor fancy himself the friend of mankind, because in his heart he wishes well to the prosperity of the world. That he may call forth the whole vigour of his soul, and strain every nerve, in order to produce those ends which it is the purpose of his being to advance, nature has taught him, that neither himself nor mankind can be fully satisfied with his conduct . . . unless he has actually produced them.
(TMS II.iii.3.3)

XV

The Treatment of the Principles of Public Finance in *The Wealth of Nations*

ALAN PEACOCK*

I

ONE of the direct consequences of the dominance of positive economics in contemporary economic training and research has been a sharp increase in the opportunity cost of including the history of economic thought as part of the equipment of the 'compleat economist'. In the specialized area of public finance, decline in scholarly interest in the work of past masters was arrested, it is true, by the inspiration derived from the pioneer work of Wicksell, Lindahl, and some Italian writers which led to the development of the modern theory of public goods,[1] but this may only be the exception, although an outstanding one, which proves the rule. The scant references to the work of the classical economists in textbooks and treatises have now a ritualistic air about them, and the days when it was felt necessary to devote a chapter to discussion of the Smithian 'canons of taxation' have gone.

If professional judgement of public financiers avers that Adam Smith requires no more than a passing mention, what purpose is served by an exegesis and commentary on the relevant sections of *The Wealth of Nations*? No *vade mecum* is needed for those simply interested in intellectual history, for there are his views set out, crystal clear, in Book V of his masterpiece. From time to time, the economics profession renews its interest in the history of economic thought because of some remarkable discovery, such as the Overstone papers, or some extraordinary feat of literary detection, such as the identification by Professor Fetter of the authorship of articles on economics in the various nineteenth-century reviews. I have no such major discoveries to report and my incursions into scholarly sleuthing[2] produced no results of any consequence.

* Professor of Economics at the University of York. The author is a member of the Public Sector Studies Group, University of York, which is supported by a programme grant of the SSRC. I am grateful for this support, and also for comments from Collison Black, Tony Culyer, Andrew Skinner, and Donald Winch.

[1] See the frequent references in public finance literature to their work which is translated in Musgrave and Peacock, *Classics in the Theory of Public Finance* (1958).

[2] According to Rae, *Life of Adam Smith* (1895), Smith's period of office as a Commissioner of Customs and Excise from 1781 until his death was characterized by punctilious

Perhaps sufficient reason for reappraisal is to be found in the shortcomings of 'positive economics' itself as a framework for the discussion of the public finances. The analytical skills which positive economics develops, important though they are, do not train us to identify problems of interest and significance in economic policy. Nor do they necessarily help to develop the talent for devising workable economic institutions and instruments (such as new forms of taxation and methods of expenditure control) adapted to policy requirements.

The Wealth of Nations is a compelling advertisement for an approach to public finance which avoids the arid scholasticism often associated with the analytical refinements of positive economics and a narrow outlook which can even on occasion lead to methodological error. I hope to show in this contribution that Adam Smith treated issues in public finance which receive close attention in the current literature with a good deal more sophistication than is often found today. Inevitably, the development of this thesis calls for a selective treatment of his views,[3] and those who would do full justice to them will find no substitute for reading Smith's pithy prose for themselves.

II

An important aspect of the modern theory of public finance is its domination by Paretian welfare economics, particularly in the theory of public (social) goods. The familiar Paretian analysis indicates that, in the absence of externalities, but in the presence of competition in both the product and factor markets, an economic equilibrium can be reached which is compatible with individual consumer choice. It is easy to draw the conclusion from this analysis that the fulfilment of the Paretian assumptions, particularly the belief in the sanctity of individual choice and maintenance of competition, would create an economy fully acceptable to liberal economists in the Smithian tradition.[4] The formal model has been developed in recent years to take account of the problem that some goods have the character of 'publicness'.[5] To maximize the welfare of an individualistic society, subject

devotion to duty (*Life*, 330), but he did not appear to have developed further his ideas on public finance. A check on the records of the Customs and Excise Department and of Register House, Edinburgh, confirms this view.

[3] Clearly this contribution is incomplete, for it covers Smith's views on the effects of public finance on the allocation and distribution of resources but says little about growth and development. I believe it impossible to provide an adequate treatment of Smith's position without reference to the alternative forms of government intervention affecting development which Smith examines, e.g. usury laws, labour legislation, debt, and monetary policy. In any case, the subject is fully covered in the admirable work by S. Hollander, *The Economics of Adam Smith* (1973).

[4] That this is a false conclusion is shown in A. T. Peacock and C. K. Rowley, 'Pareto Optimality and the Political Economy of Liberalism', *Journal of Political Economy*, lxxx (1972).

[5] That is to say, goods which, using fashionable terminology, are non-excludable and

to this further condition, requires that the vertical sum of the indifference curves of each member of society is tangential to the transformation function representing the alternative production opportunities of private and public goods. To achieve Pareto optimality, all individuals would have to agree on the division of the cost of public goods which each would have to bear, and also on the amount of each public good which is to be provided. Thus arises the familiar dilemma that, as public goods can be equally enjoyed by all, there is no way in which the market can force individuals to reveal their preferences for such goods. The problem posed by this situation is to find some alternative decision-making process which individuals will all accept and which at the same time allows the Paretian optimum to be achieved.

It would take us far away from our subject to do justice to all facets of the mammoth literature on 'Pareto-relevant' decision-making processes. However, those who have followed the Wicksellian tradition have tried to devise voting systems which simulate, if they do not replicate, a perfect market. Broadly speaking, these have diverged markedly from straight 'one man one vote' systems, but have required some initial distribution of voting power, coupled with freedom to trade votes, including the payment of compensation (bribery) between voters in order to obtain majority support for particular decisions about the amount and the financing of public goods, all in the interests, it must be noted, of preserving the Paretian rule.[6]

Even with the elaborate seventeenth-century discussion of the idea of a 'social contract' before him, Smith can hardly be criticized for not deriving the proper functions of government from the tastes and preferences of individual consumers, when in his day the very notion of the basic Paretian precondition for efficient operation of the economy—perfect competition—was suspect.[7]

For Smith the important preoccupation was to devise a system of public

non-rival. Once provided to one person they are provided to all and consumption by one person does not prevent equal consumption by others. For a useful summary of public goods theory, see M. Peston, *Public Goods and the Public Sector* (1972), Ch. 2.

[6] For a perceptive analysis of these problems, see David M. Winch, 'Pareto, Public Goods and Politics', *Canadian Journal of Economics*, ii (1969).

[7] Interestingly enough, David Hume's discussion of the origin of government closes with a passage which is reminiscent of modern explanations of the need for political action to cope with the problem of indivisible services: 'Two neighbours may agree to drain a meadow which they possess in common, because it is easy for them to know each other's mind; and each must perceive that the immediate consequence of his failing in his part is the abandoning of the whole project. But it is very difficult, and indeed impossible, that a thousand persons should agree in any such action; it being difficult for them to concert in so complicated a design, and still more difficult for them to execute it; while each seeks a pretext to free himself of the trouble and expense, and would lay the whole burden on others. Political society easily remedies both these inconveniences.' See David Hume *Treatise on Human Nature* (1740), III.ii.7.

finance and other measures of public policy which did not destroy markets, either by intervention in the private economy or through the economic operations in the public economy, for the destruction of markets was incompatible with the pursuit of Smith's ultimate aim—the preservation of 'natural liberty'. Thus in a famous passage which heralds the introduction of his system of public finance, Smith writes:

All systems either of preference or restraint, therefore, being thus completely taken away, the obvious and simple system of natural liberty establishes itself of its own accord. Every man, as long as he does not violate the laws of justice, is left perfectly free to pursue his own interest his own way, and to bring both his industry and capital into competition with those of any other man, or order of men. The sovereign is completely discharged from a duty in the attempting to perform which he must always be exposed to innumerable delusions, and for the proper performance of which no human wisdom or knowledge could ever be sufficient; the duty of superintending the industry of private people, and of directing it towards the employments most suitable to the interests of the society . . .

and he adds:

According to the system of natural liberty, the sovereign has only three duties to attend to; three duties of great importance, indeed, but plain and intelligible to common understandings: first, the duty of protecting the society from the violence and invasion of other independent societies; secondly, the duty of protecting, as far as possible, every member of society from the injustice or oppression of every other member of it, or the duty of establishing an exact administration of justice; and thirdly, the duty of erecting and maintaining certain public works and certain public institutions, which it can never be for the interest of any individual, or small number of individuals, to erect and maintain, because the profit could never repay the expense of any individual or small number of individuals, though it may frequently do much more than repay it to a great society.[8]

Smith may avoid the important question, who shall decide the amount and form of government expenditure on goods and services, for there is no discussion in his work of voting systems or principles of Parliamentary control over expenditures.[9] At the same time, his range of interests extends to questions which are hardly touched on in books on public finance, even those in which the theory of public goods is regarded as no more than a point of departure for discussion of practical issues. Thus the 'polar case' of indivisibility is seen by Smith as the exception rather than the rule, and he seeks other, equally cogent, reasons for market failure as the basis for public provision of goods. He does not fall into the trap of assuming that 'public-

[8] Adam Smith, *The Wealth of Nations*, IV.ix.51. All references are to the (fifth) Cannan edition, reprinted by Methuen and Co., 1961.

[9] This point is considered further in section VI below.

ness' of goods makes the case for public production, as distinct from public *finance* of goods and service by the state. Finally, he is conscious of the need to ensure that in cases where public production is inevitable, some attempt must be made to simulate market conditions in order to prevent inefficiency.

We can illustrate Smith's eclectic approach by looking at each of the 'three duties' which are laid out in the quotation above. Smith accepts that defence is a pure public good in the Samuelsonian sense, but this fact does not rule out the possibility that defence can be provided by voluntary action or imply that it necessarily requires public organization of the production of defence. Smith lays considerable emphasis on the 'state of society' as the important determinant of the form of defence provision. Thus during the second 'stage' of economic development, represented by pastoral communities,[10] the common pastimes, such as wrestling, cudgel playing, etc., develop complementary skills for conduct of warfare. Furthermore,

> when a Tartar or Arab actually goes to war, he is maintained by his own herds and flocks which he carries with him, in the same manner as in peace. His chief or sovereign . . . is at no sort of expense in preparing him for the field; and when he is in it, the chance of plunder is the only pay which he either expects or requires.
>
> (WN V.i.a.4)

With the development of technical changes in weapons, not only does defence production become more capital intensive, but specialized skills have to be developed which are no longer complementary with alternative occupations. But, during the very period when improvements in agriculture and manufacture—the third stage—are taking place, resulting in economic progress which excites the jealousy of neighbours and provokes invasion, the 'natural habits of the people render them altogether incapable of defending themselves' (WN V.i.a.15) because of the high opportunity cost of voluntary engagement in learning the new arts of war. It is at this stage that the state has to choose between enforcing military exercise through the creation of a militia or taxing the community in order to finance a standing army. Adam Smith arrives at the conclusion that the second alternative of 'public production of defence' is to be preferred, not because defence is a public good, but because, following the principle of division of labour, a standing army is more efficient. Furthermore, contrary to the contemporary republican belief that a standing army is a danger to liberty, Smith argues that the 'degree of liberty which approaches licentiousness can be tolerated only in countries where the sovereign is secured by a well-regulated

[10] For a detailed analysis of Smith as a student of the stages of the development of society, see Meek, 'Smith, Turgot and the Four Stages Theory', *History of Political Economy*, iii (1972).

standing army' (WN V.i.a.41),[11] that is to say the important public good 'liberty' can only be secured when an army firmly under government control has no rival domestic producers to contend with. As a tailpiece to his discussion, he predicts that defence becomes progressively more expensive as society advances in civilization. Technically more effective weapons not only escalate the cost of war and training costs in peace,[12] but, more important still, require the development of more expensive fortification of towns to counteract the employment of those same weapons by actual or potential enemies.

The mode of discharge of the 'second duty', the administration of justice, likewise cannot be explained solely by the necessity of making it equally available to all. The prima facie case for public production of justice rests on the poor quality of private production. Resolution of disputes over property rights can sometimes be decided by private arbitration, but to make the administration of all justice depend on private enterprise could lead to abuse. For, as Smith puts it:

> The person who applied for justice with a large present in his hand was likely to get something more than justice, while he who applied for it with a small one, was likely to get something less. Justice might be too frequently delayed, in order that this present might be repeated. The amercement, besides, of the person complained of, might frequently suggest a very strong reason for finding him in the wrong, even when he had not really been so.
>
> (WN V.i.b.14)

However, if 'quality control' is made possible only by making it impossible to buy justice, there remains for Smith, as for several important eighteenth-century liberal thinkers, one significant difficulty in turning production over to the state, how to prevent justice from being 'sacrificed to what is vulgarly called politics', for

> The persons entrusted with the great interests of the state may, even without any corrupt views, sometimes imagine it necessary to sacrifice to those interests the rights of a private man. But upon the impartial administration of justice depend the liberty of every individual, the sense which he has of his own security. In order to make every individual perfectly secure in the possession of every right which belongs to him, it is not only necessary that the judicial should be separated from the executive power, but that it should be rendered as much as possible independent of that power.
>
> (WN V.i.b.25)

[11] For a fuller analysis of the distinction between 'publicness' of goods and 'public provision of goods', with particular reference to defence, see Francesco Forte, 'Should Public Goods be Public?', *Papers on Non-Market Decision Making*, viii (1967).

[12] 'The powder, which is spent in a modern review, is lost irrecoverably, and occasions a very considerable expense. The javelins and arrows which were thrown or shot in an ancient one, could easily be picked up again, and were besides of very little value' (WN V.i.a.43).

Such a view is hardly exceptional in eighteenth-century liberal writing, but what is interesting are the institutional methods which Smith considered might give it practical expression. Thus courts might be financed largely by fees without danger of corruption, with judges paid by piece-work—and in arrear to make them diligent![13] But, as Smith realizes, defining the 'piece' is not easy, and instances how judges in some countries, whose emoluments were regulated by the number of pages they had occasion to write in court, easily found it possible to 'multiply words beyond all necessity'. He wonders whether freedom from executive power could be ensured by payment out of, say, the income of landed property managed by the courts themselves, but concludes that: 'The necessary instability of such a fund seems, however, to render it an improper one for the maintenance of an institution which ought to last for ever' (WN V.i.b.23).

If Smith's discussion of ear-marking sources for revenue for judicial services outside the control of the executive and legislature is tentative, he is unwilling to go any further than to admit that defraying the expenses of justice out of general taxation would involve no 'impropriety' (in WN V.i.c).

The discussion of the 'third' duty—the provision of certain public works and institutions—is often instanced as giving the lie to the charge that Smith was a proponent of *laissez-faire*.[14] The charge, of course, is false, but it must be noted that he is unimpressed by the view that such services as the transport system (and particularly canals), health, education, might be run by government departments, and is very careful in his examination of the nature and amount of general revenue which should be assigned to the support of the organizations which operate them. The only public service of a mercantile character which Smith believes can be successfully run by a government department is the Post Office because 'there is no mystery in the business. The returns are not only certain, but immediate.'[15]

In the important case of transport systems, for example, Smith anticipates modern discussion. The State has to provide finance for the building of roads and must supervise financial methods for their maintenance and

[13] 'By not being paid to the judges until the process was determined, [fees] might be some incitement to the diligence of the court in examining and deciding it. In courts which consisted of a considerable number of judges, by proportioning the share of each judge to the hours and days which he had employed in examining the process . . . public services are never better performed than when their reward comes only in consequence of their being performed' (WN V.i.b.20). Smith observes immediately after this quotation that a system of this sort operated in the France of his day.

[14] See the notable attack on those who have so labelled Smith and his followers, by Lionel Robbins, *The Theory of Economic Policy in English Classical Political Economy* (1952), Lecture 1.

[15] There is some doubt in Smith's exposition about the exact role of the state in the production of primary education and of certain recreational facilities, but I am inclined to agree with Stigler that the Post Office is the only case where government *management* is specifically mentioned. 'Smith's travels on the Ship of State', above, 237.

improvement, because of the external benefits which would not otherwise be captured if roads were left to individual enterprise. This familiar argument is supplemented by the observation that roads break down local monopolies, in itself a further benefit to the economy, and hence their development will require state encouragement in order to overcome the opposition of interest groups.[16]

In the search for principles of operation for common transport policies, the EEC Commission have suggested that transport systems should be operated independently of the government budget, but subject to pricing rules based on the marginal cost principle which, broadly speaking, would require transport authorities to charge vehicles differentially according to their use of the system, taking account of the social costs, e.g. congestion costs, which they impose on others.[17] These ground rules may take a lot of swallowing by UK government officials, but find more than an echo in *The Wealth of Nations*, Book V. Smith rejects the proposition that revenue from tolls should be made to operate 'as a very great resource which might at some time or other be applied to the exigencies of the state', for 'the turnpike tolls being continually augmented in this manner, instead of facilitating the inland commerce of the country, as at present, would soon become a very great incumbrance upon it' (WN V.i.d.12). The national system should be operated by trustees, whereas local street paving and lighting should be conducted by local public authorities and financed by local taxes because the benefits of such services are specific to inhabitants of the locality. The trustees should be instructed to charge vehicles exactly in proportion to the wear and tear they inflict on the system. It is at this juncture that Smith makes specific mention of tax shifting. The tax or toll is 'advanced' by the carrier, though the consumer bears the tax in full. But the *net* benefit to the consumer, it is argued, is positive for the provision of roads lower the 'expense of carriage' so that the price of the goods bought, even after allowing for the toll, is lower than it would otherwise be. Even if such a result rests on special assumptions which are not explored by Smith, the argument shows a ready appreciation of a cost-benefit approach (WN V.i.b.4).

The problem of maintaining incentives in non-market-oriented activities which are provided directly by the state or supported by public funds is one of the dominating themes of that part of the 'third duty' which is concerned with 'public institutions', now termed the problem of avoiding 'X-

[16] 'Though they introduce some rival commodities into the old market, they open up many new ones to its produce. Monopoly, besides, is a great enemy to good management, which can never be universally established but in consequence of that free and universal competition which forces everybody to have recourse to it for the sake of self-defence' (WN I.xi.b.5).

[17] See EEC Commission 'Draft Decision on Common System of Charging for Transport Infrastructure' (1971).

inefficiency'. Smith is primarily interested in the case where, following the usual arguments for under-provision of a service through the market, the state supports, say, educational and religious institutions by some form of endowment or earmarked revenue such as income from state properties or the yield of a particular tax. We have already reviewed his suggestions for regulating the payment to judges, and his views on the economics of education are treated elsewhere in this volume by Mark Blaug.[18] Here we only review Smith's treatment of a familiar dilemma in public expenditure control. If the state allocates funds to higher and secondary education establishments which represent the bulk of their income, the 'discipline of colleges and universities is in general contrived, not for the benefit of the students, but for the interest, or more properly speaking, for the ease of the masters' (WN V.i.f.15). But unless the state combines such a system of public finance with detailed control and supervision of the institutions concerned, ignorant administrators with wide discretion may at best exercise ineffective control and, at worst, act in an arbitrary and capricious manner. Nothing is more likely to degrade the teaching profession, whose attention will be directed towards toadying to the government authorities. Smith never resolves the dilemma, although he is aware that he is making a powerful case for an education system financed by fees. There is much to admire here in the vigour of the prose, the wealth of illustration from both ancient and contemporary history, and the deft touches of satire, but not much practical guidance, other than for the public finance of education to be so arranged that no teacher is paid wholly from the public purse (WN V.i.f.55).

III

Having established that the optimal allocation of resources would require both some forms of public production on a limited scale, varying with the stage of development of society, and also state subsidies to private or quasi-public institutions, Smith has to consider the implications of transferring resources to the state to give effect to his public expenditure proposals. He dismisses the possibility of financing these proposals by the patrimony of the state or by state trading mainly on the grounds of their insufficiency, and turns to examine taxes.

Smith adopts a simple expository procedure in examining the tax system. First of all certain normative 'maxims' (Smith does not call them 'canons') are stated: the famous maxims of equality, certainty, convenience, and economy. Taxes are then classified into those which are *intended* to be borne by the three sources of 'private revenue', wages, profit, and rent, and those which 'fall indifferently' upon any of these three sources of private revenue. Ignoring some classificatory peculiarities of Smith, these two broad categories cover respectively taxes on incomes and

[18] See below, pp. 568–74.

taxes on expenditure. Examples of each kind of taxation are culled from the experience of several European countries as well as Britain[19] and appraised in the light of the maxims, having regard to the problem of tax shifting which complicates the appraisal procedure. What is noticeably missing from his exposition is any attempt to weight the importance of each maxim, so that no final conclusion is drawn either about the relative merits of different forms of taxation or about the 'package of taxes' which would best accord with Smith's own normative propositions. But the exposition is full of practical suggestions on the operation of particular taxes which were deservedly influential in his own time.[20] We now examine the 'maxims' more closely, and consider one important example of their application before considering a more fundamental criticism of Smith's approach.

IV

The maxim of 'equality' entails the acceptance of income as the relevant measure of tax to be paid by individuals, who in relation to the services of government are like 'joint tenants of a great estate, who are all obliged to contribute in proportion to their respective interests in the estate' (WN V.ii.b.3). That Smith meant that taxes should as far as possible be proportional to income is clear enough, but his technical examination of taxes leads him to conclude that any tax falling on subsistence wages must of necessity be shifted, so that there are good practical reasons for having an exemption limit.[21] Taking all taxes into consideration, we can define Smith's optimal tax schedule (after allowing for taxes paid and with shifting taken into account) as one in which the marginal tax rate remains constant, but the average rate would rise with income in consequence of the exemption limit: in short, a mildly progressive tax structure. Proportionality has to be modified on practical rather than on equity grounds.[22]

[19] Smith's main source of information was a remarkable book written by one Moreau de Beaumont called *Memoires concernant les droits et impositions en Europe* prepared for a commission on tax reform in France and published only for official use in 1768–9 in four volumes. The first volume gives an account of European tax systems and the remaining volumes review the French system in detail. According to Rae (*Life*, 344), Smith obtained his copy from Turgot and believed that there were only four copies available in Britain in his day. I have been able to track down only one copy publicly available which is in the British Museum.

[20] For evidence see Rae, op. cit., Chs. 18, 20, and Stephen Dowell, *History of Taxation and Taxes in England* (1884), 3rd ed. (reprinted 1965), particularly vol. 2.

[21] 'The middling and superior ranks of people, if they understood their own interest, ought always to oppose all taxes upon the necessaries of life, as well as all direct taxes upon the wages of labour' (WN V.ii.k.9).

[22] I do not deny, of course, that Smith elsewhere seems to support progressive taxation on grounds of fairness, but in no more than a passing reference which is hardly a strong plea for soaking the rich: 'It is not *very unreasonable* [italics mine] that the rich should contribute to the public expence, not only in proportion to their revenue, but something more than in that proportion' (WN V.ii.e.6). E. Seligman makes the point in *Progressive Taxation in Theory and Practice, American Economic Association Quarterly*, Third Series, ix (1908).

The remaining maxims amount to principles designed to minimize the real costs of raising revenue to the taxpayer. He must suffer as little as possible the 'psychic' costs of not knowing what he is to pay and how the amount is calculated which would have the side-effect of turning the tax system into a sordid bargain between the collector and the payer, encouraging evasion and violating the principle of 'equal treatment of equals'. Convenience of payment reduces the real costs of collection which would otherwise fall on the taxpayer. Economy in collection reduces the real costs of transferring resources for public use. Heavy administrative expenses of collection, being associated with inquisitorial examination of taxpayers, e.g. in detecting smuggling, imposes a double burden on the community, the extra costs of administration and the 'vexation' of inquiry which 'is not strictly speaking an expense, [but] is certainly equivalent to the expense at which every man would be willing to redeem himself from it' (WN V.ii.b.6).

Smith's maxims are not original, and were anticipated in earlier literature, notably by the cameralists, but Smith himself did not claim that they were:[23]

> The evident justice and utility of the foregoing maxims have recommended them more or less to the attention of all nations. All nations have endeavoured, to the best of their judgment, to render their taxes as equal as they could contrive: as certain, as convenient to the contributor, both in the time and in the mode of payment, and in proportion to the revenue which they brought to the prince, as little burdensome to the people.
>
> (WN V.ii.b.7)

But Smith's own analysis of European tax practice presents ample evidence to contradict this last sentence!

V

The application of Smith's maxims can be best understood by taking an example, and I propose to consider his extensive discussion of 'taxes on consumable commodities' (in WN V.ii.k).

For Smith the first maxim leads him to support taxes on 'luxuries', which might be defined negatively as taxes which do not impinge on subsistence which, by reducing the supply of labour, will, in the long run, raise labour's supply price, i.e. the tax will be shifted to other classes. Immediately this maxim calls for a whole range of reforms. In principle, taxes on fuel (e.g. coal), light (e.g. candles), on health (e.g. soap), on basic foodstuffs (e.g. corn), and clothing (e.g. leather) should certainly be reduced, although abolition

[23] For an excellent account of pre-Smithian tax principles and analysis of Smith's position, see Forte, 'History and Theory of Public Finance' (1972), *Bulletin of International Fiscal Documentation.*

might produce revenue difficulties. Simultaneously, subject to revenue constraints, taxes on consumable commodities should be reviewed in order to devise a system which would directly hit those of 'middling or more than middling fortune'.

Smith's reforms are not merely couched in general terms, and several taxes are examined in considerable detail, notably the taxes on beer and spirits which formed the bulk of the taxes on expenditure in his time.[24] His reform proposals in this case offer an insight into his method of tax analysis. Malt was an important input for spirits, and also for heavy beers. It was taxed as an input, and beers and spirits were separately taxed through the breweries and distilleries respectively. However, home brewing and distilling were common among richer country families who were exempt from the tax on 'output', and relatively lightly taxed on the 'input' of malt. An important administrative problem to be reckoned with was that opportunities for defrauding the revenue were greater in the brewery or distillery than in the malt-house. Smith puts forward the obvious solution, which is to increase the tax on malt and reduce the tax on brewed beer. This would benefit the poor at the expense of the rich in two ways: first of all, by lowering the price of beer with a low malt content and, secondly, by the differential increase in the price of distilled liquors bought by the rich and in the cost of home-brewed beer with a high malt content enjoyed by the country gentry. Furthermore, the alteration of the point of tax would ease the problem of evasion. Smith, however, realizes that his conclusion must take account of possible revenue loss and that what we now term the elasticity assumptions are crucial to the analysis. He circumvents this problem by recommending that the increased tax on malt should be accompanied by adjustments in the taxes on spirits and beer which would maintain the price of spirits and reduce that of beer. By assuming that all taxes are passed on to the consumer in full and that the price elasticity of demand for beer is greater than unity, he is able to conclude that revenue would in fact increase.[25] He goes further and considers how far the demand for barley, used along with malt in distilling, would be affected by tax changes, but having shown that the demand for malt would not be reduced by the tax changes, he concludes that the demand for barley would be unaffected so long as there was competition in barley production. (It does not occur to him that distillers might ever dare to alter the factor mix by

[24] For relevant data, see G. Eckstein, *Adam Smiths Finanzwissenschaft* (photocopy, Diplom-Arbeit, Universität Nürnberg–Erlangen (1967)).

[25] 'According to this policy, the abatement of taxes upon the distillery ought not to be so great as to reduce, in any respect, the price of those liquors. Spirituous liquors might remain as dear as ever; while at the same time the wholesome and invigorating liquors of beer and ale might be considerably reduced in price. The people might thus be in part relieved from one of the burdens of which they at present complain the most; while at the same time the revenue might be considerably augmented' (WN V.ii.k.50).

substituting barley for malt!)[26] In short, although the analysis is incomplete (no clear statement is made about production functions) and several assumptions are used without evidence, Smith shows his capacity for analytical rigour as well as for practical insight.

Public financiers have often speculated on the possibility of devising a system of taxes on expenditure which would be both equitable and efficient, having regard to the administrative defects of direct taxes on income.[27] Smith also gives this idea a good run for its money. With taxes geared to hit the consumption of the rich, equity is achieved, and such taxes, too, are certain in their assessment, and convenient to the taxpayer who pays as he purchases. 'Upon the whole such taxes, therefore, are, perhaps, as agreeable to the three first of the four general maxims concerning taxes, as any other' (WN V.ii.k.60). But they are expensive to administer, encouraging smuggling for example, and vexatious to those who have to face 'the frequent visits and odious examination of the taxgatherers' (WN V.ii.k.65). Much that has been written about the 'case' for taxes on expenditure is an amplification of Smith's analysis. The rock on which reform schemes have usually foundered is that of the difficulty of adapting the system so that it can take account of the characteristics of the taxpayer, other than his income level, which are relevant to equity, such as his number of dependants and the structure of his inter-temporal preference system. The definition of the tax-paying unit—whether the individual or the household—is not considered by Smith, but he makes an interesting passing reference to the inter-temporal equity problem. Thus a man of 'great fortune' in his minority consumes little, so pays little by way of taxation on expenditure, and if in later years he is parsimonious he can continue to avoid taxation. Even if he is not parsimonious, he can avoid taxation designed to finance the protection of his property by living abroad—like the Irish absentee landlords. Smith concludes that no system of taxes on luxuries will meet his first maxim, and that being so, the system must be supplemented, for example by a land-tax which would hit the rich (WN V.ii.k.58).

VI

The method which Smith adopts in formulating principles of economic policy conforms with an honourable tradition. Explicit normative judgements are made and translated into economic objectives which conform with his ultimate aim: the establishment of the system of natural liberty. Given his analysis of the economy, the instruments of policy are then identified and their tasks defined. However, it has been claimed by Stigler

[26] Lord North followed Smith's advice in 1780 by increasing the malt duty with a rebate to brewers for sale so that the pot of beer would 'reach the lip of the consumer untaxed'. See Dowell, op. cit.

[27] J. M. Buchanan and F. Forte, 'Fiscal Choice Through Time: A Case for Indirect Taxation', *National Tax Journal*, xvii (1964).

that this method of analysis cannot be legitimately employed by Smith. If the pursuit of self-interest—'the natural effort of every individual to better his condition'—is the best way of achieving wealth and prosperity, why should self-interest not be allowed to dominate their political as well as their economic actions? Commenting on Smith's famous maxims of taxation, he argues:

A Chancellor of the Exchequer would have found these rules most peculiar. If adopted, they would obtain for him at least the temporary admiration of the professors of moral philosophy but this is a slender and notably fickle constituency on which to build a party. The two basic canons of taxation are surely rather different:
1. The revenue system must not imperil the political support for the regime.
2. The revenue system must yield revenue.
Smith's maxims touch on aspects of a revenue system which are relevant to its productivity and acceptability, not always in the direction he wished, but they form a wholly inadequate basis for judging individual taxes.[28]

One can agree with Stigler that once having accepted the economic sophistication of Smithian man, there is no reason to doubt his political sophistication. Even then, Smith is quite clearly of the opinion that taxation brings with it the right of representation, and, in contrast to that formidable gentleman, Dr. Johnson, supported representation of the American colonies in the British legislature.[29] Did Smith not also say that taxation was the badge of freedom and not of servitude? But it is one thing to be employing one's commercial or political talents to promote self-interest in a society which has accepted the necessity for competition as a way of channelling self-interest towards the goals of society and another to do so under conditions where entrenched monopoly privileges abound. Thus, to re-emphasize a point made earlier, while Smith might be criticized for neglecting to discuss the implication of his system of political economy for political organization, so that individual preferences could be reflected in the amount and composition of public goods and in the structure of taxation, such concerns pale into insignificance alongside his need to persuade his fellow men that sectional commercial interests buttressed by legislation which prevented competition and created inefficient state enterprises and departments were inimical to economic and social progress.[30]

[28] Stigler, above, 243. I need hardly add that Professor Stigler is still one of Smith's most faithful admirers.

[29] Johnson's pamphlet *Taxation no Tyranny* appeared in 1775, the year before the publication of *The Wealth of Nations.* On the American question, see the article by David Stevens, above, 202.

[30] Professor Stigler himself has presented a persuasive case for preserving lower layers of government as a means of fostering competition in the provision of public services. *Federal Expenditure Policy for Economic Growth and Stability* (1957), 213–19. His fiscal prescriptions are put forward with Smithian fervour, and with an equal disregard for the need to seek the blessing of political support.

The technique of moral suasion through the exposure of ignorance and prejudice seems justified in such circumstances as Smith faced, yet Stigler contends that at best 'this is an extraordinary slow and uncertain method of changing policy; at worst it may lead to policies which endanger society'. History hardly bears out Stigler's prediction, for successive Chancellors found nothing 'peculiar' about Smith's maxims and espoused them with almost indecent haste. But the creation of a political analogue to the market system—Parliamentary democracy—did not result in such a ready acceptance of Smith's principles of public expenditure. This is a problem which still engages the energies of those, including Professor Stigler and myself, who owe so much to the man from Kircaldy.

XVI

The Economics of Education in English Classical Political Economy: A Re-Examination

MARK BLAUG*

THERE is a small but growing literature on the role of education in the doctrines of the English classical economists, most of which is unfortunately contradictory if not downright misleading.[1] Among its shortcomings is a failure to emphasize the fact that Adam Smith's important ideas on the economics of education were largely ignored by his followers and that the very topic itself was neglected until John Stuart Mill took it up again in the 1840s, only to repudiate most of Smith's analysis. In addition, the literature is prone to ancestor worship: it seems forever to be crediting early nineteenth-century authors with a modern grasp of the subject and, in particular, with the insights of what has been described as 'the human investment revolution in economic thought', namely, Schultz–Becker–Denison and all that. I shall argue, however, that classical political economy made virtually no contribution to the theory of human capital; indeed, in some respects it undermined its foundations. Lastly, the secondary literature is marred by a tendency to lose sight of the dates at which various classical writers made their educational pronouncements, almost as if the precise historical context had no bearing whatever on the views that they expressed. And yet it is only by paying attention to dates that we come to realize that the classical economists gradually adjusted their ideas on education in the wake of legislative changes; instead of having an influence on policy, policy had an influence on them. I have now said enough, I hope, to justify a re-examination of classical writings on the economic aspects and consequences of education.[2]

I ADAM SMITH AND THE REMUNERATION OF UNIVERSITY TEACHERS

When the National Board for Prices and Incomes (PIB) delivered its first report on the pay of British university teachers in 1968, it found that the salary structure was biased towards research: 'all the evidence we have

* Professor of the Economics of Education at the University of London Institute of Education.

[1] For references, see section 7, below.

[2] I take this opportunity to thank A. W. Coats, D. P. O'Brien, A. S. Skinner, and D. Winch for their helpful comments on an earlier version of this paper.

received shows that promotion tends to be awarded for research as measured by publication.'[3] To counter this bias, the PIB proposed a system of discretionary payments to those members of staff who taught either more or better than the average, where 'better' was judged at least in part by students responding to 'a carefully drafted questionnaire'.[4] Although the use of student assessments is a familiar feature of American higher education, the PIB proposal was greeted in Britain with jeers about 'gearing salaries to popularity polls' and soon came to be rejected first by the universities and then by the government. The participants in this acrimonious controversy, virtually all of whom rejected the notion of relating salaries in any way to student opinions, divided neatly into a minority who flatly denied that the quality of teaching could be objectively assessed and a majority who asserted that it was already being assessed informally by heads of department as an essential element in deciding on promotions.[5]

It must be conceded that there is in fact very little firm evidence that 'publish or perish' is the basic principle of promotion in British universities. On the other hand, casual empirical observation confirms the PIB view and one would have thought that the burden of proof is on those who deny the research bias. In any case, as soon as it is argued that the quality of teaching is actually taken into account in making promotions, it remains only to decide how to assess that quality as objectively as possible. In that case, encouraging students to express their views can only aid assessment, serving in addition as an expression of faith in their essentially sound judgement. It goes without saying, of course, that a really comprehensive judgement of teacher effectiveness would combine student assessments with tests of student learning and with assessments by colleagues.[6]

None of the contenders in this debate cited Adam Smith, although he had indeed addressed himself at some length to precisely the same problem: how should we reward teachers so as to best induce them to perform their tasks with maximum efficiency? In the fear that any summary of his argument would meet with incredulity, I cite his own words:

In some universities the salary makes but a part, and frequently but a small part, of the emoluments of the teacher, of which the greater part arises from the honoraries or fees of his pupils. . . . In other universities the teacher is prohibited from

[3] N.B.P.I., Report No. 98, *Standing Reference on the Pay of University Teachers in Great Britain*, Cmnd. 3866 (1968), 13.

[4] Ibid. 14.

[5] The majority view is well expressed by D. C. Corner and A. J. Culyer, the only British economists to have written at length on the P.I.B. Report: 'University Teachers and the P.I.B.', *Social and Economic Administration*, iii, (1969), 138–9.

[6] It is interesting to ask oneself how British university teaching is now evaluated, given the absence of student assessments and the prevailing taboo against attending a colleague's lectures: obviously, it is done, if it is done at all, by talking to students on a casual basis or by inference from a colleague's performance in a staff seminar. Is it conceivable that anyone could oppose the use of supplements to such crude devices? Apparently yes.

receiving any honorary or fee from his pupils, and his salary constitutes the whole of the revenue which he derives from his office. His interest is, in this case set as directly in opposition to his duty as it is possible to set it. It is the interest of every man to live as much at his ease as he can; and if his emoluments are to be precisely the same, whether he does, or does not perform some very laborious duty, it is certainly his interest, at least as interest is vulgarly understood, either to neglect it altogether, or, if he is subject to some authority which will not suffer him to do this, to perform it in as careless and slovenly a manner as the authority will permit. If he is naturally active and a lover of labour, it is his interest to employ that activity in any way, from which he can derive some advantage, rather than in the performance of his duty, from which he can derive none.

If the authority to which he is subject resides in the body corporate, the college, or university, of which he himself is a member, and in which the greater part of the other members are, like himself, persons who either are, or ought to be teachers; they are likely to make a common cause, to be all very indulgent to one another, and every man to consent that his neighbour may neglect his duty provided he himself is allowed to neglect his own. In the university of Oxford, the greater part of the public professors have, for these many years, given up altogether even the pretence of teaching.[7]

Clearly, this is the PIB model: although universities are not profit-making institutions, nevertheless the behaviour of university teachers as utility-maximizers gathered together in a kind of syndicalist club to pursue common ends is broadly predictable.[8] So is the behaviour of students, which Adam Smith described with a generosity rarely encountered these days among university dons:

The discipline of colleges and universities is in general contrived not for the benefit of the students, but for the interest, or more properly speaking for the ease of the masters. Its object is, in all cases, to maintain the authority of the master, and whether he neglects or performs his duty, to oblige the students in all cases to behave to him as if he performed it with the greatest diligence and ability . . . Where the masters, however, really perform their duty, there are no examples, I believe, that the greater part of the students ever neglect theirs. No discipline is ever requisite to force attendance upon lectures which are really worth the attending, as is well known wherever any such lectures are given . . . Such is the generosity of the greater part of young men, that, so far from being

[7] A. Smith, *The Wealth of Nations*, ed. E. Cannan (1937), V.i.f.6–8. Glasgow in 1776 was one of those universities where 'the salary makes but . . . a small part of the emoluments of the teacher'. Smith's own salary at Glasgow may have been £70 a year with a house, while his fees amounted to about £100. J. Rae, *Life of Adam Smith* (1895; 1965), 48–9. Several witnesses testify to Adam Smith's own pedagogic zeal: see E. G. West, *Adam Smith* (1969), 112–13.

[8] For an attempt to develop the model in a twentieth-century context see A. J. Culyer, 'A Utility-Maximising View of Universities', *Scottish Journal of Political Economy*, xvii, (Nov. 1970) and R. Layard, R. Jackman, 'University Efficiency and University Finance', *Essays in Modern Economics*, ed. M. Parkin and A. R. Mobay (1973).

disposed to neglect or despise the instructions of their master, provided he shows some serious intention of being of use to them, they are generally inclined to pardon a great deal of incorrectness in the performance of his duty, and sometimes even to conceal from the public a good deal of gross negligence.[9]

II ADAM SMITH AND THE ORGANIZATION OF EDUCATION

What distinguishes Adam Smith's views on economic development from later nineteenth-century and even twentieth-century efforts is the emphasis that he placed on the organization of economic institutions that harness the self-interests of individuals to the interests of society as a whole. He never lost sight of the fact that the remuneration of individuals working in public institutions, insulated as they are from ordinary market pressures, raises special difficulties. 'Public services', he pronounced, 'are never better performed than when their reward comes only in consequence of their being performed, and is proportioned to the diligence employed in performing them' (WN V.i.b.20). He goes on to argue, however, that to define and measure 'diligence' in a strictly quantitative sense in such fields as law, education, and the Church may create more problems than it solves; the principles that govern pay in these areas can only be guidelines of a qualitative nature. Virtually the whole of the first chapter of Book V, 'Of the Expenses of the Sovereign or Commonwealth', is taken up with the question of devising techniques for rewarding lawyers, clerks, judges, clergymen, and teachers which will force them to advance social interests even as they pursue their own interests.[10]

We have already considered Adam Smith's views on university teaching and particularly university teaching in England. The situation in the English independent schools was much better than in the universities, he believed, because 'the reward of the schoolmaster in most cases depends principally, in some cases almost entirely, upon the fees or honoraries of his scholars' (WN V.ii.f.17). On balance, however, he favoured the Scottish system: the cost of school buildings in rural parishes was met by a tax on the local heritors and tenants (in towns these costs were financed out of municipal funds); the teachers received a small fixed stipend from the same source, supplemented by private fees which frequently varied with the range of the subjects they offered to teach. 'In Scotland', he noted, 'the establishment of such parish schools has taught almost the whole common people to read, and a very great proportion of them to write and account.

[9] WN V.i.f.15. It is evident that there is a missing link in the argument. Smith assumes as a matter of course that teachers do not have exclusive control of their own examinations; if they did, the quality of teaching would justify itself, whatever it was. The system of internal and external examiners in Glasgow in the eighteenth century was not unlike that of British universities today. See G. Davie, *The Democratic Intellect. Scotland and her Universities in the Nineteenth Century* (1961), 14–25.

[10] For a brilliant exegesis of Book V, see N. Rosenberg, 'Some Institutional Aspects of *The Wealth of Nations*.' *Journal of Political Economy*, lxviii, (Dec. 1960).

In England the establishment of charity schools has had an effect of the same kind, though not so universally' (WN V.ii.f.55). Some suggestions for curriculum changes in those schools, to include geometry and mechanics,[11] and a proposal for a system of occupational licensing completed his recommendations for educational reform.[12]

Adam Smith's marked preference for private over public education is evident throughout Book V. Nor is there a hint of the argument that education can only be competently judged after it has been received and not before, which was to become so popular in the last half of the nineteenth century. On the contrary: 'Those parts of education, it is to be observed, for the teaching of which there are no public institutions, are generally the best taught . . . The three most essential parts of literary education, to read, write, and account, it still continues to be more common to acquire in private than in public schools' (WN V.ii.f.16). Nevertheless, the effects of occupational specialization are such as to deprive 'the labouring poor' of their 'intellectual, social, and martial virtues', or, in the language of today, to 'alienate' workers.[13] For that reason, state aid to education is justified and perhaps so is compulsory attendance:

For a very small expence the public can facilitate, can encourage, and can impose upon almost the whole body of the people, the necessity of acquiring those most essential parts of education ['to read, write, and account']. The public can facilitate this acquisition by establishing in every parish or district a little school, where children may be taught for a reward so moderate, that even a common labourer may afford it; the master being partly, but not wholly paid by the public; because, if he was wholly, or even principally paid by it, he would soon learn to neglect his business.

(WN V.ii.f.54–5)

Driving the argument home, Adam Smith summed up by advancing an entirely new reason for state aid to education derived from an unformulated theory of 'social control':

[11] Concern about the social and economic 'relevance' of curricula was very common in eighteenth-century Scotland: see D. J. Withrington, 'Education and Society in the Eighteenth Century', *Scotland in the Age of Improvement*, eds. N. T. Phillipson and R. Mitchison (1970).

[12] WN V.ii.f.55–7. E. G. West, drawing on a long private letter by Adam Smith, shows that Smith objected to a medical or for that matter a teaching profession confined to university graduates and he implies that Smith rejected the general principle of occupational licensing. 'Private versus Public Education. A Classical Economic Dispute', *Journal of Political Economy* (1964), reprinted in *The Classical Economists and Economic Policy*, ed. A. W. Coats (1971), 126–8. However, the wording in *The Wealth of Nations* on the licensing of mechanical trades, as distinct from the learned professions, is unambiguously favourable. See also J. Viner, 'Guide to John Rae's Life of Adam Smith', in Rae, *Life of Adam Smith*, 10–13.

[13] WN V.ii.f.50. With the exception of the invisible-hand paragraph in the second chapter of Book IV, this is perhaps the most frequently cited passage in the whole of *The Wealth of Nations*, and the commentaries on its meaning would fill several library shelves.

Though the state was to derive no advantage from the instruction of the inferior ranks of people, it would still deserve its attention that they should not be altogether uninstructed. The state, however, derives no inconsiderable advantage from their instruction. The more they are instructed, the less liable they are to the delusions of enthusiasm and superstition, which, among ignorant nations, frequently occasion the most dreadful disorders. An instructed and intelligent people besides, are always more decent and orderly than an ignorant and stupid one. They feel themselves, each individually more respectable, and more likely to obtain the respect of their lawful superiors, and they are therefore more disposed to respect those superiors. They are more disposed to examine, and more capable of seeing through, the interested complaints of faction and sedition, and they are, upon that account, less apt to be misled into any wanton or unnecessary opposition to the measures of government. In free countries, where the safety of government depends very much upon the favourable judgment which the people may form of its conduct, it must surely be of the highest importance that they should not be disposed to judge rashly or capriciously concerning it.

(WN V.ii.f.61)

The thoughts contained in this passage made a lasting impression on the members of the classical school. The rest of Smith's views on education—the role of fee-paying as an incentive device for teachers; the harmful effects of educational endowments on schools and universities; the stress on a more practical syllabus in elementary schools; the plea for a system of occupational licensing of manual trades—were soon forgotten and even the issues raised by them simply dropped out of English classical political economy.

Likewise, the brief hint at the concept of human capital in the famous chapter on relative wages in Book I, while reproduced in almost identical words in every classical text, was never developed in any substantial way by any of Smith's disciples.

When an expensive machine is erected, the extraordinary work to be performed by it before it is worn out, it must be expected, will replace the capital laid out upon it, with at least the ordinary profits. A man educated at the expence of much labour and time to any of those employments which require extraordinary dexterity and skill, may be compared to one of those expensive machines. The work which he learns to perform, it must be expected, over and above the usual wages of common labour, will replace to him the whole expence of his education, with at least the ordinary profits of an equally valuable capital.

The difference between the wages of skilled labour and those of common labour, is founded upon this principle.[14]

In modern language, this passage says that monetary rewards in any

[14] WN I.x.b.6–7; see also II.i.17 where the 'maintenance' of someone during 'his education, study or apprenticeship' is defined as 'capital fixed and realized, as it were, in his person'.

occupation must in equilibrium suffice to indemnify individuals for the costs of any education and training they have acquired. As such, it amounts not to a finished piece of analysis but rather to an invitation to examine the problem of skills differentials from a new angle. Fruitful theorizing only begins when it is recognized that such dissimilar phenomena as formal schooling, on-the-job training, the consumption of medical care, geographical migration, and the general process of job search are all essentially similar ways of investing in oneself by incurring present costs for the sake of future benefits. In some circumstances, these purely personal investments in human beings also become social investments in the quality of the labour force. A necessary but not sufficient condition for this coincidence between private and social returns is the existence of perfectly competitive labour markets. In this sense, the analysis of wage differentials, which of course constituted an essential element of classical economies, remains incomplete without an investigation of the economic value of education. But the classical economists, as we shall see, simply failed to explore the implications of a human capital view of labour supply. Adam Smith made a start; John Stuart Mill carried it a little further; and Marshall certainly began to do justice to the theme of human capital formation. Nevertheless, these three authors between them did no more than to open the door to Becker's *Human Capital* (1964), which actually constructed the foundations of the subject for the first time.

III MALTHUS AND MCCULLOCH ON STATE EDUCATION

It has been aptly observed that 'the economics of education in English classical economics could be presented as a discussion of material in the works of Adam Smith and John Stuart Mill'.[15] To be sure, Malthus, James Mill, Chalmers, McCulloch, Jones, Chadwick, Senior, Cairnes, and Fawcett, to mention only English members of the classical school, each had something to say about education. In almost every case, however, what they said consisted either of *obiter dicta* or of general but impractical pronouncements in favour of a 'national' system of education. The absence of the name of Ricardo from the list is itself revealing: the leading economist of the day never addressed himself directly to any educational question. Likewise, Torrens hardly ever mentioned education. In another context, Bentham's vast educational treatise, *Chrestomathia*, would warrant discussion and Malthus and Senior, in particular, deserve our attention if only because the former was the most widely read economist of the nineteenth century and because the latter took a leading part in several Royal Commissions which dealt with educational problems. Nevertheless, practically nothing new was added and a great deal was lost in the seventy years that

[15] W. L. Miller, 'The Economics of Education in English Classical Economics', *Southern Economic Journal*, xxxii (Jan. 1966), 294.

separate the publication of *The Wealth of Nations* from the appearance of Mill's *Principles*. In those years, Parliament launched its first tentative efforts to subsidize the education of the poor, private schooling grew by leaps and bounds to a point where most children were attending school many weeks of the year, most working-class adults having by then achieved rudimentary literacy with or without the benefit of schooling, while all the time the debate on the Religious Question—Church schools or lay schools—raged on without being resolved.[16] It is not too much to say that one can read all the great names in English classical economics without learning anything about these questions. Clearly it is not only in the twentieth century that economists have neglected the economic aspects and economic consequences of education.

The standard treatment of educational issues by early nineteenth-century economists was firmly established by Malthus in the second edition of the *Essay on Population* (1803). His remarks are characterized by an exaggerated regard for the achievements of the Scottish parochial system, a fervent but vague plea for the adoption of something like it in England, in opposition to the Tory view that popular instructions endangered the security of property,[17] and a pronounced emphasis on the tendency of education to promote self-reliance with hardly a mention of the formation of productive skills. Where Malthus goes beyond Adam Smith is in suggesting that the curriculum of elementary schools should include political economy, and particularly 'the real state of the lower classes of society, as affected by the principle of population'. This too was a point which was echoed by virtually every classical economist who ever mentioned education.[18]

Charity day schools, Sunday schools, Dame schools, and factory schools

[16] See Historical Appendix below.

[17] Malthus is known to have advised Whitbread whose Poor Law Bill of 1807 sought a national system of education incorporated in the structure of parish relief, appealing for authority chiefly to Scotland.

[18] Here at any rate they succeeded in having an impact on events. In 1821, James Mill and Bentham, among others, were instrumental in forming the Society for the Diffusion of Useful Knowledge for the express purpose of producing cheap literature for the poor, including the *Penny Magazine*, full of homely truths about political economy. See R. K. Webb, *British Working Class Reader, 1790–1848*, (1955), 85–92; M. Blaug, *Ricardian Economics*, (1958), 145–6. Then in 1833, Richard Whately published his immensely influential *Easy Lessons on Money Matters for the Use of Young People* and a year later Harriet Martineau took the reading public by storm with her *Illustrations of Political Economy*. See J. M. Goldstrom, 'Richard Whately and Political Economy in School Books, 1833–80', *Irish Historical Review*, xv (Sept. 1966); Blaug, *Ricardian Economics*, Ch. 7; R. K. Webb, *Harriet Martineau* (1960), Ch. 4; and H. Scott Gordon, 'The Ideology of Laissez Faire' in Coats, ed. *The Classical Economists and Economic Policy*, (1971), 189–97. In fact, as J. M. Goldstrom has now shown, *The Social Content of Education 1808–1870. A Study of the Working Class School Reader in England and Ireland* (1972), political economy conquered all the elementary school books in Britain between 1830 and 1860; after that date, the vogue for teaching economics to children seems to have passed away as quickly as it came.

(the latter dating from the Health and Morals of Apprentices Act of 1802) all saw a rapid growth in the first few decades of the nineteenth century and even in Scotland, as we shall see, private schooling had long ago caught up and surpassed the statutory school provision. Nevertheless, Malthus mentioned only Sunday Schools and these pages were left unrevised between the second edition of 1803 and the sixth and last edition of 1826. 'It is surely a great national disgrace', he wrote, 'that the education of the lower classes of people in England should be left merely to a few Sunday schools, supported by a subscription from individuals, who can give the course of instruction in them any kind of bias which they please. And even the improvement of Sunday schools (for objectionable as they are in some points of view, and imperfect in all, I cannot but consider them as an improvement) is of very late date.'[19] He concluded his comments by pronouncing: 'no government can approach to perfection that does not provide for the instruction of the people. The benefits derived from education are among those which may be enjoyed without restriction of numbers; and as it is in the power of government to confer these benefits, it is undoubtedly their duty to do so' (ibid. 441).

Malthus's failure to make any reference to the Religious Question, at least in the sixth edition, is somewhat surprising. The British and Foreign School Society was launched in 1814 to encourage local efforts in establishing schools that would provide non-denominational religious teaching. This came hard on the heels of the formation of the National Society for Promoting the Education of the Poor in the Principles of the Established Church Throughout England and Wales, and by the 1820s every educational issue was fought out in terms of the two rival organizations.[20] Malthus's recommendation of a public system of elementary education, without any indication of how the problem of religious teaching was to be resolved, must have meant little to his readers.

In the last chapter of the *Essay on Population*, significantly entitled 'Our Rational Expectations Respecting the Future Improvement of Society', Malthus returns to the question of education. He touches briefly on what we would now describe as one of the external effects of schooling, namely, its tendency to promote a climate of opinion conducive to family limitation, and adds: 'The practical good effects of education have long been experienced in Scotland . . . education appears to have a considerable effect in the prevention of crimes, and the promotion of industry, morality, and regular conduct.'[21]

[19] T. R. Malthus, *An Essay on the Principle of Population* (1878), 437 (Bk. IV, Ch. 9). Sunday schools, first launched in 1879 by Robert Raikes, enrolled by 1803 some 850,000 pupils in 7,000 schools throughout Great Britain.

[20] The title of an early pamphlet by James Mill conveys the flavour of the debate: *Schools for All, Not Schools for Churchmen Only* (1812).

[21] Malthus, *Essay on Population*, 470, 478 (Bk. IV, Ch. 13).

The contrast between law-abiding Scotland and unruly England became one of the clichés of the period, as much with the Scottish as with the English members of the classical school. It appears in some of the early essays of James Mill,[22] although not in the more famous article on education for the Supplement to the fifth edition of the *Encyclopaedia Britannica*, and it is one of McCulloch's recurrent themes. McCulloch, however, was more realistic about the law-and-order argument for education than either Adam Smith or Malthus. He always took the view that factory employment would make workers less deferential and compliant but he accepted this consequence as part of the price of economic growth. After endorsing 'a really useful system of public education', which would join reading and writing to the teaching of religion, morality, and political economy, with the object of persuading the poor that 'they are really the arbiters of their own fortune', he added the comment that 'we are not of the number of those who expect that any system of education will ever ensure tranquillity in periods of distress, or that it will obviate the vicissitudes and disorders inherent in the manufacturing system'.[23]

Once again one is struck by the failure to explain what particular system of public education is being advocated. Nevertheless, it is clear from other references that McCulloch's model is that of the parochial system of Scotland: 'there cannot be the shadow of a doubt that were government to interfere so far as to cause a public school to be established in every parish in England, where the fees should be moderate, and where really useful instruction should be communicated to the scholars, its interference would be in the highest degree beneficial.'[24] Elsewhere, he endorsed all that Adam Smith had said on the appropriate method of remunerating school teachers.[25]

IV HUMAN CAPITAL AND THE ECONOMIC VALUE OF EDUCATION

McCulloch is frequently singled out among classical economists for his explicit recognition of the concept of human capital, linking the provision of education to economic growth. But as a matter of fact, all that McCulloch did was to go one step further than Adam Smith in defining capital to include not only the 'skill, dexterity, and judgement' of workers, but also workers themselves as measured by the accumulated costs of rearing them.[26] No doubt, this was perfectly consistent with the general logic of classical

[22] J. Mill, 'Education of the Poor', *Edinburgh Review*, xxi (Feb. 1813).

[23] J. R. McCulloch, *Principles of Political Economy* (3rd edn., 1843), 431–2; a similar, but less explicit statement appears in the 1st edn., 1825, 360–1.

[24] *Quarterly Journal of Education* (1831) quoted in D. P. O'Brien, *J. R. McCulloch, A Study in Classical Economics* (1970), 346. O'Brien's book gives a brief but informative account of McCulloch's views on education (ibid. 344–7).

[25] See McCulloch's edition of *The Wealth of Nations* (1828), 589.

[26] See B. F. Kiker, *Human Capital: In Retrospect* (1968), 30–1.

wage theory, which treated the supply of labour as being perfectly elastic at the going wage rate. But the point is that McCulloch made no analytical use of the idea. He never committed himself to anything as clear-cut as Chadwick's assertion in 1862 that educated workers are at least 20 and perhaps 25 per cent more productive than uneducated workers[27]—and nor did any of the other classical economists.

The question whether to categorize either human beings themselves or the acquired skills of human beings as fixed capital has actually very little economic significance *per se*. As we know, Marshall rejected Fisher's idea of counting the skills of the labour force as part of the capital stock of an economy but that did not prevent him from exploring Adam Smith's suggestion that an investment motive makes itself felt in the demand for education.[28] Contrariwise, many classical economists defined capital to include human skills and even described the earnings differentials between skilled and unskilled labour as 'profit on capital' and yet drew no inferences from such statements with respect to either the private demand for education or the effects of subsidizing elementary education.

McCulloch is a case in point but an even better one is Senior. Senior was of course insistent on the notion that the time-consuming acquisition of a special skill requires 'abstinence', which must earn the going rate of return in the economy on physical capital. Nevertheless, he denied that the personal motive of 'a gentleman's son' in acquiring education was primarily that of investment in future earning power.[29] Similarly, in his unpublished lectures of 1847–52, while asserting that 'good elementary schools' will pay for themselves via improvements 'in diligence, in skill, in economy, in health', he declined to include knowledge and skills in the definition of 'capital' (*Industrial Efficiency*, ii. 328–9; i.170); indeed, he went out of his way to deny that the most powerful influences of schools lie in the domain of either cognitive or manual skills.

The word 'education' may be defined, he observed, as the sum of

the influences which one person intentionally exercises over another by precept

[27] E. Chadwick, 'Opening Address of the President of Section F of the British Association of the Advancement of Science', *Journal of the Statistical Society of London*, xxv (Mar. 1862), 519. McCulloch did lay stress on the diffusion of knowledge as a source of economic growth (O'Brien, *J. R. McCulloch*, 280, 346) but it is not clear that he regarded schooling as such as a significant element in the diffusion of knowledge.

[28] See my *Introduction of the Economics of Education* (1870), 2–6. Kiker, after a comprehensive survey of eighteenth- and nineteenth-century doctrines of human capital, concludes that 'the concept of human capital was somewhat prominent in economic thinking until Marshall discarded the notion as "unrealistic"' (op. cit. 112). But this is doubly misleading: the concept was by no means prominent in nineteenth-century economic thought and Marshall only discarded it in his definition of capital; elsewhere in his treatise he came back repeatedly to its economic implications and contributed more to the analysis of the idea than any other economist since Adam Smith.

[29] N. W. Senior, *An Outline of the Science of Political Economy* (1836), 205–7. Also N. W. Senior, *Industrial Efficiency and Social Economy*, ed. S. L. Levy (1928) ii. 334–5.

or by example ... These influences are of two kinds: first, the imparting of knowledge, which may be called *teaching*; secondly, the creation of habits, which may be called *training* ... As between teaching and training, there can be no doubt that training is by far the more important ... Training, therefore, or the formation of habits, rather than teaching, or the imparting of knowledge, is the great business of society.

(Op. cit., ii.329–31)

This passage, asserting unambiguously that the economic value of schooling is much more a matter of effective behaviour than of cognitive knowledge, undoubtedly expresses the more or less implicitly held belief of all the classical economists. What was critical, they seemed to be saying, was to disseminate among workers the behavioural traits appropriate to an industrialized society. Indeed, the 'left' and the 'right' in this period, if we can use such words, were entirely united on the principal effect of education: Tory extremists were convinced that elementary schooling would cause the poor to question the necessity of their poverty and therefore opposed the spread of education, while liberal Whigs were equally convinced that education would 'tame' the poor and therefore favoured its extension. What is striking in all this is the failure to take any explicit account of the role of education in the formation of so-called 'vocational skills'.

John Stuart Mill's treatment of education is an even more striking example of the failure to develop the main implications of the human capital concept. In his discussion of 'the degree of productiveness of productive agents', he lays great stress on 'the economical value of the general diffusion of intelligence among the people' and draws an unflattering comparison between Continental and English workers: 'If an English labourer is anything but a hewer of wood and a drawer of water, he is indebted for it to education, which in his case is almost always self-education.'[30] This sounds indeed as if Mill saw a vital connection between education and economic growth, but when he came later in the book to make his case for government intervention in education, he made no reference of any kind to the economic value of education. The emphasis in the famous 1845 essay on 'The Claims of Labour' and in the chapter 'On the Probable Futurity of the Labouring Classes' in the *Principles* is altogether on character-formation and self-improvement.[31]

Similarly, after denying that the expenses of rearing children are motivated

[30] J. S. Mill, *Principles of Political Economy*, ed. W. J. Ashley (1909), 109 (Bk. I, Ch. 7, § 5).

[31] The sentence which hails education as 'not the principal, but the sole remedy' for poverty in the 1845 essay (*Collected Works of John Stuart Mill. Essays on Economics and Society*, ed. J. M. Robson, (1967) iv. 378) is not repeated in the *Principles* where the accent is as much on 'spontaneous education' and 'newspapers and political tracts' as on 'the quantity and quality of school education' (*Principles*, 757–8).

by investment considerations, Mill concedes that the costs of acquiring 'technical or industrial education' are incurred for 'the sake of the greater or more valuable produce thereby attained, and in order that a remuneration equivalent or more than equivalent, may be reaped by the learner' (*Principles*, 40). This is a clear statement of the fundamental axiom of the theory of human capital but it is as far as Mill went, probably because he had come to doubt the significance of the Smithian principle that the labour market tends to equalize the net advantages of different occupations. Believing as he did that professional men constitute a non-competing group with manual workers, he drew attention to the fact that clerks earn more than bricklayers in violation of Smith's theory: 'The higher rate of his [the clerk's] remuneration . . . must be partly ascribed to monopoly' (op. cit., 392–3). But he did agree that the diffusion of education was beginning to erode these monopoly rents, which is easier to square with Smith's theory than with his own:

> Until lately [writing in 1848], all employments which required even the humble education of reading and writing, could be recruited only from a select class, the majority having had no opportunity of acquiring those attainments . . . Since reading and writing have been brought within the reach of the multitude, the monopoly price of the lower grade of educated employment has greatly fallen, the competition for them having increased in an almost incredible degree.
>
> (Op. cit., 392)

In short, throughout this period the theory of human capital remained more or less in the embryonic form in which it appears in *The Wealth of Nations*, a suggestion of a theory rather than a theory properly so-called. Senior denied it outright and even McCulloch and John Stuart Mill only glanced at it in passing.

V COMPULSION AND TUITION FEES

In analysing classical views on matters of educational policy, it is essential to distinguish opinions expressed before 1833 from those expressed after that date. The year 1833 constitutes a natural dividing line as marking the year in which Edwin Chadwick and Southwood Smith introduced the 'Prussian' principle of compulsory education under cover of a Factory Act, albeit for a strictly limited category of children, and in which Parliament was persuaded for the first time to make an annual grant to approved schools. The Factory Act of 1833 prohibited the employment of children under the age of 13 in textile mills unless they produced a certificate of their attendance in a school in the previous week; it said nothing about how the schooling in question was to be provided or how it was to be paid for; certainly there was no intention to make it free except on the basis of charity to the very poorest children. This point deserves some emphasis.

When Charles Roebuck earlier in the same year had laid the educational programme of the Philosophical Radicals before the Reformed Parliament, he shocked the House by demanding compulsory education for all children between the ages of 6 and 14. But even he emphasized the importance of retaining school fees for all but the poorest.[32] Of course, outside the Radical camp literally nobody entertained the idea of elementary education that was both compulsory and free.

Some reformers, however, seem to have soon moved beyond the position adopted by Roebuck. At any rate, the *Report on the Hand-Loom Weavers in 1841* contained the following remarkable statement:

> The merit . . . of the education clauses in the Factory Act is, not what they have done, but what they have acknowledged. It is obvious, at first sight, that the legislature, which fines a parent for sending a child to work at a power loom without having sent it the day before to school cannot consistently exempt from the same obligation the parent who sends his child to . . . any employment beyond his own doors. And we think that, on reflection, everyone must feel that the mere accident of the child's being employed in the house of a stranger, or in that of his own parent, and to go a step further, of his being or not being employed at all, does not affect the parent's obligation, or the duty of the state to enforce it. It is equally obvious that, if the state be found to require the parent to educate his child, it is bound to see that he has the means of doing so. The voluntary system, therefore, . . . has been repudiated; and we trust that in a matter of this importance . . . a system which has been repudiated in principle will not be permitted to continue in practice.[33]

The Report was largely written by Senior, one of the four commissioners, and the language in this paragraph is unmistakably that of Senior. It defines a position from which, as we shall see, he was later somewhat to retreat. The passage just cited is, to my knowledge, unique in the period in publicly recommending something close to the twentieth-century remedy of compulsory elementary education for all, provided by the state without fees of any kind.[34] Nevertheless, it is noteworthy that even this statement does not go quite so far as to recommend abolition of all fees as a matter of principle.

To demonstrate that it is nevertheless unrepresentative of advanced opinion in the day, let us consider John Stuart Mill's application of the

[32] J. E. G. de Montmorency, *State Intervention in English Education, A Short History from the Earliest Times Down to 1833* (1902), 347. The whole of the speech is reprinted in this book, which is incidentally an invaluable primary source for the period before 1833.

[33] *Report of the Commissioners for Inquiring into the Condition of the Unemployed on the Hand-Loom Weavers in the United Kingdom*, Parliamentary Papers (1841), x.122. The report goes on to recommend a school inspectorate, a system of teacher training to be financed from 'the national revenue' rather than from local rates, and a Royal Commission to investigate the entire question of educating the poor (ibid. 123).

[34] The passage is discussed by M. Bowley, *Nassau Senior and Classical Economics* (1937), 262, but without emphasis on its startling character.

'Non-Interference Principle' to education. For the first time since Adam Smith, we meet here with an entirely original contribution to the classical theory of educational policy. Furthermore, having first advanced his ideas in the *Principles* in 1848, Mill went on to develop them further in the essay *On Liberty* (1859) and returned to them once again ten years later in an essay on 'Endowments'.

The new contribution is the notion that the commodity 'education' represents a clear-out case of market failures on the grounds that its production is inherently plagued by problems of consumer ignorance. In a nutshell: 'The uncultivated cannot be competent judges of cultivation' (*Principles*, 953). The modern phrase 'market failure' is used advisedly as Mill's words leave no doubt of his meaning: 'It will continually happen, on the voluntary system, that, the end not being desired, the means will not be provided at all, or that, persons requiring improvement having an imperfect or altogether erroneous conception of what they want, the supply called forth by the demand of the market will be anything but what is really required' (ibid.). It is perhaps misleading to label this argument as being one of consumer ignorance. Here ignorance in making choices can be remedied, in principle at any rate, by the provision of information, but the assertion that the opinions of uneducated people about education are necessarily worthless is really a proposition about the effects of education on the formation of tastes and hence on the ultimate foundation of choice. At first glance, this proposition appears to be a value judgement but on further examination it is seen to be an empirical generalization for which there is indeed a good deal of evidence.[35] At any rate, education seems to be a commodity the demand for which 'grows by what it feeds on'.

Nevertheless, Mill's thesis is liable to self-contradiction when combined, as he wished to combine it, with a belief in the desirability of enfranchising the lower classes. If the uneducated are incompetent judges of education, why are they regarded as competent judges of parliamentary representatives that vote funds for education? To be sure, people may be unwilling to indulge 'the irrational passion for rational calculation', preferring to delegate certain difficult choices to parliamentary representatives, but it takes an argument of some kind to make the case. Without directly facing the difficulty inherent in his position, Mill nevertheless recognized the logical necessity of claiming a quasi-paternalistic role for government:

any well-intentioned and tolerably civilized government may think, without

[35] I am reminded of the Hollywood argument that commercial film producers make bad films because the public wants bad films, to which some retort: 'Make better films and tastes will soon improve'. When generalized, this sounds like a reason for ignoring consumer sovereignty in everything, leaving us only to argue over the selection of sovereign taste-makers. But inasmuch as it is a testable proposition about the influence of supply on the formation of tastes, it is far from general: it may be true of films and even of education but on the other hand it may not be.

presumption, that it does or ought to possess a degree of cultivation above the average of the community which it rules, and it should therefore be capable of offering better education and better instruction to the people, than the greater number of them would spontaneously demand. Education, therefore, is one of those things which it is admissable in principle that a government should provide for the people.

(Ibid.)

He now moves on to 'elementary education' in particular, by which phrase he and other nineteenth-century authors always meant, not first-stage education for children, but rather education for the poor as a social class, whether children or adults. What he advocated was compulsory instruction either at school or at home, while relegating the role of the state to the provision of financial assistance to permit all parents to comply with this requirement: 'It is therefore an allowable excerise of the powers of government to impose on parents the legal obligation of giving elementary instruction to children. This, however, cannot fairly be done, without taking measures to insure that such instruction shall be always accessible to them either gratuitously or at a trifling expense' (ibid. 954). It is significant that at this point he found it necessary to confront the contemporary belief in the positive virtues of fee-paying: 'This is not one of the cases in which the tender of help perpetuates the state of things which renders help necessary.' Holding that the poor could not be expected to defray the full cost of elementary education, he concluded:

The education provided in this country on the voluntary principle has of late been so much discussed, that it is needless in this place to criticise it minutely, and I shall merely express my conviction that even in quantity it is [in 1848], and is likely to remain, altogether insufficient, while in quality, though with some slight tendency to improvement, it is never good except by some rare accident, and generally so bad as to be little more than nominal. I hold it the duty of the government to supply the defect, by giving pecuniary support to elementary schools, such as to render them accessible to all the children of the poor, either freely, or for a payment too inconsiderable to be sensibly felt . . . the remainder of the cost to be defrayed, as in Scotland, by a local rate.

(Ibid. 955–6)

Having said this much, he qualified it immediately by attacking the idea of a state monopoly of education:

Though a government . . . may, and in many cases ought to, establish schools and colleges, it must neither compel, nor bribe any person to come to them; nor ought the power of individuals to set up rural establishments to depend in any degree upon its authorization. It would be justified in requiring from all the people that they shall possess instruction in certain things, but not in prescribing them how or from whom they shall obtain it.

(Ibid.)

Mill wrote as if the principles of state subsidies to elementary education was yet to be established. But, of course, Treasury grants to voluntary schools amounted in 1849 to £125,000, having risen sixfold from the date of their inception in 1833. The argument by 1848 was not so much over the very principle of state assistance but rather over the religious character of aided schools. By 1851, when the *Census of Education* produced the first reliable figures for the nation as a whole, the Church of England provided 90 per cent of all elementary school places in the country; in rural areas, its monopoly was almost complete. In consequence, Church schools had been receiving the lion's share of government grants to elementary education,[36] and this is perhaps the reason that Mill, firmly opposed as a Radical Utilitarian to the Established Church, took a poor view of the growth of voluntary schooling. This is, of course, a pure speculation. But consider what it would have meant to have endorsed the voluntary system. That would be to imply that there was nothing wrong with the powerful grip which the Anglican Church had by then secured over the school system. Surely, this must have been too much to swallow for the son of James Mill and the pupil of Bentham?

According to Mill then the duties of the state are to set minimum educational standards; thereafter, private schools operating their own subsidized fee system, in competition with State schools waiving the fee payment for poor children, can be relied on to provide education. But how is such a scheme to be enforced? Mill does not tell us in the *Principles*: he makes no reference to the central education inspectorate, which had been created by 1848 as an essential element in the Whig programme of state-aided elementary education, and he says nothing about how the income of parents is to be discovered for purposes of remitting fees. In the last chapter of the essay *On Liberty*, however, he becomes slightly more explicit.

The treatment of education in the essay begins with a clear assertion of the central doctrine: 'Is it not almost a self-evident axiom, that the State should require and compel the education, up to a certain standard, of every human being who is born its citizen?'[37] This 'self-evident axiom' seemed to Mill both to resolve the vexed Religious Question and to avoid the dangers of the Leviathan state.

> Were the duty of enforcing universal education once admitted there would be an end to the difficulties about what the State should teach, and how it should teach, which now convert the subject into a mere battlefield for sects and parties . . . If the government would make up its mind to require for every child a good education, it might save itself the trouble of providing one. It might leave the

[36] In addition, the Anglican Church's National Society raised £870,000 in 1851 from its own resources, while the secular British Society, together with Wesleyan, Baptist, and Congregational schools, managed to raise only £125,000.

[37] J. S. Mill, *Utilitarianism, Liberty and Representative Government* (Everyman Library, 1910), 160.

parents to obtain the education where and how they pleased, and content itself with helping to pay the school fees of the poorer classes of children, and defraying the entire school expenses of those who have no one else to pay for them. The objections which are urged with reason against State education do not apply to the enforcement of education by the State, but to the State's taking upon itself to direct that education; which is a totally different thing. That the whole or any large part of the education of the people should be in State hands, I go as far as anyone in deprecating . . . A general State education is a mere contrivance for moulding people to be exactly like one another . . . An education established and controlled by the State should only exist, if it exists at all, as one among many competing experiments, carried on for the purpose of example and stimulus, to keep the others up to a certain standard of excellence.[38]

The scheme he proposed runs as follows: children are to be tested at an early age in the ability to read; failure to pass the examination subjects the parents to a fine and, thereafter, to compulsory schooling at their own expense; these examinations are to be held annually and the range of subjects is to be gradually extended up to some unspecified age; apart from these, all examinations are to be voluntary and designed merely to certify competence in a field. The implied strictures against occupational licensing, by the way, are made to apply explicitly to the teaching profession (*Utilitarianism*, 162).

Mill's final statement on educational questions came in 1869 in an essay on 'Endowments', undoubtedly provoked by the publication of the Report of the Taunton Schools Inquiry Commission. This paper largely goes over the same ground as the *Principles* and the essay *On Liberty* but it does add some new points. Firstly, Mill took the next step in the steady tendency to deprecate fee-paying by rejecting Adam Smith's view that the quality of teaching must deteriorate if teachers' salaries are unrelated to the number of pupils they succeed in attracting; since teachers serve consumers who are essentially ignorant of the product they are buying, Mill argued, pecuniary incentives will fail to produce desirable results.[39] These remarks had a special contemporary relevance because the Revised Code of 1862 had recently intoduced the principle of payments-by-results. Secondly, Mill extended his earlier views on state subsidies to elementary education and now proposed free secondary and university education for those members

[38] Ibid. 161. It is curious how few historians of economic thought have drawn attention to these striking sentences. But see E. G. West, 'Liberty and Education: John Stuart Mill's Dilemma', *Philosophy*, xi (Apr. 1965); and J. M. Robson, *The Improvement of Mankind. The Social and Political Thought of John Stuart Mill* (1900), 209–12. It requires only one addition, the substitution of education vouchers for subsidized fees, to be pure Milton Friedman. See M. Friedman, *Capitalism and Freedom* (1963), 85–108.

[39] Mill, *Collected Works*, v.624. Mill had denied the full force of Smith's objections to endowed schools even earlier in an essay on 'Corporations and Church Property' (1833): ibid. iv.214ff.

of the working class who exhibited 'capacities . . . for the higher departments of intellectual work'.[40] No other economist, not even Fawcett,[41] ever went so far.

VI SENIOR'S LATER VIEWS

To round off our discussion, it remains only to say a few words about Senior's views in later years. There is almost nothing original to report and were they the views of anyone else they would hardly deserve comment. The Newcastle Commission on the State of Popular Education, appointed in 1858 with Senior as one of its members, was split between a minority who opposed subsidization of fees but approved central grants for the construction and maintenance of school buildings and a majority who insisted on an extension of the annual Parliamentary grant specifically designed to allow fees to be set well below costs. Senior clearly took the majority view. Rejecting a colleague's eloquent statement of free-market principles applied to education, he wrote in a private memorandum: 'I agree with Mr. G. Smith in thinking that part of the money paid directly for the child's education ought to be paid by the parent. The payment of school pence promotes regularity of attendance, adds in the parent's mind to the value of what is purchased, and gives a feeling of independence. But a small fee is sufficient for these purposes.'[42] He calculated the costs of elementary education at not less than 30*s*. a year and declared: 'there is no reason to believe that now, or at any time that can be defined, that sum is or will be obtainable from the parent' (ibid., 185).

In 1861 he published a volume of his notes and resolutions submitted to the Commission, entitled *Suggestions on Popular Education*. Once again, he reiterated his belief that the poor could not afford cost-covering fees, this time adding to the expense of tuition fees 'the much greater expense of foregoing the child's wages'.[43] He now borrowed from Mill the notion that poor parents would neglect the education of their children even if they were not poor and he combined this idea with his own long-standing dislike of working-class organizations. Someone had proposed the introduction of

[40] Ibid. v.627–8. But the passage begins with the maxim: 'The State does not owe gratuitous education to those who can pay for it. The State owes no more than elementary education to the entire body of those who cannot pay for it.'

[41] Writing in 1871, Fawcett came out strongly in favour of compulsory elementary education. Nevertheless, he opposed the total abolition of fees although by this time, as he said, 'free and compulsory education has come to be the watchword of a party': *Pauperism: Its Causes and Remedies* (1871), 61–6, 123ff.

[42] Quoted in S. L. Levy, *Nassau W. Senior 1790–1864* (1970), 184. Ch. 22 of this book contains a garbled and entirely ahistorical account of Senior's views on education.

[43] N. W. Senior, *Suggestions on Popular Education* (1861), 3–5; also 18, 44. An almost identical statement is found in *Industrial Efficiency and Social Economy*, ii.334–5. It appears that virtually the whole of Senior's book of 1861 derives from his lecture notes of 1847–52. Bowley, *Nassau Senior*, 268, supplies a succinct precis of the 1861 book and deals elsewhere with Senior's general views on educational questions (ibid. 267–9, 330–1).

parents into the management of schools; Senior violently rejected this proposal on the grounds that the 'lower classes' were not even competent to run their own benefit societies or trade unions: 'For fifty years they have been managing their own trades' unions. There is not one which is not based on folly, tyranny and injustice which would disgrace the rudest savages. They sacrifice their wives', their children's, and their own health and strength to the lowest sensuality. The higher the wages the worse seems, in general, to be the condition of the families.'[44]

The shrill paternalistic tone of these remarks is consistently maintained in all the notes and resolutions of *Popular Education*. As in the case of John Stuart Mill, there is some reason to believe that Senior shared the increasing tendency of Dissenters to despair of ever competing successfully with Church of England schools. The average parent, he observed, simply would not accept non-denominational education.[45] Detailing the deplorable quality of most private schools, he concluded: 'yet to these dens of ignorance and malaria one third of the labouring classes still send their children . . . although good and cheap public schools are at their door' (ibid., 29). Nevertheless, the earlier principal rejection of the 'voluntary system' is missing in this book, although there are many passages which suggest that it is only political expediency which prevented Senior from again recommending possibly free and certainly compulsory schooling for all.

VII CONCLUSION

A brief review of the secondary literature will serve to underline some of the points I have been making about the educational doctrines of the classical economists.

The subject first came into prominence with the publication of Lord Robbins's masterly volume of lectures on the classical theory of economic policy. Robbins devoted a few pages to the question of education, passing quickly from Adam Smith to Malthus to the Hand-Loom Weavers Report with a passing glance at McCulloch. Adam Smith, according to Robbins, 'urged that the government should provide subsidized, but not quite free, elementary education'.[46] I would have thought that a better summary is: Adam Smith urged that local government should provide subsidized, but definitely not free, elementary education. After noting Malthus's endorse-

[44] Senior, *Popular Education*, 31–2; an identical statement is found in *Industrial Efficiency*, ii.340.

[45] Senior, *Popular Education*, 19–20. It is perhaps odd that he should regret this fact. He was the son of a Berkshire clergyman of the Church of England and remained an Anglican throughout his life, although a sceptical one (Levy, *Nassau Senior*, 57–9). I can throw no light on this apparent contradiction but it may be similar to his position on Philosophical Radicalism: he worked with the Benthamites and clearly agreed with most of their social views and yet he never committed himself explicitly to their cause.

[46] L. Robbins, *The Theory of Economic Policy in English Classical Political Economy* (1952), 90.

ment of Adam Smith's views, Robbins quotes the Hand-Loom Weavers Report as a 'typical illustration of opinion some forty years later'. 'After which', he remarks, 'nothing surely remains to be said' (ibid. 93). Curiously enough, Robbins does not even mention John Stuart Mill's repudiation of the principle of free, compulsory schooling. We must conclude therefore that a great deal more remains to be said—a thought which appears to have struck other commentators.

The next round in the discussion is by Blitz, an essay which first appeared in Spanish in 1961 but which was soon translated and circulated privately.[47] Blitz's treatment is distinguished by a clear grasp of the central element in the classical economists' approach to education: 'the early classicists saw little place for mass education as a strictly *economic* investment—except as it might contribute indirectly through effects on population and civic order'; the nineteenth-century literature 'seems to show much greater concern over the problem of the discipline of the labour force than over the problem of skill' (ibid. 37, 46). Before the creation of a national police force and the development of small arms weapons, there was a widespread fear of rioting mobs, inspired by the example of the French Revolution. The classical economists, Blitz points out, did take what was then the enlightened view that the spread of education among the poor would promote rather than endanger political stability. Malthus, a Tory in respect of the Corn Laws, nevertheless played an important role in establishing what might be described as the Whig attitude of the classical economists to popular education.

Unfortunately, Blitz exaggerates the role of Senior and attributes views to him which are in fact due to John Stuart Mill. In a sense it is true to say that Senior of all the classical economists showed 'the greatest explicit concern for education' but Senior published nothing on education until 1861. So far as the printed word is concerned, it is clearly John Stuart Mill who is the key figure and Blitz has little to say about him. This brings us to the first chapter in Vaizey's pioneering textbook on the economics of education. His treatment of Adam Smith is excellent, although it is marred by some serious historical inaccuracies, such as the statements that education was compulsory in eighteenth-century Scotland and that all Scottish schoolmasters in 1776 were university graduates.[48] Vaizey emphasizes the Malthusian tradition which linked the spread of education to family planning and then cites John Stuart Mill as favouring state provision of and

[47] R. C. Blitz, 'Some Classical Economists and Their Views on Education', *Economica*, 1961, partly reprinted in English in the UNESCO *Readings in the Economics of Education*, eds. M. J. Bowman and others (1968).

[48] J. Vaizey, *The Economics of Education* (1962), 18, 19, Primary education became compulsory in Scotland in 1891; many eighteenth-century Scottish schoolmasters were university graduates but by no means all were. See M. Cruickshank, *History of Teacher Training in Scotland* (1970), 16–17.

assistance to elementary education, alongside private schooling, possibly but not necessarily financed by compulsory levies (ibid. 20–1). But he makes no reference to the passages in Mill's *Principles* which distinguish between minimum educational standards and school attendance as such. Having cited Smith, Ricardo, Malthus, McCulloch, and Marshall, but not Senior, he concludes: 'Thus there is a long and honourable tradition from Adam Smith to Alfred Marshall which assigns to publicly supported education a major role not only in promoting social peace and harmony, and self-improvement, but in the process of wealth-creation itself' (ibid. 23). To label the bits and pieces that can be collected from writers other than Adam Smith, John Stuart Mill and Marshall as 'a long and honourable tradition' is, surely, something of an exaggeration. Furthermore, if there was such a tradition, it certainly did not assign a major role to education in the process of wealth-creation, although it did assign a definite role to education subordinate to that of law and legislation in 'promoting social peace and harmony, and self-improvement'.

Two remarkable articles by West in 1964 threw a new light on the view of the classical economists. West is basically concerned to demonstrate that Mill and Senior departed radically from Adam Smith in respect of the applicability of free market principles to education: whereas Smith held that the market mechanism merely required financial assistance from the state to make it more effective, Mill and Senior denied the relevance of the principle of freedom of choice in the field of education.[49] Although Mill did in the the end come down in favour of private schooling, he did not do so because of the classic liberal argument that the experience of making choices in education is itself an education in the art of choices, but rather because he was afraid that the state would abuse its monopoly of education. In short, Mill and Senior moved a long way towards educational paternalism. Nevertheless, West summarizes their views in these words:

While the early economists argued for *some* State education, they conceived it in very qualified terms indeed. If we were asked to select the most conspicuous of the main features which distinguished them from current practice, it would probably be their insistence that fees should not be abolished and should always cover a substantial part of the education ... there is indeed nothing in the evidence of their writings to suggest that any one of them would have supported the degree of State predominance in education that is experienced in our own times.[50]

[49] Bowley, *Nassau Senior*, 276, noted long ago that Mill and Senior marked a breach with the preceding generation respecting the question of state intervention. West's contribution was to relate this insight to educational issues.

[50] E. G. West, 'The Role of Education in Nineteenth-Century Doctrines of Political Economy', *British Journal of Educational Studies*, xii, (May 1964), reprinted in E. G. West, *Education and the State* (2nd. edn., 1970), Ch. 8. See also E. G. West, 'Private versus Public Education' in Coats, ed., *The Classical Economists and Economic Policy* (1971).

Even this apt summary errs by omission as both Mill and Senior did call for the selective abolition of fees in elementary education, or, more accurately expressed, for a means-tested scale of fees.

Central to West's argument is his contention that the quantity of private schooling in the period was much greater than most modern historians would credit and that even its quality was tolerable given the circumstances of the time. In that connection, the views of Mill and Senior present something of an obstacle since it is perfectly clear that they had a very low opinion of the private schools of their own day. West's attempt to deal with their objections is not, I think, altogether convincing. 'The fact was', he writes, 'that neither Senior nor Mill liked the type of school that the free market was providing by the middle of the nineteenth century. This was undoubtedly due to their opinion that these schools were inferior to the large scale models which the poor law institutions were dutifully producing to the order of their Benthamite supervisors.'[51] This appears to be a reference to workhouse schools conducted in accordance with the precepts of 'the monitorial system', in which case it is an elliptical comment as both Mill and Senior envisaged standard-sized state schools outside the jurisdiction of the Poor Law Commissioners; by 1848, the earlier enthusiasm for the economic-of-scale features of the monitorial system had long since waned.[52]

Two years after West's articles there appeared what is undoubtedly the best single, certainly the least misleading, commentary on the theme in question: 'The Economics of Education in English Classical Economics' by Miller. His review is topical rather than chronological but he does not disguise the fact that the classical economists were generally not at their best on the topic of education. Here, for the first time, John Stuart Mill commands the centre of the stage and the classical stress on 'better men rather than better workers' is continuously kept in mind.[53]

There followed a curious paper by Hollander in which he begins by posing a spurious question and ends by answering it to his own satisfaction.[54] The classical economists generally favoured government intervention in elementary education, Hollander declares, but why did they not extend this principle explicitly to vocational training in specific skills? In view of the fact that John Stuart Mill was worried about monopoly rents in earnings, he might be expected to have advocated government support of vocational training as a device for equalizing incomes. That he did not do

[51] West, *British Journal of Educational Studies*, 170–1.

[52] In the 2nd edn. of his *Education and The State*, xxxiii, West reiterates his belief that Senior was a paternalist who sought to impose 'Benthamite and Protestant' schooling on less-than-willing parents. This comment sounds nearer the mark.

[53] Miller, *Southern Economic Journal*, xxxii (1966), 296–300.

[54] S. Hollander, 'The Role of the State in Vocational Training: The Classical Economists' View', *Southern Economic Journal*, xxiv (Apr. 1968).

so must have been due, Hollander argues, to his preoccupation with Malthusian considerations on the labour supply side.

It is not altogether clear what Hollander means by vocational training but it appears that he is thinking of formal vocational training in educational institutions rather than on-the-job training. In that case, it is worth noting that the distinction between general and vocational training is something which would never have occurred to the classical economists. When they wrote on education they were usually thinking of elementary education, and as Hollander himself admits: 'starting from an illiterate base it is difficult to distinguish elementary from vocational training since, frequently, the former is a necessary prerequisite of the latter' (ibid. 520). In those instances where they addressed themselves to secondary and higher education, they took it as a matter of course that the State had no obligations in these matters; it is true that John Stuart Mill went so far as to advocate free higher education to bright working-class children, and even government subventions to universities for purposes of encouraging research (*Principles*, 976–7), but he is a singular exception in this regard. In any case, whatever the stage of education under consideration, the classical economists paid little attention to the tendency of schools to develop vocationally useful skills. Instead they threw all their weight behind the law-and-order argument for education. It is significant the Hollander is in fact driven to argue that the classical writers recognized, not just the social and political benefits, but also the 'specifically economic advantages' of elementary schooling; he even asserts that McCulloch was by no means exceptional in relating education to economic growth (op. cit. 520). In some sense, therefore, Hollander's article loses all the ground gained by Blitz and Miller.

It remains only to add that Robbins's earlier treatment of the classical theory of economic policy was deepened and extended by Samuel's full-scale study.[55] Parts of this book analyse the classical economists' conception of the role of education as a type of 'nondeliberative social control', after which the issue may be said to have been settled.

The last and most recent contribution to the debate begins provocatively enough: it denies that either Robbins, Vaizey, West, or Miller have done justice to 'the richness, detail and consistency of the Classical analysis' and baldly asserts that 'qualitatively they [the classics] said, though often in general and non-technical language, everything that is to be said about the economics of education'.[56] The impact of these remarks is somewhat lessened when we learn that the author defines the term 'Classical economists' as Keynes did to refer to all pre-Keynesian economists and that

[55] W. J. Samuels, *The Classical Theory of Economic Policy* (1966).

[56] P. N. V. Tu, 'The Classical Economists and Education', *Kyklos*, xxii fasc. 2 (1969), 691, 716.

much of the article is concerned with the views of Sidgwick, Marshall, Wicksteed, Taussig, Pigou, Dalton, and Cannan. Although the essay is a useful compendium of opinions arranged in chronological order, the treatment of the classical economists as such is not entirely satisfactory and once again does less than justice to the ideas of Mill and Senior.

Let us sum up our 'review of the troops'. All the classical economists, without a single exception, approved of state assistance to locally provided schools and usually they justified such proposals in terms of the role of education as a more or less deliberate method of 'social control'; at least until John Stuart Mill, no definite argument was ever advanced to suggest that education would fail to be optimally provided by a pure market mechanism. However, neither before nor after Mill did any leading classical economist advocate compulsory and completely free elementary, much less secondary, education—the only possible exception is Senior, but of course the public was unaware of his role in drafting the Hand-Loom Weavers Report—and none of them entertained the idea of confining the teaching force to a state-licensed profession. What is true is that from Mill onwards there was increasing dissatisfaction with the voluntary system and a growing desire to see public schools competing with private schools, how much this has to do with the great Religious Question we can only conjecture.

With respect to the details of educational policy, there was a general tendency to be wise after the event: no classical economist suggested that the employment of children should be made conditional on prior school attendance until the Factory Act of 1833 had actually established this principle; no one called for the central training and recruitment of teachers until the pupil-teacher system had been invented in the early 1840s; and even the proposal to import the Scottish parochial system into England was left vague and unrelated to the steady growth of the English voluntary system before and after 1833. In short, the classical economists had no impact on the history of education in the century between the publication of *The Wealth of Nations* and Forster's Education Act of 1870, but the history of education certainly made an impact on them.[57]

So much for policy questions. What about theory and, particularly, the theory of human capital? Far from it being true that the classical economists had said 'everything that is to be said about the economics of education', I have been arguing that economic analysis of education systems had hardly begun. To be sure, the concept of human capital has a long history going back to the seventeenth century, largely connected with such questions as measuring the costs of wars and evaluating preventive health programmes,

[57] A similar observation applies to the history of factory legislation: see my paper, 'The Classical Economists and the Factory Acts—A Re-Examination', *Quarterly Journal of Economics* (1958), reprinted in Coats, ed., *The Classical Economists and Economic Policy* (1971).

all of which has little to do with the demand for education or with the contribution of education to economic growth. Statements to the effect that education pays for itself by making people more productive, which one occasionally encounters in the classical literature, are actually of little import as the same may be said with equal force of sanitation, housing, food, and clothing at low levels of economic development. In fact, until Lyon Playfair wrote his famous letter to the Taunton Commission, attributing Britain's poor performance at the 1862 Paris Exhibition to inferior educational provision in Britain as compared to the Continent,[58] it never occurred to anyone to relate the quantity and quality of schooling directly to a country's economic performance.[59] Where the classical economists did make a contribution is in the area of welfare economics applied to education; and here it is all in John Stuart Mill. But as for human capital and education as investment in human beings, one can pass straight from Adam Smith to Marshall without the slightest loss.

Perhaps this is too severe. Although they rarely entertained the notion that education affects economic growth directly, they did think of the provision of education as a kind of national investment; it is simply that they interpreted this proposition in a way which we would now label 'sociological' rather than 'economic'. Modern economists are sometimes accused of attributing the economic value of education entirely to the effects of cognitive learning in schools. But this does less than justice. It would be more accurate to say that modern economists view schooling as a 'black box': without pretending to know precisely what goes on in classrooms, they nevertheless do know that passing through schools increases the earning power of people. The classical economists did know, or thought they knew, what went on inside the box: schooling effectively altered the behaviour of students, breeding attitudes of punctuality, persistence, concentration, obedience, and at the same time self-reliance; employers recognized this tendency of education to inculcate definite social values and hence were willing to pay educated workers more than uneducated ones, even if what they had learned was of no specific use to employment.[60] It may well be that the classical accent on values and attitudes, rather than on manual or intellectual skills, is closer to the heart of the matter than we like to think, particularly in societies that have not yet

[58] The letter is reprinted in W. H. Court, *British Economic History, 1870–1914; Commentary and Documents* (1965), 168–9.

[59] Alas, Mill is once again the exception. See the passage in Mill's *Principles*, 109, quoted above.

[60] There is a good deal of evidence that employers during the Industrial Revolution were deeply concerned with the problem of 'labour commitment'; see S. Pollard, 'Factory Discipline in the Industrial Revolution', *Economic History Review*, 2nd ser. xvi (1963), and his *Genesis of Modern Management. A Study of the Industrial Revolution in Great Britain* (1965), 181–92; see also N. J. Smelser, *Social Class in the Industrial Revolution. An Application of Theory to the Lancashire Cotton Industry, 1770–1840* (1959), 105–7.

become fully industrialized.[61] It would certainly be far-fetched to argue that industrialization necessarily produces a growing demand for literate and educated workers and that these 'manpower requirements' provide the key to the role of education in the Industrial Revolution.[62] There is still something to be learned from reading the classical economists, even if, as in this case, it has to be a reading between the lines.

HISTORICAL APPENDIX

We have so far ignored a hidden presumption in most of the commentaries on our period, namely, that there was little schooling in the heyday of the British Industrial Revolution and that most of it was bad. It has become evident from recent research, however, that literacy rates in early nineteenth-century Britain were astonishingly high, which raises the question how this could have been achieved without widely diffused schooling. Furthermore, it appears that private schooling, far from stagnating, grew at a phenomenal rate right up to the 1870s, which is precisely why men like Mill and Senior were alarmed about its unsatisfactory quality. The fact is that if we are properly to understand the views of the classical economists, we must begin by putting to one side the standard histories of nineteenth-century education, which seem to have been largely written to prove that education is only adequately provided when the state accepts its responsibility to furnish compulsory education *gratis*.[63]

We take up first the question of literacy. An article by Sargant, published as early as 1867, first recognized the potentialities of the marriage register as a crude index of literacy rates during the Industrial Revolution.[64] Since then other evidence on birth and death registers, spot surveys of literacy in particular towns and the sale of unstamped working-class newspapers have led to the conclusion that 'by 1840, two-thirds to three-quarters of male adult workers were literate (the percentage for women being slightly

[61] See my 'Correlation Between Earnings and Education: What Does It Signify?', *Higher Education*, i (Feb. 1972), for a discussion of alternative theories of the content of the 'black box'.

[62] Most British economic historians have argued that the early stages of the Industrial Revolution generated very little demand for literate workers. This seems to be correct judging at any rate from the contemporary experience of developing countries (Blaug, *Economics of Education*, 252–3). It does not follow, however, that education during the Industrial Revolution was therefore unimportant from an economic standpoint. M. Hartwell, *The Industrial Revolution and Economic Growth* (1971), Ch. 11, attacks leading British economic historians for neglecting the role of education in the Industrial Revolution but his attack is spoiled by a very simple-minded view of the relationship between education and economic growth. For an antidote to Hartwell, see M. D. Shipman, *Education and Modernisation* (1971), Ch. 3; Goldstrom, *Social Content of Education*, Ch. 5, and particularly, M. Sanderson, 'Literacy and Social Mobility in the Industrial Revolution in England', *Past and Present* (Aug. 1972), 89–95.

[63] Mr. D. J. Davies provided valuable research assistance in combing the literature.

[64] W. L. Sargant, 'On the Progress of Elementary Education', *Journal of the Statistical Society* (Mar. 1967).

smaller), with rates in towns regularly above those of rural areas'.[65] When we consider that the world mean literacy rate in 1970 is abour 60 per cent and that the whole of Tropical Africa, the Middle East, and large stretches of Latin America fail to attain even 40 per cent, the statistics cited above for adults in Britain in 1840, and working-class adults at that, are nothing short of extraordinary.

A careful reading of the classical economists would of course have prepared us for the new view on literacy during the Industrial Revolution. We recall that Adam Smith noted in passing that 'In Scotland, the establishment of . . . parish schools has taught almost the whole common people to read, and a very great proportion of them to write and account. In England the establishment of charity schools has had an effect of the same kind, though not so universally.'[66] Similarly, there are sentences in John Stuart Mill that show that he took it for granted that most contemporary workers could read and write: 'Since reading and writing have been brought within the reach of the multitude, the monopoly price of the lower grade of educated employments has greatly fallen . . .'[67] There are similar hints of high literacy rates among the poor in the writings of James Mill, Bentham, Brougham, and McCulloch.

If schooling was as insufficient in quantity and as poor in quality as most modern historians of education allege, how did so many workers learn to read and write? It is true that it is not uncommon for literacy to run ahead of schooling, and in any country at any stage in its history there are always more literate people than individuals who have gone to school. Nevertheless, the apparently large gap between the literacy rate and the school enrolment rate during the British Industrial Revolution does raise some intriguing questions. Conventional histories of education neatly dispose of the problem by simply ignoring the literacy evidence.[68] But as a matter of

[65] Hartwell, *The Industrial Revolution*, 238, and the references cited, 236–8.

[66] Cited above in the text. [67] Cited above in the text.

[68] See e.g. J. W. Adamson, *English Education 1789–1902* (1930); F. Smith, *A History of English Elementary Education* (1931); C. Birchenough, *History of Elementary Education in England and Wales* (3rd edn., 1938); B. Simon, *Studies in the History of Education 1780–1870* (1960); H. C. Barnard, *A History of English Education from 1760* (2nd edn., 1961); W. G. Armytage, *Four Hundred Years of English Education* (1964); S. J. Curtis, *History of Education in Great Britain* (6th edn., 1965); S. J. Curtis and M. E. Boultwood, *An Introductory History of English Education Since 1800* (4th edn., 1966); M. Sturt, *The Education of the People. A History of Primary Education in England and Wales in the Nineteenth Century* (1967); and D. Wardle, *English Popular Education 1780–1970* (1970). None of these books even mentions the word 'literacy' in their index. But some of them, such as Simon and Curtis, at least discuss the problem of literacy rates from Tudor to Victorian times (Curtis, *History*, 196). A few specialist studies do weave the new evidence in their story but turn it around so as to allow for expressions of dismay that as much as a quarter of the working class was illiterate around 1850. See J. F. C. Harrison, *Learning and Living 1790–1960. A Study in the History of the English Adult Education Movement* (1961), 42. However, G. Sutherland, *Elementary Education in the Nineteenth Century* (The Historical Association, 1971), makes up for the deficiences of all the rest.

fact, it is generally conceded that nearly universal literacy was achieved in Victorian England by 1900 or thereabouts, and it is easy to show that unless literacy rates around the middle of the nineteenth century were about 40 to 50 per cent, 100 per cent literacy rates could not have been achieved in two generations.

The simple truth is that formal education was much less important in the nineteenth century than it now is and much reading and writing was acquired without benefit of formal schooling. Out-of-school education and particularly the adult educational movement is certainly discussed in all the standard educational histories but it is rarely emphasized; moreover, the subject is usually raised in order to show to what lengths people had to go to make up for the inadequacies of state provision.[69] Examples of out-of school education in the period are, first of all, mutual improvement societies and Dissenting Academies, particularly in northern towns, of which the best known are the Literary and Philosophical Institutes, the Mechanics' Institutes and the Owenite Halls of Science.[70] Secondly, there were the libraries, reading rooms, and working-class newspapers, which flourished despite the stamp duties.[71] Thirdly, freelance lecturers travelled the towns and stimulated self-study among the poor, which in such cases as the Welsh Circulating Schools reached the point of being formally organized;[72] those were the days when, in the words of one economic historian, 'the towns, and even the villages, hummed with the energy of the autodidact'.[73] All of this amounts to an impressive array of devices and arrangements outside the formal educational system, none of which is given proper credit in promoting the knowledge of reading and writing by most historians of education.

This brings us to part-time formal education, such as Sunday Schools and adult evening schools, which figure prominently in all the histories of the period. Less frequently mentioned are the factory schools, which pro-

[69] The tone of Adamson's chapter on 'The Workman's Self-Education' (*English Education*, Ch. 6) illustrates the point. But see Smith, *English Elementary Education*, 36–7; Birchenough, *History*, 52; and Armytage, *Four Hundred Years*, 51–60. Armytage in fact concentrates on informal and part-time formal learning, and refers only incidentally to formal elementary education; nevertheless, his treatment leaves much out of account. But R. D. Altick, *The English Common Reader 1800–1900* (1957), 149–66, provides just the right emphasis.

[70] See e.g. Harrison, *Learning and Living*, 43–57; Simon, *Studies*, 235–53.

[71] Altick, *Common Reader*, 198–293; Webb, *Working Class Reader*, Ch, 1; and particularly P. Hollis, *The Pauper Press. A Study in Working-Class Radicalism of the 1830s* (1970).

[72] A. E. Musson and E. Robinson, *Science and Technology in the Industrial Revolution* (1969), is rich in detail on self-education; see in particular their essay, 'Training Captains of Industry' on the education of Boulton and Watt. See also Simon, *Studies*, 183–93.

[73] E. P. Thompson, *The Making of the English Working Class* (1968), 781. Ch. 16 of this book provides an excellent treatment of working-class literacy in the first half of the nineteenth century.

liferated in the northern textile industry long before the 1833 Act made them mandatory.[74] And, finally, we come to full-time day schools for children, which is where we do face what appears to be an almost unresolvable controversy.

There was actually little controversy until the publication of West's *Education and the State* (1965), inasmuch as most historians of education are agreed that the figures of the Newcastle Commission of 1861 can be dismissed as absurdly optimistic. The Newcastle Commission attempted the first comprehensive survey of school attendance in nineteenth-century England and it concluded that almost every child received some school education during the year, largely in private, charity and proprietary schools, and that there were no serious geographical gaps in the physical provision of schools. In brief, West's argument is that the Newcastle Commission gives a much more reliable picture of educational provision around the middle of the century than the hurriedly assembled report of conditions in four selected industrial towns that served Forster as his main evidence in urging the Education Bill of 1870.[75] Every piece of statistical evidence, he contends, points to a spectacular spontaneous growth in private voluntary education in the first half of the nineteenth century, and the Act of 1870, far from multiplying schools, largely replaced private schools by state schools. He sums up his case in these words: 'in 1869 most people were literate, most children had some schooling, and—what may come as the biggest surprise of all—most parents [working-class included] were paying fees for it.'[76]

Since then he has taken the argument a little further by producing the striking finding that the percentage of national income which was spent on full-time education of children of all ages in 1833 actually exceeded that of 1920! What is even more amazing is that the 1833 figure for children below the age of eleven is nearly the same as that for 1965. Furthermore, these calculations, initially carried out on the assumption of a drop-out rate of 20 per cent in 1833, survive the assumption of a 50 per cent drop-out rate.[77]

Replying to West on behalf of traditional historians of education, Hurt largely gives up the argument about numbers, instead asserting that the day schools of the period were nothing more than baby-minding créches,

[74] M. Sanderson, 'Education and the Factory in Industrial Lancashire, 1780–1840', *Economic History Review*, 2nd ser. xx (Aug. 1967); also G. Ward, 'The Education of Factory Child Workers, 1833–1850', *Economic History, Supplement to the Economic Journal*, iii, (Feb. 1935).

[75] West, *Education and the State*, Ch. 10. For a counter-view, see W. P. McCann, 'Elementary Education on the Eve of the Education Act', *Journal of Educational Administration and History*, ii, (Dec. 1969).

[76] West, *Education and the State*, xvii.

[77] E. G. West, 'Resource Allocation and Growth in Early Nineteenth-Century British Education', *Economic History Review*, 2nd ser. xxiii (1970).

not educational institutions as we would now understand them.[78] The dispute about quality is as old as the Newcastle Commission itself: the reports of the inspectors of the Commission held that the standard of teaching in most elementary schools was 'excellent, well and fair', while the assistant commissioners pronounced an almost wholly unfavourable verdict on the quality of instruction, particularly for the younger children. This debate is unlikely to be ever effectively settled. Contemporary opinion was in each case no more than a judgement based on casual impressions, and the variance in quality between individual schools must have been enormous; it always is at early stages of educational development. Besides, the problem of fairly assessing these judgements now without the hindsight of twentieth-century standards is almost insuperable. Suffice it to say that a fair summary of the evidence about quantity leads to the view that one-half to two-thirds of all children in Britain around the middle of the century attended full-time schooling for about two and possibly three years, few remaining after the age of eleven.[79] Granted that the schooling was probably of very low quality, it nevertheless remains an impressive achievement for what was then an underdeveloped country. Consider, for example, that there are few poor countries today where as many as half the children complete the first six grades of primary school; the average years of schooling in Africa, Asia, and Latin America nowadays is not more than two to three years. Perhaps England did not compare favourably with France and Russia in the nineteenth century in terms of formal schooling; informal schooling, however, probably made up the whole of the difference.

It is part and parcel of West's thesis that the growth of education in Scotland in this period under the impact of the Act of 1696 has been widely misunderstood. It is generally acknowledged that the Scottish Lowlands achieved almost universal literacy by 1760 before the 'take-off' into the Industrial Revolution, and of course this remarkable feat is usually attributed to the Scottish parochial system. Be that as it may, once the Industrial Revolution started, the shifts of population from rural areas to the towns seem to have relegated the parochial schools to a minor role. At any rate, by 1818 fee-paying private schools enrolled twice as many children as did the parochial schools and, when we add charity day schools and Sunday Schools, four times as many children as the parochial system. Furthermore, the government's returns of 1833/4 showed that the proportion of the population receiving schooling was practically the same in the two halves of Britain; thus, if we can assume identical population age structures in

[78] J. S. Hurt, 'Professor West on Early Nineteenth-Century Education', *Economic History Review*, 2nd ser. xxiv (1971), and E. G. West, 'Interpretation of Early Nineteenth-Century Educational Statistics', *ibid.*

[79] The evidence for a model period of four years, which goes further than what is endorsed by received opinion, is argued by E. G. West in a forthcoming book, *Education and Industrial Revolution.*

Scotland and England, we may conclude that the growth of education in Scotland during the Industrial Revolution was largely unaffected by the statutory provision of the Act of 1696.[80] In short, the fondly held belief of the classical economists that the law-abiding conditions of Scotland could be traced directly to Scotland's superior school provision consequent on the Act of 1696 is now seen to have been nothing less than a total misunderstanding of the actual course of events.

A final word about fees must bring the discussion to an end. We have seen that none of the classical economists advocated free elementary education except for the children of the poor. It is remarkable how the early nineteenth-century presumption that parents in general are perfectly willing to pay directly for education but that some cannot afford to do so is lost sight of in most modern histories of education. To quote only one authority: 'Education, universal, compulsory, gratuitous . . . this formula describes the aim in the educational sphere which English Radicals and Liberals strove to attain throughout the nineteenth century.'[81] Impelled by recent experience to believe that only compulsion can ever make education universal and that compulsory education logically implies free education, modern historians find the views of the early nineteenth-century writers strangely self-contradictory. If West is to be believed, however, elementary education during the Industrial Revolution was neither compulsory nor free, but it was practically universal. Similarly, Forster in 1870 retained school fees with free tickets for the poor, and most schools only became completely free in 1891; however, elementary education became compulsory in 1881 so that for ten years education was compulsory but not free. Even the organized working class did not begin to demand a free system of secular elementary education until 1847.[82] But middle-class opinion did not come round to 100 per cent publicly financed education until after the Revised Code of 1862 and all through the period under examination fee-paying was widespread, no less among the working-classes than among the middle classes: 'Working-class parents in Bristol, which had a population of 120,000 [in 1834], were paying over £15,000 a year for their children's education, a sum over half that reluctantly granted by Parliament in 1833 to aid the building of schools throughout England and Wales. This gives a glimpse of the extent to which the working class supported schools out of their own pockets.'[83] Were the uncultivated really incompetent to be judges of cultivation, or were they simply too poor to do much judging?

[80] West, *Education and the State*, 73–5; also T. C. Smout, *A History of the Scottish People, 1560–1830* (1969), 452–72.

[81] Adamson, *English Education*, 7. It would be easy to cite other examples.

[82] Simon, *Studies*, 340–6. 'Free education for all children' was one of the ten immediate objectives in the *Communist Manifesto* of 1848.

[83] Ibid. 254.

Some Concluding Reflections

THOMAS WILSON

I

THE essays in this volume on Adam Smith have reviewed the range and shown the subtlety of his system of thought. Any concluding summary of so vast an area would be unwieldy and cumbersome. A full summary even of this second part alone which is mainly concerned with Smith's economics would be hard to construct and would probably contribute little. If, nevertheless, some final comments seem appropriate, the best course may be to take a central theme and to comment on this theme in the light of preceding essays. Some concluding observations, if so fitted together as to form a pattern of this kind, may serve to complement and to extend what has been said in the Introduction.

Difficult as any summary, however devised, may be, there can be little difficulty about the choice of such a central theme. That theme selects itself: the role of the market and the state in the conduct of economic affairs. An attempt will therefore be made in these concluding pages to bring together some of Smith's views and, in doing so, to make some passing references to certain aspects of this many-sided topic that are relevant and important two centuries after the publication of *The Wealth of Nations*.

Caricature is one of the penalties of greatness, and it is a penalty which Smith has not been allowed to escape. In popular culture Smith is the extreme and uncompromising exponent of *laisser faire*. He is the apologist for capitalism, the mouthpiece of the new bourgeoisie. In his own day those who wished to be so convinced may have been prepared to believe that in his works selfishness had indeed been hallowed by metaphysics. Two centuries later, few people may be inclined to place so much reliance on the Invisible Hand or to accord the same respect to an economic philosophy in which so much reliance was placed upon it. The caricature now fails to appeal. That this is in fact a caricature, and a rather crude one, will be apparent enough to anyone who has read these essays—or, of course, the works of Smith himself. There is always a danger, however, that in attempting to correct this caricature, one may produce another. It would be foolish if, in reminding ourselves of the qualifications, we allowed ourselves to lose sight of the central ideas themselves.

Caricatures distort and the distortions may, indeed, mislead; but by definition caricatures do not misrepresent their subjects in all respects even when the drawings are bad ones. For the fact remains that Smith did place great emphasis on the socially beneficial effects of the attempts by individuals to better themselves, he did believe that the competitive market was an immensely useful social mechanism and he did envisage a role for the state which, if less severely restricted than the caricature suggests, was nevertheless meagre by our contemporary standards two centuries later.

Under these circumstances, it is perhaps appropriate to try and answer, with this particular context in mind, the general question posed by Professor Boulding: 'After Samuelson, Who Needs Adam Smith?' (*History of Political Economy*, iii, 1971).

II

Smith's starting point was the remarkable growth that had already taken place, even by the latter part of the eighteenth century, in the wealth of nations. As he was at pains to stress, this growth was not the outcome of any conscious plan on the part of Governments or people but was rather the consequence of the propensity to truck, barter and exchange. In saying this he was not simply adopting an ideological viewpoint but was accepting an undeniable fact of history. For one as interested as he was in the stages of historical development, this was a natural attitude. It was also a natural attitude for the author of TMS with his interest in human psychology. The argument may be fundamentally simple; yet it may be suggested that there is a case for recalling his emphasis on unintended and unforeseen social outcomes in an age when success and failure are so often attributed almost exclusively to the conscious efforts of Governments. Perhaps no one would advance explicitly so exclusive a claim for the power of official policy but, implicitly, it lies behind much of what is said and written about economic affairs in the latter part of the twentieth century. We may, therefore, need to be reminded that even in economies far more planned than any Smith could have envisaged—even indeed in Communist countries where very detailed planning enforced by controls is at the centre of economic philosophy—the actual course of events will follow lines which lie in part beyond this control. We may after all need to be reminded periodically of the fact of uncertainty, of the importance of unforeseen and unforceable developments. To say this is not to surrender wholly to economic determinism. Smith himself would not have gone as far as that. But there is, in effect, a strong element of economic determinism in his work. What is interesting is to observe that determinism in his case led to a free-enterprise market economy, whereas Marx's determinism led him beyond the liberal economy to Communism.

While the propensity to truck, barter and exchange permits an intricate division of labour which is one of the causes of economic growth, the interdependence which this entails requires some machinery for communication and control, some means of affording incentives and of rewarding success.

In Smith's view, the market met this need, if not completely, at least over a wide range of activities. Unfortunately there is a modern tendency to distinguish between 'economic' and 'social' considerations as though the market itself was not a piece of social machinery and an exceedingly important way of achieving social objectives. To Smith, this would, we may infer, have seemed exceedingly odd. The market is a social mechanism which can be relied upon to perform much of the work of communication and control. In the modern world, this work can also be performed in part, though never completely, by preparing official plans and by seeking to enforce these plans by official commands. The contemporary debate revolves around the choice in any particular situation of the right combination of plans and prices, for the cocktail may be mixed in different ways. What is, however, quite irrational is any suggestion that a complex economy with an elaborate division of labour could operate without *either* markets or official plans. Yet it is necessary to report that this strange view has had some vocal supporters in the later part of the twentieth century. (See, for example, the criticism of this view in *The Political Economy of the New Left* by Assar Lindbeck, (1971); and in 'Market Socialism and Its Critics' by A. Nove, *Soviet Studies*, July 1972.)

There is no need to stress Smith's dislike of controls. He attacked with vigour attempts by state or guilds to regulate prices and wages, to specify the characteristics of the goods to be produced, and to obstruct the free movement of goods and people. In part these controls were designed to support the general strategy of the mercantilist system; in part their origin was so traditional that they no longer had, in his day, any clear contemporary *raison d'être*. But the controls he condemned were not related to an economic plan of the modern kind which specifies programmes for production and for the inputs required to make it possible. In this sense, there were no plans in his day whether of the Soviet or the French indicative variety. Thus, in modern terms, what Smith was criticizing were, in effect, controls without plans. We may therefore find ourselves tempted to ask whether he would have been equally hostile if he had been able to envisage an economy with plans enforced by controls or regulated by some mixture of controls and prices. There is little point, perhaps, in indulging in speculation of this kind, but it is proper to remind ourselves of his scepticism about the wisdom and foresight of Government, his cynical realism about the distortions that might arise from the 'clamorous importunity of vested interests', and his belief that the system of 'natural liberty' made detailed supervision and control by central authority both unnecessary and undesirable.

The analysis of the price system has been described by Professor Arrow as 'one of the most significant intellectual achievements of mankind.' (*Human Values and Economic Policy*, ed. by Sidney Hook (1967), 10.)

Professor Hollander and others have shown that Smith's own contribution to this achievement was greater than has always been recognized. Although he was writing without the insights of 'the marginal revolution', the WN contains what is, in effect, quite a sophisticated account of how a market economy adjusts to change both from the side of demand and that of supply. Smith was much interested in 'natural' price and thus in movements towards equilibrium but he did not allow his attention to be so much absorbed by the contemplation of some final state of equilibrium as to neglect the forces making for change. There were two aspects of his dynamic approach which may call for particular attention: first, his predictions about different elasticities of supply in a growing economy and the corresponding adjustment of demand to take account of what would now be described as elasticities of substitution; secondly, his stress on the way in which competition would stimulate efficiency and thus, in modern terminology, shift the position of the cost curves.

Although Smith had quite a lot to say about the probable effects of different forms of business organization, and even predicted certain aspects of the separation between ownership and management, he did not develop any very precise theory of the pricing and output policies of the firm. This is an obvious deficiency although, with the history of economics from the early thirties until quite recent years in mind, the debit mark may seem less serious than it would have done at one time. For Smith, if he did not succeed in producing a rigorous analysis that was right, he at least avoided the danger of producing a rigorous analysis that was in some ways seriously misleading—and his shade may therefore be commended by another shade, that of Alfred Marshall! Thus the practice of analysing competition on the assumption of given cost-curves is infinitely removed from the tenor of the WN. For Smith, competition implied rivalry and the most powerful stimulus to efficiency both in reducing costs and in responding to consumers' preferences that could be devised. 'Good management' was of central interest to Smith and it 'can never be universally established, but in consequence of that free and universal competition which forces everyone to have recourse to it for the sake of self-defence' (WN I.xi.b.5). This aspect of competition, if not forgotten, was too little stressed during the heyday of comparative statics. Today such issues have at last been made theoretically respectable by the introduction of the term 'X-efficiency'.

Although so much interested, as a social philosopher, in social welfare, Smith was prepared to accept the fact that people will pursue their own interests. What he was at such pains to stress was that personal interests need not always conflict. *Mutual* advantage may result from a bargain. Before this is set aside as a mere truism, it is necessary to recall how widely the doctrine of confrontation is accepted in practical affairs today both in dealing with domestic issues and, not least, in foreign trade. If, however, a reasonable degree of harmony is to be achieved, then economic affairs need to be conducted in a proper environment and, for Smith, a crucial aspect of their environment was the existence of competition. This need not indeed be 'perfect' competition in the special sense accorded to that expression in the nineteen-thirties. But what is required is rivalry and workable competition.

If, however, competition should be seriously undermined in an important market, what verdict can then be given about the price system? The outstanding contemporary market where competition is most severely restricted is, of course, the labour market. Here the situation is vastly different from that with which Smith was familiar. When he observed the economic environment of his own day, he was naturally impelled to condemn the greater severity with which the combination acts were enforced against the men as compared with the masters. It was then the workers who would always be in the weaker position; but two centuries later, the situation has changed dramatically. Notwithstanding the importance of large firms and the perennial attempt to establish 'combinations', whether explicitly or by means of information agreements, the competitive pressures in the product market remain strong. It is rather in the market for labour that the monopolistic organizations controlling supply are so powerful. It is this, of course, that has led to attempts to devise incomes policies of one sort or another. What is of particular interest to us is that attempts of this kind have occasionally been condemned, not merely by the interested parties, but by some of those who claim to be following in the tradition of Adam Smith. It is, therefore, of some importance to remind ourselves that Smith's reliance on the market was conditional upon there being competition. 'Competition' he said 'will regulate much better than any assize' (WN I.x.c.62). Or again: 'The real and effectual discipline which is exercised over a workman is not that of his corporation, but that of his customers' (WN I.x.c.31). If, however, competition has been undermined and cannot readily be restored, is an assize better than nothing? This is one of the central questions of economic policy in the second half of the twentieth century. If it would be unreasonable to expect to find much clear guidance in a great treatise written two centuries ago, it would also be unreasonable to invoke the authority of the master out of context in order to condemn all attempts to set up and to use an 'assize' in countries where it is politically impossible to restore competition in the labour market.

III

Money is indispensable in any economy where the division of labour has advanced significantly. Indeed, as we now appreciate, some kind of money plays a part even in what appear to be quite primitive economies. In the more developed world, the importance of money is not confined to economies where private enterprise is predominant, for it also performs critically important, if more limited, functions even in Communist countries notwithstanding their great reliance upon central planning by the state. To Smith money was 'the great wheel of circulation, the great instrument of commerce' (WN II.ii.23). This may appear to be another obvious point, too simple to be of much interest in modern times; but it is salutary to remember that there is a long-standing suspicion of money on the part of some of the critics of the capitalist system and a corresponding inclination to suppose that money can be dispensed with when capitalism has gone. This view is still held in some quarters and, in the not so very distant past, it found practical expression. Thus during the period of War Communism the all-Russian congress of economic councils 'expressed the desire to see the final elimination of any influence of money upon the relation of economic units' (*An Economic History of the USSR* by Alex Nove, (1972), 64). Russia learned her lesson in due course but much distress might have been avoided if the teaching of Smith—which received so much attention in an early phase of Russian history—had not been forgotten.

Money is indispensable but money can get out of hand and become, not only an engine of commerce, but a cause of serious economic difficulties as we all know to our cost. On this issue, Smith was undeniably weak. He did not envisage the possibility of deflation because he held that 'what is saved is as regularly consumed as what is usually spent, and nearly in the same time too' (WN II.iii.18). This was a view that was, of course, to dominate the classical tradition. It is true that, in the long-run, he may have been nearer the truth than Malthus for, in the event, growth was not checked by chronic long-run deflation. Intended saving may diverge from intended investment in the short-run but, over a longer period, there may be a closer link, as Denis Robertson was wont to stress. We are touching at this point on an issue that still requires more attention than it has received and one may even be tempted to give Smith marks for superior insight about the longer run. These marks cannot, however, really be very high for Smith did not analyse these matters in any sophisticated way whether with regard to the short-run or the long. There is another point which must be made at this stage. Smith's failure to appreciate the danger of deflation is well-known. What has received less attention is his failure to say much about inflation resulting from an excess of paper money. For he held to the view that any issue in excess of a country's needs would simply return to the banks. Of course he was partly following Hume's teaching on monetary matters, but with less sophistication.[1] Subsequently the theory of demand

[1] Thus, in discussing the implications for international finance, Viner has observed that Hume, for his part, did not neglect rising prices as Smith had done. 'One of the mysteries of the history of economic thought is that Adam Smith, although he was intimately acquainted with Hume and his writings, should have made no reference in *The Wealth of Nations* to the self-regulating mechanism in terms of price levels and trade balances, and should have been content with an exposition of the international distribution of specie in

inflation was to be developed by Smith's successors, notably Ricardo, Thornton, and Joplin, and, in doing so, they turned their attention to one part of the price mechanism which, in *this* connection, Smith had also neglected: the role of the rate of interest and the effect of a divergence between the market rate and the 'natural' rate which would equate saving and investment.

We can sum up this section by saying that the effective operation of the market on which Smith placed so much emphasis requires appropriate planning of changes in the money supply and in fiscal policy. Smith may be excused for failing to recognize the importance of fiscal policy but it must also be acknowledged that he was not one of the pioneers in monetary theory.

IV

Let us now return to the question of economic growth and consider the respective roles of the state and the market. Although Smith did not explain very clearly the nature of the factors that could call a halt to the process of economic growth, his view that a limit might in fact be reached finds an echo today in the writings of the Club of Rome and similar 'doomsters'. When growth was continuing, real wages would rise; when it was checked the continuing rise in population would reduce real wages to 'the lowest rate which is consistent with common humanity' (WN I.viii.16). This is the pessimism to which Professor Heilbroner has drawn attention.

It need not be assumed, however, that the subsistence level itself will be unaffected by the experience of growth and will thus be as low at the end of the period of expansion as at its beginning. Smith saw clearly enough that poverty is, in part at least, a relative concept and he might have applied his reasoning to his discussion of the ending of growth. In fact it was left to Ricardo to do so at a later date. Admittedly, even if real wages were to be no higher after an era of growth than at the outset, it would not be reasonable to infer that the whole process of expansion had therefore been pointless. While the expansion lasted people would enjoy higher standards, and it might after all last for a very long time indeed. Even if a halt were finally called and real wages dropped back, the total number of people alive would be larger when the process of expansion finally came to an end. It is with considerations of this kind that Mr. Eltis has been concerned.

Our immediate concern is with the respective roles of the market and the

the already obsolete terms of the requirement by each country, without specific reference to its relative price level, of a definite amount of money to circulate trade.' *Studies in the Theory of International Trade*' (1937), 87. As Professor Bloomfield has pointed out in his essay above, 478–80, Smith's position appears similar to that adopted by some modern economists of the monetarist school; but in order to rationalize Smith's position fully, it is necessary to make some special assumptions: (a) no inflation from paper money elsewhere in the world, (b) fixed exchange rates, and (c) no non-tradable goods.

state in this process of growth. As we have observed, the growth which had already taken place and that which Smith expected to take place in the future were not the result of special efforts directed to this end by Government. It was the system of 'natural liberty' which permitted change and development and this was clearly, in Smith's view, a high mark in favour of that system, even if his primary objective was to describe and explain rather than to recommend. That modern school of thought which opposes economic growth might perhaps want to accord a lower mark; but it is hard to believe that even those economists who hold this view about the undesirability of growth in the latter part of the twentieth century would really urge that growth should have been checked in the latter half of the eighteenth century. For that matter it is not easy to discern the means by which a *halt* could then have been called. Many of those modern economists who take a different view and wish to see the rate of growth sustained, and even accelerated, would accord a larger role to the state than Smith thought proper, although there would be marked differences of opinion about both the nature and the scale of the official policies thought to be required. Smith, it need scarcely be said, was deeply sceptical of what the state might achieve in this regard, although assistance with education and the like might help to create conditions favourable to growth. It is fair to add that British experience in recent years has left a good many observers sceptical about the possibility of altering the 'underlying rate of growth'. Thus there have been some signs of a reversion to determinism in this context. There may, however, be other ways in which Governments and perhaps international bodies can do something to extend the period of growth and to protect living standards. Here we are touching upon such large issues as conservation and population policies and it would be unreasonable to expect that the WN would be an appropriate guide.

Growth has its costs. There is little need to emphasize that fact at a time when so much stress is being placed on the damage to the environment. It was, however, the human costs that particularly concerned Smith as it did several of his contemporaries. He developed what we would now call a theory of alienation many years before Marx. This is one of the darker sides of the WN to which Professor Heilbroner has drawn attention. But, as Professor West has observed, alienation may be interpreted in various ways and Smith's position differed somewhat from that of Marx. What most needs to be stressed, perhaps, is the fact that alienation, in one sense at least, is the consequence of the division of labour and is a necessary penalty of industrialization. This is true whether the industrial economy is capitalist or socialist. It is, indeed, far from clear that increased central planning by a more powerful state bureaucracy would lessen this sense of alienation. Smith, for his part, felt that these ills could at least be eased a little, and it was here that the state had a role to play in fostering education and promoting entertainments of one kind or another. The proposal may seem sensible enough, though hardly sufficient to cope adequately with the problems of alienation.

V

As Professor Peacock has reminded us, both Hume and Smith had a clear idea of the nature of what we now describe as 'public goods' and recognized the importance of there being an adequate supply of such goods. Similarly Smith's proposal about elementary education implies a recognition of the case for what have come to be known as 'merit goods'. Smith was, however, very conscious of the danger of an extravagant and ill-advised use of resources and was in general convinced that the strength of demand should be tested through the market. It is true that in modern economic literature a good deal of attention has been given to possible voting systems as democratic tests, but Smith could scarcely, in his day, have been expected to anticipate much of this later line of inquiry. It remains true, however, that the scope for using such devices is limited and, over the range of issues which the market is capable of handling, the market can be so used as to obtain the most 'democratic' answer, even two centuries after the WN.

Although 'voting through the market' is democratic, inequality implies plural voting. The radical resentment felt against this plural voting has, of course, often encompassed the market itself in condemnation. Smith's own views on inequality were ambivalent, and indeed it might be said that the WN was a mixture of conservatism and radicalism. As Professor Spengler has recorded, Smith had many sharp things to say about businessmen; he was impatient, for example, of their tendency to blame high wages for lack of competitiveness in foreign trade but to neglect high profits (WN I.ix.24). As Professor Rees has pointed out, he was one of the first to lay stress on the economy of high wages and to warn against the danger of excessively long hours and over-work. This emphasis, together with his concern with education, is what would now be described as an interest in 'human capital'. This modern term is not particularly attractive and it may be misleading. For Smith was not merely anxious to ensure that the proletariat was properly cared for in order to ensure that it would be appropriately efficient. It must be clear to any reader of the TMS and the WN, that his human interest was warmer and deeper than that. Although his moral philosophy was not narrowly 'utilitarian', he expresses at times what reads like a radical Benthamite concern for the greatest happiness of the greatest number: for example, '. . . what improves the circumstances of the greater part can never be regarded as inconveniency to the whole' (WN I.viii.36). Some of his strongest expressions of view were to be found in the Early Draft of the WN and, in the Lectures, he points out that the unpleasantness of particular lines of work and the rewards obtained vary inversely.[2] But the WN itself, if less forthright on the whole, contains several passages that are far too radical to warrant the view that he was indifferent to the question of fairness in distribution. Thus one may quote: 'For one rich man, there must be at least five hundred poor, and the affluence of the few supposes the indigence of the many' (WN V.i.b.2). Nor was his radicalism confined to questions of income and wealth. A wider sympathy—and one that should not be regarded as merely an expression of his Whiggery—is contained in remarks such as the one to the effect that: 'All the innocent blood that was shed in the civil wars, provoked less indignation than the death of Charles I' (TMS I.iii.2.2). Why then did he not propose more radical measures in the WN itself?

In assessing his views on inequality in *earned* incomes, it is necessary to recall Smith's firm belief that the effort exerted by anyone in any particular occupation will depend very much upon the relationship between reward and effort. This, he believed, held true of the academic professor and of the cleric as well as the worker and the farmer. This view was not necessarily inconsistent with the belief that, if *different* occupations are compared, there is no positive correlation between reward and effort. He was also very conscious of an important point that is sometimes overlooked in modern political discussion: that is, the way in which differences in pay will draw people into occupations where their talents can be put to better use. Thus the market performs an allocative function which would otherwise have to be performed by means of controls, with less efficiency and less freedom for the individual. This movement of people from some occupations to others that offered more would tend to reduce inequalities between occupations. The system of natural liberty would therefore even out differences to some extent and this equalizing force should not be impeded by monopolistic restraints. Differences in productivity between different individuals would remain. But Smith did not believe that these in the main reflected innate differences. The explanation lay rather in education and training and here, as we have already observed, the state had a contribution to make.

Even in a shorter period, competition would remove inequities created by monopolistic restrictions. But, as Professor Bowley has observed: 'No attempt was made in *The Wealth of Nations* to show that this freedom (of the market) would lead to a distribution of wealth consistent with Adam Smith's ideal of social justice or welfare whatever that is believed to be. It has led, however, to the view that the prices of the factors in a fully competitive market are *fair* as between individuals in the markets rather in

[2] 'The opulence of the merchant is greater than that of his clerks, though he works less; and they again have six times more than an equal number of artisans, who are more employed. The artisan who works at his ease within doors has far more than the poor labourer who trudges up and down without intermission. Thus, he who as it were, bears the burden of society, has the fewest advantages.' LJ (B) 213, ed. Cannan; 163; cf. ED 2.3.

the sense in which *fair* is used in the concept of *fair play*, in contrast to the *unfairness* of imperfectly competitive markets' (*Studies in the History of Economic Theory before 1870*, (1973), 131). Competition would thus prevent 'exploitation' in this sense but not 'exploitation' if this is taken to mean that all incomes from property constitute 'exploitation'. Smith, of course, did not deny that land and capital are productive or that their contribution to output benefits the workers as well as the owners. But, even if privately owned, the ownership of capital and land may be highly concentrated or more widely distributed. If, for example, Smith has recommended a policy of land reform, this would have been quite consistent with the radical views expressed throughout his works[3]. It may be that his more conservative attitude reflected his emphasis on historical evolution which, if it did not entail historical determinism in the full sense, may at least have made him inclined to view with caution the practical scope for radical change. This attitude may perhaps be detected in his remarks about the appropriation of property and the accumulation of stock: '. . . it would be to no purpose to trace further what might have been its effects (i.e. the effects of this change) upon the recompense of wages on labour' (WN I.viii.5). There is also a further but related question of obvious importance: this is the extent to which the WN was intended to be a normative as well as a positive work.

The redistribution of income and wealth, which in turn affects the ways in which markets operate, involve problems of a kind that many modern writers on welfare economics have found particularly troublesome. Apart from the difficulty of assessing the consequences of changes in distribution for the general functioning of the economy, there is the question of how to make interpersonal comparisons of utility that will be generally acceptable, and there is the further question of value judgements. The shifts in income and wealth need not, of course, consist only of those between rich and poor but may well be between different occupational groups, i.e. horizontal changes as well as vertical ones. Thus growth itself may entail both gainers and losers; or, to take another example, a change in foreign economic policy may have similar effects. Again the choice between different forms and rates of taxation for the financing of public goods will have effects for distribution, and the whole question of merit goods raises basic questions of social ethics. It may be that modern analytical welfare economics has made too much heavy weather of these difficulties and produced a cautious agnosticism which has been accompanied, not perhaps surprisingly, by an unduly uncritical and implicit treatment of these issues in much applied welfare economics. The fact that there are real analytical difficulties is apparent enough.

[3] That is to say a proposal for reform more far-reaching than his proposal for freer trade in land.

Smith, for his part, was not daunted by the problem of making interpersonal comparisons. On the contrary, 'sympathy', in the sense of fellow-feeling, is the central theme of the TMS. Or, to use modern terminology, this work is very much concerned with describing and analysing considerations relevant to the making of interpersonal comparisons. Moreover Smith felt that human beings were so constituted for it to be reasonable to expect a tolerable measure of agreement in this field. Admittedly this reasoning must not be pushed too far in dealing with economic matters. The common features in human nature were rather broad characteristics. As has been observed in the Introduction, his approach did not exclude differences in human experience and these, we must now observe, might be reflected in difficulties in the making of interpersonal comparisons of utility. It is, after all, the very diversity in preferences that lies behind the propensity to trade, barter and exchange that constitutes one of the basic reasons for wishing to use the market as a social mechanism. When the importance of such diversity is conceded, it follows that problems may be encountered in comparing the effects on different people of economic changes which, though significant, are limited and do not involve basic matters of life and death. One cannot, therefore, claim that the analysis in the TMS provided Smith with a way of dealing adequately with the problem of verifying interpersonal comparisons or with that of obtaining near unanimity in support of any particular comparisons that might be made. In the WN Smith was clearly enough content to make broad judgements and leave it at that.

When we turn to value judgements we do not find in Smith the sharp, perhaps over-simplified, distinction between such judgements and empirical statements that we find in much modern welfare economics. Again Smith would appear to have been more hopeful about the possibility of reaching a tolerably good consensus, at least in any given age and society. The achievement of this consensus would, however, have required that those who passed judgement were reasonably disinterested, or at least capable of taking a disinterested view. The same condition is necessary in making any statements involving interpersonal comparisons of utility which, if ostensibly factual, may be biased by self-interest. The safeguard against this danger, which is a central feature of the TMS, is the notion of the 'impartial spectator', a notion which could have been put to much greater use in the WN. Moreover greater agreement might be reached on moral issues by the exchange of opinions. Smith's position was clearly far removed from the view that different value judgements simply reflect differences in 'taste' that cannot usefully be discussed.

The role of the impartial spectator in Smith's moral philosophy has been discussed by Professors Raphael and Campbell in their essays in the first part. The possible usefulness of this notion in analytical welfare economics cannot be further explored here, but a brief comment can be made in conclusion.

The Introduction has emphasized the extent to which Smith's views on moral philosophy were carried over into his writings on economics; but it would be going too far to claim that the synthesis was complete. This is not merely because the WN is a more empirical and less metaphysical work than the TMS, as Viner, for example, so rightly stressed in his essay, *Smith and Laisser-Faire*. (*Adam Smith, 1776–1926*, (1928), chapter 5.) On the analytical plane itself the ideas in the two works were not fully integrated. Whether a fuller integration would have been achieved if Smith had completed the vast intellectual task he had set himself can be no more than a matter for speculation.

Table of Corresponding Passages of *The Wealth of Nations*

THE first column gives part and paragraph numbers from the Glasgow edition of *The Wealth of Nations*. The second and third columns give the corresponding pages in the (5th) Cannan edition (Methuen, 1930) and in the Modern Library version (New York, 1937).

I.i	1930	1937
1	5	3
2	5–6	3–4
3	6–7	4–5
4	7–9	5–7
5	9	7
6	9–10	7–8
7	10	8–9
8	10–11	9–10
9	12	10
10	12–13	11
11	13–14	11–12

I.ii		
1	15	13
2	15–16	13–14
3	17	15
4	17–18	15–16
5	18	16

I.iii		
1	19	17
2	19–20	17–18
3	20–21	18–19
4	21	19
5	21–22	19–20
6	22	20
7	22	20
8	22–23	20–21

I.iv	1930	1937
1	24	22
2	24–25	22–23
3	25	23
4	25–26	23–24
5	26	24
6	26	24
7	26–27	24–25
8	27–28	25–26
9	28	26
10	28–29	26–28
11	29–30	28
12	30	28
13	30	28
14	30	28
15	30	28
16	30	28
17	30	29
18	30–31	29

I.v		
1	32	30
2	32–33	30–31
3	33	31
4	33	31
5	33–34	31–32
6	34	32
7	34–35	32–33
8	35	33
9	35	33
10	35–36	33–34
11	36	34

I.v	1930	1937
12	36	34
13	36–37	34–35
14	37	35
15	37–38	35–36
16	38	36
17	38–39	36–37
18	39	37
19	39	37
20	39–40	37–38
21	40	38
22	40	38
23	40–41	38–39
24	41	39
25	41	39
26	41	39–40
27	42	40
28	42–43	40–41
29	43	41
30	43	42
31	43–44	42
32	44	42
33	44	42–43
34	45	43
35	45	43–44
36	45–46	44
37	46	44
38	46	44–45
39	47	45
40	47–48	45–46
41	48	46
42	48	46

I.vi	1930	1937
1	49	47
2	49	47
3	49	47
4	49–50	47–48
5	50	48
6	50–51	48–49
7	51	49
8	51	49
9	52	50
10	52	50
11	52	50
12	53	51
13	53	51
14	53	51
15	53	51–52
16	54	52
17	54	52
18	54–55	52–53
19	55	53
20	55	53
21	55	53
22	55	53
23	55	53–54
24	56	54

I.vii		
1	57	55
2	57	55
3	57	55
4	57	55
5	57–58	55–56
6	58	56
7	58	56
8	58	56
9	58–59	56
10	59	57
11	59	57
12	59	57
13	59	57
14	60	57–58
15	60	58
16	60	58
17	60–61	58–59
18	61	59
19	61	59
20	62	59
21	62	60
22	62	60
23	62	60
24	62–63	60–61
25	63	61
26	63	61
27	63	61

I.vii	1930	1937
28	63–64	61
29	64	62
30	64	62
31	64	62
32	64	62
33	65	62–63
34	65	63
35	65	63
36	65	63
37	65	63
I.viii		
1	66	64
2	66	64
3	66	64
4	66–67	64–65
5	67	65
6	67	65
7	67	65
8	67	65
9	67–68	65–66
10	68	66
11	68	66
12	68	66
13	68–69	66–67
14	69	67
15	69–70	67–68
16	70	68
17	70	68
18	70–71	69
19	71	69
20	71	69
21	71	69
22	71–72	69–70
23	72–73	70–71
24	73–74	71–72
25	74	73
26	74–75	73
27	75	73–74
28	75	74
29	76	74
30	76	74
31	76–77	74–75
32	77	75

I.viii	1930	1937
33	77–78	75–76
34	78–79	76–78
35	79–80	78
36	80	78–79
37	80–81	79
38	81	79
39	81	79
40	81–82	80
41	82–83	80–81
42	83	81
43	83	81
44	83–84	81–82
45	84	82–83
46	85	83
47	85	83
48	85	83–84
49	86	84
50	86	84
51	86–87	84–85
52	87	85
53	87	85
54	87	85–86
55	87–88	86
56	88	86
57	88	86
I.ix		
1	89	87
2	89	87
3	89	87
4	90	88
5	90–91	88–89
6	91	89
7	91	89–90
8	92	90
9	92–93	90–91
10	93–94	91–92
11	94–95	92–93
12	95	93–94
13	95–96	94
14	96	94–95
15	96–97	95
16	97	95–96
17	97	96

I.ix	1930	1937
18	97–98	96
19	98	96
20	98	96–97
21	98	97
22	98–99	97
23	99	97
24	99–100	97–98

I.x.a (Of Wages and Profit in the different Employments of Labour and Stock)

1	101	99
2	101	99
3	101	99

I.x.b (Inequalities arising from the Nature of the Employments themselves)

1	102	100
2	102	100
3	102–03	100–01
4	103	101
5	103	101
6	103	101
7	103	101
8	103–04	101–02
9	104	102
10	104	103
11	105	103
12	105	103
13	105	103–04
14	105–06	104
15	106	104
16	106	105
17	107	105
18	107	105
19	107	105
20	107	105
21	107	106
22	107–08	106
23	108	106–07
24	108	107
25	108–09	107

I.x.b	1930	1937
26	109	107
27	109–10	108
28	110	108–09
29	110–11	109
30	111	109
31	111–12	109–10
32	112	110
33	112–13	110–11
34	113	111
35	113	112
36	114	112
37	114–15	112–13
38	115	113–14
39	116	114
40	116	114
41	116	114
42	116	114–15
43	116	115
44	117	115
45	117	115
46	117–18	115–16
47	118	116
48	118	116
49	118	116–17
50	119	117
51	119	117
52	119–20	117–18

I.x.c (Inequalities occasioned by the Policy of Europe)

1	120	118
2	120	118
3	120	118–19
4	120	119
5	120–21	119
6	121	119
7	121–22	120
8	122	120
9	122–23	120–21
10	123	121
11	123	121
12	123	121–22
13	123–24	122
14	124	122

I.x.c	1930	1937
15	124	122–23
16	124–25	123
17	125–26	123–24
18	126	124
19	126–27	124–25
20	127	125
21	127	125–26
22	127–28	126
23	128	126–27
24	128–29	127
25	129	127–28
26	129–30	128
27	130	128
28	130	128–29
29	130	129
30	130–31	129
31	131	129
32	131	129
33	131	129
34	131–33	129–31
35	133	131
36	133	131
37	133	131–32
38	133–34	132
39	134–35	132–34
40	135–36	134
41	136	134
42	136	134
43	136–37	134–35
44	137	135
45	137	135
46	137	135–36
47	137–38	136
48	138	136
49	138	136–37
50	138	137
51	138–39	137
52	139	137
53	139	137–38
54	139–30	138
55	140	138–39
56	141	139–40
57	141	140
58	141–42	140

I.x.c	1930	1937
59	142	141
60	142–43	141
61	143–44	141–42
62	144	142–43
63	144	143

I.xi.a (Of the Rent of Land)		
1	145	144
2	145–46	144–45
3	146	145
4	146	145
5	146	145
6	146	145
7	146	145
8	147	145–46
9	147	146

I.xi.b (Part I)		
1	147	146
2	147	146
3	147–48	146–47
4	148	147
5	148–49	147–48
6	149	148
7	149	148
8	149–50	148–49
9	150	149
10	150	149
11	150	149
12	150–51	149–50
13	151	150
14	151	150–51
15	152	151
16	152	151
17	152	151
18	152	151
19	152–53	151–52
20	153	152
21	153	152
22	153	152
23	153	152
24	153	152
25	153–54	152–53

I.xi.b	1930	1937
26	154	153–54
27	155–56	154–55
28	156	155
29	156	155
30	156	155
31	156–57	155–56
32	157–58	156–57
33	158–59	157–59
34	159	159
35	159–60	159
36	160	159
37	160	159–60
38	160	160
39	161	160
40	161	160
41	161–62	160–61
42	162	161

I.xi.c (Part II)		
1	162	161
2	162	161
3	162	161–62
4	163	162
5	163–64	162–63
6	164	163
7	164–65	163–64
8	165	164
9	165	164–65
10	165	165
11	165	165
12	166	165
13	166	165
14	166	165
15	166	165
16	166–67	165–66
17	167	166
18	167–68	166–67
19	168	167
20	168	167
21	168	167–68
22	168–69	168
23	169	168
24	169	168
25	169–70	168–69

I.xi.c	1930	1937
26	170–71	169–70
27	171	170
28	171–72	170–71
29	172	171
30	172	171–72
31	172–73	172
32	173	172–73
33	173–74	173
34	174	173
35	174	173–74
36	174–75	174

I.xi.d (Part III)		
1	175–76	174–75
2	176	175
3	176	175
4	176	176
5	176	176
6	177	176
7	177	176

I.xi.e (Digression on Silver. First Period)		
1	177	176
2	177–78	176–77
3	178	177–78
4	178–79	178
5	179	178
6	179	178–79
7	179	179
8	179	179
9	180	179
10	180	179
11	180	179–80
12	180–81	180
13	181	180
14	181–82	180–81
15	182	181
16	182	181
17	182–83	181–82
18	183	182
19	183	182–83
20	183	183
21	183–84	183

I.xi.e	1930	1937
22	184	183–84
23	184–85	184–85
24	185–86	185
25	186–87	185–86
26	187	186
27	187	186
28	187	186–87
29	187–88	187
30	188	187–88
31	188	188
32	188	188
33	188–89	188
34	189	188–89
35	190	189–90
36	190	190
37	190	190
38	190–91	190
39	191	190–91

I.xi.f (Second Period)		
1	191	191
2	191	191
3	191–92	191
4	192	191–92
5	192	192

I.xi.g (Third Period)		
1	192	192
2	192–93	192
3	193	192–93
4	193–94	193
5	194	194
6	194–96	194–96
7	196	196
8	196	196
9	196	196
10	196–97	196–97
11	197	197
12	197	197
13	197	197
14	197	197
15	197–98	197–98
16	198	198
17	198–99	198–99

I.xi.g	1930	1937
18	199–200	199–200
19	200	200
20	200	200–01
21	201	201
22	201	201
23	201–02	202
24	202	202
25	202	202
26	202–04	202–04
27	204–05	204–05
28	205–07	205–07
29	207	207
30	207	207–08
31	207	208
32	208	208
33	208–09	208–09
34	209	209
35	209	209–10
36	209–10	210
37	210	210

I.xi.h (Variation in . . . the respective values of Gold and Silver)		
1	210–11	211
2	211	211
3	211	211–12
4	211	212
5	211–12	212–13
6	212–13	213–14
7	213	214
8	214	214–15
9	214	215
10	214–15	215
11	215	215–16
12	215	216
13	215	216

I.xi.i (Grounds of the Suspicion that the Value of Silver still continues to decrease)		
1	216	216
2	216	216–17
3	216	217

I.xi.j (Different Effects of the Progress of Improvement upon . . . different Sorts of rude Produce)	1930	1937
1	216–17	217

I.xi.k (First Sort)		
1	217–18	218–19

I.xi.l (Second Sort)		
1	219	219–20
2	219–20	220
3	220–22	220–22
4	222–23	222–23
5	223	224
6	223	224
7	223	224
8	223–24	224–25
9	224–25	225–26
10	225	226
11	225–27	226–27
12	227	227–28
13	227	228

I.xi.m (Third Sort)		
1	228	228
2	228	228–29
3	228	229
4	228	229
5	228	229
6	228–29	229–30
7	229–30	230
8	230	230–31
9	230–31	231
10	231–32	231–32
11	232–33	232–33
12	233–34	233–34
13	234	234
14	234	234–35
15	234–35	235
16	235	235
17	235	235–36

I.xi.m	1930	1937
18	235	236
19	235–36	236
20	236	236
21	236–37	236–37

I.xi.n (Conclusion of the Digression)		
1	237–38	237–39
2	238	239
3	238–39	239
4	239	239–40
5	239–40	240
6	240	240
7	240	240
8	240	240–41
9	240	241
10	241	241–42
11	242	242

I.xi.o (Effects of the Progress of Improvement upon . . . manufactures)		
1	242	242–43
2	242	243
3	242	243
4	242–43	243
5	243	243–44
6	243	244
7	243–44	244
8	244	244
9	244	245
10	245	245
11	245	245
12	245–46	246
13	246	246
14	246	246–47
15	246	247

I.xi.p (Conclusion of the Chapter)		
1	247	247
2	247	247
3	247	247–48
4	247	248

I.xi.p	1930	1937
5	247	248
6	248	248
7	248	248
8	248	248–49
9	248–49	249
10	249–50	249–50
II		
1	258	259
2	258–59	259
3	259	260
4	259	260
5	259	260
6	259–60	260–61
II.i		
1	261	262
2	261	262
3	261	262
4	261–62	262–63
5	262	263
6	262	263
7	262	263
8	262	263
9	262	263
10	262–63	263–64
11	263	264
12	263–64	264–65
13	264	265
14	264	265
15	264	265
16	264	265
17	264–65	265–66
18	265	266
19	265	266
20	265	266
21	265	266
22	265	266
23	265	266
24	265–66	266–67
25	266	267
26	266	267
27	266	267

II.i	1930	1937
28	266–67	267–68
29	267	268
30	267	268
31	267–68	268–69
II.ii		
1	269	270
2	269	270
3	269	270
4	269–70	270–71
5	270	271
6	270	271
7	270–71	271–72
8	271	272
9	271	272
10	272	273
11	272	273
12	272	273
13	272	273
14	272–73	273–74
15	273	274
16	273	274
17	273	274
18	273–74	274–75
19	274	275
20	274	275
21	274	275
22	274–75	275–76
23	275	276
24	275	276
25	275	276
26	275	276
27	276	277
28	276	277
29	276	277
30	276–77	277–78
31	277	278
32	277	278
33	277–78	278–79
34	278	279
35	278	279
36	278	279
37	278–79	279–80
38	279	280

II.ii	1930	1937
39	279	280
40	279–80	280–81
41	280	281
42	280–81	281–82
43	281	282
44	281–82	282–83
45	282	283
46	282–83	283–84
47	283	284
48	283–84	284–85
49	284	285
50	284	285
51	284–85	285
52	285	285–86
53	285	286
54	285	286
55	286	286–87
56	286–87	287–88
57	287	288
58	287	288
59	287	288
60	288	288–89
61	288	289
62	288–89	289–90
63	289–90	290–91
64	290–91	291–92
65	291–92	292–93
66	292	293
67	292–93	293–94
68	293	294
69	293–94	294–95
70	294–95	295–96
71	295	296
72	295–96	296–97
73	296–98	297–99
74	298–99	299–300
75	299	300
76	299	300
77	299–300	300–01
78	300–01	301–02
79	301	302
80	301	302–03
81	302	303
82	302	303

II.ii	1930	1937
83	302	303–04
84	303	304
85	303	304
86	303–04	304–05
87	304	305–06
88	305	306
89	305–06	306–07
90	306	307
91	306	307
92	306	307
93	306–07	307–08
94	307	308
95	307	308
96	307–08	308–09
97	308	309
98	308–09	309–10
99	309	310
100	309–10	310–11
101	310	311
102	310	311–12
103	310–11	312
104	311	312
105	311–12	312–13
106	312	313

II.iii		
1	313–14	314–15
2	314	315
3	314	315
4	315	315–16
5	315	316
6	315	316
7	315–16	316–17
8	316	317
9	316–17	317–18
10	317	318
11	317–18	318–19
12	318–19	319–20
13	319–20	320–21
14	320	321
15	320	321
16	320	321
17	320	321
18	320–21	321–22

II.iii	1930	1937
19	321	322
20	321	322
21	321	321–23
22	322	323
23	322	323
24	322–23	323–24
25	323	324
26	323	324
27	323	324
28	323–24	324–25
29	324	325
30	324–25	325–26
31	325	326
32	325–26	326–27
33	326	327
34	326	327
35	326–27	327–28
36	327–28	328–29
37	328	329
38	328–29	329–30
39	329–30	330–31
40	330	331
41	330	331–32
42	331	332

II.iv		
1	332	333
2	332–33	333
3	333	334
4	333	334
5	333–34	334–35
6	334	335
7	334–35	335–36
8	335	336
9	335–36	336–37
10	336	337
11	336–37	337–38
12	337–38	338–39
13	338	339
14	338	339
15	338–39	339–40
16	339	340
17	339	340

II.v	1930	1937
1	340	341
2	340	341
3	340	341
4	340	341
5	340–41	341
6	341	342
7	341–42	342–43
8	342	343
9	342	343
10	342–43	343–44
11	343	344
12	343–44	344–45
13	344	345
14	344	345
15	344	345
16	344–45	345–46
17	345	346
18	345	346
19	346	346–47
20	346	347
21	346–47	347–48
22	347	348
23	347	348
24	347–48	348–49
25	348	349
26	348	349
27	348	349
28	349	350
29	349–50	350–51
30	350–51	351–52
31	351–52	352–53
32	352	353
33	352	353
34	352–53	353–54
35	353	354
36	353	354
37	354	355

III.i		
1	355–56	356–57
2	356	357
3	356–57	357–58
4	357–58	358–59
5	358	359

III.i	1930	1937
6	358	359
7	358–59	359–60
8	359	360
9	359	360
III.ii		
1	360	361
2	360	361
3	360–61	361–62
4	361	362
5	361–62	362–63
6	362	363
7	362–63	363–64
8	363–64	364–65
9	364	365
10	364–65	365–66
11	365	366
12	365–66	366–67
13	366–67	367–68
14	367–68	368–69
15	368	369
16	368	369
17	368	369–70
18	368–69	370
19	369	370
20	369–70	370–71
21	370	371–72
III.iii		
1	371	373
2	371–72	373–74
3	372–73	374–75
4	373	375
5	373	375
6	373–74	375–76
7	374	376
8	374–75	376–77
9	375–76	377–78
10	376	378
11	376	378–79
12	376–77	379
13	377–78	379–80
14	378	380

III.iii	1930	1937
15	378	380
16	378	380–81
17	378–79	381
18	379	381
19	379–80	381–82
20	380–81	382–83
III.iv		
1	382	384
2	382	384
3	382–83	384–85
4	383	385
5	383–84	385–86
6	384	386
7	384–85	386–87
8	385–86	387–88
9	386	388
10	386–87	388–89
11	387	389
12	387–88	389–90
13	388	390
14	388	390
15	389	390–91
16	389	391
17	389–90	391–92
18	390	392
19	390–91	392–93
20	391–92	393–94
21	392–93	394–95
22	393	395
23	393	395
24	393–94	395–96
IV		
1	395	397
2	395	397
IV.i		
1	396	398
2	396–97	398–99
3	397	399
4	397	399

IV.i	1930	1937
5	398	400
6	398	400
7	398	400
8	398–99	400–02
9	400	402
10	400–01	402–03
11	401–02	403–04
12	402	404
13	402–03	404–05
14	403	405
15	403	405–06
16	404	406
17	404	406
18	404–05	406–07
19	405–07	407–09
20	407	409
21	407	409
22	407	409
23	407–08	409–10
24	408	410
25	408	410
26	408–09	410–11
27	409	411
28	409–10	411–12
29	410–11	412–13
30	411–12	413–15
31	413	415
32	413–14	415–16
33	414–15	416–17
34	415–16	417–18
35	416	418
36	416	418
37	416	418
38	416	418
39	416	418
40	416	418–19
41	416	418–19
42	417	419
43	417	419
44	417	419
45	417	419

IV.ii	1930	1937
1	418	420
2	418–19	420–21
3	419	421
4	419	421
5	419	421
6	419–20	421–22
7	420	422–23
8	421	423
9	421	423
10	421	423
11	421–22	423–24
12	422	424
13	422–23	425
14	423	425
15	423–24	425–26
16	424	426
17	424–25	426–27
18	425	427
19	425	427–28
20	425–26	428
21	426–27	428–29
22	427	429
23	427	429
24	427	429–30
25	427	430
26	428	430
27	428	430
28	428	430
29	428–29	430–31
30	429	431
31	429–30	431–32
32	430	432
33	430	432–33
34	430	433
35	431	433
36	431	433
37	431	433–34
38	431–32	434
39	432–33	435
40	433	435–36
41	433–34	436
42	434–35	436–37
43	435–36	437–38
44	436	438–39
45	436	439

IV.iii.a (Part I)

	1930	1937
1	437–38	440–41
2	438–39	441–42
3	439	442
4	439	442
5	439–40	442–43
6	440	443
7	440–41	443–44
8	441	444
9	441–42	444
10	442	445
11	442–43	445–46

IV.iii.b (Digression concerning Banks of Deposit)

1	443	446
2	443–44	446–47
3	444	447
4	444–45	447
5	445	447–48
6	445–46	448–49
7	446–47	449–50
8	447	450
9	447–48	450
10	448	451
11	448–49	451
12	449	451–52
13	449	452
14	449–50	452–53
15	450–51	453–54
16	451	454
17	451–52	454–55

IV.iii.c (Part II)

1	452–53	455
2	453	456
3	453	456
4	453	456
5	454	456–57
6	454	457
7	454–56	457–59
8	456–57	459–60
9	457–58	460

IV.iii.c	1930	1937
10	458	461
11	458–59	461–62
12	459–60	462–63
13	460	463
14	461	463–64
15	461	464
16	461	464
17	461–62	464–65

IV.iv	Vol. 2	
1	1	466
2	1–2	466
3	2	466–67
4	2	467
5	2	467
6	2–3	467
7	3	467–68
8	3	468
9	3–4	468–69
10	4–5	469–70
11	5	470
12	5	470
13	6	470–71
14	6	471
15	6	471
16	6	471

IV.v.a (Of Bounties)

1	7	472
2	7–8	472
3	8	473
4	8	473
5	8–9	473–74
6	9	474
7	9	474
8	10–11	475–76
9	11	476
10	11	476
11	11	476
12	11	476–77
13	11–12	477
14	12	477
15	12	477

IV. v.a.	1930	1937
16	12	477–78
17	12–13	478
18	13	478
19	13–15	478–80
20	15	480–81
21	15–16	481
22	16	481
23	16–17	481–82
24	17–18	482–83
25	18–19	483–84
26	19	484
27	19	484
28	20	485
29	20	485
30	20	585
31	20–21	485–86
32	21	486
33	21–22	486–87
34	22	487–88
35	22–23	488
36	23	488–89
37	24	489
38	24	489
39	24	489–90
40	24	490

IV.v.b (Digression concerning the Corn Trade)		
1	25	490
2	25	490
3	25–26	490–91
4	26–27	491–92
5	27	492–93
6	27–28	493
7	28	493
8	28–29	493–94
9	29	494
10	29	494
11	29–30	494–95
12	30	495
13	30–31	495–96
14	31	496
15	31–32	496–97
16	32	497

IV.v.b.	1930	1937
17	32–33	497–98
18	33	498
19	33	498
20	33	498–99
21	33–34	499
22	34	499
23	34	499
24	34	499–500
25	34–35	500
26	35	500–01
27	36	501
28	36	501
29	36	501
30	36	501
31	36	501
32	36–37	501–02
33	37–38	502–03
34	39	504
35	39	504
36	39–40	504–05
37	40	505
38	40–41	505–06
39	41–42	506–07
40	42	507
41	42	507
42	42	507–08
43	42–43	508
44	43	508
45	43	508–09
46	44	509
47	44	509
48	44	509–10
49	44–45	510
50	45	510
51	45	510
52	45	510
53	45	510

IV.vi.		
1	46	511
2	46–47	511–12
3	47	512
4	47	512
5	47–48	512–13

IV.vi.	1930	1937
6	48	513
7	48	513
8	48	513–14
9	49	514
10	49	514
11	49	514
12	50	515
13	50	515
14	50–51	515–16
15	51	516
16	51	516
17	51	516
18	51–52	516–17
19	52–53	517–18
20	53	518
21	53–54	518–19
22	54	519
23	54–55	519–20
24	55	520
25	55	520
26	55	520
27	55	520
28	55–56	520–21
29	56	521
30	56–57	521
31	57	521–22
32	57	522

IV.vii.a (Part I)	1930	1937
1	58	523
2	58	523
3	59–60	523–25
4	60	525
5	60	525
6	60–61	525–26
7	61	526
8	61–62	526–27
9	62	527
10	62	527
11	62	527
12	62	527
13	62–63	527–28
14	63	528
15	63	528
16	63–64	528–29
17	64	529
18	64–65	529–30
19	65	530
20	65–66	530–31
21	66	531
22	66	531

IV.vii.b (Part II)	1930	1937
1	66	531–32
2	67	532
3	67–68	532–33
4	68	533
5	68	533–34
6	68–69	534
7	69–70	534–35
8	70–71	535–36
9	71	536
10	71	536–37
11	71–72	537
12	72	537–38
13	72–73	538
14	73	538
15	73	538
16	73	538
17	73	538–39
18	73–74	539
19	74–75	539–40
20	75–76	540–41
21	76	541–42
22	76–77	542
23	77–78	542–43
24	78	543
25	78	543–44
26	78	544
27	79	544
28	79	544
29	79	544
30	79	544–45
31	79–80	545
32	80	545
33	80	545
34	80	545–46
35	80–81	546

IV.vii.b	1930	1937
36	81–82	546–47
37	82	547
38	82	547
39	82	547
40	82	547–48
41	82–83	548
42	83	548
43	83	548–49
44	83–84	549
45	84	549
46	84	549
47	84	549–50
48	84–85	550
49	85–86	550–51
50	86	551
51	86–87	551–52
52	87	552–53
53	87–88	553
54	88	553–54
55	89	554
56	89	554–55
57	89	555
58	89	555
59	90	555
60	90	555
61	90	555
62	90	555–56
63	91	556
64	91	556

IV.vii.c. (Part III)	1930	1937
1	91	557
2	91	557
3	91–92	557
4	92	557
5	92	557
6	92	557
7	92–93	557–58
8	93	558
9	93–94	558–59
10	94	559
11	94	559
12	94	559–60
13	94	560
14	95	560
15	95	560–61
16	95	561
17	95–96	561
18	96	561–62
19	96–97	562
20	97	562
21	97	562
22	97–98	562–63
23	98–99	563–64
24	99	564
25	99	564–65
26	100	565
27	100	565
28	100	565
29	100	565–66
30	100	566
31	100	566
32	100–01	566
33	101	566
34	101	566
35	101	566–67
36	102	567
37	102	567
38	102–03	567–68
39	103	568
40	103–04	568–70
41	105	570
42	105	570
43	105–06	570–71
44	106–07	571–72
45	107–08	572–73
46	108	573
47	108	573
48	108–09	574
49	109	574
50	109	574–75
51	109–10	575
52	110	575
53	110	575–76
54	110–11	576
55	111	576
56	111	576–77
57	111	577
58	112	577

IV.vii.c.	1930	1937
59	112	577–78
60	112	578
61	112–14	578–79
62	114	579
63	114–15	579–80
64	115–16	580–81
65	116	581
66	116–17	581–82
67	117–18	582–83
68	118	583
69	118	583–84
70	118–19	584
71	119	584–85
72	119–20	585
73	120–21	585–86
74	121	586–87
75	121–22	587–88
76	122–23	588
77	123–24	588–89
78	124	589
79	124	589–90
80	125	590–91
81	125–26	591
82	126	591–92
83	126–27	592
84	127	592
85	127	592–93
86	127–28	593
87	128–29	593–94
88	129	594–95
89	129	595
90	129–30	595
91	130	595–96
92	130	596
93	130	596
94	130–31	596
95	131	596
96	131	596–97
97	131–32	597
98	132	597–98
99	132–33	598–99
100	133–34	599–600
101	134–36	600–01
102	136	601–02
103	136–37	602–03

IV.vii.c.	1930	1937
104	137	603
105	138–39	603–04
106	139–40	604–05
107	140	605–06
108	140	606

IV.viii.		
1	141	607
2	142	607–08
3	142	608
4	142–43	608–09
5	143	609
6	143	609
7	143–44	609–10
8	144	610
9	144	610
10	144	610
11	145	611
12	145	611
13	145	611
14	145–46	611–12
15	146	612
16	146	612
17	146	612
18	146–47	612–13
19	147	613
20	147–48	613–14
21	148	614
22	148–49	614–15
23	149	615
24	149–50	615–16
25	150	616
26	150–51	616–17
27	151–52	617–18
28	152	618
29	152	618
30	152	618
31	152	618–19
32	153	619
33	153	619
34	153–54	619–20
35	154	620
36	154	620–21
37	155	621

IV.viii.	1930	1937
38	155	621
39	155	621
40	155–56	622
41	156–57	622–23
42	157	623
43	157–58	623–24
44	158	624
45	158	624
46	158	624
47	158	625
48	159	625
49	159	625
50	159	625
51	159	625
52	159–60	625–26
53	160	626
54	160	626

IV.ix.	1930	1937
1	161	627
2	161	627
3	161–62	627–28
4	162	628
5	162–63	628
6	163	629
7	163–64	629–30
8	164	630
9	164	630
10	164–65	630–31
11	165	631
12	165–66	631–32
13	166–67	632–33
14	167	633
15	167–68	633–34
16	168	634
17	168	634
18	168	634
19	168	634
20	168–69	634–35
21	169	635
22	169	635
23	169–70	635–36
24	170	636
25	170	636–37
26	171	637
27	171–72	637–38
28	172	638
29	172	638–39
30	172–73	639
31	173	639
32	173–74	639–40
33	174	640
34	174	640–41
35	174–75	641
36	175	641
37	175–76	641–42
38	176–77	642–43
39	177	644
40	177–78	644
41	178–79	644–45
42	179	645
43	179	645–46
44	179	646
45	180–81	646–47
46	181	647
47	181–83	647–49
48	183–84	649–50
49	184	650
50	184	650–51
51	184–85	651
52	185	651–52

V.i.a. (Part I)		
1	186	653
2	186	653
3	186–87	653–54
4	187	654
5	187–88	654–55
6	188	655
7	188–89	655–56
8	189	656
9	189–90	656–57
10	190	657
11	190–91	657–58
12	191	658
13	191	658
14	191–92	658–59
15	192	659

V.i.a.	1930	1937
16	192	659
17	192–93	659–60
18	193	660
19	193	660
20	193	660
21	193–94	660–61
22	194	661
23	194	661
24	194–95	661–62
25	195	662
26	195	662
27	195–96	662–63
28	196	663
29	196	663
30	196	663
31	196–97	663–64
32	197	664
33	197	664
34	197	664
35	197–98	664–65
36	198–99	665–66
37	199	666
38	199–200	666–67
39	200	667
40	200	667
41	200–01	667–68
42	201	668
43	201–02	668–69
44	202	669

V.i.b (Part II)		
1	202	669
2	202–03	669–70
3	203	670
4	203	670
5	204	671
6	204	671
7	204–05	671–72
8	205	672–73
9	206	673
10	206	673
11	206	673–74
12	207	674
13	207–08	674–75

V.i.b.	1930	1937
14	208	675
15	208–09	675–76
16	209–10	676–77
17	210	677
18	210	677
19	210	677
20	210–11	677–78
21	212	679
22	212–13	679–80
23	213	680
24	213–14	680–81
25	214	681

V.i.c (Part III)		
1	214	681
2	214–15	681–82

V.i.d (Article 1st)		
1	215	682
2	215	682
3	215	682
4	216	683
5	216	683
6	216	683
7	216–17	683–84
8	217	684
9	217–18	684–85
10	218	685
11	218	685
12	218–19	685–86
13	219	686
14	219	686
15	219	686–87
16	220	687
17	220–22	687–89
18	222	689
19	222	689

V.i.e.		
1	223	690
2	223	690–91
3	224	691

V.i.e.	1930	1937
4	224	691
5	224	691
6	224–25	691–92
7	225	692
8	225	692
9	225–26	692–93
10	226–28	693–95
11	228–29	695–96
12	229	696
13	229–30	696–97
14	230–32	697–99
15	232	699
16	232	699
17	232	699
18	232–33	699–700
19	233	700
20	233–34	700–01
21	234–35	701–02
22	235–36	703
23	236	703
24	236–37	704
25	237	704–05
26	237–44	705–11
27	244	711
28	244	711–12
29	244–45	712
30	245–46	712–13
31	246	713
32	246	713
33	246	713–14
34	247	714
35	247	714
36	247	714–15
37	247	715
38	248	715
39	248	715
40	248	715–16

V.i.f (Article 2d)		
1	249	716
2	249	716
3	249	716
4	249–50	717
5	250	717
6	250	717

V.i.f.	1930	1937
7	250	717–18
8	250–51	718
9	251	718–19
10	251	719
11	252	719
12	252	719
13	252	719–20
14	252–53	720
15	253	720–21
16	253–54	721
17	254	721
18	254	721
19	254	722
20	254–55	722
21	255–56	722–23
22	256	723
23	256	723
24	256	723–24
25	256–57	724
26	257	724–25
27	258	725
28	258	725–26
29	258	726
30	259	726
31	259	726–27
32	259	727
33	259–60	727
34	260	727
35	260	727–28
36	260–61	728
37	261	728
38	261	728
39	261	728–29
40	261–62	729–30
41	262–63	730
42	263	730
43	263–64	730–31
44	264–65	731–32
45	265–66	732–33
46	266	733
47	266–67	734
48	267	734
49	267	734
50	267–68	734–35
51	268–69	735–36

V.i.f.	1930	1937
52	269	736–37
53	269	737
54	270	737
55	270	737–38
56	270	738
57	270	738
58	271	738
59	271	738–39
60	271–72	739
61	272–73	739–40

V.i.g (Article 3d)		
1	273–74	740–41
2	274–75	741–42
3	275	742
4	275	742–43
5	275–76	743
6	276	743
7	276–77	743–44
8	277–78	744–45
9	278–79	746
10	279	746–47
11	279–80	747
12	280	747–48
13	280	748
14	281	748
15	281	748
16	281–82	748–49
17	282–83	749–50
18	283	750
19	282–84	750–51
20	284–85	751–52
21	285	752
22	285–87	752–54
23	287	754
24	287–88	754–55
25	288	755–56
26	289	756
27	289–90	756–57
28	290	757
29	290	757
30	290–91	757–58
31	291	758
32	291	758–59

V.i.g.	1930	1937
33	291–92	759
34	292–93	759–60
35	293	760
36	293–94	760–61
37	294–95	761–62
38	295	762
39	295–96	762–64
40	296–97	764
41	297–98	764–66
42	299	766

V.i.h (Part IV)		
1	299	766
2	299	766
3	299	766–67

V.i.i (Conclusion)		
1	300	767
2	300	767
3	300	767
4	300	767–68
5	300–01	768
6	301	768

V.ii		
1	302	769

V.ii.a (Part I)		
1	302	769
2	302	769
3	302	769
4	302–03	769–70
5	303	770–71
6	304	771
7	304	771
8	304	771
9	304–05	772
10	305	772
11	305	772–73
12	306	773
13	306	773
14	306	773

V.ii.a	1930	1937
15	306–07	773–74
16	307–08	774–75
17	308	775
18	308–09	775–76
19	309	776
20	309	776
21	309	776–77

V.ii.b (Part II)		
1	310	777
2	310	777
3	310	777
4	310–11	778
5	311	778
6	311–12	778–79
7	312	779

V.ii.c (Article 1st)		
1	312	779–80
2	313	780
3	313	780–81
4	313–14	781
5	314	781
6	314	781–82
7	314–15	782
8	315	782
9	315	782
10	315	782
11	315	782–83
12	315–16	783
13	316	783
14	316	783
15	316–17	783–84
16	317	784
17	317	784
18	317–18	784–85
19	318	785
20	318	785–86
21	318–19	786
22	319	786
23	319	786
24	319	786–87
25	320	787

V.ii.c	1930	1937
26	320	787
27	320–21	787–88

V.ii.d (Taxes which are proportioned . . . to the Produce of Land)		
1	321	788
2	321	788–89
3	322	789
4	322	789
5	322–23	789–90
6	323	790
7	323	790
8	323–24	790–91
9	324	791

V.ii.e (Taxes upon the Rent of Houses)		
1	324	791
2	324–25	791–92
3	325	792
4	325	792
5	325–26	792–93
6	326–27	793–94
7	327	794
8	327–28	794–95
9	328	795
10	328	795–96
11	329	796
12	329	796
13	329	796–97
14	330	797
15	330	797
16	330	797
17	330	797
18	330–31	797–98
19	331	798
20	331	798

V.ii.f (Article 2d)		
1	331	798
2	331–32	798–99
3	332–33	799–800

V.ii.f.	1930	1937
4	333	800
5	333	800
6	333	800
7	333–34	800–01
8	334	801
9	334	801
10	334–35	801–02
11	335	802
12	335–36	802–03
13	336	803
14	336	803

V.ii.g (Taxes upon the Profit of particular Employments)		
1	336	803–04
2	336–37	804
3	337	804
4	337–38	804–05
5	338	805
6	338–39	805–06
7	339–40	806–07
8	340	807
9	340–41	807–08
10	341	808
11	341	808
12	341–42	809
13	342	809

V.ii.h (Appendix to Articles 1st & 2d)		
1	342	809
2	343	810
3	343	810
4	343–44	810–11
5	344	811
6	344	811
7	344–45	811–12
8	345	812
9	345	812
10	345	812–13
11	345–46	813
12	346	813
13	346–47	813–14

V.ii.h.	1930	1937
14	347	814
15	347	814
16	347	814
17	347–48	814–15
18	348	815

V.ii.i (Article 3d)		
1	348–49	815–16
2	349	816–17
3	350	817
4	350	817
5	350	817
6	350	817–18
7	351	818

V.ii.j (Article 4th)		
1	351	818–19
2	351–52	819
3	352	819
4	352	819
5	352	819–20
6	352–53	820
7	353	820–21
8	353	821
9	354	821

V.ii.k (Taxes upon Consumable Commodities)		
1	354	821
2	354	821
3	354–55	821–22
4	355	822
5	355	822–23
6	355–56	823
7	356	823–24
8	356–57	824
9	357	824–25
10	357	825
11	358	825
12	358	825–26
13	359	826
14	359–60	826–27

V.ii.k.	1930	1937
15	360	827
16	360	827
17	360	827–28
18	360–62	828–29
19	362	829
20	362	829–30
21	362	830
22	363	830
23	363–64	830–31
24	364–65	831–32
25	365	832
26	365	832
27	365	832–33
28	365–66	833
29	366	833
30	366–67	833–34
31	367	834
32	367	834
33	367	835
34	367	835
35	367–68	835
36	368	835
37	368	835–36
38	368–69	836
39	369–70	836–37
40	370	837
41	370	837
42	370	837–38
43	370–71	838
44	371–72	839
45	372	839–40
46	372	840
47	372–73	840
48	374	840–41
49	374	841–42
50	374–75	842
51	375	842
52	375	843
53	376	843
54	376–77	843–44
55	377	844–45
56	377–78	845
57	378	845–46
58	378–79	846–47

V.ii.k.	1930	1937
59	379	847
60	379–80	847
61	380	847
62	380–81	847–48
63	381	848–49
64	381–82	849
65	382–83	849–50
66	383	850
67	383–84	850–51
68	384	851
69	384	851–52
70	384–85	852
71	385	853
72	385–86	853
73	386	853–54
74	387	854
75	387–88	854–55
76	388	855
77	388–89	855–56
78	389–90	856–57
79	390	857
80	390–91	857–58

V.iii.		
1	392–93	859–60
2	393–94	860
3	394	861
4	394–95	861–62
5	395	862
6	395	862
7	395–96	862–63
8	396	863
9	396	863
10	396–97	863
11	397	863–64
12	397–98	864–65
13	398	865
14	398	865
15	398	865
16	398–99	865
17	399	865–66
18	399	866
19	399	866
20	399	866

V.iii.	1930	1937
21	399	866
22	399	866
23	400	866–67
24	400	867
25	400	867
26	400–01	867–68
27	401	868
28	401	868
29	401	868
30	402	868–69
31	402–03	869–70
32	403	870
33	403	870
34	403–04	870–71
35	404	871
36	404–05	871–72
37	405	872
38	405–06	872–73
39	406	873
40	406	873
41	407	873–74
42	407	874
43	407	874
44	407	874
45	407–08	874–75
46	408–09	875–76
47	409–10	877
48	410–11	877–78
49	411	878
50	411	878–79
51	412	879
52	412	879
53	412	879
54	412–13	879–80
55	413	880
56	413	880–81

V.iii.	1930	1937
57	414	881
58	414–15	881–82
59	415	882
60	415–16	882–83
61	416–17	883–84
62	417	884
63	417–18	884–85
64	418	885
65	418	885
66	418–19	885–86
67	419	886
68	419	886–87
69	419	887
70	420	887
71	420	887
72	420–21	887–88
73	421	888
74	421–22	888–89
75	422	889
76	422–24	889–91
77	424–25	891–92
78	425	892
79	425	892–93
80	426	893
81	426	893–94
82	427	894
83	427	894
84	427	894–95
85	427–28	895
86	428	895
87	428–29	896
88	429–30	896–97
89	430	897
90	430–31	897–98
91	431	898
92	431–33	898–900

Index

H

I

J

K

L

M